BEHAVIORAL SCIENCE AND
EDUCATIONAL ADMINISTRATION

BEHAVIORAL SCIENCE AND EDUCATIONAL ADMINISTRATION

The Sixty-third Yearbook of the National Society for the Study of Education

PART II

By
THE YEARBOOK COMMITTEE
and
ASSOCIATED CONTRIBUTORS

Edited by

DANIEL E. GRIFFITHS

Editor for the Society

HERMAN G. RICHEY

19 NSSE 64

Distributed by THE UNIVERSITY OF CHICAGO PRESS • CHICAGO, ILLINOIS

The responsibilities of the Board of Directors of the National Society for the Study of Education in the case of yearbooks prepared by the Society's committees are (1) to select the subjects to be investigated, (2) to appoint committees calculated in their personnel to insure consideration of all significant points of view, (3) to provide appropriate subsidies for necessary expenses, (4) to publish and distribute the committee's reports, and (5) to arrange for their discussion at the annual meeting.

The responsibility of the Society's editor is to prepare the submitted manuscripts for publication in accordance with the principles and regulations approved by the Board of Directors.

Neither the Board of Directors, nor the Society's editors, nor the Society is responsible for the conclusions reached or the opinions expressed by the Society's yearbook committees.

Published 1964 by

THE NATIONAL SOCIETY FOR THE STUDY OF EDUCATION

5835 Kimbark Avenue, Chicago, Illinois 60637

Copyright, 1964, by HERMAN G. RICHEY, *Secretary of the Society*

First printing, 10,000 Copies

Printed in the United States of America

The Society's Committee on
Behavioral Science and Educational Administration

RICHARD O. CARLSON
Acting Director, Administrative Science Center
University of Pittsburgh
Pittsburgh, Pennsylvania

JACK A. CULBERTSON
Executive Director
University Council for Educational Administration
Ohio State University
Columbus, Ohio

DANIEL E. GRIFFITHS
(Chairman)
Associate Dean, School of Education
New York University
New York, New York

LAURENCE D. HASKEW
Professor of Educational Administration
University of Texas
Austin, Texas

RICHARD C. LONSDALE
Professor of Education
School of Education, Syracuse University
Syracuse, New York

Associated Contributors

H. WARREN BUTTON
Assistant Professor
State University of New York at Buffalo
Buffalo, New York

RAYMOND E. CALLAHAN
Professor of Education
Graduate Institute of Education
Washington University
St. Louis, Missouri

ROALD F. CAMPBELL
Reavis Professor of Educational Administration
University of Chicago
Chicago, Illinois

W. W. CHARTERS, JR.
Professor of Education and Lecturer in Sociology
Washington University
St. Louis, Missouri

WILLIAM R. DILL
Associate Dean
Graduate School of Industrial Administration
Carnegie Institute of Technology
Pittsburgh, Pennsylvania

BERTRAM M. GROSS
Professor of Political Science
Maxwell Graduate School of Citizenship and Public Affairs
Syracuse University
Syracuse, New York

JOHN K. HEMPHILL
Director, Executive Study
Educational Testing Service
Princeton, New Jersey

LAURENCE IANNACCONE
Associate Director
Graduate Institute of Education
Washington University
St. Louis, Missouri

JAMES M. LIPHAM
Associate Professor of Educational Administration
University of Wisconsin
Madison, Wisconsin

HOLLIS A. MOORE, JR.
Dean, College of Education
University of Arizona
Tucson, Arizona

Editor's Preface

This part of the Yearbook to which is appended a record of the Society's activities and a list of its members could not appropriately be presented without mention of the distinguished services of Dr. Nelson B. Henry, Secretary-Treasurer of the Society and Editor of its yearbooks from 1941 to 1959, and Co-editor from 1959 to his retirement in 1963. Although the content of the twenty-two yearbooks that he edited was the work of hundreds of outstanding educators, each volume published reflected Dr. Henry's technical skill and consistent adherence to high standards of workmanship. It is a privilege to record in this preface this acknowledgment of his effective contribution to the plan and program of the Society.

The minutes of the Board of Directors for 1959 and 1960 reveal the growing awareness of the Board to the ferment in the field of administration. In October, 1960, Laurence D. Haskew, a member of the Board, summarized the activities in the field and the Board's previous discussions of them. He recommended that the Society schedule for publication a yearbook that would present postwar developments in administrative practice and theory. The Board voted that Mr. Daniel E. Griffiths, New York University, be asked to prepare a proposal for such a yearbook. On the invitation of the Board, Mr. Griffiths attended the February meeting of 1961 to present his views relating to the nature of the proposed yearbook. The Board approved the proposal submitted by Mr. Griffiths and appointed him Chairman of the Society's Committee on Educational Administration. Mr. Griffiths convened the Committee for an extended planning session. The excellent and superbly organized volume now presented is the work of the Committee and Associated Contributors.

The Society is grateful to the Free Press of Glencoe for permission to present as chapter iii of this yearbook, a condensation of chapters vi and vii of *The Managing of Organizations: The Administrative Struggle*, a two-volume text on the theory and practice of administration by Bertram M. Gross. The text is to be published in the Autumn of 1964. The condensation was prepared by Daniel E. Griffiths, Chairman of the Society's Committee on *Behavioral Science and Educational Administration*.

This yearbook is and will remain for years a landmark in the development of administrative theory and practice.

HERMAN G. RICHEY
Editor for the Society

Table of Contents

CHAPTER I

The Theme

DANIEL E. GRIFFITHS, RICHARD O. CARLSON,
JACK CULBERTSON, and RICHARD C. LONSDALE

The last yearbook of the National Society for the Study of Education dealing with administration appeared in 1946 and was entitled *Changing Conceptions in Educational Administration*. What is most remarkable in comparing the present yearbook with its predecessor is the lack of similarity. Only one topic, the professional preparation of administrators, is common to both, and the recommendations made concerning it in 1946 may well be urged anew in 1964. A good example of this point is the situation with regard to internship: some programs of good quality do exist, but many more are needed, and the need for new thinking in this area is unremitting. The 1946 yearbook did not point the way to the future; rather, it marked the end of an era in educational administration. Shortly after its publication, a series of events was initiated which culminated in the present state of affairs in educational administration. The treatment of these events, plus their historical antecedents and the events succeeding them, forms the core of the 1964 yearbook on administration.

One cannot pass by a book so mistakenly named *Changing Conceptions in Educational Administration* without comment. The book was written as the country emerged victorious from World War II. The basic theme of the book, democratic administration, had "carried over" from the 1930's. With the victory of the democracies over the totalitarian states there was no doubt in the minds of the authors that the value base of democratic administration was not only correct for the times but would continue to be the trend for years to come. The 1946 yearbook represents also the high-water mark of insularity in educational administration. All of the authors were educationists, men who devoted their lives to professional education. They appear to have been little affected by the thoughts and work of scholars in philosophy, history, or in any of the behavioral sciences. The format of the book is generally in the classical educational administration tradition: the statement of a principle, followed by either argument or one or more illustrations from the public schools. References to theory are completely missing; references to research nearly so.

Eighteen years later it must be said that few of the predicted changing conceptions emerged, but that educational administration did change and in ways which differed greatly from those forecast in 1946.

Behavioral Science and Educational Administration is not intended to forecast new directions but, rather, to plot present trends in as careful a manner as possible. The authors attempt to say what has happened and what it means.

What the Book Is About

Except in chapters ii and iii, the authors present the new developments which have occurred in educational administration since the end of World War II. These developments are not always easy to discuss since they generally have not come to full realization. There is, for example, considerable activity in administrative theory; yet a large number of professors and practitioners have little or no interest in the topic. The same is true of many other developments, yet educational administration has made obvious progress in a number of directions.

Since this book presents an *interpretation* as well as a *description*, it would be well to read it as a whole and not skip from one chapter to another in random order. The book is designed to present new developments in educational administration and to interpret them to workers in the field of education. The new conceptions and developments are discussed in the paragraphs which follow:

Administration is susceptible to empirical research.—Administration is not entirely a common-sense, fly-by-the-seat-of-the-pants art which can only be passed on from practitioner to practitioner; it can be studied, using the tools of the behavioral scientist. These tools include concepts and theories of human behavior, research designs, statistical insights, computers, and the logic of these modes of inquiry.

Probably the most critical failure of past efforts in the study of administration was that there was no confrontation of evidence and principles. This resulted largely from the value orientation of the writers who felt that it was sufficient to assert that they believed in something. Attempts to operationalize the concepts contained in the principles or the values held have been fruitless so that "theories" advanced have faded away to nothing.

The present posture is toward operationalizing concepts, testing propositions, and developing theories based upon evidence. There is still much being written that could have been written thirty years ago, and there is much research being published which ignores entirely the operationalizing of concepts, related research outside education, the use of computers, and advances in research design. But a change in the direction of thought in educational administration is discernible and it may well be *the* direction for the coming decades.

Administrators in all organizations are confronted with a common set of tasks.—The opinion that educational administration is a unique activity, differing greatly from business, military, hospital, and other varieties of administration, has largely given way to the idea that there is more that is common about the varieties of administration than is different. Lazarsfeld has argued that all administrators are confronted by four major tasks and that these tasks vary in little other than emphasis from organization to organization. These tasks are:

1. The administrator must fulfil the *goals* of the organization.

2. The administrator must make use of *other people* in fulfilling these goals, not as if they were machines, but rather in such a way as to release their initiative and creativity.

3. The administrator must also face the humanitarian aspects of his job. He wants people who work for him to be happy. This is *morale*— the idea that under suitable conditions people will do better work than they will under unsuitable conditions.

4. The administrator must try to build into his organization *provisions for innovations*, for change, and for development. In a changing world people and organizations must adjust to changing conditions.

The conditions for change must be incorporated into the organization so that there may be a steady process of development rather than a series of sudden, disruptive innovations.[1]

It may well be that educational administration does differ in significant ways from other types of administration. As yet, these differences have not been clearly delineated; however, once educators have learned what they can from other varieties of administration, programs of research should be initiated which would enable them to identify different kinds of educational organizations, different kinds of environments in which these organizations operate, and implications of the varieties of organizational purpose, form, and environment for the design and administration of school systems.

Administrators now view the human being in a different light.— Human beings may be said to have been viewed by administrators in two ways in the past and are now tending to be viewed in a third way. The first of the past views was that of classical, administrative science. This view was evident in the writings of Frederick Taylor and, in educational administration, in such works as the Twelfth Yearbook of the National Society for the Study of Education. Man was viewed as an inert instrument, performing tasks assigned to him. During this period, roughly 1900 to 1930, little thought was given to motivation or differences in human behavior; in fact, few, if any, of the attributes of man as man were considered.[2]

The second view of man in organizations was typified by Western Electric studies of Mayo and Roethlisberger in industrial management and possibly by the book *Democracy in School Administration*.[3] During this period, roughly 1930 to 1955, man was viewed in the context of a group; in industry it was the informal work

1. Paul F. Lazarsfeld, "The Social Sciences and Administration: A Rationale," in *The Social Sciences and Educational Administration*, pp. 3, 4. Edited by Lorne Downey and Frederick Enns. Edmonton: University of Alberta, 1963.

2. For a more detailed account of this period, see James March and Herbert Simon, *Organization* (New York: John Wiley & Sons, 1958) and Raymond Callahan, *Education and the Cult of Efficiency* (Chicago University of Chicago Press, 1962).

3. G. Robert Koopman, Alice Miel, and Paul J. Misner, *Democracy in School Administration*. New York: Appleton-Century-Crofts, 1943.

group, in education it was the committee. Practical administration was characterized by emphasis upon human relations, group dynamics, and permissiveness. Small group research and the writings of Carl Rogers provided much of the basic thought for the view of man during the latter part of this period.[4]

The present view takes more fully into account the various qualities of man: intellectual, emotional, motivational, and perceptual. Man is seen as devoting only a portion of his life to the organization in which he works and it is recognized that his role there is often in conflict with the role he plays in other organizations such as the family, church, political party, and the like. The values man holds are considered as variables which condition his organizational behavior. The structure of the organization is seen to be influential in shaping his behavior, and the importance of the informal group to which he pays allegiance is also recognized. The present view of man is not a simple picture; it is, rather, a view of complexity.

The foregoing may be called the major changes which have occurred in recent years. There have been several other changes which are now obvious and which have had their genesis in the research of the past ten years. Statements indicative of these changes follow:

1. Leadership and administration are not the same behaviors. It has been fashionable for some fifteen years to equate leadership and administration, but whenever attempts have been made to operationalize the two concepts the difference has become obvious. While this point is made clear in chapter vi, it can be said here that when the dichotomy between leadership and administration is elucidated, the elucidation has great implications for the practice of administration not only in terms of behavior but also in terms of organizational structure.

2. The formal structure is seen as a beginning for the study of organizational behavior. With the formal structure established, the researcher views the informal structure and its effect upon the attainment of the goals of the organization and the goals of the individual.

4. For a more detailed discussion of this period see Daniel E. Griffiths, "The Case Method of Teaching Educational Administration: A Re-appraisal, 1963," in *Journal of Educational Administration* (Australia), I (October, 1963).

The complexity of organizational processes is thus put into proper perspective.

3. Scholars from the behavioral sciences have become increasingly interested in the study of administration.

4. Both the practice of administration and the preparation of administrators are seen to be influenced by the foregoing changes.

The Plan of the Book

The text which follows is divided into four sections containing fourteen chapters. Probably to a greater extent than in most yearbooks, the chapters were written to be read consecutively. The committee met and planned the theme and topics to be covered. The authors wrote drafts of their chapters, exchanged them, and then met for two days to criticize each other's work and to note ways in which chapters could relate to one another. Chapters were then revised and again exchanged.

Section I, *Historical Perspective*, treats the background in which administration is viewed. It comprises three chapters. Moore opens the section with a discussion of the ferment in school administration. This is largely a first-hand recapitulation of the events from the end of World War II through 1960, interpreting them so as to enable the reader to understand recent activities which have changed administration.

Gross and Griffiths study the ideas of a number of scholars upon whose work is based the present scientific view of administration.

Callahan and Button present the changing view of man in the organization, using the tools of the historian in the development of their exposition.

The second section is entitled *Some New Scientific Bases of Administration*. While not comprehensive and all-inclusive, the chapters cover a variety of topics indicative of present-day scholarly activity in administration.

In chapter v, Griffiths investigates of the nature of theory, its definition, its components, and its development, together with a number of illustrations drawn from present-day theories.

Lipham discusses the research on administrative leadership and clearly points to the dichotomy between administration and leadership.

Lonsdale synthesizes current research on organizational purposes, structure, inducements, climate, and survival and discusses them in terms of maintaining the organization in dynamic equilibrium.

Hemphill confines himself to a single study which explores the psychological variables related to various styles of administrator performance.

Dill devotes chapter ix to an examination of decision-making as a key concept in the study of organization.

Charters and Iannaccone, in two separate chapters, take hold of the concepts of formal and informal organization and reshape them into more usable concepts. These chapters demonstrate the point that, when one studies and analyzes the school, he begins to conceptualize at a higher level; and concepts, which once were quite acceptable and sufficient, lose their utility and are replaced by concepts of a different order and, indeed, kind.

In the last chapter of this section, Carlson develops a typology of organization-client relationships in service organizations and then suggests some of the consequences and implications of the type of relationship clients have with public schools.

Section III is entitled *Implications of the New Scientific Bases for the Profession*.

In chapter xiii, Campbell discusses the implications of the new scientific bases for practice.

Culbertson draws upon the preceding chapters to indicate the type of preparation program which would reflect presentations made in earlier chapters.

In Section IV, *Implications of the New Scientific Bases for Education*, Haskew discusses the implications of the scientific bases of administration for the profession of education.

SECTION I

HISTORICAL PERSPECTIVE

CHAPTER II

The Ferment in School Administration

HOLLIS A. MOORE, JR.

Anyone who has tried his hand at writing history knows better than to claim that the beginning of a long-time, continuing trend can be dated with precision, but if a date is selected to mark the beginning of a "ferment in school administration," 1947 is probably the best choice.

As a separate subject of study, school administration has been recognized for about fifty years.[1] Departments of education were established as early as the 1870's. These departments often offered courses relating to school management as well as to philosophy and were a part of the curricula at the University of Michigan; Teachers College, Columbia University; Ohio State University, and others.

In 1887, an article in the *Political Science Quarterly* by Woodrow Wilson, then assistant professor of history at Bryn Mawr College, reviewed, for what has been claimed to be the first time, the importance of the study of the science of administration in the peculiarly democratic context of the American ethic.[2] Entitled "The Study of Administration," the article began with an observation that "the eminently practical science of administration is finding its way into college courses in this country." At that time the process of administration appeared to some observers to be in conflict with the concept of democracy—so much so, in fact, that Wilson found it necessary to reassure his readers that the study of administration could, after all, be in the American tradition, that administration was not necessarily a "European, bureaucratic con-

1. See chapter iv of this yearbook; also, Raymond E. Callahan, *Education and the Cult of Efficiency*, p. 188. Chicago: University of Chicago Press, 1962.

2. Woodrow Wilson, "The Study of Administration," in *Political Science Quarterly*, II, No. 2 (June, 1887).

cept." In one passage, he wrote: ". . . in answer to critics who say we shouldn't borrow the science of administration from Europe . . . [I believe] we have only to filter it through our constitutions, put it over a slow fire of criticism and distill away its foreign gases." Wilson was, as generally, decades ahead of his time, describing in one part of the article a goal which still stands for us in 1964: "The object of administrative study is to rescue executive methods from the confusion and costliness of empirical experiment and set them upon foundations laid deep in stable principle."

The period of sixty years, extending from the appearance of Wilson's article to the beginning of recent ferment, saw many changes. Colleges of education employed professors of school administration, textbooks giving advice on management of schools filled many shelves, and administration became a foremost area of graduate study in education. Some university professors were known throughout the nation for their teaching and writing in school administration—Snedden, Cubberley, Engelhardt, Strayer, Mort, Moehlman.

During the 1920's and 1930's, programs of educational administration were initiated by many colleges and universities throughout the country. By the end of World War II approximately three hundred institutions of higher education claimed programs of preparation for school administration.

School Administration—1947

To see in perspective the developments in administration during the period of just less than two decades which began at the end of World War II, an examination of the status of school administration at that time is appropriate.

There were more than 60,000 school districts in the United States, many of them nonoperating and most of them too small for any kind of efficient administration. They required not an administrator, in the true sense of the word, but rather a teacher who was willing to send a few reports to the county school office or to the state superintendent.

The roll of school administrators carried some noted names: Willard Goslin was in Minneapolis; A. J. Stoddard was Philadelphia's superintendent; Herold Hunt was in his last year at Kansas

City; and James Spinning had already been in Rochester for 13 years. Yet, the ranks of school superintendents were severely depleted of young men who would take over the major jobs a few years later. During the war years the flow of new talent into school administration had markedly diminished.

The profession's national organizations needed direction and a new vision of their roles. An independent association for school superintendents had been established in 1867 and joined the National Education Association a few years later as a department, becoming the American Association of School Administrators (AASA) in 1937. A department of the NEA for elementary principals was created in 1921; for secondary principals in 1927. In the period immediately after the war, there was widespread discontent among rural administrators; they saw little evidence that the AASA was concerned about their needs. The National Association of County and Rural Area Superintendents was organized to serve this special group.

Over the years, the AASA has been the largest and most powerful of the administrator organizations. Described as an organization for all school superintendents, it was dominated, until the late 1940's by the chiefs of large city school systems. School administrators from small towns, rural areas, and suburbs were rarely given posts of prominence in the organization. The election of John Bracken, superintendent at Clayton, Missouri, to the presidency of the AASA in 1949 broke many years of domination by superintendents of large cities.

Membership in 1946 was approximately 6,000, only a little more than half of whom were bona fide school superintendents. (Other members were teachers, principals, college professors, book-company employees, and vendors interested in the school market.) In 1937 when the organization changed its name (from Department of Superintendence), it hoped to attract a somewhat more diversified group and to bring into its ranks the deputy and assistant superintendents of the larger cities, a group thought by AASA leaders to be growing rapidly. However, elementary- and secondary-school principals were "off limits" to membership-proselyting by the AASA (this is still true today), thus preventing the development of any single voice for school administration.

The first executive secretary of the AASA was Sherwood Shankland. Throughout his tenure, the AASA struggled for recognition and adequate support. Neither was easy to achieve. During the depression years, Shankland borrowed against his personal insurance policies to keep AASA going.

Worth McClure, superintendent at Seattle for many years, succeeded Shankland in 1946. Through McClure's leadership, the role of the AASA in determination of professional policy expanded dramatically. In spite of his oft-declared "passion for anonymity," he played a central role on the national scene for the next ten years.

Other elements contributed to the composite picture of educational administration in 1947. Many states issued certificates for administrators, but none of these required more than the master's degree. There was cursory accreditation of teacher education, but no special attention was given to the field of administration.

Some of the ferment in school administration, particularly as it touched college preparation for the job, grew directly out of discontent with what the colleges were doing. College courses proliferated to an alarming degree, forming and reforming around aspects of "the job" as defined by the practitioners or "the subject" as defined by professors. It was difficult to tell the difference. In either case the result was largely folklore, experiences recounted by professors to students in summer sessions, with little research into the process or theory of administration.

School administrators who seriously studied the scene could conclude with Nathan Glazer's comments made years later that "a very large part of what students and teachers do in the best universities is sheer waste. It is not particularly vicious waste, except insofar as it dulls minds and irritates and frustrates students and teachers." [3]

While graduate courses in school administration increased, leaders emerged here and there who tried hard to establish educational administration as a subject of scholarly study. The outlines of present-day theory of administration were not yet sharp or clear, but important groundwork was being laid.

3. Nathan Glazer, "The Wasted Classroom," *Harper's Magazine*, CCXXII-CCXXIII (October, 1961), 147.

The Ferment Begins

In 1946 and 1947, three events occurred to disturb the setting described in the preceding paragraphs: (*a*) The Kellogg Foundation received a recommendation from its education advisory committee that school administration was a field which deserved Foundation support; (*b*) the planning committee of the AASA included in its statement of goals for the association "the initiation of studies and programs looking toward further professionalization of the superintendency," and (*c*) the professors of educational administration formed an organization which was to focus on the scientific study of administration, the elements of leadership, and the dissemination of practices encountered in the preparation of school administrators.

Kellogg Foundation.—In 1930, after having served as a delegate to President Hoover's White House Conference on Children, W. K. Kellogg established a foundation to "improve the health, happiness and well-being of children and youth, without discrimination as to race, creed, or geographical distribution." [4]

Interest in the preparation of school administrators was revealed as early as the 1930's by the Kellogg Foundation. Funds were then expended toward the improvement of seven rural counties in Michigan. Believing that school programs in these areas might be improved through more complete understanding of child development by teachers and administrators, the Foundation conducted a summer training period for some of the administrators from schools of those counties.

The Foundation's report describes its early interest as follows:

Nearly a quarter-century ago when the newly born W. K. Kellogg Foundation was aiding seven counties of southwestern Michigan in the highly experimental Michigan Community Health Project, the citizens of these counties saw the improvement of their schools as a prime community objective. They asked and received from the Foundation aid for local efforts toward community studies of school needs, consolidation of school districts, teacher training through scholarships, school construction and modernization and short courses for school boards. And not

4. *The First Twenty-five Years*, p. 5. Battle Creek, Michigan: W. K. Kellog Foundation, 1955.

the least significant of their activities were considerations of the problems of the school administrator.[5]

When its advisory committee on education (Paul Hanna of Stanford; Maurice Seay and Ralph Tyler of the University of Chicago) recommended that the Foundation enter the field of public school administration, the reason given stressed the role of administrators in community leadership. The Foundation had long been interested in means of improving community living (starting originally with a concern for health practices and facilities) and, in carrying out its projects, the Foundation staff members had noted that the success of community projects frequently turned on the degree of leadership shown by local school administrators. Too often this leadership was faulty, unimaginative, and grossly out of tune with the hopes and desires of a community. Many school administrators showed a lack of knowledge about community processes and the role of the school in the improvement of every-day living.

Thus, the advisory committee's recommendation reasoned that to improve schools in a major sense meant, first, to affect the quality of its leaders. In-service programs which would upgrade the performance of superintendents was a central theme at this early stage of Kellogg interest.

American Association of School Administrators.—The second of the three events was the presentation of a report by the AASA's planning committee which had been charged with the job of "projecting the AASA program of concerns for ten years into the future." Willard Goslin, superintendent in Minneapolis, was chairman of the committee, and the report touched on all aspects of the AASA. Included was "initiation of the studies leading to . . . professionalization." [6]

It would be an exaggeration to say that the AASA planning committee had in mind the dimensions of a grand design supported by Foundation funds when it requested the initiation of studies. Yet, the report does list three areas which became major concerns during the period of the Cooperative Program in Educational Ad-

5. *Ibid.*, pp. 99–100.

6. Hollis A. Moore, Jr., *Studies in School Administration*, p. 2. Washington: American Association of School Administrators, 1957.

ministration (CPEA): improved training programs, refined standards of selection by school boards, and wider participation by the AASA in the activities of the profession.

National Conference of Professors of Educational Administration.—Formation of the National Conference of Professors of Educational Administration (NCPEA) was the last of the three developments which converged almost simultaneously to create the ferment in school administration. For many years professors of educational administration had participated in many educational organizations, including the AASA, but they seemed to be far removed from the center of professional activities. For a time in the 1920's and early 1930's, professors and textbook authors dominated the program of annual AASA conventions, but that arrangement was deliberately changed in favor of more "practical" speeches and panels by "firing-line" superintendents.[7]

The question of acceptance and participation was not the crucial one, however. What was needed—and not provided by the AASA —was a planned procedure through which professors could exchange knowledge of teaching and research practices and could expand scientific inquiry relating to educational administration.

The NCPEA was born as an idea during the 1947 convention of the AASA in Atlantic City. Beginning with a discussion of the problems relating to the teaching and practice of educational administration, the group formed a special committee on arrangements for a summer conference. Members were Walter Cocking, editor of the *School Executive*, E. B. Norton, executive secretary of the Council of Chief State School Officers, and Worth McClure.

In August, 1947, 72 men gathered at Homestead, the country club of International Business Machines near Endicott, New York, for the first professors' conference. The conference was aided not only by free space from IBM, but by a gift of $3,500 from the General Education Board. By the time the conference was over, NCPEA was launched. (It became official the following year.)

The NCPEA has never pushed hard for a large membership. (There were 72 persons in attendance at the first meeting in 1947;

7. A survey of convention programs in the 1930's and 1940's will reveal the shift.

ten years later at Fayetteville, Arkansas, there were 142.) It has never assessed dues nor formed a secretariat; it has not even elected officers, except a planning committee of nine members.

The Co-operative Program in Educational Administration

Exploratory conferences.—Following up the Goslin committee recommendations, a request for funds was submitted to the Kellogg Foundation by a special subcommittee of the AASA.[8] The proposal was denied. Viewed years later and in the light of subsequent events, this decision was probably fortunate for the profession. The original project had requested an outlay of approximately $75,000 for the appointment of a national commission to "study the school superintendency."

The proposal envisaged a commission of fifteen members, a director and staff, and six regional lay-professional planning conferences. Four major concerns were listed: professional preparation; working relations between superintendents, school boards, and staffs; conditions of service, such as tenure, and retirement; and attraction of able men to school administration. On the last point, a nation-wide campaign of selective recruitment was called for.

The four areas of concern were important ones, but it was clear that the project as proposed would be principally in the hands of the AASA. The national commission would make pronouncements and might even mount an effective "recruitment campaign," but collegiate institutions could remain relatively unaffected by such a project. What the proposal did not recognize was the need to affect college and university programs directly.

Foundation officials, in rejecting the proposal, made a counter-offer. They were unwilling to underwrite more than an exploratory project until the scope of need for a study in school administration could be determined. And they asked for inclusion of the National Association of County and Rural Area Superintendents and the Council of Chief State School Officers. The Foundation agreed to finance a series of five exploratory conferences. These meetings would investigate the various issues which had been raised

8. Committee members were: Worth McClure, Herold C. Hunt, Henry Hill, Alfred D. Simpson, Hobart M. Corning, and John K. Norton.

and develop a rationale for a major, nation-wide effort to improve educational administration.

The final regional meeting adjourned in New York on April 27, 1949, and proposals soon were on their way to the Kellogg Foundation. The proposals asked for more money over a longer period of time than had the earlier ones and also asked that the project be centered in universities having a regional or national leadership character. The proposals by-passed the possible approach of a national commission. This move obviously cast the project into a wholly new context: It was not a "study," as such, but a large-scale improvement program. Undoubtedly the grants would result not so much in discovery or pronouncements as in changes in the institutions which prepare school administrators.

Co-ordination of the project.—During the first few years of the program there was a demand for increased co-ordination and for direction from some single source. But control of the program continued to be diffused—the result of deliberate decision on the part of the Kellogg Foundation. The Foundation expressed disinterest in establishing a national co-ordinating committee. Certainly, from the beginning, the Kellogg Foundation refused as a matter of policy to exercise any large measure of control over the program. Therefore, it was perfectly natural from the Foundation point of view that each university regional center should give direction to its own project.

It was no secret that some leaders of the AASA were less than enthusiastic about the turn taken by the proposals—toward the universities instead of toward a national commission. In part to represent the interests of the practitioners (some of whom felt by-passed), a Development Committee was appointed by the AASA executive committee. Ostensibly, the committee was to have broad policy-making responsibilities. Some members considered it their responsibility to review proposals and to advise the Foundation as to grants which should be made. Such clear-cut channels for decision-making, however, never materialized. One of the regional centers was established without any review of its proposal by the Development Committee.

Although the Development Committee was a creature of the AASA, one member represented rural-area superintendents, and one was a chief state school officer. During the ensuing years, the AASA more and more became the dominant organization, with a corresponding decline in influence by the Council of Chief State School Officers and the County and Rural Area Superintendents until, in 1955, a central committee was established and was placed within the AASA organization, almost completely ignoring the other two organizations.

The CPEA in action.—During the next ten years the Kellogg Foundation was to put more than six million dollars into projects for the improvement and study of school administration. The projects, called Cooperative Program in Educational Administration (CPEA), began with the opening of the 1950-51 academic year in five universities: the University of Chicago; Teachers College, Columbia University; Harvard University; George Peabody College for Teachers; and the University of Texas. Grants during the following year to the University of Oregon, Ohio State University, and Stanford University rounded out the eight major regional centers. In 1955, subsequent grants to these and other institutions raised the number of recipients to almost 30, and in the early 1960's grants were made for the study of a special kind of educational leadership —the administration of junior colleges.

How were the funds used? A detailed account would take several volumes; probably any generalization does the program an injustice by being selective. The funds made possible many conferences of administrators and college faculties to analyze issues relating to school administration and particularly to assess pre-service and in-service programs for administrators. An important use of funds was the purchase of research efforts of scholars from the social and behavioral sciences to identify and examine administrative problems of schools. The grants also were responsible for underwriting instructional changes, such as internships, interdisciplinary seminars, and special field studies.

Each of the eight regional centers had a small, full-time staff, sometimes regular members of the faculty and sometimes an outside group without rank or tenure. Each center used funds to attract superior graduate students for study and work on projects related to the CPEA. Dozens of dissertations—some of them excellent additions to administrative research—came from projects initiated and carried on by Kellogg funds.

But there were serious gaps and failures, too. No nation-wide data were ever assembled, because each center was on its own. It is amazing in light of the original concern over "the waning supply of young administrators" that at no time was a comprehensive national supply-and-demand study completed. Nor did the CPEA thoroughly survey either existing practices or promising innovations in administrator-preparation programs. At one time the directors of the eight centers, spurred to action by an unrelenting impatience exhibited by the Development Committee for some unity of approach, promised to meet annually. They elected one of the directors (H. F. Alves, of Texas) chairman, but nothing much came from the effort.

Evaluation of results.—In 1957, the situation was described as "one of improvements for school administration across the country. The outcomes which are the process kind . . . are among the most valuable." [9]

In 1960, Griffiths optimistically observed: "Many changes have occurred recently, with remarkable rapidity and with almost a single stimulus (CPEA) . . . the emphasis on preparation is moving away from bonds, buildings, and buses towards the true content of administration—people." [10] Tope, later in 1960, wrote: "It is generally recognized that one of the most important outcomes of the Cooperative Program in Educational Administration was the development of a national concern for adequate preparation programs for school administrators and the accompanying development of national organizations concerned with the development of a profession of educational administration." [11]

It is extremely difficult even yet to "step back" a sufficient distance from the CPEA in order to evaluate its real impact. Several claims were made, however, concerning its influence.

9. Moore, *op. cit.*, p. 21.

10. Daniel E. Griffiths, "New Forces in School Administration," *Overview*, I (January, 1960), 48-51.

11. Donald E. Tope, *A Forward Look: The Preparation of School Administrators*, 1970, p. 105. Eugene, Oregon: Bureau of Educational Research, University of Oregon, 1960.

1) *School administration preparation programs in universities closely identified with CPEA were permanently altered because of the grants.* Clearly, the existence of sizable Kellogg grants on the eight campuses permitted employment of new personnel, helped to attract students, and gave visibility on the national scene. The projects at the University of Oregon established a new curriculum in school administration oriented heavily toward the social sciences, one which has continued beyond the last Kellogg grant. The content of the University of Chicago's program, likewise, appears to be changed, as does its "staff-associate" recruitment procedure. Stanford's present internship arrangements can be traced directly to the CPEA, as can Harvard's "career program." Less lasting impact on the curriculum in educational administration is observable in the other four institutions, least perhaps at Peabody. The University of Texas, Ohio State, and Teachers College, Columbia, were all institutions of such size and complexity that some aspects of the programs for administrator preparation were relatively untouched throughout the decade of Kellogg activity. (This observation is not meant to be a judgment of the worth of contributions from these four institutions. Peabody, Teachers College, and Texas gave stronger leadership at times to the surrounding region than to their own campus, and many important studies came from those institutions and from Ohio State.)

2) *The national program produced a new literature of school administration.* It is as hard to generalize on this as it is to trace origins. Most publications which bear the clear stamp "CPEA" on the title page are either narrow in scope or are "progress reports," such as those submitted to the Foundation. A glance at the 303 titles reported by 1957 will reveal few lasting, landmark contributions to the literature of educational administration.[12] Yet, during the CPEA decade and immediately after, the literature of school administration showed new life. Four or five excellent books of case studies emerged; textbooks focused on important human and conceptual skills; and the impact of behavioral science on educational administration began to be felt. While *the* good research journal in the field

12. Moore, *op. cit.*

still has not been established, there are good reasons to expect the establishment of such a journal within the near future.

3) *The several regional centers produced able, young leaders in school administration.* The validity of this claim is clear if we define terms. If by "able, young leaders" the statement means superintendents, then the claim is exaggerated. True, there are superintendents who were discovered by selection procedures developed in CPEA projects, and a few owe their doctorate to the regional centers, but the number is probably not substantially greater than it would have been without CPEA. It is another story when one considers the preparation of professors of school administration. The experience of the Southern region is reported by Pierce and Albright:

Well over 200 graduate students had substantial responsibilities in the [Southern States] Program, of whom 101 served as graduate assistants and received their doctoral degrees in educational administration.

Although the CPEA came into being because of concerns related to the superintendency, it will be noted that less than 10 per cent of the doctoral graduates who received their training through the program accepted positions as school superintendents. The nine who became assistant superintendents may be assumed to have as their goal service as a superintendent. There is no evidence to indicate whether or not the 10 who accepted positions as principals aspire to the superintendency. Only 27 of the 101 doctoral graduates went into public school administration. Nearly two-thirds of the graduates went into higher education either as teachers or in administration, or both.[13]

It seems safe to say that there is, indeed, a new breed of leader in school administration. Typically, he is on the faculty of a multipurpose university which prepares school administrators, he is a student of the behavorial sciences, and he is an interpreter of research applied to educational processes and institutions.

4) *The CPEA established professional solidarity and sanctions.* —Two organizations were offspring of the Kellogg grants—the Committee for Advancement of School Administration (CASA) and the University Council for Educational Administration (UCEA).

13. Truman M. Pierce and A. D. Albright, *A Profession in Transition,* p. 181. Southern States Cooperative Program in Educational Administration. Nashville, Tennessee: George Peabody College for Teachers, 1960.

These two residual organizations carry the burden of continuing the work started by the CPEA. One is an arm of the superintendents' professional association, a kind of committee-in-charge-of-revolution, if it remains true to its high purpose. The other is a self-perpetuating body of first-rate, multipurpose universities dedicated to improving instructional practices, scientific inquiry, and curriculum development in the graduate study of educational administration.

In addition to CASA and UCEA, the Kellogg grants indirectly gave strength and vitality to the National Conference of Professors of Educational Administration. The NCPEA, admitting persons from all grades of institutions, is not selective in membership as is the UCEA. But it has given a strong voice to the professors of educational administration. Many observers credit the NCPEA with much of the influence which brought the Cooperative Program in Educational Administration into being in 1950. Whether or not this is true, the NCPEA was a spark which set off research studies, critical appraisals of preparation programs, and the production of an impressive array of books, monographs, and articles on the subject of educational administration.

Early publications, either inspired or sponsored by NCPEA, stressed "democratic administration" concepts. By the mid-1950's, the stress shifted to the contribution of the several social-science disciplines. The high-water mark of the later development was the 1954 conference at Denver, where representatives from the social sciences attended the conference for the first time. As the 1960's began, the third major shift in emphasis occurred: This time it was "administrative theory" which occupied the center of the stage, supported by an earlier, major NCPEA publication, *Administrative Behavior in Education*.[14]

Committee for Advancement of School Administrators

From 1950 until 1955 the Development Committee for the CPEA continued to have difficulty in finding its precise role. Near the end of the CPEA's fifth year, the Committee sent members on

14. *Administrative Behavior in Education.* Edited by Roald F. Campbell and Russell T. Gregg. Sponsored by the National Conference of Professors of Educational Administration. New York: Harper & Bros., 1957.

so-called "inspection trips" to the eight centers to evaluate the effectiveness of the projects. But this was clearly not the approach which would mend the split between the practitioners' interests and those of the projects, which were essentially university operations.

As the first five years of the CPEA drew to a close, the demand for some co-ordination became more pronounced. Such requests also received a more favorable ear at the Kellogg Foundation than they had previously. Maurice F. Seay had become director of the Foundation's Division of Education in 1954 and was receptive to the idea of a committee which would provide some direction and co-ordination for the various projects.

In July, 1955, negotiations between the AASA and the Kellogg Foundation brought into being the Committee for the Advancement of School Administration. The first issue was one of membership. Officials of the AASA wanted one director of a regional CPEA to represent the centers on the new committee. The center directors protested, pointing out that it was "all or none." The AASA executive committee feared domination of the Committee by the colleges. A compromise was offered by Worth McClure: membership would go to all eight regional directors, three members of the AASA executive committee, a chief state school officer, a school board member, an official representative of the NCPEA, the executive secretary of the AASA, a county or rural-area superintendent, and two persons chosen at large, one of whom would be chairman.

After two years of operation with a membership of eighteen, the Committee was reorganized on a more workable basis to consist of the president and president-elect of AASA, a chief state school officer, two university administrators, two professors of educational administration, a school board member, and the chairman (a superintendent of schools). Membership designation has remained unchanged since 1957, and Committee personnel has been rather stable.

The Committee has served under three chairmen: Herold C. Hunt, Harvard University professor who resigned to become under-secretary of Health, Education, and Welfare in the Eisenhower administration; second, Lawrence G. Derthick, superintendent of schools at Chattanooga, Tennessee, who resigned to become United States Commissioner of Education, and Paul J. Misner, superintendent of schools at Glencoe, Illinois, who has served continuously as chairman since 1957.

In 1955 Hollis A. Moore, Jr., associate editor of *The Nation's Schools*, was selected as executive secretary. He was succeeded in 1961 by J. C. Wright, superintendent of public instruction in Iowa. Roderick F. McPhee served for two years as associate secretary of the Committee and, for the six-months interim between Moore and Wright, as acting executive secretary.

The Committee began operation with little to guide it except a general agreement that there needed to be "a diffusion of results from the several CPEA centers." No formal, written proposal in the usual sense was submitted to the Foundation.

With an absence of clear-cut directives, the Committee faced a conflict of expectations: Foundation officials expected the Committee to be a dissemination center,[15] AASA officers expected the Committee staff to evaluate the effectiveness of the regional projects, and the CPEA centers themselves expected the Committee to influence AASA policy. The Committee's history reflects an attempt to do each of these, with greatest success in the third area.

In spite of pressure from the AASA executive committee, the centers understandably objected to any after-the-fact evaluation of their effectiveness by the new Committee. They refused to be measured either against a single instrument or against each other. They considered stewardship of the funds to be directly to the Foundation and not through the new Committee.

The chief handicap in fulfilling the dissemination function was that there were little new data relating to the practice of school administration directly traceable to CPEA. More could be done in disseminating information about the practices of collegiate institutions, but this function soon became more appropriately that of the UCEA than of the Committee.

In summarizing the various studies and publications made in the regional centers of the CPEA, the committee published and widely

15. *The First Twenty-five Years, op. cit.*, p. 104. "This committee is the agency through which the two organizations will attempt to increase the use of the results of CPEA through more extensive reporting in professional meetings, in professional literature, and in some of the major mass media of communications."

circulated *Studies in School Administration*. Later the Committee's executive secretary was chairman of the 1960 AASA yearbook, *Professional Administrators for America's Schools*. The yearbook was the best summary available of the recommendations for changes in preparation programs.

The job of the Committee, which rapidly took precedence over all others, was, of course, to throw into the wheels of progress of the American Association of School Administrators the insights, understandings, findings, and perceptions generated by the CPEA. In essence, this meant trying to change the AASA from a convention-and-yearbook organization, almost exclusively concerned with practicing superintendents and their day-to-day problems, to one which was concerned with professional preparation, maintenance of standards, and stimulation of research.

Perhaps the most significant work of the Committee revolved around the establishment (through political/professional sanctions) of standards for the preparation of school administrators. Essentially, this took the Committee into areas of state certification regulations and professional accreditation. Eventually it affected the policies of the AASA itself.

Easily the most significant publication of the Committee was *Something To Steer By*,[16] a succinctly-stated platform of 35 goals to be pursued by the total profession. More than 25,000 copies of this document were distributed, and it became extremely influential in the formation of standards of preparation, programs of in-service education, school board procedures for selecting superintendents, and some broad outlines of badly needed research.

The Committee was barely six weeks old when a representative of the National Council for Accreditation of Teacher Education (NCATE) approached the Committee's executive secretary with a proposal that a study be made which would result in the development of a document establishing criteria for the accreditation of graduate programs of study which prepare school administrators. The NCATE had been in operation only a year but already had projected some future accrediting of special programs in addition

16. *Something To Steer By*. Washington: American Association of School Administrators, 1958.

to accreditation of teacher education, its first line of responsibility. The Council had expected to appoint a special committee to propose standards in school administration and was about to do so when the Committee for the Advancement of School Administration was formed. The NCATE then asked the Committee if it would perform this function, thereby eliminating the necessity for appointing a separate committee.

The CASA worked on the accreditation project for several years. First it presented to the NCATE a guide which spelled out the important features of preparation programs for administrators which should be considered in any accreditation visit. The guide was a refinement of an earlier document prepared for New York State by the staff of the Middle Atlantic CPEA at Teachers College, Columbia University.

Later the Committee was instrumental in working with a sub-group of the NCATE to establish specific standards. During the academic year 1959-60 the Council used the administration standards for the first time. Accreditation visits to appraise the administrator-preparation program occur only when an institution undergoes general accreditation of its teacher-education program.

An important principle was established through the AASA-NCATE co-operative effort: The AASA would not try to perform an accrediting function but would rely, instead, on the agency recognized as the sole accrediting body in teacher education.

The Committee was soon to promote another development which would draw the AASA and the NCATE closer together than ever anticipated—the action to limit active membership in the AASA after 1964 to graduates of two year graduate programs in school administration accredited by the NCATE. This action, in the form of an amendment to the constitution of the AASA, was approved at the annual convention of the Association in Atlantic City in 1959.[17] The AASA, now with membership close to 15,000, was—through this action—taking aggressive, active leadership in the promotion of high professional standards, even to the extent of limiting its own membership. The Committee for the Advancement

17. *Your AASA in 1958-59*, p. 9. Washington: American Association of School Administrators, 1959.

of School Administration, after seeing that the standards were written, took to the road to explain such institutional accreditation to school superintendents and professors of educational administration. The Committee even contributed funds to help the NCATE achieve early review of programs.

Obviously the action on membership did several things. It put the organization on record as requiring quality preparation for its members and it also gave great strength to accreditation under NCATE. More than that, it tied the hopes of administrators for professional advancement to the success of the accreditation movement. This is not an inevitable blessing. Haskew points out in a later chapter that whether the NCATE can use accreditation "constructively is open to serious question on the basis of accreditation history. . . . the accreditation agency can become an institutional protectorate rather than an arm of professional advancement." It will be necessary for the Committee for the Advancement of School Administration to judge the contributions of accreditation as the movement spreads.

Probably the greatest danger for the CASA is that it will lose its character as an agent of change. It can easily slip into the fabric of the AASA, become one of its several standing committees and spend most of its efforts in consolidating gains and justifying the policies of the Association. To maintain its unique role as prompter-of-revolution will require some resistance against the usual pressures for conformity.

The University Council for Educational Administration

As the period covered by the first grants by the Kellogg Foundation drew to a close in 1955, the original eight centers began to formulate plans for continuation of their projects, including the making of requests to the Foundation for additional funds. One of the centers (Teachers College, Columbia University) proposed an organization which later developed into the University Council for Educational Administration (UCEA).

The Teachers College prospectus described a co-operative organization of colleges dedicated to the improvement of preparation programs. Membership was to consist not of persons but of universities, those institutions quite clearly leaders in the field of preparing school administrators. A group somewhat larger than the eight regional center institutions was anticipated, but it was to be small enough to be an "elite group." Kellogg Foundation funds were requested to get the organization going, but in the long run it was expected that the institutions themselves would finance the operation through dues, assessments against the institution, and grants obtained from governmental and foundation agencies.

In the fall of 1956 an exploratory conference was held on the Teachers College campus to which representatives of approximately 30 universities were invited. All of the participating institutions invited were active in the first five years of the Cooperative Program in Educational Administration. All of them offered doctor's degrees with majors in school administration, and most of them had made some substantial mark in administrative research.

An organization was formed after the usual difficulty with constitution and by-laws, and it was called University Council for Educational Administration. The membership, at first, numbered thirty-two, later raised to thirty-five, and now amounts to more than forty. One of the obviously knotty problems faced by the UCEA was how to expand its membership—if expansion were desirable—and how to establish criteria which would be defensible in terms of the purposes of the organization.

After a three-year period on the Columbia campus the organization was moved to permanent quarters at Ohio State University; the first executive director, Daniel R. Davies, professor of educational administration, Teachers College, Columbia, was succeeded by Jack Culbertson, an associate professor of educational administration at the University of Oregon. A board of trustees was formed, including unofficial liaison representatives—the executive secretary of the AASA, the secretary of the CASA, and certain representatives of the United States Office of Education.

As Anderson has pointed out in the Sixty-first Yearbook of the National Society for the Study of Education, "reform [in professions] is essential from time to time. A principal point of reform in a profession is at the point of education for it." [18] The purpose of

18. G. Lester Anderson, "Professional Education: Present Status and Continuing Problems," in *Education for the Professions*, p. 17. Sixty-first Yearbook of the National Society for the Study of Education, Part II. Chicago: Distributed by the University of Chicago Press, 1962.

the UCEA has been to work at the point of education for school administration. The Council has developed co-operative research projects relating to the problems of better instruction in school administration. The impact of the UCEA has been felt chiefly by member institutions, but other institutions are also permitted to purchase such important artifacts of teaching as tapes, films, case studies and simulated materials, and other aids.

A research approach has characterized the UCEA endeavors. Career-development seminars concentrate on relevant topics. "Position papers" prepared for the UCEA seminars are among the most thoughtful and provocative publications in the field of educational administration. Other UCEA projects are publication of case studies, task forces on major investigations, and research studies.

As the period covered by its second grant from the Kellogg Foundation drew to a close (the original grant to Teachers College was followed in 1960 by a grant specifically to the UCEA), the organization faced serious problems of financing; membership fees from the institutions still provided only a minor part of its costs, and foundation support was undoubtedly available only for a brief period. It was yet to be proved that the organization could attract substantial continuing research grants, although its one major research grant from the United States Office of Education—the "criteria of success in administration" project directed jointly by the Educational Testing Service—had been a solid success.[19]

Summary

These have been exciting days for people at the heart of school administration—exciting even for those on the periphery. Yet, much that has happened has been undirected and haphazard. What is taught in administration courses is discouragingly like what was taught before the "period of ferment," and research is still largely pedestrian. Since 1947 there has been more ferment than accomplishment, more that is tentative than proved.

Perhaps the chief contribution of the period 1947-63 was its

19. John K. Hemphill, Daniel E. Griffiths, and Norman Frederiksen, *Administrative Performance and Personality*. New York: Bureau of Publications, Teachers College, Columbia University, 1962.

success in focusing the spotlight on educational administration. Many of the rewarding outcomes of the CPEA came after its books had been closed, but probably would have come either much later or not at all had there been no CPEA. These significant outcomes were: (*a*) administration was established as a scientific study; (*b*) the profession of school administration took a clear, open stand for high standards of quality; (*c*) curriculum innovations in preparation programs slowly became or began to become widespread; and (*d*) a new breed of leaders in educational administration were taking over important posts and bringing about changes that would shape the future.

CHAPTER III

The Scientific Approach to Administration[1]

BERTRAM M. GROSS

A major contention of this book is that the study and practice of administration has been becoming more scientific. While chapter iv traces the history of school administration through its formative periods, this chapter undertakes the task of noting certain major efforts toward establishing a scientific base for administration. This is done by an analysis of the work of men and women who pioneered in administrative theory and research. The chapter is thus organized in terms of people rather than ideas. It might be subtitled: *From Taylor to Simon.*

Although this chapter deals with many of the most important administrative thinkers, it does not try to identify the hundreds of others who have also helped develop the scientific approach to administration. A full canvass of the vast activity currently going on in this area would also have to deal with the contributions from each of the social sciences, from other established disciplines, and from such new fields as information theory, operations research, and general systems theory.[2]

It should also be pointed out that, although administrative thought has made tremendous advances, the greatest advances still lie ahead. In comparison with any mature science, administrative

1. This chapter is reprinted in a condensed form from chapters vi and vii of *The Managing of Organizations: The Administrative Struggle*, by Bertram M. Gross, to be published in the autumn of 1964 by The Free Press of Glencoe. These two chapters appear as part of a larger section in "The Development of Administrative Thought." This condensation has been prepared by Daniel E. Griffiths for inclusion in this yearbook.

2. These other areas of administrative thought are dealt with in "The Contributors from Other Fields" (chap. vii) and "The Rising Flood" (chap. ix) in Gross, *The Managing of Organizations: The Administrative Struggle* (see footnote 1).

theory is still relatively undeveloped. "After babbling and crawl-
ing, it is learning how to talk and walk. It now faces a long period
of accelerating and exuberant growth." [3]

The Pioneers: The Gospel of Efficiency

Two clearly defined streams of thought developed during the
first half-century of the 1900's. The first of these can be called
administrative efficiency. In fact, it would be more accurate to call
this stream of thought the *gospel of efficiency*. The intensity of
verbal dedication to the efficiency goal was scarcely impaired by
the equal interest of administrators in many other goals or by the
lack of equal interest in the precise analysis of efficiency itself.

Although there were many who wrote in the efficiency vein,
the sense of the movement can be gained by a study of four men:
Taylor, Fayol, Gulick, and Urwick. Before reviewing the work
of these men, it is interesting to note certain facts concerning them:

Frederick Taylor (1858–1915)   USA   Engineering, private business,
                                     middle management

Henri Fayol (1841–1925)   France   Engineering, private business,
                                    top management

Luther H. Gulick (1892–   )   USA   Political science, public service
                                    —research and consulting

Lyndall Urwick (1891–   )   USA   Engineering, military service,
                                   middle management, public
                                   service

The predominance of engineering backgrounds, and the personal involvement in management are the common characteristics
of these men. Only Gulick studied in a nonengineering field.
Although Fayol was the only one of the four to be personally involved in a top-management position, the others engaged in administration at somewhat lower levels.

TAYLOR: MORE FROM WORKERS

How do we get more work out of workers who are naturally
lazy and engage in systematic "soldiering"? This was the question

3. Bertram M. Gross, "The Emergence of Administrative Science," in *The
Managing of Organizations: The Administrative Struggle*, chap. xxx.

which concerned Frederick Taylor in the early 1880's when he rose
to be foreman of the Midvale Steel Works in Philadelphia. He first
attempted to answer the question by the improvement of the tools
which workers used and by developing more efficient use of the
tools. From this he jumped directly into the analysis of work methods, a field which previous engineers had rarely entered.[4]

Analysis and planning of work processes.—Before Taylor, many
manufacturers had used "piece work" systems under which workers received higher wages for producing more output. Taylor
heaped scorn on these systems, charging that the employers had no
way of knowing how much work could really be accomplished in
a given period of time. The incentive effect of higher wages was
vitiated by being dependent on the initiative of the workers themselves.

Taylor proposed that managers use scientific research methods
in discovering the best way of performing every piece of work.
There would also be changes in the specifications for tools and materials, the selection and training of workers, and in the supervision
of work. With all of this done it would then be possible to make
proper use of bonuses and premiums for higher individual output.
He maintained—and demonstrated—that through this combination
of methods it would be possible to obtain dramatic increases in efficiency. Taylor summed up his stand on these points as follows:

> It is only through *enforced* standardization of methods, *enforced*
> adaptation of the best implements and working conditions and *enforced*
> cooperation that this faster work can be assured, and the duty of en-
> forcing the adoption of standards and of enforcing this cooperation rests
> with *management* alone.[5]

Taylor's first innovation was to gather together the detailed
knowledge of methods of work, record it, and improve upon it
through analysis and experimentation, and finally reduce it to
"laws, rules and even mathematical formulae." Taylor did this by

4. The written record of Taylor's achievements are found in three documents: "Shop Management," "The Principles of Scientific Management," and
"Testimony before the Special House Committee," all published in *Scientific
Management* (Foreword by Harlow S. Person. New York: Harper & Bros.,
1947).

5. *Ibid.*, p. 53.

applying to the movements of workers' bodies the same methods of careful observation which he had used in studying metal-cutting machines. In one of his first experiments he gave a young man a stop watch and a carefully prepared set of forms. This man spent two and a half years analyzing the motions of individual workers. Through analysis of detailed records of every movement "the one best method" for accomplishing the most work in the shortest time was discovered. Taylor was tremendously encouraged by the fact that after three years, average output per man in the machine shop doubled.

Taylor maintained that it was also necessary to standardize tools for specific jobs. In a historic experiment at the Bethlehem Steel Works on the shoveling of coal, Taylor found that the average shovel-load varied from 16 to 38 pounds. Further experiments showed that good workers were able to shovel more tons per day if they used a shovel carrying a load from 21 to 22 pounds. Subsequently, Taylor found that with different types of material to be shoveled, about 15 different types of shovels were needed. From then on, when workers arrived in the morning, they received written instructions on what to shovel and what shovels to use. After three and a half years, 140 men were doing the work formerly done by 400 to 600 men.

Taylor insisted that each worker should be given the job for which he was best suited and, in addition, be trained to use prescribed motions with standardized tools and materials. Taylor's own words best give his ideas on selection:

Now one of the very first requirements for a man who is fit to handle pig iron as a regular occupation is that he shall be so stupid and so phlegmatic that he more nearly resembles in his mental make-up the ox than any other type. . . . There is work for each type of man, just as, for instance, there is work for the dray-horse and work for the trotting horse . . . there is no type of work, however, that suits all types of man.[6]

Taylor came to the conclusion that his system required foremen different from those required for the traditional methods. He devised the "functional" foreman. Taylor divided the task of foremanship into eight separate functions, four on the shop floor: in-

6. *Ibid.*, pp. 5, 175.

spector, repair foreman, speed boss, and gang boss; and four in the planning room who dealt with routing, preparation of instruction cards, time and cost records, and discipline. Each worker received orders from eight supervisors rather than one as under the previous system.

Having indicated how the rate of production could be improved, Taylor developed new systems of paying workers in accordance with their output instead of the number of hours worked. The essence of all these plans was the payment of extra sums to workers who met or exceeded the defined task otherwise known as "standard time," "norm," or "bogy." Above all, each worker was paid in accordance with his individual output rather than the output of the group to which he belonged since Taylor said:

> When workmen are herded together in gangs each man in the gang becomes far less efficient than when his personal ambition is stimulated. . . . Individual efficiency falls almost invariably down to or below the level of the worst man in the gang. . . .[7]

The opposition to Taylor.—Taylor's methods were deeply resented by both management and workers. Managers took umbrage because he insisted they were unqualified unless assisted by highly-trained experts. The resentment of the workers was even deeper. They resisted being asked to behave like machines and move mechanically in accordance with predetermined patterns. They disliked having comradely work-relationships broken by wage systems which put every worker on his own. They reacted against Taylor's effort to transfer to management the craftsman's knowledge of his trade.

The unions in 1912 obtained an investigation of his methods by a special committee of the House of Representatives, and in 1915 an amendment was added to the Army Appropriations Act which forbade the use of stop watches or the payment of premiums or bonuses in Army arsenals. This law stayed on the statute books until World War II.

The strongest blow, however, was struck by the investigation conducted for the United States Commission on Industrial Relations by Professor Robert Hoxie. The report concluded that Taylor

7. *Ibid.,* pp. 72, 73.

dealt with only the mechanical and not the human aspects of production and that time-study and task-setting were largely arbitrary rather than scientific pursuits.[8]

The scientific management movement.—In his earlier days Taylor usually referred to his bundle of administrative techniques as "the task system" or "task management." In 1910, a new and more popular label was provided by Louis Brandeis (later a Supreme Court Justice) who represented eastern shipping concerns in a struggle against a projected increase in railroad rates. He contended that the railroads could maintain their profits without an increase in rates if they would introduce more efficient methods of operation, and he used Taylor's ideas to support his position. Brandeis felt that a more popular term than "task system" was needed, and he hit upon "scientific management" (a term previously used only occasionally by Taylor.)

The railroad rate case gave Taylor's ideas not only a popular label but also a tremendous amount of popular attention. His closest associates, Henry Gantt, Frank B. and Lilliam Gilbreth, Horace Hathaway, Sanford Thompson, and Harrington Emerson published countless articles and many books. They and innumerable followers served as advisers to hundreds of companies, thus developing the profession of "efficiency expert" or "management consultant." Engineering schools began to give courses on "shop management" and "industrial management." Schools of business management followed suit. Many special disciplines, each partly rooted in "scientific management," emerged from the welter: production engineering (or production management), cost accounting, personnel management, and industrial psychology. The movement became international and gained its greatest support in Russia where it was accepted by Lenin and Trotsky and influenced the training of engineers.

FAYOL: MORE FROM MANAGERS

Like Taylor, Henri Fayol was an engineer whose technical achievements were impressive. In his earlier days he performed

---

8. Robert Hoxie, *Scientific Management and Labor*. New York: D. Appleton & Co., 1915.

outstanding work in overcoming the fire hazards in coal mining
and in analyzing the geological formation of French coal deposits.
Like Taylor, he concentrated on industrial administration but maintained that the basic principles of administration were applicable to
all forms of organizations. But here the similarity ends and the differences between the two men (who might be called the founders
of modern administrative thought) begin. The problem faced by
Fayol in 1888, when he rose from a technical post to become general manager of his company, was how to save a mining company
which was on the verge of bankruptcy. This was a much broader
problem than any ever faced by Taylor. To deal with it, he could
not limit himself to work methods and work planning. He focused
more and more on what is to be expected from managers. He based
his conclusions not on laboratory-style observations, but on personal experience during many years of high administrative responsibility.

A general approach to administration.—Fayol was the first writer
to develop what might be called a "general approach" to administration.[9] As a top executive himself, he looked at administration
from the top down. This gave him a broader perspective than
Taylor, who was first and foremost a technician. This wider perspective is found in his views on the essence of administration and
on the need for administrative training and theory.

Fayol defined administration as "to plan, to organize, to command, to co-ordinate, and to control." [10] These have come to be
known as "Fayol's Elements" and are further delineated as follows:

To plan means to study the future and arrange the plan of operations.
To organize means to build up the material and human organization of
    the business, organizing both men and materials.
To command means to make the staff do their work.
To co-ordinate means to unite and correlate all activities.

9. Fayol's major work is *General and Industrial Management* (translated by
Constance Storrs, with an introduction by L. Urwick. London: Sir Isaac Pit-
man & Sons, 1949). His other major publication is "The Administrative
Theory of the State" (translated by Sarah Greer and published in *Papers on
the Science of Administration,* edited by Luther Gulick and L. Urwick. New
York: Institute of Public Administration, 1937).

10. Fayol, *General and Industrial Management, op. cit.,* pp. 6-7.

To control means to see that everything is done in accordance with the rules which have been laid down and the instructions which have been given.[11]

Fayol contended that administration was not the exclusive privilege or responsibility of a few people, but was spread throughout the organization. Everyone should participate to some extent in administration, but the degree of responsibility and participation increases as one moves up in the hierarchy.

Administration, however, is only part of governance. To govern is to conduct the undertaking toward its objectives by seeking to derive optimum advantage from all available resources. This calls for smooth working of six essential functions: (*a*) technical activities, (*b*) commercial activities (buying, selling, and exchange), (*c*) financial activities (search for and optimum use of capital), (*d*) security activity (protection of property and persons), (*e*) accounting activities (stocktaking, balance sheet, costs, statistics), (*f*) administration (which operates only on personnel and not directly on either materials or machinery). At times, however, Fayol seems to depart from this initial categorization and to write about administration as something which itself deals with the integration of the first five activities.

Fayol was a strong advocate of the teaching of administration not only to potential "managers" but to everyone, since he believed administration was present in all organized human activity. Teaching administration should take place from primary school through the university, and the task should then be taken up by the all employing institutions. He attributed the lack of teaching on the fact that there was no theory of administration, and he devoted much of his later life to the development and advocacy of what he called *the* theory.

Flexible principles.—Fayol was resolved that, unlike other top managers of his acquaintance, he would not depart without leaving a body of doctrine behind him. Accordingly, he set out to propound a considerable number of principles. He listed 14 principles in his *General and Industrial Management*: division of work, authority, discipline, unity of command, unity of direction, subordina-

11. *Ibid.*, see pp. 6, 43-110.

tion of individual interests to the general interest, renumeration, centralization, scalar chain (line of authority), order, equity, stability of tenure of personnel, initiative, and *esprit de corps*. He also formulated a number of principles in analyzing the five elements of administration.

Fayol went to considerable length to stress the flexibility of the principles. He maintained that "there is nothing rigid or absolute in management affairs; it is all a question of proportion." [12] All principles of administration are flexible, and their proper adaptation to specific circumstances "is a difficult art requiring intelligence, experience, decision and proportion." [13] In addition, Fayol contended that there is no limit to the number of administrative principles. There is a place for any new principle whose worthiness is confirmed by experience, and old ones can be changed in the light of experience.

Principles, to Fayol, were assertions based upon his own experience. He considered science to be an accumulation of these assertions collated under a number of headings which he deemed appropriate.

GULICK-URWICK: THE ARCHITECTURE OF ORGANIZATION

World War I gave a tremendous impetus to the gospel of efficiency. At a technical level the followers of Taylor developed more mature techniques of work-study and production management, of testing and selection of workers, and of cost accounting. At a more general level the principles of Fayol were developed into more precisely articulated principles of formal organization.

For examples of the principles of formal organization, one can hardly do better than turn to the work of Luther Gulick and Lyndall Urwick. Both of them authored significant formulation of organizational principles—formulations far superior to those of a host of lesser imitators. Although they concentrated on certain formal aspects of administration, they were both aware of broader approaches to the subject and even encouraged the presentation of other viewpoints. Both served on public bodies charged with pro-

12. *Ibid.*, p. 19.

13. *Ibid.*

ducing state papers on important aspects of administration. Both were indefatigable publicists, propagandists, and promoters of the gospel of neutral principles directed at raising the level of organizational efficiency.

In 1937 Gulick and Urwick co-operated in editing *Papers on the Science of Administration*.[14] Of the eleven papers in this collection, two ("Notes on the Theory of Organization" and "Science, Values and Public Administration") were authored by Gulick and two ("Organization on a Technical Problem" and "The Function of Administration, with Special Reference to the Work of Henri Fayol") were written by Urwick. From among the long list of their other publications, special reference might also be made to Gulick's, *Administrative Reflection on World War II*[15] and Urwick's *The Elements of Administration*.[16]

From Fayol's elements to POSDCORB.—As a framework for his neutral principles, Urwick uses Fayol's five elements of administration: planning, organization, command, co-ordination, and control. In so doing, however, he separates forecasting from planning in order to give it special emphasis. In addition, Urwick expands Fayol's categories to make them more inclusive. His answer to the questions, "What is the work of the chief executive? What does he do?" is POSDCORB, a verbal artifact made up of the initial letters of seven types of administrative activities:

Planning, that is working out in broad outline the things that need to be done and the methods for doing them to accomplish the purpose set for the enterprise;

Organizing, that is the establishment of the formal structure of authority through which work subdivisions are arranged, defined and co-ordinated for the defined objective;

Staffing, that is the whole personnel function of bringing in and training the staff and maintaining favorable conditions of work;

Directing, that is the continuous task of making decisions and embodying them in specific and general orders and instructions and serving as the leader of the enterprise;

14. *Papers on the Science of Administration, op. cit.*

15. Luther Gulick, *Administrative Reflection on World War II*. University, Alabama: University of Alabama Press, 1948.

16. L. Urwick, *The Elements of Administration*. New York: Harper & Bros., 1943.

Co-ordinating, that is the all important duty of interrelating the various parts of the work;

Reporting, that is keeping those to whom the executive is responsible informed as to what is going on, which thus includes keeping himself and his subordinates informed through records, research and inspection;

Budgeting, with all that goes with budgeting in the form of fiscal planning, accounting and control.[17]

In this list of seven activities, three (planning, organizing, and co-ordinating) were taken over bodily from Fayol. His command appears under the heading of direction, and control is covered by budgeting and reporting, which serve as instruments of both planning and control. In staffing, Gulick separates out for special mention an activity which Fayol largely included as part of organization.

Whatever its merits or demerits, POSDCORB served as a convenient starting point for innumerable writers interested in dealing with different aspects of administration or, to use a term which soon came into wide use, with different administrative processes. Many writers on public or business administration took this list and through additions, subtractions, and amendments adapted it to meet their own tastes and needs.

Organizational principles.—Despite their interest in dealing with administration as a whole, most of the Gulick-Urwick principles deal with the architectonics of formal organization. A look at three of their principles gives the flavor of their work.

Gulick reiterates Fayol's maxim that "A man cannot serve two masters." Although rigid adherence to this principle may have its absurdities, these are "unimportant in comparison with the certainty of confusion, inefficiency and irresponsibility which arise from the violation of this principle." [18] He himself, however, provided an exception to this principle in the case of field office specialists. According to the principle of "integrated dual supervision," for example, an engineer in a field office can be subject to the "admin-

17. Luther Gulick, "Notes on the Theory of Organization," *Papers on the Science of Administration, op. cit.,* p. 13.

18. Gulick, *ibid.,* p. 9.

istrative supervision" of the field office manager and to the "technical supervision" of the chief engineer in the central office.[19]

While Fayol in discussing the exercise of authority emphasized the need to promote responsibility, Urwick deals with both sides of the relationships. It is not enough to hold people accountable for certain activities, it is also essential to delegate to them "the necessary authority to discharge that responsibility." On the other side, "the responsibility of all persons exercising authority should be absolute within the defined terms of that authority. They should be personally accountable for all actions taken by subordinates." In contrast to Fayol's observation that the measurement of responsibility eludes all calculation, he sets forth the widely quoted principle that "at all levels authority and responsibility should be coterminous and coequal." [20]

According to Urwick, "No supervisor can supervise directly the work of more than five, or at the most, six subordinates whose work interlocks." [21] When the number of subordinates increases mathematically, there is a geometrical increase in all the possible combinations of relationships which may demand the attention of the supervisor. Gulick identifies various factors that may influence the optimum span, particularly the capacity of an individual executive, the nature of the work performed, the stability of an organization, and the geographical proximity to those who are supervised. He is less categorical about the maximum number of subordinates but no less confident concerning the general validity of the principle.[22]

The Pioneers: The New Beginnings

Although the gospel of efficiency obtained a wide following, it never achieved a monopoly. Indeed, from the very beginning it provoked intellectual competition, if not outright opposition. The trade-union attack on Taylorism was followed by an increasing

19. Gulick, *Administrative Reflection on World War II, op. cit.,* pp. 91-96.

20. All quotes in this paragraph are from Urwick, *Elements of Administration, op. cit.,* pp. 45-46, 125.

21. *Ibid.,* pp. 52-53.

22. Gulick, *"Notes on the Theory of Organization," op. cit.,* pp. 7-9.

awareness of the limitations of "scientific management." Both teachers and practitioners grew restless with the narrowness of the principles presented so confidently by Fayol, Gulick, and Urwick. At first, it was charged that their principles, although theoretically sound, simply did not work out in practice. It was not long, however, before their theoretical validity was also challenged. Still more significant, entirely apart from the revolt against the gospel of efficiency, many new lines of thought were initiated.

These new beginnings are much harder to categorize than the gospel of efficiency. The new pioneers did not dispute the importance of efficiency as a goal, but they held that other goals must also be considered. They did not challenge the ultimate desirability of laws and principles, but they suggested that the previously promulgated laws and principles were premature and should be revised, if not rejected *in toto*. In part, it might be said that the second group of pioneers demanded a new approach to "human relations." In part, it might be said that they went farther in developing the "process approach" to administration, with attention to such fundamental processes as communication and decision-making. Yet, each of these characterizations is incomplete. No label more specific than "new beginnings" is broad enough to encompass the multilinear content of this second stream of administrative thought.

Perhaps the best way to illustrate the richness of these new beginnings is to summarize the work of five people: Mary Parker Follett, Elton Mayo, Fritz Roethlisberger, Chester Barnard, and Herbert Simon. Each of these made seminal contributions to the growth of a new discipline.

Before reviewing the work of each, it is interesting to note their personal backgrounds, and especially interesting to compare this group with the disciples of efficiency.

Mary Parker Follett (1868-1933)	USA	Political science and economics
		Community work and public service
		Occasional lectures on business administration
Elton Mayo (1880-1949)	USA	Psychology and philosophy
		Industrial research
		University professor

Fritz J. Roethlisberger (1898-)	USA	Chemical engineering, philosophy Industrial research University professor
Chester I. Barnard (1886-1961)	USA	Private business, top management Philanthropic institution, top management
Herbert A. Simon (1916-)	USA	Political science, business administration and psychology Occasional government service University professor

As with the disciples of efficiency, each of the foregoing had close contact with administrative life—although Barnard, like Fayol, was the only one with sustained personal experience in top-level administrative responsibility. Unlike the previous list, not one of the five was an engineer. It is significant to note that three of the five were university professors and that the disciplines of political science, economics, sociology, and psychology are represented. Although Follett did some of her work in England and Mayo emigrated to the United States from New Zealand, each person on the list is an American. The United States has become the world center of modern administrative thought, and there are few, if any, thinkers of comparable rank in other countries.

FOLLETT: THE DYNAMICS OF HUMAN INTEGRATION

Administration is one of the very few fields of human thought in which a woman has been an outstanding pioneer. Although less known to the public than Florence Nightingale and Madame Curie, her achievements are no less significant.

Mary Follett was one of the first to recognize the psychological aspects of administration and to deal with them on the basis of modern psychological thought instead of glib reference to the mysteries of human nature. She was the first to perform the unladylike task of inserting the nasty word "power" into the vocabulary of administration. She breathed a sense of dynamism and creative democratic spirit into the more static concepts of scientific management and organizational principles. She was one of the first to indicate how business management might develop into a genuine profession.

Like many others, Follett came to administration in a round-
about way. After studying economics, she entered political science
by preparing an intensive historical survey of the post of Speaker
of the United States House of Representatives and the growing
political power associated with it.[23] She then became active in
many forms of community work, particularly adult education and
vocational guidance. Her interest in social problems led to a book
on democratic government and community activity.[24] Her community work brought her into public service as a member of the
Massachusetts Minimum Wage Board. Here she met many businessmen and labor leaders and became familiar with management-labor
disputes. These experiences led to a book on the psychological processes by which the views and interests of conflicting groups may
be integrated.[25]

By this time her attention was drawn more and more to business
administration. She made contact with many thoughtful businessmen in both the United States and England, men who were seeking
an ideology more satisfying than mere money-grubbing and
broader than Taylor's scientific management. In trying to develop
new ideas of administration, she produced a series of lectures and
articles replete with practical wisdom, deep flashes of intuition,
undepartmentalized thinking, and an all-pervading spirit of democratic dynamism. The most complete and representative set of her
papers was published under the title, *Dynamic Administration: The
Collected Papers of Mary Parker Follett*.[26]

To present a summary of Follett's thinking on administration is
a baffling task, since she never attempted a systematic formulation.
Her thinking was very much akin to what she conceived to be the
process of social action, continuous emerging and becoming. Never-

23. Mary Parker Follett, *The Speaker of the House of Representatives*.
London: Longmans, Green & Co., 1896.

24. Mary Parker Follett, *The New State*. London: Longmans, Green &
Co., 1920.

25. Mary Parker Follett, *Creative Experience*. London: Longmans, Green
& Co., 1924.

26. *Dynamic Administration: The Collected Papers of Mary Parker Follett*.
Edited by Henry C. Metcalf and L. Urwick. New York: Harper & Bros., 1940.

theless, within the iridescent stream of her writings, it is possible to single out certain concepts that have been particularly influential.

Administrative concepts.—Follett's discussion of conflict is typical of her approach to administration, and an understanding of its resolution is a key to her thought. She conceives of conflict as "not necessarily a wasteful outbreak of incompatibilities, but a normal process by which socially valuable differences register themselves for the enrichment of all concerned." [27] She posits three ways of dealing with conflict. One is domination, which means a victory for one side or the other. The second is compromise, which means that each side gives up something in order to have peace. The third, and most constructive, is integration. In a true integration of conflicting views, a place is found for each desire, and neither side sacrifices anything. In fact, both sides gain.

The first steps toward integration are to bring a conflict into the open and to discover its most significant aspects rather than merely the most dramatic ones. This requires a judicious examination of the symbols that are used and the realities to which they actually refer. It involves both breaking the demands and interests of both sides into their constituent parts and finding the whole or real demand. It involves dropping the general dispute and centering upon proposed activities. The parties to the conflict should never allow themselves to be forced into an either-or situation, but should seek a solution which is better than either of the two given alternatives. Above all, integration requires an understanding that human behavior is not linear but circular. *B* does not merely react to what *A* does. He also reacts to his own anticipation of what *A* may do on his own and of how *A* may react to something *B* does. Yet the actual response is still more circular: "I can never fight you. I am always fighting you plus me. . . . Employees do not respond only to their employers, but to the relation between themselves and their employer. . . . Circular behavior on the basis of integration gives us the key to constructive conflict." [28]

Follett's concept of authority leads her to an interesting revision of the traditional concept of responsibility which she calls "cumu-

27. Follett, *Creative Experience, op. cit.*, p. 300.
28. *Dynamic Administration, op. cit.*, p. 45.

lative responsibility." She raises the question, "How can the work of different people and units in an organization be unified?" The answer is found in the ideas of cross-functioning, group responsibility, and cumulative responsibility. Each individual function should not be seen in isolation; rather, it must be seen in terms of its interdependence with, and contribution to, other functions. Each sub-executive, because of his function, has the responsibility to integrate his work with other sub-executives rather than merely pass on the task of co-ordination to hierarchical superiors. This requires organizational arrangements for intimate cross-relations, rather than too much reliance on "always running up and down a ladder of authority." [29]

Follett draws two significant conclusions from this analysis of responsibility. The first is that lower-level executives should be regarded as responsible for helping to formulate general policy. The second is that workers also have a role in management. Employees and their elected union representatives have a major contribution to make to the management of a company. This contribution should be solicited and given, not on the basis of the Golden Rule, but on the higher principle of genuine community of interest.

This pluralistic conception of responsibility should not, however, lead to laziness. For example, a works council may be regarded as an advisory, a judicial, or even a legislative body, but never an executive body. In dealing with executive functions, responsibility must be "fixed" so that, in case of failure, those who caused it can be located. This is not for the purpose of reprisals, but rather that the situation may be improved.

A profession in the making.—Follett saw certain tendencies in the direction of the professionalization of business management. Among these were the developments of "scientific management," the growth of specialization, the decline of arbitrary authority, the trend toward conscious control of business cycles, and the recognition that management is a more fundamental element in industry than either stockholders or bankers. But a true profession is based on the motive of service and a foundation of science.

29. *Ibid.*, p. 158.

The real service of businessmen is not just the production and distribution of manufactured articles. It is "to give an opportunity for individual development through the better organization of human relationships. . . . The *process* of production is as important for the welfare of society as the *product* of production." [30]

With respect to science, two major steps are needed. First of all, the scientific standard must deal not only with the technical side, but also with the personnel and human relations side. In fact, the technical side itself cannot be properly understood if divorced from the human side. The second step is to develop an organized body of knowledge. This involves intensive and continued research and the "organization of the knowledge obtained by research." [31] Analysis should be made of managers' jobs "somewhat corresponding to the analysis of workers' jobs in the Taylor system." [32] Above all, there should be systematic recording of executive experience in individual plants. It is also essential to compare the experience and experiments of different companies and different countries. In the difficult pioneer work of developing standards of service and building a body of organized knowledge, managers themselves must play the major role. "All professions have been developed by the work of their own members." [33] The manager must contribute to the development of his profession in addition to activity in a management organization. "The way in which you give every order, the way in which you make every decision, the way in which you meet every committee, in almost every act you perform during the day, you may be contributing to the science of management." [34]

MAYO-ROETHLISBERGER: RESEARCH ON WORKERS' BEHAVIOR

In 1925, when Follett issued her call for intensive research within organizations, an ambitious research project was already under way at the Western Electric Company's Hawthorne plant in Chicago. Its purpose was to measure the effect on workers' production of

30. *Ibid.*, p. 141.
31. *Ibid.*, p. 125.
32. *Loc. cit.*
33. *Ibid.*, p. 139.
34. *Loc. cit.*

different intensities of illumination. Although the investigators conducted their study with the thoroughness of Taylor himself, after two and a half years of experiments they sadly reported that they found no direct statistical relationship between illumination and workers' output. Still eager to pin down the effect on productivity of physical conditions of work, they turned to the Harvard Graduate School of Business Administration. They obtained the help of Elton Mayo, professor of industrial psychology, and Fritz Roethlisberger, a sociologist.

The Hawthorne researchers started a second project in 1927. This time they decided to measure the influence of rest pauses of different lengths and frequencies, with and without lunches, and different lengths of both workday and workweek. It was assumed that these would influence productivity through their effect on fatigue and monotony. They placed five girls in a separate room and gave them each the standardized task of assembling small pieces of telephone equipment called "relays." They provided for the automatic counting of hundreds of relays produced each day. They arranged to give the girls continuous physical examinations and to study their home environments. They placed an observer in the room to keep accurate records of all that happened and to maintain a friendly atmosphere.

Although the project was initially designed on a rather simple basis, one thing led to another and four supplementary studies were also undertaken. Instead of lasting a year or two, it lasted more than five years. Preliminary conclusions were published by Mayo in 1933.[35] The materials collected were so vast that the authoritative summation of the project was not published until 1939.[36] Both Mayo and Roethlisberger published later works based upon the Hawthorne studies.[37]

The Hawthorne studies.—During the first few months of the

35. Elton Mayo, *The Human Problems of an Industrial Civilization*. Boston: Harvard Business School, 1933.

36. Fritz J. Roethlisberger and William J. Dickson, *Management and the Worker*. Cambridge: Harvard University Press, 1939.

37. Elton Mayo, *The Social Problems of an Industrial Civilization*. Boston: Harvard Business School, 1945.

relay assembly test room, physical conditions were maintained without change in order to get the girls accustomed to the test room. In this period hourly output rose. Then conditions were gradually improved: hours of work were decreased below 48, rest periods of different lengths and frequencies were introduced. Hourly output rose steadily, usually more than enough to counterbalance the decline in hours per week. Weekly output declined only when hours per week fell below 42. After a year and a half of charting these changes it was decided to withdraw all of the improvements and return to the original conditions at the beginning of the experiment. Contrary to reports of many of the popularizers of the Hawthorne study, hourly production fell somewhat. Nevertheless it remained far higher than at the beginning of the experiment. Moreover, the return to a 48-hour week brought the weekly output to new heights.

In the next period, hours were reduced from 48 to 45:40, and two rest periods (one with refreshments) were brought back. Hourly output then rose very sharply, so much so that, despite the decline in hours, it brought weekly output to its peak.

By this time, the investigators were puzzled:[38]

The general upward trend in output independent of any particular change in rest pauses or shorter working hours was astonishing. The improvement in mental attitude throughout the first two years of the experiment was also perplexing. Neither one of these developments could be related to the kind of working day in any simple one-one correlation. . . . To what could this improved output, on the one hand, and improved mental attitude or morale, on the other be related?

Two supplementary experiments were then performed, and, in the light of these, the investigators concluded that neither wage incentives alone nor all the changes in physical conditions taken together could explain the increases in output in the first two years of the Relay Assembly Test Room. More important, they concluded that they had been mistaken in the first effort to maintain a controlled environment in which they could test for the effect of a

---

Elton Mayo, *The Political Problems of an Industrial Civilization*. Boston: Harvard Business School, 1945.

Fritz J. Roethlisberger, *Management and Morale*. Cambridge: Harvard University Press, 1941.

38. Roethlisberger and Dickson, *op. cit.*, pp. 86-87.

single variable while holding other factors constant. The effort to keep all other factors constant was, in itself, the biggest change of all.

One source of this change was a radical change in the nature of supervision. Previously the girls had been under strict supervision, but in the test room the atmosphere was more relaxed. The girls were allowed to talk freely, and changes in working conditions were discussed with the girls in advance instead of being arbitrarily announced by superior authority. It thus became obvious that:

> In the endeavor to keep the major variables in the situation constant and the girls' attitude cooperative, the investigators inadvertently altered the social situation of the group. Thus, as a consequence of setting up an experiment to study the factors determining the efficiency of the worker, they abrogated most of the rules intended to promote and maintain efficiency.[39]

Second, the girls received more attention. The fact that they were being studied became a source of pride. Important visitors streamed through the test room. They even "became the focus of considerable attention from top management."[40]

Third, the girls grew into a close-knit group. They co-operated not only with their experimenters but with each other. They grew more and more to enjoy their interpersonal relationships at work, and out of this grew new group loyalties and solidarities.

In short, the conclusion was that people work better if treated like human beings, with some specifications as to what is meant by "human beings." It was this idea which some commentators hailed as "the great illumination." One can hardly help speculating whether its revolutionary character testifies more to the brilliance of the research or more to the blindness of the industrial psychologists and engineers who had been preaching the gospel of efficiency in accordance with Frederick Taylor's conceptions of human motivation. Many years later Roethlisberger suggested that the Hawthorne studies simply represented "the systematic exploitation of the simple and the obvious."[41]

39. *Ibid.*, pp. 182-83.
40. *Ibid.*, pp. 180-81.
41. Roethlisberger, *Management and Morale, op. cit.*, p. 7.

In 1928, the investigators decided it was important to make a special study of human attitudes and sentiments in the plant. They employed a special group of interviewers and intended to use the results for corrective action. The interviewers soon found great difficulty in staying with the interview schedule and shortly developed a technique called the *indirect approach*. With this technique the employee followed his own lead. The interviewer listened attentively and displayed interest in everything the employee said.

Here, as in the relay assembly test room, it was the unforeseen results that led to success. It was soon found that the data acquired by the interviewer could not be used to remedy conditions. On a number of occasions the conditions objected to were changed, but the complaints continued anyway. It was found, however, that the indirect interviews led to decreasing tensions, raising morale, and changing methods of supervision. Further, the interviewers felt they had obtained new insights into employee behavior.

As a result of their interviewing experiences, some of the interviewers started to analyze the social situation in various departments. But it was soon decided that any careful analysis of social relations among workers called for a concentrated study of a single group. In November, 1931, the project leaders established the bank wiring observation room. Here fourteen men worked together for seven months under careful observation. Instead of taking over the supervisory duties themselves, the investigators included as data the behavior of the four supervisors who came into contact with the workers.

The findings on output might seem, at first blush, to substantiate Taylor's charge that workers engage in "systematic soldiering." While the workers were capable of producing at a high level, they did not do so. In fact, by restricting output they deliberately held down their own wages. This was at odds with Taylor's conception of worker behavior. In attempting to explain the restriction of production, Roethlisberger and Dickson arrived at the "logic of sentiments," which is defined as a system of ideas and beliefs which express values residing in the interhuman relations of the different groups in the plant. The ideas and beliefs stem not only from the formal organization but also from the informal groups.

The great depression worsened during the period of the bank

wiring room study and was a factor not reckoned with when the experiments started in 1927. The question, "Was restriction of output also a way of resisting the depression and warding off unemployment?" was never fully dealt with. Data presenting output in good times was not contrasted with output in bad times. In contrasting the company-oriented sentiments in the relay assembly test room with the company-resistant sentiments in the bank wiring observation room, the drastic change in the economic situation and the resulting change in the company's employment policies is not even mentioned.

Human relations.—The most significant effect of the Hawthorne studies was to make the "human relations" of Mayo and Roethlisberger a major concern in administrative thought and practice. This was human relations as seen mainly from the viewpoint of top administrators interested in obtaining the co-operation of their employees. It did not deal directly with the behavior of the managers themselves, the organization of employees into unions, or the thorny human problems of management-union relations. Thus, it was quite different from the human relations of Follett, who was interested in the behavior of managers as well as workers, who dealt directly with interest conflicts, and who favored union participation in management. The Mayo-Roethlisberger approach was thus more open to abuse and perversion by managers who saw human relations as merely a new device to get more work out of employees by social and psychological manipulation.

Although there are some differences in emphasis between Mayo and Roethlisberger, both see human relations as based on two fundamental concepts: equilibrium and the social skills of the elite. Equilibrium is regarded as a state in which "if a small (not too great) modification different from that which will otherwise occur is impressed on the system, a reaction will at once appear tending toward the conditions that would have existed if the modification had not been impressed." [42]

The skills to which Mayo and Roethlisberger refer are those held by the practical administrator. The most specific skills which

42. Roethlisberger and Dickson, *op. cit.*, p. 567.

they identify are those of diagnosis and communication. Managers must learn how to think of co-operative phenomena in terms of social conditioning, of informal patterns of behavior, sentiments, and beliefs, and of equilibrium analysis. Above all, they must learn the skills of patient listening.

BARNARD: LEADERSHIP IN CO-OPERATIVE SYSTEMS

One is always surprised when a highly successful man of affairs plays the role of a theoretician, and even more so if he succeeds. This happened with Henri Fayol, the first genuine theoretician of modern administrative thought. It happened again with Chester Barnard, the first outstanding theoretician in the field. Barnard came to administrative theory after many years of experience as president of the New Jersey Bell Telephone Company. In 1937, he was invited to give a series of lectures on administration at the Lowell Institute in Boston. He was subsequently urged to publish these lectures in book form. This was done in *The Functions of the Executive*, which is one of the great classics in administrative literature.[43] Ten years later he published *Organization and Management*, a more loosely organized collection of papers and lectures.[44]

In these two books Barnard tries to build a rounded theoretical system. While he does not achieve the simplicity and clarity of Fayol's uncompleted work, he goes far deeper than anything ever hinted at by Fayol. He also brings to bear upon administrative theory his powers of intellectual analysis that have been invigorated and sharpened by contact with philosophy, political science, economics, sociology, psychology, and the physical sciences. Barnard divided his conceptual scheme into two parts: (*a*) a theory of organization and co-operation, and (*b*) the functions and methods of the executive.

The theory of organization.—In the preface to *The Functions of the Executive*, Barnard bewails the lack of attention to formal organization. Most social scientists, he maintains, have "just reached

43. Chester I. Barnard, *The Functions of the Executive*. Cambridge: Harvard University Press, 1938.

44. Chester I. Barnard, *Organization and Management*. Cambridge: Harvard University Press, 1948.

the edge of organization as I experienced it, and retreated." [45]
They have failed to give sufficient recognition to formal organization "as a most important characteristic of social life, and as being
the principal structural aspect of society itself." [46] Among political
scientists, the legalistic approach to the nature of authority has pre-
vented "the acceptance of essential facts of social organizations." [47]
Among economists the exaggeration of the economic phases of human behavior has obscured the emotional and physiological aspects.
Students of administration have given only a superficial description
of "the topography and cartography of organization." [48] Much
more is needed if we are to understand the organizational framework for executive functions.

Barnard discusses his theory under the following headings: An
organization as a co-operative system, the contribution-satisfaction
equilibrium, the multiplicity of satisfactions and incentives, formal
and informal organization, and the functions and pathology of
status systems. Two of these topics are discussed in this chapter to
give the flavor of the theory.

In presenting an *organization as a co-operative system*, he first
points out that the usual concept of an organization is that of "a
group of persons, some or all of whose activities are coordinated." [49]
This is an unworkable concept since it implies "membership."
Every person is a member of various groups. Moreover, some of
the most important participants in certain organizational activities,
such as stockholders, creditors, customers, suppliers, and subcon-
tractors, can hardly be called members. If the group concept means
anything at all, the hard core of meaning is the "system of interactions." [50] To obtain a workable concept, therefore, it is better to

45. Barnard, *The Functions of the Executive, op. cit.*, p. ix.

46. *Loc. cit.*

47. *Loc. cit.*

48. *Ibid.*, p. viii.

49. *Ibid.*, p. 68.

50. *Ibid.*, p. 70.

focus directly on the interactions and regard an organization as "a system of consciously coordinated activities or forces of two or more persons." [51]

In this sense, an organization is not a material object. It can be only indirectly symbolized by reference to the equipment or the people that may be involved. It is a system composed of the activities of human beings, a system in which the whole is always greater than the sum of its parts and "each part is related to every other part in some significant way." [52] As a system, it is held together by some common purpose, by the willingness of certain people to contribute to the operation of the organization, and by the ability of these people to communicate with each other.

The basic unit in any organization, "if measured by the number of persons simultaneously contributing to it, is usually quite small—from two to fifteen or twenty persons, and probably not having an average of more than ten." [53] The key limitation on size is the difficulty of effective communication among large numbers of people. The growth of organizations, therefore, is usually accomplished by the addition of small units. Thus it is that nowhere in the world "can there be found a large organization that is not composed of small units." [54]

With the exceptions of the state and the church, all organizations are partial systems. They are dependent upon larger and more comprehensive systems. The most comprehensive formal organizations are included in "an informal, indefinite, nebulous, and undirected system usually named a 'society.' " [55]

Barnard's discussion of formal and informal organization was the most definitive to his time and is still basic to the work of theorists. In analyzing informal organization, Barnard goes much beyond the conclusions drawn by Mayo and Roethlisberger from the bank wiring observation room. He maintains that there are

51. *Ibid.*, p. 73.

52. *Ibid.*, p. 77.

53. *Ibid.*, p. 105.

54. *Ibid.*, p. 110.

55. *Ibid.*, p. 79.

"informal organizations related to formal organizations every-where." [56] This includes the organization of executives as well as workers. The difference between formal and informal organizations is that while the former is a system of consciously co-ordinated ac-tivities, the latter is unconscious, indefinite, and rather structureless. The relationship between the two forms of organization is very intimate. On the one hand, it is informal organization which gives rise to formal organization. On the other hand, once formal organ-izations are established, they inevitably create and require informal organizations, which not only condition them, but vitalize them. Thus, one can scarcely exist without the other.

At times, informal organizations may operate against either the purposes or the methods of the formal organization with which they are associated. Yet, there are three positive functions that in-formal organizations alone can perform for formal organizations. One is "the communication of intangible facts, opinions, suggestions, decisions that cannot pass through formal channels without raising issues calling for decisions, without dissipating dignity and objec-tive authority, and without overloading executive positions." [57] The second function is to maintain cohesiveness in formal organiza-tion through regulating the willingness to serve and the stability of objective authority. The third is the maintenance of the feeling of personal integrity, of self-respect, of independent choice. This feel-ing may be regarded as "a means of maintaining the personality of the individual against certain effects of formal organization which tend to disintegrate the personality." [58] In this connection, Barnard also points out that individuals who cannot maintain a sense of self and a sense of ability to make choices of their own are incapable of functioning effectively in a co-operative system. This is, indeed, a far cry from those principles of Taylor's scientific management which, if effectively carried out, would destroy the individual's sense and reduce him to the status of a machine.

The role of executives.—The basic role of the executive, in

56. *Ibid.*, p. 115.

57. *Ibid.*, p. 225.

58. *Ibid.*, p. 122.

Barnard's eyes, is to preserve the internal and external equilibrium of the organization. However, Barnard does not pin down this role in more specific terms. At one point he maintains that, "It is precisely the function of the executive to facilitate the synthesis in concrete action of contradictory forces; to reconcile conflicting forces, instincts, interests, conditions, positions and ideals." [59] At another point, in his introduction to *The Functions of the Executive*, he says, "The functions of the executive with which the last part of this treatise is concerned are those of control, management, supervision, administration in informal organization." [60] Yet, when we identify the specific types of activities which Barnard analyzes, we find that they are neither so general as that of synthesizing contradictory forces nor so specific as control, and so forth. Those aspects of executive activity to which he gives the most attention— and perhaps for which we are most indebted to him—are leadership, communication, decision-making, authority, and responsibility. An examination of leadership and decision-making will give an indication of his insights.

Although placing great emphasis on *leadership*, Barnard does not regard it as the only element in organizational performance. Leaders merely serve as catalysts to help stimulate the activities of all those who contribute to an organization. "The work of cooperation is not a work of leadership, but of organization as a whole. . . . Cooperation, not leadership, is the creative process; but leadership is the indispensable fulminator of its forces." [61]

He is also careful to distinguish between "leadership" as referring to prominence or excellence in some special field of activity and "leadership" in the sense of the guidance of people in organizations. This confusion has led to an exaggeration of the importance of intellectual capacity in leadership. Actually, he maintains, intellectual capacity is less significant in the guidance of people than are four other basic qualities: vitality and endurance, decisiveness, persuasiveness, and the sense of responsibility. Although intellectual abilities may be an important element in leadership, they are by no

59. *Ibid.*, p. 21.
60. *Ibid.*, p. 6.
61. *Ibid.*, p. 259.

means sufficient to maintain it. At times, they may serve to wreck it—for intellectuals may "prove to be irresponsible (absent-minded, non-punctual), non-decisive (ultra-judicial, see so many sides that they can never make up their minds), non-persuasive (a little 'queer,' not interested in people)." [62] Moreover, the more men concentrate upon techniques, machines, processes, and abstract knowledge, the more they are "necessarily diverted to a considerable extent from experience with men, organizations and the social situations, the distinctive fields of application of leadership ability." [63] Yet, it is precisely the intellectual qualities which are most suitable for training through formal processes of instruction and education. This is why leaders are now secured chiefly by selection rather than by formal preparation.

Responsible experience in leading is the only fundamental preparation for leadership. Yet, experience is not merely a matter of living through a given number of years in a certain position. Significant experience is obtained only by adaptation and learning—things that do not necessarily come automatically with the passage of time. Moreover, the refined specialization and technical complexity of modern organizational life limit leadership experience to very narrow spheres. Few opportunities exist for general experience in leadership. Hence, we need to develop "artificial methods" of giving wide experience. Apart from suggesting that experience can be gained informally in "extracurricular" activities, Barnard does not develop further the nature of the so-called "artificial methods."

Concern with the training and selection of leaders, however, should not lead one to assume that the capacities of individual leaders are the exclusive component of leadership. Leadership is always a function of "at least three complex variables—the individual, the group of followers, the conditions." The person who may be ideally suited for leadership in certain groups under certain conditions may be entirely unsuitable for the leadership of other groups, or of the same groups under different conditions. Thus, stable conditions call for the qualities of "self-restraint, deliberation and definement of

62. Manuscript.

63. *Ibid.*

technique." On the other hand, conditions of great instability and uncertainty require more in the way of "physical or moral courage, decisiveness, inventiveness, initiative, even audacity." [64]

Barnard identifies *decision-making* as a fundamental part of the administrative process. In so doing he looks at an organization not only as a system of communication but as a system of logical decision-making. In fact, organizational decision-making is far more rational than individual decision-making. In organizations, purposes are formulated with a greater degree of clarity than in the case of individuals. More organizational action is based upon deliberation and calculation rather than upon unconscious and automatic response. Even automatic responses in organizations may be the result of carefully analyzed organizational decisions on procedures and methods.

It is difficult to study organizational decision-making because "there is little direct opportunity to observe the essential operations of decision." [65] Many people participate in any one decision; a single decision is usually merely a small point in a long sequence of decisions. Only a small part of decisions may be identified as a result of formally given orders. Most of them "produce no direct evidence of themselves and . . . knowledge of them can only be derived from cumulation of indirect evidence." [66]

Nevertheless, according to Barnard, it is possible to set forth a few general principles concerning administrative decision-making. First of all, decisions are always made within a framework of certain organizational purposes which themselves embody the product of previous decisions. It is these purposes which make it possible for the decision-maker to operate selectively upon the huge mass of facts which may possibly bear upon his decision. Second, the decision-maker must distinguish between those facts which may affect the accomplishment of an organization's purpose and those which are more or less immaterial. This can be done only through a search for "strategic factors." The strategic factor is "the one

64. *Ibid.*
65. *Ibid.*
66. *Ibid.*

whose control, in the right form, at the right place and time, will establish a new system or set of conditions which meets the purpose. . . . The determination of the strategic factor is itself the decision which at once reduces purpose to a new level, compelling search for a new strategic factor and a new situation." [67]

The aim of technique, according to Barnard, is to assist in the accurate discrimination of strategic facts. "Chemical analysis, mechanical analysis, telescopes, microscopes, statistical processes, balance sheets, are the means by which the strategic factors hidden in the superficial are magnified to observable dimensions and are brought into significant focus." [68] Unfortunately, there has been uneven development of these techniques. The technical methods of discriminating among physical parts of the environment are far more developed than those relating to economic factors. "A similar disparity exists between the economic and the other social factors of the environment. There exists in the social field no such powerful magnifier as the balance sheet which rivets the attention on the significance of the difference between income and outgo, nor any invention of general applicability that approximates in precision money of account that lies back of the balance sheet." [69]

This imbalance in the discrimination of the facts of the environment has serious consequences. Since we have fewer methods of analyzing the present, we often turn to the past instead. Instead of asking what something is *now* worth, we ask, "What did it cost?" Instead of looking at the past and the future as simply a means of trying to understand the present, we often confuse *what has been* with *what is*.

Yet, the solution of this difficulty cannot be found merely in the multiplication of logical technique. It is also essential to develop nonlogical mental processes. These are the processes of mind which are "not capable of being expressed in words or as reasoning. . . . This may be because the processes are unconscious or because they are so complex and so rapid, often approaching the instantaneous,

67. *Ibid.*, p. 203.

68. *Ibid.*, pp. 206-7.

69. *Ibid.*, pp. 207-8.

that they could not be analyzed by the person within whose brain they take place." [70] The rigorous, logical work of the exact scientist, the mathematician, the lawyer, and the accountant is relevant only to materials that consist of precise information. For materials of a speculative type or of a hybrid character, it is to a large degree irrelevant to apply the logical reasoning processes. Such material cannot bear the weight of ponderous logic. Moreover, in organizational situations the mere logical formulation of a problem or statement of a hypothesis may itself have a major effect in changing the situation that is being analyzed and rendering the formulation or the hypothesis inaccurate.

SIMON: THE BEHAVIOR OF ADMINISTRATIVE MAN

The work of the last pioneer on our list, Herbert Simon (1916-   ), can be regarded as a significant extension of that of his immediate predecessors. He goes further than Follett, Mayo, and Roethlisberger in analyzing some of the psychological and social aspects of administration. He picks up and develops some of Barnard's basic ideas on equilibrium, decision-making, communication, and authority. Finally, he extends still further the practice of his predecessors in skipping across interdisciplinary boundaries. Yet, more than any of the other pioneers, Simon is a systematic theory-builder. He gives more attention to rigorous definition and the precise formulation of relationships. He is more concerned with the methodology of the social sciences. In fact, his interest in helping develop a "science of human behavior" has led him to such philosophic considerations as the nature of causality and the "proof" of logical theorems.

Simon's central goal has been to develop a *value-free* science of administrative behavior, if not indeed a "science of man." In his later writings, particularly, he shows little of the warmth and depth of understanding which characterize Follett, Mayo, Roethlisberger, and Barnard. In his effort to escape values, he has much more in common with Taylor and Gulick.

Nevertheless, Simon feels it necessary to sweep away the premature principles of the earlier pioneers. In positive terms he be-

70. *Ibid.*, p. 302.

lieves that a science of man must "accommodate his dual nature as a social and as a rational animal." In the light of this dualism, he rests the foundations of his work on "two principal mechanisms— the mechanism of influence and the mechanism of choice." He believes that the full analysis of these extremely complex mechanisms is impossible without the use of mathematics, which to his ears is "the most dulcet of languages."

Of all the pioneers, Simon has unquestionably been the most prolific. His work includes half a dozen books or monographs and over a hundred journal articles, quite a number of which were written in collaboration with others. His first work on administration was done as a young political scientist working with Clarence Ridley on problems of municipal government. The Simon-Ridley booklet, *Measuring Municipal Activities,* is still a minor classic in municipal administration.[71] Then, at the University of California's Institute of Public Administration, he published various studies on the ideal case load for social workers, the measurement of fire-insurance risks, and metropolitan consolidation. These detailed investigations, together with personal experience in various government agencies, contributed an important underpinning to his two major volumes: *Administrative Behavior, a Study of Decision-making Processes in Administrative Organizations,*[72] and *Public Administration.*[73] Extensions and applications of the views developed in these two volumes are provided in *Models of Man,*[74] a collection of sixteen mathematical journal articles, together with a series of unifying comments, and *Organizations,*[75] a summary in "propositional" form of different approaches to organization theory.

71. Herbert A. Simon and Clarence Ridley, *Measuring Municipal Activities.* Chicago: International City Managers' Association, 1938.

72. Herbert A. Simon, *Administrative Behavior* (preface by Chester I. Barnard). New York: Macmillan Co., 1947. (A second edition, with a new introduction by Simon, was published in 1957.)

73. Herbert A. Simon, Donald Smithburg, Victor Thompson, *Public Administration.* New York: Alfred A. Knopf, 1950.

74. Herbert A. Simon, *Models of Man.* New York: John Wiley & Sons. 1957.

75. James G. March and Herbert A. Simon, *Organizations.* New York: John Wiley & Sons, 1958.

The attack on "classical organization theory."—In their *Organizations*, March and Simon distinguish between classical or traditional organizational theory and subsequent theories which deal with organization members in terms of attitudes and motivations or in terms of decision-making and problem-solving.

The classical theory, in turn, is divided into two parts. "Classical administrative science" is represented by Gulick and Urwick. "Physiological organization theory" is represented by Taylor and his followers.

Simon will long be re-read with pleasure for his zestful, free-swinging attacks on Gulick and Urwick. He brands many of their most sacred principles as homely proverbs, myths, slogans, pompous inanities, and "terms not unlike those used by a Ubangi medicine man to discuss disease." He finds that their work suffers from "superficiality, oversimplification, lack of realism." He charges them with giving too little attention to human motivations, conflicts of interest, information-processing, decision-making, and program formation.

In launching this attack Simon, gave expression to the widespread disenchantment of many people, both academicians and practitioners, who were disturbed by the yawning gulf they often saw between the prescribed principles and effective practice. He, thus unwittingly, contributed to a deep undercurrent of skepticism toward the *possibility* of useful generalization on administration. For his own part, however, he has consistently maintained that valid principles *can* be developed. But this *requires divorcing* administrative theory from value-judgments, developing concepts that can serve as criteria in describing and diagnosing administrative situations, and assigning weight to these criteria. The Gulick-Urwick principles "represent only a fragmentary and unsystematized portion of these criteria."

Although earlier using Taylor's "functional foremanship" in his attack on the unity of command, in *Organizations*, Simon joins with March in criticizing Taylor's "scientific management" as a whole. They refer to this body of thought as limited to such physiological variables as physical capacity, motion, speed, and fatigue.

For March and Simon, "scientific management" would "transform a general-purpose mechanism, such as a person, into a more efficient special-purpose mechanism." [76] In so doing, it concentrates on repetitive tasks involving a minimum of problem-solving and presupposes monetary motivation exclusively. Even within these limitations, it suffers from serious defects. Only in a minority of cases have production engineers succeeded in synthesizing time standards from standard data on component units. Nor have they established clear specifications for data analysis. The human organism, even when regarded as merely a neurophysiological machine, has proved too complex for even the best of Taylor's followers. The ideas of scientific management are probably better adapted to genuine, rather than human, machines. As such, indeed, they have contributed significantly to the development of modern machine building and automation.

The mechanism of influence.—For Simon, the people in organizations are not passive instruments or neutral means, they are decision-making organisms or mechanisms. Yet somehow or other administrators engage in certain types of behavior which cause other types of behavior by these decision-making mechanisms. In other words, administrators exercise "power" or "influence" over them. This is done through actions which affect the environment of decisions by helping to change the factual or value premises on which decisions are based.

The first decision which an organizational participant (whether employee, consumer, or stockholder) must make is *whether or not to participate*, that is, whether or not to contribute his work or money. Here Simon takes Barnard's idea of equilibrium and restates it as follows: "Each participant will remain in the organization if the satisfaction (or utility) he derives from the net balance of inducements over contributions (measured in terms of their utility to *him*) is greater than the satisfaction he could obtain if he withdrew. The 'zero point' in such a 'satisfaction function' is defined, therefore, in terms of the opportunity cost of participation." [77]

Simon defines authority initially as "the power to make decisions which guide the actions of another." But he disputes the traditional

76. *Ibid.*, p. 13.

77. Simon, *Administrative Behavior, op. cit.*, chap. vi.

ideas that authority can be fully understood as a legal phenomenon or that authority is based on formal sanctions alone. He finds that a person will accept orders not merely because of the fear of punishment but also because of willingness to achieve the organization's purpose, a disinclination to accept responsibility, a psychological willingness or desire to follow a leader, or the social sanctions imposed by the group to which he belongs. Moreover, many subordinates will often ask themselves "how would my superior wish me to behave under these circumstances?" He thus anticipates the exercise of authority, a phenomenon referred to as the "rule of anticipated reactions." [78] Under such circumstances authority may be exercised only to reverse an incorrect decision where reactions are improperly anticipated. Where no corrections are made, the evidences of authority in terms of sanctions will be very slight.

Simon defines communications as "any process whereby decisional premises are transmitted from one member of an organization to another." This is a two-way process, including both the transmittal *to* a decisional center and the transmittal of the decisions reached *from* the center to other parts of the organization. This process moves "upward, downward and laterally throughout the organization." Placing much less emphasis than Barnard upon the formal network of authority, Simon finds that informal channels are much more important in the transmission of information.

In *Organizations*, March and Simon summarize recent thinking on individual or group conflict within organizations, with some attention to conflict within individuals and between organizations. They maintain that an organization reacts to conflict by four major processes: problem-solving, persuasion, bargaining, and "politics." They defer problem-solving to their consideration of rational choice and more or less ignore both persuasion and "politics." They survey efforts to develop criteria for bargaining through the theory of games. They come to the pessimistic conclusion that, with rare exceptions, bargaining theory has operated in an empirical vacuum. They maintain that no general theory of bargaining can be developed unless serious empirical research is developed to "match, in

78. Simon, *Administrative Behavior, op. cit.*, p. 129.

terms of energy and competence, the mathematical efforts of the past 10 years." [79]

The mechanism of choice.—In dealing with human choice, Simon settles down to wrestle with his greatest love, the decision-making process. For him the theory of administration and a theory of rational choice depend one upon the other. On the one hand, human behavior in organizations is "intendedly" rational. On the other hand, most rational decision-making takes place in social groups. Or, put another way, the purpose of organizations is to compensate for the limited rationality of individuals. The purpose of administrative theory is to fill a gap in the rationality of organizations.

Nor is Simon at all satisfied with the theories of choice developed in economics, the theory of games, or statistical decision-making. In his later writings, he smites them hew and thigh with all the zest with which he had earlier attacked Gulick and Urwick. He then sets out seriously on his own road toward developing a theory of human choice.

Simon slices the process of individual and group decision-making into the following phases:

1. The perception of behavior alternatives.
2. The anticipation of various consequences resulting from different behavior alternatives.
3. The evaluation of these consequences in terms of the "satisfaction," "utility," or "welfare" they may yield.
4. The selection of one or another behavior alternatives on the basis of the foregoing evaluation.

Simon maintains that the theories of rational choice contained in the economists' theory of the firm and in statistical decision-making are all founded upon at least three unrealistic assumptions: (*a*) the assumption that the decision-maker is omniscient concerning the existence of all possible alternatives and the future consequences of all possible alternatives, or at least the probability distribution of consequences of each alternative; (*b*) the assumption of the unlimited computational ability of the decision-maker; and (*c*) the assumption that every one carries in his head a complete and consistent

79. March and Simon, *Organization, op. cit.*, p. 134.

preference-ordering of all possible consequences. Simon asserts that any theory based on such assumptions is fundamentally wrong as either a descriptive or a normative model. He supports this position by demonstrating that the assumption of rationality in the economics of the firm leads not to "a unique determinate solution but to a whole set of 'viable solutions.' " [80] Of all possible alternatives, people perceive only a few. Of all possible consequences, they only predict a few and may be wrong at that. Nor is the aspirational level inflexible. "As the individual in his exploration of alternatives finds it *easy* to discover satisfactory alternatives his aspirational level rises; as he finds it *difficult* to discover satisfactory alternatives his aspirational level falls." [81] Thus, he need not compare marginal increments in order to get the maximum results. Instead of insisting upon "optimal" solutions, he is satisfied with "good enough" or "somehow muddling through." Since he has not the wit to "maximize," he is obliged to "satisfice."

It is clear that, for Simon, the administrator's task is influencing the decision-making process. Administrative activity determines not the content of an organization's work, but rather "how the decision-making function is to be advocated and influenced in that particular organization." Nevertheless, sound organizational decisions require knowledge of the content. Moreover, administrators are also involved in the activity (which Simon prefers to call non-administrative) of working on content itself.

This leads Simon to two conclusions concerning the training of higher administrators. First, subject-matter competence is essential except at the very highest levels of the hierarchy. Second, the proper training of genuine administrators lies, not in the narrow fields of administrative theory, but in the broader fields of the social sciences generally.

Measurement and mathematics.—Simon has probably gone farther than anyone else in applying advanced mathematical analysis to the social sciences. His interest in the subject was first revealed in his work on municipal affairs in which he and Ridley tried to

80. Simon, *Models of Man, op. cit.*, pp. 197-98.

81. *Ibid.*, p. 253.

identify the units of output for local municipal departments of fire, police, and public health. Unfortunately, this important work was not systematically continued. His later work on the mathematical analysis of influence and decision-making is on an incomparably higher level of elegance and maturity, although less directly related to concrete administrative problems. Here he still searches for units of measurement but is now prepared to use not only cardinal numbers but also ordinal numbers and vectors. He also carries mathematical analysis to a point where he is involved much less with measurement than with symbolic logic.

Against those who may regard his mathematical approach to administration as esoteric, Simon vigorously defends his position. Mathematical language, he maintains, makes it much easier to handle a large number of variables, thus avoiding the many logical gaps and unstated assumptions of verbal language. Because of the ease of manipulation, it is also psychologically advantageous.

Simon is quick to confess the poverty of mathematical resources in their application to the social sciences. But this is an honest poverty, in contrast with the pretensions of verbal languages. "If this poverty is less visible in nonmathematical theorizing, it is because it never becomes explicit and not because it is absent." [82]

As Simon sails off into the stratosphere of abstract mathematical speculation, one might easily come to the conclusion that he has left far behind him the mundane ideas with which his predecessors were occupied. And yet when one examines his latest writings closely, one can see in his emphasis upon mechanisms and measurements at least a partial return to the spirit of Taylor and of "physiological organization theory." When one contemplates his model of intendedly rational man "muddling through" as he balances conflicting considerations, one cannot help but suspect that this is a sophisticated way of saying that man acts in accordance with proverbs. In this sense the iconoclast of an earlier generation comes back, somewhat older, to worship at the feet of the idols he once set out to destroy.

The difference, of course, is that Simon's mechanistic approach

82. *Ibid.,* p. 94.

operates at a higher level. It is buoyed up by the achievements of experimental psychology, learning theory, and information theory. It is expressed with exquisite mathematical refinement. How much it may bring to the theory and practice of administration, it is too early to tell. Too much should not be expected too quickly. The adventure is a difficult one. Nor will the world be the loser if it turns out that his future contributions to human knowledge should be less in administration and more in mathematics and machine-building.

CHAPTER IV

Historical Change of the Role of the Man in the Organization: 1865-1950

RAYMOND E. CALLAHAN
and
H. WARREN BUTTON

In this chapter an attempt will be made to briefly describe historic American concepts of school administration. These concepts have been based on general philosophies of education and have been influenced by prevailing public thought of their time. Descriptions of these are presented as background for this chapter.

Although it is sometimes so alleged by administrator-harried teachers, the first administrator did not appear on Tuesday of the first week of operation of the first school in America. There was no need for school administration until there were sizable schools and school districts and a consequent need for the co-ordination of activities. Until after the Civil War, the school administrator was a rarity. In 1870 there was only a handful of city superintendents, and their duties were limited; most often they served only as clerks to the board and administered teacher examinations.[1] There were about two dozen state superintendents by 1870, and their duties also were usually limited.

The Administrator as Philosopher-Educator, 1865-1900

Shortly after 1870, as the number of administrators began to increase rapidly, some little thought was given to the nature of the organization of schools and school systems. Representative of this

---

1. United States Bureau of Education, "School Supervision," *Report of the Commissioner of Education Made to the Secretary of the Interior, with Accompanying Papers*, pp. 434-37. Washington: Government Printing Office, 1870.

first development were E. E. White,[2] W. N. Hailman,[3] and Francis Wayland Parker.[4] Although they arrived at their conclusions by somewhat different paths, they would have agreed that the purpose of the school was to develop the innate abilities of each individual pupil. Education was a process of "unfolding," a development of the unique qualities of each individual. The accomplishment of this development was an art, and the teacher was to be an artist. "[Methods] must bear the impress of the teacher's image, and pulsate with the life which he breathes into it," said White. Parker's and Hailman's beliefs were similar.

But even as White, Parker, and Hailman were writing and speaking, the circumstances in which administrators found themselves were changing. Enrolment in the elementary schools was increasing rapidly, particularly in the large cities. We lack what seems to be a completely adequate explanation of this. Undoubtedly, one reason was the rapid growth of the cities themselves in the early stages of our growing urbanization. The growth of industry and commerce gave elementary education a dollar value it had not had when the economically self-sufficient farm had been more nearly universal. In any event, the size of enrolment and the rate of increase in enrolment made new and more demands upon the organization and administration of the school.

The rapidly increasing number of centralized city systems provided tests of and rewards for administrators.[5] The value of a ra-

2. White expressed his views several times. Typical are: "Proceedings of the Ohio Superintendent's Association," *National Teacher*, I (1871), 515; "The Freedom of the Teacher," *National Teacher*, I (1870), 67-69; Emerson E. White, "School Supervision" [continued], *Fifty-fourth Annual Meeting of the American Institute of Instruction: Lectures, Discussions, and Proceedings*, pp. 185-94. (Boston: the Institute, Board of Directors, 1884).

3. W. N. Hailman, "Emancipation of Teachers," *Education*, II (March, 1882), 339-45.

4. *Notes of Talks on Teaching, Given by Francis W. Parker* ... Reported by Leila E. Patridge (New York: E. L. Kellogg & Co., 1883; published in 1903, and subsequently, with title: *Talks on Teaching*); Francis W. Parker, "The School of the Future," *National Education Association Journal of Proceedings and Addresses* (Session of the Year 1891) (New York: the Association, 1891).

5. It appears that the highly centralized city system was primarily a western innovation and spread eastward. This development and movement needs to be investigated.

tionale of administration which supported centralized control increased. New figures in administration came into prominence.

Typical of those writing about a new concept of school administration were William Torrey Harris and William H. Payne. Less well known, perhaps, but holding similar views were N. A. Calkins, Andrew Edson, and Josiah L. Pickard. Harris had become superintendent of the St. Louis system in 1868. After twelve years in that city, he retired to Concord, Massachusetts, to study and teach philosophy. In 1889 he was named United States Commissioner of Education, a post he held until 1906. In addition to his prominence as an educator, he was undoubtedly the leading American Hegelian philosopher. As a writer, he was enormously productive; as an administrator, he was interested in the problem of school organization.

Payne was superintendent of schools in Adrian, Michigan, in 1875 when he wrote *Chapters on School Supervision,* the first book dealing with what we know as educational administration. He was appointed professor of education at the University of Michigan in 1879 and taught there what has been claimed to be the first college-level course in school administration. Later, Payne was president of Peabody Institute. Before his death in 1907, he returned to the University of Michigan. While Harris was a thoroughgoing philosopher, Payne tended to be eclectic, to draw as a scholar upon various sources, religious and secular.

Generally, the philosophies of education of Harris and Payne were similar. They were idealists, in the Platonic sense. For them, the first problem of the superintendent was to discover by philosophical or scholarly inquiry the appropriate purposes of and methods for education. (Sears would later differentiate between the power of knowledge and the power of authority; for the school of thought represented by Harris and Payne, this was a unity.) Purpose and method would be discovered by the superintendent whose superior knowledge fitted him for this task. Then it only remained to execute the superintendent's plans. There was little specialized knowledge and skill involved in the process, and hence there was little to be gained by establishing staff positions. The principal was the deputy of the superintendent, transmitting directives and seeing that they were carried out. Teaching was defined as making the pupil master small daily doses of the accumulated knowledge selected by the superintendent. The nature of the individual pupil, which had been the first concern of White, Hailman, and Parker, was of less concern to Harris and Payne. The pupil was judged to be a potentially rational being and was to be molded to fit the requirements of society. The task of the teacher was simply to retail knowledge to a captive audience. For this, the teacher needed knowledge only of that which was to be retailed.[6] Although there was some similarity in the American and German concepts of school organization and administration and, although there was knowledge of German school administrative practice in this country, it appears that the development of administration here was little influenced by outside forces. The development was largely indigenous.

The pattern of school organization advocated and then employed could be defended on the grounds of effectiveness and practical necessity. The education of teachers, general and professional, was in fact limited; few teachers even in the cities had more than twelve years of formal education. The most urgent objective of the schools was simple literacy. The high rate of early drop-out frequently almost precluded the attainment of other goals. In these circumstances, it could be argued that the decisions made by the teacher ought logically to be kept at a minimum, since the tasks of the teacher did not require the making of decisions and his limited knowledge did not enable him to make sound ones.

The Transition Period, 1900-1913

Beginning about 1900, the conception of the role of the chief administrator of the schools began to change. This change occurred not because of any change in the nature of the work of the teachers (Harris, and others, shunted aside suggestions that psychological knowledge was pertinent for the teacher) nor because of any basic changes in the purpose of the school. Rather, the changes were a direct result of the impact of powerful social forces on the one side

6. See Payne's test for the selection of teachers: William H. Payne, *Chapters in School Supervision* . . . (Cincinnati, 1875), pp. 38, 40-41. New York: Wilson, Hinkle & Co., 1875.

and the weakness of educators, especially the public school superintendent, on the other.[7]

In this period as in the decades immediately preceding it, the greatest force was industrialization—the application of mechanical power to the production of goods. Of great influence also was the economic philosophy of the free-enterprise, capitalistic system under which industrialism developed in America. The great material achievements of industrial capitalism in the late nineteenth century were directly responsible for two developments which were to have a great effect on American society and education after 1900. One of these was the rise of the business and industrial group to a position of great prestige and influence, resulting in the subsequent saturation of America with business-industrial values and practices. The other was the great reform movement identified historically with Theodore Roosevelt and spearheaded by the muckraking journalists.

The strength of business values in American society at the turn of the century made it inevitable that these values would greatly influence educational administration, but the extent of this influence was increased by certain aspects of the great reform crusade which occurred at this time. The reform movement was primarily an attempt to cope with the problems which were a product of rapid industrialization; the consolidation of industry and the concentration of wealth; the ruthless exploitation of the country's natural resources; the corruption and inefficiency which existed in government; the tremendous growth of urban centers; the flood of immigrants who added to the complexity of the social and political problems of cities in which most of them settled; and finally, the fear among the middle-class groups that America would react to these problems in an extreme or radical way. This reaction had, of course, been predicted by Karl Marx and had been realized, to an extent, in the growth of the various forms of socialism in America.

That genuine problems existed in American society at the turn

7. This is due to the pattern of local support and control which characterizes the American public schools. Without tenure and being dependent on the good will of the school board and powerful groups in the community not only for his job but also for adequate financial support, the administrator in the schools is especially vulnerable.

of the century, there can be no doubt. But the generation of wide-spread public enthusiasm and indignation necessary to give force to a reform movement in a democratic society required that the public be aroused and informed. This function was performed effectively by the muckraking journalists whose articles appeared in the low-priced periodicals. S. S. McClure demonstrated in 1902-03 that exposure of corruption and waste was profitable, and other popular journals followed his lead. In the next decade, America was flooded with exposures by the muckrakers, as every aspect of American life came under attack to such extent that even the most complacent were prodded into discontent. Some of the muckrakers, such as Steffens, Baker, and Tarbell, combined the accuracy and thoroughness of the research scholar with the qualities of a good reporter. Others, however, were neither so painstaking nor so responsible, and many of the articles were nothing more than sensational. From this time on one of the realities of life for public school administrators was the existence of a powerful, profit-seeking (and not always responsible) press which was capable through its mass circulation of stirring the American people to action.

As Richard Hofstadter has pointed out, the muckrakers were politically moderate men, not radicals, and they were working in a period, despite its problems, of general prosperity.[8] They did not intend to stir the American people to drastic action which would transform American society. They did not attack the business system; indeed, and very important to our story, *their solution of many of the problems was through the application of modern business methods.* This was especially true in regard to corruption and inefficiency in government. So the business ideology was spread continuously into the bloodstream of American life. It was strengthened, not weakened, by the muckrakers as they extolled "modern business methods" and "efficiency" and connected these with progress and reform in the public mind. It was, therefore, quite natural for Americans, when they came to reforming the schools, to apply business methods to achieve their ends.

By 1910, after years of subjection to the steadily growing busi-

8. Richard Hofstadter, *"The Age of Reform,* p. 196. New York: Alfred A. Knopf, Inc., 1955.

ness influence and about the time that the momentum of reform had reached its peak and Americans had become accustomed to a critical view of all their institutions, the schools, especially in the larger cities, were facing problems that would have taxed a professionally excellent, richly endowed, educational system. No such system existed, and the schools and teachers available were overwhelmed by the new problems which arose. Some fourteen million immigrants had come to America between 1865 and 1900. After 1900, they came at a rate of about one million per year. The majority of these people remained in the eastern cities where their children were entered— with increasing frequency because of the improvements in child labor laws and compulsory-attendance legislation—into the public schools. Coming predominantly from the poorest socioeconomic groups in southern and eastern Europe, these uprooted, non-English-speaking children from semiliterate families with diverse cultural backgrounds created an educational problem of great magnitude and most serious import.

On the physical side alone, thousands of additional classrooms and teachers were needed. Even without the flood of immigration, greater expenditures for education had become necessary due to the normal increase in population and the increasing responsibilities placed upon the schools. With the vast numbers of new students, taxes had to be raised greatly to provide even the minimum essentials. Unfortunately, this need for large increases in school funds occurred not only at a time when the country had been roused to a concern for economy and conditioned to suspect that all public institutions were inefficient and wasteful but also in an inflationary period in which the cost of living had risen more than 30 per cent. The result was that administrators, who needed additional funds, were forced to deal with a suspicious, economy-minded public which wanted to cut costs.

It is against this background of social and educational conditions that an event must be seen which was to have far-reaching consequences for educational administration. This was the spectacular entrance upon the American scene, in the autumn of 1910, of Frederick Taylor and his system of scientific management. In the months and years that followed, the country was saturated with hundreds of articles, and scores of books were written on scientific management and efficiency. As a result, the country became even more efficiency-conscious. Demands were made that Taylor's system be applied to education, and these were always coupled with statements concerning the financial savings which would be forthcoming.[9]

The publicity given to the scientific management movement and the great claims made in its behalf intensified the feeling on the part of the public that great waste existed everywhere and that means were at hand for eliminating it. One result was that a new wave of criticism was directed against many institutions, and especially those which were large enough to be suspected of gross managerial inefficiency and those which were supported by public taxation. The schools, particularly in the larger cities, qualified for criticism on both of these criteria. Beginning early in 1911, hardly a month passed for two years in which articles complaining about the schools were not published either in popular or in professional journals. Gradually the criticism grew in volume, reaching a peak in the summer and fall of 1912. In these months a series of incendiary articles were published in two of the popular journals with tremendous circulations, *The Saturday Evening Post* and *The Ladies Home Journal*.[10] In June, 1913, the editor of the *American School Board Journal* reported, "*No recent year has seen such wholesale changes in superintendencies and other high school positions as the present year—1913. In the Middle-West there has been a perfect storm of unrest culminating in wholesale resignations, dismissals and new appointments.*"[11]

The School Administrator as Business Manager, 1913-15

So far as the conception of the nature of administration and especially of the superintendency was concerned, there was evidence of change from the notion of the administrator as scholar-statesman, or at least a teacher of teachers, to that of a business manager even

9. For a detailed account of the Taylor system, its introduction into American society, and its influence on educational administration, see Raymond E. Callahan, *Education and the Cult of Efficiency: A Study of the Social Forces That Have Shaped the Administration of the Public Schools*. Chicago: University of Chicago Press, 1962.

10. For an account of the nature and extent of this criticism, see *ibid.*, chap. iii.

11. *American School Board Journal*, XLVI (June, 1913), 28.

before the efficiency mania hit the country late in 1910. This change is evident in the reports of professional meetings, in the journals, and in major books on administration by W. E. Chancellor in 1904 and 1908.[12] This change was probably a natural result of the rapid growth of city school systems into mass organizations, the growing admiration for the managers of large business and industry, and the increasing tendency to apply business concepts to all areas of human experience. Even so, Chancellor does at times refer to the superintendent as a scholar and at one point writes that his relationship to the school board "stands somewhat as an attorney to a client." [13] And Dutton and Snedden in their text, which was published in 1908 and which was rivaled only by Chancellor's book as the most important textbook on educational administration before 1910, present the superintendent as an educational leader and statesman who needed, above all, a broad liberal and professional education.[14]

The difference between the two concepts of administration was brought to the attention of educators in March, 1910. The occasion was a meeting of the National Society of College Teachers of Education, which was devoted to a consideration of university study of educational administration. The main paper was read by Frank Spaulding, superintendent of schools in Newton, Massachusetts. Charging that the administration of public education was "grossly inefficient" and "the weakest phase of our great educational enterprise," he urged that the training of the administrator emphasize the practical aspects of the job and be based on "simple and sound business principles." [15] Spaulding's paper was criticized by William Burris, dean of the College for Teachers of the University of Cincinnati, who argued that the administrator of the highest type was "first of all a philosopher." [16] Paul Hanus, professor of education at

12. Willard Estabrook Chancellor, *Our Schools: Their Administration and Supervision* (Boston: D. C. Heath, 1904); *Our City Schools: Their Direction and Management* (Boston: D. C. Heath & Co., 1908).

13. *Our Schools, op. cit.*, p. 10.

14. Samuel T. Dutton and David Snedden, *The Administration of Public Education in the United States*, chap. xiv. New York: Macmillan Co., 1908.

15. Frank E. Spaulding, *The Aims, Scope, and Method of a University Course in Public School Administration*, pp. 3-26. Iowa City, Iowa: National Society of College Teachers of Education, 1910.

16. *Ibid.*, p. 72.

Harvard and the man who planned the program, was disappointed because of the criticism of Spaulding's paper and was discouraged because many members of the group "were apparently looking for the principles of school administration elsewhere than in administration." This fact, he said, lent support to the cynic's view that "most of us are not yet ready to study school administration, much less to give a university course in that subject." [17]

Ready or not, in the years immediately following, educators were forced to devote a great deal of attention to administration, and not only courses but whole programs were developed in that field in the universities. On the question of what the nature of these courses should be, the issue was decided in Spaulding's favor, and not by the logic of his argument but by the course of events. The American people, stirred by sensational criticisms in the popular magazines and convinced that the schools were grossly inefficient (many leading educators had boarded the critics' bandwagon), demanded administrators who could operate the schools efficiently, and by "efficiently" they meant economically. At the first meeting of the Department of Superintendence of the National Education Association after the storm of criticism descended, it was Spaulding, not Burris, who was invited to give a major address. His topic was "Improving School Systems through Scientific Management." [18]

Despite the title, Spaulding's version of scientific management bore little resemblance to Taylor's scheme. What he did was to report on the procedures which he had used with great success in Newton. These consisted of ways and means of lowering costs. He had eliminated small classes, increased the size of others, and reduced the number of classes offered. The result was that fewer teachers were needed, but those who remained had a heavier pupil load. In his presentation, Spaulding used several graphs and charts which, together with his title, provided a façade of "science" over what was essentially simple cost accounting. Although a conception of the role of the administrator was obvious from his remarks, he

17. Paul H. Hanus, "Editorial Notes," *School Review*, XVIII (June, 1910), 426-27.

18. Frank E. Spaulding, "Improving School Systems through Scientific Management," *Proceedings of the Department of Superintendence, National Education Association, 1913*, pp. 249-79. Washington: National Education Association, 1913.

dealt with the problem directly only at the very end of his address. He criticized those educators who advocated separating the business aspects of administration from the educational. These men, he said, "give evidence of about as sound and comprehensive a grasp of the real problem of educational administration as the would-be manufacturer of shoes must have of industry who would put his factory in charge of two independent experts. . . ." [19]

Whatever harmful educational consequences ensued from Spaulding's practices (and questions on this point were brushed aside) his conception of administration and his recommendations for practice made sense to men who were trying to keep their jobs. Superintendents who adopted his suggestions were able to reduce education to financial terms and to meet their economy-minded critics on their own ground. At the same time, by giving to the work of the administrator the appearance of scientific respectability, Spaulding not only contributed to the improvement of the status of the administrator but also provided him with a professional rationalization for an overemphasis upon the financial aspects of education. And if there were any who doubted the effectiveness of Spaulding's approach, he could dispel his doubts by noting Spaulding's successful career. He had kept his job at Newton, which had the reputation of being the "burial ground of superintendents," for ten years at a salary of $4,000.[20] In Massachusetts, only the superintendency at Boston paid more.[21] In 1914 he was appointed superintendent at Minneapolis at $8,000 per year. Three years later he moved to Cleveland at an annual salary of $12,000.[22]

The other major effort to change educational administration over to the business-industrial model was made by John Franklin Bobbitt. The ideas were presented in the Twelfth Yearbook of the National Society for the Study of Education. In this volume, published early in 1913, Bobbitt applied to educational administration some of the major elements of Taylor's system of management,

19. *Ibid.*

20. Frank E. Spaulding, *School Superintendent in Action in Five Cities,* pp. 222-23. West Rindge, New Hampshire: Richard R. Smith, Publisher, Inc., 1955.

21. *Ibid.,* p. 382.

22. *American School Board Journal,* LIV (February, 1917), 61.

which had been dramatically introduced to the public in 1910. Administration was to be based on a body of science, but the administrator was the chief interpreter of that science, which he used in making all major decisions; setting standards for the "product"; determining the task to be performed and the incentive (salary) to be provided; determining the methods of instruction, together with providing detailed instruction for the use of the "workers"; selecting and training the "workers"; and choosing tools and appliances to be used. Like Taylor, Bobbitt believed that efficiency depended on "centralization of authority and definite direction by the supervisors of all processes performed." Both systems reduced the "workers" to automatons and placed heavy responsibility for "production" on management. For Bobbitt, purpose and economy determined organization and teacher role.

The evidence from the professional journals shows that it was Spaulding's ideas, not Bobbitt's, which were accepted by most of the men who wrote on educational administration after 1913. The reasons for this are rather obvious. His ideas were easy to apply and they got the job done, i.e., economy was achieved and the schools had the *appearance* of being run efficiently. Bobbitt's system required an elaborate and expensive research and planning division. Even the largest school system had neither the money nor the talent for such an operation. Besides, the public was not primarily concerned with real efficiency (even if we grant that Bobbitt's system would have produced it) but with cost. Furthermore, although Bobbitt's work produced little public opposition within the profession (in fact, one of the leaders in educational administration, Ellwood Cubberley, praised his work), his description of children as raw material and products and of teachers as workers was undoubtedly too extreme even for politically conscious, business-oriented administrators. But it was difficult to publicly oppose the sacred cow, scientific management, in 1913. Probably Bobbitt's work contributed in a general way to the acceptance by administrators of the business-industrial organizational patterns in education, and his effort certainly strengthened the authoritarian concept of administration.

The School Executive and His Professional Preparation, 1915-29

By 1915, a great change in educational administration was well under way, and in the next decade the basic patterns were extended and institutionalized through the development of graduate programs in administration. The two men who led in this development were Ellwood Cubberley, dean of the School of Education at Stanford, and George Strayer, professor of educational administration at Teachers College, Columbia. Cubberley's major influence was exerted through his texts, especially his *Public School Administration* published in 1916, while Strayer's influence was exerted through his teaching and research direction at Teachers College and through the many major surveys which he directed.

Cubberley's conception of administration as presented in his 1916 textbook is an interesting combination of the ideas of Chancellor, Dutton and Snedden, Spaulding, and Bobbitt. The superintendent is pictured as a heroic, almost superhuman figure. His is the office "up to which and down from which authority, direction, and inspiration flow." He is "the organizer and director of the work of the schools in all their different phases. . . ." He is "the executive officer of the school board, and also its eyes, and ears, and brains." He is "the supervisor of the instruction in the schools, and also the leader, adviser, inspirer, and friend of the teachers." [23] On the other hand, little attention is given to the teachers and this is directed toward the mechanical aspects of their selection and management by the supervisory staff. In some respects, Cubberley's system of administration can be described as benevolent authoritarianism. His superintendent is not a scholar or a philosopher, but neither is he Bobbitt's engineer nor Spaulding's cost accountant, although much of his text is devoted to the financial and mechanical aspects of education. He is, rather, an executive, a director of large enterprises, one might almost say a captain of education. As he is described by Cubberley he would be almost identical, trait by trait, to the paragons of virtue, energy, and ability who constitute the ideal "successful" men in the success-story literature.[24]

23. Ellwood P. Cubberley, *Public School Administration*, p. 132. Boston: Houghton Mifflin Co., 1916.

24. Compare, for example, the personal qualities which Cubberley (*op. cit.*, pp. 137-38) describes as being necessary with those listed by Orison Marden in *A Young Man Entering Business* (New York: Thomas Y. Crowell & Co., 1907).

Cubberley did not discuss teachers as factory-workers, as Bobbitt did, but neither did he discuss them as professional workers. They are treated, rather, in a humane and paternalistic way.[25] If the administrator filled the role Cubberley set out for him, the teacher was not to make professional decisions. He might advise, but his role was a subordinate one. Perhaps, since the purpose and task of the school was a more complicated one than three decades before, the teacher was expected to have more skills; still, he was a technician, rather than a professional person.

In the 1920's, probably the most influential figure in the development of administration was George Strayer, the leader in educational administration at the institution which awarded more advanced degrees in administration than all other graduate schools in the country between 1910 and 1930. He was the first to apply Thorndike's basic statistical techniques to the work of educational administration, and he sought to achieve for his graduate program the professional respectability of medicine and law. In this he fell far short, and by 1925 it was clear that the work at Teachers College was clearly lacking in the scientific and scholarly foundations essential for a high-quality professional school.[26] What emerged, instead, was a fairly high-level service station which provided students with the practical skills (primarily in finance, business management, public relations, and "plant" management) which enabled them to acquire and keep jobs in a business society.

There were several factors responsible for this development. Most important was Strayer's conception of the nature of professional training and the translation of this conception into a program for preparing school administrators. Strayer believed, along with Spaulding and his dean at Teachers College, James E. Russell, that professional training should provide the student with the specific

25. See, for example, Cubberley's chapter, "The Teaching Corps," in *Public School Administration, op. cit.*

26. Evidence for this statement can be seen in the nature and quality of the doctoral dissertations in administration done at Teachers College between 1910 and 1930 or in the types of problems included and the manner in which they are handled in the volume entitled *Problems in Educational Administration*, which Strayer produced (with N. L. Engelhardt *et al.*) in 1925.

skills he needed to do the job. Russell, for example, in writing about medicine stated that "the binding of a wound or the tying of an artery is not a superlative test of intelligence, but no medical school thinks of graduating a physician without giving that ability." [27] He argued that there was "no room for academic instruction in a professional curriculum once professional training really begins." [28] and, he said, "no professional school should be controlled by an academic or research faculty." [29]

Strayer applied these ideas to the graduate work in administration at Teachers College. He believed that students should have experience in drawing graphs, in operating calculating machines and film projectors, and in making entries and checking accounts.[30] And this emphasis upon the specific and immediate tasks was carried to the doctoral dissertation as Strayer contended that "there is no detail of the work of the administrator that may not properly become the subject of intensive investigation by those who are candidates for the doctors' degree in the professional school." [31] The result was an emphasis upon the techniques and the mechanics of administration. While this kind of program did not require extensive study in the disciplines upon which a real understanding of education must be based and was not oriented toward basic inquiry and the production of knowledge, it did provide students with the knowledge and skills necessary to operate the schools in a business-like way—a prerequisite for job survival in most school districts in

27. James E. Russell, *The Trend in American Education*, p. 232. New York: American Book Co., 1922.

28. *Ibid.*, p. 226.

29. *Ibid.*, p. 233.

30. George D. Strayer, "Professional Training of School Executives in the University," *National Education Association Proceedings of the Sixty-sixth Annual Meeting*, pp. 755-60. Washington: National Education Association, 1928. (Also in Department of Superintendence, National Education Association, *Official Report, 1928*, pp. 96-100.)

31. George D. Strayer, N. L. Engelhardt, and Others, *Problems in Educational Administration*, p. viii. New York: Bureau of Publications, Teachers College, Columbia University, 1925.

the twenties.[32] However, it is interesting to note that the great majority of these men who were trained as practitioners went into college or university teaching.[33]

There were other factors which operated to make the establishment of a high quality professional school at Teachers College difficult. The dedication to service and to meeting the needs of society had been a part of the school's philosophy since its founding.[34] This commitment was manifested not only in the work in administration but also in the large number of courses which were offered in the practical arts. These offerings were so extensive that one of the school's historians noted that programs were offered to prepare students "for every sort of educational work imaginable." [35]

Equally important and, in part, making it all possible was the fact that Teachers College had, for all practical purposes, cut its ties with Columbia University. President Nicholas Murray Butler tried, in 1914, to bring Teachers College into the University, as had been done with the medical school. Butler believed and stated that there was "no place outside of a university for a high-grade professional school of any kind. . . ." His effort failed and Teachers College became a "sovereign state" very loosely connected to the University.[36] This meant that the College was free to set its own standards. It also made it difficult for the school to draw upon the resources, both scholarly and financial, of the University. Lacking financial support, the most important institution in professional education was forced to operate almost entirely on tuition income.[37] For this reason and also because of its service orientation, the administration of Teachers College encouraged and accepted increases in student enrolment. By 1926-27, Teachers College had 5,333 students; and

---

32. See Callahan, *op. cit.*, chap. viii.

33. *Ibid.*, pp. 248-49. See also, Lawrence A. Cremin, David A. Shannon, and Mary Evelyn Townsend, *A History of Teachers College, Columbia University*, p. 119. New York: Columbia University Press, 1954.

34. See Cremin, Shannon, and Townsend, *op. cit.*, chaps. i and iv.

35. *Ibid.*, p. 114.

36. *Ibid.*, pp. 71-73.

37. *Ibid.*, p. 120.

in that year, 1,383 Master's degrees were awarded.[38] So Teachers College became a mass-production institution with a student body made up largely of part-time students[39]— a development in sharp contrast to other types of professional schools and one that made a high quality of work extremely difficult to achieve.

A Search for New Concepts of School Administration, 1930-50

In the 1930's, concepts of administration shifted in two respects. First, there was a reappearing interest in the purpose of public education as a proper concern of the administrator and as a predicator of school organization and administration. Second, there was less interest in supervision and teaching effectiveness. However, there was continued attention to the management and operation of the school, and continued investigation and exposition in such areas as finance, public relations, school plant. In these fields the techniques and procedures borrowed or adapted from business methods were still applied.

The reappearance of interest in purpose grew, perhaps, from popular interest in social planning during the depression of the 1930's. The status of the businessman was not, of course, as high during this period as it had been in the preceding decades, and perhaps this too acted to alter the rationale of school administration. The administrators' reawakening social conscience is reflected by the titles of the yearbooks of the Department of Superintendence at the time. The eleventh yearbook, in 1933, was *Educational Leadership* and was dedicated to William Torrey Harris, whose name had gone unspoken for a quarter-century. The thirteenth yearbook, in 1935, was *Social Change in Education*. Another statement of the relevance to the administrator of the purpose of the school and the problems of society was Newlon's *Educational Administration as Social Policy*.[40] Possibly it marks the apogee in the 1930's of that interest.

38. *Ibid.*, pp. 115-16.

39. *Ibid.*, p. 118.

40. Jesse H. Newlon, *Educational Administration as a Social Policy*. New York: Chas. Scribner's Sons, 1934.

There are several tentative explanations for the decrease of interest by writers on administration in the supervision of teachers. In general, the empirical investigations of the preceding decade in the field of teacher effectiveness had not been fruitful. Attempts to replicate experiments and substantiate findings had generally not been successful; it was not possible to generalize from research in this area.[41] The problems of supervision and of teaching method were not readily amenable to investigation in the management frame of reference nor with the techniques available. Second, the field of supervision had become one of the major interests of a new group of specialists and of a new organization, the Association for Supervision and Curriculum Development (this is the latest of several names). The rationale for relating supervision with curriculum development in brief explanation was this: If the purpose of supervision is to improve instruction, and if the means of improving instruction is by curriculum development, then supervision becomes largely a matter of aiding in curriculum development.

A prominent and seemingly typical figure in the continuing inquiry in administration during the 1930's and early 1940's was Arthur B. Moehlman. He was an administrator in Detroit in the 1920's; later he was professor of educational administration at the University of Michigan. He was one of the most industrious and prolific scholars in the field of education since Harris, and his bibliography includes literally hundreds of items. He published in the fields of the history of education, school finance, "social interpretation" or public relations, the school survey, child accounting, and school plants, to name a few which come to mind. As editor of *The Nation's Schools*, he expressed himself on almost every topic related to school administration and management. His knowledge of the literature in the fields in which he was interested was encyclopedic. His *School Administration* presents a statement of his views in 1940. It opens with one hundred and twenty pages devoted to a consideration of the school in the light of its social environment,

41. For research on teacher effectiveness to about 1935, see, for example, Gilbert L. Betts, "Education of Teachers Evaluated through Evaluation of Teacher Ability," *National Survey of the Education of Teachers*, V, *Special Teacher Studies*, pp. 87-154. United States Office of Education Bulletin, 1933, No. 10. Washington: Government Printing Office, 1935.

before going on to the formulation and presentation of sixteen "principles of organization." These principles were "derived from the purposes of education and generally accepted practice." There is no clear distinction as to which source supplied each principle, but apparently most of them were based primarily on the latter. Although their purpose was to serve as a taxonomy, they were certainly imperfect for that purpose. They did, however, provide part of the framework for the book, served to unify its presentation, and had didactic value at least. Within this framework, the matters dealt with were generally those which had been of concern in the preceding decade; school boards, child accounting, plant, textbooks, finance, and so on. Interestingly, a brief definition of administration[42] in the body of the book does not refer to the purpose of the school; the administrator was still a manager, proficient in the techniques of management and school operation.[43]

It may have been, however, that Moehlman's attempt to reanalyze school administration was a step toward the concepts of administration and related empirical research to which most of this book is devoted. The treatment of administration by Mort[44] and Sears[45] in 1946 and 1950, respectively, seem to rise logically from the same general sort of approach as that employed by Moehlman. Each saw administration as mediating between classroom teaching-learning and the purpose or function of the school, and each made a considerable attempt to develop systemic concepts of administration. Mort's and Sears' approaches both appear flawed now. Mort relied too heavily upon "common sense," and Sears upon "authority." Neither term is adequately defined; they were "primitives" upon which expositions rested rather precariously.

Considering the variety of concepts of administration current or employed over the last century, it may be possible to make a few

42. Arthur B. Moehlman, *School Administration*, p. 261. Boston: Houghton Mifflin Co., 1940.

43. For a detailed treatment, see Callahan, *op. cit.*

44. Paul R. Mort, *Principles of School Administration*. New York: McGraw-Hill Book Co., 1946.

45. Jesse B. Sears, *The Nature of the Administrative Process*. New York: McGraw-Hill Book Co., 1950.

generalizations. First, whether or not any concept of administration is generally accepted and employed depends upon the demands placed upon it by the existing organization of the schools, on the one hand, and upon the administrator's relation with the community, on the other. (However, this applies only to the general acceptance of a concept of administration. An individual may hold and employ a concept of administration out of its time; the development of a concept of or relating to administration by an individual we have not dealt with. This would seem to be a problem of another order and to be outside our purpose in this chapter.) We have been interested in the influences which have shaped administration in inquiry and practice, but the reason we have been interested in administration is that administration not only is influenced but influences. The application of the behavioral sciences to the study of administration should influence administration and administration's influence.

SOME NEW SCIENTIFIC
BASES OF ADMINISTRATION

CHAPTER V

The Nature and Meaning of Theory

DANIEL E. GRIFFITHS

There is much confusion concerning the concept of "theory" in education since most educationists use the term much more loosely than do those who are working to develop administrative theory. Modern administrative theorists limit the zone of their interests and define in a rigorous fashion the area of their inquiry. Theorists in administration see themselves as social scientists who are greatly influenced by the methodology, the purposes, and the orientation of physical scientists. This chapter aims to set forth the position of administrative theorists as regards the nature, the meaning, and the construction of theory. Since a fundamental belief of these workers is that the adjectival varieties of administration have more in common than not, the substance of this chapter is drawn from business, public, industrial, and educational administration. The methodology is derived from both the social and the physical sciences.

The Nature of Theory

One approach to definition is to state what the concept is *not*. By attempting to exclude certain commonly accepted meanings in an explicit fashion, it may be possible to focus upon the meaning actually accepted.[1]

WHAT THEORY IS NOT

When the urban superintendents of the country were asked to name the outstanding weaknesses of their preparation programs in graduate school, the one which ranked at the top of the list was, "too much theory; courses not practical."[2] Letters were sent to a

1. For a more detailed discussion of this topic, see Daniel E. Griffiths, *Administrative Theory*. New York: Appleton-Century-Crofts, 1959.

2. *Professional Administrators for America's Schools*, pp. 34-35. Washington: American Association of School Administrators, 1960.

sampling of superintendents who responded in this way asking what
was meant by "too theoretical." The answers to these letters were
quite revealing, since they demonstrated many misuses of the word
theory. Some thought theory was the opposite of practical, thereby
equating *theory* with *impractical*. Others had the interesting notion
that if a course was *poor*, it was *theoretical*. (The search for the
origin of this idea would be a fascinating research project!) The
most common use of the concept *theory* was as a synonym for
speculation, supposition, or the *ideal*. These men said that graduate
work in school administration was little related to reality, that it
was concerned with what "ought to be" rather than what "is."
This dichotomy will be discussed in more detail later. To say that
theory is not impractical, not poor, nor is it speculation, supposition,
nor the ideal, clears away some of the obfuscation which surrounds
the concept.

There are other prominent misunderstandings regarding the
meaning of theory. It is often contended that theory is a personal
affair, a dream, a philosophy, a taxonomy, or common sense, but it
is none of these. Since the confusion between theory and philosophy
is more prevalent than the others, let us examine the two concepts.

The most commonly held belief regarding theory of administration is that it is a set of "oughts," that is, a set of rules that tells
one how to administer. Now, a well-developed set of values, having
logical consistency and related to reality, is of crucial importance to
the administrator. But this set of values is not a theory. The difference between theory and values is usually discussed in terms of the
"is-ought" dichotomy.

Possibly the use of an example from the physical sciences will
clarify the difference. If a person jumped out of a window in the
thirtieth story of a building, the exact speed at which his body
would hit the sidewalk below could be predicted. The force of the
impact could be calculated, and it could be predicted that the person would die upon hitting the sidewalk. All this is in the realm of
theory. It can be said, "If a person leaps from the thirtieth story of
a building, he will die." There is no implication of "oughtness" in
this statement. There are no values in the statement. Values can be
put in as variables, however. A person might raise the question,
"Do I want to die?" If his answer is "yes" (a value judgment), then

he might consider the efficiency of leaping from a thirty-story window. Theory tells him this would be very effective (his goal would be achieved in an economical manner).

It can be seen that the "is" deals with two functions of theory. Most obviously it is concerned with *description*. In the above example, an accurate description of the speed of the man's falling body and the force with which he hits the sidewalk can be obtained by reference to the theory of gravitation. In addition, an adequate *explanation* of why the man falls at a certain speed and why the force is what it is can also be obtained from the theory of gravitation. The "is" of the "is-ought" dichotomy refers to both a description and an explanation of the event being considered.

When philosophy is equated to a set of values, the term "philosophy" is being used very loosely. If theory is to be used in a precise fashion, then so too must philosophy. As Butler so concisely states, one would need to deal with the three great problems of philosophy:

(1) The problem of reality is this: What is the nature of the universe in which we live? Or, in the last analysis, what is real? The branch of philosophy which deals with this great problem is called *metaphysics*. (2) The problem of knowledge is this: How does a man know what is real? That is to say, how do we come by our knowledge and how can we be sure it is true, not error or illusion? The area of philosophy which is devoted to solving this problem is named epistemology. (3) The third great problem, the problem of value is this: What are the important values which are to be desired in living? Are there values rooted in reality? And how can they be realized in our experience? The branch of philosophy dealing with such questions as these is named *axiology*. In addition to these three, but most closely related to *epistemology*, is another branch of philosophy which deals with the exact relating of ideas. This area of philosophy is commonly referred to as the science of *logic*.[3]

Theory is not a set of values, and neither is it a philosophy. Halpin has summed up this argument very cogently:

. . . some writers have used this term [theory] in the sense of "value theory," to refer not to how administrators *do* behave, but to how they

3. Donald Butler, *Four Philosophies*, p. 15. New York: Harper & Bros., 1957.

ought to behave. This confoundment between the "is's" and the "oughts" of behavior is responsible for a greater failure in communication between educators and social scientists than any other issue. No one will deny that we need normative standards—in the ethical meaning of the term—for how administrators *ought* to behave, but these prescriptions do not constitute a theory.[4]

WHAT THEORY IS

A definition.—The confusion as to what constitutes theory has brought forth a motley array of progeny. So that some order might be brought out of chaos, Halpin and Griffiths issued calls asking that there be common acceptance of Fiegl's definition.[5] This definition is rather narrow and is highly restrictive in its scope, but is, however, what is needed, since a word has no value if it can be used to cover all sorts of academic exercises. Fiegl defines theory as follows:

In order to provide for a terminology which will not constantly involve us in a tangle of confusions, I propose to define a "theory" as a set of assumptions from which can be derived by purely logico-mathematical procedures a larger set of empirical laws. The theory thereby furnishes an explanation of these empirical laws and unifies the originally relatively heterogeneous areas of subject matter characterized by those empirical laws. Even though it must be admitted that there is no sharp line of demarcation (except a purely arbitrary one) between theoretical assumptions and empirical laws, the distinction, at least in the sense of a gradation, is illuminating from a methodological point of view.

One more terminological suggestion may help: Let us speak of scientific explanation wherever more specific or more descriptive statements are derived from more general or more hypothetical assumptions.[6]

In essence, Fiegl proposes that theory be defined as a set of assumptions from which can be derived by purely logico-mathematical procedures a larger set of empirical laws. A number of

4. Andrew W. Halpin, "The Development of Theory in Educational Administration," in *Administrative Theory in Education*, p. 6. Edited by Andrew W. Halpin. Chicago: Midwest Administration Center, University of Chicago, 1958.

5. Halpin, *op. cit.*; Griffiths, *op. cit.*, chap. ii.

6. Herbert Fiegl, "Principles and Problems of Theory Construction in Psychology," in *Current Trends in Psychological Theory*, p. 182. Pittsburgh: University of Pittsburgh Press, 1951.

questions might be raised concerning the definition: What is the meaning of set? What is the difference between assumptions and laws? Must a theory be tested before any indication of its value is known? What would be a theory which meets this definition?[7]

Terminology.—The language of theory-building is very confusing. Since concepts are used differently by practically all writers and there appear to be no authorities, it would seem that an agreement on basic terminology is essential. With this in mind, the following is offered.

As the term *set* is used here it means a group of assumptions such that (1) no other assumption can be derived from any other combination of assumptions in the group, and (2) the empirical laws cannot be derived without the inclusion of every member of the group.

Presumptions are basic to and precede assumptions in the thinking of the theorist. Some writers call presumptions "principles," but this appears to be too confusing. Let presumptions remain presumptions. What can be said about presumptions? They are not empirical findings and are not directly derived from empirical findings, but they are ways of directing empirical findings. Often they are decisions. The only criterion that can be employed in the selection of presumptions is usefulness. If a presumption gives rise to assumptions upon which theory can be built, then it is retained; if not, it is abandoned. An example of a useful presumption is that administration may be viewed from the perspective of decision-making.

Assumptions grow out of presumptions. One should strive to create a set of assumptions which explains a law in the most elegant and most parsimonious, the neatest, most revealing, and the most relevant fashion possible.

Laws are statements of empirical regularities of phenomena. They have the same form as hypotheses, but have withstood more testing. Examples of well-known laws are the Hawthorne Effect and Boyle's Law.

7. I should like to acknowledge the help in clarifying the concept of theory received from participation in the Faculty Seminar on Educational Theory at Teachers College, Columbia University, sponsored by the Horace Mann—Lincoln Institute of School Experimentation, 1960-61. The work of the Seminar was reported in *Proceedings* and other unpublished documents.

In an attempt to clarify the terminology of theorists, let us take the terms *assumption* and *laws* and consider them together with some other terms with which they are commonly used. Brodbeck points out that a statement of fact, a concept, a law, and a theory are all different things.[8] A fact is a particular thing, such as Johnny's I.Q. To state a fact is to state that a concept has an instance or a number of instances. When a fact is connected with other facts, a generalization or law is formed. As Brodbeck says, "A law states that whenever there is an instance of one kind of fact, then there is also an instance of another."[9] As an example of a law, note the following: the distance a released body falls varies directly with the square of its time, that is, $d = 16 \ t^2$. A law is always an empirical generalization. To move along with the argument, a theory is a deductively connected set of laws. Certain of the laws are the axioms or postulates of the theory and are usually called assumptions. Their truth is not so much self-evident as it is taken for granted, so that the truth of other empirical assertions called theorems can be determined.

The basic terminology of theory-building is comprised of such words as *fact, concept, presumption, assumption, theory*, and *law*.

Test of theory.—Since a number of physical-science theories have stood for years (sometimes centuries) without empirical proof, the question arises as to the urgency and necessity of proof. Does a formulation have to be tested to be called a theory? The answer is probably "no." What is needed is that the theory must be *logically* capable of proof or disproof whether or not the tools for testing are available at the time of formulation. For example, while the Copernican Theory awaited the invention of a powerful telescope to ascertain parallax, the *logical* test of the theory could have been made at any time. It is not as difficult as it may seem to apply this criterion. Certain theories can be rejected out of hand, for example the following:

1. Theories written so as to make testing impossible as, for

8. May Brodbeck, "Models, Meanings, and Theories" in *Symposium on Sociological Theory*, pp. 373-403. Edited by Llewellyn Gross. Evanston, Illinois: Row, Peterson & Co., 1959.

9. *Ibid.*, p. 337.

example, the caloric theory of heat which postulated "caloric" as an odorless, weightless, invisible substance.

2. Masked tautologies which assume the form of theories; for example, "opium puts people to sleep because it contains a dormative power."

The test (at this stage) of a theory is whether or not it is logically capable of proof even if the necessary instruments have not been devised.

An illustration.—Probably the best illustration of a theory in educational administration which approximates the Fiegl definition comes from Getzels.[10] This theory is hypothetico-deductive in nature and describes administration as a social process in which behavior is conceived as a function of both the nomothetic and the idiographic dimensions of a social system.

Getzels first presented a set of assumptions and then derived a series of hypotheses from the model. Administration is conceived structurally as the hierarchy of subordinate-superordinate relationships within a social system; and functionally this hierarchy of relationships is the locus for allocating and integrating roles and facilities in order to achieve the goals of the social system. The social system is comprised of two dimensions: the nomothetic which consists of institution, role, and expectation; and the idiographic which consists of the individual, his personality, and his need-disposition. Two sets of definitions are presented, namely: *institution* is used to designate agencies established to carry out "institutionalized functions for the social system as a whole," [11] and *roles* are the "dynamic aspects" of the positions, offices, and statuses within an institution. Roles are defined in terms of role expectations, and roles are complementary.

The set of assumptions is presented diagrammatically in the chart following. In this diagram each term on the two axes is the analytic unit for the term preceding it. In the idiographic dimension, for example, institution is defined as a set of roles, role as a set of expectations.

10. Jacob W. Getzels, "Administration as a Social Process," in *Administrative Theory in Education, op. cit.,* pp. 150-65.

11. *Ibid.,* p. 153.

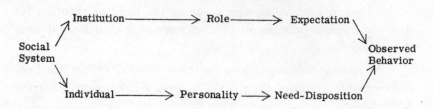

Nomothetic Dimension[12]

Idiographic Dimension

It can be seen that a given act is derived simultaneously from both the idiographic and the nomothetic dimensions. The general equation for this relation is $B = f\ (R \times P)$, where B is observed behavior, R is an institutional role, and P is the personality of the particular role incumbent.[13]

The proportion of role and personality factors determining behavior will vary according to several variables. The accompanying chart should clarify the nature of the interaction between role and personality in various situations.[14] It is obvious that, in the military, behavior is influenced more by role than personality, while, with the artist, behavior is influenced more by personality than by role. The proportions should be considered as illustrative and not precise.

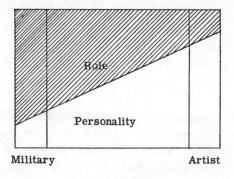

$$B = f\ (R \times P)$$

12. *Ibid.*, p. 156.
13. *Ibid.*, p. 157.
14. *Ibid.*, p. 158.

Getzels hypothesized that there are three types of conflict to be found in organizations: role-personality conflict, role conflict, and personality conflict.

Role-personality conflicts occur as a function of the discrepancies between the pattern of expectations attached to a given role and the pattern of need dispositions characteristic of the incumbent of the role. *Role conflicts* occur whenever a role incumbent is required to conform simultaneously to a number of expectations which are mutually exclusive, contradictory or inconsistent, so that adjustment to one set of requirements makes adjustment to another impossible or at least difficult. *Personality conflicts* occur as a function of opposing needs and dispositions within the personality of the role incumbent himself. It could be demonstrated (or at least contended) that these hypotheses could be called laws, since they appear to be statements of empirical regularities which now have sufficient proof to be so accepted. In terms of Getzels' theory, these three types of conflict represent incongruence in the nomothetic dimension, in the idiographic dimension, or in the interaction between the two. Within the framework of the theory, it may be generalized that such incongruence is symptomatic of administrative failure and leads to loss in productivity in both the individual and the organization.

Contemporary Theory

There are many stages in the development of a science. It is rare that any science develops in a sequential set of steps, and administration is no exception to this observation. Contemporary work is proceeding at all of the various stages. There are many ways to discuss scientific work, one of which might be called the "level approach." [15] This means that there are different levels of scientific work, all of which have some value. At the lowest level there are what might be called "sensitizing concepts." They are rather primitive, but serve the purpose of identifying certain specifics which occur in administration. The middle level in the scientific hierarchy may be called the "integrating concept" level. These concepts serve

15. Daniel E. Griffiths, "Response to Paul Lazarsfeld, 'The Social Sciences and Administration: A Rationale,'" in *The Social Sciences and Educational Administration*, pp. 13-19. Edited by Lorne Downey and Frederick Enns. Edmonton: University of Alberta, 1963.

the purpose of relating several lower-level concepts into complex concepts of great power. At the top of the hierarchy is "theory," defined as above by Fiegl.[16]

A PARADIGM

The levels of stages of the development of theory can be incorporated into a paradigm (Fig. 1). Theory development begins with certain presumptions in the mind of the investigator. This leads him to make observations of administrative situations, the result being one or more descriptions. The investigator then attempts to explain

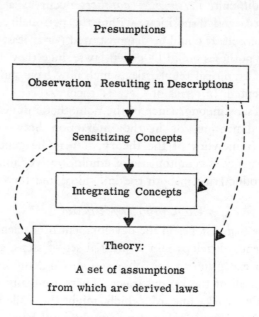

FIG. 1.—Paradigm for theory development

his observation. He can do this on one of three levels: sensitizing concepts, integrating concepts, or theory. Should he explain his observations at the level of theory, he would create a set of assumptions, would derive laws from these assumptions, and would be able to predict administrative behavior with a rather high degree of probability.

16. Fiegl, *op. cit.*

One should not get the idea that theory-making proceeds in a regular manner through the steps in Figure 1. Generally everyone starts with presumptions. Some skip the descriptive phase, but the resulting work is generally poor when this is done. Some start with sensitizing concepts and jump to theory, while others stay at the level of sensitizing concepts. Some start at presumptions, move to observations, skip to theory, then work back to sensitizing and integrating concepts and then back to description to test their theoretical formulations. The paradigm is used in this chapter merely to aid in visualizing the work of the theoretician.

The remainder of this chapter is devoted to a discussion of concept development and current work at each of the three levels.

CONCEPT DEVELOPMENT

Theoretical studies in administration are plagued with the consequences of ill-defined concepts and are thus handicapped in efforts to *describe* administrative situations. Even the most sophisticated students of school administration often resort to homely parables and analogies to talk about administration. As Simon says of administration in general:

> We talk about organization in terms not unlike those used by a Ubangi medicine man to discuss disease. At best we live by homely proverbs: "The important thing about organization is to have the right man in the right place." At worst we live by pompous inanities: "The relationship between delegant and his deputy arises from delegation and is invariable in character." [17]

The first and major task in the construction of a science of administration is the development of concepts which will permit the description of administrative situations. Although considerable progress has been made in recent years, there is still a long way to go before an adequate body of concepts is built.

A definition.—What is meant by a concept? A concept is simply a term to which a particular meaning has been attached. Once the meaning has been attached to the term, the term should always be used with this particular meaning; and, conversely, whenever a

17. Herbert Simon, *Administrative Behavior*, p. xiv. New York: Macmillan Co., 1957 (second edition).

particular meaning is intended, the same term should be used. If this single step forward could be made—that is, the use of the same concept by all to describe the same meaning—it would be a giant step. To illustrate what is meant in this situation let us quote a recent book on theory in educational administration. The following two sentences are in consecutive order: "The terms adaptability and quality are used interchangeably in this book. Of course they are not the same." This is an example of what we are talking about. If the two terms are not the same, why should they be used interchangeably? And if the two terms are used interchangeably, why are they not the same?

Operationism.—The lack of appropriate concepts has made it very difficult to adequately describe administrative situations or administrative behavior. In order to solve this problem, theoreticians have turned to *operationism.* This approach is generally credited to Bridgman, a physicist whose book, *The Logic of Modern Physics*, presents the basic tenets of operationism. The idea is very simple and is stated by Bridgman as follows: "In general, we mean by any concept nothing more than a set of operations; *the concept is synonymous with the corresponding set of operations.*" [18] In other words, operationism is the way of thinking which holds that (*a*) concepts are given their meaning by the methods of observations or investigations used to arrive at them, and (*b*) concepts have no meaning apart from their operations. This rigid formulation has been modified slightly, and a concept is now considered to be operational if a link to other operational concepts can be clearly demonstrated. For example, the I.Q. is operational because it is obtained by dividing mental age by chronological age, both of which are operational concepts.

SENSITIZING CONCEPTS

Lazarsfeld has contended that the way to approach the relationship between administration and the social sciences is to hold some over-all view of administration and to relate social science to that

18. Percy W. Bridgman, *The Logic of Modern Physics*, p. 5. New York: Macmillan Co., 1927.

view.[19] He states that "the social sciences have relevance for administration on a purely empirical level." [20] As a result of his research, Lazarsfeld has developed a number of concepts which can be classified as sensitizing concepts. These concepts are well defined and serve the purpose of drawing attention to specific behaviors associated with administrative activity.

The concept of *visibility* serves as an illustration. This concept is based upon the observation that individuals within an organization are differentially aware of what is going on within the system. Lazarsfeld points out that this is so because organizations are usually set up so as to give the administrator greater access than his subordinates to information about role-performance. He "sees" more, partly because he wants to "see" more and partly because the organization was so designed. Lazarsfeld points out, however, that not all things are equally visible to the administrator: subordinates may act to reduce the visibility of their role-performance, the administrator may not be motivated to try to increase his area of vision, or the organization may lack mechanisms for making certain aspects of role-performance visible.

Lazarsfeld describes a study done by Stouffer to show the significance of the concept of visibility in understanding an aspect of organizational behavior:

. . . a number of top level people in business organizations were interviewed to find out who it was that helped each of them get to the top. After these "helpers" had been identified, a survey was conducted to find out where they themselves were then located within the organization. Surprisingly, it was discovered that none of these "helpers" had gotten anywhere. It would seem that such people should have been rewarded for their work in developing junior talent. But there was no provision for making this behavior *visible*. If the president of the organization had wanted to do justice to the people who were developing junior talent, in accordance with his wishes, he should have made some provisions for finding out what individuals were doing this part of their jobs. As it was those individuals who spent less time developing their subordinates and more time on their own tasks were the ones rewarded through promotions. An important aspect of role-performance was not

19. Lazarsfeld, *op. cit.*

20. *Ibid.*, p. 6.

visible because there were no mechanisms for making it visible and also, perhaps, because the top administrators were not motivated to make it visible.[21]

From this example, it is clear that the sensitizing concept when well defined is a basic ingredient in the scientific study of administration. There are several examples of sensitizing concepts in the chapters which follow. Carlson, in chapter xii, creates the concepts of the "domesticated" and "wild" organizations so as to better understand the school dropout and other types of commonly observed behavior. In chapter viii, Hemphill discusses numerous scoring categories, which are operational concepts, that help to explain the behavior of school principals. Charters, in chapter xi, discusses the concepts of task, position, authority-relation, and department—each a concept at the sensitizing level.

INTEGRATING CONCEPTS

The integrating concept is complex in that it orders the relationships among a number of sensitizing concepts. It is powerful in that it enables us to see relationships not suggested by the sensitizing concepts taken singly and, further, in that it offers paths to future inquiry by researchers and theoreticians and guidance to the performance of administrators. The illustration is the concept of anticipated and unanticipated consequences as formulated by Gouldner.

Lazarsfeld's definition of the task of the administrator was presented in chapter i and forms the basis for the present discussion of Gouldner's concept. To summarize the four phases of the task:

1. The administrator must fulfil *the goals* of the organization.
2. The administrator must make use of *other* people in fulfilling these goals, not as if they were machines, but rather in such a way as to release their initiative and creativity.
3. The administrator must be concerned about *morale* and the idea that under suitable conditions people will do better work.
4. The administrator must build into his organization *provisions for innovation,* for change, for development.[22]

21. *Loc. cit.*

22. This presentation of the Gouldner Model borrows from James G. March and Herbert Simon, *Organization,* p. 45 (New York: John Wiley & Sons, 1958). The method of presentation was suggested by W. W. Charters, Jr., Washington University, St. Louis.

When an administrator attempts to achieve a goal he takes precautions to ensure that the people in an organization act in ways that will gain the goal. This is often called *control*. The administrator, further, would like to have the people feel "good" while they function in the prescribed manner. This is called maintaining a *low level of interpersonal tension*. He would also like to keep the *visibility of power relations* low and so relies on the *use of general and impersonal rules* rather than on confronting employees personally. The administrator's action and the anticipated consequences of his action can be diagrammed as in Figure 2.

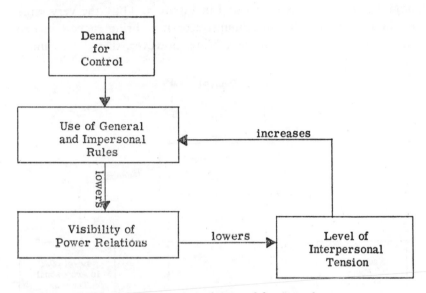

Fɪɢ. 2.—Anticipated consequences of demand for control

The diagram is read as follows: a *demand for control* results in the *use of general and impersonal rules*, which lowers the *visibility of power relations* between the administrator and other members of the organization while compliance with rules is attained. The lower *visibility of power relations* lowers the *level of interpersonal tension*, which, in turn, increases the *use of general and impersonal rules*.

However, the demand for control may not result in achievement of the desired goal. Something totally *unanticipated* by the administrator may occur. A rule cannot be written to achieve maximum achievement. For instance, a rule concerning the time when teachers should be on the job can state only a reasonable minimum, not **a** maximum. Therefore, rules give employees *knowledge of minimum acceptable behavior.* Should the employee act on the knowledge of minimum acceptable behavior, this would increase the *difference between organizational goals and achievement.* In order to minimize this difference, the administrator usually, but not always, increases the *closeness of supervision.* This results in an increased *visibility of power relations,* which raises the *level of interpersonal tension* and decreases the value of the *use of general and impersonal rules.* This is pictured in Figure 3. Thus, the very same methods employed by an administrator may bring success in one situation and failure in another. Note, however, that there cannot

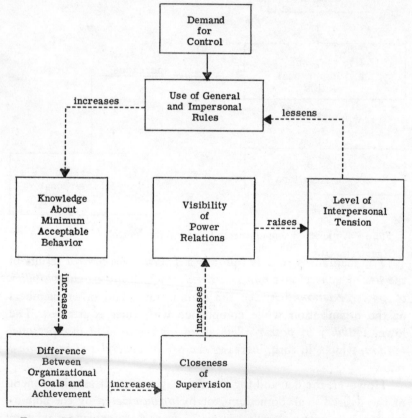

FIG. 3.—Unanticipated consequences of administrative act

be "unanticipated" consequences unless there are first "anticipated" consequences. The concept has meaning only in the over-all context of the total administrative performance.

Figure 4 indicates the value of the concept of *unanticipated consequences* when viewed in the context of an administrator's anticipated consequences. It gives a way of *ordering* several less complex concepts. One might say that a large segment of administrative behavior takes on meaning when viewed in the context of this major concept.

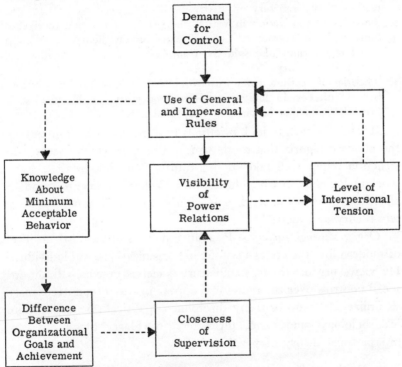

Fig. 4.—Unanticipated consequences viewed in the context of an administrator's anticipated consequences. (Gouldner model from March and Simon, *op. cit.*, p. 45.)

Several integrating concepts are used in succeeding chapters of this book. Hemphill, in chapter viii, presents eight basic factors and two secondary factors which are integrating concepts, each of which order a number of sensitizing concepts. Both Iannaccone and Charters, in chapters x and xi, respectively, present integrating concepts which order several concepts in ways which give these simpler concepts greater meaning. Charters, for instance, uses "organization maintenance" in this way.

THEORIES

A number of theories of administration have been proposed in the past fifteen years. March and Simon[23] have categorized these theories as follows:

1. Theories of conflict, i.e., role conflict, personality conflict, and role-personality conflict. The Getzels theory, described above, is an illustration of this category of theory.
2. Theories of motivation in which the needs, drives, and motives of individuals are considered. The Barnard-Simon theory of organizational equilibrium discussed by Campbell in chapter xiii illustrates this type of theory.
3. Theories of decision-making in which man is considered as a rational being with certain limitations. The theory of decision-making by Griffiths is an illustration of this approach.[24]

It might be well to look briefly at two theories which go beyond the above categorization to show the direction which theory construction might well take in the future. The first of these is the work of Presthus, in which he uses the Weber bureaucratic model,[25] and the second is the work of Griffiths, in which he employs system-theory as a model.[26]

Organizational society.—Presthus analyzes three distinct levels of modern life: society as a whole, big organizations, and individuals. He views organizations as miniature societies in which traditional social controls over the individual appear in sharp focus. His analysis utilizes the tools of many disciplines—political science, economics, sociology—and turns, ultimately, to Harry Stack Sullivan's interpersonal theory of psychiatry.[27]

23. March and Simon, *op. cit., passim.*

24. Griffiths, *Administrative Theory*, chap. iv.

25. Robert Presthus, *The Organizational Society*. New York: Alfred A. Knopf, Inc., 1962.

26. Daniel E. Griffiths, "Administrative Theory and Change in Organizations," in *Innovation in Education*. Edited by Matthew B. Miles. New York: Teachers College Bureau of Publications, 1964.

27. Harry Stack Sullivan, "Tensions, Interpersonal and International," in *Tensions That Cause Wars*, p. 95. Edited by H. Cantrill. Urbana: University of Illinois Press, 1950. Quoted in Presthus, *op. cit.*

Sullivan developed the theory that each person's personality is the result of his pattern of accommodation with people who are significant to him. How the individual accommodates is strongly influenced by the social setting in which the interpersonal relations occur. Sullivan defines personality, then, as a consistent way of reacting or accommodating to interpersonal situations, where social values and institutions play a powerful role. He argues that most behavior is the result of the individual's search for relief from tension induced by conforming to authority. *Anxiety* is the most compelling of tensions, and much behavior is seen as an effort to escape from it. Sullivan declares: "I believe it fairly safe to say that anybody and everybody devotes much of his lifetime and . . . energy . . . to avoiding more anxiety than he already has, and if possible, to getting rid of some of this anxiety." Sullivan concludes that our personalities are formed as we work out ways of getting along with persons in authority—our parents, our teachers, the police, our bosses—and we bring that method of accommodating with us when we come to work in an organization.

Presthus, in defending the argument that large organizations induce anxiety in their members, first defines a "large organization," using as a model Max Weber's theory of bureaucracy. According to Weber, a bureaucracy is the most efficient form of organization devised by human beings. The personal, irrational, and emotional elements are minimized and the members tend to work with speed, precision, discretion, and technical know-how, without ambiguity or friction. The bureaucracy has the following characteristics:

1. Fixed and official jurisdictional areas, regularly ordered by rules, policies, regulations, by-laws.
2. Principles of hierarchy and levels of graded authority that ensure a firmly ordered system of super- and subordination in which higher offices supervise lower ones.
3. Administration based upon written documents.
4. Administration by full-time, trained officials.
5. Administration by stable and comprehensive general policies.[28]

28. Presthus, *op. cit.*, p. 5.

Clearly Weber's formulation does not completely describe modern organizations. Weber ignores the psychological elements, the goals of individuals, the informal groups, and the influences of the larger society—all of which are taken into account by Presthus. As Presthus says:

Members are expected to be loyal to the organization, to behave consistently and rationally according to technical and professional criteria and to defer to the authority of the organization's leaders. The social and psychological basis of this accommodation is the major concern of this book.[29]

The big organization, says Presthus, induces anxieties in its members simply because of its fundamental characteristics. Let us examine some of them:

Size becomes a factor when an organization becomes so large that any given member does not have face-to-face contact with most other members. The larger the organization, the lower morale drops as individuals tend to feel unimportant.

As organizations increase in size and complexity, members must begin to specialize. Such division of labor has both advantages and disadvantages. On the one hand, the technical quality of the work improves. On the other hand, interpersonal relationships deteriorate; so also does the sense of identification with the organization.

"The main function of hierarchy is to assign and validate authority along a descending scale throughout the organization." [30] The hierarchy is of vital importance, since the individual's participation in an organization is always affected by his place in the hierarchy. The weight attached to suggestions, the influence of each member, even the order in which members of a group walk through a doorway is determined by one's hierarchical position.

The importance of status and status symbols is well known. The organization constantly reminds members of their status by the way it distributes salaries, offices, expense accounts, vacations, staff, secretarial help, and titles.

Most bureaucracies are run by a few people; thus they are

29. *Ibid.*, p. 7.

30. *Ibid.*, p. 34

oligarchies. The "few" are set off from the rest by their "preponderance of power." Their presence in an organization constantly reminds the members that here is a small group with more power than all the others combined. Their presence tends to accentuate the anxieties of the other members.

Presthus states that members accommodate to the demands of the organization in three ways—upward mobility, indifference, and ambivalence.

1) *Upward-mobiles.* These persons are the most successful organization members. The upward-mobile feels friendly toward his superiors and believes that they are friendly and sympathetic toward him. He has little difficulty making decisions in conflict situations because he accepts the organization's values as decisive. He is extraverted and gets along with other people, yet he regards his subordinates with considerable detachment, which leads him to make decisions in terms of the organization rather than the individual. Upward-mobiles enjoy organization life, are successful at it, and reap the rewards of status and salary.

2) *Indifferents.* While the upward-mobile revels in the competition of the organization, the "indifferent" refuses to compete for the organization's favors. The indifferent person comes from one of two backgrounds. Some enter the organization with great expectations but are unsuccessful and react by turning their backs on the organization. Others have a working- or lower-class origin and are taught not to expect much from the organization. The "indifferent" accommodates to organizational demands by doing his work, arriving on time, and leaving on time—but by developing his major interests *outside* of the organization. His anxieties are reduced to a minimum because he refuses to become involved in the organizational race for rewards. He separates his work from the rest of his living. As Presthus says, "He sells his time for a certain number of hours and jealously guards the rest."

3) *Ambivalents.* The last group is a small minority who can neither resist the appeals of power and success nor play the role required to gain them. The ambivalent finds it hard to get along with authority and cannot play the organization game. As contrasted with the upward-mobile, he places individual friendships above the good of the organization. When confronted with a con-

flict, he decides in favor of the individual as against the organization. His is, indeed, a miserable lot in the modern large organization.

The Presthus theory deals largely with conflict and motivation yet it also discusses man as a rational being. It is an attempt to explain the behavior of man within an organizational context.

System theory.—The work of Griffiths does not fit the categories either, but for another reason. The model employed, system theory, is designed to be all-inclusive. It is a way of looking at a social organization as a whole. Griffiths uses system theory as a model to investigate the problem of change in organizations.

A system is simply defined as a complex of elements in mutual interaction. Systems may be open or closed. An open system is related to and exchanges matter with its environment, while a closed system is not related to nor does it exchange matter with its environment. Further, a closed system is characterized by an increase in entropy, while open systems tend toward the steady state. (Given a continuous input, a constant ratio among the components of the system is maintained.) All systems except the smallest have subsystems, and all but the largest have suprasystems, which are their environments.

System theory deals only with open systems having the properties of systems in general, together with certain characteristics which distinguish them from closed systems.[31]

1. Open systems exchange energy and information with their environment; that is, they have *inputs* and *outputs*.

2. Open systems tend to maintain themselves in *steady states*. A steady state is characterized by a constant ratio being maintained among the components of the system. A burning candle is often used as an example of a steady state. Upon being lighted the flame is small, but it rapidly grows to its normal size and maintains the size as long as the candle and its environment exist.

3. Open systems are *self-regulating*. In the illustration above, a sudden draft will cause the flame to flicker, but with the cessation of the draft the flame regains its normal characteristics.

4. Open systems display *equifinality;* that is, identical results

31. For an elaboration of these characteristics, see Gordon Hearn, *Theory Building in Social Work*, pp. 44-50. Toronto: University of Toronto Press, 1958.

can be obtained from different initial conditions. Hearn points out that equifinality in human beings (they are open systems) is illustrated by the case of two babies, one born prematurely, the other full-term. While at birth they may look very different and may be in different stages of development, within a few months the differences will have disappeared. Even though the initial states may differ, human beings generally achieve the same stages of development.

5. Open systems maintain their steady states, in part, through the *dynamic interplay of subsystems operating as functional processes*. This means that the various parts of the system function without persistent conflicts that can be neither resolved nor regulated.

6. Open systems maintain their steady states, in part, through *feedback* processes. In general, feedback refers to that portion of the output of a system which is fed back to the input and affects succeeding outputs, and to the property of being able to adjust future conduct by past performance.

7. Open systems display *progressive segregation*. This process occurs when the system divides into a hierarchical order of subordinate systems which gain a certain degree of independence of each other.

A number of propositions concerning conditions aiding or inhibiting change have been derived from the model:

—The major impetus for change in organizations is from the outside.

—The degree and duration of change is directly proportional to the intensity of the stimulus from the suprasystem.

—Change in an organization is more probable if the successor to the chief administrator is from outside the organization than if he is from inside the organization.

—When change in an organization does occur, it will tend to occur from the top down, not from the bottom up.

—"Living systems respond to continuously increasing stress first by a lag in response, then by an over-compensatory response, and finally by catastrophic collapse of the system." [32]

32. J. G. Miller, "Toward a Theory for the Behavioral Sciences, *American Psychologist*, X (1955), 525.

—The number of innovations expected is inversely proportional to the tenure of the chief administrator.

—The more hierarchical the structure of an organization, the less the possibility of change.

—The more functional the dynamic interplay of subsystems, the less the change in an organization.

System theory is the result of an attempt to develop a general theory which enables the researcher to describe, explain, and predict a wide range of human behavior within organizations. It deals with conflict, motivation, and decision-making so that, like the work of Presthus, it cuts across the three categories of March and Simon. The two theories represent the direction in which theoreticians might move in the coming years.

Conclusion

This chapter is the result of an attempt to depict the place of theory in the scientific study of administration. Stereotyped notions of the nature of theory were discussed, and Fiegl's definition of theory was offered as one which could be accepted. Since the scientific study of administration proceeds on several levels, a set of categories was offered as a way of organizing this work. Sensitizing concepts, integrating concepts, and theories were discussed and illustrated.

CHAPTER VI

Leadership and Administration

JAMES M. LIPHAM

Paralleling, if not antedating, the recent development of administrative theory has been an unprecedented concern with the study of leadership. The national preoccupation with leadership on the part of researchers and practitioners alike has been no less than phenomenal. Scholars in such distinct yet related fields as anthropology, business management, educational administration, industrial relations, psychology, public administration, and sociology have conducted numerous, intensive investigations which focus upon leadership and leader behavior. Although these investigations represent diverse approaches to the study of leadership, they have produced a number of significant findings which illuminate the study and the practice of educational administration.

The primary purpose of this chapter is to summarize recent studies of leadership which have implications for administrative theory and practice. As an introductory focus, the organizational setting for educational leadership will be described briefly. Since the point of view taken here is that leadership and administration are, indeed, not synonymous, these terms will be defined. The closing paragraphs of the chapter will include a discussion of some problems concerning leadership which are in need of further clarification.

The Organizational Setting

In examining the setting for leadership, we may, after Getzels,[1] conceive of an organization as a hierarchy of superordinate-sub-

---

1. J. W. Getzels, "Administration as a Social Process," in *Administrative Theory in Education*, pp. 150-65. Edited by Andrew W. Halpin. Chicago: Midwest Administration Center, University of Chicago, 1958. (For a more detailed treatment of Getzels' theoretical formulation, see chap. v.)

ordinate relationships—a structured social system. This hierarchy of relationships serves to facilitate the allocation and integration of roles and resources in order to achieve the goals of the system. That is, a social system exists to discharge certain institutionalized functions; these functions are the goals or ends toward which behavior within the organization is directed. To attain the goals, the workflow of the organization is designed to produce an identifiable commodity that is useful to the larger social system. The school, for example, exists to produce educated students for the more comprehensive social system of which the school is a part. From these relationships, it is important to note that the concept of social system may be applied at any level of organizational analysis. As Getzels has stated:

. . . within this framework, for one purpose, a given community may be considered a social system with the school a particular organization within the more general social system. For another purpose, the school or even a single class within the school may be considered a social system in its own right.[2]

The organization, as a social system, may be viewed analytically in terms of two dimensions, the sociological and the psychological. The important analytical and conceptual unit of the sociological dimension of an organization is the role: the dynamic aspects of positions, offices, and statuses which define the behavior of individuals within the organization. Roles are defined in terms of expectations, the normative obligations and responsibilities which govern proper or legitimate modes of action. Roles, also, are complementary and interdependent; that is, each role derives its meaning in terms of other related roles within the organization. Thus, the school system, for example, is structured in terms of such complementary roles as board members, superintendents, supervisors, principals, teachers, and pupils.

In terms of the psychological dimension, an organization is always interpersonal in nature; that is, individuals are involved. In order to understand and predict social behavior, we must take into account the need-dispositions of the individual as well as the

2. J. W. Getzels and E. G. Guba, "Social Behavior and the Administrative Process." *School Review*, LXV (Winter, 1957), 423-41.

hierarchical-role structure of the organization. As noted by Hemphill, "If we concern ourselves with the persons or individuals, we must consider, among other factors, their values, their traits, and their need-dispositions." [3] Thus, in any given school viewed as a social system, Principal A perceives the appropriate relationship to Student X, Teacher Y, or Administrator Z in part as a function of his own personality; likewise, each individual may be expected, in part, to respond in terms of his own personality.

In summary, the foregoing description of the organizational setting stresses the primacy of both the sociological (institutional role) and the psychological (individual personality) dimensions. These two dimensions, which are of equal importance, bear a striking similarity to the evaluative concepts or organizational "effectiveness" and organizational "efficiency" advanced by Barnard who defined these terms as follows: "Effectiveness relates to the accomplishment of the co-operative purpose, which is social and nonpersonal in character. Efficiency relates to the satisfaction of individual motives, and is personal in character." [4]

Leadership and Administration Defined

Perhaps the most significant—and certainly the most frequent—description of the school superintendent is that of "leader." As Halpin has noted, "in ordinary parlance the term 'leadership' is used in an evaluative sense. To say that a man displays leadership implies that this is 'good' or 'effective' leadership." [5] Even so, it is not unusual to find that the practicing superintendent, when faced with what seem to be contradictory results of traitist, situationist, and behavioral approaches to the study of leadership, may have come to regard the once-halo-surrounded term "leadership" with a certain uneasiness, if not downright antipathy. The term "leadership,"

3. John K. Hemphill, "Administration as Problem Solving," in Andrew W. Halpin, *Administrative Theory in Education*, p. 107. Chicago: Midwest Administration Center, University of Chicago, 1958.

4. Chester I. Barnard, *The Functions of the Executive*, pp. 60-61. Cambridge, Massachusetts: Harvard University Press, 1938.

5. Andrew W. Halpin, *The Leadership Behavior of School Superintendents*, p. 12. Chicago: Midwest Administration Center, University of Chicago, 1960 (reprinted).

particularly when coupled with the word "instructional," may connote to the practitioner a whole set of actual and imagined prescriptions for his behavior—"absolutely musts," "certainly oughts," and "positively shoulds"—which, in the daily operation of his organization, somehow seem to get overlooked. The ambivalence toward leadership thus sensed, but seldom openly expressed because of guilt feelings and value connotations, provides a clue that, while administration and leadership may have many factors in common, they are, indeed, not synonymous.

Although leadership has been defined in a number of ways, the definition proposed here derives additional meaning when viewed in terms of the organizational context presented in the foregoing paragraphs. We may define leadership as the initiation of a new structure or procedure for accomplishing an organization's goals and objectives or for changing an organization's goals and objectives.[6] Note that the emphasis here is upon initiating change. Presumably, two routes are open to the leader who would attempt to change established organizational relationships and goals. He may utilize delegated status and exert authority in terms of his role, or he may utilize achieved prestige and exert influence in terms of his individual personality.[7] Perhaps both role and individual strengths would be brought to bear. In either event, the leader is concerned with initiating changes in established structures, procedures, or goals; he is disruptive of the existing state of affairs.

The administrator, on the other hand, may be identified as the individual who utilizes existing structures or procedures to achieve an organizational goal or objective. As in the case of the leader, the administrator may bring to bear the authority of his role or the influence of his personality in his relationships with other members of the organization. But the administrator is concerned primarily with maintaining, rather than changing, established structures, procedures, or goals. Thus, the administrator may be viewed as a stabilizing force.

6. Hemphill, *op. cit.*, p. 98.

7. Egon G. Guba, "Research in Internal Administration—What Do We Know?" in *Administrative Theory as a Guide to Action*, p. 124. Edited by Roald F. Campbell and James M. Lipham. Chicago: Midwest Administration Center, University of Chicago, 1960.

In view of the foregoing distinction between administration and leadership, it becomes apparent that the oft-used term "administrative leadership" is something of a paradox. To characterize a given behavioral act as "administrative leadership" is to fail to recognize a source of conflict inherent in most superordinate organizational roles—conflict between the administrative role and the leadership role. Except, perhaps, for a few complex institutions of very large size, leadership functions and administrative functions are usually combined in a single-role incumbent. The superintendent of schools, for example, must, at times, wear an "administrative hat" and, at other times, wear a "leadership hat." Having but one head, the superintendent should, indeed, be aware of which "hat" he is wearing, since he undoubtedly is expected both to administer and to lead.

The distinction made here between leadership and administration carries no implication that one is universally more appropriate, more important, or more difficult than the other. In both leadership and administration, the same organizational and individual variables are involved. Although the initiation of change within an organization is usually perceived as a complex and energy-consuming process, adherence to existing goals, structures, and procedures in a kaleidoscopic field of forces can be equally as demanding.

In an attempt to distinguish between "head men" and "leaders," some writers have suggested that the "head man" is concerned primarily with means and that the "leader" is concerned with ends or goals. A primary weakness of the means-ends dichotomy is that it fails to recognize, according to our definition, that leadership, initiating new structures, is concerned with means as well as ends. Likewise, administration, maintaining existing structures, requires close attention to ends as well as means.

The latitude for leadership—the extent to which leadership expectations are held for the school superintendent's role—may vary greatly from community to community.[8] Consider, for example, the recent request for a school superintendent made to a university placement office by a board of education which wanted,

8. Richard O. Carlson, *Executive Succession and Organizational Change.* Chicago: Midwest Administration Center, University of Chicago, 1962.

"An 'educational leader' who will maintain the excellent program of our school system." The request from this board conveys in muted language the following message, "We don't want a leader at all, but an administrator—someone who will not alter our goals, structures, or procedures." The attitude of this particular board might well be appropriate. Remembering that leadership, like change, is neither "good" nor "bad," they simply may have had enough leadership. Of course, this is only one explanation; there could be many reasons, ulterior and otherwise, why some communities do not, in fact, want a superintendent who is a leader.

The frequency of leadership acts, that is, how often the superintendent engages in leadership behavior, is a crucial factor. As Hemphill has noted, leadership behavior includes the following classes of acts:

1. *Attempted leadership:* acts which are accompanied by an intention of initiating a structure-in-interaction.
2. *Successful leadership:* acts that have initiated a structure-in-interaction during the process of mutual-problem solution.
3. *Effective leadership:* acts that have initiated a structure-in-interaction that has contributed to the solution of a mutual problem.[9]

Since leadership involves a series of steps, time is required to assess the extent to which an attempted leadership act is *successful* or *effective.* Thus, in terms of frequency, the practitioner might err in either of two directions. At the lower frequency extreme, the failure to attempt leadership could result in inadequate structures, ineffective procedures, and archaic goals. At the upper extreme, repeatedly attempting leadership, it would be difficult to assess the effectiveness of any given leadership act because of the interposition of successive leadership acts. That is, frequent, continuous changes in an organization's structures, procedures, and goals could result in disorganization, disintegration, and disorientation.

Just as frequency is an important aspect of leadership, so also is the factor of potency. Potency refers to the extent to which an initiated change represents a significantly different departure from that which exists, i.e., the magnitude of an initiated change. It is in

9. Hemphill, *op. cit.,* pp. 105-6.

terms of potency, for example, that a person such as Dewey, who drastically affected the teaching-learning situation, was eminently qualified to be called an "educational leader." In the field of education, a common observation is that the structures and procedures of the schools have changed very little over the past several decades. Perhaps a safe generalization is that the leadership acts of most educators are of low potency and are limited primarily to that of tinkering with the organizational structure—of the variety, "When in doubt, elect another committee."

Leadership roles in structured organizations are, indeed, complex. Thus, the methodology and the findings of leadership studies concerned with small, unstructured, randomly selected groups are likely to be of only limited value when transplanted indiscriminately to large, complex, hierarchical organizations. An example which may be cited is the notion of "democratic" leadership, which has been so eminently popular in the field of educational administration for many years. Derived largely from White and Lippitt's[10] classic studies of five-member hobby clubs composed of ten-year-old children, the concept of "democratic" leadership was yanked from its referents in research, equated with all that is "good" and persistently preached as the only appropriate leader behavior for solving all operational problems within complex educational organizations. Needless to add, the meaning of the term, hence its usefulness, suffered. It was found that this loosely defined political concept, which had been seized as a panacea, indeed hindered more potential leaders than it helped. The major source of error, however, resided in the fact that a host of organizational realities were usually ignored—if not zealously scorned.

Studies dealing with the leadership of organizations usually have failed to distinguish between leadership and administration. With but few exceptions, most studies of leadership conducted to date begin with a rather arbitrary statement somewhat like the following: "For the purposes of this study we will assume that all superintendents (or principals) are leaders." This is a sweeping assumption,

10. Ralph White and Ronald Lippitt, "Leader Behavior and Member Reaction in Three 'Social Climates,' " in *Group Dynamics, Research and Theory*, pp. 585-611. Edited by Dorwin Cartwright and Alvin Zander. Evanston, Illinois: Row, Peterson & Co., 1953.

in terms of the definitions of leadership and administration prof-
fered here, yet the results of such studies provide useful insights
concerning the nature of leadership in the educational organization.
Let us examine, in turn, these leadership studies which may be
classified according to psychological, sociological, and behavioral
approaches to the study of organizational leadership.

Psychological Studies of Leadership

The psychological approach to the study of leadership is based
largely upon the common recognition that an individual's behavior
is determined in part by his unique personality structure. That is,
what a person "is" may be fully as significant a behavioral determinant as what he "is expected to do."

Much of the early research on leadership was characterized by
intensive efforts to distinguish leaders from other people. Regarding the personal construct required for effective leadership in the
educational organization, some investigation and much speculation
was reported in the literature. From self-report tests of personality
and from descriptions of leaders by superiors and subordinates,
long lists of desirable personality traits were derived. These lengthy
lists became not unlike descriptions of the good Boy Scout. In the
absence of a suitable taxonomy, such lists, furthermore, frequently
included mutually contradictory traits—kind but firm, pensive but
active, steady but flexible, forceful but co-operative. Somewhat
disappointed with these results, authorities in the field assumed the
stance that some persons were "natural-born leaders" and that others were not; they frequently reminded the neophyte that "a pleas-
ing personality" was the *sine qua non* for anyone who would
attempt to lead his organization.[11]

Historically, the search for desirable personal qualities next
turned from a listing of traits to the use of "scientific" measures of
personality. Believing that the failure to discover significant personality characteristics of leaders was due primarily to the naïve
use of faulty procedures, many investigators adapted or developed
a variety of ingenious devices to measure leadership qualities.

11. Ward G. Reeder, *The Fundamentals of Public School Administration*,
p. 21. New York: Macmillan Co., 1958.

Thurstone,[12] for example, administered a figures test of perception and a card-sorting test to federally employed executives. Using the relationship of salary to age as a criterion of successful leadership, he discovered that successful executives scored higher than unsuccessful ones both in accuracy of perception and in ability to differentiate among categories in sorting cards. Chapple and Donald[13] constructed a machine, called an interaction chronograph, which measured certain verbal and nonverbal behaviors of an individual during a structured interview. From use of the chronograph in interviews held with supervisory and nonsupervisory personnel, they concluded that supervisors excelled in the following characteristics: initiative, dominance, speed of interaction, and adjustment to the interview situation. Henry[14] turned to a projective technique, the *Thematic Apperception Test*, to supplement interview and test data obtained from one hundred successful business executives. On the basis of their responses, he concluded that the successful executives were high in achievement drive, mobility drive, emotional alertness and activity, ability to organize unstructured situations, and tendencies to identify with superiors but not with subordinates.

After numerous psychological investigations of leadership had been conducted, concerted efforts were directed toward synthesizing the results of these studies in order to discover a personality syndrome universally characteristic of leaders. Stogdill examined 124 leadership studies conducted in both organizational and experimental environments. He concluded: "A person does not become a leader by virtue of some combination of traits, but the pattern of the personal characteristics of the leader must bear some relationship to the characteristics, activities, and goals of the followers." [15]

12. L. L. Thurstone, *A Factorial Study of Perception*, pp. 140-41. Chicago: University of Chicago Press, 1944.

13. Eliot D. Chapple and Gordon Donald, Jr., "A Method for Evaluating Supervisory Personnel," *Harvard Business Review*, XXIV (Winter, 1946), 201-3.

14. William E. Henry, "The Business Executive: The Psychodynamics of a Social Role," *American Journal of Sociology*, LIV (January, 1949), 286-91.

15. Ralph M. Stogdill, "Personal Factors Associated with Leadership: A Survey of the Literature," *Journal of Psychology*, XXV (1948), 35-71.

In a synthesis of the literature to 1954, Gibb stated that "numerous studies of leaders have failed to find any consistent pattern of traits which characterize leaders." [16] Pierce and Merrill likewise concluded: "Perhaps one of the results of the research is the conclusion drawn that the study of personal characteristics, *per se*, is only one aspect of the study of leadership." [17]

The consistent failure to find a generalized personality syndrome typical of leaders in any or all leadership settings may have been due to many factors. The following, for example, are the possibilities noted by Gibb: inadequate measurement, lack of comparability of data from different kinds of research, and the inability to describe leadership adequately.[18]

In view of present theoretical conceptualizations concerning administration and leadership, the failure to discover a universally applicable set of personality characteristics of the leader seems more logical than it does surprising. Increasingly the focus must be upon the relationship of the individual to the organization. While the extent to which "the man makes the job" or "the job makes the man" may be a relative matter, the fact remains that a major source of conflict derives from discrepancies between the basic personality structure of an individual and the demands of his organizational role. Every practicing school superintendent could, no doubt, cite numerous instances of this type of conflict. For example, he may, as a person, immensely dislike speaking before groups, yet, as a superintendent, he seems constantly to be mounting some podium. Or, at a somewhat deeper level, he may be an intense and introspective person, yet on the job each train of thought seems to be abruptly shattered.

The relationship of personality variables to performance in the role of public school principal was recently investigated by Lip-

16. Cecil A. Gibb, "Leadership," in *Handbook of Social Psychology*, p. 889. Edited by Gardner Lindzey. Cambridge, Massachusetts: Addison Wesley Publishing Co., 1954.

17. Truman M. Pierce and E. C. Merrill, Jr., "The Individual and Administrator Behavior," in *Administrative Behavior in Education*, p. 332. Edited by Roald F. Campbell and Russell T. Gregg. New York: Harper & Bros., 1957.

18. Gibb, *op. cit.*, p. 889.

ham.[19] From an analysis of this role, it was argued that the principal normatively could be expected to engage in purposeful activity, to strive for positions of higher status, to relate well to others, and to feel secure in the face of highly affective stimuli. It was hypothesized, therefore, that principals having a personality structure tending to produce the aforementioned behaviors would suffer less strain in fulfilling their roles; they would be rated more effective than those whose personal needs were incongruent with the role expectations. By the use of interviews, observations, and quasi-projective techniques, data were obtained from 84 principals in a Midwestern city school system. The hypotheses were substantiated. Those principals rated more effective by the superintendent of schools and members of the central office staff scored significantly higher in activity drive, achievement drive, social ability, and feelings of security than did the principals who were rated less effective.

Studies such as the foregoing are subject to numerous limitations. Guba[20] has noted, for example, that an adequate terminology for relating psychological or personal characteristics to sociological or organizational characteristics does not exist at the present time. Another limitation concerns the extent to which the data are generalizable. That is, the personal construct required for effective role performance in School X may differ markedly from that required in School Y. Likewise, the personal construct required for effective performance as a school principal may differ substantially from that required of the superintendent of schools, the business manager, or the instructional supervisor. In sum, the recent emphasis on commonalities in all fields of administration notwithstanding, care must be exercised when generalizing from situation to situation and from one leadership role to another.

At the present time, the extreme reaction to the failure of the traitist approach to isolate the personality syndrome of the universal leader appears to have abated. Having rescued both "the baby and the bath water," researchers may now, without apology, consider in a fresh perspective the importance of the psychological dimen-

19. James M. Lipham, "Personal Variables of Effective Administrators," *Administrator's Notebook*, IX (September, 1960), 1-4.

20. Guba, *op. cit.*, p. 129.

sion. In examining such an important factor as the motivation on the part of an individual to attempt leadership acts, for example, such personality variables as energy, need achievement, self-esteem, and attraction to the group are of importance, perhaps bearing a predictive relationship to whether or not the would-be leader will display task-oriented, interaction-oriented, or self-oriented leadership behavior.[21] Just as the focus upon the psychological dimension is essential in assessing the motivation of the leader, so also is this focus useful in assessing such important variables within the work group as morale, satisfaction, influence, esteem, involvement, and identification. Recently, however, many researchers have utilized these factors as criterion variables in studying a dimension of leadership that is equally as important as that of the psychological dimension—the sociological dimension.

Sociological Studies of Leadership

Recognizing that psychological factors were not entirely sufficient to account for leadership phenomena, many researchers during the past decade devoted increased study to sociological factors. Thus, the focus shifted from a study of personal needs and dispositions to a study of organizational roles and relationships—from a concern with the characteristics of the individual to a concern with the characteristics of the group. This shift in focus was rapid and drastic. Bearing some similarity to ancient nature-nurture, heredity-environment, and instinct-training controversies, a struggle ensued between the "traitists" and the "situationists," the latter emerging victorious from the fray.

Like the psychological investigations which preceded them, the sociological studies also were subject to many limitations. Indeed, many of the earlier sociological studies were concerned with group phenomena primarily and with leadership only incidentally, yet they do provide data concerning a host of organizational variables which the would-be leader dare not ignore.

Perhaps the most extensive comparison among groups, designed to distinguish the major dimensions by which groups differ and

21. Bernard M. Bass, *Leadership, Psychology, and Organizational Behavior*, pp. 146-57. New York: Harper & Bros., 1960.

thereby measure the impact of the leader, has been set forth by Hemphill.[22] He identified the following fifteen group dimensions: size, viscidity, homogeneity, flexibility, stability, permeability, polarization, autonomy, intimacy, and control (pertaining to the group as a unit); and position, participation, potency, hedonic tone, and dependence (expressing a respondent's relation to his group). Hemphill found two dimensions, viscidity (the feeling of cohesion in the group) and hedonic tone (the degree of satisfaction of group members) to correlate more highly with leadership adequacy than did the other dimensions. Guetzkow's[23] investigation of decision-making conferences and Katz, Maccoby, and Morse's[24] study of high- and low-production groups, likewise, emphasized the fact that working with people in groups is a complicated undertaking and that there are many differences among groups which are of crucial importance to the leader.

A major source of conflict for the leader of an organization is the situation in which he frequently finds himself attempting to fulfil simultaneously the expectations of two or more reference groups which may be contradictory in nature. Consider, for example, the position of the school superintendent with regard to providing supplies or equipment—only one of a multitude of functional problems with which he is faced daily. From the viewpoint of the teachers, the superintendent may legitimately be expected to maximize—or at least endorse—requests for supplies, materials, repairs, or facilities which they deem essential for their instructional needs. On the other hand, the board of education, or perhaps some frugal taxpayer, may view the appropriate role of the superintendent as one of reducing—or at least minimizing—educational expenditures. In effect, any final decision by the superintendent, even one of compromise, may be viewed by either or

22. John K. Hemphill, *Situational Factors in Leadership*. Columbus: Ohio State University, 1949.

23. Harold Guetzkow, *Groups, Leadership, and Men*. Pittsburgh: Carnegie Press, 1951.

24. Daniel Katz, Nathan Maccoby, and Nancy C. Morse, *Productivity, Supervision, and Morale in an Office Situation*. Ann Arbor, Michigan: University of Michigan, 1950.

both of the reference groups as largely unsatisfactory. The list of dilemmas, of which the foregoing is typical, might be expanded indefinitely, since the complexity of decisions concerning the educational enterprise is increasing.

Conflicts in expectations, moreover, transcend such specific functional concerns as program, plant, or personnel; they are related to generalized expectations for leadership as well. Moser[25] investigated the extent of conflict in generalized expectations held for the school principal's role. Intensive interviews designed to stimulate subjective responses concerning the principal's leadership were held with school personnel in twelve school systems. It was discovered that the teachers and the superintendent subject the principal to markedly different sets of leadership expectations and that the principal's behavior varies according to whether he is with superiors or subordinates. Finding that the principal emphasized "nomothetic" behaviors (stressing goal achievement, institutional regulations, and centralized authority) in his relations with the superintendent, and "idiographic" behaviors (stressing individual needs and wants, minimum rules, decentralized authority) in his interactions with teachers, Moser concluded that the principal is in a delicate position as a member of two organizational families.[26] Similar findings have been reported by Gross and others[27] concerning the school superintendent's role.

Just as conflict in expectations for the role of the leader may occur among reference groups, so also may conflicts occur within a reference group. In a study of the type of leadership teachers want, Moyer[28] had teachers react to eighty statements dealing with "leader-centered" and "group-centered" behavior on the part of

25. Robert P. Moser, "The Leadership Patterns of School Superintendents and School Principals," *Administrator's Notebook*, VI (September, 1957), 1-4.

26. *Ibid.*, p. 4.

27. Neal Gross, Ward S. Mason, and Alexander W. McEachern, *Explorations in Role Analysis: Studies of the School Superintendency Role*. New York: John Wiley & Sons, Inc., 1958.

28. Donald C. Moyer, "Leadership That Teachers Want." *Administrator's Notebook*, III (March, 1955), 1-4.

the principal. At the same time, they were asked to rate the personal and professional satisfaction they derived from their working situation. One of his major findings was that the greater the unity within a group in attitudes toward leadership, the higher the satisfaction in the group. When faculties were compared on the basis of their solidarity or homogeneity of attitudes toward leadership, those school faculties high in homogeneity were also high in overall satisfaction derived from the work situation.[29] Evidently, congruence in expectations among the members of a group emerges as a factor which is fully as significant as that of actual leadership style, which, until recently, has received the primary attention of researchers.

Thus far in this chapter, research has been examined concerning both the individual and the organizational dimensions of leadership. Research concerning the individual dimension represents the psychological approach to the study of leadership; research concerning the organizational dimension represents the sociological approach. The most recent approach to the study of leadership, however, is concerned with both dimensions and recognizes that both role and personality are determinants of observed behavior within an organization. These investigations may be subsumed under the title "behavioral studies of leadership."

Behavioral Studies of Leadership

Halpin provided a succinct explication of the behavioral approach to the study of leadership when he stated:

First of all, it focuses upon observed behavior rather than upon a posited capacity inferred from this behavior. No presuppositions are made about a one-to-one relationship between leader behavior and an underlying capacity or potentiality presumably determinative of this behavior. By the same token, no a priori assumptions are made that the leader behavior which a leader exhibits in one group situation will be manifested in other group situations. . . . Nor does the term . . . suggest that this behavior is determined either innately or situationally. Either determinant is possible, as is any combination of the two, but the concept

29. Moyer, *op. cit.*, p. 3.

of leader behavior does not itself predispose us to accept one in opposition to the other.[30]

Out of the work of the Personnel Research Board at Ohio State University, two dimensions of leadership—initiating structure and consideration—have emerged as significant dimensions for describing leader behavior. These two dimensions were delineated by Halpin and Winer,[31] from a factor analysis of responses to the *Leader Behavior Description Questionnaire* of Hemphill and Coons.[32]

These dimensions have been defined as follows:

1. Initiating structure refers to the leader's behavior in delineating the relationship between himself and the members of his work group, and in endeavoring to establish well-defined patterns of organization, channels of communication, and methods of procedure.

2. Consideration refers to behavior indicative of friendship, mutual trust, respect, and warmth in the relationship between the leader and the members of his staff.[33]

In a study of the leadership behavior of aircraft commanders, Halpin[34] discovered that the effective leaders were those who scored high on both dimensions—initiating structure and consideration. Hemphill[35] came to a similar conclusion from a study of departmental administrators in a liberal-arts college. In a subsequent study

30. Andrew W. Halpin, *The Leadership Behavior of School Superintendents*, p. 12. Chicago: Midwest Administration Center, University of Chicago, 1959 (reprinted).

31. Andrew W. Halpin and B. James Winer, "A Factorial Study of the Leader Behavior Descriptions," in *Leader Behavior: Its Description and Measurement*. Edited by Ralph M. Stogdill and Alvin E. Coons. Columbus: Ohio State University, 1957.

32. John K. Hemphill and Alvin E. Coons, "Development of the Leader Behavior Description Questionnaire," in *Leader Behavior: Its Description and Measurement, op. cit.*

33. Halpin, *The Leadership Behavior of School Superintendents, op. cit.*, p. 4.

34. Andrew W. Halpin, "The Leader Behavior and Effectiveness of Aircraft Commanders," in *Leader Behavior: Its Description and Measurement, op. cit.*

35. John K. Hemphill, "Patterns of Leadership Behavior Associated with Administrative Reputation in the Department of a College," *Journal of Educational Psychology*, XLVI (November, 1955), 385-401.

of school superintendents, Halpin[36] secured descriptions of the leadership behavior of school superintendents from the superintendents themselves, from members of their administrative staff, and from members of their boards of education. Results of the study revealed effective or desirable leadership behavior to be characterized by high scores of both initiating structure and consideration. Similar results were obtained by Evenson[37] in a study of high-school principals.

Noting, after Hemphill, that "an outside observer can be aware of consistent behavior occurring during an interaction that has not been perceived by the parties to the interaction," [38] the staff associates of the Midwest Administration Center at the University of Chicago conducted an intensive study of on-the-job behavior of school superintendents in four Midwestern communities.[39] At intermittent periods throughout the school year, staff associates trained in the nonparticipant-observation technique visited, observed, and recorded verbal and nonverbal behaviors of the school superintendents in interaction with others. Reports of the observations were prepared and subjected to individual and group analyses utilizing the leadership dimensions of initiating structure and consideration. In addition to serving as a scheme for postanalysis of observed interaction, the dimensions were utilized on a limited number of occasions as a perceptual screen for observing on-the-job behavior of the superintendents. Use of the dimensions as a perceptual screen was directed toward providing an answer to the following question: "How does one behave when one is initiating structure or showing consideration?"

The dimensions were, indeed, useful for describing leader behavior. For example, the superintendents were found to initiate

36. Halpin, *The Leadership Behavior of School Superintendents, op. cit.*, p. 79.

37. Warren L. Evenson, "Leadership Behavior of High School Principals," *National Association of Secondary-School Principals Bulletin*, XLIII (September, 1959), 96-101.

38. Hemphill, "Administration as Problem Solving," *op. cit.*, p. 96.

39. James M. Lipham, "Initiating Structure and Consideration," *Observation of Administrator Behavior*, pp. 27-68. Edited by Staff Associates, Midwest Administration Center. Chicago: University of Chicago, 1959.

structures such as the following: a joint committee of maintenance supervisors and instructional supervisors to establish a school for custodians, a new procedure for assigning utilization of school facilities during evening hours, and a change in responsibility for revising student handbooks from a committee of principals to a representative committee of principals, teachers, and students.

Of the total observed behaviors of the superintendents in the study, 671 interactions, it was surprising to discover that the leadership dimension of initiating structure could be inferred in less than *3 per cent* of the superintendents' interactions; the dimension of consideration, in *23 per cent*. Two reasons were believed to account for such a variation in these percentages. The first concerned the methodology of the study; the second, the nature of the dimensions themselves.

In analyzing the interactions of the superintendents, the researchers found it easier to infer the dimension of consideration than to infer the dimension of initiating structure. This was contrary to expectations, since the definition of the initiating structure dimension had been made more explicit by Hemphill[40]—to include *attempted, accepted*, and *effective* leadership—than had the consideration dimension. A detailed examination of the circumstances under which the dimension of initiating structure may be inferred, however, provided an explanation for this finding. The difficulty, in the Midwest Center study, was not in the explicitness of the dimensions, but in the use of observation as a technique for obtaining evidence. Since the focus in this study remained upon the superintendent, evidence of the initiating structure dimension was limited primarily to recording *attempted* leadership acts. There was obtained certain limited evidence that an *attempted* structure was *accepted* when an individual responded to the superintendent: "Yes, we will try this new way." But to obtain immediate evidence that an *accepted* structure was *effective* would have required that observation be made of many people in addition to the superintendent.

As indicated above, the assessment of behavior through observational procedures is subject to numerous limitations and the nature

40. Hemphill, "Administration as Problem Solving," *op. cit.*, pp. 105-6.

of this assessment was believed to account for the low frequency, 3 per cent, of leadership behaviors by the school superintendents observed in the Midwest Center study. However, an entirely different procedure, in-basket performance in a simulated school situation, was utilized by Hemphill, Griffiths, and Frederiksen[41] to assess the behavior of school principals. This study, which is described in chapter viii by John Hemphill, reached a major conclusion that no factor clearly recognizable as leadership appeared in the analysis of the principals' work.

Regarding the nature of the two dimensions, the consideration dimension was found in the Midwest Center study to possess both positive and negative components, whereas the initiating structure dimension possessed only one. That is, negative initiating structure was difficult, if not impossible, to discover. Let us see why this is true. Suppose that a superintendent attempts to initiate a structure and that this structure is accepted. If subsequent events reveal the attempted and accepted structure is ineffective, it may be logical to assume that the parties involved would again bring this fact to the attention of the superintendent. To the extent that he takes a new action to amend the structure, a new series of leadership acts would be attempted. To the extent that the leader takes no additional action in such a circumstance, it may be surmised only that he fails to initiate structure. Thus, scores on the dimension of initiating structure may vary from no action to positive action. Consideration, on the other hand, possesses both positive and negative components. Some behaviors may be scored as highly considerate; others, highly inconsiderate.

The Midwest Center study also revealed that the leadership dimensions of initiating structure and consideration were interactive. Many behaviors could be classified appropriately in both dimensions. Structure was usually initiated in some manner with regard to consideration. Concerning this circumstance, Halpin has concluded:

The correlation between the two dimensions—*consideration* and *ini-*

41. John K. Hemphill, Daniel E. Griffiths, and Norman Frederiksen, *Administrative Performance and Personality.* New York: Teachers College Bureau of Publications, Columbia University, 1962.

tiating structure—shows that an effective leader can initiate structure without sacrificing consideration. Yet we repeatedly encounter superintendents who fear to take a stand, who hesitate to initiate structure, lest they be accused of being anti-democratic. This is nonsense, for the superintendents who adopt this attitude lose the respect of their staffs; teachers can quickly spot the phony who tries to hide his own ineptness in the soggy oatmeal of a pseudo group-process.[42]

In sum, the results of the Midwest Center study revealed that the dimensions of initiating structure and consideration were useful for classifying leader behavior, accounted for a relatively small percentage of the on-the-job behavior of school superintendents, were not of the same order, and were interactive in nature. The findings of the study, moreover, tended to reveal that the dimension of initiating structure is particularly useful for distinguishing between leadership and administration.

Numerous other studies have isolated or hypothesized dimensions similar to those of initiating structure and consideration. In a recent summary of the evidence to substantiate these dimensions, Bass,[43] for example, has cited over twenty such studies which were conducted in organizational environments, primarily military and industrial settings. Within the educational setting, the theoretical derivation by Getzels and Guba [44] of "nomothetic" and "idiographic" styles of leader behavior bears some similarity to initiating structure and consideration dimensions. Getzels and Guba have defined the nomothetic leadership style as one which places emphasis upon organizational role-expectations; the idiographic leadership style places emphasis upon individual need-dispositions. Willower[45] utilized the nomothetic-idiographic conceptualization to investigate the relationship between leadership styles and leaders' perceptions of subordinates. Among other relationships, he found that the school principal whose leadership style was characterized

---

42. Andrew W. Halpin, "The Superintendent's Effectiveness as a Leader," *Administrator's Notebook*, VII (October, 1958), 3.

43. Bass, *op. cit.*, pp. 101-5.

44. Getzels and Guba, *op. cit.*, pp. 435-38.

45. Donald J. Willower, "Leadership Styles and Leaders' Perceptions of Subordinates," *Journal of Educational Sociology*, XXXIV (October, 1960), 58-64.

as idiographic tended to regard teachers as professional persons to a greater extent than did the principal whose behavior was described as nomothetic.

The behavioral approach to the study of leadership has provided additional insights into the nature of leadership, the distinction between administration and leadership, the relationship between sociological and psychological dimensions of leadership, and the relationship between emerging theories of administration and theories of leadership. Perhaps the greatest contribution of the behavioral approach, however, is that it has highlighted the need for developing a better understanding of leadership.

Toward an Understanding of Leadership

In view of the multitude of studies which have been concerned with leadership, it seems somewhat anomalous to suggest that our knowledge in this area is still limited. Of the completed investigations, however, only a limited number have been concerned with leadership in complex organizational settings; still fewer have drawn any distinction between administration and leadership. The definition of leadership we have proposed—the initiation of a new structure or procedure for accomplishing an organization's goals or for changing an organization's goals—reveals a number of problems in need of further clarification.

First, we may consider the term "initiating," which is embodied in our definition of leadership. Like most process words, "initiating" is multidimensional in nature. The following question might, therefore, be raised: "Just what is involved in initiating?" Prior to initiating, for instance, would surely lie the decision to initiate. Such a decision would, perforce, be concerned with a problematic situation viewed in terms of decision alternatives each of which, for the leader, might have such positive and negative valences as the desire to be right and the desire to co-operate.[46] Once the decision has been made to initiate or not to initiate, then plans must be made to implement the decision; plans for activities would need to be communicated, co-ordinated, and eventually evaluated. Thus, the

---

46. Daniel E. Griffiths, "Administration as Decision-making," in *Administrative Theory in Education, op. cit.*, pp. 119-49.

initial concept used to define leadership, "initiating," appears to contain many of the elements of the well-documented "process" approach to the study, not of leadership behavior, but of administrative behavior. Further research might well be directed, therefore, toward determining the extent to which the processes involved in both leading and administering are similar in nature.

Another important problem relates to the concept "structure" which is also included in our definition of leadership. As indicated earlier in this chapter, much of the research on leadership has been concerned with randomly-selected, *unstructured* groups. Of those leadership studies which have dealt with organizational leadership, moreover, the focus primarily has been upon intra-organizational structures and relationships. To better understand leadership, we can no longer afford to ignore extra-organizational variables—the relationship of the leader to the larger social structure of which the organization is a part.

A third problem which is raised by our distinction between administration and leadership concerns evaluation. The term "accomplish" demands that the question, "In terms of what criteria?" be raised. The absence of an ultimate criterion for assessing the extent to which an organization is attaining its goals has caused many researchers to focus attention upon process outcomes, rather than product outcomes. In educational organizations particularly, the emphasis has not been upon the nature of the product of the school but upon how smoothly the school operates—the extent to which "the ship is well-oiled." Unfortunately, most researchers have utilized only one or two intermediate criteria, such as morale or satisfaction, as a basis for drawing conclusions concerning leadership. They have failed to recognize that, conceivably, it is precisely these "happiness" indices that are temporarily jeopardized most by a given leadership act. The absence of an ultimate criterion of organizational accomplishment renders it particularly difficult to determine the extent to which any given leadership act represents an accomplishment. It is not suggested that subsequent research on leadership should be directed toward establishing an ultimate criterion of effectiveness; it is suggested, however, that additional research is needed which utilizes a multiple-criterion approach for the evaluation of leader effectiveness.

The final concept to be considered is that of "goals." As indicated earlier, both organizational and individual goals are important; the relationship between the two seems crucial. Numerous social scientists[47] have expressed concern regarding the extent to which the individual has internalized organizational goals and, in the process, has become an "organization man." In this regard, leadership may constitute an interesting paradox. The leader, viewed in one context, is less an "organization man" than the nonleader. The leader's commitment to individualistic goals may be so strong that he must challenge the existing organization. When viewed in a broader context, however, the leader becomes an "organization man's organization man." His commitment to organizational goals may be so strong that he must challenge the existing organization for the good of the organization. Clearly, additional studies are needed concerning the extent to which leaders are modified by organizational goals and the extent to which organizational goals become modified by leaders.

In summary, the position has been taken in this chapter that while leadership and administration may have many factors in common, they basically are mutually exclusive. To some, restriction of either of the terms will be viewed as not only unnecessary but also undesirable. But to understand better the nature of leadership in complex organizations, such restriction of definitions serves a useful purpose at present—that of revealing how limited our knowledge of organizational leadership is.

47. See, for example: Chris Argyris, *Personality and Organization* (New York: Harper & Bros., 1957); E. Wight Bakke, *The Fusion Process* (New Haven, Connecticut: Labor and Management Center, Yale University, 1953); Al Wheelis, *The Quest for Identity* (New York: W. W. Norton Co., 1958); and W. H. Whyte, *The Organization Man* (New York: Simon & Schuster), 1956.

CHAPTER VII

Maintaining the Organization in Dynamic Equilibrium

RICHARD C. LONSDALE

Perspective

"Maintaining the organization" can have at least four different meanings [1] at different levels of generality. At the most particular level it can mean satisfying the personal and social needs of the participants (e.g., employees, owners, clients) in an organization in order to retain their support and to hold the organization together. In this sense, the term stands for one of the two basic purposes of organizations which shall be referred to as "needs-satisfaction." At a more general level, "maintaining the organization" can include both basic purposes of organizations: "task-achievement" as well as needs-satisfaction. Here it means keeping the organization functioning by meeting its broad purposes. On another level, "maintaining the organization" can contrast with "changing the organization," the former connoting the static organization and the latter the dynamic organization. Most useful for the purpose of this chapter is a fourth meaning, combining the second with an adaptation of the third. In this chapter, therefore, "maintaining the organization" means sustaining the organization in dynamic equilibrium through a developing integration of task-achievement and needs-satisfaction. This meaning will be expanded in the last section of the chapter.

Given this definition, "maintaining the organization" includes, in part, the interaction between the individual and the organization, an interaction which involves five levels. Thus, (1) the individual or self occupies or enacts (2) a role or roles in (3) a work group

---

1. Charters gives it still another meaning in his chapter where he denotes "organization maintenance" as comprising input-output functions and work-co-ordination functions.

within (4) the organization, which in turn functions within (5) a culture. Figure 1 represents these five levels, the point of tangency symbolizing the interaction involved.

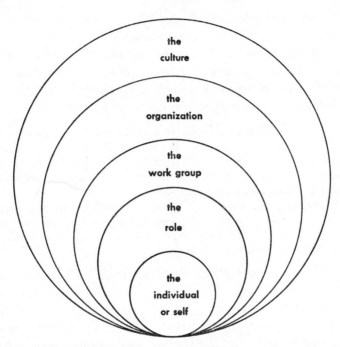

FIG. 1.—Levels of interaction of the individual and the organization. (Adapted from Daniel E. Griffiths, "Administrative Theory and Change in Organizations," in *Innovation in Education*. Edited by Matthew B. Miles. New York: Bureau of Publications, Teachers College, Columbia University, 1964.)

The remainder of the chapter presents an analysis of organizational purposes, role theory in relation to task-achievement, organizational inducements in relation to needs-satisfaction, organizational climate, and system theory in relation to organizational survival.

Organizational Purposes

In the development of organizational theory, many writers have pondered the question, "What are the purposes of organizations?" The emergence of a fairly high degree of consensus can be seen as a common theme running through the analyses of a number of authors over the past quarter-century.

ILLUSTRATIVE ANALYSES

Barnard, 1938.—In 1938 Barnard formulated his now-familiar concepts of "effectiveness" and "efficiency." "Effectiveness" was the "accomplishment of the recognized objectives of cooperative action." [2] "Efficiency" was the capacity of an organization to maintain itself by the individual satisfactions it affords. In further analysis of efficiency, he introduced the concept of equilibrium:

> This may be called its capacity of equilibrium, the balancing of burdens by satisfactions which results in continuance. Efficiency or equilibrium can be secured either by changing motives in individuals (or securing substitute individuals of appropriate motives), which is cooperation on a social factor, or by its *productive* results which can be distributed to individuals. These productive results are either material or social, or both. As to some individuals, material is required for satisfaction; as to others, social benefits are required. As to most individuals, both material and social benefits are required in different proportions.[3]

Roethlisberger and Dickson, 1939.—In a book published the next year, growing out of the same Harvard fount, Roethlisberger and Dickson observed: "An industrial organization may be regarded as performing two major functions, that of producing a product and that of creating and distributing satisfactions among the individual members of the organization." [4]

Homans, 1950.—Homans, another one of the Harvard group, related the same two dimensions of purpose to the concepts of authority and control:

"Authority—the acceptance of orders—and control—obedience to the norms of the group—are not different in kind from one another but are two forms of the same process. And the job of a leader is twofold: (*a*) to attain the purposes of the group, and (*b*) in so doing to maintain a balance of incentives, both reward

---

2. Chester I. Barnard, *The Functions of the Executive*, p. 55. Cambridge: Harvard University Press, 1938.

3. *Ibid.*, p. 57.

4. F. J. Roethlisberger and William J. Dickson, *Management and the Worker*, p. 552. Cambridge: Harvard University Press, 1939.

and punishment, sufficient to induce his followers to obey him." [5]

Cartwright and Zander, 1953.—In 1953, in their first compilation of research and theory on group dynamics, Cartwright and Zander [6] claimed that most or perhaps all group objectives fit under the two headings of "goal achievement behaviors" and "group maintenance behaviors." This conclusion was based upon their synthesis of research with small nonformal groups.

Ohio State University Personnel Research Board, 1940's-50's.— Meanwhile, in the late forties and early fifties, the Ohio State University Personnel Research Board was conducting its leadership studies in which the "Leadership Behavior Description Questionnaire" was developed as a tool for assessing two dimensions of leadership, "initiating structure in interaction" and "consideration." Halpin defined the former as referring to the behavior of the leader "in delineating the relationship between himself and members of the work-group, and in endeavoring to establish well-defined patterns of organization, channels of communication, and methods of procedure." [7] "Consideration" he described as referring to "behavior indicative of friendship, mutual trust, respect, and warmth in the relationship between the leader and the members of his staff." [8]

Getzels and Guba, 1950's.—Also during the 1950's Getzels, working at the University of Chicago with Guba (his first doctoral candidate there), formulated his social-process model of behavior, now widely used in training programs and research in educational administration and described in chapter v by Griffiths. Although not developed as an analysis of organizational purposes, this social-process model, with its nomothetic (task-achievement) and idiographic (needs-satisfaction) dimensions, clearly fits into the stream of thought being traced here concerning organizational purposes.

5. George C. Homans, *The Human Group*, p. 423. New York: Harcourt, Brace & Co., 1950.

6. *Group Dynamics: Research and Theory*, p. 541. Edited by Dorwin Cartwright and Alvin Zanders. Evanston, Illinois: Row, Peterson & Co., 1953.

7. Andrew W. Halpin, *The Leadership Behavior of School Superintendents*, p. 4. The School-Community Development Study Monograph Series, No. 4. Columbus: College of Education, Ohio State University, 1956.

8. *Ibid.*

For example, in the report of the second (1959) University of Chicago conference on theory in educational administration, Guba, drawing upon his theoretical work with Getzels, wrote:

> The unique task of the administrator can now be understood as that of mediating between these two sets of behavior-eliciting forces, that is, the nomothetic and the idiographic, so as to produce behavior which is at once organizationally useful as well as individually satisfying. Action which will lead to such behavior on the part of personnel is the highest expression of the administrator's art.[9]

Stogdill, 1959.—Both Stogdill and McGregor (the latter writing in more popularized form especially for an audience of business executives) integrated the two major purposes of organizations, thus emphasizing the point made by Guba. Stogdill [10] presented a theory of organizational achievement in which he saw "member inputs" (behaviors) comprising performances, interactions, and expectations which worked through mediating variables of a formal structure (function, status, and purpose and norms) and a role structure (responsibility, authority, and operations) to yield "group outputs" (achievement) composed of productivity, morale, and integration. He defined "productivity" as "the degree of change in expectancy values resulting from group operations"; "morale" as "freedom from restraint in action toward a group goal"; and "integration" as "capacity to maintain structure and function under stress." [11]

McGregor, 1960.—McGregor [12] contended that too many business organizations still conduct their affairs in accordance with a

---

9. Egon G. Guba, "Research in Internal Administration—What Do We Know?" in *Administrative Theory as a Guide to Action*, p. 121 (edited by Roald F. Campbell and James M. Lipham. Chicago: Midwest Administration Center, University of Chicago, 1960). For one of the latest presentations of the model described above, see Jacob W. Getzels, "Conflict and Role Behavior in the Educational Setting," in *Readings in the Social Psychology of Education*, pp. 309-18 (edited by W. W. Charters, Jr., and N. L. Gage. Boston: Allyn & Bacon, 1963. A note on p. 310 of that chapter lists prior formulations of the model).

10. Ralph M. Stogdill, *Individual Behavior and Group Achievement: a Theory*. New York: Oxford University Press, 1959.

11. *Ibid.*, pp. 277-78.

12. Douglas McGregor, *The Human Side of Enterprise*. New York: McGraw-Hill Book Co., 1960.

traditional view of direction and control based on task-achievement only, with no real recognition of the importance of satisfying individual needs for self-development and growth. He labeled as "Theory X" a set of assumptions about human nature and human behavior underlying this traditional view: that people dislike and will avoid work if they can; that they therefore have to be coerced, controlled, directed, and even threatened with punishment to get them to work toward organizational objectives; and that they treasure security above all else because they have little sense of responsibility or ambition and simply want to be directed.

In contrast, he described the more enlightened view of the task of organization as based on "Theory Y": that people like work and find it as natural as play or rest; that they will use self-direction and self-control in working toward organizational objectives they accept; that working toward organizational objectives can yield a variety of rewards, of which the most significant are ego-satisfaction and self-actualization; and that, given proper conditions, people will even seek responsibility and use a high degree of their potentiality of imagination, ingenuity, and creativity in solving problems of organization.

Likert, 1961.—In a volume summarizing the major findings of the research program of the Institute for Social Research at the University of Michigan, Likert formulated what he called an integrating principle which "provides a fundamental formula for obtaining the full potential of every major motive which can be harnessed in a working situation." [13] This "principle of supportive relationships" is as follows:

> The leadership and other processes of the organization must be such as to ensure a maximum probability that in all interactions and all relationships with the organization, each member will, in the light of his background, values, and expectations, view the experience as supportive and one which builds and maintains his sense of personal worth and importance. [14]

Further, because of the finding concerning the central role of

---

13. Rensis Likert, *New Patterns of Management,* p. 103. New York: McGraw-Hill Book Co., 1961.

14. *Ibid.*

the work group, "management will make full use of the potential capacities of its human resources only when each person in an organization is a member of one or more effectively functioning work groups that have a high degree of group loyalty, effective skills of interaction, and high performance goals."[15]

THE CONTINUING CONTROVERSY

If there has been achieved a fair degree of consensus on the two basic purposes of organization, there certainly has not been achieved any consensus on the relative importance of each. Thus, in one of three articles published during the summer of 1962, Dale[16] contended that human relations is not the *sine qua non* for executive success; rather, he called for men who know the field, who have technical skills, in contrast to generalized management skills. In a second article, Leavitt[17] cited the need for differentiated sets of subsystems within organizations, in some of which Taylor's approach of routinizing and controlling would be used, while others would use the participative approach of making the jobs more challenging and novel. "In so doing we may end up being efficient and at once human and unhuman, depending on where, within the large organization, we choose to focus."[18] On the other hand, in a third article,[19] Argyris saw industrial personnel relations now entering a new era concerned with helping workers become self-realizing by assisting them to enlarge and express their full potentialities, thereby increasing their responsibility, commitment, competence, self-respect, and respect for others.

Organizational analysis has helped the administrator understand the alternative purposes of organization and some of the consequences of choosing each. The choice is still his: whether to emphasize one and subordinate the other or to work toward the higher

15. *Ibid.*, p. 104.

16. Ernest Dale, "Men Who Can't Manage," *Atlantic Monthly*, CCX (July, 1962), 58-62.

17. Harold J. Leavitt, "Unhuman Organization," *Harvard Business Review*, XL, (July-August, 1962), 90-98.

18. *Ibid.*, p. 97.

19. Chris Argyris, "A New Era in Personnel Relations," *Dun's Review and Modern Industry*, (June, 1962), 40-41, 177-78.

level of integrating the task-serving and needs-serving purposes of organization.

Role Theory in Relation to Task-Achievement [20]

To achieve the task of an organization, whatever that task may be, requires the combined efforts of a number of people working in a hierarchy of superordinate-subordinate relationships with each other and carrying out varying duties and responsibilities. A significant contribution to an understanding of the nature and operation of that organizational structure is the set of concepts and constructs drawn from role theory, an area of theory bringing together analyses and findings from the fields of sociology, anthropology, and psychology.

ELEMENTS OF ROLE THEORY

According to role theory, organizations are social systems made up of people who occupy various "positions" in vertical (hierarchical) and horizontal relationship to each other. Any given position is the location of one individual or class of individuals within the social system. The way people behave in these positions depends

20. This section is a synthesis drawn from a number of sources, especially the following:

Irwin Deutscher, "Role Theory and Role Conflict." Lecture during Administrative Interns' Seminar on Educational Change, Syracuse University, July 17, 1963.

Getzels, *op. cit.*, chap. ix.

Neal Gross, Ward S. Mason, and Alexander W. McEachern, *Explorations in Role Analysis: Studies of the School Superintendency Role.* New York: John Wiley & Sons, 1958.

Raymond Hunt, "Role and Role Conflict." Lecture during Administrative Interns' Seminar on Educational Change, University of Buffalo, July 6, 1962.

Ralph Linton, "Status and Role," in *Human Relations: Concepts and Cases in Concrete Social Science*, I, *Concepts*, pp. 98-110. Edited by Hugh Cabot and Joseph A. Kahl. Cambridge: Harvard University Press, 1953. (Reprinted from Ralph Linton, *The Study of Man.* New York: D. Appleton-Century Co., 1936.)

Henry A. Murray and Clyde Kluckhohn, "Outline of a Conception of Personality," in *Personality in Nature, Society, and Culture*, chap. i. Edited by Clyde Kluckhohn and Henry A. Murray, with the collaboration of David M. Schneider. New York: Alfred A. Knopf, 1953 (second edition).

Theodore R. Sarbin, "Role Theory," in *Handbook of Social Psychology*, I, *Theory and Method*, chap. vi. Edited by Gardner Lindzey. Reading, Massachusetts: Addison-Wesley Publishing Co., 1954.

partly on how they think they are expected to behave and on how others actually expect them to behave. These expectations are called "roles." The behavior of people in these social roles is also affected by their personalities.[21]

A deeper penetration of the concept of "role" reveals a number of possible ramifications. Thus, a "role prescription" is a social norm for a role, abstractly defined by the culture. A "role stereotype" is an individual's own personalized perception of a role, which may be largely shared with other people or be idiosyncratic. A "role description" is a report of behaviors actually performed by role incumbents. A "role expectation" is an anticipation of a behavior or set of behaviors of another person in a role, a set of evaluative standards. An expectation may have direction, in that it may be either a prescription or a proscription, and it may have intensity, on a continuum ranging from the permissive through the preferential to the mandatory. Role expectations are often complementary, one role carrying with it certain expectations of the other role, as with teacher and student or school board member and administrator. Expectations for a role may include personal attributes desired in the role incumbent as well as anticipated behaviors. A "role perception" is an estimate of another person's expectation for one's own role. If the other person is seen as having a right to hold this expectation, it is regarded as "legitimate"; if he is seen as not having such a right, then it is regarded as "illegitimate." Similarly, one's expectations for another role may be viewed as "rights," while another person's expectations for one's own role are "obligations." Since many people may have expectations for a given focal position or role, a particular set of expectations coming from a single counter position or role may be described as applying to a "role sector." Finally, any particular role behavior which has primarily a gratificational or deprivational significance is called a "sanction."

"Role-playing" is a term usually used to describe the overt social behavior of a person, what he does in his role. "Role-taking" pertains to one's empathizing with another's role, usually in a passive, nonovert manner. "Playing at a role" is pretending that one is act-

---

21. From this brief description it may be seen that the Getzels-Guba social behavior model (*supra*) is really a part of role theory.

ing out a role, as in a training situation. Because of the possible confusion between "role-playing" and "playing at a role," the former is often better referred to as "role enactment."

The "status" of a position or role is the rank or prestige it has within its social structure. The individual's perception of his own status is his "subjective status," which is in contrast with his "objective status" (that which is accorded to him by others). This pair of terms is somewhat related to "ascribed" and "achieved" status, where "ascribed" refers to status assigned to an individual because of his position, regardless of his abilities or differences; such ascribed status attaches to the role itself. "Achieved status" is that earned by the particular incumbent in a role because of his special qualities and performance. Any given occupied role may, therefore, have a portion of both ascribed and achieved status.

Sarbin [22] identified three factors influencing the variations in role enactment of an individual: the validity of his role perception, his skill in enacting the role, and the influence of his own cognitive structure on his perception and enactment of the role.

Murray and Kluckhohn concluded that each individual has "the *need for roleship*, that is, the need to become and to remain an accepted and respected, differentiated and integrated, part of a congenial, functioning group, the collective purposes of which are congruent with the individual's ideals. So long as the individual feels this way about the group that he has joined, he will try to abide, as best he can, by its *schedule* of role functions." [23]

ROLE DIMENSIONS

Roles have a variety of dimensions which are useful in explaining and predicting role behavior. Thus, a role may be "manifest" or "latent." A manifest role is one's overt or apparent role, e.g., the role of secondary-school principal. A latent role usually refers to a social role which might emerge as a result of some social characteristic or to a secondary role subordinated to a primary role. For example, a secondary-school principal who was 62, with 25 years experience as a principal, a widower, and president of the Rotary

22. Sarbin, *op. cit.*, p. 255.
23. Murray and Kluckhohn, *op. cit.*, p. 19.

Club, would have latent roles dependent upon his age, experience, sex and marital status, and position in the social structure of the community which could have a special influence upon his behavior as principal.

One pair of latent roles of significance in administration is the "local" and the "cosmopolitan." Among teachers, a "pure local" would be one born, reared, and educated in the same community in which he has done all of his teaching, while a "pure cosmopolitan" would be, for example, a teacher appointed to a position of chairman of the English department from outside the school system and who felt his allegiance to be to English as a discipline. Most teachers would represent various midpoints along this continuum. Locals tend to have a stronger allegiance to the vertical, institutional subculture; cosmopolitans, to the horizontal, professional subculture embracing various separate associations. Studies, such as those by Merton,[24] Gouldner,[25] and Suttoff,[26] reveal the influences of local or cosmopolitan orientations on role enactment.

"Specific" roles are those clearly defined with sharp boundaries, such as a priest at Mass or a clerk in a postoffice. "Diffuse" roles, in contrast, are defined with great leeway for variation in role behavior by individual incumbents, such as the role of wife in American society or of counselor in schools.

A "universalistic" role pervades many areas of experience and of life; the incumbent cannot easily set aside the expectations the role carries. This is again illustrated especially well by the role of clergyman or of teacher in a small town. A role is "particularistic" when it is specific to one area of experience and life, as with a commercial pilot or a cook in a school cafeteria.

Roles may be "sequential" when they succeed one another along a life cycle or career pattern; or they may be "concurrent" when

24. Robert K. Merton, *Social Theory and Social Structure*, pp. 387-436. Glencoe, Illinois: The Free Press, 1957.

25. Alvin W. Gouldner, "Cosmopolitans and Locals: Toward an Analysis of Latent Social Roles," *Administrative Science Quarterly*, II (December, 1957), 281-306; II (March, 1958), 444-80.

26. John Suttoff, "Local-Cosmopolitan Orientation and Participation in School Affairs," *Administrator's Notebook*, IX (November, 1960), 1-4.

one individual fills several roles simultaneously. Sequential family roles would include child, youth, adult bachelor, husband, father, grandfather; sequential professional roles would include student, teacher, vice-principal, principal, assistant superintendent, superintendent. Concurrent roles would be school business manager, father of three children, superintendent of the Methodist church school, and chairman of the Community Chest drive. Normally, among concurrent roles one of them has to be "salient" at any given time.

ROLE CONFLICT

Role theory has particular utility in clarifying the nature of some of the conflict within organizations. Role conflict may stem from a number of sources.[27] One of these is the possible conflict between cultural values and institutional expectations. The secondary-school principal may recognize the general cultural value placed upon a well-balanced program of education while feeling distinct pressure from the school board and the community for public display activities by the musical and dramatic organizations and the athletic teams.

Conflicts within roles and between roles are the most common of role conflicts. One kind occurs when the manner in which a person thinks he is expected to behave (role perception) is different from the manner others really expect him to behave (role expectation). An administrator may think the board of education wants him to refer most problems to it for consideration during meetings, while the board really thinks its meetings are too cluttered and wishes the administrator himself would make more decisions. Another kind occurs when two reference groups have conflicting expectations of a role incumbent, as when the teachers' association expects the superintendent to press for higher salaries while the school board expects him to keep the school taxes down. Or there may be conflict among members within a particular reference group concerning their expectations for a role. One group of teachers may expect their principal to be an idea man and an initiator; but another group may simply want the principal to stay out of their way and be ready to supply the art paper and chalk when needed.

27. See Getzels, *op. cit.*; Murray and Kluckhohn, *op. cit.* Part of this subsection necessarily duplicates part of Griffiths' chapter v.

Dalton proposed a type of conflict in perceptions between incumbents of co-ordinate or related roles. Formal roles always embrace supplemental informal roles, and individuals will vary in their capacity to assume these informal roles, especially in those "clashes between formalists and informalists over when and how far to depart from a formal role." [28]

Conflict can occur over the relative saliency accorded two or more concurrent roles at a given point in time. This is the plight of the married woman teacher who at 4:30 may be torn between giving further help to a small group of students and going home to get an early supper for her husband who has an evening meeting.

A separate category includes conflict between role expectations and personality dispositions. For example, the operation of the daily schedule and the constant flow of required reports may cause real role strain for teachers disinclined toward punctuality and systematic work habits. A special case of this kind of conflict is that deriving from personality disorders.

CONFLICT RESOLUTION AND THE PROCESS OF CHANGE

Some degree of conflict within organizations is inevitable; indeed, a certain amount of it is healthy and may be quite productive of change, since it may bring about creative transformations and inventions resulting in the improvement of the structure and functioning of the organization. Some administrators, perhaps intolerant of ambiguity, seem bent on attempting to resolve all conflict or at least on covering it up. They miss the fact that some amount of social disorganization makes for stimulating relationships and positive change. But the question is, "How much?" And there is no pat answer to it. Only further study of the antecedents and consequences of role and other kinds of conflict can begin to supply the answer.

Meanwhile, wasteful and pointless role conflict can certainly be reduced by analyzing and studying roles and communicating more objectively with respect to them. Participants in the organization can observe role behavior of others and learn from them. They can

28. Melville Dalton, *Men Who Manage, Fusions of Feeling and Theory in Administration*, p. 257. New York: John Wiley & Sons, 1959.

read and talk about roles and their meaning. They can practice and then evaluate their own role behavior, using the language of role theory. For role theory provides a means for conceptualizing some of the problems of individual performance within the organization in a way which provides more insights and a more rational view of organizational behavior than have commonly been available.

This section on role theory as a conceptualization of organizational structure has related to the task-achievement dimension of organizational purpose. A discussion of organizational inducements in relation to the needs-satisfaction dimension is in order.

Organizational Inducements in Relation to Needs-satisfaction

To satisfy the needs of its workers, an organization offers certain inducements or incentives, hoping that thereby the workers will be motivated to carry out their roles with sufficient effectiveness to achieve the tasks of the organization. The resulting job-satisfaction and productivity constitutes what is known as morale. This section will treat these concepts.

INDIVIDUAL NEEDS AND MOTIVATION

Needs.—In a monumental study of personality, Murray described a "need" as "a hypothetical process the occurrence of which is imagined in order to account for certain objective and subjective facts." [29] He more fully defined it as "a force which organizes perception, apperception, intellection, conation and action in such a way as to transform in a certain direction an existing, unsatisfying situation." To continue the quotation:

A need is sometimes provoked by internal processes of a certain kind . . . arising in the course of vital sequences, but more frequently (when in a state of readiness) by the occurrence of one of a few commonly effective press [plural, also "press"]. . . . Thus, it manifests itself by leading the organism to search for or to avoid encountering or, when encountered, to attend and respond to certain kinds of press.[30]

29. Henry A. Murray *et al., Explorations in Personality,* p. 54. New York: Oxford University Press, 1938.

30. *Ibid.,* p. 124.

A need, then, may be generated internally or externally. Murray used the term "press" to designate this directional tendency in an external object or situation. A press has both a qualitative and a quantitative power for harming or benefiting, which varies widely. Murray further stated:

The process in the subject which recognizes what is being done to him at the moment (that says "this is good" or "this is bad") may be conveniently termed *pressive perception*. The process is definitely egocentric, and gives rise almost invariably to some sort of adaptive behavior.[31]

Stern, who has built some of his research around a framework based upon Murray's concepts, defined needs as "organizational tendencies which appear to give unity and direction to personality." [32] They are, he pointed out, revealed by an individual's modes of behavior or inferred from observations of an interaction. He has devised an elaborate instrument for identifying an individual's structure of needs, which he has used in a number of studies of educational environments.

In an analysis which served as one of the sources for Getzels' later development of the social-process model of behavior, Parsons and Shils gave this meaning of "need-dispositions":

Need-dispositions . . . are tendencies to orient and act with respect to objects in certain manners and to expect certain consequences from these actions. The conjoined word *need-disposition* itself has a double connotation; on the one hand it refers to a tendency to fulfill some requirement of the organism, a tendency to accomplish some end state; on the other hand, it refers to a disposition to do something with an object designed to accomplish this end state.[33]

Maslow [34] formulated a theory of motivation based upon a

31. *Ibid.*, p. 119.

32. George G. Stern, "The Measurement of Psychological Characteristics of Students and Learning Environments," in *Measurement in Personality and Cognition*, p. 28. Edited by Samuel Messick and John Ross. New York: John Wiley & Sons, 1962.

33. Talcott Parsons and Edward A. Shils, "Personality as a System of Action," in *Toward a General Theory of Action*, pp. 114-15. Edited by Talcott Parsons and Edward A. Shils. Cambridge, Massachusetts: Harvard University Press, 1951.

34. A. H. Maslow, *Motivation and Personality*. New York: Harper & Bros., 1954.

hierarchy of needs, instinctoid in their nature, i.e., constitutional or hereditary in their determination. His taxonomy of basic needs places the physiological needs (such as hunger and thirst) at the bottom of the hierarchy. Going up the scale of needs are the safety needs (with psychological safety higher than physical safety), the need for love and belongingness, the need for esteem for others and for self, the need to know and to understand, the aesthetic needs (the latter two categories precede the highest one by original implication and later interpretations of his theory), and, finally, the need for self-actualization. This last and highest category "refers to man's desire for self-fulfillment, namely, to the tendency for him to become actualized in what he is potentially. This tendency may be phrased as the desire to become more and more what one is, to become everything that one is capable of becoming." [35] An important part of the theory is that other and higher needs emerge as soon as lower needs are satisfied, but not until they are satisfied. Thus, the need for self-actualization emerges only as the lower needs are satisfied. Maslow has speculated that perhaps as few as one per cent of the population have achieved a level of self-actualization in their needs-satisfaction.

Although an administrator might at first be challenged to try to help as many individuals as possible within his organization to reach the self-actualization level, according to Maslow's theory, there is as yet probably insufficient testing of the theory to estimate the consequences to an organization of having a number of its personnel operating at the self-actualized level. The organization might not be able to tolerate the amount of individualism, autonomy, spontaneity, and resistance to enculturation, which may be among the characteristics of the self-actualized person.

Schutz,[36] using a quite different rationale from those of Murray, Parsons and Shils, or Maslow, derived a theory of interpersonal behavior built around a basic postulate that each person has three interpersonal needs: inclusion, control, and affection. Each person has the need to establish and maintain a satisfactory relationship

35. *Ibid.*, pp. 91-92.

36. William C. Schutz, *FIRO: a Three-Dimensional Theory of Personal Behavior*. New York: Holt, Rinehart & Winston, 1958.

with other people in each of these three areas, where "inclusion" means "interaction and association"; "control" also includes "power"; and "affection" includes love and refers to a close, personal relationship. In each of these areas any given behavior may be ideal, deficient, excessive, or pathological, and tends to be conditioned by the nature of interpersonal relations experienced in childhood between parents and children. In the development of a group, the same three needs must be met in the same sequence. Another postulate in his 1958 formulation posited a relationship between compatibility and goal-achievement, such that a group high in one would tend to be high in the other. "Compatibility is a relation between two or more persons, between an individual and a role, or between an individual and a task situation, that leads to mutual satisfaction of interpersonal needs and harmonious existence." [37] As of the present writing, Schutz is directing an extensive study among some 80 public school districts in California in an effort to test the utility of these and other derived propositions for explaining and predicting the behavior of school administrators.

Motivation.—In this analysis, motivation is viewed as closely related to needs, indeed, as stemming from needs. Correspondingly, therefore, motivation may be stimulated internally or externally and may be seen as "the complex of forces starting and keeping a person at work in an organization." [38] Like needs, motives must generally be inferred from the observation of behavior or the measurement of attitudes. Viteles [39] saw motives as persistent behavior directed toward an end state or goal. Primary motives are biological; secondary motives are social. Following Maslow, motives have a prepotency, or a differential order of strength.

In the same study, Viteles reviewed two outmoded motivational theories. The concept of "economic man" regarded behavior as wholly rational and volitional, with the employee responding in orderly fashion as a rugged individualist to the pressure of material

37. *Ibid.*, p. 105.

38. Robert Dubin, *The World of Work, Industrial Society and Human Relations*, p. 213. Englewood Cliffs, New Jersey: Prentice-Hall, 1958.

39. Morris S. Viteles, *Motivation and Morale in Industry*. New York: W. W. Norton & Co., 1953.

needs and self-interest, making his decisions by calculations of incremental utility. This theory overlooked the fact that the worker seeks more than financial rewards from his work. The instinctive theory of economic activity held that man's economic activities are motivated by instinctive wants. This theory has been discounted, since human social behavior seems to stem little, if at all, from any sources which may be called instincts. Rather, there is an increasing tendency to view the problem of motivation in terms of the person as a whole, to focus upon a total personality in interaction with a total social environment.

Usually businessmen identify themselves with the firm they manage. For them the firm has a psychological reality. This identification with their firms also may satisfy the personal motivation of the executives to satisfy their ego, to gain power and security, and to increase their income.[40]

Reporting on a study of almost 13,000 men and women serving in the civilian and military services of the American federal government in 1959, Martin [41] concluded that the key motivational characteristic of these persons was their feeling of dedication to the public service. The job of the federal executive "requires above all the capacity, and these men have this capacity, to internalize the needs of the organization so that its needs become the needs of the self." [42]

Martin's conclusions fit with those of Herzberg, Mausner, and Snyderman,[43] who made an intensive study of about 200 accountants

40. George Katona, "The Motivations of Businessmen," in *Industrial Man: Businessmen and Business Organizations*, pp. 168-88. Edited by W. Lloyd Warner and Norman H. Martin. New York: Harper & Bros., 1959. (Reproduced from *Psychological Analysis of Economic Behavior*, pp. 193-210. New York: McGraw-Hill Book Co., 1951.)

41. Norman H. Martin, as reported in "Our Public Servants," *Carnegie Corporation of New York Quarterly*, XI (July, 1963), 3 [a pre-publication review of W. Lloyd Warner, Paul P. Van Riper, Norman H. Martin, and Orvis F. Collins, *The American Federal Executive: a Study of the Social and Personal Characteristics of the Civilian and Military Leaders of the United States Federal Government*. New Haven: Yale University Press, 1963].

42. *Ibid.*

43. Frederick Herzberg, Bernard Mausner, and Barbara B. Snyderman, *The Motivation To Work*, pp. 113-19. New York: John Wiley & Sons, 1959 (second edition).

and engineers in nine companies in the Pittsburgh area who answered the question, "What do people want from their jobs?" They found two kinds of answers. One involved the potentiality of the occupation as a source of personal growth. These job factors they called the "motivators." The second answer related to extra-job factors. These they called the factors of "hygiene."

> The factors that lead to positive job attitudes do so because they satisfy the individual's need for self-actualization in his work. . . . Man tends to actualize himself in every area of his life, and his job is one of the most important areas. The conditions that surround the doing of the job cannot give him this basic satisfaction; they do not have this potentiality. It is only from the performance of a task that the individual can get the rewards that will reinforce his aspirations. It is clear that although the factors relating to the doing of the job and the factors defining the job context serve as goals for the employee, the nature of the motivating qualities of the two kinds of factors are essentially different. Factors in the job context meet the needs of the individual for avoiding unpleasant situations. In contrast to this motivation by meeting avoidance needs, the job factors reward the needs of the individual to reach his aspirations. These effects on the individual can be conceptualized as actuating approach rather than avoidance behavior. Since it is in the approach sense that the term motivation is commonly used, we designate the job factors as the "motivators," as opposed to the extra-job factors, which we have labeled the factors of hygiene. [44]

On the basis of their research they urged that the one most significant goal in raising the mental health of most of our citizens must be to increase the potential for motivation in their work. In this, Herzberg, Mausner, and Snyderman stated the positive goal, while such writers as Viteles [45] and Argyris [46] have pointed to the negative consequences of failing to achieve that goal. For instance, they have seen unions as possible adaptive mechanisms, helping workers eliminate obstacles to gratification of needs and as substituting satisfactions outside industry for the needs and wants which management does not provide—or perhaps can never provide.

44. *Ibid.*, p. 114.

45. Viteles, *op. cit.*, pp. 85-93.

46. Chris Argyris, *Personality and Organization: The Conflict between the System and the Individual.* New York: Harper & Bros., 1957.

Motivation in occupational choice.—Anne Roe has made a motivational theory of needs fundamental to her development of a psychology of occupations:

Occupations as a source of need satisfaction are of extreme importance in our culture. It may be that occupations have become so important in our culture just because so many needs are so well satisfied by them. Whether the relation is causal or not, and if so which is cause and which is effect, does not particularly matter. It is probably a sort of feedback arrangement anyway. What is important is that this relationship exists and is an essential aspect of the value of the occupation to the individual.[47]

Similarly and more recently, Thompson concluded that "the degree of satisfaction an individual obtains from his work is proportionate to the degree to which it enables him to implement his self concept and satisfy his salient needs." [48]

Kuhlen and Dipboye,[49] among others, have noted the special motivational patterns that seem to attract people to teaching rather than to other occupations. They have also noted the differing patterns even between elementary- and secondary-school teaching. They proposed the need for reshaping the image of teaching as a career to make it more appealing as a continuing career, with outward symbols of progress up a career ladder within teaching—perhaps by the institution of academic ranks, as in universities—so that individuals no longer will have to leave teaching in order to get ahead, even within the field of professional education.

INCENTIVES

The inducements-contributions balance.—Incentives are the usual motivating instrumentalities used by formal organizations to elicit the co-operation from workers necessary to get them to enact

47. Anne Roe, *The Psychology of Occupations*, p. 33. New York: John Wiley & Sons, 1956.

48. A. S. Thompson, "Personality Dynamics and Vocational Counseling," *Personnel and Guidance Journal*, XXXVIII (1960), 350-57.

49. Raymond G. Kuhlen and Wilbert J. Dipboye, *Motivational and Personality Factors in the Selection of Elementary and Secondary School Teaching as a Career*. Syracuse: Syracuse University Institute of Research, 1959 (mimeographed).

their roles in the organizational structure which will make possible the achievement of the task of the organization. In one of the best-known theories about incentives, Simon built upon the work of Barnard to create a theory of organizational equilibrium based on the maintenance of a balance between inducements and contributions in an organization. According to this theory,[50] the participants in an organization receive inducements from the organization in exchange for their contributions to the organization. Each participant will continue in this exchange as long as the inducements offered are as great as or greater than the required contributions in return. The participants' contributions constitute the materials out of which the organizations' inducements are manufactured. Therefore, the organization remains solvent as long as there are enough contributions to make possible sufficient inducements to draw forth the contributions. A measure of the utility to the participant of the inducement-contribution balance is his desire to move plus his perception of the ease of moving from one job to another.

Cyert and March [51] extended this theory by the introduction of the concept of "organizational slack," which they defined as the difference between total resources available to the organization and total payments necessary to maintain the organizational coalition. In strong boom periods, organizations accumulate slack and use it to meet revised demands of its members, while retaining some of it as slack. During an economic downturn, this slack becomes a cushion, permitting the firm to survive in the face of adversity. Slack thus stabilizes the system in two ways: "(1) by absorbing excess resources, it retards upward adjustment of aspirations during relatively good times; (2) by providing a pool of emergency resources, it permits aspirations to be maintained (and achieved) during relatively bad times." [52]

Commenting on the Barnard-Simon theory, Krupp cautioned, "Unless consent is clearly explained and employee resistance to

50. James G. March and Herbert A. Simon, *Organizations*, pp. 84-86. New York: John Wiley & Sons, 1958.

51. Richard M. Cyert and James G. March, *A Behavioral Theory of the Firm*, pp. 36-38. Englewood Cliffs, New Jersey: Prentice-Hall, 1963.

52. *Ibid.*, p. 38.

management engineering established within the framework of organization analysis, the equilibrium that emerges may merely be a managerially engineered equilibrium in a world of docile organization men." [53]

Kinds of incentives.—Barnard [54] formulated a kind of taxonomy of incentives divided into the specific and the general ones. His subcategories ranged from such tangible inducements as money, things, and physical conditions to the most intangible which he called the "condition of communion," or comradeship, social integration, solidarity, and mutual support in personal attitudes.

By far one of the most interesting and unusual treatments of the subject of incentives is that of Dalton,[55] in which he described the system of official and unofficial rewards and incentives which he found in three manufacturing firms and a department store where he served in part as a participant-observer. He identified the following as unofficial incentives for managers: the employment of friends and relatives of plant and community associates, plush offices, a margin or slush fund for use in emergencies, expense-accounting, pay-backs and split fees, services and materials from the company garage, long-distance telephone calls, and even such an item unrelated to the company's business as an eleven-unit aviary for the back lawn of one of the executives constructed on company time by one of the plant workers. He noted how various unofficial incentives and rewards are granted workers as well as managers and concluded:

. . . however well defined official tasks may be, and however neatly we think we have fitted our personnel to these roles, the inescapably fluid daily situation distorts expected working conditions. Regardless of formal rankings, which are often only nominally based on potential for such action, some personnel more aptly do what is essential than do others. Tacitly or not, both they and their rewarders are aware of who solves problems and sustains the organization. Through time they are compensated as resources and situations allow. The process may seem

53. Sherman Krupp, *Pattern in Organization Analysis: a Critical Analysis,* pp. 110-11. Philadelphia: Chilton Company Book Division, 1961.

54. Barnard, *op. cit.,* pp. 142-53.

55. Dalton, *op. cit.*

to overlap with theft, or it may escape control and become theft, but able executives both utilize and contain unofficial rewards.[56]

A correspondingly realistic study of the incentive system in other organizations, including institutions of elementary, secondary, and higher education, would be not only revealing but also more explanatory of the total range of material, social, and psychic inducements included in the motivational pattern of those organizations.

MORALE

Lewis Carroll, had he been a contemporary writer, could well have been thinking of such a word as "morale" when he had Humpty-Dumpty say, "When I use a word, it means just what I choose it to mean—neither more nor less." Few words used in administration or in organizational theory have accumulated such a conglomeration of connotations. Some examples illustrate the variety of meanings and associations attributed to "morale": "absence of conflict," "collection of job-related attitudes," "ego-involvement in one's job," "feeling of happiness," "feeling of togetherness," "freedom from restraint in action toward a group goal," "generalized feeling state," "good personal adjustment," "motivation and incentives," "personal acceptance of goals of group," "we-feeling or cohesiveness of group," and "zeal with which goal-directed activity is carried out." As Walker [57] has pointed out, too many definitions of morale treat it as if it were an underlying condition with many symptoms, such as high or low productivity, low or high rate of absence, few or many complaints, few or many quarrels, few or many strikes, and few or many accidents.

Nor is this confusion in meaning just a recent phenomenon. Writing in 1941, Roethlisberger made a plea for dropping the word "morale" from the vocabulary of administration. He called for the substitution, instead, of "effective classifications of human situations and skillful methods of treating them" and, in the study of a work group, for attention "to *particular* human beings in *particular* places

56. *Ibid.*, p. 215.

57. Nigel Walker, *Morale in the Civil Service*. A Study of the Desk Worker, pp. 57-63. Edinburgh, Scotland: Edinburgh University Press, 1961.

with *particular* feelings and sentiments for which they need concrete social expression." [58]

But there is a way out of this definitional problem that is consistent with the rationale of this chapter, starting with the preferred
definition of "maintaining the organization." It is a way out, which,
incidentally, has support among various other analysts.[59] By this
view, morale is a feeling of participants in an organization stemming
from a combination of (*a*) perceived productivity or progress
toward the achievement of the tasks of the organization, and (*b*)
perceived job satisfaction or the satisfaction of individual needs
through the interaction of the participant in his role within the
work group and the total organization. Further, high morale is
the participant's perception of a successful task-needs integration.
Since task-needs integration is the ultimate purpose of administration, it follows that high morale is the participant's perception of
the consummation of administrative purpose. As Walker put it, the
key questions about any new practice or policy are these: "How
will it affect individual or collective efficiency?" and "How will it
affect the employees' enjoyment of their jobs?" [60]

Operationally, then, the measurement of morale consists in

58. F. J. Roethlisberger, *Management and Morale*, p. 194. Cambridge:
Harvard University Press, 1941.

59. See Franklyn S. Barry, "Administrative Morale: a Study of Selected
Factors Related to the Morale of the Administrative Staff of Public Schools."
Unpublished Doctor's dissertation, Syracuse University, 1956.
   Eric F. Gardner and George G. Thompson, *Social Relations and Morale
in Small Groups*. New York: Appleton-Century-Crofts, 1956.
   Egon G. Guba, "Morale and Satisfaction: a Study in Past-Future Time
Perspective," *Administrative Science Quarterly*, III (September, 1958), 195-209.
   Egon G. Guba and Charles E. Bidwell, *Administrative Relationships:
Teacher Effectiveness, Teacher Satisfaction, and Administrative Behavior*. A
Study of the School as a Social Institution. Chicago: Midwest Administration
Center, University of Chicago, 1957.
   Robert L. Kahn and Daniel Katz, "Leadership Practices in Relation to
Productivity and Morale," in *Group Dynamics: Research and Theory*, pp. 612-
28. Edited by Dorwin Cartwright and Alvin Zander. Evanston, Illinois: Row,
Peterson & Co., 1953.
   Roger F. Moran, "An Analysis of Industrial and Military Morale Research
with Implications for Assessment of Morale on College and University Cam-
puses." Unpublished Doctor's dissertation, Syracuse University, 1954.
   Stogdill, *op. cit.*
   Walker, *op. cit.*

60. Walker, *op. cit.*, pp. 57-63.

measuring the participant's perception of the accomplishment of the two major purposes of the organization. This can be done by interview, questionnaire, observation, and other conventional techniques. Concerning the two purposes, the resulting finding can indicate a low-low, low-high, high-low, or high-high evaluation. Whether the two middle combinations (low task-achievement with high needs-satisfaction or high task-achievement with low needs-satisfaction) are equivalent in morale value, remains to be determined by further experimentation. But a high evaluation of both task-achievement and needs-satisfaction, *as perceived by the individual participant*, is the desideratum where morale is the focus.

The virtue of this conceptualization of morale is that it relates morale centrally to other basic concepts concerning organizational purpose rather than leaving it at least somewhat detached from such other concepts. It makes morale, in part, a measure of the successful interaction among individual needs, motivation, and incentives. It becomes a measure of the favorable achievement in the view of the participant, of the inducements-contribution balance. With relation to the preceding section on role theory, it makes morale, additionally, a measure of effectiveness in role enactment, of congruence between role perceptions and role expectations, and of congruence between role expectations and need-dispositions.

Organizational Climate

A consideration of organizational climate follows easily after a discussion of morale, since the two are somewhat related. Just as morale has been related to organizational purposes, so also can organizational climate be related. Indeed, organizational climate might be defined as the global assessment of the interaction between the task-achievement dimension and the needs-satisfaction dimension within the organization, or, in other words, of the extent of the task-needs integration. In general usage the term has a psychosocial flavor which reflects more concern with the needs-satisfaction dimension than with the task-achievement dimension, but the meaning that gives relatively equal attention to both is preferred. Two analyses of the impact of organizational climate upon workers and three studies evaluating aspects of organizational climate are now discussed.

THE IMPACT OF ORGANIZATIONAL CLIMATE UPON WORKERS

An extensive review of research done on organizational behavior by others and reflection upon the meaning of his own research in industrial organizations led Argyris [61] to the proposition that the needs of healthy individuals are in conflict with the demands of the formal organization. Since the needs of healthy individuals are not congruent with the traditional requirements of formal organizations, a disturbance will result which will tend to manifest itself in some one or some combination of four kinds of behavior: (a) quitting the organization, (b) moving up the ladder of organization, (c) adopting defense mechanisms, or (d) turning apathetic and losing interest. The possible remedy is to decrease the incongruency noted by enlarging the job and/or the role as one way of changing the nature of the organizational structure or by using employee-centered leadership as a modification of directive leadership.

As already described by Griffiths in chapter v, Presthus [62] saw the bureaucratic organization producing three patterns of accommodation: the "upward mobiles," the "indifferents," and the "ambivalents." Of particular interest here is his characterization of the innovating role of the ambivalents:

Despite his inability to meet bureaucratic demands, the ambivalent type plays a critical social role, namely, that of providing the insight, motivation, and the dialectic that inspire change. The upward-mobile honors the status quo and the indifferent accepts it, but the ambivalent is always sensitive to the need for change. [63]

Neither of these formulations by Argyris or Presthus grew out of any analysis of the special characteristics of the educational organization, and neither is directly transferable to that kind of organization. But both suggest what Presthus called "social dysfunctions of organization" and may lead us to new diagnoses of organizational maladies. Further, as Presthus hoped, they may activate us to develop more humanistic values and a more permissive work

61. Argyris, *Personality and Organization, op. cit.*

62. Robert Presthus, *The Organizational Society: An Analysis and a Theory.* New York: Alfred A. Knopf, 1962.

63. *Ibid.,* p. 258.

climate for at least certain creative areas of organization, such as those in education, art, and scientific research.[64]

EVALUATIONS OF ORGANIZATIONAL CLIMATES

Some of the most interesting recent studies relating to organizational theory are those evaluating aspects of organizational climates. For instance, in a study of nine Western hospitals, Mathews [65] measured five dimensions of administrative climate (decision-making, leadership, goal-integration, influence, and personal relations) on a continuum ranging from a social philosophy of administration to a technological philosophy of administration. As she used the terms, a social philosophy of administration refers to a wide use of the participatory process, with staff members up and down the line involved in decision-making and generally supportive interactions, while a technological philosophy refers to a typical hierarchical organization where decisions, rules, and regulations are made at the top and procedures are standardized for the personnel at various levels. She found important contradictions in the administrative philosophies of these hospitals as they leaned toward the social orientation on some of the test dimensions and toward the technological orientation on others. She also found a significant correlation between the tenure of nurses and the degree of philosophic contradiction; hospitals at either end of her continuum, with a more clearly social *or* technological orientation in their organizational climates, were marked by a pattern of higher tenure among their nurses, while hospitals arrayed near the middle of the continuum, a position reflecting philosophic contradictions, had a lower tenure among their nurses. Thus, it may be that hospitals at the two extremes retained personnel more inclined toward their particular philosophic orientation of the organizational climate, or it may be that the nurses in the hospitals with more philosophic conflicts rejected that kind of organizational climate by leaving it.

64. *Ibid.*, p. 323.

65. B. Phelps Mathews, "Inconsistency: a Complex Problem in Administration," *Hospital Administration*, VII (Fall, 1962), 21-35.

Drawing upon Murray's concepts of need and press,[66] Stern [67] and his associates developed the "Activities Index" to measure individual needs and the "College Characteristics Index" (CCI) to measure organizational press, where press is "an external situational counterpart to the internal personality needs . . . [and] . . . refers to the phenomenological world of the individual, the unique and inevitably private view which each person has of the events in which he takes part." [68] They have used these instruments in measuring the pressive aspect of the organizational climate of a number of colleges and universities. From the analyses of the findings of the CCI in 69 colleges and universities, they derived the following six factors describing the effect of the organizational climate of those institutions upon students: intellectual orientation, social effectiveness, play, friendliness, constraint, and dominance-submission. High scores on these factors were obtained by various types of colleges as follows: liberal-arts colleges, on intellectual orientation; liberal-arts colleges and several select denominational colleges, on social effectiveness; several large state universities and private universities, on play; a mixed group of schools, on friendliness (informal social organization); denominational colleges, on constraint (compliance); and state teachers' colleges, on dominance-submission (or custodial care). The major source of diversity in the colleges studied was the level of their intellectual press. Using new instruments, Stern and his associates are now extending their studies to evening colleges and high schools.

Halpin and Croft [69] administered an "Organizational Climate Description Questionnaire" to 1,151 teachers and principals in 71 schools in six states in six different regions of the United States to study the organizational climates of elementary schools. They defined organizational climate as the "organizational personality" of

66. *Supra.*

67. George G. Stern, "Characteristics of the Intellectual Climate in College Environments," *Harvard Educational Review,* XXXI (Winter, 1963), 5-41.

68. Stern, "The Measurement of Psychological Characteristics . . . ," *op. cit.,* p. 29.

69. Andrew W. Halpin and Don B. Croft, *The Organizational Climate of Schools.* Washington: U.S. Office of Education, July, 1962 (multilithed). (See also Halpin and Croft, "The Organizational Climate of Schools," *Administrator's Notebook,* XI (March, 1963), 1-4.)

a school. Their factor analyses yielded six profiles or organizational climates arranged on a continuum ranging from "open" through "autonomous," "controlled," "familiar," and "paternal" to "closed." They found three parameters useful in describing the organizational climates or social interaction within elementary schools: authenticity, or the openness of the behavior of leaders and group members; satisfaction, an "attainment of conjoint satisfaction in respect to task accomplishment and social needs"; and leadership initiation, the "latitude within which the group members, as well as the leader, can initiate leadership acts." [70] From their study they drew the implication that there is a need to provide training for administrators that will give them insight into the nature of different organizational climates through training in psychoanalysis and clinical psychology as well as in the social psychology of groups.

It would appear likely that some of our most heuristic studies of the next few years will be those examining and assessing various dimensions of organizational climates within educational organizations as well as other kinds of organizations.

System Theory in Relation to Organizational Survival

Up to this point, the evolution of consensus concerning the two principal purposes of organization and their integration has been traced, the application of role theory to the purpose of task-achievement shown, the nature of organizational inducements in relation to the purpose of needs-satisfaction analyzed, and organizational climate as a measure of task-needs integration considered. It remains, now, to give attention to the first part of the definition of "maintaining the organization," where it is proposed that it means "sustaining the organization in dynamic equilibrium. . . ." The conceptual framework best suited for this analysis is that supplied by the system model.

In these times and with the present state of development of organizational theory, no administrator can be excused for failing to give high priority in his planning to the problem of organizational survival. Consequences of such failure are most readily observable among business organizations, the "wild" organizations conceptual-

70. *Ibid.*, p. 102.

ized by Carlson in chapter xii. The recent disappearance of the Underwood Corporation as a separate corporate entity [71] illustrated the failure of that company's management to adapt to the changing conditions of the office-equipment industry, while the contrasting rejuvenation of the Coca-Cola Company [72] demonstrated the success of its management in adjusting to just as important changes in the beverage industry. Meanwhile, it remains to be seen whether the efforts of the Endicott Johnson Company to maintain a significant position among shoe manufacturers [73] will have proved too little and too late or just soon enough.

Chin [74] has provided an outline of system theory around which, in part, shall be built the present description.

THE BOUNDARY OF THE ORGANIZATION

One use of system theory is in defining the boundary of the organization as a system. As applied to a public school district, for instance, it requires administrators and others to define the school "system," to decide to what extent parents and parent organizations shall be included within the system or left outside it, to decide whether the local government (in a fiscally dependent district) shall be included or left outside. Tilles noted that the system approach causes the business executive "to raise his sights above the hurly-burly of current in-company operations and understand how his company relates to its complex environment—to the other great systems of which it is a part." [75]

ORGANIZATIONAL EQUILIBRIUM

Static and dynamic equilibrium.—Central to system theory is the concept of organizational equilibrium. Equilibrium may be

71. "My Name Was Underwood," *Forbes*, XC (July 1, 1963), 15.

72. "The Change That Refreshes," *Forbes*, XC (September 1, 1963), 25-26.

73. "What Happened at Endicott Johnson after the Band Stopped Playing," *Fortune*, LXVI (September, 1962), 126-30 ff.

74. Robert Chin, "The Utility of System Models and Developmental Models for Practitioners," in *The Planning of Change: Readings in the Applied Behavioral Sciences*, pp. 201-14. Edited by Warren G. Bennis, Kenneth D. Benne, and Robert Chin. New York: Holt, Rinehart & Winston, 1961.

75. Seymour Tilles, "The Manager's Job—a Systems Approach," *Harvard Business Review*, XLV (January-February, 1963), 73-81.

static, as viewed originally by Pareto,[76] or dynamic. In a condition of static equilibrium a system responds to a stimulus or a change in its environment by a reaction or adjustment which tends to restore the system to its original state. In a condition of dynamic equilibrium the system may respond to such a stimulus or a change in its environment by a shift to a new balance or by a modification of its goals. It is apparently this kind of dynamic shift which was made successfully by the management of the Coca-Cola Company.

Homeostasis.—The biological processes of homeostasis are being applied conceptually in organization theory to help fathom the nature of equilibrium. Homeostasis is the self-regulating property of a living process. It is a dynamic state, an open rather than a closed system.[77] Examples of homeostatic processes in human beings are the tendency toward constant balance in the concentrations of sugar, salt, oxygen, and carbon dioxide in the blood; the tendency of blood volume to maintain itself, through the coagulating mechanism where there is a break in the circulatory system; mechanisms for maintaining constant body temperature; and mechanisms for removal of foreign particles and invading organisms from the circulatory system. Beer has provided a succinct clarification of the concept of homeostasis:

> In a homeostat a critical variable is held at a desirable level by a self-regulatory mechanism. It is not even meaningful to say that the value for this critical level must be invariable. . . . What is important to a natural control system is that the variation occur within physiological limits. This means to say the value is always at its mean desired level to a known standard of approximation, and that there is a compensatory mechanism in the system which edges it back towards that mean whenever it begins to wander away.[78]

76. Vilfredo Pareto, "On the Equilibrium of the Social System," in *Theories of Society: Foundations of Modern Sociological Theory*, II, 1288-92. Edited by Talcott Parsons *et. al.* New York: Free Press, Division of Crowell-Collier Publishing Co., 1961. (Reprinted from Vilfredo Pareto, *The Mind and Society*. Edited by Arthur Livingston. Translated by Andrew Bongiorno and Arthur Livingston. New York: Harcourt, Brace & Co., 1935.)

77. Anatol Rapoport, "Homeostasis Reconsidered," in *Toward a Unified Theory of Human Behavior*, chap. xvii. Edited by Roy R. Grinker. New York: Basic Books, 1956.

78. Stafford Beer, *Cybernetics and Management*, pp. 22-23. New York: John Wiley & Sons, 1959.

Feedback.—Essential to the understanding of homeostasis, and therefore also of equilibrium, is the concept of feedback, which, in turn, is the central idea of cybernetics. Pfiffner and Sherwood described it as follows:

> In its simplest form, feedback is the kind of communication an actor receives from a live audience. If the crowd is enthusiastic, the performer reacts with similar enthusiasm. There is in a way a closed circuit between performer and audience with continuing interchange of information. . . . Essential to feedback is the notion that the flow of information is actually having a reciprocating effect on behavior. This is why the term *loop* is frequently associated with feedback. This circular pattern involves the flow of information to the point of action, a flow back to the point of decision with information on the action, and then a return to the point of action with new information and perhaps instructions. A primary element in this process is the sensory organ, the instrument through which information is obtained. Until recently only the animal organism, particularly the human brain and nervous system, was sufficiently developed to possess this capacity.[79]

As applied to organization, feedback is the process through which the organization learns: it is the input from the environment to the system telling it how it is doing as a result of its output to the environment. This feedback-input is then used to steer the operation of the system. The sensory organs of the organization functioning to process the information feedback are the individuals or groups within the administrative hierarchy assigned the roles of assessing the information and then sending the right signal back to the action points to continue or modify behavior, as necessary. Obviously, this is a conceptualization related to the standard administrative process of evaluation. One of the attendant problems, if the feedback loop is to work properly, is sensitizing the organization's "sensory organs" so as to decrease any blockage and increase receptivity. To accomplish this is in part the purpose of the kind of in-service development program for administrators which is frequently called "sensitivity training." [80]

79. John M. Pfiffner and Frank P. Sherwood, *Administrative Organization*, p. 299. Englewood Cliffs, New Jersey: Prentice-Hall, 1960.

80. Robert Tannenbaum, Irving R. Weschler, and Fred Massarik, *Leadership and Organization: A Behavioral Science Approach*, Part II. New York: McGraw-Hill Book Co., 1961.

Entropy.—A final concept relating to equilibrium is that of "entropy," a concept taken from the field of statistical mechanics and classical thermodynamics. Entropy is a measure of ignorance, disorder, disorganization, randomness, or chaos. In interpreting the significance of this concept for organizational theory, Rothstein noted "that organization is essentially a negative entropy just as information is." [81]   Thus, maximum entropy is zero organization, and zero entropy is maximum organization.

Responses to disturbance.—In summary of this set of concepts, the system may respond to disturbances from the outside (*a*) by resisting or disregarding the disturbances or protecting and defending itself against them; (*b*) by using homeostatic forces to restore the former balance; or (*c*) by accommodating to these disturbances by achieving a new equilibrium.[82] It is the view of this chapter that administrators should assist the organization in responding in the third of these three ways.

Organizational Change

Clearly, an organization needs stability in order to survive. It is the function of the administrator, as Lipham uses the term in chapter vi, to assure this stability. But too much stability can lead to rigidity, and rigidity can mean a fragility resulting in disintegration under the stress caused by disturbances from inside or outside. What is needed for organizations in the present era is flexibility to accommodate to these disturbances—to initiate new structures or procedures, or to revise the goals of the organization, as Lipham puts it in his definition of "leadership" as differentiated from "administration." The ideal, then, as Stogdill concluded, is the "median range within which flexibility and stability optimize the capacity for survival." [83]

Like all ideals, this one is difficult to achieve. Cyert and March [84]

---

81. Jerome Rothstein, *Communication, Organization, and Science*, p. 34. Indian Hills, Colorado: Falcon's Wing Press, 1958. Note the use of "entropy" by Griffiths, in his discussion of system theory in chapter v, with an opposite meaning of "an ordering process" as also used by Beer, *op. cit.*, p. 26. Unfortunately the term has these two contrasting usages in the literature.

82. Chin, *op. cit.*, p. 205.

83. Stogdill, *op. cit.*, p. 286.

84. Cyert and March, *op. cit.*, pp. 118-20.

have identified the tendency toward "uncertainty avoidance" among business firms. Coser [85] has noted the disintegrating effect of conflict upon the organization which is intolerant of conflict or has not "institutionalized" it, and he has set forth the functionality of conflict in helping bring about new adjustments in norms or the development of new norms, in permitting the readjustment of power relationships, and in maintaining boundary lines. Thompson [86] has argued for more co-ordination and a recognized mutual interdependence to resolve the basic conflict between hierarchical roles (line) and specialist roles (staff) in organizations. McGregor [87] has recognized a similar need for line-staff collaboration. Carlson [88] has found a greater inclination toward effecting organizational change on the part of "career-bound" than "place-bound" superintendents of schools. Dalton [89] has dichotomized administrators into "routinizers" (which he called "weak") and "adapters" ("strong"), on the basis of his intensive study of three industries and a department store. Selznick, like Lipham, using the fulcrum of change, has called for executives, if they would be statesmen, to make "the transition from administrative management to institutional leadership." [90]

It may be, as Lindblom [91] observed, that "incremental change" using the "branch method" of changing the current situation in organizations by small degrees is both more feasible and more healthy than comprehensive change using the "root method" of always

85. Lewis A. Coser, *The Functions of Social Conflict*. Glencoe, Illinois: Free Press, 1956.

86. Victor A. Thompson, *Modern Organization*. New York: Alfred A. Knopf, 1961.

87. McGregor, *op. cit.*, pp. 157-75.

88. Richard O. Carlson, *Executive Succession and Organizational Change: Place-Bound and Career-Bound Superintendents of Schools*. Chicago: Midwest Administration Center, University of Chicago, 1962.

89. Dalton, *op. cit.*

90. Philip Selznick, *Leadership in Administration*, p. 154. Evanston, Illinois: Row, Peterson & Co., 1957.

91. Charles E. Lindblom, "The Science of 'Muddling Through,'" *Public Administration Review*, XIX (Spring, 1959), 79-88.

starting from fundamentals. But the important point is that organizations should strive to develop a favorable orientation toward change, a willingness to change, and a readiness for change. In the years ahead, leaders of organizations must be trained to be sensitive to the need for change, to be able to recognize when change will be beneficial or when stability is to be preferred, and to be skilled in accomplishing the change when it is needed. If they would function as change-agents within the organization, leaders must have an understanding of the forces within individuals, within the organization, and surrounding the organization which, using the language of Lewin, must be unfrozen, changed, and then refrozen.[92] When major changes are needed, they must be able to develop strategies of change, realizing that large-scale change is a process, not an event, and that it takes place over a period of time.[93]

Is all of this the contamination of a theoretical discussion by a large dose of value? Probably not, although there is a danger that the choice of words may convey that idea. Rather, we are living through a period of history when change is necessary for survival. This necessity is imposed upon formal organizations, as well as upon individuals and upon the culture. Even though change or atrophy may not be so dramatically revealed among Carlson's "domesticated" organizations (e.g., educational institutions) as among his "wild" ones (e.g., business firms), the former must ultimately change also in order to survive. If there is a value involved in what has been said, it is that organizational leaders should be ready to act to bring about change and not simply to react to forces demanding change. To use Griffiths' taxonomy of decision-making,[94] executives would initiate more creative decisions concerning change instead of simply responding to pressure for change by intermediate or appellate decisions.

92. See also Floyd C. Mann, "Studying and Creating Change: a Means to Understanding Social Organization," in *Research in Industrial Relations, a Critical Appraisal*, p. 162. Edited by Conrad M. Arensberg *et. al.* New York: Harper & Bros., 1957.

93. See Eli Ginzberg and Ewing W. Reilley, *Effecting Change in Large Organizations*. New York: Columbia University Press, 1957.

94. Daniel E. Griffiths, *Administrative Theory*, pp. 98-102. New York: Appleton-Century-Crofts, 1959.

Conclusion

"Maintaining the organization in dynamic equilibrium," therefore, is a complex process which involves achieving the tasks of the organization and meeting the needs of the individual participants in the organization. The application of role theory will contribute to the former; an understanding of the nature of individual needs, motivation, and incentives is bound up in the latter. The highest success in maintaining the organization is reached when there is an integration of task-achievement and needs-satisfaction. Morale is a measure of the individual's perception of the extent of this integration; organizational climate is a more global index of the same dimension. System theory provides the concept of dynamic equilibrium, which is the desired state if the organization is to survive. It is the organizational leader's challenge to effect this change in a manner which maintains a balance between stability and flexibility.

CHAPTER VIII

Personal Variables and Administrative Styles

JOHN K. HEMPHILL

Introduction

In order to consider an area of human activity as broad and as complex as that of the relationships between the qualities of personality and administrative behavior, one must focus upon some specific part of the area and must assume a definite point of view. In this chapter no attempt will be made to cover the entire spectrum of either human personality or of educational administration. This chapter will be focused upon the administrative styles of 232 elementary-school principals, each of whom worked for one week as the principal of the same simulated school—Whitman School—and whose personal qualities were studied by means of a large battery of cognitive ability, interest, and personality tests.

In the first section of this yearbook (Historical Perspective) and in many of the chapters in other sections, authors have made clear the importance of the developing scientific body of knowledge about educational administration. A predominant concern is with theory and the conceptual analysis of significant parts of total area spanned by educational administration. These theories and analyses must remain speculations, however, if they are not subsequently tested against empirical facts obtained by careful observation of relevant behavior of administrators.

The point of view in this chapter is empirical. We shall be looking at facts from a research study and attempting to understand what they imply. The facts to be examined have been reported in detail elsewhere, but a brief introduction to the study in which they were obtained will be necessary to provide a setting for the discussion which follows. For details, the interested reader must consult the original report.[1]

1. John K. Hemphill, Daniel E. Griffiths, and Norman Frederiksen, *Admin-*

The Basic Study

With support from the Cooperative Research Branch of the United States Office of Education, Educational Testing Service and Teachers College conducted a research project directed toward the development of criteria of performance in school administration. The major objective of the project was to determine how one might describe the differences between performances of elementary principals. Satisfactory answers to this seemingly simple question were not to be found by review of the large accumulated literature on the problem of selecting school administrators. Most previous studies were subject to the fundamental criticism of having completely confounded differences due to the unique properties of a specific school situation and those due to the unique personality of the principal. No two principals had ever attempted to run the same school or to handle the same administrative problems, nor had they ever been subjected to the same methods of research observation. In a fundamental sense, no two principals' administrative performance had ever been compared, since no two had worked within fully comparable organizational settings. In fact, it appears unlikely that two principals in real life can ever be expected to run the *same* school.

In order to make it possible to compare the administrative performance of different principals, it appeared necessary to simulate a school in a manner that made it possible for different persons to encounter the same administrative problems, in the same settings, and in a manner that permitted systematic observations of their different performances. This was the approach adopted.

The school simulated was called Whitman School and was located in Jefferson Township of the state of Lafayette. Whitman School was based upon a carefully selected real school, and many of its administrative problems were drawn directly from this real school.

During the week that each of 232 principals served at Whitman School they performed a variety of administrative tasks. They (*a*)

istrative Performance and Personality. New York: Teachers College Bureau of Publications, 1962.

wrote short articles for the school paper and the local paper; (*b*) delivered an address to the PTA; (*c*) handled a large assortment of problems presented as items in their in-baskets; (*d*) observed and evaluated probationary teachers at work (on film); (*e*) participated in discussion of educational problems; and so on. Reports from the 232 principals who worked in this simulated situation testify to the "reality" of their experience.

In addition to requiring that principals actually do administrative work in a standardized situation, the design of the study provided a way of securing information about the principals as persons and about how they were regarded in their home schools. Each principal completed approximately fifteen hours of psychological tests. He took a battery of sixteen ability tests, completed a personality questionnaire, filled out a lengthy biographical form, took four special tests of professional and general knowledge, and completed two interest inventories. In addition, each principal was rated on 13 items by three of his supervisors, and each of his teachers described her impressions of his behavior as a leader and as a supervisor.

By operating Whitman School, the principals provided an extensive body of data concerning their administrative performance. We shall concentrate upon only one part of these data—how these principals handled their in-basket work.

Three separate in-baskets were used in the simulation of Whitman School. Together they contained a total of 96 items, i.e., separate letters, memos, reports and other documents typical of those that school administrators encounter in their day-to-day work. Each in-basket represented a two- to three-days' accumulation of work. The principals assumed they were actually on the job and handled the in-basket's contents in exactly the same manner as they normally would, except that everything they did had to be put in writing. At the end of the two-hour-and-fifteen-minute "test" period the principals completed a "Reasons for Action Form." They left behind, as data for the research, a vast array of written products—letters they had drafted, replies to requests, schedules for future discussion, notes to their secretaries and teachers, and similar items. This written output was available for scoring and analysis.

Analyses of the Data

In order to score the responses the principal had made in handling the in-basket problems, a 68-category scoring schema was developed. Sixty-eight categories seemed to cover quite adequately the different ways one might wish to view the work of an administrator. These categories are listed in Table 1.

TABLE 1

LIST OF SCORING CATEGORIES

1. Estimated number of words
2. Number of items not attempted
3. Usual courses of action
4. Rejection of test conditions

5. Number of subordinates involved individually
6. Number of subordinate groups involved
7. Number of superiors involved
8. Number of outsiders involved individually

9. Number of outside groups involved
10. Unusual courses of action
11. Gives recognition for ability or good work
12. Shows awareness of poor work

13. Carelessness or minor error
14. Socially insensitive
15. Relates to background materials or other items
16. Conceptual analysis

17. Prejudges, makes unwarranted assumption, or largely inappropriate perception
18. Uses human or personal values in analysis
19. Uses physical values in analysis
20. Uses program values in analysis

21. Discusses with subordinates
22. Discusses with other principals
23. Discusses with superiors or outsiders
24. Asks for information, opinion, advice, or permission from subordinates

25. Asks for information, opinion, advice, or permission from superiors
26. Asks for information, opinion, advice, or permission from outsiders
27. Requires further information
28. Delays or postpones decision or temporizes

29. Arrives at a procedure for deciding
30. Contingent decision
31. Concluding decision
32. Makes tentative or definite plans only

33. Work scheduled for same or following day, for himself
34. Work scheduled for same or following week
35. Work scheduled: indefinite time or no time specified
36. Takes leading action

37. Takes terminal action
38. Follows lead by subordinates
39. Follows lead by superiors
40. Follows lead by outsiders

41. Follows a pre-established structure
42. Coordination of the work of others
43. Initiates a new structure
44. Delegates completely

45. Delegates partially with control
46. Delegates partially, but without control
47. Gives directions and/or suggestions
48. Refers to superiors

49. Communicates face-to-face; plans to do so
50. Communicates by telephone
51. Communicates by writing
52. Gives information to subordinates

53. Gives information to superiors
54. Gives information to outsiders
55. Explains actions to subordinates
56. Explains actions to superiors

57. Explains actions to outsiders
58. Courtesy to subordinates
59. Courtesy to superiors
60. Courtesy to outsiders

61. Informality to subordinates
62. Informality to superiors
63. Informality to outsiders
64. Backs up teachers or staff officers

65. Improves staff; plans to do so
66. Attempts to improve the working conditions of the staff
67. Imposes controls: sets a deadline
68. Imposes controls: follow-up or feedback planned

A manual giving explicit and detailed directions for the application of the categories to the responses of the principals was prepared. Trained scorers used these categories and the manual to score the outputs of the principals. The scorer first read a principal's response to an item, including the reasons he gave for taking his course of action, and, after achieving as good a grasp as possible of the response that had been made and what had motivated it, proceeded to indicate which ones of the 68 categories described the response.

Figure 1 shows an item and the response made to it by one principal. This particular response to this item was scored for: "Estimated number of words written" (code 2, short), "Number of subordinates involved individually" (one), "Number of subordinate groups involved" (one), and as having involved a "Concluding decision," a "Terminal action," as giving "Directions and/or suggestions," and as "Communicating by writing." None of the other categories were judged to apply to this response.

After all responses to the 96 items had been scored, the total frequency of use of each category by the principal was ascertained. A principal theoretically could obtain any score from zero through 96 on most of the categories, but actually no principal earned a score as high as 96 on any category. Table 2 shows the average score for the 232 principals on 10 selected categories.

TABLE 2

MEAN SCORES EARNED BY 232 PRINCIPALS ON TEN SELECTED
SCORING CATEGORIES

CATEGORY	MEAN SCORE
Gives recognition for ability or good work	2.77
Conceptual analysis	8.78
Discusses with subordinates	23.16
Delays, postpones decision or temporizes	8.13
Concluding decision	44.44
Makes tentative or definite plans *only*	30.75
Work scheduled: indefinite time or no time specified	35.30
Follows lead by subordinates	18.94
Delegates completely	.75
Courtesy to subordinates	19.82

From Table 2 we note that, on the average, the principals made concluding decisions on less than half of the items and did planning

ITEM:

JEFFERSON TOWNSHIP PUBLIC SCHOOLS
JEFFERSON, LAFAYETTE

MEMO

DATE: **August 28, 1958**

TO: All Principals

FROM: Assistant Superintendent for
      Business Management

SUBJECT: Supplies

I am very sorry to say that some unaccountable delay in shipping
will prevent this year's supply of pencils from reaching your
school before September 12.

This office regrets to add to your burdens at this busy time of
the year, but the situation is, unfortunately, beyond our control.
I trust that you can make some provisions for coping with this
problem.

A-5

RESPONSE:

OFFICE OF THE SUPERINTENDENT OF SCHOOLS
JEFFERSON TOWNSHIP PUBLIC SCHOOLS

*Post this notice.
Teachers may
deal with it
in their own way.*

REASON FOR ACTION:

Problem	What I Did	Why
A5	Note attached to post	Teachers can deal with this

FIG. 1.—An in-basket item and a principal's response to it.

only on about one-third of them. Action on about 10 per cent of the items was delayed or postponed, and a similar proportion of items was analyzed beyond their immediate implications. Very little work was delegated completely, but about one-quarter of the items were to be discussed with subordinates.

The next step in the data analysis was to look for patterns of responses in the category scores. How could this large mass of specific data be reduced to permit it to be readily comprehended?

It was found that 28 of the categories could be discarded because few principals used them often enough to earn significant scores. The remaining 40 scores were intercorrelated and their interrelationships examined by means of factor analysis. The result was the discovery of 10 factors (or clusters of items with high mutual relationships) which provide a basic framework for viewing administrative work. A list of the categories that grouped together to define each factor is shown in Table 3.

TABLE 3

CATEGORIES GROUPING BY FACTORS

Major factors:

Factor X: *Preparation for decision vs. taking final action*

Arrives at a procedure for deciding
Requires further information for deciding
Work scheduled for same or next day
Discusses with subordinates
Asks subordinates for information or advice
Communicates face-to-face
Initiates a new structure
Work scheduled for same or next week
Concluding decisions (negative)
Terminal action (negative)

Factor Y: *Amount of work done in handling items*

Number of words written
Number of usual courses of action
Number of outsiders involved
Gives directions or suggestions
Number of subordinates involved
Communicates by writing
Takes leading action

TABLE 3 (Continued)

Gives information to subordinates
Follows lead by superiors

Additional factors:

Factor A: *Exchanging information*

Asks subordinates for information, opinion, or advice
Gives information to subordinates
Requires further information for deciding
Gives information to outsiders
Number of subordinate groups involved
Number of usual courses of action

Factor B: *Discussing before acting*

Work scheduled—time unspecified
Discusses with subordinates
Communicates face-to-face
Initiates a new structure
Arrives at a procedure for deciding
Tentative or definite plans only
Number of items attempted
Discusses with superiors or outsiders
Number of usual courses of action
Requires further information for deciding
Number of subordinate groups involved
Follows lead by subordinates
Follows lead by superiors
Terminal action (negative)

Factor C: *Complying with suggestions made by others*

Concluding decision
Number of items attempted
Follows lead by subordinates
Terminal action
Follows lead by superiors
Follows pre-established procedure
Communicates by writing
Number of words written
Number of subordinates involved
Gives directions or suggestions
Gives information to subordinates
Number of usual courses of action
Informality to subordinates
Number of subordinate groups involved

Factor D: *Analyzing the situation*
>   Uses program values
>   Conceptual analysis
>   Aware of poor work

Factor E: *Maintaining organizational relationships*
>   Number of superiors involved
>   Discusses with superiors or outsiders
>   Number of outsiders involved
>   Relates to background materials or other items
>   Follows lead by outsiders
>   Communicates by telephone
>   Delays, postpones (negative)

Factor F: *Organizing work*
>   Work scheduled for same or next week
>   Work scheduled for same or next day
>   Follows pre-established procedure
>   Relates to background information or other items
>   Work scheduled—time unspecified (negative)

Factor G: *Responding to outsiders*
>   Gives information to outsiders
>   Courtesy to outsiders
>   Follows lead by outsiders
>   Number of outsiders involved
>   Carelessness or minor error
>   Awareness of poor work

Factor H: *Directing the work of others*
>   Leading action
>   Communicates by writing
>   Courtesy to subordinates
>   Gives directions or suggestions
>   Courtesy to outsiders
>   Carelessness or minor error
>   Number of subordinates involved
>   Communicates by telephone (negative)
>   Tentative or definite plans only (negative)

The first two factors are major factors and may be regarded as underlying or generating the remaining eight. In another sense these two major factors represented very general descriptions of what the principals did in handling the items; the remaining eight describe what they did in more detail.

The first of the two major factors was identified as, *"Preparation for decision vs. taking final action"* (Factor X). The factor is double-ended or *bipolar*, suggesting that principals tended to stress either preparing for action or taking action. The principal who took final action most frequently did so on nine times as many items as did another principal who took action least frequently.

The second major factor was identified as, *"Amount of work done in handling items"* (Factor Y). Differences among principals in carrying out their administrative work can be described in terms of how much energy they expend in doing it. The most industrious of the principals did four times as much work as the least industrious and did it within the same two hours and 15 minutes and on the same 96 administrative items or problems. A major factor in these principals' administrative work was clearly the volume of work they were able to turn out.

In general terms, the major differences in what the principals did was that they worked at different rates (expended energy in different amounts) on the problem and placed different emphasis upon preparing for decisions as opposed to taking immediate actions. The remaining eight factors that were discovered in the analysis refer to more specific differences among the principals in their styles of administrative performance.

One of the factors, descriptive of a way administrative work was done, was identified as Factor A, "Exchanging information." Principals who typically worked in the way described by this factor stressed the passing of information from subordinate to superior or vice versa. Their style of administration was to function as good communication channels in the organization. In contrast, other administrators played "close to the vest" and told others very little about what was going on.

A second factor, Factor B, was called "Discussing with others before acting." This was a style of administrative life that characterized the work of many principals. It seemed that it is standard procedure for many principals to discuss almost every problem with someone, perhaps a superior or a subordinate, before a decision is made or an action taken.

The third factor, Factor C, was "Complying with suggestions made by others." This was a characteristic of administrative behav-

ior of many younger principals. Whenever someone, either a subordinate, superior, or outsider, had suggested a course of action
which they thought would solve or help solve a problem, principals whose style of work was described by this factor simply went
along with the suggestion. These principals seemed not to lead,
but rather preferred to *follow* others in carrying out their administrative responsibilities.

The fourth factor, Factor D, was identified by the label "Situational analysis." A principal whose style was characterized by an
emphasis on situational analysis tended to examine each problem
for its broad or long-range implications. He was concerned with
effects of his actions or possible action upon morale, or about setting
examples, or about what might be the roots of an issue. A principal
less concerned with situational analysis did not go beyond the problem at hand. He simply chose to deal with the obvious parts of the
problems and seemed to get less involved with what might be their
deeper implications.

"Maintaining organizational relationships," a fifth specific factor
in administrative work, was characterized by a tendency to consult, to defer to superiors, to follow leads from outsiders, and to
act promptly rather than postpone or delay. This style of administration placed weight upon getting along with others and doing
the right things to keep the organization running smoothly.

The sixth factor was identified as "Organization of work"
(Factor F). It refers to the amount and specificity of scheduling
and planning that was evident in the principal's work. For example,
some principals whose work was characterized by this style were
careful always to specify the day and the hour of conferences they
wished to have with their teachers or with others. Other principals
never did so, but only indicated that they would have a conference
or take care of a problem at some unspecified time in the future.

A seventh factor was identified as Factor G, "Responding to
outsiders." Principals given to so responding typically displayed an
unusually high sensitivity to parents or other persons outside the
school system. It appears that they regarded outsiders as having
a legitimate demand on a principal's time. Other principals seemed
far less concerned with problems coming to them from outside and
confined their attention to the immediate school system.

The eighth factor, Factor H, was "Directing the work of others." A principal whose administrative style is described by this factor typically handled his administrative chores by giving them to someone else as tasks to be done. Principals who were low with respect to this factor were less often directive and explicit in suggesting administrative tasks for others to do, and perhaps did more of these tasks themselves.

Administrative Performance vs. Leadership

It is important to distinguish between (a) the behavior of an administrator, (b) administrative behavior, and (c) leadership behavior. All three are important in evaluation of the performance of an administrator. By the behavior of an administrator, we refer to anything and everything that a person who holds an administrative post may do both on and off his job. It is clear that an administrator may earn a poor reputation by engaging in some form of off-the-job behavior that is socially disapproved just as readily as he can by poor performance on the job. The school principal is particularly vulnerable to this kind of negative evaluation. In fact, it may be difficult at times to draw a clear line between what is properly considered "on the job" and what is private and "off the job." Failure to make this distinction is responsible for some of the confusion with regard to evaluation of school administrators.

Another important distinction is that between leadership behavior and administrative behavior. The reasons and importance of this distinction are discussed in detail by Lipham in chapter vi. Failure to make this distinction may be the cause of much confusion which exists today. To lead is to initiate a new form or procedure for accomplishing an organizational or group objective. To administer is to carry out existing or established procedures for reaching such objectives. School principals are expected both to lead and to administer, but in some respects these two expectations can be in conflict. The initiation of a new procedure that promises to meet problems more effectively may imply abandoning an established one which is known to work. The distinction among the behavior of administrators, leadership behavior, and administrative behavior has been cited here to make clear what is meant by *administrative behavior*. It is important to note that *no* factor clearly recognizable as *leadership* appeared in the analysis of principals' work.

Relationship of Personal Characteristics and Administrative Performance

Armed with the ten factors as concepts that describe administrative work of principals, it is possible to begin to answer such questions as the following:

1. What kind of principal stresses preparation for decision above taking final action?
2. What kind of principal tends to follow suggestions made by others rather than to act independently?
3. What kind of principal stresses maintaining organizational relationships?
4. What kind of principal earns high ratings from his superiors? From his teachers?

There are innumerable questions of this type that can now be considered. The data that were gathered by the administration of the battery of psychological tests and the rating forms allow us to formulate some tentative answers. Table 4 presents, in a simple tabulated form, some of the more important findings that emerged from an analysis of the complex relationships between (*a*) the ten factors in school administration and (*b*) the personal qualities and performance ratings of the principals.

Principals who characteristically stressed preparation for decisions in their administrative work (at least in the simulated school) and who resisted the temptations to act precipitously were also the principals who earned high ratings from their superiors in their home schools. These principals were better prepared professionally, as was evident from their scores on tests of general and professional knowledge. They did better on tests of reasoning, were above average in fluency, and were able to learn new material quickly. Their values and interests tended to be more strongly concerned with the educational needs of pupils. In general, these principals were able to understand more completely the complex nature of the individual administrative problems and then, apparently, to recognize their need to seek further information and otherwise make preparations before they could take appropriate action.

TABLE 4

SUMMARY OF RELATIONSHIPS WITH THE UNIQUE
COMPONENTS OF IN-BASKET PERFORMANCE FACTORS

Performance on In-Basket Problems	Cognitive Abilities and Knowledge	Personality, Interest, and Values	Biographical Data	Evaluations
Factor X, Preparation for decision	Fluent; facile with symbolic material; sees associations quickly; good at reasoning; knows school administration, elementary education, science, and facts about the general culture; learns new material rapidly	Values educational needs of pupils. Interests similar to psychologists and lawyers	(Not related)	Superiors—positive
Factor Y, Amount of work	Over-all high ability; fluent with words and ideas; knows elementary education, school administration, cultural, and scientific material; learns new material rapidly	(Not related)	(Not related)	Superiors—neutral to slightly positive
Factor A, Exchanging information	Has great verbal knowledge and facility; knows elementary education, school administration, and facts about the general culture	Sociable, sensitive, trusting, confident, and relaxed. Interests like superintendents, lawyers or psychologists; unlike policemen	More characteristic of women	Superiors—very positive; teachers—positive
Factor B, Discussing before acting	(Not related)	Mature, self-confident, and relaxed. Interests like policemen and public administrators	Little administrative experience	Superiors—negative; teachers—negative

TABLE 4 (continued)

Performance on In-Basket Problems	Cognitive Abilities and Knowledge	Personality, Interest, and Values	Biographical Data	Evaluations
Factor C, Complying with suggestions	Ability to reason and sees relationships; knows general cultural facts, science, and mathematics; learns new material rapidly	Aloof, shy, practical, skeptical, independent, insecure, unstable and tense. Interests like policemen; unlike school superintendents	Young, little experience, more characteristic of men	Superiors—very negative; teachers—negative
Factor D, Analyzing the situation	Ability to reason and sees relationships, knows general cultural facts, science, and mathematics	Aloof, dominant, practical, shrewd, feels pressure. Interests like policemen and public administrators	Has administrative experience, more characteristic of men	Superiors—negative; teachers—negative
Factor E, Maintaining relationships	Slow in seeing relationship; lacks knowledge of science and mathematics	Sociable, lively, sensitive, confident, dependent, and relaxed. Interests of superintendents and lawyers	More characteristic of women	Teachers—very positive
Factor F, Organizing work	(Not related)	Easily frustrated, inflexible, shy, skeptical, insecure, unstable, and tense. Interest unlike superintendents, administrators, and psychologists	(Not related)	Superiors—generally negative; teachers positive regarding initiating structure
Factor G, Responding to outsiders	Lacks general ability; lacks knowledge of science and mathematics, school administration, and general culture	Submissive, subdued, shy, naive, stable and relaxed. Interests unlike public administrators and lawyers	Has large amount of teaching experience, older, more characteristic of women	Superiors—neutral to slightly negative
Factor H, Directing others	Lacks knowledge and ability; unable to learn new material quickly	Sober and stable. Interests unlike school superintendents and lawyers	Has experience in education; older	Teachers—negative

High work output seems also to be characteristic of the better prepared and more able principals, but a large volume of work was not necessarily an indication that the principal would be well regarded by his supervisors. Perhaps the most significant implication of the many relationships between good performance on tests of ability and high work output lies in the negative direction. Principals who are low in general ability and basic professional knowledge were also low in ability to cope with the administrative work found in their in-baskets. They handled fewer items, spent less effort in examining the various aspects of each problem and in general appeared to have done a less thorough job.

It is of interest to contrast two classes of principals that can be formed by combining Factors X and Y. On one hand there are those principals who were high on both these factors, i.e., those who stressed preparation for decisions and did a lot of work in the process. These principals were characterized by their success in organizing and accomplishing a lot of work that seemed to them to be necessary in order to be able to make a good decision. On the other hand, those principals who were low on both factors were characterized by their tendency to act summarily and without preparation. These principals in everyday life would likely be those who would find it easy to endorse the attitude that good administration consists of a promptly rendered "yes" or "no" on all problems requiring a decision. When these two polar types of principals were compared, it became abundantly clear that the more able and better prepared principals, those most concerned with educational values, and those highly regarded by both the superiors and the subordinates were those who accomplished a large amount of preparatory work.

In terms of what the able and well-regarded principal does, we may summarize the results of the research succinctly in the words —*he works at organizing preparations for his decisions*. This in no way implies that such principals never reach a decision, but it may imply that good decision-making involves a large amount of preliminary work, i.e., seeking more information, determining what is fact and what is opinion, obtaining the views of others, and related activities.

Let us now turn to some findings related more directly to how the principals carry out their work, i.e., to the styles of their administrative preformance.

Those principals who stress communication (Factor A) in their style of work tended to be more verbal (use words well) and to be better professionally prepared than those who did not. Their personalities were distinctly more social; they were more sensitive, trusting, and relaxed. For some reason such principals were more likely to be women; they tended to be more highly regarded both by their superiors and their teachers.

Principals who preferred to discuss problems with others before they acted (Factor B) were often those who were less experienced in administration. They tend to be relatively mature, self-confident, and relaxed, and to have interests suggesting needs to conform (like public administrators or policemen). These principals tended not to be as well regarded by either their superiors or their teachers as were those who worked with less emphasis upon having a discussion before action could be taken.

A style of administration described by compliance with suggestions (Factor C) was most characteristic of the younger man who had recently become a principal. Perhaps this is a realistic adjustment for such a young man to make, if he is to assume a role of authority and power in a group of teachers who are senior to him both in age and experience. This style of administration was associated with such personal qualities as aloofness, being practical, independent and skeptical, but also with being anxious. Nevertheless these principals seemed able to reason and to learn quickly. Such a style of administrative behavior did not earn high regard from either superiors or teachers for the principal who had adopted it.

Ability to reason and to see relationships, as measured by cognitive tests, were personal qualities of principals whose style of administrative behavior included an emphasis upon "analyzing the situation" (Factor D). These principals also tended to have distinctive personalities. They were more dominant, shrewd, practical, and sensitive to pressure. They tended to have more administrative experience and to possess superior general knowledge. Stress on situational analysis, however, does not seem to be a way of achieving high regard from either superiors or teachers.

"Maintaining relationships" (Factor E) as a style of administrative behavior seemed to have earned principals high regard from their teachers. However, this behavior does not appear to place high demands upon cognitive or general intellectual ability, and it is somewhat more characteristic of women principals. In terms of personality, such a style is associated with a person who is sociable, lively, dependent, relaxed, sensitive, and confident. "Maintaining relationships" is a way of doing administrative work that can be utilized by the principal who is fortunate enough to have a *pleasant and social* personality even though he lacks real basic ability.

The principals who were the more insecure, unstable, inflexible, shy, and tense seemed to need to place greater emphasis upon "organizing work" (Factor F). Such persons could easily be described as compulsive. This style of administrative performance was not associated with high regard by either the principal's superiors or his teachers, but it is not likely that superiors or teachers disapprove of organization in the work of the principal. Rather, the negative evaluation may have resulted from reactions to the personality traits associated with this style of performance.

It is of interest to note that it was the weaker, more submissive principal of lower ability whose style of administrative performance was marked by responsiveness to the demand of persons outside the organization (Factor G). This seems to imply that the able administrators were more capable of resisting pressure from outside their own organization.

"Directing others" was associated with such personal qualities as lower ability, less professional knowledge, and also age and experience. It would appear that principals who emphasized this style of work have found, through long experience, assigning tasks to others to be a useful method of getting work done which they themselves are not capable of doing well. Their approach to administration is to use power and authority to parcel out tasks to others, tasks that principals of greater ability might do on their own.

It is important to point out that, in discussing the relationships between personal qualities and styles of administrative performance, we have engaged in some degree of overstatement and oversimplification. Only on rare occasion could one find an actual principal who would exhibit behavior in complete agreement with one of these styles. Far more often principals would be found whose work would be best described as a mixture of two or more of these styles. It would also be expected that many principals would show flexibility in their behavior, so that on some occasions their behavior would correspond with one of the styles and on other occasions would fit another. However, the value of the analysis here described lies in the fact that concepts are provided through which differences in the behavior of different administrators can be understood. These concepts provide tools by which a complex set of relationships between personal qualities and organizational behavior may be teascd apart and clearly recognized for what they are.

Summary

This chapter has been a summary of the results of a relatively large investigation of how 232 elementary-school principals perform administrative tasks. A further summary is of necessity, therefore, a highly abstracted account of the results of the many findings produced by the original study.

Differences among principals in their performances of administrative tasks were described in most general terms by large variations in the amount of work they accomplished in a fixed time period and in the emphasis they placed either upon making preparations for future decisions or upon immediately taking action upon the problems. These two general characteristics of differences among performances were supplemented by noting differences in styles of work.

Eight administrative styles were identified as follows:

1. *High communication style.* Principals characterized by this style of work stressed communicating with others about the problems they encountered in their work.
2. *High discussion style.* Principals characterized by this style placed unusually high emphasis upon the use of face-to-face discussion in administration.
3. *High compliance style.* This style characterizes principals who generally followed suggestions made by others.
4. *High analysis style.* Principals who were high with respect to this style spent relatively more effort than others in analyzing the situation surrounding each administrative problem.

5. *High relationships style.* This style refers to a high concern with maintaining organizational relationships, especially relationships with superiors.
6. *High work-organization style.* This refers to the principal's emphasis upon scheduling and organizing his own work.
7. *High outside-orientation style.* Principals high on this style of administrative performance displayed greater readiness than others to responding to pressures from outside the school.
8. *High work-direction style.* Principals who followed this style tended to stress giving directions to others as an important part of their work.

A study of the relationship between patterns of administrative performance and personal variables associated with the principals, disclosed many specific associations. The style of administration of a principal may be understood in part as an expression of measurable personality characteristics. The different patterns of administrative performance also appear to lead to differences in the way the principal is regarded by his superiors and his teachers. The facts established by this research study provide a part of the empirical information needed to bring into focus the growing concern with theory and to stabilize the concepts in educational administration.

CHAPTER IX

Decision-making [1]

WILLIAM R. DILL

Why decision-making, which received almost no attention in the last yearbook of the National Society to deal generally with theories of administration, deserves a full chapter in this volume may be sensed from assertions by specialists in administration, such as the following:

The essential process of adaptation in organizations is decision, whereby the physical, biological, personal, and social factors of the situation are selected for specific combination by volitional action.[2]

The task of "deciding" pervades the entire administrative organization quite as much as the task of "doing." [3]

. . . the central function of administration is directing and controlling the decision-making process. It is not only central in the sense that it is more important than other functions, as some writers have indicated, but it is central in that *all* other functions of administration can best be interpreted in terms of the decision-making process.[4]

I shall find it convenient to take mild liberties with the English language by using "decision-making" as though it were synonymous with "managing." [5]

The executive is a decider and not a doer.[6]

---

1. For helpful comments on an earlier draft of this chapter, the author is particularly indebted to J. V. Culbertson and T. L. Hilton.

2. Chester I. Barnard, *The Functions of the Executive.* Cambridge, Massachusetts: Harvard University Press, 1938.

3. Herbert A. Simon, *Administrative Behavior: A Study of Decision-making Processes in Administrative Organization.* New York: Macmillan Co., 1957 (second edition).

4. Daniel E. Griffiths, *Administrative Theory.* New York: Appleton-Century-Crofts, Inc., 1959.

5. Herbert A. Simon, *The New Science of Management Decision.* New York: Harper & Bros., 1960.

6. David W. Miller and Martin K. Starr, *Executive Decisions and Operations Research.* Englewood Cliffs, New Jersey: Prentice-Hall, Inc., 1960.

Decision-making, even for those who doubt its centrality to the theory and practice of administration, has become too important to ignore. More is involved than a simple relabeling of old concepts and experiences. The interest in decision-making symbolizes a fundamental reorientation in our view of organizations and the rapidly developing liaison between theories of administration and ideas from economics, statistics, mathematics, and the behavioral sciences. As a basic framework for organizational analysis, the decision-making approach has power, breadth, and sympathetic connections with other disciplines.

Advantages of Decision-making as an Organizing Framework

In the days of POSDCORB (Planning, Organizing, Staffing, Directing, Coordinating, Reporting, and Budgeting),[7] it was fashionable to focus on the activities of administrators—on the "functions" they performed and on the way they spent their time. Yet even from charts of activities as detailed as the ones which Carlson and Burns have given us, it is hard to infer what holds organizations together and makes them progress.[8]

The essential difference in the decision-making approach is that it highlights the goals, the tasks, and the choices that determine activities in organizations. What administrators do and how they allocate their time is a product of what they want to achieve and how they decide to proceed. The decisions which individuals make to join, to support, or to quit an organization and the decisions which they make as participants to solve the problems confronting it largely determine the organization's chances for survival and growth. Single decisions can be isolated for study and analysis, and sequences of decisions—related one to the other by their contribu-

7. Luther Gulick, "Notes on the Theory of Organization," in *Papers on the Science of Administration*, p. 13. Edited by Luther Gulick and L. Urwick. New York: Institute of Public Administration, Columbia University, 1937.

8. Sune Carlson, *Executive Behaviour* (Stockholm: Stromberg, 1950); and Tom Burns, "The Direction of Activity and Communication in a Departmental Executive Group," *Human Relations*, VII (1954), 73-97.

tion toward a common goal, by their contiguity in time, or by their sharing of the same subunit's agenda—provide a skeleton outline of an organization's history. Few other approaches have shown the same power to illuminate the dynamics of organizational life.

The breadth comes from the way decisions are defined. A decision involves more than the simple choice among well-defined alternative solutions to a well-defined problem. Decision-making covers several stages, from the discovery and definition of problems and the search for alternatives to choose among, through commitment, to the implementation of the choice and the evaluation of results. The *agenda-building* phase (which Simon has called "intelligence" activity)[9] covers the time administrators spend defining goals and tasks and assigning priorities for their completion. The *search* phase (Simon's "design" activity) encompasses efforts to find or invent alternative courses of action and to find information that can be used to evaluate them. The *commitment* phase (Simon's "choice" activity) involves testing proposed alternatives to choose one for adoption or, as is often appropriate, to postpone making the choice. The *implementation* phase includes clarifying the meaning of a commitment for those who are to help carry it out, elaborating the new tasks or decision problems that the commitment leads to, and motivating people to help put the commitment into effect. The *evaluation* phase involves examining the results of previous commitments and actions in order to find new tasks for the agenda and to help the organization learn how to make decisions more effectively. These phases, performed at different levels in interlocking sequences of decisions, cover the range of administrative activity.[10]

In addition to its power and breadth, a decision-making orientation has helped bring a *rapprochement* of organization theory and practice to concepts from economics, the quantitative disciplines,

9. This and the following categories are from Simon, *The New Science of Management Decision, op. cit.,* p. 2.

10. For elaboration of this framework, see William R. Dill, "Administrative Decision-making," in *Concepts and Issues in Administrative Behavior,* pp. 29-48. Edited by Sidney Mailick and Edward H. Van Ness. Englewood Cliffs, New Jersey: Prentice-Hall, Inc., 1962.

and the behavioral sciences. Traditionally, economists have been concerned with decisions as they try both to describe how people choose to allocate scarce resources and to prescribe how these resources should be allocated. In the real-life decisions that organizations face, statisticians and mathematicians have found analogies to problems they were already working with: how to evaluate limited samples of information, how to define and measure relationships and use these measurements to attribute causality and make predictions, how to deal with uncertainty, and how to find and verify the "best" of a set of possible answers to a problem. The success of early applications of these ideas to administrative problems has stimulated the development of such new mathematical and statistical tools as linear programing and sampling techniques that are especially applicable to managerial decision-making.[11]

Behavioral scientists have long been interested in how individuals and groups perceive their world, set goals, solve problems, and resolve conflicts. They have simply extended the range of their inquiries to study these processes in real or simulated administrative settings. Thus, studies of perception range from the fundamental work being done in experimental psychology to studies like Dearborn and Simon's analysis of the effects of departmental affiliations on administrators' definitions of a decision problem.[12] Notions about level of aspiration have relevance not only for abstract laboratory exercises, but also for the behavior of college presidents setting development or enrolment goals. The same hypotheses that help explain how experimental subjects learn nonsense syllables or how high-school Sophomores prove geometry theorems help us predict better how a school board and professional educators will respond to the challenge raised by new developments in teaching methods or new scientific achievements by the Russians.

11. Abraham Charnes and William W. Cooper, *Management Models and Industrial Applications of Linear Programming* (New York: John Wiley & Sons, 1961); Robert Schlaifer, *Introduction to Statistics for Business Decisions* (New York: McGraw-Hill Book Co., 1961); W. Edwards Deming, *Sampling Design in Business Research* (New York: John Wiley & Sons, 1960).

12. DeWitt C. Dearborn and Herbert A. Simon, "Selective Perception: A Note on the Departmental Identifications of Executives," *Sociometry*, XXI (July, 1958), 140-44.

The General Scope of Decision-making Research

The fruitfulness of the decision-making framework as a guide for theory, research, and practical advice has encouraged many kinds of exploration. In place of one comprehensive theory of decision-making, we have a number of partial theories. These have developed mostly from attempts to answer three questions:

1. *How are decisions made?* Psychologists, sociologists, and economists have studied individuals, groups, and organizations at work in laboratory settings and in real life as they dealt with problems and made choices and commitments. The aim of these studies was to understand more clearly the limits of rationality in human action and to develop models that will let us make more accurate predictions of decision-making behavior.

2. *Who should make decisions?* Behavioral scientists have been very interested in exploring different arrangements for the participation of individuals and groups in making decisions, sometimes with the goal of improving the quality of decisions and the efficiency of the process, but most often with the goal of finding more effective ways to implement decisions.

3. *How can we get better decisions?* Economists, statisticians, mathematicians, and management scientists have been interested in developing rules and strategies for making decisions that will yield better results (e.g., lower costs, higher profits, better utilization of plant and equipment) than the methods which administrators now use.

There is not space in this chapter to summarize all the interesting things that have been done to find answers to these questions. For a general and fairly recent review of the literature, there is a very comprehensive annotated bibliography on decision-making by Wasserman and Silander.[13] Other general references (and the questions they pertain most directly to) include: Simon, *The New Science of Management Decision* (1, 3);[14] Miller and Starr, *Execu-*

13. P. Wasserman and F. S. Silander, *Decision-making: An Annotated Bibliography.* Ithaca, New York: Cornell University Press, 1958.

14. Simon, *op. cit.*

tive Decisions and Operations Research (3);[15] Mailick and Van Ness (editors), *Concepts and Issues in Administrative Behavior* (1, 2);[16] Rubenstein and Haberstroh (editors), *Some Theories of Organization* (1, 2);[17] essays by Edwards (1, 3);[18] and, within the field of educational administration itself, the essay by Griffiths.[19]

Rather than duplicate what these surveys have done, I have tried in the remainder of this chapter to highlight a few developments in each area of inquiry that seem especially relevant to the problems of educational administration. This has been difficult, both because there is a lack of closure and integration among the three lines of research and because most of the work that has been done has not been done with educational organizations. The lack of integration results in incongruities that are hard to resolve. As the descriptive theorists, for example, present us with good analyses of how decisions are now being made, the normatively oriented students of decision-making are training administrators to make decisions differently. Among the normatively oriented, too, the men who are concerned with the more effective use of human resources in decision-making tend to ignore new developments in the technology by which decisions are made; on the other hand, the men who are developing new mathematical and statistical decision rules and designing computers to help make managerial decisions have often been naïve about the problems of persuading and training an organization to use these new techniques.

We can approach the analysis of a school's decision to buy new equipment, like teaching machines, via three kinds of studies, none of which makes explicit reference to the others. The first are studies

15. Miller and Starr, *op. cit.*

16. *Concepts and Issues in Administrative Behavior, op. cit.*

17. *Some Theories of Organization.* Edited by Albert H. Rubenstein and Chadwick J. Haberstroh. Homewood, Illinois: Dorsey Press, Inc., 1960.

18. Ward Edwards, "The Theory of Decision-making," in *Some Theories of Organization, op. cit.,* pp. 385-430; and Ward Edwards, "Behavioral Decision Theory," in *Annual Review of Psychology,* XII (1961), 473-98 (Edited by Paul R. Farnsworth *et al.* Palo Alto, California: Annual Reviews, Inc., 1961).

19. Griffiths, *op. cit.*

which map out how such decisions have been made but which ignore the problem of specifying more rational decision procedures. The other two are studies which recommend either who should be involved in making the decision or how the economic return of different alternatives should be calculated, but which seldom look at both issues at once and which usually ignore questions of building these decision policies into existing school systems.

Our second difficulty, the paucity of basic work on decision-making in educational organizations, is less obvious but perhaps more serious. Despite Litchfield's arguments that much of a science of administration will be applicable to all kinds of organizations,[20] laboratory groups, business firms, and government administrative agencies differ in important respects from schools, colleges, and universities. Most of what we know about decision-making we have learned by looking at problems and processes in the former settings. What we need now is more attention to problems and processes in the latter. One of the purposes of this chapter is to suggest some of the unique attributes of educational organizations that make generalizations from existing research difficult but which make the prospects for future research exciting.

Limits to Rationality

To understand how decisions are actually made, we need knowledge about the environments in which decision-makers work, about individuals and groups as decision-makers, and about the complexities of interpersonal and intergroup relations in decision-making. Unfortunately for the task of a chapter as brief as this one, these specifications cover almost the total range of knowledge about human behavior. One can only summarize some of the lines of research that have been connected directly with the analysis of how people decide; there is not space to treat them all or to suggest new links that may develop between general sociological or psychological studies and research on decision-making. Neither is there space to describe the mathematical models and computer simulations that

20. Edward H. Litchfield, "Notes on a General Theory of Administration," *Administrative Science Quarterly*, I (June, 1956), 3-29.

are providing us with powerful new languages for describing and predicting decision-making behavior.[21]

THE ORGANIZATIONAL ENVIRONMENT

With respect to the environments in which decision-makers work, four features stand out. The first is their ambiguity for the people who must deal with them. Organizations do not receive problems for decision clearly defined, ready for deliberation. Even the small number of problems that seem clearly formulated by the external environment may be misleadingly defined. It is only recently that we have begun to recognize in both theory and practice that agenda-building and search activities may have greater effects on the future of an organization than the actual choice or commitment does. The benefits of any choice that is made are constrained by the "problem" and the "alternatives" that the organization has defined.

The second feature of organizational environments is their factorability. The world is complicated to analyze, but not all of the interactions that make up the environment have to be considered at once. There is evidence both from the successes of operations research models and from the heuristic methods of problem-solving used by skilled administrators that relatively simple "images" of the world can serve very effectively as the basis for predictions and actions in administration, just as simplified models serve to approximate reality in chemistry and physics.

To tie these first two points together with an example, consider the many hints and demands with which the principal of a modern public high school must deal. Conant, Bruner, and the authors of this yearbook are only a few of the many "sources" in his environment that provide him with indirect suggestions or clear statements of problems on which he ought to work. As we watch him try to map the course of action his school will take, we will see that it obviously makes a big difference whether he gives first attention to Conant's recommendations about better vocational training for the students who will not go on to college or to the PTA's complaints about the school's extracurricular programs. He must decide

---

21. G. H. Orcutt, Martin Shubik, G. P. E. Clarkson, and Herbert A. Simon, "Simulation: A Symposium," *American Economic Review*, L (December, 1960), 893-932.

for himself what questions Conant's book or the PTA's complaints really pose for him to consider, and his assignment of priorities determines where the school will head.

On the other hand, although the problems are not obvious in their original presentation by the environment, a principal who is willing to try to find the significant problems and to predict the likely outcomes of various decisions should be able to do reasonably well. He may be able to predict the gross effects of a new program of vocational training, for example, by looking at a few variables like the basic properties of the job market into which graduates will move and by looking at the basic attitudes that prospective students have toward such a curriculum. If he knows the main sources of job opportunities that are available, he does not need a complete catalogue. If he knows only who supports and who opposes his program, he may not need to know the exact nature of their feelings.

Most environments provide strong cues that help organizations build simplified models of what their environments demand and what the outcomes of action will be. One set of cues is associated with the sources of environmental inputs. School administrators learn—sometimes too well—which of the sources of information in the community have expert knowledge of how certain inputs should be interpreted, which have power to make their definitions of goals and tasks "stick," and which can be ignored or overruled. Another set of cues is associated with the manner by which cues are transmitted to the organization. Many letters are ignored; but as Western Union is fond of pointing out in its advertisements, few telegrams are. A third set is associated with the clarity of the information and the frequency with which it is repeated to the organization. The effect of Russia's *sputnik* on science education comes at least in part from the extent to which its "lessons" were clearly and repeatedly stated to the people who control our school systems. One wonders what the effect of similarly clear and repeated statements of our lag in foreign language instruction might accomplish. A final set of cues are the models which the environment has provided ready made—through formal education, professional journals and meetings, and popular folklore—for analyzing what the world demands of an organization and how the world will react to what the organization does.

A third major characteristic of the environment that affects decision-making behavior is its heterogeneity when viewed from different points in an organization. In a significant sense, we cannot talk about the environment of information to which a school (as a total organization) has access. We must talk instead about a set of overlapping environments to which subgroups in the organization (the school board or the trustees, the principals or the president and his aides, the teachers or professors in various departments or colleges, and the students) have access. These different environments reinforce for various groups in the organization their own ways of perceiving the world and their specialized backgrounds of experience for interpreting what they find. It matters who discovers that there is a decision to be made. He has special power in defining the problem. By defining it and deciding how to communicate it to others, he determines how it will be handled and what the eventual outcome will be. The student who hears and believes, for example, that a certain faculty member has Communist leanings may not be able to do much about it; the school board member who hears and believes such a report is usually much more able to take action.

The fourth feature of the environment is its long-run impact on the people who make up an organization and on their approach to decision-making. This includes effects on people's decisions to join or to stay with the organization, effects on the formal and informal structure of the organization, and effects on the goals and strategies which people learn to use in finding, making, and implementing decisions. An environment which is committed to certain kinds of educational programs is likely to drive out of a school organization the administrators, teachers, and students who are interested in alternative kinds of programs. It is likely to produce a school system which is organized to handle the favored programs efficiently but which may not be well adapted to handle other kinds of programs. And it is likely to encourage among members of the organization a tendency to judge new challenges and opportunities from a local point of view. This is why in many attempts to set up new educational ventures at home or overseas, sponsors have set up entirely new schools rather than try to remake old ones.

These characteristics of organizational environments stem from a basic conception of environments as information systems and from a conception of the environments' contacts with organizations as series of information channels. This point of view lets us experiment with the kinds of quantitative measures of information that information and communication theory provide; and, more especially, it permits us to describe the interactions of organizations and their environments in ways that permit us to duplicate and extend the interactions by computer simulations. More precise languages for the description and characterization of environments should help in the problems of comparing different organizations and of predicting organizations' future behaviors as their environments change.[22]

INDIVIDUALS AS DECISION-MAKERS

Although some limits to rationality in decision-making can be traced to qualities of the environment, others are properties of the men and groups of men who make the decisions. Three of these characteristics of people seem worth mentioning. First is the notion which Simon's writings have helped to bring into prominence: that men approach most decisions with the goal of "satisficing" rather than "optimizing." [23] This does not mean that administrators have low aspirations or that they are disinterested in the best solution, if one exists. Over the long run, men often do try to "optimize" their situation; and by appropriate manipulation of incentives, we can certainly strengthen or weaken men's desires to get something close to an optimal decision.

But still, most of our evidence about human behavior suggests that administrators (and people in general) have more in common with Sancho Panza than with Don Quixote. We make decisions for the present, with the idea that we can remake them in the future. We tend to accept alternatives that at most can be described as

22. William R. Dill, "The Impact of Environment on Organizational Development," in *Concepts and Issues in Administrative Behavior, op. cit.*, pp. 94-109. For another approach to the analysis of environment which stresses the role of the environment as a source of goals and standards for the organization, see James D. Thompson and William J. McEwen, "Organizational Goals and Environment: Goal-setting as an Interaction Process," *American Sociological Review*, XXIII (1958), 23-31.

23. Simon, *Administrative Behavior, op. cit.*, pp. xxiv-xxvii.

"satisfactory for the time being" because we are better judges of what is "better" than of what is "best." For complex problems, like revamping our educational program to match the Russians, we do not know how to optimize; and even in cases in which we do, as we can in case of many kinds of scheduling problems, it may take too long or cost too much to work out the optimum. Time pressures and the total network of incentives under which administrators work often put emphasis on fire-fighting behavior—on carrying decisions far enough so that a problem can be set aside for a while and so that new and more urgent tasks can be dealt with.

The notion that men are "satisficers" means that research in psychology on perceptual processes, learning, goal-setting, and level of aspiration phenomena become very important as elements in a theory of organizational decision-making.

The second main idea about individual behavior is that it can be described effectively in terms of strategies or programs for action, using many of the same concepts that we might use to describe the instructions that govern the behavior of an electronic computer. "Program" descriptions of behavior let us use the power and flexibility of the computer to simulate human decision processes and to predict what the response to different kinds of environmental inputs will be.[24]

The third main idea about individual behavior is that, by use of the programing concept, we can analyze what decision-makers do into a sequence of fairly simple elements. The evidence we have so far suggests that the basic elements in the thought processes of skilled and less skilled decision-makers are not necessarily dissimilar. The difference lies in the ways by which these basic component strategies are combined into tools for modifying goals, interpreting the environment, and developing and evaluating alternative courses of action.

GROUPS AS DECISION-MAKERS

Decision-making in organizations involves an understanding of interpersonal as well as of intrapersonal aspects of behavior. Almost every brand of modern organization theory emphasizes the non-

24. Allen Newell and Herbert A. Simon, "Computer Simulation of Human Thinking," *Science*, CXXXIV (December 22, 1961), 2011-17.

monolithic character of organizations; and we are moving, even in our analysis of business organizations, toward theories that characterize firms as essentially political aggregations of individuals and groups in coalition or in conflict with one another.[25] Within a school system, it is often easier to describe the goals of the teachers versus the school board or the goals of School A versus School B in the system than it is to describe the goals of the system as a whole.

Much of the research that has been done has been aimed toward discovering what encourages and maintains these smaller subunits. We have explored the effects on organizational cohesiveness of many factors: environmental constraints, technology, the physical layout of offices and other facilities, communication media and restrictions, the origins and outside loyalties of different groups of organizational participants, struggles for power and control, and many others.

As subunits interact in considering a decision, there are processes of communication, of influence, and of negotiation and bargaining which affect the outcome. To understand these, we can draw from a variety of kinds of organizational research. For communication processes, the most interesting studies contrast the differences between what one group intends to transmit and what a second group receives,[26] explore effects that different amounts and kinds of information have on problem-solving behavior,[27] and investigate the limits on communication that various organizational constraints impose.[28] For influence processes, there are many stud-

25. See chapters in Richard M. Cyert and James C. March, *A Behavioral Theory of the Firm.* Englewood Cliffs, New Jersey: Prentice-Hall, Inc., 1963.

26. Jerome S. Bruner, "Social Psychology and Perception," in *Readings in Social Psychology*, pp. 85-94 (Edited by Eleanor E. Maccoby, Theodore M. Newcomb, and Eugene L. Hartley. New York: Henry Holt & Co., 1958 [third edition]); Erving Goffman, *The Presentation of Self in Everyday Life* (Garden City, New York: Doubleday-Anchor Books, 1959).

27. Donald M. Johnson, *The Psychology of Thought and Judgment* (New York: Harper & Bros., 1955); Richard M. Cyert, James G. March, and William H. Starbuck, "Two Experiments in Bias and Conflict in Organizational Estimation," *Management Science*, VII (April, 1961), 254-64.

28. Harold J. Leavitt, "Some Effects of Certain Communication Patterns on Group Performance," in *Readings in Social Psychology, op. cit.,* pp. 546-64; Murray Glanzer and Robert Glaser, "Techniques for the Study of Group Structure and Behavior. II, Empirical Studies of the Effects of Structure in Small Groups," *Psychological Bulletin*, LVIII (January, 1961), 1-27.

ies of the factors that induce or inhibit conformity behavior.[29] There are comparative studies of the outcomes of different strategies for influence and persuasion, both in intimate small-group situations and in more formal and more distant organizational relationships.[30] And there are case studies of many attempts to change behavior in organizations.[31]

Research on the processes of bargaining and negotiation is more recent; but stimulated by developments like game theory and by the theoretical proposals of men like Blake, Shubik, Schelling, Thompson and Tuden, and Cyert, March, and Simon, the ways in which disagreements and conflicts are resolved are getting increasing attention.[32] Perhaps the most important proposition so far is that the initial nature of the conflict puts strong limits on the means available to resolve it and on the solution that is likely to be reached. As Thompson and Tuden argue, for example, a situation which involves disagreement between two groups either on what will result from a particular alternative or on what they wish would result from their action is not likely to be resolvable by rational, analytic discussion. There is no basis for agreement in this way.

29. *Conformity and Deviation* (Edited by Irwin A. Berg and Bernard M. Bass. New York: Harper & Bros., 1961); Edward L. Walker and Roger W. Heyns, *An Anatomy for Conformity* (Englewood Cliffs, New Jersey: Prentice-Hall, Inc., 1962).

30. *The Planning of Change*. Edited by Warren G. Bennis, Kenneth D. Benne, and Robert Chin. New York: Holt, Rinehart & Winston, Inc., 1961.

31. E. Ginsberg and E. Reilly, *Effecting Change in Large Organizations* (New York: Columbia University Press, 1957); Robert H. Guest, *Organizational Change: The Effect of Successful Leadership* (Homewood, Illinois: Dorsey Press, Inc., 1962).

32. Robert R. Blake and Jane Srygley Mouton, "Reactions to Intergroup Competition under Win-Lose Conditions," *Management Science*, VII (July, 1961), 420-35; Martin Shubik, "The Use of Game Theory in Management Science," *Management Science*, II (October, 1955), 40-54; T. C. Schelling, "An Essay on Bargaining," *American Economic Review*, XLVI (1956), 281-306; James D. Thompson and Arthur Tuden, "Strategies, Structures, and Processes of Organizational Decision," in *Comparative Studies in Administration*, pp. 195-216 (Edited by James D. Thompson *et al.* Pittsburgh: University of Pittsburgh Press, 1959); Cyert and March, *op. cit.*; James G. March and Herbert A. Simon, *Organizations* (New York: John Wiley & Sons, 1958).

Blake and Mouton have designed an ingenious experiment which shows in a measurable fashion that "open" and "secret" bargaining or diplomacy lead almost inevitably to different outcomes.

Participation in Decision-making

Studies of rationality in decision-making have focused mainly on the processes of agenda-building, search, and commitment that lead up to a choice. A largely separate group of studies, though, has been concerned with the problems leading away from a choice—studies stimulated by the frequent experience that it is easier to make than to carry out a commitment when the understanding and co-operation of other people are involved.

Implementation has not always been seen as a major problem. Gulick, for example, largely ignores it when he defines the work of chief executives as: "the continuous task of making decisions and embodying them in specific and general orders and instructions and serving as the leader of the enterprise." [33] Compliance with decisions was expected, even if it was not always achieved. The resistance which occurred was not viewed as a challenge to the basic theory.

Others, though, have interpreted problems of implementation as evidence that new strategies for making decisions were needed. Their work has been guided most conspicuously by the proposals of Lewin and his students for involving the people who are to be affected by decisions more fully in the process of defining the problem, developing alternatives, and making the choice.[34] They have found in experiments and field studies that many groups (such as teachers) in organizations want more chance to participate in making decisions that affect their activities and opportunities. They have found that by giving groups an opportunity to participate, administrators not only get more co-operation in implementing the

33. Gulick, *loc. cit.*

34. K. Lewin, "Group Decision and Social Change," in *Readings in Social Psychology*, pp. 197-211; L. Coch and J. R. P. French, Jr., "Overcoming Resistance to Change," *ibid.*, pp. 233-50; Ralph K. White and Ronald Lippitt, *Autocracy and Democracy* (New York: Harper & Bros., 1960).

choices that are made but also may get better quality decisions.[35] They have found, in studies such as Gordon's, that participative methods can lead to greater production and efficiency as well as to higher morale.[36]

There has been a great deal of discussion about the role of different distributions of decision-making responsibilities in schools and colleges. There have been studies which show that both teachers and students want a more active role in decisions, and there have been a few attempts to measure the effects of participative methods on the educational process.[37] There have even been studies which suggest a major problem concerned with obtaining approval from the community for new tax measures or bond issues for education at the local level has been the alienation of large blocs of voters in the community.[38] The hypothesis is that the lower socioeconomic groups, cut off from full participation in the life of the community, vote against these measures simply to protest their alienation—not because they disapprove of the measures or their cost.

Still, the applicability of ideas about participative decision-making no longer seems as obvious as it once did. Inviting wider involvement does not always bring positive results. We have learned, for example, that experiments in participation will sometimes be seen, correctly or incorrectly, as false invitations to come in and discuss commitments which have already been made. We have learned that participation, like any other incentive, generally does not work if other aspects of the environment conflict with the effects it is supposed to produce.[39] In analyzing an experiment with participa-

---

35. Russell T. Gregg, "The Administrative Process," in *Administrative Behavior in Education*, pp. 278-80. Edited by Roald F. Campbell and Russell T. Gregg. New York: Harper & Bros., 1957.

36. Thomas Gordon, *Group-centered Leadership*. (Boston: Houghton Mifflin Co., 1955); Rensis Likert, *New Patterns of Management* (New York: McGraw-Hill Book Co., 1961.

37. Gregg, *loc. cit.*

38. J. E. Horton and W. E. Thompson, "Powerlessness and Political Negativism," *American Journal of Sociology*, LXVII (1962), 485-93.

39. Coch and French, *op. cit.*, p. 250; William R. Dill, "Environment as an Influence on Managerial Autonomy," in *Comparative Studies in Administration, op. cit.*, pp. 131-61.

tion that had not been a complete success, Strykker pointed out two such counteracting factors. First, the decision to start a participative experiment was essentially nonparticipative—it was imposed by a zealous superior on the managers who had to operate it. Second, the president vitiated many of the effects of participation by inviting numerous outside consultants (without requests from lower management) to advise management on what to do.[40]

Other problems in theory and practice have arisen from a failure to distinguish organized, participative patterns of decision-making from unstructured, laissez-faire approaches. Both give employees a chance to help make decisions, but only the first recognizes the need for some central direction and action in organizational decision-making. The two approaches are not equivalent, either in efficiency or in the satisfactions which people feel with the results.[41]

We are also discovering that the opportunity to participate in decision-making is not as highly prized by many people as the first experiments led us to believe. Administrators are usually not just showing authoritarian attitudes when they complain that the people who work for them are not interested in responsibility. Many studies show employees quite willing to let superiors make decisions for them.[42] Some disinterest in participation can be traced to basic personality characteristics.[43] Some can be traced to the fact that in accepting employment in American society, people are accepting roles—and they recognize that these roles include constraints on their autonomy on the job. They may be indifferent to opportunities for greater involvement in decision, they may not feel that the opportunities are legitimate for the role

40. Perrin Strykker, "How 'Participative' Can a Company Get?" *Fortune*, LIV (September, 1956), 134-36 ff.

41. White and Lippitt, *op. cit.*

42. William R. Dill, Thomas L. Hilton, and Walter R. Reitman, *The New Managers*, pp. 94-96, 187-89 (Englewood Cliffs, New Jersey: Prentice-Hall, Inc., 1962); J. R. P. French, Jr., Joachim Israel, and Dagfinn Ås, "An Experiment on Participation in a Norwegian Factory," *Human Relations*, XIII (1960), 3-20.

43. Victor H. Vroom, *Some Personality Determinants of the Effects of Participation*. Englewood Cliffs, New Jersey: Prentice-Hall, Inc., 1960.

they are playing, or they may be willing to forego opportunities they would like to have on the job because activities outside of work provide the major interest and satisfaction in their lives.[44]

We still have need for considerable amounts of research to find, for different kinds of organizations and different sorts of decisions, patterns of participation which will meet the following goals:

1. *Control goal:* Insure that decisions do get made and that, for control purposes, there be someone to talk with when it comes time to evaluate decisions or seek explanations for their results.
2. *Motivation goal:* Bridge the gap that often exists between making and implementing decisions by making them in ways that make the people who will have to help carry them out feel identified with their successful implementation.
3. *Quality goal:* Improve the quality of decisions by involving those who have most to contribute to the decisions.
4. *Training goal:* Develop skills for handling problems in the men who will move eventually into administrative positions, and test for the presence of these skills.
5. *Efficiency goal:* Get decisions made as quickly and with as little waste of manpower as possible.

Goals 1 and 5 might be said to argue for fairly limited participation in decision-making. Goals 2, 3, and 4 argue for more extensive participation—but in different ways: 2 for participation by the people who may be affected by the decision; 3 for participation by the people who are expert in solving it; and 4 for participation by people who may be neither personally involved nor expert, but who are being prepared for advancement.

Finally, all of the work that has been done on studies of participation in decision-making needs to be extended to take into account the new developments in strategies for making better decisions, especially those which suggest that computers may become important elements in the decision-making network of an organization.[45]

44. Barnard, *op. cit.*, pp. 167-70; Simon, *Administrative Behavior, op. cit.*, pp. 115-17.

45. Simon, *The New Science of Management Decision, op. cit.*; *Management Organization and the Computer* (Edited by G. P. Shultz and T. L. Whisler. Glencoe, Illinois: Free Press, 1960); *Management and the Computer of the Future* (Edited by Martin Greenberger. New York: M.I.T. Press and John Wiley & Sons, Inc., 1962).

New Ways To Make Decisions

The quest for better ways to make decisions goes on at many levels. The strength and diversity of the quest suggests that we are not really satisfied by "satisficing." At the simplest level, the last few decades have seen rapid advances in our capacity to define and collect data that are relevant to the complex decisions that organizations must make. The study of markets in industry is no longer an informal assemblage of experts' opinions. It involves sophisticated questionnaire and interview techniques to probe the attitudes and intentions of consumers. It involves the use of statistical sampling theory to guide the selection of information sources. It may involve the study of social diffusion processes to understand the spread of acceptance of a product over time. The assessment of student performance, despite criticisms which may be leveled against our methods, has been greatly improved by the development of more reliable procedures for generating ratings and grades and by the developments of standardized tests of aptitude and achievement. "Teaching machines" can provide even more frequent and perhaps more useful samples of learning behavior than periodic testing programs can provide.

Increasing sophistication can also be seen in our ways of measuring the costs of running educational programs, of estimating the return on an investment in new facilities or new programs, and of using budgets and other standards as a basis for judging many aspects of individual and organizational performance. New techniques in performance rating may help insure the fairness of merit-based salary systems. New approaches to sociometric analysis of the kind Coleman has used can give us more precise information about communication, power, and value structures within a school system.[46] Such progress in developing and teaching better systems of measurement is the first stage in improving decision processes.

At a second level, there has also been great progress in turning our experience with decisions into "models" for predicting what the consequences of new decisions might be. It is well known that if we have experience with the relationship of test scores and high-

46. James Coleman, *The Adolescent Society*. Glencoe, Illinois: Free Press, 1961.

school grades to college performance, we can develop regression or discriminant "models" to predict for new applicants what their college grades should be. But in research being done for industrial and military organizations, we are attempting much more ambitious kinds of predictions. By means of computer simulations of how a factory operates, for example, we can explore what will happen if the pattern of incoming orders changes or if various scheduling rules are applied.[47] This is analogous to, and not intrinsically more complicated than, trying to simulate an educational facility and to explore different rules for scheduling classroom use. Interesting attempts are being made to develop models that will predict voting results and the outcomes of community elections on special issues such as the fluoridation of water or the construction of a school or library.[48] These studies, if successful, may eventually help school administrators anticipate community reactions to proposed decisions.

Other models of direct interest to educators are those which are being developed to predict population trends or those which are being used in marketing to predict consumer-brand loyalties (something in which alumni secretaries, for example, might be interested). Some of these forecasting models are based on statistical methods, some on mathematical models, and some on carefully prescribed, but essentially nonmathematical computer programs. The common characteristic of all of them is not necessarily a high degree of analytical complexity; some, in fact, are rather simple. The main characteristic is that they generate specific predictions which can later be labeled as true or false; and if they do not predict well, they can be modified to try again.

The third level is the development of models which will explore alternatives, evaluate them, and propose a decision which is the equal of what human managers could propose and which sometimes, within the limits of certain assumptions and constraints, can be defined as "optimal."

Techniques like linear programing are already being used to

47. Charles P. Bonini, *Simulation of Information and Decision Systems in the Firm.* Englewood Cliffs, New Jersey: Prentice-Hall, Inc., 1963.

48. Work is being done by Robert Abelson at Yale University, James Coleman and others at Johns Hopkins University, and Robert Crain at the University of Chicago.

determine lowest-cost routings for fleets of school buses. They are being tried on the problem of devising more efficient plans for classroom utilization. Someday they will probably be used in educational organizations to help decide the optimal size of local school units or to map out long-range programs of investment, construction, and resource utilization. Such methods already are being used for complicated scheduling and planning decisions in business, government, and the military services; and they have an impressive record for producing decisions that have been much less costly or much more profitable than the best that human managers have been able to produce by using intuition and experience.

Where the problems are too complex or too unstable to permit the development of optimal decision rules, we are now making progress on another class of techniques: the so-called "heuristic strategies" for decision-making. These are refined and improved versions of the rules of thumb which human managers use on complex problems; and when developed so that they can be applied and used by a modern electronic computer, they have already shown a capability for finding better decisions more quickly than can be found by traditional methods.

The final stage comes when these decision-making systems become complete enough to collect data on the outcomes of their decisions, to evaluate the results, and to modify themselves to produce better decisions in the future. Computers, like executives, must be able to learn from experience if they are to reach their full potential. One of the first learning machines to be perfected in the educational realm will probably be an advanced version of today's "teaching machines." Already there are some fairly promising proposals for developing teaching devices which not only record student responses but which use these responses to vary the order of presentation of new material to the student and to learn new rules for organizing the presentation of material. The men working in this field argue that there is nothing in principle to keep such machines from "learning" to be at least as adaptive to the personalities and aptitudes of particular students as most teachers can be, particularly in classes of 20-50 people.

There also seems to be nothing in principle to prevent computer programs from doing at least as good a job of evaluating applicants for admission to college as most admissions officers now do or to keep them, at some time in the future, from automatically using college performance data effectively periodically to revise admission criteria and choice rules.

Some Special Problems in Educational Administration

As indicated earlier, very little of the basic research on decision-making that has been done has been based in school or college organizations. In building theories, educational administrators have borrowed heavily from ideas that developed from the study of industrial or governmental organizations. The political control of school systems, the reluctance of academicians to dissect their own home environments, and the limits on resources for supporting either descriptive or normative research have all helped prevent the kind of direct and unhampered attack that is needed on decision-making in educational organizations.

What are some of the things which might be done? First, to improve our theories of how decisions are made, we ought to take advantage of the special nature of most schools as organizations.

The educational field is one of the few in American society where we can make direct comparisons of decision-making procedures among systems pursuing the same goals but under different kinds of control. Some schools are public and much like other public agencies; some are private and governed by the philosophies of American business; some are private and governed by the traditions of church organizations. In both public and private schools, we should know more about the problems of making decisions that meet internal desires for progress and that at the same time satisfy school boards, trustees, legislative groups, and alumni who hold the purse strings.

These groups are not the same as the customers, suppliers, bankers, and directors of business firms. In the case of schools, objections by outsiders are often to the decisions themselves, because the basic issue is a contest over whose values, preferences, and subjective experience will prevail. In the case of business firms, the response of outsiders is less often to the decisions and the premises on which they rest than it is to their outcomes. And the outcomes can more easily and more legitimately be measured in economic terms.

In educational organizations, we also have an opportunity to explore the effects of limited financial resources on decision-making. What are schools able to substitute for the money which business and military groups invest to insure that key decisions are recognized and made, to provide incentives for participants in an educational system to co-operate in elaborating decisions and putting them into effect, and to develop or adapt new techniques for making decisions? What are the costs to our schools of not being able freely to hire decision-making specialists, of not being able to sponsor more research on decision problems and practices, of not being able to spend more time searching for better decision-making strategies?

In a school or college, we have some unusual relations among the major groups involved in its operation. There is often a larger gap between directors or trustees and the full-time administrative officers than there is between directors and top management in industry. In industry, the directors may sometimes include members of management; and they are usually men who themselves have had considerable experience as managers. In educational organizations, directors or trustees have seldom been full-time educators themselves; yet, particularly in the case of some public institutions, they may have more real administrative power than most industrial boards of directors possess.

There are also gaps in many school systems between the administrators and the teaching and research faculty. It is less likely in schools than in industry that administrative posts will be filled on a seniority basis from within the faculty. Faculty members are often reluctant to take time from their preferred occupations of teaching and research to become administrators; yet, as highly trained professionals, they generally feel quite competent to second-guess their colleagues who do take administrative assignments. Teachers may resist administrators, partly because the opportunity for autonomy is traditionally an incentive to draw men into teaching and partly because schools can seldom offer salaries and fringe benefits that would compensate for the sacrifice of autonomy which industry can demand.

Students pose special problems. They are sometimes treated as subordinates, but they are not subordinates in ability and ambition as are some worker groups in industry. Their subordination rests mainly on considerations of age and experience, a combination which generates protests and reactions among young persons in business as well as in the educational system. Students are also transients. This means that even in cases where they are held captive by compulsory attendance laws, they may well resist strong identification with the goals and values of the system. The most stable aspect of their experience from year to year lies in their relations with the classmates with whom they move from grade to grade rather than with the teachers who change from year to year and eventually from hour to hour. When transient loyalties and strong peer-group ties combine with resentment about subordination, students, as every administrator knows, will keep aggressively raising issues that their predecessors have also raised and pushed.

Because of the tight limits on their financial resources, educational organizations have more to gain than most institutions in our society from intensive investment in finding ways to use these resources more efficiently. This is why the study of decision-making practices and potentialities is critical for schools and colleges in the years ahead. Increasingly, we should be taking the lead in reporting new knowledge and suggesting innovations rather than relying on industry and government to provide us with ideas for action.

CHAPTER X

An Approach to the Informal Organization of the School

LAURENCE IANNACCONE

Orientations to Informal Organization

The organization chart, the published constitution, and the typical high-school textbook in civics convey information concerning one aspect of the organizations with which they are respectively concerned. This aspect of organizational life has often been called the formal organization. For centuries, some students of organization have thought that the formal organization is only what appears on the surface of organizational life and is given lip service. They have felt that beneath the formal organization and obscured in part by it, there lies a "real" world consisting of the way things actually get done and how people truly behave in organizations. Paying attention to this aspect of organizations was more important than studying the formal organization for understanding how the collective activities of people are directed toward accomplishing organizational goals. This approach may be seen in Aristotle's discussion of what "really went" on in the decision-making of the Spartan state under a legal constitution and following formal debate. The procedures of Herodotus, Machiavelli, and Lincoln Steffens display a similar approach. They looked beneath the legal operations and forms of the organizations they studied to better comprehend the underlying forces which influenced decisions. Later this interest was shared by students of economic organizations. It is of current interest to students of educational organizations. The concept and theory of informal organization were developed by this approach.

Three orientations may be distinguished in the writing on informal organization. One of these views the informal organization as primarily subversive of the formal organization. A second tends to see the informal organization as a healthy supplement to the formal organization. A third orientation is less concerned with the formal organization's goal achievement and sees the informal organization as providing for the psychological welfare of organization members. It is largely interested in human relations.

The subversive orientation stresses the significance of the fact that informal organization disposes of social power which is supposed to belong only to legal offices and agencies. It takes particular note of the extent to which the informal organization hampers the work of the formal organization. The early development of this orientation resulted from studies of political organizations. Lincoln Steffens' position after years of muckraking illustrates this orientation. "My conclusion was," he wrote, "that there was indeed such a thing in America as sovereignty, a throne, which, as in Europe, had slipped from under the kings and the president and away from the people too. It was the unidentified seat of actual power. . . ." [1] In the present century, studies concerned with the restriction of output in business and industry frequently share this "subversive" orientation.

In contrast is the work of students such as Peter Blau in his studies of the operations of public agencies. Blau lays stress on the extent to which extralegal arrangements among the organizational members helped in the fulfilment of organizational goals. This orientation views informal organization as a complex network of interpersonal relations among organization members which functions to accomplish the organization's tasks in ways more effective than those formally determined by the paper specification of functional roles.[2] These students are concerned with the satisfaction of individual needs only as this relates to organizational task accomplishment.

Griffiths, who shares this orientation, has taken Herbert Simon's position with respect to informal organization and applied it to schools. For them the concept of decision-making is the key to the

1. Lincoln Steffens, *The Autobiography of Lincoln Steffens*, p. 588. New York: Harcourt, Brace & Co., 1931.

2. Peter M. Blau, *The Dynamics of Bureaucracy*. Chicago: University of Chicago Press, 1955.

study of organization. In Griffiths' words, the informal organization is "the system of interpersonal relations which forms within an organization to affect decisions of the formal organization and this system is omitted from the formal scheme or is in opposition to it." [3] Although the function of informal organization influencing decision-making is central to this position, such influence need not be subversive. Indeed, as Griffiths *et al.* point out, it is probably more often beneficial than harmful to the formal organization in furthering the accomplishment of its tasks.[4]

The orientation toward informal organization which stressed its function as providing for the psychological welfare of organization members was given major impetus by the now famous Mayo studies in the Western Electric Company. The Mayo studies began with a concern for physiological factors influencing worker output. However, the discovery of other underlying regularities in the behavior of work group members, especially the influence of the work group upon the development of individual worker attitudes toward their work and toward the organization, redirected the attention of the investigators and made them students of informal organization. They used the concept of informal organization for that complex network of interpersonal relations within the organization which meets the individual's needs for satisfactory human relationships but which are not taken into consideration by the formal organization.

Each of these orientations has proven valuable despite their inevitable oversimplification of reality. To the extent that they refer to different phenomena under the common phrase, informal organization, they can lead to misunderstanding. Even more serious, they tend to share a common weakness in the use of the terms formal and informal organization as dichotomous concepts. Carlson, speaking of the literature on informal organization wrote:

3. Daniel E. Griffiths, "Towards a Theory of Administrative Behavior," in *Administrative Behavior in Education*. Edited by Roald Campbell and Russell T. Gregg. New York: Harper & Bros., 1957.

4. Daniel E. Griffiths, David L. Clark, Richard Wynn, Laurence Iannaccone, *Organizing Schools for Effective Education*. Danville, Illinois: Interstate Printers & Publishers, 1962.

It creates a mental image of two separate and distinct organizations in purposive organizations. It sets up mental categories of formal and informal organization and implies that all observations must be sifted into one or the other category.[5]

The single organization to which Carlson alludes can be viewed usefully in a number of different frameworks, each of which gives emphasis to different aspects of its operations. So Carlson, writing for this volume, stressed the relationship of the organization to its environment, its client relationships in particular (see chap. xii). Charters abstracted elements of formal organization, concepts of work-flow, and division of labor and specialization (see chap. xi). The concepts essential to our orientation toward informal organization are legal power and extralegal power in the system for making decisions and establishing policy for the organization—in our case, the school.

Legal Power and Decision-making

LEGAL POWER

Social power is the capacity to control stimuli impinging upon other individuals which produce an effect phenomenologically observable as compliant behavior. Virtually every individual has some power with respect to those with whom he interacts. This is true even of a newly born infant. Legal power is a subcategory of social power. It is the capacity to bring to bear the machinery of government in controlling the stimuli impinging upon individuals.

The source of the legal power which operates in the school is the state. The form and nature of a school district and its operations are, in large part, determined by state law and state agencies. These may be viewed as providing the framework and limits within which the legal power of a school district exists and operates. The way in which the legal power of a school district is allocated may be seen as a result of two sets of conditions. One of these exists within the school and is related especially to its work-flow. The

5. Richard O. Carlson, "Informal Organization and Social Distance: A Paradox of Purposive Organization," *Educational Administration and Supervision*, XLIV, No. 6 (November, 1958), 367.

other stems from the school's relationship to its legal environment and is especially related to its public nature.

The school exists as a public agency to accomplish certain instructional tasks. Charters has discussed how this is done using the concepts of work-flow, division of labor, and role-specification for teachers. But, as he has pointed out, the problem of certifying that teachers do perform in accordance with their role-specification is not met by the specification of roles itself (see chap. xi, p. 259). Accordingly, the responsibility for certifying the performance of organizational members must be allocated somewhere. Moreover, certification of performance implies more than mere evaluation of performance. Somewhere in the organization of society, there must be the ability to insure performance by teachers and other organizational members in accordance with their role-specifications. Vesting the offices and agencies of society which hold responsibility for certifying performance in schools with the legal power to insure performance solves this problem to a great extent.

School districts are local units governed by school boards which are responsible directly, or sometimes indirectly, to voters. Within the limits of state law, school boards are agents of the state and dispose of the legal power of the state over their respective schools and over the activities of organizational members, administrators, teachers, pupils, and others. Characteristically they make decisions which are hierarchically superordinate to the decisions made by organizational members and are binding on members of the school system. The board needs this legal power to discharge the responsibility for certifying performance which is vested in them. School boards, in making decisions, dispose of areas of discretion within legal limits. This provides for flexibility in the application of general state law to the particular local instance and specific tasks involved.

This legal discretion also creates a set of problems which would be less likely to be found at the board level of operations were there no such discretion vested in the board. Since the legal power of the state stands behind the board's actions and since the board may exercise discretion in its actions, the capacity to influence or control school board behavior provides a tempting prize for organizational members, individually or collectively. For example, control of board action with respect to its responsibility for certifying satisfactory performance would permit teachers, within the limits of state law, to redefine "satisfactory" in conformity with what they enjoy doing.

Typically, the school board uses a chief school administrator, the superintendent, to act as its agent in discharging most of its responsibilities for certifying performance. As the agent of the board he too disposes of legal power over the activities of organizational members. The grant of legal power vested in the superintendent's office is largely dependent upon the board. The superintendent disposes of less legal power and has a narrower area of discretion than the board. Ignoring other possible offices between the superintendent and the building principal, the legal power and the legal obligation for certifying and insuring the performance of teachers flows from the state to the school board, thence to the superintendent, and from the superintendent to the principal.

These successive pairs of positions connect the organizational personnel of the school district in hierarchical chains culminating in the school board. Each position in these chains is serially related to another, so that a flow of legal power exists from the school board, acting as an arm of the state, to the classroom teacher, who also acts as an agent of the state vested with legal power with respect to the pupil. Each position in this chain disposes of some area of discretion. Legal power, while inherent in a series of organizational positions, is wielded by people who occupy those positions and who are allowed judgment in carrying out their responsibilities. The legal discretion present in each position in this chain presents organizational members with similar tempting prizes as noted above in connection with the board's discretion.

There is in the school, then, a complex pattern of paired relationships between persons who occupy offices in a legally determined series of hierarchical positions, terminating at one end in the school board and at the other in the teacher. This set of relationships may be seen as providing the school with a structure which is social, in that it involves people as its elements. This social structure provides the channel through which legal power flows from the state ultimately to the teacher in her relationship to the pupil. Hence, we shall call it the legal structure of the school. It exists, in the first instance, to provide a means for certifying that teachers and other organizational members will perform in accordance with their role specifications.

ORGANIZATIONAL DECISION-MAKING

A variety of mechanisms of co-ordination exists to preserve the coherence of the system of tasks associated with work-flow. But, as Charters points out, "The most generally useful mechanism of work co-ordination is the allocation of decision-making functions to various offices and committees" (see chap. xi, pp. 258-59). This provides a means for resolving conflicts among organizational participants. Conceivably, a structure of social relationships fulfilling these functions but completely distinct from the legal structure could exist. This would entail obvious duplication of effort. It would also create a series of problems concerning the relationship between the legal and decision-making structures. Hence, the function of making decisions to preserve organizational coherence has been vested to a large extent in the legal structure supplemented by advisory committees, faculty meetings, and so forth. The legal structure functions both for certifying organizational performance and as the structure for decision-making in the school. This means, for example, that teachers may go to the same position for information concerning what is necessary to maintain co-ordination between their work and that of other teachers and to determine what behavior is required in order for their work to be certified as satisfactory. However, this combination of functions in the same offices and the existence of overlap between authority and decision-making structures may be seen as a source of several kinds of problems.

Information-flow.—The quality of decision-making in an organization is related to the amount of relevant information available concerning the issues under consideration. Ordinarily we would wish to maximize the information available to improve the quality of decision-making. But to the extent that the administrator, the person playing a key role in organizational decision-making, is also legally responsible for certifying the performance of other organization members, the latter are faced with a quandary. The more information they give decision-makers, the more effective may be the decision-making system, but also the more vulnerable they become before the legal power-holders. Faced with this dilemma, teachers are likely to select the information they give their principals so as to reduce their potential jeopardy before the legal power structure. It can be hypothesized, for example, that the lesson plans filed by a teacher with the principal's office will more closely approximate state requirements than will the activities in the teacher's classroom.

Rigidity vs. flexibility.—The school administrator, acting to insure teacher performance according to law and its progeny, school policy, must uphold the policy, the regulation, or the tradition of past practice. This may result in a tendency toward rigid behavior on the part of the administrator. The law also demands that its agents be consistent in their application of the law. Without consistency in law, there can be no justice. The administrator's habit of consistency in applying regulations and his tendency to uphold them may militate precisely against the flexibility needed for creative decision-making.

Confusion in delegation and shared decision-making.—Confusion with respect to delegation may easily occur when an administrator seeks to share his decision-making activities with organization members. While the administrator may delegate some of his decision-making activities, he cannot delegate his legal responsibility. Too often neither the administrator nor the teacher distinguishes between his position in the legal structure and in the decision-making structure. When, for example, a principal seeks to share his decision-making activities with his teachers, they may assume he has delegated some of his legal power. Teachers at faculty meetings not infrequently make decisions, the implementation of which depends upon legal power neither they nor the principal hold. The resulting disillusionment is sometimes attributed to poor faith.

Over time the combination of the three developments sketched above are likely to result in poorer decision-making and a static organization. The selection of information given an administrator by teachers helps him to perceive the organization as operating in closer conformity to the legal structure than it indeed does. This will result in his underestimating the need for changing that structure. His decisions will continue to be made in terms of a structure which is becoming outmoded by ongoing activities in the school and events around it. This set of misperceptions will also be reinforced by the habit of consistency which legal fairness demands.

If, in addition, faculty meetings and committee assignments are not fruitful in correcting this set of misperceptions, there will be a decreasing amount of change of the legal structure. The result of this will be either an increase in the gap between the organization's daily activities and the legal structure or a reduction of organizational achievement to the minimum legal requirements. The one presents us with the classic conflict between formal and informal organization documented by many researchers. The other finds the organization in a dysfunctional feed-back cycle which lowers the school's achievement of its goals.

MOBILIZING LEGAL POWER TO INSURE COMPLIANCE

An example from the realm of teacher-pupil relations may illustrate briefly the typical pattern used to mobilize the flow of authority over organizational participants and thus insure compliance.

A recent study of the changing perspectives of student teachers noted that they learned to use "increasing doses of institutional pressures and sanctions to make the child conform to the organizational pattern in the room." [6] The study found that the teacher at first applied sanctions in the room, then sent the pupil away from the class, then to the office, and finally called upon the family for support. The pattern involved reaching for more and more legal power to bring to bear on the recalcitrant pupil to produce compliance.

This pattern is followed on a much larger scale in the complex organization of the school itself. An initial mild reprimand from the principal to a teacher may lead to a longer "discussion," which may culminate in a specific order. Noncompliance at this point may easily lead to "talking things over" with the superintendent. Eventually, agencies of the state other than the school board, such as the courts, may come into play to insure compliance on the part of organizational members. Thus, two characteristic modes of operating appear in the legal system. (a) Faced with continued noncompliance, the holder of legal power reaches farther and

6. Laurence Iannaccone and H. Warren Button, Co-operative Research Division of U.S. Office of Education report, Project 1029 (in process).

farther toward the source of his legal power for more power in order to insure compliance. (*b*) In this process, as the legal power-holder reaches farther toward the source of his power, other agencies of the state holding legal power are brought into play, thus broadening as well as deepening the base of legal power brought to bear to insure compliance.

The Extralegal Power Structures of the School

EXTRALEGAL SOCIAL POWER

Four concepts have been central to the study of informal organization. It has been commonly seen as *extralegal* in nature, structurally involving primary *groups* (and cliques). Functionally, informal organization has been seen as providing a source for the satisfaction of idiosyncratic *psychological needs* and, as acting to channel *social power* to influence organizational policy and decision-making. The source of extralegal power in the school may be found in its necessary social relationships. The work-flow of which Charters speaks brings people together in ways specified by the job description. Human interaction in face-to-face settings is inevitable. Almost equally inevitable is the development of a series of complex human interactions beyond those required by the job and resulting from choices made by people. Social power, as defined above, resides in such interaction.[7] These not only knit people to one another more tightly but also increase their capacity to control the stimuli which influence others, i.e. their social power.

Students have long noted the development of primary groups among workers. Individuals exercising choice become members of extralegal groups of workers for a complex variety of reasons. It may be sufficient for our purposes to note that such groups provide for the satisfaction of idiosyncratic psychological needs, many of which are ignored by the structure of legal power and work-flow. One result, however, of the existence of primary groups is the creation of what may be called group power.

The members of primary groups share norms, or statements of what ought to be, concerning the behavior of a "good" group

7. *Supra*, p. 226.

member. Such norms help to control the behavior of group members. The group may be seen collectively as having more social power than any single group member. The social power of the individuals whose behavior most closely approximate the group norms is enhanced by those norms. The individual who speaks and acts in conformity with such group norms may be viewed as acting for the group and as supported by the power of the group, indeed, as wielding the power of the group. In a sense, without formal voting, he represents the group both with regard to other group members and to persons outside the group.

Factors which influence the formation of primary groups anywhere may be seen at work in the formation of groups of teachers also. Studies on primary group formation among teachers have found that such groups not only exist from September to June in a school but that they are reconstituted with no appreciable change when the school reassembles the following year. The coffee "klatch," the lunch group, the car pool, and the various other primary groups of teachers in a school are brought into existence by a variety of factors. Organizational factors which influence the formation of primary groups of teachers include proximity of teaching stations, the schedule of free periods, and similarity of teaching assignments. Personal characteristics which influence group formation among teachers include age, sex, marital status, and previous training.

Whatever the reasons for the formation of particular primary groups of teachers, once they have come into being, they dispose of social power. This may be seen in the influence a group and its norms exercise over group members. The power of the group may also be brought to bear upon other persons in the school, including school administrators. The extralegal power generated in the primary group may then conflict with the legal power held by the school administrator. The teacher whose behavior violates the school regulations, whether in spirit or letter, constitutes a problem for the organization and, specifically, the administrator. The problem becomes altogether different and more serious for the organization when such a teacher is supported by a primary group. This is particularly true when the teacher who comes into conflict with the administrator holds a position of leadership in his group. The conflict becomes still more serious and universal when the extralegal power of more groups are brought into play in the confrontation with legal power.

THE COMPLEX POWER STRUCTURE OF THE SCHOOL

However prone the administrator may be to treat teachers as isolated individuals or the school's faculty as a single primary group, neither of these is generally possible. Instead, the school's faculty tends to consist of several primary groups. The groups generally are linked together. There are two kinds of linkages. The occurrence of a common member in two primary groups of teachers constitutes one such link between the two groups involved. Such a link we may refer to as an *articulation* between groups. Or two groups of teachers may be knit by a pattern of interaction between the group members which does not involve the existence of a member common to each. This occurs when a member of one group of teachers regularly interacts with a member of a second group of teachers, and we refer to this as a *bridge*. The bridge spans the gap between the two groups but is sufficiently limited to prevent the two groups from merging into one.[8]

The primary groups of teachers in a faculty form a complex structure knit by articulations and bridges. There may be an occasional primary group which is isolated from the rest of the groups in the school. Similarly, there may be individual teachers who do not regularly interact with other teachers and who are not part of any primary group in the school. Indeed, the extralegal nature of such groups permits people to remain outside them if they choose. The same extralegal nature permits the group to choose its members also. The links of interaction which unite a faculty need not knit each group directly to every other. Depending in part on the size of the faculty, we would expect some groups to be linked indirectly to a second group by an intervening third group. But, just as we would expect most teachers to be related by regular interaction with some other teachers, so we would expect most groups of teach-

---

8. The author is indebted to Frank W. Lutz for help with this section in particular. For a more complete discussion of these concepts, see Frank W. Lutz, "Social Systems and School Districts: A Study of the Interactions and Sentiments of a School Board." Doctoral dissertation, Washington University, St. Louis, Missouri, 1962.

ers to be connected with other groups by a chain of regular interaction.

Again, as in the case of the social power resulting from the
existence of the group, we need not assume that articulations or
bridges come into existence in order to unite these groups. It is
more parsimonious to assume that they are produced by the same
social processes which give rise to voluntary social relationships
among people.

Once such relationships exist, the persons who interact with one
another play a key role in the complex group structure. Information
flows through such articulations and bridges, and mutual adjustment between groups faced with common problems is facilitated
by them. Groups of teachers so related may more readily present
a united front when confronted with common vexations. It would
be surprising indeed if such linkages were not used by teachers to
facilitate co-operation. In particular, we should expect these extralegal linkages to be useful in achieving mutual support for dealing
with common problems when the source of vexation lies in the legal
power structure or when proposed solutions to problems take an
extralegal turn.

We have pointed out that extralegal social power arises out of
the basic facts of social existence, not from the law nor its agents,
and is not recognized by the law or the authority structure of the
school. Nevertheless, it may be used to influence the behavior of
persons who occupy positions in the authority structure. The influence of the legal power structure tends to be visible to organization
members. Less visible, but no less potent, is the influence of the
extralegal power structure. As suggested above, the administrator[9]
—a principal, for instance—faced with noncompliance by an individual teacher may reach up the legal power structure in an attempt
to insure compliance. This almost inevitably requires him to "make
a case" for such support. He runs the risk that his call for support
will be evidence to his superiors that he cannot handle his job. The
initial impasse may result in a re-examination of an administrator's
decision. It may result in a principal's using discretion to avoid bringing the problem to his superiors' attention. Sometimes the confron-

9. See p. 230.

tation of legal power with even the little amount of social power a single teacher holds with respect to her principal can produce a decision which will better accomplish the organization's goals. Unfortunately, some face-saving way for the administrator to surrender the issue may be easier for him, at the cost of organizational goals.

Suppose that our hypothetical situation does not involve an isolated teacher but, instead, the representative of a group acting with the support of the group and its norms. The principal in this case is confronted not with the social power of an individual but with group power. The group's norms, however, are not likely to support noncompliance unless a major problem in the regulations or the organization exists. The principal faced with noncompliance which is supported by group norms confronts a problem considerably more serious than if he dealt with an isolated teacher. Some alternative to calling for more legal power is now more likely to be selected by the administrator even though it may not be what he and others would consider an optimum solution to the problem. The situation becomes still more serious when the administrator is confronted by a clash with a teacher who occupies an articulation or bridge in the social structure of the school.

Primary groups make for an increase in the power of individual teachers or, as we have called it, group power. Articulations and bridges between groups create a complex social structure with further enhanced power. When the complex social structure is engaged in adjusting differences among teacher groups with respect to changing the work or the operations of the school, and especially when it operates to unify the staff in order to influence administrator decision-making, it becomes fruitful to view it as a power structure. Its power may be used to bring a teacher's behavior in line with general norms shared by several primary groups. As groups of teachers converge upon specific norms held by the faculty in general, the position of the deviant becomes less tenable. Likewise, the extralegal power structure may influence the behavior of the principal as, for example, getting the principal to redefine his procedures for certifying teacher performance or even to redefine satisfactory performance. Thus, the school's extralegal power structure may change the meaning of law at its point of application.

Just as the legal structure for certifying performance provides the organization with the core of a general mechanism for decision-making in the organization, so the complex group structure resulting from the linking of primary groups of teachers, provides a general mechanism for influencing decision-making. In general, it may be enough for the principal to be aware of the complex social structure which exists in his school. But when it operates to influence decisions, he had better learn more about it and take that knowledge into consideration as he acts. The complex group structure of the faculty may be used not only to influence the principal's exercise of his discretionary legal power but also to influence his decision-making with respect to co-ordination.

However, the legal power and decisions of the central office and board restrict the scope of the principal's discretion. Many problems faced by teachers may be solved only by going beyond the principal. When communication up the legal structure does not result in a response satisfactory to the teachers, it becomes necessary for them to influence legal structure above the principal.[10] As an illustration, we mention the case of a school staff which considered unfair a decision by a principal concerning a teacher's sick leave. The principal's decision conformed to past policy and the regulations. It was necessary to change the regulations in order to prevent a repetition of the situation. Since the source of the regulations was the school board, not the principal, it was necessary for the teachers to reach up the legal structure, above the principal, to influence a change in the regulations. In such instances it is frequently necessary to use more social power than that which the power structure of a single school building has. The utilization of existing linkages and the possible creation of new linkages between groups of teachers in different school buildings provides a solution. The linkages between buildings will most often be bridges rather than articulations. Factors which induce articulations, such as proximity of teaching stations and the need for frequent communication in co-ordinating the work-flow, are largely absent between build-

10. For a case study illustrating a structure and process such as we have described and its impact on policy-making, see Griffiths *et al.*, *op. cit.*, pp. 227-93.

ings. It is thus less likely that articulations between groups in different buildings will come into existence. Although not many bridges spanning the gap between groups of teachers in two different buildings are likely to exist without considerable effort on the part of the teachers, common need for mutual support to reach past the principals up the legal structure may produce between-building linkages.

To maintain continued interaction in between-building linkages requires deliberate action by the individuals involved in them. Fixed meeting dates, formal committee assignments of professional organizations, planned agendas, and the paraphernalia of formal organizations help to keep such interaction going. Links between buildings which might otherwise snap are kept in existence. Mutual support among teacher groups in different buildings is more readily available by means of such continued linkages than if they had to be built each time a problem was met. Again, the power of the complex social structures is enhanced by linkage points. Power remains potential until a common problem requiring a mutual adjustment among the groups of teachers arises, but, when activated, the power to affect central office or board personnel is likely to be overwhelming. To the extent that the behavior of individuals at the linkage points conforms to the general norms held by the teachers in the system, such individuals dispose of immense power with respect to their colleagues' behavior. In effect, they represent the total staff in relation to the top of the authority structure.[11] They may, indeed, be viewed as having the capacity to control stimuli impinging upon the chief school administrator which produces an effect phenomenologically observable as an increase or decrease in anxiety. (At this point it may even be observable as blood pressure.)

THE MOBILIZATION OF SOCIAL POWER TO
INFLUENCE DECISION-MAKING

When a teacher seeks to influence the making of a decision in the organization, he begins with that point in the authority structure nearest him. Only after a teacher finds that the authority structure does not respond as he wishes does he expend the energy it takes

11. *Loc. cit.*

to utilize the extralegal power structure instead. Even where there has been a long history of using this structure, the practice persists of going first—if somewhat skeptically—to the legal structure directly. The teacher who gains the support of his primary group in seeking to influence a decision is engaged in mobilizing power. This involves using his network of interpersonal relations to add group power to his own. Such a process obliges the teacher to persuade his group. The group (which may exist as a coffee klatch, a lunch group, or a car pool) may be usefully viewed now, when it behaves to influence decisions, as a small unit of group power. The behavior of group members in relation to each other, to other teachers, and to the administrator changes as needed to influence the decision involved.

The power which a primary group of teachers applies to influence a decision may not be enough. If the decision they seek to influence is important enough for them to invest more energy and time, they can add to their power by obtaining the support of other teachers. This requires communication, persuasion, and mutual adjustments both within and between groups. It entails energy and time. The articulations and bridges which already exist, for whatever original reasons, will now be used. The necessary investments of energy for mutual adjustments are not likely to be made unless the decision involved is important to the teachers concerned. Thus, for example, a change in sick leave policies cannot usually be made at the school-building level. The teachers from one building are unlikely to wield sufficient influence to bring about a change in policies which requires school board action. To be effective they would have to use the network of bridges and articulations throughout the school system. This, in turn, will require mutual adjustment among the groups in the complex social structure which disposes of extralegal power. But when a staff spends the energy needed for mutual adjustments among its groups to present a relatively united front on an issue, they mobilize more power than can any component group in the power structure.

A complex extralegal power structure is likely to be well knit only when it faces problems, issues, or decisions which are important to many teachers from the various school buildings in a given district. Problems which can be solved at the building level will not produce a district-wide extralegal structure. The amount of energy needed to get voluntary groups of teachers throughout a whole school system to work together to influence a given decision is very great. A large amount of discussion and persuasion is necessary. A variety of groups of teachers must develop shared norms with respect to influencing a specific decision. When bridges which knit a whole system are established, the individuals at such bridge points dispose of correspondingly great amounts of social power. They may speak as representatives of the teachers to the representatives of the legal structure, even to the citadel agency of law in the district, the school board. Their effectiveness in influencing decisions will depend in no small part on how much extralegal power they can mobilize.

The administrator, using legal power, may have to reach up farther and farther toward the source of his power in order to insure compliance. The representative of the teachers may likewise have to reach farther and farther toward the source of his power, the primary group of teachers, to make his influence effective upon decision-making. As the legal structure reaches farther toward its source, it brings other legal power structures, agencies of the state, into play. So also, as the extralegal power structure reaches farther toward its source, it brings to bear the far-flung network of primary groups and their linkages. These are not now only interacting around coffee or sharing lunch or a ride together; they interact around common organizational problems, share perceptions, and support each other to influence decision-making. As in the case of mobilizing legal power, so the mobilizing of extralegal power involves a process of broadening and deepening its base. Together they may be viewed as parallel social structures. They are linked to each other by interaction at bridge points between the two structures. The one disposes of legal power and makes decisions in the school. The other disposes of extralegal power and influences the decision-making.

Implications for School Administration

The parallel existence of legal and extralegal power structures in the school provides an obvious potential source of conflict. But social conflict need not be harmful. When the energy which goes into the conflict is directed by intelligence toward the discovery of mutually acceptable solutions to problems, it may result in a more effective fulfilment of the school's tasks than would occur without the conflict. The parallel power structures with their respective sources of power at opposite ends can check the other. The combination of legal and extralegal structures into an interdependent organization may help avoid some of the difficulties which were noted earlier in this chapter as resulting from the overlap between legal power and decision-making structures.[12]

Information flow.—The legal power in the decision-making structure tends to reduce its effectiveness as the flow of information is reduced by that power. But the existence of a parallel extralegal power structure knit together by bridges and articulations involving the mutual adjustments among teachers helps to compensate for that reduction in effectiveness.

The gap between the legal and extralegal power structures is typically bridged by interaction between persons who occupy linkage positions in their respective structures. This interaction provides a series of bridges between the legal and extralegal power structures. Decision-making at such points in the organization can capitalize upon the strength of each structure and can bring to bear the information available to each structure. The teacher who is a bridge between these does not stand unprotected before legal power.

Rigidity vs. flexibility.—The habit of consistency built into positions in the legal structure may be offset to some extent by the interaction occuring at a bridge between the legal and extralegal power structures. Conscious that the teacher with whom he interacts represents an organized staff, the administrator may be led to re-examine the policy, the regulations, or the tradition of past practice in terms of its current usefulness. The confrontation of power structures requires the administrator to engage in a more extensive search for a satisfying solution than would otherwise be the case.

Shared decision-making.—Strengthening such bridges may also be the most realistic way to involve teacher participation in decision-making. Too often and too long, attempts at obtaining teacher

12. See pp. 229-31.

participation have rested on a rabble hypothesis. The assumption implicitly or explicitly present in most participation schemes is either that teachers will participate in decision-making as individuals or that the faculty may be treated as a single group. The importance of the various primary groups to which teachers belong is thus ignored. Capitalizing upon the bridges between the legal and extra-legal power structures, instead, gives due recognition to these groups. It should never be forgotten that they are basically voluntary in nature. They and their representatives more truly display the exercise of choice by the staff than do many votes taken at faculty meetings. Much more time is spent by teachers discussing school policies in primary groups than is available for committee or faculty meetings. Such discussions are considerably less fettered than are those which go on in committees.

Strengthening of the bridges between the two power structures will bring the fruit of free faculty discussion to bear upon decision-making. The network of articulations and bridges through which discussion by teachers must progress to influence policy development insures a process of careful consideration which will improve the quality of decision-making. This distillation of untrammeled discussion is the essence of democracy, whether it be in the nation, the state, or a school system.

CHAPTER XI

An Approach to the Formal Organization of the School

W. W. CHARTERS, JR.

Concepts of Formal Organization

Since classical times man has sought to describe underlying regularities in the forms by which people combine their efforts for a purpose. In the quest for understanding, the idea of *formal organization* has been a highly fruitful conceptual tool. It singles out a few features from an infinitely complex ongoing situation which permit him to see similarities and regularities where otherwise he would see only diversity.

The fundamental concepts of formal organization, as it has been developed in recent years, are four: *task, position, authority relations*, and *department*.

1. The most fundamental of the four is the *task*, or job. It requires that a distinction be drawn between the work which men do and the men who do the work. The job is taken as an element worthy of discussion in its own right.

Once the idea of task is abstracted, it is possible to conceive of an organization of tasks involved in the accomplishment of some purpose. To quarry a block of limestone, for example, one can say that it requires Tasks 1, 2, 3 . . . *n*, and he can describe the order in which they must occur, without reference to the people who do the work. The tasks must, of course, be performed by persons, but so long as they are done properly and in the right order, it is a matter of indifference as to who does them.

2. *Position* refers to a grouping of tasks, usually of just the right number and related to the extent that they can be performed by one individual. The particular tasks associated with a position may be specified by the job description for the position.

3. *Authority relationships* specify (for a pair of positions in a co-operative enterprise) who may legitimately initiate action for whom. This concept has proved to be useful in describing regularities, especially at the executive level and between supervisors and operating personnel. Authority relationships typically connect all personnel of the enterprise in a hierarchical form so that they culminate in a single officer or governing body.

4. The concept of the administrative unit, or *department*, is built upon the preceding concepts. It refers to the way positions and their associated tasks are assembled under a unitary authority system. Administrative units may be conceived at different levels of inclusiveness, from the small work group of operatives to the production division, from the platoon to the regiment, from the science department to the high school, and so on.

These concepts of formal organization are gross over-simplifications of reality, but they allow man to apply rational thought to ways in which tasks might be better organized. He can begin to question whether goals might be achieved more readily by a different distribution of tasks among positions or of positions among departments. Further, the concepts are sufficiently general to allow him to see similarities among enterprises as discrete in operations and purpose as an army division, an ecclesiastical order, and a toy factory or differences among enterprises as similar as two adjacent school systems. He is able to discern problem areas which enterprises have in common and can hope to learn solutions from one enterprise which are applicable to others.

FORMAL ORGANIZATION IN EDUCATION

"Formal organization of the school" has come to mean the various ways of distributing administrative tasks among positions and the patterns for forming administrative units.

One of the most prominent lines of educational research has been that of developing typical job descriptions. Given an administrative position, such as guidance director, curriculum co-ordinator, or assistant principal, the researcher seeks to describe the tasks typically performed by position incumbents in a number of school districts. Such descriptions, when compared with a priori conceptions of what tasks should be performed, may suggest shortcomings which "need to be" corrected in administrator training or else-where. Or the researcher may turn the problem around. Given a set of administrative tasks which need to be performed by some-one, he may attempt to discover whether they are performed at all in a school district and, if they are, by the incumbents of what posi-tions. The list of presumably essential tasks might include such matters as selecting and inducting teacher personnel, co-ordinating and revising the curriculum, and maintaining relationships with the community.[1]

Other problem areas suggested by the concepts of formal organ-ization have not received much empirical study but are, neverthe-less, matters of intense interest in education. One problem is that of the proper locus of major decision-making responsibilities in the school system. What are the relative merits of a centralized as op-posed to a decentralized authority structure? How much and what kind of autonomy should the building unit have? Other issues relate to the aggregation of administrative units, "staff" as well as "line." The issues appear in connection with such topics as the intermediate district, the advantages of school consolidation and of district organization, the expansion of central office personnel and the appropriate distribution of functions served by them, the 6-3-3 versus the 8-4 or the 6-2-4 plans, and the optimum size of the ele-mentary or high school or of the entire school system.

All of these issues are congruent with the mode of abstraction proposed by the concepts of task, position, authority relations, and department. The analysis is "formal" in the sense that it treats the structure of relationships among tasks and positions independently of the people who staff or participate in the enterprise.

As fruitful as the concepts of formal organization have been in pointing out regularities in co-operative enterprise and in suggesting problem areas, they have limitations. For one thing, the concepts are entirely static. They do not refer to anything that moves or changes. They can suggest problem areas, but they offer no propo-

---

1. One such list which has been influential in the description of formal organization is Luther Gulick's POSDCORB—Planning, Organizing, Staffing, Directing, Co-ordinating, Reporting, and Budgeting. Luther Gulick, "Notes on the Theory of Organization," in *Papers on the Science of Administration*, p. 13. Edited by Luther Gulick and L. Urwick. New York: Institute of Public Administration, 1937.

sitions regarding how one thing leads to another. As a result, they lend themselves only to description. At least, as the concepts are applied in education, they also tend to treat administration as though it had nothing to do with the basic work operations of the school—the teaching-learning process—which administrators are supposed to administer.

In the remainder of this chapter we will describe a different mode of analysis which, nevertheless, remains consonant with the general idea of formal organization. Also, it connects at various points with concepts from the social-psychological, or "human relations," approach to school affairs which have been applied so powerfully to education in recent years. Social-psychological concepts regarding the "informal organization" leave untouched the question of how the work of the school gets done, just as the concepts of formal organization disregard the people who do the work. Perhaps the wedding of the two approaches will be beneficial.

The Work Structure of the School

WORKFLOW

The first concept we will introduce is *workflow*, which we have borrowed unabashedly from industrial engineering. It represents the sequence in which work operations are performed and techniques applied in order to transform material from its original state to a more desirable or valuable state. It envisions a unit of material moving through a succession of processes designed to form it to the desired model.

While it may appear to violate humanistic conceptions of the educative process, our view of the pupil as "material" to be "processed" by school personnel provides a useful starting point for analyzing the work structure of the school. A child enters the public school roughly at age six and, during the next twelve years, is exposed to a succession of events designed to have a lasting effect upon his cognitive capacities and behavioral propensities. He moves through a sequence of work processes, each presumably helping to shape him in accordance with an envisioned outcome—the educational goals of the school. How much connection there is between the various work operations and the goals is another matter, but, in principle, all of the teaching acts to which he is exposed are organized toward achieving a desired end.

The uniquely human attributes of the "material" shaped by the educative process have important consequences for the organization of work. Certainly the pupil is not malleable in the same sense that a piece of metal is. On the contrary, the pupil is a selective and reactive organism, perfectly capable either of ignoring what the teacher sets before him or of actively resisting the teaching. The teacher cannot literally mold a child as he might forge a piece of heated iron, every blow of the hammer making a visible difference in the material.

The task of teaching, then, consists of two kinds of operations. (a) The teacher must make learning events available. He must provide visual and auditory stimuli in the form of written and spoken words, implements, social circumstances, and other facilities, along with directions for their use. All of these he arranges in an order which he hopes will produce the kinds of change he wishes to achieve in the child. (b) At the same time, the teacher must induce the pupil to come to terms personally with the events he has arranged. The child must be "motivated" to see, read, listen, reflect, respond, and perform at a level sufficiently deep within himself to engage and, hopefully, change his cognitions and behavioral inclinations.

The selective and reactive properties of the "material" with which the teacher works represent, in some respects, an advantage. Learning can occur without the direct presence of the instructional agent. Pupils may be sent to the library or study hall and assigned homework, and, to the extent that the teacher is successful in inducing them to take seriously the events he suggests, desired changes can occur in the "material" in his absence.

But these same attributes of the "material" can confound the work of education. The pupil is necessarily exposed to a tremendous variety of events in his environment other than those arranged for him by teachers. In some instances these events produce changes contrary to those sought by the school, while in other instances their effects are consonant with those sought through the educative process. It is therefore exceedingly difficult to establish unequivocally the extent to which instructional personnel are responsible for whatever changes occur. Physical materials rarely display this spontaneous metamorphosis toward (or away from) the finished product. While the bulldozer operator has indisputable evidence regarding the changes he has wrought on a pile of earth, the teacher's evidence of changes wrought is meager indeed.

The central task performed in the school, then, consists first in arranging sets of events from which learning is expected to occur and second in inducing pupils to expose themselves to the events. The sets of events are graduated in complexity and cover a variety of subject matter. Some are designed to be preparatory for subsequent learning experiences. The various sets of events through which pupils move during their schooling constitute elements of the workflow.

DIVISION OF LABOR

Another concept for describing the organization of work is *division of labor*, meaning the manner in which tasks in the school's workflow are broken up and distributed among a number of different instructional agents. It has several advantages over the somewhat parallel concept of the administrative unit, or department, in the classical idea of formal organization. It does not require us to introduce the concept of authority prematurely as "department" does. Furthermore, as a term of far-reaching importance in sociology, it connects on the theoretical level with a number of other terms relating to the social order and to the sociology of bureaucracy. One of these, of which we will make use, is *specialization*.

The efforts of a number of participants in a co-operative enterprise may be combined in one of two fundamental ways—in a *duplication* of labor or in a *division* of labor. In the duplication of labor, the materials processed by the enterprise are allocated to various participants, and then each participant performs all of the operations in the workflow for his portion of the material. An educational illustration of this would be the elementary-school district, consisting of several one-teacher schools scattered around the district, in which each teacher performs all of the instructional tasks (through the elementary level, at least) for those pupils within his particular attendance area. In the division of labor, the workflow is divided into its constituent operations and assigned to participants, each of whom performs just his operations for all of the materials processed by the enterprise. A parallel illustration of this is the consolidated elementary school where first-grade pupils from all over the district are taught by one teacher, second-grade pupils by another, and so on.

In analyzing the modern school, however, the critical questions relate to the bases upon which the instructional labor is divided. As the basis for dividing the labor varies, so will the locus of problems associated with workflow and, more generally, with the organization of work.

In education the basis for dividing the work of instruction varies along a bi-polar continuum. One pole of the continuum corresponds to the case of the graded elementary school, in its pure form. Here the work of instruction is divided according to the age-grade of the pupil who is the object of the teaching act, without regard for the subject matter taught. The teacher specializes in children of a given age and grade level. The pure case at the other pole of the continuum is the strictly departmentalized high school, where instruction is divided according to subject matter, without direct regard for the age-grade of the pupil. In this case the teacher is a specialist in a given subject. It is noteworthy that teachers in both circumstances are specialists, but in different things.

In Figure 1 the three forms of combining efforts of instructional personnel in education are illustrated—the duplication of labor, the division of labor according to age-grade, and the division of labor according to subject matter. Participating teachers are entered on the vertical axes of the charts, and the constituent tasks of the workflow are shown on the horizontal axes. An "X" at the intersection of the axes represents the particular tasks for which a teacher is responsible. The arrow entering the chart represents the pupils for whom the teacher furnishes instruction.

It has interested us to observe that many of the curriculum reforms and organizational innovations proposed for the schools through the years represent moves away from either pole of the continuum. In the high school, innovations such as the core curriculum, correlated studies, the home-room assignment, and the like, are attempts to lessen subject-matter specialization in favor of encouraging greater concern for pupils at a particular stage in their

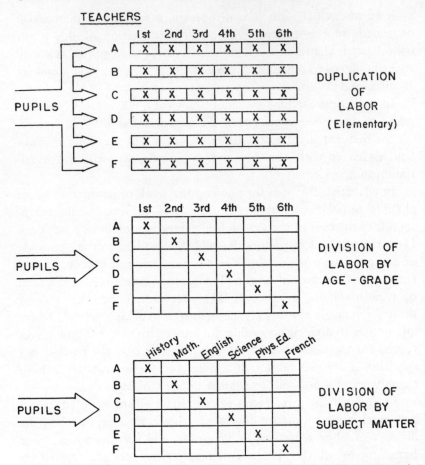

FIG. 1—The duplication of labor and two forms of the division of labor in instruction.

educational development. Proposals in the elementary school, on the other hand, often constitute moves away from the strict age-grade division of labor toward subject-matter specialization. The introduction of special teachers for foreign language, art, music, and remedial reading are illustrative. More radical moves toward departmentalization are contained in the Dalton Plan, the dual progress plan, and other curricular proposals, both old and new.

NONINSTRUCTIONAL ACTIVITIES OF THE SCHOOL

There are other tasks besides instruction which must engage the energies of participants in the educational enterprise. One class of these is comprised of the various noninstructional *services* rendered to pupils, parents, and citizens of the community by the modern school system. Bus transportation, meals, medical services, recreational programs, athletic and musical displays, aid in community solicitations, and observance of ceremonials are a few of the services which make the public school such a complex institution.

In any enterprise, some energy must be diverted from the central work itself to activities which enable work operations to proceed. We call these overhead activities the *organization maintenance* functions. They arise in even the simplest of work systems involving only a single participant. The solitary worker, for example, must devote some of his time to assembling materials and facilities he needs, planning his operations, caring for his tools, and, if it is an economic venture, marketing his product. As the enterprise becomes larger, more complex, and more enduring, the organization maintenance functions multiply at a disproportionate rate.

While there are a variety of organization maintenance functions, two major types relevant to an analysis of the work of the school are: the *input-output* functions, which serve to maintain the school system in a satisfactory relationship with its environment; and *work-co-ordination* functions, which serve to maintain and enhance the coherence and effectiveness of the organization of tasks within the system.[2]

Input-output activities.—Input-output functions relate to such matters as recruiting teachers, providing for and assuring the presence of pupils, constructing and maintaining quarters in which instruction may proceed, purchasing of and accounting for supplies, submitting records of pupil attendance and other forms required by state and federal agencies, and, above all, assuring an adequate flow of funds to support the school. They also relate, on the output side, to the matter of certifying a reasonable degree of correspondence between the school's "product" and the demands made by parents and other interested parties. This problem of the goals of the school is an especially pressing one. In a complex enterprise like the school,

2. This distinction roughly parallels the terms "external" and "internal" administration commonly used in the literature of school administration.

goals are multiple, competing, and sometimes mutually incompatible. Widely varying definitions may be held by interested parties and even by participants. Since all goals cannot be optimally realized, they must somehow be ordered in priority, and the political process this entails is one of the input-output activities of organization maintenance.

Work-co-ordination activities.—Work-co-ordination functions relate directly to preserving the coherence of the system of tasks associated with workflow. When a workflow is separated into its constituent parts and the tasks allocated to different people, it must nevertheless remain a coherent whole if it is to achieve its ends. The work of one participant must be made to fit with the work of others, and the total must be oriented to the goals which give it its *raison d'etre* in the first place. Following sections of this chapter will discuss the work-co-ordination function in greater detail.

Interdependence of organization maintenance functions.—The input-output function and the work-co-ordination function are closely related. Thus, when the input of funds for the school is reduced, necessitating a reduction in the number of teaching personnel, a reallocation of the work load or a rearrangement of the workflow or some other alteration in the internal organization of work must occur. Or when there are major changes in output demands, such as the recent stress placed upon science and mathematics training, the work structure within the school may be reordered accordingly.

Rearrangement of the internal work processes is only one means of adapting to variability in the outside environment. There is another choice. Another means is for school personnel to pay greater attention to input-output activities and to take steps to dampen the effects of a variable environment. By anticipating possible changes in environmental conditions, school personnel can act to forestall them or, if this is impossible or unwise, to spread their consequences over time. By foreseeing a drastic increase in the pupil population, for example, the school may be able to make the necessary internal changes gradually.

All of this points to an important and fruitful conception of the school's formal organization. It points to the tendency for the work organization to retain a coherence and stability of its own even in the face of violent and excessive fluctuations in the environment. By virtue of organization maintenance activities of school personnel, the work structure displays the characteristics of a quasi-autonomous system.

THE DIVISION OF NONINSTRUCTIONAL LABOR

Another feature of the division of labor has accompanied the dramatic growth in the magnitude and complexity of American public schools over the years. A more or less clearly delineated separation has occurred between instructional and noninstructional tasks. Personnel who engage in no instructional work whatsoever appear in the school. Included, among others, are custodians, cooks, bus drivers, and nurses. A whole corps of administrative officers, some responsible for noninstructional services and some primarily responsible for organization maintenance functions, also have made their appearance. The subdivision of labor within the noninstructional realm in some instances may be more elaborate than that within the instructional realm itself.

The separation of organization maintenance and service activities from instructional tasks, however, is far from complete. It certainly cannot be said that instructional personnel have been freed from all noninstructional functions. This can be seen in the number and variety of duties which take teachers' time away from teaching —duties such as collecting milk money, making reports of pupil attendance, supervising hallways and lunchrooms, and taking tickets at athletic events. Less obvious is the fact that critical functions of organization maintenance—particularly in the realm of the internal co-ordination of work—cannot be removed from teaching personnel. In some degree, these functions *inevitably* rest in the hands of the instructional staff, a matter to which we next turn.

Co-ordination in the Workflow

The various concepts regarding the structure of work in the school allow us now to focus our attention upon one of the principal problems of the organization of work, the co-ordination of effort. In devoting our attention to the work-co-ordination functions of the school, we have no intention of depreciating the significance of other "overhead" activities, such as public relations, teacher recruitment, and the like. The matter of maintaining the school in a satisfactory position with respect to its environment is treated elsewhere in this yearbook.

If teaching were an entirely routine, entirely determined process occurring in an unchanging environment, few problems of co-ordination would arise. Under such circumstances, a goal could be established, a series of work operations specified which would invariably lead to the goal, and co-ordination would be built into the master plan by which the whole "machine" was put together. The only remaining problem would be to find teachers willing and able to do precisely what the plan called for, no more and no less.

But the educative process is far more complicated. For one thing, there is a very large discrepancy between an educational goal and our knowledge of precisely what work operations are required to achieve it. While the desired outcomes in some enterprises can be readily translated into a sequence of concrete activities, the goals of education are notoriously difficult to so translate. This is why educators place so much emphasis upon having well-trained, intelligent people to carry out the instructional tasks; they must rely heavily upon the teachers' moment-to-moment judgments in deciding what next must be done. They expect them, too, to discover better ways of teaching—to innovate and to change. Maintaining coherence in the work structure, consequently, becomes a paramount issue.

For another thing, teachers are not automatons, nor are they exclusively and single-mindedly concerned with the goals of the enterprise in which they are employed. They are human beings, with all the passions and capacities characteristic of the species. They have their own conceptions of what is and is not important for the school to do. They have their own personal aspirations and wishes and behavioral inclinations which they express through their work. The human character of human organization poses additional problems for the co-ordination of effort in the school.

THE LOCATION OF CO-ORDINATION PROBLEMS

Whenever the work which one participant must do is contingent upon what another participant is doing or has done, a potential problem for co-ordination exists. In a global way, of course, every teacher in a school system is dependent upon every other teacher. If a few fail in doing their jobs, the effectiveness of the whole enterprise is diminished. The compelling problems of co-ordination, however, are not found at this level but in the more direct dependence of the performance of one task upon the performance of another task. One form of this direct dependence is a familiar one. It occurs whenever, in the performance of a task, the teacher must command scarce resources in order to meet his responsibilities, whether the resources are physical facilities and equipment or the time of pupils. Another kind of contingency relates to the movement of pupils through the workflow. Co-ordination issues arise whenever pupils are passed from the hands of one teacher to those of another for the next stage in their "processing." Directly, we will become more concrete about the location of potential problems, but first we must complete our discussion of the workflow in school systems.

Up to now we have talked as if a school system had only one workflow channel through which all pupils moved. This may be true in some schools, but in others there may be a number of more or less discrete channels. Some of the channels are for children of differing ability—children who, we might say, require different amounts of "processing" to bring them up to standard. Such process channels may be quite distinct, with their own separate teaching personnel and little pupil interchange among the channels, or they may be barely discernible as separate programs. The elementary school which groups pupils homogeneously from year to year is a case in point. Not infrequently separate channels are established to produce somewhat different final products. An illustration of such product channels is the trade, commercial, general, and academic courses of study side by side in the high school.

The point is that multiple workflow channels, which permit pupil transfer from one channel to another, complicate the co-ordination problem if the interchange entails pupil movement between teachers. The transfer of pupils from one reading group to another within the classroom poses no co-ordination problems for the school, but the transfer between homogeneously grouped classrooms does.

In any particular instance, the location of potential co-ordination problems requires a careful examination of the various workflow channels in the system. Nevertheless, we can point to some of the more salient areas which may demand special co-ordinative effort on the part of the school personnel.

The content of instructional events.—What the teacher hopes to teach his pupils is often contingent upon their having learned something earlier. This is most obviously the case in connection with the "tool" subjects. It would be extremely difficult for a high-school-science teacher to succeed in inducing expected changes in students who, in earlier years, had failed to learn to read. It is also assumed to be the case in the so-called cumulative subjects. Capacity to profit from "Spanish II" depends upon skills acquired in "Spanish I"; plane geometry may be said to depend upon the concepts and skills acquired in algebra. "Horizontal" as well as longitudinal contingencies are sometimes regarded as important. The elementary-music teacher's instruction may be designed to supplement and reinforce objectives of the grade teacher; objectives in the general science course may relate to those of the civics course. We are led to believe, however, that many of these longitudinal and horizontal contingencies are more matters of traditional assumption than evident fact. If what precedes has little bearing upon what follows or if the concepts and skills taught in science make no difference in the work of the civics teacher, co-ordination of course content is hardly a pressing problem.

Timing in movement through the workflow.—Closely related to the preceding area is the matter of the progression of pupils from one "processing" stage to the next. The predominant criterion in public education for deciding whether or not a pupil is ready to move on is a *time-of-exposure* criterion, which holds that if a pupil has been exposed to a set of instructional events for a given length of time he is ready. Even when this is coupled with a *content-mastery* criterion, based upon tests and other sources of feedback, movement normally occurs at standard time intervals—at the semester's end or year's end. Hence, longitudinal co-ordination in timing is not a severe issue in schools. It can arise when one teacher, finding time on his hands at the end of a year, covers material the next teacher expects to include in his course of study. Horizontal co-ordination is more problematic. Where pupils are interchanged between workflow channels, some attention to the timing of movement may be necessary to prevent them from missing out on important prior instructional developments in the host classroom. And when departmentalization exists in a school, the problem of scheduling pupils, teachers, and classroom space can assume massive proportions, as any high-school principal knows.

Classroom management.—Contingencies in the manner of inducing pupil exposure to learning events often are more apparent to teachers than contingencies in instructional content. One instructor who expects his pupils simply to "read and recite" may create severe problems for another teacher of the same pupils who counts on their taking a more active and independent part in the learning process. An elementary-art teacher who "lets the children get out of hand" can make life difficult for their regular teacher upon his return to the classroom.

Competing demands on pupils' time.—If, as in the departmentalized school, one pupil has several instructional agents, a danger exists that the agents independently make demands on his time which exceed the amount the pupil has available. Heavy homework assignments, for example, may be demanded of him on the same day by each of his different teachers; the skills of a musically talented athlete may be sought simultaneously by the coach and the band director.

Use of scarce instructional resources.—Co-ordination is an issue where simultaneous demands are made upon scarce resources and facilities, such as gymnasium and playground space, audio-visual equipment, library materials, clerical services, bus transportation for field trips, and so on.

There are two additional areas where co-ordinative issues arise but which are outside the instructional realm itself, i.e., in the various service projects undertaken by school personnel and in organization maintenance functions. These are particularly important since the failure of co-ordinated effort in their performance is often far more evident than failure in the co-ordination of instructional operations. If the school play goes on with some of the props still unpainted, if certain teachers do not submit their attendance records in time to be forwarded to the state, the consequences are easily observed, and responsibility is readily allocated. As a result, it is not unusual for the performance of these noninstructional tasks to become *the* criterion by which both teacher and school are judged rather than performance in the less tangible areas of instruction, a clear case of what Carlson, in chapter xii, calls *goal displacement,*

MECHANISMS OF CO-ORDINATION

In any enduring enterprise the co-ordination of work is sought in a variety of ways. All three of the following major classes of co-ordinating mechanisms will be found in public schools.

Specification of functional role.—As we suggested earlier, no school system could depend exclusively upon the co-ordination which is "built into" the master plan by which the work is divided and instructional operations are assigned to teachers. Nevertheless, an important co-ordinating function is supplied by the impersonal specifications of what the teacher is expected to do. Such specifications come in the form of the school-adopted textbook series, course syllabi and curriculum guides, statements of standard operating procedures and detailed instructions found in teachers' manuals, and so on. Obviously, every last detail of educating pupils cannot be planned in advance, and even in those school systems which rely upon highly detailed role specifications, this mechanism must be supplemented by others which provide for flexibility, unforeseen circumstances, and innovation.

Exchange of information.—Communication channels which link participants in various parts of the workflow serve as another mechanism of co-ordination. Through the exchange of information, participants can alert one another to contingencies and problems which arise so that they may make mutual adjustments in their operations—an exceptionally flexible co-ordinative procedure. Norms of the small work groups are implicated in the process, too. Groups of interacting teachers may develop shared understandings as to who should and should not do what, and these normative agreements have the power of informal group sanctions behind them. But the co-ordinative effects achieved in these ways are severely limited in scope. In a large and complex school system, it is physically impossible for all teachers to interact with all others, much less to consummate mutually agreeable adjustments simultaneously. No modern school system could depend upon person-to-person interaction exclusively to achieve co-ordination, despite its effectiveness within its limited jurisdiction.

Investment of authority for decision-making.—The most generally useful mechanism of work co-ordination is the allocation of decision-making functions to various offices and committees. Decisions regarding how work operations are to be adjusted must be binding on those whose work is affected. Therefore, control prerogatives (or legitimate authority) normally are vested in these offices, too. The utility of this mechanism lies in the diversity of functions it can serve in work co-ordination. Communication channels can be centralized in the officers, promoting greater effectiveness in the exchange of information among teachers. Decision-makers are more than passive transmission points, however; they seek information, process it, select among alternative courses of action, and initiate change in work operations. By vesting the decisions in legitimate authority, a means is provided for resolving conflicts of interest among participants (a problem not met in the second mechanism of co-ordination, above) and for certifying that teachers will perform in accordance with their role specifications (a problem not met in the first mechanism). The creation of an authority system, however, introduces into the school a kind of interpersonal relationship which has profound psychological consequences, a fact fully treated in the human-relations approach to school administration.

VARIATIONS IN THE DEMAND FOR CO-ORDINATION

The extent to which mechanisms of co-ordination must be employed in a school system seems to vary with certain identifiable conditions, some of which we have alluded to earlier in the chapter. Only a few additional ones can be mentioned in the space available.

Instability in the school's environment and the gross size and complexity of the enterprise certainly are matters imposing strong requirements for co-ordinative effort. Where school systems have high rates of teacher turnover or must draw upon the services of relatively untrained, inexperienced teaching personnel, we might also expect a heavy demand upon the co-ordinative mechanisms.

Of particular interest is the effect upon co-ordination requirements which a highly intricate division of instructional labor introduces. A division of labor, by definition, means specialization. Notably where specialization is along subject-matter rather than age-grade lines, conditions are present for the development of *specialized perspectives* among the various participants. The social backgrounds of persons recruited into the teaching of shop, social studies, and mathematics are likely to be quite different; their training experiences are likely to be diverse; their career patterns and current problems of work may have little in common; and their circles of intimate friends and colleagues tend to differ. Consequently, their perspectives on the tasks of education—on what is important to teach, on what is the proper way to teach, and on what constitutes a problem for the school—may be governed principally by the views of the specialized nook in the educational world which they occupy. Conflicts in points of view among participants require stern measures if co-ordination in work is to be preserved.

If these propositions are true, education faces something of a dilemma. Increased school size supports a more complex division of labor, bringing into the school a more heterogeneous array of highly trained instructional specialists—persons who desire and are competent to exercise independent judgment within their realms of expertness. And yet these very same forces increase the necessity of delimiting their autonomy in the interests of co-ordination.[3] Resolution of the dilemma is one of the most important challenges confronting school administration.

A Note on School Administration

To conclude, we would like to emphasize two implications in the preceding analysis of formal organization which bear upon school administration. First, our mode of analysis holds that the administrative structure of the school arises out of the nature and complexity of the co-operative enterprise itself. We find in error the position of some observers who decry the school's inclination to "take over from business and the military" the line-and-staff pattern of administrative organization. The authority structure was not arbitrarily imported into the school. If a similarity exists, it is due to the similarity of organization problems with which the enterprises must cope.

3. Thanks are due to Roland Keene, who helped the author develop this issue. See his "Operational Freedom in Complex Organizations." Unpublished Doctor's dissertation, Washington University, 1962.

Second, the analysis suggests that work-co-ordination functions are not exclusively the province of administrative personnel. Some of the important functions of co-ordination in the workflow are served by the interchange of information among teachers without any administrator intervention whatsoever. It is incumbent upon administrators to cultivate and nurture such channels of communication. Furthermore, much of the co-ordination is achieved through wholly impersonal means, whose significance we are likely to underestimate. Under some circumstances, at least, co-ordination through textbooks, curriculum guides, standard operating procedures, and common understandings of functional role are sufficient to maintain coherence in the workflow, again without the personal intervention of administrators. All of this suggests, however, that administrative personnel need to be thoroughly knowledgeable regarding the basic work operations under their jurisdiction, not just in order to "supervise" the instruction of individual teachers, but in order to facilitate the "fit" of all parts of the work—to assure coherence of the entire instructional program.

CHAPTER XII

Environmental Constraints and Organizational Consequences: The Public School and Its Clients

RICHARD O. CARLSON

Propositions are needed in administrative science about the impact of environmental factors upon organizations. We need to know the ways in which organizational structure and behavior are constrained and facilitated by forces in the environment of an organization. There are a great many factors in what can be called the environment of an organization. Some are quite obvious, such as financial ties, material dependencies, recruitment limitations; others are less obvious, such as prestige. The area of organization-environment relations, however, is one of the least-developed areas in the study of organization. This is true in the case of public school systems[1] as well as in that of other kinds of organizations.

So that we begin with some common understanding of what is meant by the constraining or facilitating influence of environmental factors upon an organization, let us consider an example. Anyone familiar with school systems in California and Pennsylvania will know that, in the former, citizen committees are extensively used in connection with the building of new schools and rarely used in the latter. Even though the literature about citizen committees emphasizes the notion that to use citizen committees is to be "democratic," it does not seem reasonable to attempt to explain the exten-

---

1. For selective summaries of the literature in this area, see Roald F. Campbell, "Situational Factors in Educational Administration," in *Administrative Behavior in Education* (Edited by Roald F. Campbell and Russell T. Gregg. New York: Harper & Bros., 1957); and L. L. Cunningham, "Research in External Administration—What Do We Know?" in *Administrative Theory as a Guide to Action* (Edited by Roald F. Campbell and James M. Lipham. Chicago: Midwest Administration Center, University of Chicago, 1960).

sive use in California and the rare use in Pennsylvania by suggesting that school administrators and board members are more "democratic" in the one state than in the other. What seems to be a reasonable explanation, however, is that in respect to the building of new schools, the school systems in the two states are confronted with different relevant environmental factors. For one thing, California school systems must gain the approval of the voters in order to float bonds to secure money for new buildings. Pennsylvania school systems do not need to secure voter approval; they are free to create a building authority to arrange for the necessary funds. Thus, it can be argued that California school systems have a factor in their environment which constrains them in such a way that they find the strategy of the use of citizen committees to be effective. Lacking this factor (and perhaps others) in their environment, the Pennsylvania school systems do not find the citizen committee to be of strategic use in acquiring new school buildings.

As stated in the opening paragraph, the relationship between an organization and its environment has received little systematic attention in the study of organizations. It has, however, not been totally neglected. Some good studies have been made in connection with public schools, and should be mentioned to provide further illustrations. For example, McDowell has documented the observation that, as an aspect of the school's environment changes, the job of the principal also changes. He has shown that when the environment contains largely lower-social-class children, principals encourage parent participation in school affairs, and when the environment contains mostly upper-middle-class children, principals attempt to suppress parent participation in school affairs.[2] And Clark has indicated how a service character in which professionals are dominated by clients has emerged in adult education in Los Angeles because of the environmental factors of open-ended goals, organizational marginality, and what he calls an enrolment economy.[3]

2. Harold D. McDowell, "The Principal's Role in a Metropolitan School System." Unpublished doctoral dissertation, University of Chicago, 1954.

3. Burton R. Clark, *Adult Education in Transition: A Study of Institutional Insecurity.* Berkeley and Los Angeles, California: University of California Press, 1956.

What is proposed in this chapter is to focus on a single factor in the environment of the public school system and suggest, by way of propositions, some of the ways in which this factor influences the structure of the school and the behavior of its members. The environmental factor is the nature of the relationship between the organization and the clients.[4]

In order to do this, it is necessary to suggest a way of conceptualizing the relationship of clients to an organization. That is, it is necessary to point out what appear to be important variables in the relationship and some extreme values of the variables and to develop a typology of organizations within these variables and values. After doing this, we can go on and raise questions about the impact of the client-organization relationship on organizational structure and behavior.

Domesticated Organizations

Attention will be restricted to service as opposed to production organizations. In the former, but not the latter, a social relation is established with the "objects" of work, and motivation is frequently an important concern.

One way of looking at the relationship of a client to a service organization is to bring into focus the extent to which the relationship contains the element of selectivity on the part of the members of the relationship: the organization and the clients. From this perspective, it is clear that some service organizations select their clients and some do not, and that in some service organization-client relationships, clients must (in the legal sense) participate in the organization and in others they can refuse to participate.[5]

4. The organizational relevance of this environmental factor has been demonstrated by Burton R. Clark, in both *Adult Education in Transition, op. cit.,* and *The Open Door College: A Case Study* (New York: McGraw-Hill Book Co., 1960).

5. Blau has demonstrated the relevance of another typology of client-organization relationships which involves power of the client as a variable. He has shown in one social work agency that those clients with power as opposed to those without power were rendered more attention from the professional case workers, were provided with more stable relationship with the case workers, and were served by more case workers with culturally preferred ethnic characteristics. See P. Blau and W. R. Scott, *Formal Organizations,* pp. 77-79 (San Francisco: Chandler Publishing Co., 1962).

If we put the variables of selectivity on the part of the organization and on the part of the client together, we get the possibility of four types of service organization-client relationships as seen below.

SELECTIVITY IN CLIENT-ORGANIZATION RELATIONSHIP
IN SERVICE ORGANIZATIONS

Client Control over Own
Participation in Organization

Organizational Control over Admission		Yes	No
	Yes	Type I	Type III
	No	Type II	Type IV

Most of the service organizations we know in the United States are probably Type I organizations: organizations which, either by formal or informal means, select the clients they wish to deal with and are participated in by clients on a voluntary basis. The private university is a good example. Hospitals and doctors' offices also are of this type. In addition, many of the public welfare service units belong to this type. They apply stringent criteria in the selection of clients, and the potential client is not compelled to accept the service.

Type II service organizations do not select their clients, and participation in the organization is nonmandatory. The state university whose charter specifies that it accept (but not continue to serve) all high-school graduates who are at least 17 years old and who wish to enrol fits in this type, for it is not mandatory for high-school graduates to attend college. In addition, most junior colleges and adult-education units fit within this type.

Service organizations of Type III are seemingly very rare or nonexistent. This type of organization selects clients and is one in which clients are compelled to participate. An organization which has such a relationship with its members (not clients) is the citizen army, but it is not a service organization. When laws specify that individuals having certain characteristics must embrace a given service, it seems that the service is always provided by an organization that has no control over admission of clients.

There are a number of service organizations of Type IV, such as public schools, state mental hospitals, reform schools, and prisons. The clients of these organizations receive the service on a mandatory basis, and prisons, public schools, and state mental hospitals cannot exercise choice in the matter of clients.

This chapter is concerned with only Type IV organizations and specifically with only one of them, the public school. Something can be gained, however, by attempting to see some of the essential differences between Type I and Type IV organizations (the extreme ideal types of the typology) and thinking about the consequences of the differences.

First, though all service organizations, by general definition, establish a social relationship with their clients and thus face a motivation problem, the typology makes it clear that an equal necessity to motivate clients is not placed on all service organizations. It may perhaps be unnecessary to remark that the problem of inducing clients to participate would seem to be most pronounced in Types III and IV, because these organizations are most likely to be in contact with some clients who have no real desire for their services. This factor undoubtedly has many organizational ramifications. To mention only a few, it would seem to bear upon the attitudes which staff members and clients hold toward each other,[6] personality make-up of staff, prestige of the work, and deployment of organizational resources.

Further, it seems appropriate to call Type IV organizations "domesticated." By this is simply meant that they are not compelled to attend to all of the ordinary and usual needs of an organization. By definition, for example, they do not compete with other organizations for clients; in fact, a steady flow of clients is assured. There is no struggle for survival for this type of organization. Like the domesticated animal, these organizations are fed and cared for. Existence is guaranteed. Though this type organization does compete in a restricted area for funds, funds are not closely tied to quality of performance. These organizations are domesticated in the sense that they are protected by the society they serve. Society

6. Consider Erving Goffman's work on "staff-inmate split" in "Characteristics of Total Institutions," *Symposium on Preventive and Social Psychiatry*. Washington: Walter Reed Army Institute of Research, 1957.

feels some apprehension about domesticated organizations. It sees the support of these organizations as necessary to the maintenance of the social system and creates laws over and above those applying to organized action in general to care for domesticated organizations.

Type I organizations, on the other hand, can be called "wild"; they do struggle for survival. Their existence is not guaranteed, and they do cease to exist. Support for them is closely tied to quality of performance, and a steady flow of clients is not assured. Wild organizations are not protected at vulnerable points as are domesticated organizations.

It is probably obvious in using the words "domesticated" and "wild" that the writer has in mind the extensive research on organisms in domesticated and wild settings. The argument is not that organisms and organizations are alike, but that what is known about organisms under specified conditions and their responses to environments is helpful in making propositions about responses of certain organizations to their environments. Of particular relevance to this discussion is that the research has pointed out the tremendous importance and the occurrence of adaptation by wild organisms to their changing environment.

This suggests the proposition that domesticated organizations, because of their protected state, are slower to change and adapt than are wild organizations. There is some evidence to support this proposition. On one hand, Mort, a perceptive student of change in public schools, has reported that:

Educational change proceeds very slowly. . . .
After an invention which is destined to spread throughout the school appears, fifteen years typically elapse before it is found in three per cent of the school systems. . . .
After practices have reached the three per cent point of diffusion their rate of spread accelerates. An additional twenty years usually suffices for an almost complete diffusion in an area the size of an average state. There are indications that the rate of spread throughout the nation is not much slower. . . .
School systems do not seem to be geared to the fact that the knowledge of available inventions is necessary if they are to improve and that the individuals operating the schools must master this knowledge.[7]

7. Paul R. Mort, "Educational Adaptability" as quoted in *Administration for Adaptability*, pp. 32-33. Edited by Donald H. Ross. New York: Metropolitan School Study Council, 1958.

On the other hand, consider the example of diffusion of a so-called "miracle" drug among physicians. Recent research indicates that within 17 months after its introduction, about 90 per cent of the physicians in four communities were using the drug.[8]

Organizational and Client Adaptation

Up to this point a system for conceiving the relationship between clients and service organizations has been presented, and out of this the notions of wild and domesticated organizations have been developed. In addition, a proposition dealing with change in domesticated and wild organizations has been posed. With this general background behind us, let us turn to other kinds of consequences of the client-organization relationship in domesticated organizations. Even though the focus will be on the public school system, illustrations will also be offered about other Type IV organizations.

The question which is central in this and the next section of the chapter is this: How do organizations and clients adapt themselves or attempt to control their relationship when neither the client nor the organization enters the relationship voluntarily? This section will give attention to a specific part of the question: What mechanisms are used by public school systems to adapt to an unselected clientele?

Such a question stems from the assumption that Type IV organizations are geared to render what they term adequate service to only some of their clients, and that they are consequently more responsive to clients presenting one set of characteristics than to those presenting another set. Said another way, the question rests on the assumption that Type IV organizations have goals to which they are committed and their achievement is hampered by the presence of the unselected clients, and that in the course of day-to-day operations there emerge within these organizations adaptive mechanisms which tend to minimize the disruptive factors presented by the unselected clients.

It is suggested, as a proposition, that at least two adaptive

8. Elihu Katz, "The Social Itinerary of Technical Change: Two Studies on the Diffusion of Innovation," *Human Organization*, XX (Summer, 1961), 70-82.

mechanisms are present in public school systems which can be seen as responses of the organization to the environmental condition of unselected clients.

The first adaptive response of domesticated organizations to the environmental condition of unselected clients is *segregation*. Segregation takes several forms. "Dumping ground" is a term well known to educators; it signifies that some part of the school program constitutes a place where students are assigned or "dumped" for part of their program, for various reasons, to serve out their remaining school days. Students do not get dumped into the academic areas of the program but, most frequently, into the vocational areas. This practice gives clues as to the type of student the school system is most anxious to serve.

A similar mechanism prevails in mental hospitals; the term "back ward" (as opposed to "front ward") stands for the same meaning as a dumping ground.[9]

Frequently a more extreme form of segregation takes place. In California, in some school systems, there are continuation schools for those students who have proved to be too disruptive for the regular high schools. And New York City has its "600" schools. In a sense, they are the dumping grounds' dumping ground.

The writer is not passing judgment on the practice of segregation but is merely pointing to it as an adaptive response on the part of domesticated organizations to the problem of unselected clients.

Segregation in domesticated organizations frequently may lead to or is accompanied by goal displacement. Goal displacement is a process whereby the original or overriding goal is abandoned (completely or partially) and another goal substituted. In this sense it has frequently been said that government bureaucrats lose sight of the goals of the agency and make the means (rules, regulations, etc.) the goals. Goal displacement is probably common in most

9. Thomas J. Scheff, "Differential Displacement of Treatment Goals in a Mental Hospital." Paper read at the American Sociological Association meetings, 1961. Also, see R. H. McCleery, "Authoritarianism and the Belief System of Incorrigibles," in *The Prison: Studies in Institutional Organization and Change* (edited by D. R. Cressey. New York: Holt, Rinehart & Winston, Inc., 1961), pp. 266-67, for reference to segregation and administrative segregation in prisons.

types of organizations, but it is suggested as a proposition that its occurrence in domesticated organizations is often directly related to the problem of unselected clients.

As far as the writer knows, no one has taken a systematic look at the service of public schools with the notion of goal displacement in mind. In tracking down preferential treatment in public schools, however, Hollingshead pointed out what seems to be a case of goal displacement. After showing that when teachers counsel with parents of lower-class children (children who make up the majority of the students in the general and commercial courses) the emphasis tends to be on discipline problems, and that when they counsel with parents of upper-class children the emphasis is on the pupil's work, he stated:

It is paradoxical that the teachers are so much interested in the work of the children in classes II and III when on the whole these students are the ones who receive the better grades. Lower class children, on the other hand, are given poorer grades, but the teachers consult the parents about discipline far more frequently than they do about the child's work.[10]

One interpretation of this is that teachers see *education* as the goal with middle- and upper-class children but substitute *discipline* as the goal with lower-class children.

There is also some similar evidence that goal displacement occurs with segregation in public mental hospitals in the case of patients in the back wards. Scheff has stated the case as follows:

The observation that patients are more disciplined than treated on back wards is a common one, and is substantiated by almost all of the observers of mental hospitals. . . . Although there were exceptions [in the hospital reported on here], treatment procedures were converted into controls more often on back wards . . . than on front wards.[11]

Further, while most modern prison officials suggest that prisons exist to rehabilitate rather than punish, there are, nevertheless, data which indicate that punishment in a number of cases overrides the

10. A. B. Hollingshead, *Elmtown's Youth*, p. 179. New York: John Wiley & Sons, Inc., 1949.

11. Scheff, *op. cit.*, p. 5.

CARLSON   271

goal of rehabilitation. Consider the following observations about classifying prisoners.

Our impression is that Custody has a separate and independent system of classifying prisoners which has little, if anything, to do with the recommendations made by the Guidance Center. Each prisoner, who has been classified in the Center on the basis of his case record and a battery of tests is now reclassified in accordance with Custody's estimate of the prisoner as a security risk. The three degrees of security risk—minimum, medium, and maximum—are only remotely related to these earlier findings. They also have little to do with any objective standard which might enable one to distinguish between prisoners of different degrees of security risk. The custodial classification seems to be based rather on the conventional middle-class evaluation of different crimes. Crimes involving violence, sexual or other, are rated as maximum security risks, despite the fact that murderers and sex offenders have the best parole records. Similarly, former escapees from reform schools never get less than a medium security classification presumably on the ground that once an escapee, always an escapee. Yet, the individual case might well warrant less severe treatment.

. . . The custodial classification, in terms of security risk, is therefore unrelated to the program of correction. It is solely dictated by the consideration that those who have received the highest sentences must be the "most dangerous" to society and the most incorrigible—a view which coincides with that of the sensationalist press. They must be the most severely punished, therefore, not only in terms of the longer duration of their sentences, but also by the more severe treatment while they are in prison.[12]

As a second mechanism, *preferential treatment* may be suggested. There are very substantial data to support the notion that a school system typically does not treat all students alike but engages in the practice of *preferential treatment* of some students. It has been documented that the preferential treatment involves such matters as grades, withdrawal from school, discipline, punishment, and curricula and that middle- and upper-class children as opposed to lower-class children are treated preferentially.[13] Widespread familiarity with these facts eliminates the need for their detailed documentation here.

12. Harvey Powelson and Reinhard Bendix, "Psychiatry in Prison," *Psychiatry*, XIV (February, 1951), 76-77.

13. The main, but by no means the only, source of documentation of preferential treatment in public schools is Hollingshead, *op. cit.*

Preferential treatment is also practiced in public mental hospitals, as the following remarks demonstrate:

It is our thesis that, in arriving at a treatment decision, the psychiatrist explicitly or implicitly considers various socio-psychological characteristics of the patient. Specifically, we propose that the patient's age, social class, degree of custodialism, and degree of authoritarianism will influence the psychiatrist's choice of treatment. Although they are not, strictly speaking, a part of the patient's symptomatology or pathology, these characteristics constitute, as it were, a paradiagnostic basis for psychiatric treatment (p. 366).

. . . Psychotherapy is the "treatment of preference" in this hospital (p. 374).

. . . [The] facts suggest that the psychiatrists choose mainly for psychotherapy the patients who most strongly resemble themselves. In other words, the psychiatrists to some extent follow a pattern of homophilic preference in selecting patients for psychotherapy (p. 375).[14]

What this indicates is simply that domesticated organizations give preferential treatment to some of their charges. The basis of the preferential treatment may differ with the species of domesticated organizations, but nevertheless it exists. The argument here is not why the basis for preferential treatment may differ from domesticated organization to domesticated organization, nor about the value problem of preferential treatment, but merely that domesticated organizations exhibit preferential treatment and seemingly do so as an adaptive mechanism to the environmental condition of unselected clients.

The mechanisms of segregation and preferential treatment in Type IV organizations seem to make the organization-client relationship more tolerable from the point of view of the organization. Through these mechanisms the organization is able to exercise a form of subtle internal selection and sorting of clients as it goes about rendering its service. It is the argument that these mechanisms are adaptive, that they enable the protection of the valued resources of the organization and, therefore, are functional in goal achievement. In the case of the public school, this means that segregating

14. Eugene B. Gallagher, Daniel J. Levinson, and Iza Erlich, "Some Sociopsychological Characteristics of Patients and Their Relevance for Psychiatric Treatment," *The Patient and the Mental Hospital*. Edited by M. Greenblatt *et al*. Glencoe, Illinois: Free Press, 1957.

certain students protects teaching time by removing from the main stream the disruptive elements of unselected clients. And, giving partial treatment to some students protects teaching time in the sense that it channels teaching time and professional attention in general to those students for which the school is geared to supply the most adequate service. Together, these mechanisms facilitate the fulfilment of the goals to which the school commits itself.

In order for adaptive mechanisms such as indicated above to exist, some members of the organization must support the mechanisms. They do not emerge and function in a vacuum. Support of preferential treatment and segregation in the public school system would seem to flow from one set of pressures, and lack of support or sympathy for these adaptive mechanisms would seem to flow from another set of pressures. The question raised, then, is this: Is support of these adaptive mechanisms randomly distributed throughout the public school system or are some categories of school people more supportive than others? It would seem reasonable to suggest that those most concerned about protecting teaching time, the largest resource of the school system, and instructional goals would be most supportive of these adaptive mechanisms. Drawing on an elementary distinction from organization theory, this directs us to the proposition that those designated as "line" personnel—teachers, principals, and a few central office people who are in charge of instructional time and goals—will support preferential treatment and segregation as responses to unselected clients. And, on the other hand, those designated as "staff" personnel— supervisors, curriculum consultants, and guidance counselors—will be nonsupportive and unsympathetic in respect to these adaptive mechanisms.

Now take a look at the other side of the coin. Instead of looking at how the Type IV organization adapts to its unselected clients, let us examine how the clients adapt to the mandatory service of the domesticated organization. Here the question is: In adjusting to the mandatory service of the public school, what forms of adaptation do students develop?

The adaptation of those students for whom the mandatory relationship is not problematical for either the students or the school can be called a *receptive adaptation*. The other extreme of the adaptation continuum can be called the *drop-out adaptation*. (Here the client totally withdraws his participation even though it is unlawful to do so or necessitates the invoking of special arrangements.) Between these extremes there are other forms of adaptation which are somewhat problematic for either the student or the school, or both. Students exhibiting these "in-between" forms of adaptation are neither enthusiastic about receiving an education at the hands of the schools nor do they completely reject the arrangement. Such students are mainly concentrated in junior and senior high schools, and their number, no doubt, varies greatly from school to school. It is the "in-between" forms of adaptation of these students, who partially reject the school, on which the following comments center.

Central to these forms of adaptation, between the extremes of "receptive" and "drop-out," is that the adaptation rests on a redefinition of the school by the student. That is, a basic part of the adaptation is that the student defines the school in a way other than the school or the general society would define it.

One form of adaptation can be called *situational retirement*. With this adaptation, the student is physically present but not mentally present. He goes to school because to do otherwise is to be shamed; but he takes no part in what is going on around him. He defines the school as a warm, quiet place where no one will bother him. He goes to school in a manner similar to the way elderly men go to a library and unemployed men go to the movies. No one can say this type of adaptation causes the school any trouble. Attendance is good; so are citizenship and general deportment. On the behavioral side, he is a model student; on the academic side, much is to be desired. In the learning setting, this student occupies himself with inconspicuous activities. Frequently teachers come to rely on him to run errands and to perform other acts necessary in schools but which are not part of the curriculum. In a sense, this type of adaptation rejects what the school has to offer but does not reject the school. Chances are this type of student will not drop out of school.

Another form of adaptation quite unlike situational retirement is *rebellious adjustment*, because taking the rebellious line is a highly conspicuous form of adaptation. The rebellious adaptation involves some rejection of both the school and what the school has to offer. The student making the rebellious adaptation constantly tests the limits of the situation to see the extent to which he can depart from that which is expected of a student. This is an adaptation which is disruptive to and problematic for the school, and the chances of maintaining this form of adaptation over a long period of time are slim. The rebellious adaptation would seem to be a way station short of dropping out of school. The perspective taken by the student is one of seeing the whole situation as a game of wits; and the object of the game is to see how much one can get away with.

Another form of adaptation between the student and the school is one in which the student sees the school as a place to get side-payments which are not usually available elsewhere. There are many fringe benefits in going to school, and when a student continues to attend school because of these fringe benefits rather than because of the central purpose of the school, he has then made a *side-payment adaptation.* Several forms of this type of adaptation can serve as examples. One form of side-payment adaptation involves the definition of the school as a place where one can engage in competitive team sports. The school frequently recognizes this adaptation by telling the student that if he is too bad an actor in the areas of primary concern to the school, he will be deprived of what he wants out of school; a chance to play football, basketball, or what have you. Another form of side-payment adaptation derives from the fact that the school is a place where extensive contact can be made with the opposite sex. The purpose of school thus becomes interaction with the opposite sex, and the student taking this adaptation views regular schoolwork as something to put up with so long as the side-payment is available. Another form of side-payment adaptation involves the definition of the school as a place to pursue some activity (other than regular learning), such as drama or repairing radios. Here again, the activity gives meaning to the school and is the reason for attendance, and the regular work is tolerated for the sake of the activity.

These "in-between" forms of student adaptation seem to have relevance for the drop-out problem in public schools, a problem which has been labeled as one of vital concern. Their relevance lies in the fact that these forms of adaptation enable the student to gain satisfaction from the school and to remain in school, where otherwise he might not.

Even though the term "holding power" of schools is used in the research literature dealing with drop-outs, its implications have not been systematically examined.[15] The term "holding power" implies that characteristics of a school are variables in the drop-out problem and that some combination of these variables produces greater holding power than other combinations. But, as has been said, the implications of the term have not been analyzed. The term "drop-outs," on the other hand, tends to fix the problem on the characteristics of the students who drop out. It is this perspective which dominates the research literature, and it is a perspective which does not permit the researcher to think about variables within schools.

It would seem that a systematic empirical examination of "in-between" forms of adaptation might reveal some information which might be highly useful in developing recommendations for increasing the holding power of schools. And on the basis of what has been said above about the side-payment adaptation, we are directed to the following proposition. The more fringe benefits a school makes available to the "reluctant scholar" (which would probably rule out Latin clubs, and the like) and the more it understands the functions of the fringe benefits, the greater will be its holding power.

15. There are exceptions to this statement but they do not appear to be significant. One exception is that studies have been made of the differences in the holding power of the several states and of the change in holding power over time in the United States. Another exception is W. H. Gaumnitz's *Holding Power and Size of High School* (U.S. Office of Education Circular No. 322. Washington: Government Printing Office, 1950).

SECTION III

IMPLICATIONS OF THE NEW SCIENTIFIC BASES FOR THE PROFESSION

CHAPTER XIII

Implications for the Practice of Administration

ROALD F. CAMPBELL

Science is concerned with the extension of knowledge. The scientific study of administration is increasing the body of knowledge in the field. However, when the field of study is not only an academic discipline or, perhaps more accurately, a derivation of several academic disciplines but also an area of practice, there is the obligation to determine what implications, if any, new knowledge has for that practice. One might even take the position that in an applied field, such as administration, improved practice becomes the overriding purpose of such scientific study.

This is not to equate the study and the practice of administration. The student of administration must deal with theory, with concepts, with if-then propositions, and with the meticulous testing of the propositions. The practitioner, on the other hand, must deal with an organization and find means of affecting that organization and its cultural milieu in such a way that the goals of the organization are achieved. Essentially, one role is that of reflection, the other that of action.

But action without reflection is futile—even dangerous. Thus, the practitioner must also reflect. The point is that his reflection is oriented toward action, toward steps to be taken to maximize the achievement of organizational purposes. To the extent that theory and research help the practitioner reflect more significantly, more accurately, the scientific study of administration has implications for him.

These implications will be in the nature of understandings, not in ordered guides for action. Thus, one can, after reading chapter iv, appreciate the impact of the scientific-management movement upon the practice of educational administration. This illumination, to be sure, does not tell an administrator how he is to improve his own administrative behavior. Even so, increased understanding is a great boon in most administrative situations and within this context certain implications for practice will be suggested.

It should be noted that practitioners in educational administration are found in a great variety of positions. These positions may be categorized by level of school: elementary, secondary, and higher education. Administrative posts may also be characterized in terms of local, regional, state, and national units within which administrators work. Moreover, educational administrators are found in both public and private institutions. Thus, the implications suggested may have relevance for principals, deans, directors, superintendents, presidents, and other administrators.

In suggesting these implications a number of assumptions have been made; these will now be stated explicitly. It is assumed that the scientific study of administration has produced at least the beginnings of a definitive body of knowledge. Perhaps the first twelve chapters of this yearbook suggest that this assumption has some basis in fact. It should be noted that contributors to this substantive knowledge come from many disciplines; however, they share a common concern for organizations and organizational effectiveness and efficiency.

It is assumed that society itself will continue to become more complex. Indeed, the church-state and the race-relations issues now confronting both the nation and the schools of the nation serve to emphasize this trend. Clearly, the administration of educational organizations will require the administrator to deal with the forces in the organization as well as in the larger world of which the organization is a part.

It is assumed that something has been learned about the selection and preparation of administrators. While much remains to be done, the efforts of the Cooperative Program in Educational Administration under the impetus of the W. K. Kellogg Foundation [1] appear to have enabled us to advance in this area. Again, it should be noted that the study and experience dealing with selection and preparation

1. The W. K. Kellogg Foundation, *Toward Improved School Administration*. Battle Creek, Michigan: the Foundation, 1961.

of administrators have also gone forward in settings other than education. Chapter xiv deals in some detail with what is now known about selection and preparation.

Consideration of the state of administrative science leads us to suggest that implications for the practice of administration are as follows: a clarification of the organizational setting, greater precision in analysis, more effective bargaining, improved organizational direction, increased significance of staff specialization, and greater professional responsibility. Each of these implications will be discussed in some detail.

Clarify Organizational Settings

Clearly, one of the most important implications to be drawn from the study of administration is the clarification of organizational settings. While theory and research can do little by way of suggesting courses of action, they can do much to help administrators visualize the field. Random phenomena can be ordered, ways of thinking can be established, glasses through which to view events can be provided. Some areas in which this kind of understanding seems pertinent will now be suggested.

Organizations exist in the larger society. Thus, recent study of administration stresses the need to understand society. Emphasis has been given to such basic disciplines as anthropology, sociology, political science, and philosophy. Some of the understandings growing out of such study have great relevance for administration. For instance, it is clear that the United States is a culture with pluralistic values. These values may be related to religion, national origin, race, social class, occupation, level of income, political affiliation, and a number of other factors. Most school administrators are expected to organize schools and school programs in communities where school patrons differ rather sharply in their basic value positions.

To make matters more complex, a number of investigators have shown that the basic value positions of our culture are shifting from a "traditional" to an "emergent" orientation.[2] This shift, too, seems to be related to age, to social class, and to a number of other factors.

2. See George D. Spindler, "Education in Transforming American Culture," *Harvard Educational Review*, XXV (Summer, 1955), 145-56; and Jacob W. Getzels, "Changing Values Challenge the Schools," *School Review*, XLV (Spring, 1957), 97-102.

Prince found, for example, that students and teachers in public, parochial, and private schools differed significantly when categorized on the traditional-emergent continuum.[3]

In a rather extensive study [4] the value positions of educators and noneducators, as reflected in their perceptions of the goals of the school, revealed that occupation and level of schooling were strong predictors of how the goals of the school would be perceived. To college graduates and professional workers the intellectual tasks of the school were much preferred to the social, personal, and productive tasks. People with less schooling and who were blue-collar workers supported the intellectual tasks, but they favored the social and productive tasks almost as much. Region, religion, and age were also found to be fair predictors of how people would perceive the task of the school.

These studies appear to demonstrate empirically the pluralistic nature of the culture the public school, particularly, is supposed to serve. To be sure, some communities differ with respect to their heterogeneity; considerable homogeneity can still be found in some rural areas and in some suburban communities, but even these communities cannot live in isolation from the larger society.

The scientific study of administration may contribute to a clearer perception of the nature of the school organization in the society of which it is a part. Here sociology has a contribution, and the work of Parsons may be taken as an example. Parsons suggests that formal organizations have three levels or systems. These are designated the technical, the managerial, and the institutional systems. In education, the technical functions are ascribed chiefly to the teachers, and the managerial functions largely to administrators. To an extent, the controlling boards of organizations perform the institutional functions, but in another sense society itself serves as a superior agency into which organizations must articulate. To continue, in Parsons' own words:

3. Richard Prince, "Individual Values and Administrative Effectiveness." Unpublished Ph.D. dissertation, Department of Education, University of Chicago, 1957.

4. Lawrence W. Downey, The Task of Public Education. Studies in Educational Administration Monograph No. 7. Chicago: Midwest Administration Center, University of Chicago, 1960.

A formal organization in the present sense is a mechanism by which goals somehow important to the society, or to various subsystems of it, are implemented and to some degree defined. But not only does such an organization have to operate in a social environment which imposes the conditions governing the processes of disposal and procurement, it is also part of a wider social system which is the source of the "meaning" legitimation, or higher-level support which makes the implementation of the organization's goals possible. Essentially, this means that just as a technical organization (at a sufficiently high level of the division of labor) is controlled and "serviced" by a managerial organization, so, in turn, is the managerial organization controlled by the "institutional" structure and agencies of the community.[5]

No organization is ever wholly independent. In terms of the functions or purposes of the organization, in terms of the resources the organization can command, and in terms of the treatment it exercises over its customers (in education, its students), the organization is subject to higher-level controls. These controls are of three kinds: the generalized norms characteristic of the larger society, the formal structure which is interstitial between the managerial and institutional levels, and the political arrangements whereby the organization is brought into direct relationship with the larger society.

The norms of the larger society may be imposed on schools and colleges through law. Court decisions, for instance, have long upheld the right of the teacher to serve *in loco parentis* in dealing with school pupils. But if the teacher be unreasonable or neglectful in dealing with pupils, the courts may find the teacher personally liable. What is neglectful and what is unreasonable are clearly related to social norms, and they are given expression through the courts.

The board of control, whether organized for a school district, a private school, or a college, is an interstitial arrangement between the organization and the larger society. The board makes some decisions as to the nature and extent of the educational enterprise, approves personnel who are to work in the organization, seeks resources from the larger society to support the programs of the

5. Talcott Parsons, "Some Ingredients of a General Theory of Formal Organization," in *Administrative Theory in Education*, p. 44. Edited by Andrew W. Halpin. Chicago: Midwest Administration Center, University of Chicago, 1958.

enterprise, and helps the larger society understand the contributions of the organization.

The larger society often exercises very direct control over public schools when school districts seek financial support. In many states, school districts must submit operating tax levies to the electorate, and in almost all states a referendum is required for bond issues. Public colleges must make similar representations to their respective state legislatures. Private schools and colleges are required to receive approval of financial support from their own constituent bodies.

Administrative science is also providing greater understanding of organizations as such. In chapter xii, for instance, a scheme for categorizing organizations in terms of client relations was suggested, and from the simple taxonomy thus developed a number of propositions were formulated. One of these propositions suggested that domesticated organizations, such as public schools, because of their protected state, were slow to change and adapt to new conditions. Such a proposition is pertinent to the administrator, to the researcher, and perhaps even more to the larger society. If the proposition can be sustained empirically, one might ask other questions, such as, Do public schools have too much protection? The answer to this question is a policy decision, not one derived from research, but the illumination necessary to an adequate answer does grow out of concept development and research.

In chapter ix, Dill has suggested characteristics of the organizational environments in which decisions are made. These include the ambiguity and complexity of most problems, the need to reduce a complicated world to a relatively simple decision-making model, the sets of overlapping environments found in an organization, and the long-run impact of the organization on the people who make up the organization. This and other analyses of organizations give the administrator ways of viewing his own organization. For instance, the concept that the organizational environment affects those who are members of the organization may prompt an administrator to examine that environment in terms of personnel recruitment and selection. Or, the administrator may find that certain kinds of people survive but a short time in the organization because they apparently find the environment incompatible. If these selection and survival factors reinforce the environment thought to be conducive to the best functioning of the organization, clearly the administrator should retain them. On the other hand, if the organizational environment forces out those people who are needed in the organization, a major re-orientation in the organization may be necessary.

Still an additional way by which the science of administration can provide more adequate understanding of organizational concepts is well illustrated in chapter vi. Lipham draws a distinction between administration and leadership. These two terms have been viewed as synonymous by many practitioners. A recognition that most administrators seldom lead but, nonetheless, may perform a very useful service is a contribution to understanding. Moreover, to operationalize the concept of leadership removes the term from its indeterminate, cliché-ridden status and makes it useful to administration. An administrator leads when he secures a change in goals or procedures in an organization. By the very nature of organizations, leadership is required only on occasions, while administration or maintenance of the organization is a constant requirement. Frequent leadership or change would actually wreck most organizations.

Another example of the clarification of organizational concepts is found in chapter viii in which Hemphill identifies eight administrative styles. The eight styles were found to be exemplified among 232 principals whose personal characteristics and administrative behavior were examined in that chapter. Each administrative style was found to be related to a number of personal characteristics. Actually, these concepts are sufficiently clear to permit many superintendents to find them useful as an approach to the selection of school principals. These concepts themselves will not suggest which people should be selected, but the concepts do provide a way of viewing candidates. The research from which the concepts came suggests the kinds of data which might be useful in the selection process.

A more realistic picture of the nature of the culture in which schools and colleges exist, the interdependence of educational institutions as subsystems of larger social systems, and the nature of formal organizations, all appear to be areas within which greater understanding is needed by the administrator.

Give More Precision in Analysis

A second implication growing out of the scientific study of administration is that greater precision in analysis on the part of the administrator is possible. The administrator is inevitably the monitor of the decision-making process in the organization. This process, discussed in chapter ix, involves a capacity to sense a problem, to define it, to examine alternative courses of action, to make a decision, and to formulate a course of action to implement the decision. Each step in this process calls for analytical power or more skill in scientific problem-solving. Perhaps an example related to this process will serve to clarify the nature of what is now being suggested.

A school bond issue in a large suburban school district was recently defeated. Approval was being sought to permit the board of education to sell bonds in the amount of eight million dollars for the purpose of constructing and equipping a large high-school plant, to be the third high school in the district. Population projections made it very clear that the additional space would shortly be necessary. Why did the issue fail?

In retrospect, a number of questions might be asked. Had the need been adequately communicated to the people of the district? Had alternative arrangements, such as double shifts, in case more space were not made available, been adequately described to the people? Did the projected plant contain more "frills" than the people of the district thought necessary? Did this proposal follow closely bond issues for water, sewage disposal, streets, libraries, and other public facilities? Were patrons of parochial schools in the district still recovering from assessments to build separate school facilities? Did some of the neighborhoods in the district feel that the new high school was to be inappropriately located? Had the professional leaders been joined by lay leaders in advocating the bond issue?

Each of these questions, slightly re-phrased, could have been asked before the bond election. Raising and seeking objective answers to such questions is a part of the analytical power to which reference is made. As the administrator deals with his board of education and his community, he is required to be both a technical and a political analyst. Projecting population and planning physical facilities are largely technical matters. Planning strategies for communicating information and assessing community support are political and social processes, often very difficult but indispensable in the world of social action.

Of interest at this point is the study reported in chapter viii. The analysis, it will be recalled, yielded two general behavior factors: preparation for decision, Factor X; and amount of work, Factor Y. Combining these two factors, it was possible to characterize two groups of principals. On the one hand, there were those who stressed preparation for decision and did a great deal of work in the process. On the other hand, there were those who did little by way of preparation and tended to act summarily. Clearly, the decision-making behavior of the able and well-regarded principal included a large amount of preliminary work, such as seeking information, determining what is fact and what is opinion, and obtaining the judgments of other people.

A more definitive way in which administrative theory helped in analyzing an organizational problem was found in a study of a research organization. The director knew that the output of the organization was not meeting his expectations nor the expectations of his superiors, but he seemed unable to go beyond this gross evaluation. Perhaps he did not possess the concepts with which to analyze the situation in which he was placed. After a series of interviews with the researchers, it became apparent that each of the research associates was working all by himself, in what may be called a "project-centered structure." There was no "organization" as such; in fact the investigators termed it "a conglomerate of hermetically sealed cells." The associates had virtually stopped functioning as members of an organization, and, in fact, one requested that he be given a grant so that he would not need to waste his time being a corporate member.

The Barnard-Simon theory of organizational equilibrium offered some clues to an analysis of the situation and, therefore, to a clearer statement of the problems which existed. This theory is essentially a statement of the conditions under which an organization can induce its members to continue their participation and in so doing assure organizational survival. The central assumptions of the theory are:

1. An organization is a system of interrelated social behaviors of a number of persons whom we shall call the *participants* in the organization.

2. Each participant and each group of participants receives from the organization inducements in return for which he makes *contributions to* the organization.
3. Each participant will continue his participation in an organization only so long as the inducements offered to him are as great or greater (measured in terms of his values and in terms of the alternatives open to him) than the contributions he is asked to make.
4. The contributions provided by the various groups of participants are the source from which the organization manufactures the inducements offered to participants.
5. Hence, an organization is "solvent"—and will continue in existence —only so long as the contributions are sufficient to provide inducements in large enough measures to draw forth these contributions.[6]

This theory enabled the investigators to ask questions about the research organization: What inducements did the organization offer? Why should anyone offer contributions, that is, work to make the organization function rather than merely his own project? What further inducements can the organization offer so that contributions will increase?

The Barnard-Simon theory provided one way in which to view the research organization, but it was not the only way. This theory provided the concepts through which to analyze the motivational aspects of the research organization; other theories provided concepts for viewing different sides of the situation. The point is, without theory, the administrator is deprived of vital tools of operation. If an administrator is schooled in administrative theory, he may be able to make more penetrating analyses which may lead to the successful solution of organizational problems.

Extend Knowledge about Effective Bargaining

A third implication derived from the study of administration relates to increasing knowledge about bargaining on the part of the administrator. Educational institutions must compete for the resources of society. This competition may take the form of people deciding what resources are to be retained in the private realm and what are to be allocated to the public realm. Payment of more taxes for schools may mean less money for houses, cars, vacations, and other consumer goods. This competition can also extend to the

6. Discussed in James G. March and Herbert A. Simon, *Organizations*, pp. 84-111. New York: John Wiley & Sons, 1958.

selection of one public service above another. For instance, the United States Congress in recent years appears to have given road construction priority over schoolhouse construction.

While studies of organizational environment, as noted in chapter xii, have been relatively neglected, sociologists and other students of society have accumulated a considerable body of knowledge that can provide the administrator with insight as he attempts to bargain for his own organization in the larger society. Parsons, as indicated earlier, has suggested that no organization is wholly independent; every organization, whether public or private, must seek legitimation in the larger society. A grasp of this fact will convince most school administrators that the old argument about dependent and independent school districts is largely irrelevant.

Dill has suggested in chapter ix that every organization is surrounded by overlapping environments, and these various environments make a difference in the decision-making behavior of the organization. The superintendent, the principals, and many of the teachers see their colleagues in professional organizations as their reference groups even more than they see the local community. This phenomenon has caused Gouldner to designate some members of organizations as "cosmopolitans" and others as "locals." [7]

This same differentiation has also been applied to citizens. Sutthoff, in discussing his study, had this to say:

When the school administrator turns to the public for support for his educational program, he must appeal to two audiences who frequently hold conflicting values and interests. The citizen who is locally oriented would be expected to assess the policies of the local schools in terms of their conformity to commonly accepted standards and values of the community. Ideologies and techniques imported from the larger society would be suspect. Conversely, the more cosmopolitan layman would look principally to those clues which would tell him that the school system's educational program is in step with state and national trends. In many instances this divergence of views may lead to conflict. For example, many school board members consider rendering service to the community a civic duty. When change in personnel or curriculum is desired, the locally-oriented school board member would act to preserve the

7. Alvin W. Gouldner, "Cosmopolitans and Locals: Toward an Analysis of Latent Social Roles—I," *Administrative Science Quarterly*, II (December, 1957), 282-306.

norms and values of the local community. The cosmopolitan may challenge this behavior on the basis of its narrowness; he may prefer that change should be consonant with educational developments at the state and national level. Oftentimes the school administrator must reconcile the differences between these two groups.[8]

But schools and colleges are not only subject to the overlapping environments of staff members and board members, they respond to the basic socioeconomic forces of society. Actually, policy formation in education may be represented by a flow chart.[9] It seems that educational policy has its genesis in basic social, economic, political, and technological forces; its generation in nation-wide antecedent movements, such as the National Manpower Commission, and the Conant studies; its promotion by educators and lay citizens chiefly through such organizations as the U.S. Chamber of Commerce and the National Education Association; and finally, its formalization in legal expression by local, state, or national government. In short, educational organizations are affected by the total milieu of society.

If the administrator is to become a more effective bargainer in this milieu, a number of conditions seem to pertain. There is first the need to use the full resources of the organization and of the larger society in the analysis of what appears to be a desirable program for the school. The technical insights of teachers, for instance, may be indispensable in determining the lay-out for the science department of a high school. If the teachers of a particular school do not have these insights, the administrator is obligated to go beyond his own organization and consult people or examine documents where such insights are available. In any case, the recommendations of the administration should be based on the *expertise* of informed people, be they in or out of his organization.

But the administrator who would bargain effectively must do more than collect relevant data and judgments. He must use these materials to build an effective case for his program. Inevitably, at

8. John Sutthoff, "Local-Cosmopolitan Orientation and Participation," *Administrator's Notebook*, Vol. IX, No. 3 (November, 1960).

9. This idea is discussed in Roald F. Campbell, John E. Corbally, Jr., and John A. Ramseyer, *Introduction to Educational Administration*, chap. ix. Boston: Allyn & Bacon, Inc., 1962.

this point he is concerned both with what is desirable and what is possible. What is desirable ordinarily stems from certain rather objective conditions as well as from the application of certain professional values. What is possible is largely a perception of what the people involved can be persuaded to accept.

In building the case for his recommendation, it is well for the administrator to recognize that he is dealing with a variety of phenomena, some observable, some judgmental. This recognition may help him be more explicit and should contribute to the clarity of his argument. His proposal must make sense, not only to professionals but to laymen, for ultimately laymen decide the policies of public education.

At this point, the role of the controlling board of an educational institution becomes crucial. The board stands between the organization and the larger society. On the one hand, board members through service on the board develop an understanding of what it is the professionals are about. On the other hand, these board members are the representatives of the larger society in which the school exists and, as such, sense the values held by their constituents.

The partnership between the chief administrator and his controlling board is a strategic one.[10] Each has a unique role to play. Boards can err by attempting to administer the schools. Chief administrators can err by encouraging or permitting boards to become rubber stamps. Often the delineation of board-administrator roles is attempted by a set of rules and regulations. These formalized statements are useful only if they reflect understandings which derive from mutual respect and explicit discussion. The development of such an understanding should be a prime objective of every chief administrator.

Assured that some congruence of role perception on the part of the board and the chief administrator has been established, the administrator may test his bargaining skill with his controlling board. If his case is not clear, the board raises appropriate questions and requests clarity. If he over- or under-assesses the aspirations of the

10. For instance, see Thomas R. Bowman, "The Participation of the Superintendent in School Board Decision-making." Unpublished Ph.D. dissertation, Department of Education, University of Chicago, 1962.

community, board members can reflect their judgments regarding such inaccuracies. If the administrator's strategy for going to the larger community seems inappropriate, the board can and should suggest a more adequate strategy. In the end, the chief administrator and the controlling board should stand together in a program that reflects both what is desirable professionally and what seems possible politically.

With this type of solidarity, still another step can be taken in the bargaining process—the enlistment of lay or political leaders. Actually, this step may already have been partially achieved, for as administrators and board members consider goals and policies they tend to check these with opinion-leaders in the community. These opinion-leaders are found in diverse subpublics and, without their assistance, no major change in school policy can be made. The implication is clear; effective bargaining on the part of the administrator includes the enlistment of his board of control and other lay leaders in his community in the process. Only with the help of these laymen will the community respond with resources necessary for the school enterprise.

It is well to reiterate that bargaining requires political skill. Further, what one chooses to bargain for reflects a value judgment. Such judgments and such skills are essentially the province of the administrator, not the researcher. But the researcher has at least begun to describe the milieu within which the bargaining goes forward, and to explicate the nature of the bargaining process itself.

Suggest Perspective on Organizational Direction

A fourth implication stemming from the study of administration has to do with improved organizational direction. Beginning with Barnard,[11] few concepts in the scientific study of administration have been more thoroughly documented than the one that organizations must be concerned with both effectiveness and efficiency. To Barnard, effectiveness meant the achievement of institutional goals, and efficiency meant their achievement with due regard for the people in the organization. Somewhat similar dimensions, group achievement and group maintenance, were later enunciated by Cartwright

11. Chester I. Barnard, *The Functions of the Executive*. Cambridge: Harvard University Press, 1938.

and Zander,[12] as a result of their work with small groups. The Personnel Research Board at Ohio State University, in its studies of status of official leaders of organizations, found two major dimensions of effective leadership, initiating structure in group interaction and consideration,[13] and again task orientation and people orientation may be noted. Argyris has expressed much the same idea in his treatment of organization and personality conflict.[14]

The most complete and insightful development of this proposition has been the work of Getzels and Guba.[15] The theory suggested by these men is elaborated to some extent in chapter v. It will be noted that in every institution there are certain expectations which express norms for behavior in that institution. These norms are essentially goal-oriented. But since institutions are "peopled," the need-dispositions of organization members also become pertinent to the behavior of people in the organization. From this conception of administration as a social process, a number of hypotheses have been developed and tested empirically.[16] The studies have confirmed the theory and, more important for our purposes here, have yielded insights for direction of organizations.

When both institutional expectations and individual need-dispositions are seen as important, employment practices in an organization take on a different flavor. Clearly, employment becomes a time for mutual exploration on the part of the employer and the prospective employee. The employer must do his best to clarify goals and procedures of his organization and to indicate the role seen for the prospective employee. The candidate for employment is obligated

12. Darwin Cartwright and Alvin Zander, *Group Dynamics: Research and Theory*, p. 541. Evanston, Illinois: Row, Peterson & Co., 1953.

13. Ralph M. Stogdill and Alvin E. Coons, *Leader Behavior: Its Description and Measurement*. Bureau of Business Research. Columbus, Ohio: Ohio State University, 1957.

14. Chris Argyris, *Personality and Organization*. New York: Harper & Bros., 1957.

15. Jacob W. Getzels and Egon G. Guba, "Social Behavior and the Administrative Process," *School Review*, LXV (Winter, 1957), 423-41.

16. This work is reported in Jacob W. Getzels, James M. Lipham, and Roald F. Campbell, *Administration As a Social Process: Theory, Research, and Practice* (forthcoming).

to clarify as best he can his own strengths, desires, and concerns as they seem to be relevant for the organization of which he may become a member.

Two ideas expressed earlier can be at least partially implemented with a more insightful type of employment practice. With more specialization on the part of school workers, the assessment of individual strengths and aspirations before employment becomes even more necessary. Moreover, if a single school is to be given considerable autonomy within a school system, it would appear necessary that the principal and staff of that school have some part in the exploration into possible affiliation with candidates for employment.

Assignment of personnel is another important aspect of organizational direction. If employment practices have been concerned with both the organization and the person, decisions regarding initial assignments are largely effected. But over the years, both organizations and people may undergo changes. Changes in either may suggest a reconsideration of assignment. Promotion, too, within an organization always involves change in assignment. As with employment, assignment and re-assignment should be based on both organizational needs and individual propensities. Actually, the insightful administrator may see latent strength in a staff member who may not have recognized it in himself. Encouragement to make the most of such strength in a new assignment may give added zest to the staff member. Keeping staff members alive and challenged seems to be a goal sought by many administrators.

Still another function in organizational direction is that of supervision. Should the principal, for instance, employ a "high work organization" style or a "high discussion" style, as explained in chapter viii? Halpin and Croft have recently dealt significantly with this problem.[17] In terms of organizational climate, they identified six climates, from "open" at one end of a continuum to "closed" at the other. They found that a school possessing an open climate (which they deemed most effective) was a lively organization, moving toward its goals and at the same time providing satisfaction to the

17. See Andrew W. Halpin and Don B. Croft, *The Organizational Climate of Schools*. Chicago: Midwest Administration Center, University of Chicago, 1963.

members of the organization. A principal in such a school was characterized as follows:

> The behavior of the principal represents an appropriate integration between his own personality and the role he is required to play as principal. In this respect his behavior can be viewed as "genuine." Not only does he set an example by working hard himself (high *Thrust*) but, depending upon the situation, he can either criticize the actions of teachers or can, on the other hand, go out of his way to help a teacher (high *Consideration*). He possesses the personal flexibility to be "genuine" whether he be required to control and direct the activities of others or be required to show compassion in satisfying the social needs of individual teachers. He has integrity in that he is "all of a piece" and therefore can function well in either situation. He is not *aloof*, nor are the rules and procedures which he sets up inflexible and impersonal. Nonetheless, rules and regulations are adhered to, and through them, he provides subtle direction and control for the teachers. He does not have to *emphasize production*; nor does he need to monitor the teachers' activities closely, because the teachers do, indeed, produce easily and freely. Nor does he do all the work himself; he has the ability to let appropriate leadership acts emerge from the teachers (low *Production Emphasis*). Withal, he is in full control of the situation and he clearly provides leadership for the staff.[18]

Other illustrations of functions to be performed by administrators in their direction of organizations could be given. Perhaps enough has been said to suggest that when a practitioner derives insight from a theory, he has a set of spectacles through which to view all of his functions. The spectacles will not tell him where to walk, but they may delineate the paths more sharply.

Explore Nature of Staff Specialization

Schools and colleges will undoubtedly become more complex institutions. There will be substantial increases in enrolments, and in secondary schools and colleges those enrolments will include a greater cross-section of the population than is now often the case. Schools and colleges will probably seek or be required to take on more functions. For instance, the need for more early-childhood education in city slums and for more junior-college opportunity generally is readily apparent. In addition to serving more people in

18. *Ibid.*, pp. 61-62.

more diverse ways, educational institutions will be affected by the accelerated rate of growth of knowledge. These circumstances project a more complex school and thus a more diverse school staff. Enlightenment regarding the nature of increased staff specialization is thus the fifth implication growing out of the study of administration.

The technological order of the school or the implications of work-flow for the organization of the school enterprise has received insightful treatment in chapter xi. It will be recalled that more complexity in work-flow often requires a division of labor among the work force. This development is readily apparent in many school organizations. New knowledge in physical and biological sciences, for example, makes more difficult than formerly the assignment of staff members in a high school to teach both chemistry and biology. The "new" mathematics may require a special mathematics instructor for the upper grades of the elementary school. Teaching reading to youngsters from deprived neighborhoods is more difficult than such instruction to children with middle-class backgrounds.

As the work organization is formalized in terms of differentiated roles or assignments, the bureaucratic nature of the organization is increased. Bureaucracy, as students [19] of organization have found, tends to be characterized by hierarchical leadership, emphasis on set procedures, simplification of tasks, little initiative, and impersonal relations. These tendencies are not necessarily detrimental to the organization. Actually, bureaucracy may protect the enterprise from the intrusion of personal whim and become the means for reinforcing the goals of the organization.

The discussion of work-flow in chapter xi yields another point worth reiteration: The school has both instructional and maintenance functions. Many workers in the school spend all or part of their time doing tasks which facilitate but do not relate directly to instruction—the basic task of the school. Obviously, bus drivers and cafeteria workers serve in a maintenance role. Many other workers, including teachers and administrators, serve in a maintenance role part of the time. Two observations need to be made about this phe-

19. For instance, see Peter M. Blau and W. Richard Scott, *Formal Organizations*. San Francisco: Chandler Publishing Co., 1962.

nomenon. (*a*) A complex organization cannot perform its primary function without, at the same time, requiring the performance of secondary or supporting functions. (*b*) Workers in maintenance roles have their own specializations, their own work relationships, and their own occupational viewpoints.

From the nature of school organizations, as noted above, a number of implications for the administrator can be drawn. There is, first, the need for complementary staffing. In both instructional and maintenance roles specialists are required, but specialists who can work together to achieve the goals of the organization. No longer can teachers be seen as interchangeable parts; many teachers, at least, must be highly trained to do particular things. Similarly, with the decrease in number of school districts, there will be fewer chief administrators and more members of administrative staffs. The man who is to direct instruction may be quite different from the man who is to direct business affairs. Even more specialized will be the mathematics supervisor in the office of the director of instruction, and the computer programer in the office of the business manager.

Obviously, with greater specialization in school organizations, there will be increasing need for the administrator to specify the differentiated roles of school workers. Much of this can be done at the time of selection. Actually, as suggested above, the employment process should give ample opportunity to explore job demands of the institution and interests and strengths of the prospective employee. Even with the best possible matching of man and job at the time of employment, however, there will be changes in organizational demands and in individual interests, both of which will require continual assessment on the part of the administrator and the best possible matching of organizational demands and personality needs.

Another implication has to do with the exchange of information. In an organization with numerous and specialized personnel, orderly work-flow requires deliberate arrangements for exchange of information. Lateral communication, particularly, becomes a means whereby workers alert each other to the need for mutual adjustments. Thus, a teacher of a second grade can confer with a teacher of the third grade about sequential learning activities for a particular group of pupils. Or, physics and history teachers can consider homework requirements being made of pupils who are taking the two classes concurrently. While this kind of exchange of information will not solve all organizational problems, it can be useful, and administrators, through such arrangements as physical proximity and an "open" school climate can do much to facilitate it.

Still another implication for administration growing out of the work-flow in complex organizations relates to localization or decentralization of decision-making. As school organizations become larger, the question of decentralization becomes a more critical one. This is seen in the current efforts of some large city school systems to establish a number of regional or "district" superintendencies and in the efforts of many school systems to make the principal and staff of a single school a more autonomous unit in the organization. Broad participation of teachers and other staff members in decision-making can be attained in large organizations only through some plan of decentralization.

It should be noted, however, that decentralization cannot be achieved through mere tinkering with the organizational chart. If principals and regional superintendents are to make decisions in a large organization, there must be delegation of authority to them by the central office, and the principals and regional superintendents must be the kind of people who can and will perform in decision-making roles. Likewise, if teachers are to assist in planning certain aspects of the program, they must exhibit some competency for such planning.

Increased specialization of workers in organizations poses a number of dilemmas for the administrator, two of which will be noted. There is, first, the conflict between bureaucracy and professionalism.[20] As noted above, whereas bureaucracy stresses such characteristics as hierarchical leadership, set procedures, and impersonal relations, professionalism emphasizes leadership *expertise*, variability of procedures, and close colleague relationships. School organizations and school administrators are faced constantly with the challenge of making the best possible accommodation between these two opposing sets of requirements. As school workers become more

20. Studies are reviewed in Robert C. Stone, "The Sociology of Bureaucracy and Professions," in *Contemporary Sociology*, pp. 491-506. Edited by Joseph S. Roucek. New York: Philosophical Library, 1958.

professionalized, this conflict will become sharper. This can already be noted in college organizations.

A second dilemma has to do with the perspective of the specialist. Each specialist perceives the organization in terms of his own specialized knowledge, training, and interests. These differences in perception are more marked in colleges than in schools, but with increased specialization the same tendency is apparent in the schools. Thus, the physics teacher dealing with college-bound students may have little patience with programs designed to give vocational training to those who will not go on to college. The administrator is constantly challenged with finding ways of understanding and utilizing these specialists in the organization and, at the same time, mediating the viewpoints held by such specialists. The path that must be trod is not charted.

By way of summary, the growth toward increased complexity of educational organizations seems clear. Complexity in function will result in greater specialization of staff. The scientific study of administration illuminates the problem of specialization, and such illumination may help the administrator think more clearly about appropriate courses of action.

Stress Professional Responsibility

A final implication growing out of the scientific study of administration would appear to be that of increased professional responsibility. To the extent that there is an administrative science, those who study it and those who practice it have specialized knowledge, and this knowledge is being used in the continuing functioning of society. One might agree with Becker [21] that the symbol of the professions is quite different from the reality of the professions, but the fact remains that laymen do turn to administrators for certain insights and certain skills.

It is the contention here that the study of administration will bring more knowledge, and that more knowledge can result in more skill. Or, as Barnard [22] put it, there is both "scientific knowledge

21. Howard S. Becker, "The Nature of a Profession," in *Education for the Professions*, chap. iii. Sixty-first Yearbook of the National Society for the Study of Education, Part II. Chicago: Distributed by the University of Chicago Press, 1962.

22. Barnard, *op. cit.*, p. 291.

and behavioral knowledge." Katz [23] helped clarify the relationship between knowledge and skill when he spoke of technical skills, human skills, and conceptual skills. Early training in administration tended to center on technical skills, more recently human skills have received considerable attention; conceptual skills appear to have been relatively neglected. It is in this neglected area that the science of administration would appear to be called upon to make its greatest contribution.

As a group of people acquire a specialized body of knowledge and that knowledge is important to society, such people appear to be given more autonomy.[24] While medicine does not have complete autonomy, as the symbol of professionalism may suggest, those who practice medicine appear to have much greater autonomy than do members of many other occupational groups. Perhaps an even clearer illustration of the autonomy of knowledge is found among nuclear physicists. Government, the military, as well as laymen, are completely dependent upon their knowledge. It should be noted, however, in terms of the application of the knowledge, that people other than physicists help make the decisions.

But to return to administration, it is suggested that, with the growth of administrative science, the administrator and the student of administration will be given greater control in society. One need not go as far as Burnham [25] in suggesting that managers will also become the policy-makers because no one else will know enough about enterprises to make policy. Even so, it seems clear that in a complex, highly organized society those who occupy administrative roles hold strategic positions and that, as they demonstrate unique insights and skills, they will inevitably exercise greater control in society.

Control or power in an open society is of necessity accompanied by ethical responsibility. Thus, strange as it may seem at first glance,

23. Robert L. Katz, "Skills of an Effective Administrator," *Harvard Business Review*, XXXIII (January-February, 1955), 33-42.

24. The vulnerability of school administrators in the early part of this century is amply documented in Raymond E. Callahan, *Education and the Cult of Efficiency*. Chicago: University of Chicago Press, 1962.

25. James Burnham, *The Managerial Revolution*. New York: John Day Co., 1941.

more science creates the need for more ethics. This might not be true if the study of administration had nothing to do with the practice of administration. At one time, for instance, the study of the stars seemed to have little practical import. Now, however, astronomy is related to national policy, national prestige, perhaps even national survival. Even esoteric bodies of knowledge often come to have practical import. The study of administration in today's world has practical import, and thus the ethical question is continuously present.

Two deductions can be drawn from this situation. One, it is important to differentiate between the science of administration and the policy decisions in education. Science is concerned with getting a closer and closer "fix" on reality. Science deals with what "is" and the meaning of what is. Policy deals with what ought to be, with goals and directions. Goal-setting behavior of people may be studied scientifically, and indeed knowledge is necessary to perspicacious goal-setting, but the goals themselves are not the product of science. Moreover, the scientist may be motivated by his own values in deciding what to study, but his study per se must meet a public (other scientists) and not a private criterion.

A second deduction is that the administrator needs not only some knowledge of the science of administration but also some convictions about the ethics of administration. In practice he should be able to apply his scientifically derived insights ethically. This is a most difficult assignment in a pluralistic culture such as ours. Perhaps the only solution is the development of ethical standards by the emerging administrative profession. Indeed, these standards as practiced, not merely put to paper, may become the measure of the professional responsibility to which reference is made.

Summary

Administrative science offers but one major service to the practitioner: it is the service of increasing insight and understanding. This increased understanding might explain more fully the cultural milieu of organizations, give greater precision to analytical skills, extend knowledge necessary to more effective bargaining, suggest perspectives on the improved direction of organizations, provide insights regarding staff specialization, and reinforce the need for more professional responsibility. These implications appear to have relevance to the administrator as he attempts to discern and influence goals and policies basic to teaching and learning, as he stimulates and facilitates the planning and operation of programs for teaching and learning, and as he procures and manages personnel and material to implement programs of teaching and learning.

CHAPTER XIV

The Preparation of Administrators[1]

JACK CULBERTSON

Around the turn of the last century when Mark Twain noted that "training is everything . . . cauliflower is nothing but cabbage with a college education," he was not thinking of training programs for administrators. Even though Woodrow Wilson a decade earlier had defined public administration as the "detailed and systematic execution of public law," [2] general knowledge about such administration was still largely lacking. The same was true for business, hospital, school, and other kinds of administration.

Previous chapters have demonstrated that administration has been the object of much study since Mark Twain's observation about "training." The concepts and research findings, resulting from this study, have contributed much to the remarkable growth of preparatory programs for administrators. They have not been the only force shaping preparatory programs, however. Dominant societal values have also had a major impact upon preparation, since they have become closely intertwined with and have reinforced concepts of administration at various periods in this century. How the close relationships between administrative concepts and societal values have shaped programs for preparing business, government, and school administrators can be illustrated by taking a brief look at the past.

---

1. The term "administrator," as used in this chapter, refers to those who head schools, school districts, governmental units, corporations, and related organizations. It is assumed that such persons may display both administrative and leadership behavior. Administrative behavior is expressed in the execution of existing policies; when heads of organizations help create new purposes, policies or structures, they demonstrate leadership.

2. Woodrow Wilson, "The Study of Administration," *Political Science Quarterly*, II (June, 1887), p. 212.

Past Emphases in Preparation

Efficiency.—Frederick Taylor, early in the century, assumed that job performance was the focal concept in administration.[3] The controlling aim, as he saw it, was efficiency: how to divide the job and get its parts efficiently performed were central goals. In the attainment of efficiency, technology was important. Man was viewed as an adjunct to machines and as a performer of routine tasks. Time and motion studies to eliminate inefficiency were logical extensions of Taylor's concepts. Administration was concerned secondarily with human considerations; employees were seen as cogs in the wheels of production.

Taylor's concept of administration was intimately related to the dominant values of the society in which it was born. It came at a time when American industry was beginning to make impressive gains in productivity. Businessmen were well-known for their exploitative capacities; economic practices were ruggedly competitive, and high value was placed on efficiency. That the human element in business administration was not assigned a high priority is evident from, for example, the conditions which surrounded child labor. Pupil personnel administration in the schools was still guided by a "police" concept and, as Callahan and Button have demonstrated in chapter iv, the pressures for efficiency in education were strong and pervasive. Social welfare concepts had not yet influenced government administration significantly.

Taylor's concepts of administration and the societal values which nourished them had a significant influence on administrative preparation during the first quarter of this century as they permeated various fields of administration. Textbooks on school administration written by Cubberley, for example, were strongly influenced by the efficiency concept as is indicated by the fact that he compared the school to a factory and viewed children as raw materials to be shaped.[4] Authors of textbooks on government administration in the

---

3. Frederick Taylor, *The Principles of Scientific Management.* New York: Harper & Bros., 1911.

4. Daniel Griffiths, "Some Assumptions Underlying the Use of Models in Research," in *Educational Research: New Perspectives.* Edited by Jack Culbertson and Stephen Hencley. Danville, Illinois: Interstate Printers and Publishers, Inc., 1963.

mid-twenties also acknowledged their indebtedness to the concepts of Taylor and to the scientific management movement.[5]

Human relations.—Although the scientific management movement influenced preparatory programs significantly, the pendulum was to swing sharply to another view. In the early thirties a different image of administration arose from a different social climate. The famous Hawthorne experiments, which started with an interest in efficiency factors and ended with some important conclusions about human relationships, represented one of the important bridges from Taylorism to the new era.

A core facet of the new image was the human element in school administration. The administrator, according to this view, was not so much concerned with the efficient accomplishment of clearly defined units of work as he was with human relationships. Formal organization and job division, central in the scientific movement, became less important in the human-relations movement; informal relations, personnel satisfaction, and interpersonal communication became more important. Organizations were seen, not so much as rational instruments which could be neatly depicted in charts, but as dynamos of human energies and motivations, many of which were irrational in character.

That the "human-relations" view was closely related to the society that spawned it is shown by the fact that it was first voiced in the twilight period of extreme individualism. The day of the "social welfare" orientation was dawning and government and society, in pursuit of the four freedoms, were becoming more concerned with persons and less concerned with things. Co-operation rather than competition was to receive emphasis in this new movement. The school itself reflected this shift in values as teaching and administration became less efficiency-oriented and more child-centered. In the later period of the movement, the public school recognized the irrational wellsprings of behavior in students, a fact which was reflected in the "life adjustment" movement. Psychologists and social workers were added to school staffs to deal with problems of human relationships and their impact upon learning. Other organizations also

5. Dwight Waldo, *The Study of Public Administration*, p. 19. Garden City: Doubleday, Inc., 1955.

added psychologists, psychiatrists, and sociologists to their staffs to deal with human problems.

The "human-relations" view was a powerful one which infiltrated programs for preparing government, business, and educational administrators. At the Harvard Graduate School of Business Administration the development of skills in communication, co-operation, and other aspects of human relationships was central in preparation.[6] In school administration the concept of "human relations" became intimately associated with that of "democratic administration," since both emphasized group action and the value of individuals. Thus, Yauch, in a textbook entitled *Improving Human Relations in School Administration* noted that "democracy is primarily concerned with human relations," and indicated he would attempt to present "suggestions concerning the ways in which the principal can provide teachers with democratic experiences." [7]

The concepts of "human relations" and "democratic administration" made for a strong value orientation in preparatory programs. Emphasis was placed upon consensus and agreement; conflict and disagreement were viewed negatively. The focus, particularly in programs for preparing school administrators, was much more on the "ideal" treatment of personnel than upon the analysis of "real" situations. Even though the movement had its genesis in the important Hawthorne studies, it generated little research on school administration; its focus was more upon the inculcation of values than upon an objective investigation of the real world.

Some of the important assumptions underlying the "human relations" movement were made explicit in the early fifties. It was then recognized that the movement, at least in its extreme forms, fostered conformity and hindered individual creativity. In addition, the concern for human relationships was often somewhat specious, as the real purpose was increased productivity through the manipulation of group behavior. Just as Taylor's "scientific management" movement was not scientific because it left out the major variables in administration, the "human relations" movement was not always

6. J. D. Glover and R. M. Hower, *The Administrator: Cases on Human Relations in Business.* Chicago: Richard Irwin, 1952.

7. Wilbur Yauch, *Improving Human Relations in School Administration,* p. 11. New York: Harper & Bros., 1949.

humane in that many of those who accepted it were not aware of its assumptions. When these assumptions were made explicit and were carefully examined, the movement began to be viewed more critically. This undoubtedly helped to account for the fact that this highly influential movement, which had such a strong impact upon preparatory programs, began to lose its fervor in the early fifties.

Scientific emphases.—Just before the "human-relations" movement began to decline, Herbert Simon wrote a book which was to foreshadow a new era in administrative thought and new emphases in preparatory programs.[8] This era was to produce concepts which were to constitute the basis for a new science of administration. The approach was strongly influenced by logical positivism, a school of thought which Dwight Waldo has defined as follows: "Logical positivism is a would-be tough-minded school of thought that asserts its close connection with modern physical science. It abhors metaphysics, dismisses ethics, emphasizes empiricism, places a high premium upon rigorous, logical analysis." [9]

The new science of administration was to make a sharp distinction between philosophy and science; prescribing to administrators the actions they should take was seen as something distinctly different from describing and explaining administration through scientific concepts and theories. Those who adhered strictly to the new school of thought focused upon the description and explanation of administrative phenomena and avoided prescriptive statements. Thus, the authors of a major textbook on public administration published in 1950 argued that "a science (of administration) in the sense of an objective understanding of the phenomena without confusion between facts and values" is possible.[10] The authors, therefore, concentrated on the scientific aspects of administration and consciously avoided stating what government *should* do. Texts in school administration did not go to this extreme, although distinctions between

8. Herbert Simon, *Administrative Behavior: A Study of Decision-making Processes in Administrative Organization.* New York: MacMillan Co., 1947.

9. Dwight Waldo, *The Study of Public Administration*, pp. 43-44. Garden City: Doubleday, Inc., 1955.

10. Herbert Simon, Donald Smithburg, and Victor Thompson, *Public Administration*, p. 20. New York: Alfred Knopf, Inc., 1950.

the "is" and "ought" aspects of administration were made very clearly in such books as *Administrative Behavior in Education.*[11]

The new movement also placed high value on theory.[12] Contrary to the popular view that theory is for those in ivory towers, adherents of the new science maintained that theory was one of the most practical of human inventions. It was judged practical not only for those interested in studying administration but also for those interested in controlling human events, as Griffiths has demonstrated in chapter v. Therefore, courses on the "theory of administration" found their way into catalogues of different universities.

Those responsible for preparing administrators recognized clearly the complexities inherent in administration and delved into the social sciences in a search for concepts and theories to illuminate these complexities.

The core values of the movement were scientific. For the first time in history, professors of school administration and social scientists formed interdisciplinary research teams. The scientific emphasis made itself felt in preparation programs as professors sought to utilize social science concepts to illuminate such administrative processes as communication and decision-making. Systematic analysis of the important variables in actual administrative situations through cases and simulated situations became important. The administrator, as an efficient performer of a job (an image which characterized the earlier "scientific-management" movement), or the administrator as one skilled in interpersonal relations (an image which characterized the "human-relations" movement), no longer was the *central* target of training programs. Rather, the core facet of the administrator image in the new movement was that of a skilful decision-maker gifted in analysis and in the application of concepts and theories.

Again the relationship between the new movement and the scientific values of the larger society is evident. Since the late forties the pervasive influence of science and technology has been increas-

---

11. *Administrative Behavior in Education.* Edited by Roald Campbell and Russell Gregg. (New York: Harper & Bros., 1957).

12. Daniel Griffiths, *Administrative Theory.* New York: Appleton-Century-Crofts, 1959.

ingly present. Their significance has been dramatized in efforts to probe deep into the earth, on the one hand, and in the race into space, on the other. The first atomic bomb was developed just a few years before Simon's book was to initiate the new science of administration; Sputnik went into orbit just ten years later. Such dramatic events could not help but create increased concern for the teaching of sciences and mathematics in the public schools. That the scientific values which were so influential in the larger society would have a strong impact on preparatory programs for administrators is also understandable.

Conclusions.—Thus, past emphases in programs for preparing administrators have been clearly related to the dominant values of society: The emphasis on efficient management early in the century complemented society's concern for economic productivity and its support of rugged individualism; the human-relations movement, which began in the thirties, matched the shift in society to a greater concern for people and their welfare; in the late forties and early fifties the "new science" of administration came at a time when physics, chemistry, mathematics and related disciplines were reshaping not only our concepts of the universe but also our views of man's relationship to it.

That past programs would mirror dominant social values is understandable in a profession that was a mere infant fifty years ago. In one sense professional preparation for administrators during the past three or four decades has been like that of a growing, maturing adolescent. Its activities have been characterized by explorations for sound guiding values and a search for an adequate cognitive base. Since change rather than stability has been the watchword, those responsible for preparatory programs for administrators have been innovative. For example, in developing and adapting cases, field studies, internships, role playing, interdisciplinary seminars, and simulated situations into instructional methodologies, those preparing administrators have demonstrated considerable inventiveness.

All past emphases have helped point the way to a better knowledge base for preparatory programs. Taylor's scientific-management movement, in spite of its narrowness of focus, emphasized the need for careful study of worker performance. The human-relations movement, while strongly value-oriented, did draw upon the findings of those studying small groups and also applied for the first time anthropological techniques to the study of organizations. More recently, the "new science" of administration, as previous chapters have demonstrated, has contributed significantly to a research orientation in preparatory programs by clearly distinguishing between values and facts, by developing more adequate theories to encompass the complex variables in administration, and by recognizing the major significance of a multidisciplinary approach to the study of administration.

The shifting emphases of past programs have also helped illuminate the value of purposive aspects of preparation. No longer, for example, are programs so largely dominated by a single controlling value as they were in former periods. The relationships among such values as efficiency, skill in human relationship, and soundness in decision-making are now somewhat more clearly recognized; consequently, programs are developed from broader and more balanced perspectives.

To be sure, much remains to be achieved in attaining appropriate balance and needed depth in preparatory programs. In focusing more upon the study of the real world during the last decade, for example, scholars have tended to neglect the "ought" aspects of administration. This has meant that scientific content of administrative processes has been highlighted and developed during this period. Efforts to organize content which would update educational purposes and logically relate them to national goals have been much less prominent.

Other limitations have resulted from a perspective that has placed strong values in the science of administration. First, there has been a tendency to believe that basic research can solve problems which, in fact, are beyond its purview. For example, there is a widespread expectation that the criteria for selecting effective administrators can be determined by scientific methods; in fact, however, "effective" can be defined ultimately only in relation to organizational goals which represent value rather than factual postulates. Thus, science can and has provided theory for developing measures of intelligence. However, it cannot, in and of itself, provide definitive answers about how intelligent an administrator should be or indicate the precise purposes for which he should use his intelligence. The precise answers depend upon the nature of an organization's goals and desired standards of administrative performance.

The proper role of science in the selection of administrators, then, is to provide theoretical bases and scientific methodologies for developing and testing alternative means of shedding light upon potential administrative performance. Before such means could be usefully applied in the selection process, a logical relationship between the data they provide and the administrative tasks which subjects would be expected to perform would have to be demonstrated.

A second and related limitation of the new science, strictly defined, is its neutral posture on moral issues. For example, social science potentially has the capacity to describe and explain community power structure and how administrators actually cope with it; however, it cannot define what administrators *should* seek to achieve as they work with those in positions of power or how they *should* resolve moral dilemmas which they confront in the process. It seems clear, then, that even though the products of basic research are fundamental to sound preparatory programs, they are not, in and of themselves, sufficient, because administration is in part an idealistic venture performed in a setting where there are many conflicting issues and views.

Recruitment and Selection

Competition for leadership talent.—Those recruiting candidates for preparatory programs are faced with the fact that the competition for intellectual and leadership talent is becoming increasingly intense. The competition stems from several conditions. First, the proportionate number of managers and leaders needed in the various administrative organizations of society is increasing. This increase stems partly from the growth of government and other large-scale organizations and from the increased demands placed upon those who head and manage complex organizations in modern society. Second, the age group from which society's leaders will come during the next twenty years will remain constant in number while our total population will increase by one-third.[13] Third, and somewhat paradoxically, the developing science of administration itself has

13. N. B. Ryder, "Demography and Education," *Phi Delta Kappan*, XLI (June, 1960), 379.

helped bring about a more rigorous and intellectually demanding content in preparatory programs which in return has resulted in the need to recruit a higher caliber of student. Finally, great incentives to attract talented people into scientific and research careers, into military organizations, and into professional careers, such as medicine and engineering, have developed during the last decade. Since these incentives are likely to prevail and even be enhanced in the foreseeable future, special challenges confront those engaged in the recruitment of administrators.

No one has greater challenges than those recruiting candidates for government administration, including school administration. Thus, the Commission on National Goals reported to former President Eisenhower that "even the most optimistic appraisal testifies to the scarcity, not to a surplus, of the talents needed by the government, a supply which it must win in a severe competition." [14] Members of a UCEA Committee in 1962 voiced a similar view with reference to school administrators.[15] To meet the severe competition in the recruitment of school administrators, a publication of the University Council for Educational Administration [16] in 1962 stressed the need to attract talented personnel from high-school and college populations into administrative careers.

Of all the problems associated with preparatory programs, none is more basic than that of determining criteria for recruiting and selecting potential administrators.[17] It is basic because the criteria chosen influence not only recruitment and selection, but also curriculum, instruction, staffing, and evaluation since they inevitably reflect the image that a program would produce.

14. The Report of the President's Commission on National Goals, *Goals for Americans*, p. 290. Englewood Cliffs, N.J.: Prentice-Hall, 1960.

15. Report of a UCEA Committee on "Improving Preparatory Programs in the United States: Some Action Guides." Columbus, Ohio: University Council for Educational Administration, 1962 (mimeographed).

16. Jack Culbertson, "New Perspectives: Implications for Program Change" in *Preparing Administrators: New Perspectives*, pp. 151-73. Edited by Jack Culbertson and Stephen Hencley. Columbus, Ohio: University Council for Educational Administration, 1962.

17. Up to this point the discussion has focused upon aspects of preparation related to various kinds of administrators. The remainder of the chapter will focus more sharply upon the preparation of school administrators. Emphasis will be upon ideal rather than real programs.

Guides for selecting administrators.—Criteria can be expressed in terms of desired or valued administrative and leadership behaviors. However, different groups value different behaviors and place different values on the same kind of behavior. A recent study demonstrated, for example, that many of the behaviors of elementary-school principals are valued differently by teachers, researchers, raters, and administrative superiors.[18] Such findings undoubtedly help to explain why criteria for selection are typically stated in global terms. Thus, value is placed by many groups on the following behaviors: making of sound decisions, communicating effectively, maintaining morale skilfully, and coping with change constructively. These have special implications for the selection of candidates for preparatory programs.

It is widely recognized, for example, that the administrator is the central link in the many interrelated communication systems which comprise his environment. Research in various organizations suggests that the major part of his time is spent in preparing, initiating, receiving, and interpreting messages.[19] It is also clear that demands for preparing and interpreting communications are increasing in modern organizations as lines of responsibility become longer and as specialization spreads. In addition, the increasing size of organizations makes personal contacts between administrators and the administered more difficult. Therefore, the capacity to communicate and/or to learn to communicate effectively becomes an important criterion in selecting candidates for administrative preparation for modern organizations.

In assessing competence in communication, it must be remembered that the verbal environment which surrounds the administrator is comprised of many subsystems, both written and oral. All of these systems require somewhat different understandings and skills and, therefore, different measures are needed to assess required understandings and skills. Thus, written skills can be measured, for ex-

18. John Hemphill, Daniel Griffiths, and Norman Frederiksen, *Administrative Performance and Personality*, pp. 251-53. New York: Bureau of Publications, Teachers College, 1962.

19. Jack Culbertson, "Recognizing Roadblocks in Communication Channels," *Administrator's Notebook*, VII (March, 1959).

ample, by the *Cooperative English Test*; speech-making ability by rating procedures; [20] and various devices have been developed to measure interaction in small groups. However, few, if any, measures exist for measuring informal communication skills particularly in the context of large organizations.

Another kind of administrative behavior which researchers, practitioners, and theorists see as central to administration is decision-making. Barnard, for example, has pointed to the importance of this ability in executives: [21]

The occasions of decision on the initiative of the executive are the most important tests of this capacity. . . . It is clear that the most important obligation is to raise and decide those issues which no one else is in a position to raise effectively.

Special demands are placed upon decision-makers in today's world. In making decisions administrators must be able to generalize perceptively about problems which are characterized by complexity and which involve tangled and even chaotic relationships. Therefore, they need a high degree of intelligence, a liberal education, and sound professional knowledge. Certainly the capacity for making decisions and the ability to help others make decisions are important criteria of selection.

Observation is a sound technique for discovering those who are willing to take responsibility for decisions which affect others. In the words of Barnard: "Accordingly, it will be observed that men generally try to avoid making decisions, beyond a limited degree when they are rather uncritical responses to situations." [22] In addition to observation, such instruments as the *Graduate Record Examination*, the *Watson-Glaser Critical Thinking Appraisal*, and the *Miller Analogies Test* provide data on mental abilities and the capacity for judgment. "In-basket" responses in simulated situations shed light on how systematically administrators prepare for decision-making.[23]

---

20. Hemphill, Griffiths, and Frederiksen, *op. cit.*, pp. 201-18.

21. Chester Barnard, *Functions of the Executive*, p. 191. Cambridge, Massachusetts: Harvard University Press, 1938.

22. Barnard, *op. cit.*, p. 189.

23. Hemphill, Griffiths, and Frederiksen, *op. cit.*, pp. 285-89.

Finally, *The Cooperative Test of Contemporary Affairs* is one measure of general knowledge about current events, while such tests as *School Administration and Supervision* measure professional knowledge.

The building and maintenance of morale in an organization is basic to the co-operative attainment of goals. In fostering morale in modern organizations, administrators face special challenges: the high demands made upon school personnel by a society that places increasingly higher values upon education; intensive specialization and the tendencies toward separatism among teachers, supervisors, and administrators; trends toward impersonal relations in modern, large-scale bureaucracies; the rapidity of social and technological change with the attendant uncertainties which such change creates; the already existing psychological malaise in a world of hydrogen bombs, atomic missiles, increased radiation, and political uncertainties.

Personnel satisfaction is often taken as a measure of morale; however, loyalty of personnel to organizational goals and their feelings of accomplishment are more basic and significant measures. Instruments for measuring precisely an administrator's capacity for building and maintaining morale are not available, although peer ratings, personality tests, and observational techniques can provide pertinent clues.

Communication, decision-making, and morale building can be demonstrated at the level of administrative or executive action. However, the capacity to cope constructively with change is the important test of leadership. Since the policies and purposes of educational organization need to be updated continually to serve a rapidly changing society, and since new methods and structures are frequently required to meet today's challenges, the marked need for educational leadership in the modern world is obvious. Those heading schools and school districts can play a key role in shaping educational policies and in initiating innovations in schools; therefore, nothing is more essential in the selection of candidates for preparation than their leadership potential.

The capacity to cope with change involves, in part, the ability to innovate. Intelligence and general education, which are often associated with innovative ability, are susceptible to measurement through a variety of tests. However, precise predictors of innovative behavior are not available although such measures as the *Unusual Uses Test* and the *Anagrams Test* have been used in industry, and they may have some utility in education. Empirical measures of courage, energy, endurance, vision, flexibility, and other general qualities associated with leadership are not readily available. However, these qualities can be assessed in part through observational techniques.

Curriculum for Preparing Administrators

Content on administrative processes.—If decision-making, communicating, morale-building, and initiating change are important aspects of administration and leadership, it logically follows that a curriculum should help develop in potential administrators those behaviors which are appropriate for dealing with these processes.[24] This means that concepts and learning experiences are needed which will help students become more perceptive about process variables and their implications for administrative behavior.

As previous chapters have demonstrated, professors of administration, sociology, anthropology, psychology and political science have contributed significantly, during the past fifteen years particularly, to what is known about administration and leadership. The thesis is offered here that the processes of communication, decision-making, change, and morale maintenance are important not only because they have relevance for administration and leadership but also because they can provide guides for organizing much of what is known about the science of administration. Put differently, they can serve as general guides for selecting social-science content for preparatory programs. The following types of content, for example, are suggestive: [25]

Making decisions. Included would be concepts and theories pertinent to individual, group, organizational, and community decision-making;

24. The term "process" is conceived to encompass both those variables which relate to the organizational context or milieu of administration and those which relate more directly to the personal dimensions of administration.

25. For a more elaborate discussion of the concepts presented on the pages immediately following, see Jack Culbertson, "Common and Specialized Content for Preparing Administrators" in *Preparation Programs for School Administrators: Common and Specialized Learnings for Various Administrative Positions.* Edited by Donald Leu and Herbert Rudman. East Lansing, Michigan: Michigan State University Press, 1963.

the relationship of such matters as basic research, operations research, and computer technology to decision-making would also be examined, as would value dilemmas which administrators face. (For representative concepts see chapter ix.)

Communication. Theories of one-way, two-person, small-group, and organizational communication would be studied. Special consideration would be given to such matters as opinion change, mass communication, informal networks, and communication in large bureaucracies. Value issues faced by administrators would also be examined. (See chaps. viii and xi for examples of concepts which can illuminate communication.)

Coping with change. The dynamics of change in relation to individuals, groups, organizations and communities would be examined. Specific attention would be given to such matters as barriers to change, factors facilitating change, conflict in change, leadership and change, and related matters. (See chaps. v, vi and xii for pertinent concepts.)

Building morale. Bases of personnel satisfaction in the context of modern organizations would be examined. Special consideration would be given to motivation, perception, interpersonal relations, value infusion, organizational loyalty, and related topics. (See chapter vii for examples of content.)

Relevance of scientific concepts to administrative processes.— Those concepts and theories which are incorporated into preparatory programs should have more than a logical relationship to the processes noted above. Their scope and quality are also important considerations. Charters, for example, has set forth a number of criteria for gauging the value of social-science concepts and theories for administrator preparation.[26] These criteria have to do with the number and range of definitive relationships in theories: whether or not theories have dynamic and person-environment referents, the operationality of concepts, the range in the classes of phenomena they can account for, their intervention capacity, and their power to increase cognitive capacities. It should be clear that the attainment of maximum value from concepts is not entirely dependent upon the particular ones selected; their organization in the curriculum, their sequence of presentation, and the instructional methodology and materials used to teach them are all important determinants

26. W. W. Charters, "Anthropology and the Study of Administration: Response" in *The Social Sciences and Educational Administration*, pp. 85-94. Edited by Lawrence Downey and Frederick Enns. Edmonton, Alberta: Division of Educational Administration, University of Alberta in co-operation with The University Council for Educational Administration, 1963.

of their impact. Some of the recently developed concepts on the structure of the disciplines have some important implications for incorporating social-science concepts in administrative programs.[27]

Social scientists, in dealing with communication, decision-making, and related processes, have concentrated on describing and explaining actual but not ideal characteristics. However, administrators in dealing with processes also have "ought" questions to decide, and these questions often transcend science. They are represented in such queries as "Should I compromise in my decision on the budget?" or "Should I withhold certain information in my report to the Board?" Decisions on these questions frequently pose moral dilemmas for administrators. Great literature is a source for understanding such dilemmas. Plato's *Crito*, for example, provides a content that would assist potential administrators to examine and assess the problem of compromise. Ibsen's *The Wild Duck*, to take another example, dramatizes the consequences of telling the "whole truth." Thus, content from the humanities which illuminates moral issues that bear upon administrative processes can complement and reinforce social science concepts in preparatory programs.

Purpose and curriculum.—Incorporating content on administrative processes into graduate curricula is not, in and of itself, sufficient. If administrators are to exercise leadership, they will need an educational vision to which to gear processes. As leaders, they will be required to take positions on issues of educational purpose. The positions administrators take will be determined largely by the basic values which they hold on such matters as the "good" society, the "good" man, "good" government, "good" education, and "good" administration. While social and educational experiences will have already had a fundamental impact on the basic values of individuals before they enter programs, experiences can be provided during formal preparation to enable potential administrators to define more clearly and to give better order to their values. In this regard, as Harlow has noted, content from the humanities is especially pertinent in preparing administrators:

27. For example, see Jerome S. Bruner, *The Process of Education* (Cambridge: Harvard University Press, 1960), especially chap. ii, "The Importance of Structure," pp. 17-32.

For values and the making of value judgments are the domain of one of the major modes of human thought; namely, the humanities. These are the human studies, those which deal with the peculiarly human features of our experience.[28]

In providing leadership in education in our culture, the realization of two values or purposes is central: equality of learning opportunities and excellence in education. These two values, which have frequently been called the quantity and quality aspects of education, have had different meanings at different periods of history.

Changes in educational purposes.—The quantity problem has often been seen as providing enough schools and teachers to afford learning opportunities for all students. However, the specific meanings of "all" have changed many times throughout history as learning opportunities have been increased drastically by raising and lowering school age through changes in attendance laws and as compulsory education has spread from one to fifty states. In recent years, more refined issues related to equality of opportunities, such as how to provide appropriate learning experience for the culturally disadvantaged, or how to achieve effective desegregation, have offered challenges to educational leaders. In addition, policy questions have stemmed from such opposing issues as whether or not "all" students should be provided opportunities at public expense for two years of post-high-school education and whether or not compulsory age limits for high-school students should be lowered. In helping prepare administrators to deal with such issues, programs can provide opportunities for assessing changes in the meaning of "equality of learning opportunities" through a study of history. In addition, opportunities for analyzing emerging societal needs in order to discover implications for redefinitions of "equality of learning opportunities" can also be offered.

The meaning of quality or "excellence" in education is also susceptible to changing interpretations. With the tendency to view education more and more as an important national resource and with the trend toward new kinds of national commitments, such as are

28. James Harlow, "Purpose Defining: the Central Function of the School Administrator" in *Preparing Administrators: New Perspectives,* p. 68. Edited by Jack Culbertson and Stephen Hencley. Columbus, Ohio: University Council for Educational Administration, 1962.

involved in the goal of landing on the moon during the 1960's, unusual challenges are presented to those responsible for defining "excellence" in education. Policy issues related to "excellence" and their implications for preparing school leaders can be treated more specifically by raising a question such as the following: What implications do the massive national efforts to conquer and explore space have for updating the meaning of quality in education during the period ahead?

Some would maintain that the chief priority in education during the period ahead should be that of turning out enough "good" engineers, mathematicians, scientists, and technicians to insure that the race into space will be won by the Americans and not the Russians. This purpose is imposing in that more than three dozen different types of engineers, many kinds of social and natural scientists, and thousands of different classes of technicians are directly involved in the space race. They, in turn, are supported by massive numbers of personnel in supporting industries and governmental agencies. "Quality" in education within this framework is that which provides sufficient numbers of well-trained manpower to serve the national interests in space exploration.

But even within this limited definition of excellence the responsibility of the schools for supplying trained manpower is a big one because of the unprecedented numbers of personnel required and because there are frequent scientific and technological breakthroughs which create new demands for personnel and bring about marked changes in the occupational structure. Administrators need preparation which will contribute to their understandings of immediate pressures such as are involved in the current concern for trained manpower and of modes for assessing these pressures against the larger context of education and social needs. Such understandings will help them provide educational leadership in purpose determination.

A problem confronting all educational leaders is that of attaining balance in educational purposes, since strong pressures are being put upon the schools to achieve immediate and specific objectives. Even though the immediate, foreseeable, and relatively short-range national objective of landing on the moon, for example, is served by education, there is the question of the relationship of this objective to the longer-range view of educational excellence. Within the longer view, education's contribution to the enduring national goal of fostering thoughtful, wise, and creative individuals is of greater significance than the national goal of reaching the moon. The extent to which education contributes to the former goal will largely determine the extent to which citizens face creatively and resolutely the unprecedented civic, economic, and social problems which will face man *after* he has reached the moon. Thus, school leaders have the problem of relating educational purposes to more basic and longer-range goals as well as changing national concerns of a more immediate and limited character. This means that school administrators must continually seek balance between the immediate and the long-range, the shifting and the enduring, the national and individual concepts of purpose and excellence. Because of the complex issues involved in purpose-setting, the intellectual aspects of the task are becoming more important than ever. Harlow speaks to this point as follows:

In times like these, the determination of purposes is not a matter simply for an exercise in group dynamics. Neither is it a platform for the exhibition of a persuasive and charismatic personality. It is a matter for the most carefully reasoned, most carefully disciplined intellectual effort.[29]

Thus, preparatory programs require an intellectual rigor and a quality of inquiry never achieved before, if administrators are to be equipped to give needed leadership in updating the meanings of educational purposes.

Concepts for illuminating educational purpose.—Inquiry will also need to be bolstered by new advances in the breadth and depth of content in curricula, if appropriate insights about educational purposes are to be fostered. In addition to providing content from the humanities about man's enduring values, graduate curricula need to illuminate those aspects of society which have implications for updating the meaning of educational excellence and equality of opportunity. The following outline of content from the social sciences is illustrative:

29. *Ibid.*, p. 68.

Economic trends.—Such subjects as those that follow would be assessed in order to discover important implications for defining and attaining educational excellence and opportunity: (*a*) the economics of education both in this country and in developing countries, (*b*) trends in automation and technology and their effect upon the vocations and the professions, (*c*) human and natural resources in relation to future societal needs, and (*d*) the long-range economic implications of the arms and space race.

Political trends.—The following matters, among others, would be carefully examined to discover significant implications for defining and attaining educational excellence and opportunity: (*a*) changing relationships of state, local, and federal government; (*b*) governmental structures of metropolitan communities and their relationship to rural governments; (*c*) church and state relationships; (*d*) governmental responsibilities for health and welfare; (*e*) the impact of the industrial-military complex upon government; (*f*) the political struggle between the U.S.S.R. and the Western countries.

Sociological trends.—A mastery of basic sociological concepts would be sought, and such matters as the following would be given careful consideration in order to develop explicit implications for defining and attaining educational excellence and opportunity: (*a*) population trends with special consideration for (1) the mobility of minority groups, (2) the mobility of those in different social classes, and (3) distribution of people in rural, suburban, and urban areas as well as distribution in different age groups; (*b*) health, housing, vocational and educational opportunities for members of different ages, races, and social classes; (*c*) the growth of science and specialization in society; (*d*) trends in leisure and recreation patterns; (*e*) the increasing role of mass media in the American culture; (*f*) shifts in societal norms and the functions of institutions.

Operational policies and curriculum.—Operational policy relates not so much to the relationship between societal needs and educational purposes as it does to the relation between educational purposes and a program to achieve these purposes. In terms of a high-school science program, for example, operational policy should provide guides for making decisions about such matters as the procurement of teaching personnel, the purchase of instructional materials, and procedures for curriculum change. Policies should facilitate the achievement of defined purposes.

Clearly, a study of economic, sociological, and political trends would have relevance for developing operational policies. A definition of manpower needs concerning space efforts, for example, has implications for policies to guide the selection of teaching personnel, the continuing education of these personnel, science curricula, and vocational education. Therefore, the emerging needs of society should be studied to update educational purposes *and* to discover implications for defining operational policies to achieve purposes.

Knowledge provided by the scientific and scholarly inquiries of psychologists and professional educators on educational technologies is also useful for developing competence in the setting of educational policies. Of great importance in this aspect of preparation, for example, would be opportunities to develop a better understanding of such areas as learning, instructional methodologies, personnel administration, and school finance. In developing and organizing this type of content the application and organization of concepts from basic disciplines are often involved. For example, school finance is dependent, to some extent, upon economics, staff personnel administration upon sociology, and instructional methodology upon psychology.

Staffing considerations.—In incorporating content from basic disciplines to illuminate administrative purposes, processes, and technologies, problems of staff utilization are posed, particularly in regard to the involvement of social scientists. It seems clear that some progress toward the solution of this problem has been made during the last few decades, particularly in that a number of special staffing arrangements have evolved: [30] full or joint appointment of social scientists in colleges of education; interdisciplinary seminars; courses especially tailored by social scientists for students of administration; counseling of students into courses taught regularly by social scientists; special in-service and preservice education to enable professors of school administration to link their own discipline with others.[31]

30. Jack Culbertson, "Communicating Social Science Knowledge: Barriers and Beachheads," in *A Forward Look—The Preparation of School Administrators, 1970.* Edited by Donald E. Tope. Eugene, Oregon: Bureau of Educational Research, University of Oregon, 1960.

31. For a discussion of some of the important questions involved in preparing professors of school administration so that they can effectively link their discipline with others and a proposed program to prepare these professors, see Roald Campbell, "Training Research Professors of Educational Administration" in *Educational Research: New Perspectives.* Edited by Jack Culbertson and Stephen Hencley. Danville, Illinois: Interstate Printers and Publishers, Inc., 1963.

It is clear that specific staffing arrangements must be geared to the traditions and values of each institution in that the appointment of social scientists to colleges of education, for example, has been much more effective in some universities than in others. In addition, certain characteristics of social scientists also seem important: a motivation to see beyond one's discipline, an interest in the application as well as the discovery of knowledge, a desire to bridge effectively the gap between concepts and action, and an outstanding teaching ability.

Of significance for preparation is the fact that social scientists and professors of administration are beginning to achieve some synthesis of the research results on administrative processes. Thus, the concept of decision-making has become an important "organizing concept" in business administration,[32] in public administration,[33] and in school administration.[34] Important syntheses of content related to communication, change, and morale have also developed. Such work clearly needs to be continued and even enhanced.

A major challenge to those preparing administrators is to see that content directly related to educational purposes and operational policies is organized and incorporated into preparatory programs. Scientific knowledge about administrative processes tends to become organized in the natural development of the social sciences. However, systematic efforts are needed to organize data to update purposes in education. Such efforts need to be continuous and large-scale, in that data related to educational excellence and opportunity in today's world are ever susceptible to change.

The increase in the content from the social sciences and the need to see this content from within a broader framework pose special problems about how potential administrators can encompass and digest the knowledge they will need. Several measures to cope with

32. Leonard Silk, *The Education of Businessmen.* Supplementary paper, No. 11, Committee for Economic Development, 1960.

33. Herbert Simon, *Administrative Behavior: A Study of Decision-making Processes in Administrative Organization.* New York: Macmillan Co., 1947.

34. Daniel Griffiths, *Administrative Theory.* New York: Appleton-Century-Crofts, 1959.

the increasing abundance of knowledge can be taken: more systematic decisions about what is most relevant can be made; more efficient organization of relevant knowledge can be developed; research on more effective modes of teaching can be implemented; programs can be made more rigorous; part-time study in preservice programs can be sharply reduced; adequate residence requirements can be instituted; three years for preparing superintendents can and is increasingly becoming the pattern; in-service education can assume a greater role in the preparation of administrators.

Instructional Materials and Methods

The discontinuity between the study of administration and its practice is widely recognized and, as knowledge about administration increases, this discontinuity may well become greater. One way to avoid such a development is to use, in preparatory programs, those instructional methods which will effectively relate emerging concepts to practice, thus helping to insure that the latter is improved and the former is responsibly tested. It is in part to achieve this purpose that cases, simulated situations, field study, and the internship have been developed. Their use in preparatory programs has been strongly influenced by emerging social-science concepts. Therefore, they have supplemented such methods as lecture, discussion, and independent study in a special way.

The case method.—First used in programs for preparing administrators at the Harvard Graduate School of Business Administration in 1919, cases were incorporated into programs for government administrators in the 1930's and for school administrators in the 1940's. Initially, they were used to provide vicarious administrative experience and to afford opportunities for "intuitive" decision-making. However, with the emergence of pertinent content from the social sciences during the last few decades, cases have been used increasingly to relate concepts to "facts of administrative life" in order to illuminate the latter and to test the relevance of the former.

Thus, the significance of the case method in preparing administrators extends beyond the use of a series of cases with a group of potential administrators. Viewed in the longer-range perspective of a developing profession, cases can encourage and help guide the organization of relevant content about administration. In business administration, where there is the longest tradition of case teaching, considerable conceptual material has already developed in the form of case commentaries. In educational administration, where there is the shortest tradition of case use, the development of commentaries on case materials by professors of school administration and by social scientists has just begun.[35]

Simulated situations.—The use of simulation is another way of bridging the gap between facts and theories in the preparation of administrators. Even though this method for preparing administrators developed some time after the case approach, simulated materials are already available for preparing business executives,[36] school administrators,[37] and government administrators.[38] In school administration, for example, problems encountered by the superintendent, curriculum director, elementary-school principal, and secondary-school principal in the "Jefferson Township" have been simulated and used for instruction. Important media for simulating problems in these positions are "in-basket" items, which consist of letters, memoranda, notes, news-clippings, and other printed materials about which administrators must make decisions. Films, kinescopes, and tape recordings are also used to simulate administrative problems.

Background information to illuminate the context of the problems is provided by a careful description of the "Jefferson Township" schools and community. The materials which form the background for the simulated problems are rich in detail. There are, for example, more than 600 pages of written materials on the "Whitman School" and its relationship to the "Jefferson Township" community. In addition, a variety of audio-visual materials is provided.

35. For an example of a commentary which relates sociological concepts to a case in education, see Robert Alford, "Community Resistance to School Organization," Case #11 in the UCEA Case Series in Educational Administration, 65 South Oval Drive, Columbus 10, Ohio.

36. F. M. Ricciardi and C. J. Craft, *Top Management Decision-Simulation: The AMA Approach*, p. 126. New York: American Management Association, 1957.

37. *Simulation in Administrative Training.* Edited by Jack Culbertson and William Coffield. Columbus, Ohio: University Council for Educational Administration, 1960.

38. Harold Guetzkow, "A Use of Simulation in the Study of Inter-nation Relations," *Behavioral Science*, IV (July, 1959), 183-91.

Human, technical, and conceptual problems are all simulated and carefully structured to include the problem areas of school-community relations, personnel administration, funds and facilities, and educational program. Students assume the role of principal and make decisions on the problems simulated. Simulated materials provide countless opportunities for relating social science concepts to administrative situations and problems.[39]

Field study and the internship.—Still another approach to relating concepts to action is the field study. In contrast to cases and simulation, through which the "reality" of administration is transported into the classroom, the field study provides opportunities for students to observe, analyze, and study administration in its actual setting. In a number of universities, field or "community" studies have become central activities in "block-of-time" courses. Concepts from the social sciences or from areas of professional education are applied and tested in this process. Field studies not only describe but quite often analyze and evaluate selected aspects of education and administration. This contrasts with case development in which the central goal is to produce an accurate report of how an administrator grapples with a real problem.

The internship moves even closer to the "reality" of administration and, therefore, is another method which can help diminish the discontinuity between study and practice. In this aspect of preparation the potential administrator is given actual administrative responsibility while under the direct supervision of skilled practitioners and university instructors. Through this method, the intern is not only afforded opportunities to develop technical skills; he can also have experience in diagnosing organizational pathologies related to decision-making, change, morale, and communication. The method is particularly appropriate for helping administrators make the transition from preparation to practice. However, to realize the full potential of this approach to preparation, further work is needed to achieve several goals: more refined procedures for selecting school districts in which to locate interns; adequate and clear definitions of desired learnings; effective and adequate supervision; stable methods

39. For a detailed discussion of these materials see Hemphill, Griffiths, and Frederiksen, *op. cit.*

of financing; research to illuminate and improve the internship.[40]

Comparison of instructional methods.—How appropriate are existing methods and materials for effectively teaching emerging concepts about administration? Little scientific research is available on this question. However, judging from reported experience, existing simulated materials can be excellent media for effectively teaching administrators theories of change, morale, communication, and decision-making. Their capacity to provide realistic situations to apply social-science concepts related to administrative processes seems to be one of the outstanding advantages of these materials. Since they are programed to encompass the technical aspects of administration, they also have considerable utility for instructing students in specific administrative tasks. The same generalizations would apply to the use of cases, even though their background data are not as extensive and as richly detailed as are the simulated situations.

Simulated materials and cases can be used for developing competence in the creation of operational policies. However, since school system policy is already largely prescribed in simulated situations through teacher handbooks, legal codes, and board policies, instruction is more easily focused upon the making of decisions about means to implement given policies rather than upon the definition of new purposes and policies. Cases, as a rule, have also been used to diagnose variables involved in actual policy decisions rather than upon the creation of new policies. However, they can provide students opportunities to consider substantive issues of policy.

40. For detailed discussions of methods for preparing administrators, the following references are suggested: for the internship see Daniel R. Davies, *The Internship in Educational Administration* (Washington: Center for Applied Research in Education, 1962) and *The Internship in Administrative Preparation* (Edited by Stephen Hencley. Columbus, Ohio: University Council for Educational Administration, and Committee for the Advancement of School Administration, 1963); for the case method see Jack Culbertson, Paul Jacobson, and Theodore Reller, *Administrative Relationships: A Casebook* (Englewood Cliffs, New Jersey: Prentice Hall, 1960); for simulation see *Simulation in Administrative Training* (Edited by Jack Culbertson and William Coffield. University Council for Educational Administration, 1960); and for the community study see the American Association for School Administrators, *Professional Administrators for America's Schools* (Washington: The Association, 1960).

Field studies may be used for developing competence in dealing with substantive issues of policy. As a matter of fact, such studies often seek to evaluate existing policy. However, they are typically limited to smaller districts, and they encounter the resistances that often limit thorough examination of the *status quo*. Issues related to educational purpose, viewed from within a national framework, cannot be easily examined through this method. The internship, as now implemented, also provides little opportunity for grappling with broader questions of public policy.

It is evident that current instructional methodologies for preparing administrators to cope with purpose and policy in today's world are not entirely adequate. If selected policy issues facing school leaders in big city systems were simulated, and if problems which involve decisions about the relationships between educational purposes and national goals could be developed, they would add significantly to existing instructional methods. In addition, independent study could be developed to improve and enhance learning. This method would seem particularly appropriate for helping potential administrators to master concepts in the humanities and the social sciences in order to gain greater insight into educational purposes and policies. Concepts mastered through this type of study should add to the leadership potential of candidates for administrative posts and provide needed perspective for utilizing effectively emerging scientific concepts about administration and organization.

Summary

During this century, growth in preparatory programs for administrators has been matched by the development of significant foundations for a science of administration. Consequently, programs, particularly during the last decade, have had more encompassing and more rigorous types of content as bases for preparation. Thus, concepts from anthropology, economics, political science, psychology, and sociology, when incorporated into programs, can illuminate such administrative processes as communication, decision-making, change, and morale building and can help update definitions of educational excellence and equality of learning opportunities.

Such content, in and of itself, is not enough, however; administrators, in making decisions as leaders, must rely ultimately upon basic human values whose ethical dimensions are treated more adequately in philosophy and other aspects of the humanities than in the social sciences. Content produced by scholars in education on such technical aspects of administration as school finance and school housing is also required for preparing school administrators.

New and more-encompassing content in programs has raised questions about needed instructional materials and methodologies. Cases and simulated materials, developed in recent decades, are increasingly being used as concrete bases for applying and testing social-science concepts. New concepts have also had implications for other methods such as lectures, independent study, field study, and the internship.

Both the increasingly complex demands of educational administration and the new content on administration have created requirements for a higher quality of candidate for preparatory programs than ever before. These factors, plus the general competition for intellectual and leadership talent in society, make the search for candidates to enter programs more intense and more crucial. Recruitment efforts, particularly during the decade ahead, will be just as important as the effective incorporation into preparatory programs of new content, materials, and methodologies now emerging from the new science of administration.

IMPLICATIONS OF THE NEW SCIENTIFIC BASES FOR EDUCATION

CHAPTER XV

A Projective Appraisal

LAURENCE D. HASKEW

Introduction

The assignment to this author differs from those given to other contributors to this yearbook. Given access to the complete manuscript and taking into account the current scene in education, he is asked to serve as a selective projector of enduring implications.

Preceding chapters have been descriptive, valuational, occasionally hortative, or directional. They have attempted to document and delineate the phenomenon of change in one aspect of the school enterprise, educational administration. As individual presentations, these chapters stand or fall on their own merits.

But the total yearbook is more than a collection of presentations, and the phenomenon about which it testifies may yield generalizations, judgments, lessons, and questions which have value for the shaping of the future history of the educational enterprise. One man was asked to explore that possibility. This concluding chapter is the result.

The Phenomenon

The past fifteen years in this country have witnessed a redirection (some say birth) of much within school administration that is now clearly distinguishable from mere extension of precedent patterns. That redirection, both as process and as achievement, is the phenomenon under consideration in this chapter.

ITS NATURE

This phenomenon can be described more easily than it can be named. Within a context characterized by sweeping changes in both the internal and external relationships of the school enterprise in the

United States and in the roles it is called upon to undertake, there has been a distinctive response within school administration. Vehicles for this response have been the Cooperative Programs in Educational Administration and numerous institutionalized progeny, a burgeoning literature, widespread experimentation with preparation programs, and university-centered programs of organized inquiry. The ideational core of response is the conscious application of intelligence and inquiry to administration as a specialized function of institutionalized education. Collateral with the core is strong support of the method of science as *the* method of inquiry and for the creation of a theory-based discipline to undergird the art-science of professional practice of the school administrator. Completing the picture is an array of institutionalized strategies for defining and causing "improvements" in the professional practice of school administration itself. This entire picture is cast against the background of a newly urgent concern that certain values be used as criteria to distinguish improvement from regression.

ITS DEFINITION

For purposes of identification, let us call this fifteen-year-old phenomenon "The Study of Administration," using "study" in a double sense of (*a*) a setting of the mind upon inquiry leading to understanding, and (*b*) a considered, organized endeavor to reach certain ends. This title, itself, aids our perception of what is going on.

First of all, "the" connotes the project nature of this phenomenon, which has a degree of conceptual and operational unity quite rare in the history of educational movements. The *whole* typically came before the *parts*. Subprojects have stemmed from plans more often than from fortuitous circumstances; patterns of attack have been devised more often than improvised. There has been a deliberate effort to visualize the whole problem and not only to launch but to keep going a sequential, long-range, unified endeavor. Remarkable unification has been achieved in efforts, normally disparate, to apply the methods of science to a major aspect of education. These efforts are illustrated by collaborative interuniversity production of paradigms, testing of hypotheses, and joint planning of research endeavors. Similar unification has characterized the efforts of investigators, teachers, and practitioners—and this on a nation-wide rather than the customary local or regional basis. In brief, we are dealing here with a unified project much more than with the manifestations of a folk movement or discrete responses to a vaguely defined, felt need.

"Study" is used to point to three distinctive characteristics of what is transpiring. First, the focus of activity is upon a method of attack, a disciplined exploration of a defined territory with unknown features. This method differs sharply from the usual more-or-less random collecting of intriguing bits of information in the hope that someone will put them together someday. In it, production of theories is accorded prominence as the necessary precursor of truth-producing inquiry and the organization of usable knowledge. Second, an attitude is being cultivated (with some success) that administration is to be studied, not learned. That is, an undeterminate discipline is proposed as the successor to a limited accomplishment-to-be-mastered; ability and disposition to address problems is treasured more highly than memorization of the currently prevalent responses to these problems. Third, shifting semantic gears, "study" directs attention to institutionalized strategy—formation of the University Council for Educational Administration (UCEA), development of membership sanctions in the American Association of School Administrators (AASA), accreditation of collegiate preparation programs, and other programatic devices to broaden and intensify the project's impact.

"Administration" is chosen deliberately in preference to "school administration" in titling the phenomenon because of a distinctive characteristic of what goes on. There is apparent a strong effort to distinguish administration as a definable element, subject to separate attention, in a social enterprise. Let us not pose a false dichotomy here; there is no contention among the leaders in this project that "school" can or should be separated from "administration." The contention is simply that administration—as function and as process—can be studied and should be studied. Hence, there has been and continues to be a strong identification of administration as treated in this yearbook with administration in nonschool settings with the social and behavioral sciences, and with other disciplines which throw light upon the nature of administration or upon persons involved in it. Most of the chapters of this yearbook spring from such focus upon administration *qua* administration, and well typify the phenomenon whose meaning is to be ruminated upon.

The Phenomenon as Prototype

Ventures in education telesis are never-ending. As one such venture, "the study of administration" may have corporeal manifestations (at least suggestive, if not indicative) to those persons who seek to affect the evolution of the school enterprise by the injection of intelligent action. An examination of the pertinence of "the study of administration" as a prototype is in order.

IN PERVASIVENESS

In outreach and in duration, what started as "The Kellogg Project" has become a significant element in almost every phase of school administration. The endeavors and emphases of the American Association of School Administrators reflect the "study," as do projects undertaken by school-study councils, in-service conclaves, and similar self-help enterprises of practicing administrators. Firing-line, operational practices of many individual superintendents and principals have been changed, and—more important—the "proper nature" of practical school administration is acquiring new referents from definitions and priority-scales distilled by "study" activities. Consultantship operations of universities and state departments of education are being affected in character and in focus. Formal sanctions, such as certification of individuals and accreditation of university programs for preparation, are undergoing metamorphosis. Collegiate offerings for administrators are being influenced in course structures, instructional methods, subject content, and degree requirements. Research in educational administration is exhibiting some sharp breaks with its traditional rhetoric. If influence is measured by pervasion of the power structure and the institutions of a social enterprise, then "the study of school administration" may be ranked as one of the more influential undertakings in recent history. Influence is eagerly sought in efforts to change education for the better. The task of diffusing a set of ideas beyond a closed circle of devotees is particularly difficult in an enterprise as replete with special-interest "enclaves" as is schooling. Seldom is the task accomplished. It has been accomplished by "the study of administration."

Some would claim that the unusual influence of these projects stemmed from certain procedural innovations. This "study" was not directed by any master commission or other single agency. Instead, it began in autonomous regional centers, was further decentralized to subcenters, such as states, then spread to still other sponsors. Several, not one, existent organizations became promoters and developers at various times, and new organizations were devised to perform varying functions. Yet, procedure was not fortuitous; appraisal and planning occurred periodically, but the context was one in which proprietorship never crystallized.

Others would claim that procedural causation of pervasiveness was minor; that the project's genius lay in natural appeal of the intellectual discipline which began to characterize "the study" in its post-1955 phase. Emphases upon disciplinary subject matter—difficult and prestigeful concepts borrowed from other sciences, from the methods of science itself, and from noneducation disciplines—struck a widely responsive chord in post-Sputnik United States.

Perhaps all would agree, however, that the whole educational enterprise or any function within it could benefit markedly from an attempt to replicate for other endeavors the conditions which led to the pervasiveness of "the study of administration."

IN METHOD

How shall the task of educational improvement be addressed? One traditional answer has been to get as many people as possible to use rational judgment, as best they can, to agree upon (*a*) what is desirable and (*b*) what will be likely to bring about the desirable. Another traditional answer is to produce hypotheses of what might be better and to test those hypotheses in some context of evaluative control. A third approach is to investigate and record, and then to deduce; deductions may become the basis of planned and directed progress or they may become merely subject matter. The "study of administration" has used all these methods.

But, it lays unique claim to an approach superordinate to all these: the approach of scientism. Administration, it is insisted, will be advanced measurably only by employment of theory as a guide to inquiry. The search for theory becomes a conscious preoccupation, a necessary prelude to determining what administration—or any component thereof—is. Theory, in turn, becomes the prime tool for opening up *process* to productive inquiry, and process is the life-essence of administration, as it is of all education. "The study of administration" is heralded as a way (even *the* way) of addressing the unknown in education.

However, the validity of the claim itself is open to question. There is little tangible evidence that this method has been widely employed in "the study." There has been inquiry, a large volume of it. Inquiry as attitude and as reaction has been the norm, in itself a noteworthy achievement. But, most of the inquiry reported upon has been neither theory-oriented nor designed to meet the exacting rubrics of scientistic investigation. In fact, the significance of research in the total "study" is generally evaluated as minor. Further, many manifestations of "the study" (for example, advocacy of certain patterns and subject-content for preparation of administrators) depart rather sharply from what is defined ordinarily as the scientific method. Scientism as *the* method is advocated and employed vigorously by a growing coterie of influential persons, but to earmark this approach as the *essence de vivre* of "the study" is at best a questionable extrapolation.

But if scientism *could* dominate the quest for knowledge of administration, should it be the prototype for similar quest in all of education? While scientistic design has produced verifiable, significant, and usable bodies of knowledge in many fields, it has failed at such production in other fields. Attempts to apply scientistic inquiry to psychosocial phenomena are not confined to recent years; failure in previous attempts may be due to inappropriateness of the method as much as to obtuseness or ineptitude of the investigators. After all, the natural sciences have been unable to apply the methods of science to the investigation of the scientific method. The volume of "scientific" sociology, cultural anthropology, psychology of learning, cultural history, and political science is extremely small after many decades of strongly advocated scientism within those fields. If evidence is necessary for proof, it is extremely doubtful that scientism is *the* method for education. That it is *a* method, promising and underused, is both ably presented and cogently championed by various authors of this yearbook and by many others. It seems to hold particular promise as a method for disentangling and eventually controlling process, and for establishing a dependable morphology of functions. Here is where administration, and most of education, has been almost solely dependent upon folklore and revelation. Hence, in advocated method, "the study of administration" may offer a compelling prototype to those invoking telesis upon the course of education.

IN PROCEDURES

Interplay between the practice of a profession and an emerging, influential, intellectual discipline for a profession is, in significant measure, a function of procedures. In education, discipline and practice appear to be more at war with each other than in most professions. It is apparent that "the study of administration" has been characterized by unusually constructive interplay, diminution of tensions, and encouraging collaboration. Since similar results should be widely sought in the total educational enterprise, procedures in "the study" may offer some hints. Each of the five succeeding paragraphs sets forth a generalized clue deduced from the procedural manifestations of the phenomenon being examined here.

1. Involvement is standard; involvement in "study" is common; but engagement in inquiry (as contrasted with learning from or choosing "best" thoughts) is rare. Inquiry has been a dominant feature of administrator-involvement in what became "the study" almost from inception. Actually, involvement *qua* involvement was seldom the strategy and seldom mere token; inquiry was the strategy, and it caught up hundreds (perhaps thousands) of firing-line practitioners in its web.

2. Production of a discipline fits poorly into the off-hours of practitioners. Projects within "the study" assembled practitioners in large numbers as long-term members of discipline-devoted teams on university campuses. Most of them also served as liaison persons with field investigations involving other practitioners.

3. Localization, competition, and commonality must be synthesized for educational invention to be transmuted into a national movement. State studies and experimentation, regional centers, and national organizations were used in "the study" to produce a remarkable synthesis. Channels of communication quickly transferred the interdisciplinary emphasis at Oregon, the tri-dimensional con-

cept at Teachers College, the rationale for administrator-selection at
Texas into the composition of "the study" everywhere. Local loyal-
ties, uniqueness, and pride were deliberately fanned; at the same
time such conclaves as the National Conference of Professors of
Educational Administration (NCPEA), annual meetings of the
American Association of School Administrators (AASA), and the
University Council for Educational Administration (UCEA) devel-
oped a morale and common cause not bounded by geography.

4. Infusion of new theory, different strategies, additional hori-
zons add to the virile life span of organized endeavor. The Kellogg
Foundation did not wash its hands of the project at the normal time
for such an agency to bow out of the picture. Instead, it backed
the Committee for the Advancement of School Administration
(CASA), the UCEA, and other forward-moving enterprises. "Leading figures" in "the study" have found repeated means to get together, to rethink, to strike off sparks which point in new directions.
Infusion has been an enduring phenomenon.

5. The power structure of a profession must have something
practical to do if ideational constructs are to become professionally
influential. Formation of CASA was one practical response. Subsequent study and action on qualifications for membership in AASA
was another, and state associations of administrators have responded
similarly. The surface character of such responses is perturbing, but
it may be a prelude to something deeper. At least, officialdom in
the organized profession of school administration continues to ask,
"What can we do about it?" This is an unusual tribute to procedures developed by "the study."

Now, these and similar procedures are not cited as ends in themselves. The basic argument is that the school enterprise needs—perhaps more than it needs anything else—to be enlightened, rendered
more potent, and guided by a discipline. A discipline is a way of
addressing phenomena; a comprehensive, manageable, and understood derivation of content-knowledge, plus an orderly pursuit of
new knowledge. But, it is *in vacuo* until it has a professional *situs*
and professional sanction; in fact, it will hardly come into being
without these. Hence, linkage between profession and scholarship
in the drive for a discipline is essential, hard to come by, and worthy

of a conscious strategy to produce. Procedures in "the study" for production of linkage become significant in this context.

The Phenomenon's Promise

FOR DISCIPLINARY ADVANCEMENT

The purpose of this yearbook is to depict an emerging discipline of school administration as it could be described in 1963. A discipline, it has been said, consists of (a) a way of addressing phenomena, (b) a comprehensive, manageable, and understandable body of content-knowledge, and (c) an orderly pursuit of new knowledge. What has been depicted in this volume, with what promise?

1. *A way of addressing phenomena* appears as a consistent design in almost all chapters of this yearbook. This way is the point of view, the rational skeleton, of scientism. First, there is a patent attempt to identify discrete —relatively speaking, of course—factors which have demonstrable influence upon the dynamics of administration. Second, an effort is made to conceptualize each factor. Third, an approach—often experimental or tentative in nature— is made toward the construction of an analytical morphology of the factor (e.g., leadership), thus identifying variables. Finally, there are experimental attempts to manipulate one variable and trace the results of such manipulation upon the parameters of the factor itself. Overarching all of these is a repeated attempt to construct theories which appear as possibly valid explanations of the interplay between factors in producing the totality of administration.

Appearance of a "model" way is not, however, tantamount to execution of that way. Obviously, only beginnings have been reported thus far. Identification of major factors is highly tentative at this stage; for illustration, "the organization" as a factor could prove to be insufficiently discrete from other factors to be serviceable. Conceptualizations of the tentative factors are likewise far from precise; "decision-making" as presented in this volume, for example, is somewhat shadowy as a corpus. These primitivities are the natural extensions of uncertainties about theory. But, such uncertainty is healthy for "the study of administration" since it flows from deliberate use of several approaches to theory in preference to insistence upon a monolithic rationale, a point well made by

Griffiths. In total, therefore, one can conclude that a way of viewing the data of school administration *is* in view, a way which differs sharply from that in vogue during preceding decades.

That difference is significant. It consists fundamentally in viewing school administration—and hence its data—as a dynamic system which can be understood and subjected to control, rather than viewing it as a collection of entities which can only be described in terms of norms and otherwise, with control arising only from the ingenuity and art of the individual administrator translated into sermons, advice, and folklore.

2. *A body of content-knowledge meeting disciplinary criteria* emerges with less clarity. But, its proposed outlines are intriguing. Significant is the nonappearance of some traditionally "important" subject matter. Even more significant are the disciplinary subdivisions (called "factors" in the preceding paragraphs) employed as chapter titles, and the type of content found in those chapters. Administration as process, as perception of forces and of interrelations between forces, as control and leadership of energized systems, as application of knowledge by problem-solving reasoning—this quadrumvirate begins to promise understanding and management of content within subdivisions. Some of the concepts adduced have forward-reaching implications; that of workflow advanced by Charters, for example, may be widely useful in organizing all educational endeavors. In sum, one can be encouraged at the present prospect for a disciplinary morphology of school administration.

Knowledge-content presented, on the other hand, is disappointing in comprehensiveness and in depth. Alleged "great bodies of new knowledge produced by modern behavioral sciences pertinent to school administration" are not represented in the pages of this volume, except by scattered illustrations and claims that they do exist. Knowledge produced from the matrix of school administration itself is even more rare. These facts should not occasion despair or ridicule, however. Enough knowledge is visible to indicate that it can be generated and verified. The absence of "knowledge" may be more encouraging than its presence. School administration as well as of education has been plagued too long with folklore, authoritative opinion, and normative practice masquerading as knowledge; the yearbook's authors are to be congratulated upon what they ex-

cluded in adhering to standards of scientism. Also, the authors have
been more interested in examining structure than in adducing physiology. Significant bodies of physiological knowledge—what actually transpires within small groups under varying conditions of
management, for example—have been indicated only, not presented.
Necessary allocation of priorities upon space in a yearbook, however, should not mislead those who appraise. There is much more
knowledge about the physiology of administrative enterprises than
the authors have been able to illustrate; one actually finds considerable promise here for the sorely needed advancement of a content-
girded discipline for all of education, not administration alone.

However, attempts in several chapters to illustrate the practical
value of what is presented as subject matter point to the Achilles'
heel of this total endeavor. Vulnerability arises from a history-
spawned compulsion to demonstrate to practitioners that disciplinary knowledge is technology, that "how-to-do-its" emerge directly
from inquiry. Otherwise, support and involvement of the profession
may be lost. For decades, educators have successfully blocked attempts to undergird their profession with a discipline of demonstrated verifiable knowledge by saying, "but how can that be used
in the classroom?" The patent attitude is that all else is purely
theoretical play by impractical academicians. Perhaps equally, academicians have made a fetish of sharp distinction between purity
and application. "The study of administration" has been modestly
successful in healing this breach, but full recovery is far from assured. If practitioners desert discipline-searchers, or vice versa, the
breach will become as wide as it once was. In 1963, for example,
the lack of one-to-one correspondence between knowledge of role
theory and service as a school principal does not destroy the value
of the theory. But if practitioners think that it does, if they lose
their interest in, and if they withdraw their active support from
role theory, the total promise becomes minor. If disciplinarians become so enamored of fields of knowledge that they ignore the needs
arising from the practice of a profession, the loss of practitionery
support is almost inevitable. In the long run, this "study's" effective
life will be determined by what programs in the study of school administration receive the patronage of school administrators. That
outcome is still uncertain.

3. A discipline is an *orderly pursuit of new knowledge*. Few comforting signs of this aspect of disciplinary advancement appear in the preceding pages. Status of research in educational administration—as in all education—is far from promising.[1] "The study of administration" has enshrined "orderly" very successfully, but "pursuit" of new knowledge remains low in volume, disappointing in quality, and pitifully undernourished. Yet, in fairness, it must be pointed out that readiness for research is much greater in 1963 than it was in 1947, and that the sociopolitical *milieu* is more disposed toward implementation of research. Some see signs of awakening research vitality in university circles and of awakening interest (indicated by new conceptions and financial support) of government and private foundations. But one can find little significant research in educational administration actually going forward. Until that situation is changed, talk and visions hold doubtful promise for lasting disciplinary outcomes from "the study of administration."

FOR PROFESSIONAL ACHIEVEMENT

To upgrade the status and practice of school administration was the original objective of the projects which led into "the study of administration." While major attention has been concentrated upon disciplinary roads to that end, direct action has been undertaken also. Sponsored programs dealing with everyday practice—use of consultants, community study and improvement, communication with citizens, school-plant design, and numerous other programs— have been and are being conducted. Attempts to rejuvenate and professionalize state associations of administrators, school study councils, seminars for the intellectual development of administrators on the job, and principalship projects are illustrations of a wide array of change-focused enterprises. Evaluation reports from such activities are decidedly encouraging.

The chief action, however, has been that which focused upon the selection and preparation of prospective administrators. This has been a full-scale endeavor, ranging from attempts to conceptualize

---

1. See, for example, the appraisal in Daniel Griffiths, *Research in Educational Administration: An Appraisal and a Plan.* New York: Bureau of Publications, Teachers College, Columbia University, 1959.

and implement training programs themselves, to attempts to apply sanctions to the preparation component of professional stature.

Culbertson has described in this yearbook some of the drives at work in recasting formal preparation for school administration. Typical university and college practice lags far behind his description; totally redesigned university programs in 1963 hardly number ten, and two score institutions would account for all the loci of really significant innovations. The UCEA is carrying on a noteworthy series of endeavors, steadily increasing in influence, but one has only to attend the annual work-sessions of the NCPEA to become aware of a tremendous gap between advocacy and practice. The picture here is promising, however. This is to be attributed largely to the existence and the program of UCEA and to the growing collaboration between it and the AASA. An organization of such potency devoted to improvement of teaching programs is a rare phenomenon in the professions, and its existence holds decided promise for upgrading the status and practice of school administration.

While content, methodology, and quality are central concerns in preparation programs seeking to undergird a profession, ancillary problems may be more crucial. There is always the problem of logistics. How many preparation programs of requisite caliber can be built? How are adequate programs to be distinguished from inadequate programs? How may the best programs be guaranteed patronage sufficient to justify them economically? To what extent shall preparation in adequate programs be related to entrance upon practice in the profession?

"The study of administration" has evolved two prime tools for applying sanctions in the solution of problems of logistics. One is the Committee for the Advancement of School Administration inside the American Association of School Administrators. The other is a set of standards for accreditation of preparation programs for administrators (1963) under the administration of the National Council for the Accreditation of Teacher Education. Existence of these tools is both promising and dangerous.

At best, CASA or some successor can be a planning, creating, influencing agency to build a bridge between interests of the organized profession and a developing science of educational administration; it can use the skeleton of membership sanctions to build a body of support for increasing competence of administrators; it can be a vehicle for developing their competence. Or, it can be satisfied to place more skeletons in more closets, that is, merely get more state associations of administrators to adopt the token of two years of the same old preparation as a membership rule. It can ossify, turn in upon itself, become stodgy, defensive, and pedestrian, thus following the life pattern of most educational organizations. In adopting as a platform the first sentence of this paragraph, CASA would be faithful to the essence of "the study of administration" and add to the promise of that phenomenon for lasting professional achievement.

Use of the program accreditation tool for perpetuating and enhancing professional preparation is fraught with amply demonstrated difficulties. That NCATE, or any other agency, can use it constructively is open to serious question on the basis of accreditation history. Almost absurd are the expectations voiced in some quarters that NCATE will reduce the number of attempted programs to the number of institutions genuinely qualified and needed, that it will separate inadequate programs from adequate programs immediately, that its standards will at once insure meaningful new benchmarks for a mature profession, and so on. Such expectations confuse direction with achievement and are insidious in their temptation to attach labels of perfection to interim compromises. Certainly, they disregard entirely the context within which any national accreditation traditionally must function. Standards, procedures, and actions of NCATE thus far show little evidence of departure from traditional norms for institutionalized accreditation and, hence, display only long-range promise for significant change in the picture of professional preparation.

The promise of institutionalized accreditation is matched by its threat. In its use of symbols, judgments based on discrete standards rather than over-all effectiveness, fixed program patterns as descriptive norms, suspicion of the novel, demand that a single approach dominate an institution regardless of that institution's size and capability for experimentation, and pedestrian visiting teams, an accrediting agency can kill the dynamics which springs from pursuit of some goals beyond accreditation. By approval of mediocrity it can undermine collegiate institutions driving toward excellence; this is particularly true for institutions in a state-supported system of higher education where what is acceptable in one college is almost automatically imposed as the upper limit for all. In separation and self-centeredness, the accreditation agency can become a collegiate protective society rather than an instrument for advancement of professional excellence.

While NCATE may not now be subject to indictment on any such catalogue of charges, the story of its influence is yet to be written. It would be unfair to draw conclusions from the program of accreditation standards promulgated by NCATE in 1963, or from the very few applications of those standards in accrediting institutions for the preparation of school administrators. The standards are obviously empty until given qualitative content through accumulated interpretations. The few accreditations to date are, one hopes, merely pilot undertakings. But, the standards as written are not encouraging; it is difficult to see how the qualitative flavor of Culbertson's chapter can be contained within them or even stimulated by them. And, if NCATE's expectations for collegiate programs are forecast by those apparently exhibited in the pilot appraisal processes so far conducted, little positive influence by accreditation can be counted upon. Of still more concern is the fact that the current standards, "illustrations of application," and accreditation actions of NCATE are open to, if not tending toward, becoming instruments of negative influence. Therefore, this appraiser must simply wait and see what the outcomes from program accreditation will be, with little optimistic anticipation.

These notes of skepticism originating from certain institutionalizations within "the study of administration" should not cast a negative pall upon the total appraisal. After all, one of the striking features of "the study" has been its capacity to invent new institutionalizations at crucial junctures. And, foreboding is a stimulus to foresight, not foresight itself. Conscious orientation toward a long-range future remains the outstanding characteristic of the phenomenon under examination, and difficulties foreseen can become difficulties surmounted.

Therefore, this appraisal should close upon an optimistic note. That note is one of promise, promise that we have here a conception and a methodology which can add dramatically to the stature of education as professional endeavor, a stature which will grow from achievements originating in a growing scientistic discipline as the framework for artistic administrative creativity.

INDEX

Index

Sensitizing concepts: examples of, 108; Lazarsfeld quoted on, 107-8

Service organizations, grouping of, on basis of control over admission to, 264-68

Shankland, Sherwood, 14

Shared decision-making, discussion of, 241-42

Sherwood, Frank P., quoted (with Pfiffner), 173

Shils, Edward A., 156, 157

Shubik, Martin, 212

Silander, F. S., 203

Simon, Herbert A., 33, 45, 46, 69, 112, 162, 201, 202, 209, 212, 224, 287, 307; quoted, 70, 71, 105; criticism of Gulick and Urwick by, 67; major concern of, 64; scholarly production of, 65; summary of approach of, to study of administrative theory, 71-72

Snedden, David, 12, 81

Snyderman, Barbara B., 159, 160

Social and economic conditions, consequences of, for administration, 79-80

Social power: definition of, 226, 232; mobilization of, to influence decision-making, 238-40

Something To Steer By, publication of, by Comimttee for Advancement of School Administrators, 27

Spaulding, Frank E., 81, 82, 83, 84, 86; quoted, 83

Spinning, James, 13

Starr, Martin K., 203

Steffens, Lincoln, 78, 223; quoted, 224

Stern, George C., 136, 169

Stoddard, A. J., 12

Stogdill, Ralph M., 127, 146; quoted, 174

Strayer, George D., 12; conceptions of nature of professional training of, 86-87

Strykker, Perrin, 215

Sullivan, Harry Stack, 112; quoted, 113

Sutthoff, John, 152; quoted, 289-90

Stanford University: CPEA in, 20; intern arrangements of, 22

Studies in School Administration, publication of, by Committee for the Advancement of School Administration, 27

Study of administration, discussion of, 333-35

Superintendent's role, leadership expectations held for, 123-24

System theory: Griffiths' use of, to investigate changes in organizations, 116; organizational survival in relation to, 170-74; use of, in defining boundary of the organization as a system, 171

System theory and open systems, 116

Tarbell, Ida, 78

Task achievement, role theory in relation to, 149-55

Taylor, Frederick, 4, 33, 34, 38, 39, 41, 47, 50, 51, 53, 54, 64, 66, 67, 71, 81, 82, 148, 304, 305, 306; beginning of attempts of, to analyze work methods, 35; innovations by, and procedures of, 35-36; investigation of methods by government, 37; opposition of unions and others to, 37-38; proposals of, 35; views of, 34-35; quoted, 35, 36, 37

Taylorism, 305; attacks on, 44-45; theoretical validity of, challenged, 45

Teachers, role of, in administrative theory of Cubberley and Bobbitt, 86

Teachers College, Columbia University, 22, 31, 86, 87, 179, 340; CPEA in, 20; early courses in administration in, 11

Teaching of administration, Fayol's views on, 40

Technique, aim of, according to Barnard, 63

Theories of administration, categorization of, by March and Simon, 112

Theory: clarification of terminology used in building of, 100; definition of, 98-99; importance of precise terminology in building of, 99-100; misunderstandings concerning nature of, 96; levels of stages in development of, incorporated in paradigm, 104-5; nature and meaning of, 95-118; nature of contemporary work on, 103-4; unacceptable views of the nature of, 95-98

Thompson, A. S., 161

CONSTITUTION AND BY-LAWS
OF
THE NATIONAL SOCIETY FOR THE STUDY OF EDUCATION

(As adopted May, 1944, and amended June, 1945, February, 1949, and September, 1962)

ARTICLE I

NAME

The name of this corporation shall be "The National Society for the Study of Education," an Illinois corporation not for profit.

ARTICLE II

PURPOSES

Its purposes are to carry on the investigation of educational problems, to publish the results of same, and to promote their discussion.

The corporation also has such powers as are now, or may hereafter be, granted by the General Not For Profit Corporation Act of the State of Illinois.

ARTICLE III

OFFICES

The corporation shall have and continuously maintain in this state a registered office and a registered agent whose office is identical with such registered office, and may have other offices within or without the State of Illinois as the Board of Directors may from time to time determine.

ARTICLE IV

MEMBERSHIP

Section 1. *Classes.* There shall be two classes of members—active and honorary. The qualifications and rights of the members of such classes shall be as follows:

(*a*) Any person who is desirous of promoting the purposes of this corporation is eligible to active membership and shall become such on payment of dues as prescribed.

(*b*) Active members shall be entitled to vote, to participate in discussion, and, subject to the conditions set forth in Article V, to hold office.

(*c*) Honorary members shall be entitled to all the privileges of active

i

members, with the exception of voting and holding office, and shall be exempt from the payment of dues. A person may be elected to honorary membership by vote of the active members of the corporation on nomination by the Board of Directors.

(d) Any active member of the Society may, at any time after reaching the age of sixty, become a life member on payment of the aggregate amount of the regular annual dues for the period of life expectancy, as determined by standard actuarial tables, such membership to entitle the member to receive all yearbooks and to enjoy all other privileges of active membership in the Society for the lifetime of the member.

Section 2. *Termination of Membership.*

(a) The Board of Directors by affirmative vote of two-thirds of the members of the Board may suspend or expel a member for cause after appropriate hearing.

(b) Termination of membership for nonpayment of dues shall become effective as provided in Article XIV.

Section 3. *Reinstatement.* The Board of Directors may by the affirmation vote of two-thirds of the members of the Board reinstate a former member whose membership was previously terminated for cause other than nonpayment of dues.

Section 4. *Transfer of Membership.* Membership in this corporation is not transferable or assignable.

ARTICLE V

BOARD OF DIRECTORS

Section 1. *General Powers.* The business and affairs of the corporation shall be managed by its Board of Directors. It shall appoint the Chairman and Vice-Chairman of the Board of Directors, the Secretary-Treasurer, and Members of the Council. It may appoint a member to fill any vacancy on the Board until such vacancy shall have been filled by election as provided in Section 3 of this Article.

Section 2. *Number, Tenure, and Qualifications.* The Board of Directors shall consist of seven members, namely, six to be elected by the members of the corporation, and the Secretary-Treasurer to be the seventh member. Only active members who have contributed to the Yearbook shall be eligible for election to serve as directors. A member who has been elected for a full term of three years as director and has not attended at least two-thirds of the meetings duly called and held during that term shall not be eligible for election again before the fifth annual election after the expiration of the term for which he was first elected. No member who has been elected for two full terms as director in immediate succession shall be elected a director for a term next succeeding. This provision shall not apply to the Secretary-Treasurer who is appointed by the Board of Directors. Each director shall hold office for the term for which he is elected or appointed and until his successor shall have been selected and qualified. Directors need not be residents of Illinois.

Section 3. *Election.*

(*a*) The directors named in the Articles of Incorporation shall hold office until their successors shall have been duly selected and shall have qualified. Thereafter, two directors shall be elected annually to serve three years, beginning March first after their election. If, at the time of any annual election, a vacancy exists in the Board of Directors, a director shall be elected at such election to fill such vacancy.

(*b*) Elections of directors shall be held by ballots sent by United States mail as follows: A nominating ballot together with a list of members eligible to be directors shall be mailed by the Secretary-Treasurer to all active members of the corporation in October. From such list, the active members shall nominate on such ballot one eligible member for each of the two regular terms and for any vacancy to be filled and return such ballots to the office of the Secretary-Treasurer within twenty-one days after said date of mailing by the Secretary-Treasurer. The Secretary-Treasurer shall prepare an election ballot and place thereon in alphabetical order the names of persons equal to three times the number of offices to be filled, these persons to be those who received the highest number of votes on the nominating ballot, provided, however, that not more than one person connected with a given institution or agency shall be named on such final ballot, the person so named to be the one receiving the highest vote on the nominating ballot. Such election ballot shall be mailed by the Secretary-Treasurer to all active members in November next succeeding. The active members shall vote thereon for one member for each such office. Election ballots must be in the office of the Secretary-Treasurer within twenty-one days after the said date of mailing by the Secretary-Treasurer. The ballots shall be counted by the Secretary-Treasurer, or by an election committee, if any, appointed by the Board. The two members receiving the highest number of votes shall be declared elected for the regular term and the member or members receiving the next highest number of votes shall be declared elected for any vacancy or vacancies to be filled.

Section 4. *Regular Meetings.* A regular annual meeting of the Board of Directors shall be held, without other notice than this by-law, at the same place and as nearly as possible on the same date as the annual meeting of the corporation. The Board of Directors may provide the time and place, either within or without the State of Illinois, for the holding of additional regular meetings of the Board.

Section 5. *Special Meetings.* Special meetings of the Board of Directors may be called by or at the request of the Chairman or a majority of the directors. Such special meetings shall be held at the office of the corporation unless a majority of the directors agree upon a different place for such meetings.

Section 6. *Notice*. Notice of any special meeting of the Board of Directors shall be given at least fifteen days previously thereto by written notice delivered personally or mailed to each director at his business address, or by telegram. If mailed, such notice shall be deemed to be delivered when deposited in the United States mail in a sealed envelope so addressed, with postage thereon prepaid. If notice be given by telegram, such notice shall be deemed to be delivered when the telegram is delivered to the telegraph company. Any director may waive notice of any meeting. The attendance of a director at any meeting shall constitute a waiver of notice of such meeting, except where a director attends a meeting for the express purpose of objecting to the transaction of any business because the meeting is not lawfully called or convened. Neither the business to be transacted at, nor the purpose of, any regular or special meeting of the Board need be specified in the notice or waiver of notice of such meeting.

Section 7. *Quorum*. A majority of the Board of Directors shall constitute a quorum for the transaction of business at any meeting of the Board, provided, that if less than a majority of the directors are present at said meeting, a majority of the directors present may adjourn the meeting from time to time without further notice.

Section 8. *Manner of Acting*. The act of the majority of the directors present at a meeting at which a quorum is present shall be the act of the Board of Directors, except where otherwise provided by law or by these by-laws.

ARTICLE VI

THE COUNCIL

Section 1. *Appointment*. The Council shall consist of the Board of Directors, the Chairmen of the corporation's Yearbook and Research Committees, and such other active members of the corporation as the Board of Directors may appoint.

Section 2. *Duties*. The duties of the Council shall be to further the objects of the corporation by assisting the Board of Directors in planning and carrying forward the educational undertakings of the corporation.

ARTICLE VII

OFFICERS

Section 1. *Officers*. The officers of the corporation shall be a Chairman of the Board of Directors, a Vice-Chairman of the Board of Directors, and a Secretary-Treasurer. The Board of Directors, by resolution, may create additional offices. Any two or more offices may be held by the same person, except the offices of Chairman and Secretary-Treasurer.

Section 2. *Election and Term of Office.* The officers of the corporation shall be elected annually by the Board of Directors at the annual regular meeting of the Board of Directors, provided, however, that the Secretary-Treasurer may be elected for a term longer than one year. If the election of officers shall not be held at such meeting, such election shall be held as soon thereafter as conveniently may be. Vacancies may be filled or new offices created and filled at any meeting of the Board of Directors. Each officer shall hold office until his successor shall have been duly elected and shall have qualified or until his death or until he shall resign or shall have been removed in the manner hereinafter provided.

Section 3. *Removal.* Any officer or agent elected or appointed by the Board of Directors may be removed by the Board of Directors whenever in its judgment the best interests of the corporation would be served thereby, but such removal shall be without prejudice to the contract rights, if any, of the person so removed.

Section 4. *Chairman of the Board of Directors.* The Chairman of the Board of Directors shall be the principal officer of the corporation. He shall preside at all meetings of the members of the Board of Directors, shall perform all duties incident to the office of chairman of the Board of Directors and such other duties as may be prescribed by the Board of Directors from time to time.

Section 5. *Vice-Chairman of the Board of Directors.* In the absence of the Chairman of the Board of Directors or in the event of his inability or refusal to act, the Vice-Chairman of the Board of Directors shall perform the duties of the Chairman of the Board of Directors, and when so acting, shall have all the powers of and be subject to all the restrictions upon the Chairman of the Board of Directors. Any Vice-Chairman of the Board of Directors shall perform such other duties as from time to time may be assigned to him by the Board of Directors.

Section 6. *Secretary-Treasurer.* The Secretary Treasurer shall be the managing executive officer of the corporation. He shall: (*a*) keep the minutes of the meetings of the members and of the Board of Directors in one or more books provided for that purpose; (*b*) see that all notices are duly given in accordance with the provisions of these by-laws or as required by law; (*c*) be custodian of the corporate records and of the seal of the corporation and see that the seal of the corporation is affixed to all documents, the execution of which on behalf of the corporation under its seal is duly authorized in accordance with the provisions of these by-laws; (*d*) keep a register of the postoffice address of each member as furnished to the secretary-treasurer by such member; (*e*) in general perform all duties incident to the office of secretary and such other duties as from time to time may be assigned to him by the Chairman of the Board of Directors or by the Board of Directors. He shall also: (1) have charge and custody of and be responsible for all funds and securities of the corporation; receive and

give receipts for moneys due and payable to the corporation from any
source whatsoever, and deposit all such moneys in the name of the corporation in such banks, trust companies or other depositories as shall be selected
in accordance with the provisions of Article XI of these by-laws; (2) in
general perform all the duties incident to the office of Treasurer and such
other duties as from time to time may be assigned to him by the Chairman
of the Board of Directors or by the Board of Directors. The Secretary-
Treasurer shall give a bond for the faithful discharge of his duties in such
sum and with such surety or sureties as the Board of Directors shall determine, said bond to be placed in the custody of the Chairman of the
Board of Directors.

Article VIII

COMMITTEES

The Board of Directors, by appropriate resolution duly passed, may
create and appoint such committees for such purposes and periods of time
as it may deem advisable.

Article IX

PUBLICATIONS

Section 1. The corporation shall publish *The Yearbook of the National
Society for the Study of Education*, such supplements thereto, and such
other materials as the Board of Directors may provide for.

Section 2. *Names of Members.* The names of the active and honorary
members shall be printed in the Yearbook or, at the direction of the Board
of Directors, may be published in a special list.

Article X

ANNUAL MEETINGS

The corporation shall hold its annual meetings at the time and place of
the Annual Meeting of the American Association of School Administrators
of the National Education Association. Other meetings may be held when
authorized by the corporation or by the Board of Directors.

Article XI

CONTRACTS, CHECKS, DEPOSITS, AND GIFTS

Section 1. *Contracts.* The Board of Directors may authorize any officer
or officers, agent or agents of the corporation, in addition to the officers
so authorized by these by-laws to enter into any contract or execute and
deliver any instrument in the name of and on behalf of the corporation and
such authority may be general or confined to specific instances.

Section 2. *Checks, drafts, etc.* All checks, drafts, or other orders for the payment of money, notes, or other evidences of indebtedness issued in the name of the corporation, shall be signed by such officer or officers, agent or agents of the corporation and in such manner as shall from time to time be determined by resolution of the Board of Directors. In the absence of such determination of the Board of Directors, such instruments shall be signed by the Secretary-Treasurer.

Section 3. *Deposits.* All funds of the corporation shall be deposited from time to time to the credit of the corporation in such banks, trust companies, or other depositories as the Board of Directors may select.

Section 4. *Gifts.* The Board of Directors may accept on behalf of the corporation any contribution, gift, bequest, or device for the general purposes or for any special purpose of the corporation.

ARTICLE XII

BOOKS AND RECORDS

The corporation shall keep correct and complete books and records of account and shall also keep minutes of the proceedings of its members, Board of Directors, and committees having any of the authority of the Board of Directors, and shall keep at the registered or principal office a record giving the names and addresses of the members entitled to vote. All books and records of the corporation may be inspected by any member or his agent or attorney for any proper purpose at any reasonable time.

ARTICLE XIII

FISCAL YEAR

The fiscal year of the corporation shall begin on the first day of July in each year and end on the last day of June of the following year.

ARTICLE XIV

DUES

Section 1. *Annual Dues.* The annual dues for active members of the Society shall be determined by vote of the Board of Directors at a regular meeting duly called and held.

Section 2. *Election Fee.* An election fee of $1.00 shall be paid in advance by each applicant for active membership.

Section 3. *Payment of Dues.* Dues for each calendar year shall be payable in advance on or before the first day of January of that year. Notice of dues for the ensuing year shall be mailed to members at the time set for mailing the primary ballots.

Section 4. *Default and Termination of Membership.* Annual membership shall terminate automatically for those members whose dues remain unpaid after the first day of January of each year. Members so in default will be reinstated on payment of the annual dues plus a reinstatement fee of fifty cents.

ARTICLE XV

SEAL

The Board of Directors shall provide a corporate seal which shall be in the form of a circle and shall have inscribed thereon the name of the corporation and the words "Corporate Seal, Illinois."

ARTICLE XVI

WAIVER OF NOTICE

Whenever any notice whatever is required to be given under the provision of the General Not For Profit Corporation Act of Illinois or under the provisions of the Articles of Incorporation or the by-laws of the corporation, a waiver thereof in writing signed by the person or persons entitled to such notice, whether before or after the time stated therein, shall be deemed equivalent to the giving of such notice.

ARTICLE XVII

AMENDMENTS

Section 1. *Amendments by Directors.* The constitution and by-laws may be altered or amended at any meeting of the Board of Directors duly called and held, provided that an affirmative vote of at least five directors shall be required for such action.

Section 2. *Amendments by Members.* By petition of twenty-five or more active members duly filed with the Secretary-Treasurer, a proposal to amend the constitution and by-laws shall be submitted to all active members by United States mail together with ballots on which the members shall vote for or against the proposal. Such ballots shall be returned by United States mail to the office of the Secretary-Treasurer within twenty-one days after date of mailing of the proposal and ballots by the Secretary-Treasurer. The Secretary-Treasurer or a committee appointed by the Board of Directors for that purpose shall count the ballots and advise the members of the result. A vote in favor of such proposal by two-thirds of the members voting thereon shall be required for adoption of such amendment.

MINUTES OF THE ANNUAL MEETING OF THE SOCIETY

The 1963 meeting of the Society was held in the Traymore Room of the Traymore Hotel in Atlantic City at 3:30 P.M., Sunday, February 17, with Laurence D. Haskew presiding and with some three hundred members present.

The meeting is generally devoted to the presentation of Parts I and II of the yearbook. However, since Part II, *Child Psychology*, had been presented by its editor, Harold W. Stevenson, Director of the Institute for Child Development, University of Minnesota, on February 15 at a joint meeting (Chicago) with the American Association of Colleges of Teacher Education and the American Educational Research Association, only Part II, *The Impact and Improvement of School Testing Programs*, was presented. Warren G. Findley, Theodore W. Clymer, Merle M. Ohlsen, and Laurence D. Haskew participated in the program of the meeting, which was a joint meeting of the National Society and the American Association of School Administrators. The program of the presentation follows:

The Impact and Improvement of School Testing Programs
>
> Part II of the Society's Sixty-second Yearbook

Testing in Appraisal and Evaluation
>
> Warren G. Findley, Professor of Education, University of Georgia, and Editor of the Yearbook

Testing in Counseling and Guidance
>
> Merle M. Ohlsen, Associate Professor of Education, University of Illinois

Testing in the Classroom
>
> Theodore W. Clymer, Professor of Education, University of Minnesota

Discussion of Crucial Issues
>
> Laurence D. Haskew, Vice-Chancellor, University of Texas and Chairman of the Board of Directors of the National Society, speakers, and audience

SYNOPSIS OF THE PROCEEDINGS OF THE
BOARD OF DIRECTORS OF THE SOCIETY FOR 1963
I. Meeting of February 17-18, 1963

The Board of Directors met at 9:00 A.M. on February 17 in the Dennis Hotel (Atlantic City) with the following members present: Laurence D. Haskew (Chairman), Walter W. Cook, Stephen M. Corey, Edgar Dale, Robert J. Havighurst, Ralph W. Tyler, and Herman G. Richey (Secretary).

1. The Secretary reported that the election of members for the Board of Directors in December resulted in the election of John I. Goodlad and Paul A. Witty, each for a term of three years beginning March 1, 1963.

2. Officers for the Board of Directors for the year beginning March 1, 1963, were elected as follows: Mr. Dale, Chairman; Mr. Corey, Vice-Chairman; and Mr. Richey, Secretary.

3. The Secretary presented the midyear financial report and a statement concerning activities designed to increase the membership of the Society.

4. It was reported that, owing to unforseen and unavoidable circumstances, the yearbook (Part I, *Child Psychology*; Part II, *The Impact and Improvement of School Testing Programs*) could not be published before March or April.

5. The Board voted to increase the list price of Part I of the yearbook *(Child Psychology)* to compensate for publication costs which, owing to the size and the nature of the content of the volume, were larger than anticipated.

6. The Board approved the proposal for a yearbook on *Social Maladjustment among Youth* submitted by Mr. William W. Wattenberg, Wayne State University. Mr. Wattenberg's nominations for membership on the Committee (including Mr. Robert J. Havighurst of the Board of Directors) were approved. The Board directed the Secretary to make available for the use of Mr. Wattenberg and his committee funds needed for the preparation of the yearbook.

7. Progress reports were submitted on yearbooks in preparation: *Theories of Learning and Instruction* (Ernest R. Hilgard); *Behavioral Science and Educational Administration* (Daniel E. Griffiths); *Vocational Education* (Melvin E. Barlow); and *Art Education* (Reid Hastie). Reports indicated that all committees were either making normal progress of were ahead of schedule.

8. A number of proposals for yearbooks ("Developing Social Sciences in the High Schools," "Teaching Young People To Read and Speak," "Education in Foreign Countries," "National Currents in High-School English Instruction," "Outdoor Education," etc.) were discussed.

It was agreed to postpone action on all proposals until the next meeting of the Board.

II. Meeting of September 21-22, 1963

The Board of Directors met on September 21 (7:30 P.M.) and on September 22 (9:30 A.M.) in the Conrad Hilton Hotel in Chicago with the following members present: Edgar Dale (Chairman), Stephen M. Corey, John I. Goodlad, Ralph W. Tyler, Paul A. Witty, and Herman G. Richey (Secretary).

1. The members of the Board expressed their sympathy to the family of the late Walter W. Cook, a member and former Chairman of the Board of Directors, and their sorrow for the passing of an esteemed colleague and friend.

2. The Board voted to present Part II of the yearbook (Behavioral Science and Educational Administration) at Atlantic City on February 16, 1964. It was further agreed that Daniel E. Griffiths, editor of the yearbook; Sidney P. Marland, Jr., Superintendent of Schools, Pittsburgh; and Ralph W. Tyler, Director of the Center for the Study of Behavioral Sciences, should be asked to participate in the program.

3. The Board voted to schedule the annual meeting of the Society in Chicago on February 21, 1964.

4. The Board agreed that Mr. Richey should discuss with Dr. Pomeroy the possibility of a place on the program of the February meeting of the American Association of Colleges for Teacher Education for a discussion of Part I of the 1964 yearbook, *Theories of Learning and Instruction*. It was also agreed that Mr. Goodlad would negotiate with the National Society of College Teachers of Education with a view to obtaining its sponsorship of the proposed presentation. It was further agreed that, if a place for the presentation was made available, the Society would ask Professor Ernest R. Hilgard (Professor of Psychology, Stanford University, and Chairman of the committee for the preparation of the yearbook) to make the presentation.

5. The Board approved a proposal for a yearbook on the "Changing School." Mr. Goodlad was appointed chairman of the committee to prepare the yearbook. The Secretary was directed to make funds available to cover the expenses of the committee.

6. The Board asked Paul A. Witty to present a proposal for a yearbook on the exceptional child for discussion in February and for possible publication in 1967.

7. The Board asked Mr. Dale and Mr. Corey to undertake, with whatever assistance needed, the examination of the possibility and feasibility of a yearbook in the area of programmed instruction and other teaching aids. Mr. Dale and Mr. Corey were asked to make a tentative report at the February meeting.

8. Other proposals for yearbook on Adult Education, Behavioral Sciences in Education, Curriculum Development, etc., were discussed. It was agreed that these proposals should be further discussed at the February meeting.

9. The Secretary reported on finances, membership, and inventory. It was reported that the mailing lists and membership records were being transferred to IBM cards in order to take advantage of the installation of IBM machines by the Department of Education, University of Chicago.

10. Progress reports of committees preparing yearbooks were submitted: *Vocational Education* (Melvin E. Barlow, Chairman); *Art Education*, (Reid Hastie, Chairman); and *Social Maladjustment among Youth* (William W. Wattenberg, Chairman).

REPORT OF THE TREASURER OF THE SOCIETY

1962-63

RECEIPTS AND DISBURSEMENTS

Receipts:

Membership dues	$33,388.95
Sale of yearbooks	37,840.82
Interest and dividends	117.80
Miscellaneous	427.86
	$71,775.43

Disbursements:

Yearbooks:

Manufacturing	$31,733.35
Reprinting	10,851.98
Preparation	846.37
Meetings of Society and Board	2,159.92

Secretary's Office:

Editorial, secretarial, and clerical services	13,445.16
Supplies	3,214.12
Equipment	453.90

Miscellaneous:

Telephone and telegraph	2.09
Bank charges	44.30
Refunds and transfer of commercial orders	106.25
Chapter reprints (reclaimable from authors) and publications list	503.04
Filing fee	1.00
Insurance	298.40
Safe Deposit Box	4.00
Advertising	153.00
	$63,817.28

Cash in bank at beginning of year	$ 254.47
Excess of receipts over disbursements	7,958.15
Total cash on hand, June 30, 1963	$ 8,212.62
Transfer to savings account, University National Bank	5,000.00
Cash in checking account, June 30, 1963	$ 3,212.62

STATEMENT OF CASH AND SECURITIES
As of June 30, 1963

Cash:

University National Bank, Chicago, Illinois—

Checking account .... $ 3,212.62

Savings account 20,510.37

Securities: Cost

38 shares First National Bank of Boston, capital stock...... 1,063.97

Total assets $24,786.96

MEMBERS OF THE NATIONAL SOCIETY FOR THE STUDY OF EDUCATION

[This list includes all persons enrolled December 1, 1963, whether for 1963 or 1964. An asterisk (*) indicates Life Members of the Society.]

Aarestad, Amanda B., 1887 Gilmore Ave., Winona, Minn.
Aaron, Ira Edward, Col. of Educ., University of Georgia, Athens, Ga.
Abate, Harry, Board of Education, 607 Walnut Ave., Niagara Falls, N.Y.
Abbott, Frank C., Montana State University, Missoula, Mont.
Abbott, Samuel Lee, Jr., Plymouth Teachers College, Plymouth, N.H.
Abbott, Whitt K., Alice Robertson Junior High School, Muskogee, Okla.
Abel, Harold, Dept. of Human Develop., Univ. of Nebraska, Lincoln, Neb.
Abelson, Harold H., Sch. of Educ., New York City College, New York, N.Y.
Abraham, Willard, Arizona State University, Tempe, Ariz.
Abrahamson, Stephen, Sch. of Med., Univ. of So. Calif., Los Angeles, Calif.
Abramowitz, Mortimer J., Pub. Sch. 188, Queens, 218 Hartland Ave., Flushing, N.Y.
Acharlu, K. S., 1805 Temple Rd., Bangalore, India
Adair, Thelma C., 2 West 122nd St., New York, N.Y.
Adams, Mrs. Daisy Trice, 2637 Park Ave., Kansas City, Mo.
Adams, Donald K., Sch. of Educ., Syracuse Univ., Syracuse, N.Y.
Adams, Fern B., Office of Co. Supt. of Schls., Los Angeles, Calif.
Adams, Gloria T., Box 479, Cut Off, La.
Adams, Robert G., 594 Capell St., Oakland, Calif.
Adams, Mrs. Ruth R., Sch. of Educ., New York City College, New York, N.Y.
Adamson, Oral Victor, R.R. 5, Princeton Rd., Evansville, Ind.
Adatto, Albert, 14611 S.E. 15th, Bellevue, Wash.
Adelberg, Arthur J., Supt., Schl. Dist. #3, Elmhurst, Ill.
Adell, James C., 16723 Fernway Rd., Shaker Heights, Ohio
Aden, Robert C., 2509 Glenwood Lane, Denton, Tex.
Adkisson, D. F., City Public Schools, Bristol, Tenn.
Adler, Mrs. Leona K., 101 Central Park W., New York, N.Y.
Adolphsen, Louis J., 830—58th St., Hinsdale, Ill.
Adrian, Robert J., St. John's University, Jamaica, N.Y.
Ahee, Carl R., 30831 Casilina Dr., Palos Verdes Estates, Calif.
Ahrnsbrak, Henry C., 1121 Grand Ave., Wausau, Wis.
Akins, Harold S., 1300 High St., Wichita, Kan.
Alberg, Gary L., 15 S. Lexington St., St. Paul, Minn.
Albohm, John C., Supt. of Schools, Alexandria, Va.
Albrecht, Milton C., University of Buffalo, Buffalo, N.Y.
Albright, Frank S., 37 Yale Terrace, West Orange, N.J.
Alcorn, Marvin D., 4808 Atlanta Dr., San Diego, Calif.
Alden, L. Elizabeth, State University of Iowa, Iowa City, Iowa
Aldrich, Julian C., Sch. of Educ., New York Univ., New York, N.Y.
Alexander, William M., Col. of Educ., Univ. of Florida, Gainesville, Fla.
Allen, Beatrice Ona, 5347 N. Wayne Ave., Chicago, Ill.
Allen, David, 8437 Truxton Ave., Los Angeles, Calif.
Allen, Dwight W., Sch. of Educ., Stanford University, Stanford, Calif.
Allen, Edward E., Akron Central School, Akron, N.Y.
Allen, James Robert, 1249 Lake Ave., Fort Wayne, Ind.
Allen, Ross L., State University College of Education, Cortland, N.Y.
Allen, Russell L., Clark County Schools, Jeffersonville, Ind.

Allen, Warren G., State Teachers College, Minot, N.D.
Allen, William H., 1355 Inverness Dr., Pasadena, Calif.
Allison, Preston B., Box 789, College Sta., Hammond, La.
Allman, Reva White, Alabama State College, Montgomery, Ala.
Alm, Richard S., Dept. of Educ., University of Hawaii, Honolulu, Hawaii
Almcrantz, Mrs. Georgia, 402 Brown Circle, Knox, Ind.
Almroth, Frank S., 20 Hilltop Ter., Packanack Lake, Wayne, N.J.
Alt, Pauline M., Central Connecticut State College, New Britain, Conn.
Alt, Weston M., Rt. 5, Box 5174, Oroville, Calif.
Altman, Herbert H., 832 Ocean Ave., Brooklyn, N.Y.
Amar, Wesley F., Kelvyn Park High School, Chicago, Ill.
Ambrose, Edna V., 2124 N.E. 7th Ter., Gainesville, Fla.
Amershek, Kathleen, Dept. of Stud. Tchg., Univ. of Minnesota, Minneapolis, Minn.
Ames, John L., Queens College, Kissena Blvd., Flushing, N.Y.
Amidon, Edna P., 4001 North 26th St., Arlington, Va.
Anders, Mrs. Elizabeth M., 3601 Palm Dr., Riviera Beach, Fla.
Andersen, Dan W., 425 Merrill Crest Dr., Madison, Wis.
Anderson, Archibald W., Col. of Educ., Univ. of Illinois, Urbana, Ill.
Anderson, Bernard, John Spry Elementary School, Chicago, Ill.
Anderson, Clarence K., Amundsen High School, Chicago, Ill.
Anderson, Donald G., Oakland Public Schls., 1025 Second Ave., Oakland, Calif.
Anderson, Edmond C., George W. Carver Sch., 3701 Greenleaf St., Dallas, Tex.
Anderson, Ernest M., Kansas State Teachers College, Pittsburg, Kan.
Anderson, Floydelh, West Virginia State College, Institute, W.Va.
Anderson, G. Lester, University of Buffalo, Buffalo, N.Y.
Anderson, Harold, Wausau Public Schools, Wausau, Wis.
Anderson, Harold A., Dept. of Educ., University of Chicago, Chicago, Ill.
Anderson, Harold H., 340 Wildwood Ave., East Lansing, Mich.
Anderson, Howard R., Houghton Mifflin Co., Boston, Mass.
Anderson, Isabel C., Sch. of Educ., Temple University, Philadelphia, Pa.
Anderson, Jack O., 3181 Alca St., Pontiac, Mich.
Anderson, J. Paul, Col. of Educ., Univ. of Maryland, College Park, Md.
Anderson, James W., 742 Ashland Ave., St. Paul Park, Minn.
Anderson, Kenneth E., Sch. of Educ., Univ. of Kansas, Lawrence, Kan.
Anderson, Lester W., 4017 University High Sch., Ann Arbor, Mich.
Anderson, Marion A., Ginn & Co., Statler Office Bldg., Boston, Mass.
Anderson, Philip S., Wisconsin State College, River Falls, Wis.
Anderson, Robert Henry, Longfellow Hall, Harvard Univ., Cambridge, Mass.
Anderson, Ruth, 372 Central Park West, New York, N.Y.
Anderson, Stuart A., Niles Twp. High School, Skokie, Ill.
Anderson, Vernon E., Col. of Educ., University of Maryland, College Park, Md.
Anderson, Virginia, Col. of Educ., University of Arizona, Tucson, Ariz.
Anderson, Walter A., Sch. of Educ., New York University, New York, N.Y.
Andes, J. D., San Mateo City School District, San Mateo, Calif.
Andree, R. G., Rich Twp. High School, Park Forest, Ill.
Andregg, Neal B., 2553 Richmond Hill Rd., Augusta, Ga.
Andrews, Clay S., Dept. of Educ., San Jose State College, San Jose, Calif.
Andrews, Stella F., 83 Alexander Ave., Yonkers, N.Y.
Andrews, Wendell B., Public Schools, 108 Union St., Schenectady, N.Y.
Angelini, Arrigo L., University of Sao Paulo, Sao Paulo, Brazil
Angelino, Henry, Col. of Educ., University of Oklahoma, Norman, Okla.
Angell, George W., State University College, Plattsburg, N.Y.
Angelo, Mark V., Siena College, Loudonville, N.Y.
Ankeney, Margaret E., Eastern Kentucky State Col., Richmond, Ky.
Annis, Helen W., 6711 Conway Ave., Takoma Park, Md.
Ansel, James O., Western Michigan University, Kalamazoo, Mich.
Anslem, Karl R., 1105F—Sixth St., Albany, Calif.
Anthony, Elsa J., 44 Mill St., New Britain, Conn.
Apple, Joe A., San Diego State College, San Diego, Calif.
Appleton, David, City Public Schools, Conway, N.H.
Archer, Clifford P., 1381 N. Cleveland Ave., St. Paul, Minn.

Archer, Marguerite P., 137 Highbrook Ave., Pelham, N.Y.
Archer, N. Sidney, Dept. of Public Instruction, Harrisburg, Pa.
Armstrong, J. Niel, Sch. of Educ., Agric. & Tech. College, Greensboro, N.C.
Armogida, Harry, Dept. of Educ., Miami University, Oxford, Ohio
Arnaud, E. E., Our Lady of the Lake College, San Antonio, Tex.
Arnesen, Arthur E., 440 East First South St., Salt Lake City, Utah
Arnold, Dorothea, Western Michigan College, Kalamazoo, Mich.
Arnold, Eugene R., P.O. Box 308, Wilberforce, Ohio
Arnold, Gala, 740 "J" Ave., Coronado, Calif.
Arnold, J. E., Box 8540, University Station, Knoxville, Tenn.
Arnold, Marshall, 702 Greenlawn, Bowling Green, Ky.
Arnold, Phyllis D., 628 Patterson Ave., San Antonio, Tex.
Arnold, Roy W., Jr., Dept. of Educ., State University College, New Paltz, N.Y.
Arnold, William E., Sch. of Educ., Univ. of Pennsylvania, Philadelphia, Pa.
Arnsdorf, Val, Sch. of Educ., University of California, Berkeley, Calif.
Arnstein, George E., NEA Journal, 1201—16th St., N.W., Washington, D.C.
Aronfreed, Justin, Dept. of Psych., Univ. of Pennsylvania, Philadelphia, Pa.
Artley, A. Sterl., 213 Hill Hall, University of Missouri, Columbia, Mo.
Arveson, Raymond G., 38060 Logan Dr., Fremont, Calif.
Ashbaugh, H. B., Superintendent of Schools, Vermillion, S.D.
Ashe, Robert W., Dept. of Educ., Arizona State University, Tempe, Ariz.
Ashland, Homer B., Superintendent of Schools, Rutland, Vt.
Atkins, Neil P., Court Rd., Bedford, N.Y.
Atkinson, William N., Jackson Junior College, Jackson, Mich.
Auble, Donavon, Western College for Women, Oxford, Ohio
Aubrey, Roger F., Gen. Patton School, Riverdale, Ill.
Auer, B. F., 601 Cadiz Rd., Wintersville, Ohio
Aurand, Wayne O., 904 Columbia Dr., Cedar Falls, Iowa
Austin, David B., Tchrs. Col., Columbia University, New York, N.Y.
Austin, Martha Lou, University of Southern Florida, Tampa, Fla.
Austin, Mary C., 2263 Demington Dr., Cleveland, Ohio
Austin, Roy S., 300 Pompton Rd., Wayne, N.J.
Ausubel, David P., Col. of Educ., Univ. of Illinois, Champaign, Ill.
Auzenne, Mrs. Anita D., Box 225, Grambling, La.
Avegno, T. Sylvia, Sch. of Educ., Fordham University, New York, N.Y.
Ayer, Joseph C., Withrow High School, Cincinnati, Ohio

Babcock, Dorothy Boyeé, 2740 Alvingroom Ct., Oakland, Calif.
Bachar, James R., 6419 Kentucky Ave., Pittsburgh, Pa.
Bachman, Glen, Dept. of Educ., Yankton College, Yankton, S.D.
Bachman, Ralph V., South High School, Salt Lake City, Utah
Backus, Thomas A., 570—115th Ave., Treasure Island, Fla.
Bacon, William P., AF-ROTC, Kansas State University, Manhattan, Kan.
Bahn, Lorene A., Dept. of Educ., Washington Univ., St. Louis, Mo.
Bahner, John M., 89 Page Rd., Bedford, Mass.
Bailer, Joseph R., Dept. of Educ., Western Maryland College, Westminster, Md.
Bailey, Lucile, Wm. T. Machan Sch., 2140 E. Virginia St., Phoenix, Ariz.
Bair, Medill, Carmel Univ. School Dist., Carmel, Calif.
Baird, Forrest J., San Jose State College, San Jose, Calif.
Baker, Bradley, 210 Ormond Ave., Indialantic, Melborne, Fla.
Baker, Charles R., Star Route, Mountain Ranch, Calif.
Baker, Eugene H., 6855 N. Crawford Ave., Lincolnwood, Ill.
Baker, G. Derwood, Sch. of Educ., New York University, New York, N.Y.
Baker, H. Leigh, 2040 Thackery Rd., Manhattan, Kan.
Baker, Harry J., 19050 Wiltshire, Lathrup Village, Mich.
Baker, I. D., Greenville College, Greenville, Ill.
Baker, Rebecca, Southern Illinois University, Carbondale, Ill.
Baker, Robert E., Sch. of Educ., George Washington Univ., Washington, D.C.
Balassi, S. J., Patersen College, Wayne, N.J.
Baldwin, Lee E., Superintendent, Union High Sch. Dist. No. 2, Burns, Ore.
Baldwin, Rollin, 924 West End Ave., New York, N.Y.

Balian, Arthur, 6804 W. Dickinson St., Milwaukee, Wis.
Ball, George G., State College of Iowa, Cedar Falls, Iowa
Ballam, Oral L., Cache County School District, Logan, Utah
Ballantine, Francis A., San Diego State College, San Diego, Calif.
Baller, Warren R., University of Nebraska, Lincoln, Neb.
Ballou, Stephen V., Div. of Educ., Fresno State College, Fresno, Calif.
Balzer, David M., Pennsylvania State University, University Park, Pa.
Banner, Carolyn, 409 Lafayette, Jefferson City, Mo.
Bannon, Michael F., Pennsylvania State College, West Chester, Pa.
Bany, Mary, 411 N. Third St., Alhambra, Calif.
Baratta, Anthony N., Sch. of Educ., Fordham University, New York, N.Y.
Barbe, Richard H., Sch. of Educ., University of Delaware, Newark, Del.
Barbe, Walter B., Kent State University, Kent, Ohio
Barber, Anson B., Sch. of Educ., Duquesne Univ., Pittsburgh, Pa.
Barber, Grant W., 1251 Shipman St., Birmingham, Mich.
Barber, Richard L., University of Louisville, Belknap Campus, Louisville, Ky.
Barclay, Allan G., Dept. of Psych., St. Louis Univ., St. Louis, Mo.
Bardellini, Justin M., 121 Warwick Dr., Walnut Creek, Calif.
Barlow, John A., Dept. of Psych., Emory Univ., Atlanta, Ga.
Barlow, Melvin L., Univ. of California, 405 Hilgard Ave., Los Angeles, Calif.
Barnard, J. Darrell, 16 Links Drive, Great Neck, N.Y.
Barnes, Cyrus W., Beachlake, Pa.
Barnes, Elinor A., 253 Bridge St., Corning, N.Y.
Barnes, Fred P., Col. of Educ., University of Illinois, Urbana, Ill.
Barnes, Melvin W., Superintendent of Schools, Portland, Ore.
Barney, E. Martin, Barrington College, Barrington, R.I.
Barr, Charlotte A., Chicago Teachers College, Chicago, Ill.
Barr, Dixon A., Laboratory Sch., Eastern Kentucky State Col., Richmond, Ky.
Barrett, James H., Southern Colorado State Col., Pueblo, Colo.
Barros, Raymond, Catholic University of Valparaiso, Valparaiso, Chile
Barry, Florence G., 5956 Race Ave., Chicago, Ill.
Bartel, Lorena, Franklin School, 401 Military Rd., Fond du Lac, Wis.
Bartels, Mrs. Isabella, 3224 Fairway Dr., Dayton, Ohio
Barter, Alice, 4625 Booth Rd., Oxford, Ohio
Bartley, Imon, Drake University, Des Moines, Iowa
Barton, Carl L., Superintendent, Community Cons. Sch. Dist. 70, Freeburg, Ill.
Barton, George E., Jr., Tulane University, New Orleans, La.
Bartz, Amelia I., 2028 Webb St., Stockton, Calif.
Batho, Marshall G., 10236 S. Homan Ave., Evergreen Park, Ill.
Batinich, Mrs. Mary Ellen, 9215 S. Troy Ave., Evergreen Park, Ill.
Battle, John A., 11 Jones St., New Hyde Park, N.Y.
Baugher, James K., 132 W. 6th Ave., Roselle, N.J.
Baughman, Shirley, Westminster College, Salt Lake City, Utah
Baum, Paul B., La Verne College, La Verne, Calif.
Baumann, Margaret L., 1856 Sherman Ave., Evanston, Ill.
Baumgartner, Reuben A., Senior High School, Freeport, Ill.
Baumgartner, Rolla W., 749—30th St., South Bend, Ind.
Baxter, Marlin B., Moline Public Schools, 1619 Eleventh Ave., Moline, Ill.
Bayer, Les, Concordia College, Austin, Tex.
Beach, Lowell W., 1408 Univ. Elem. Sch., Univ. of Michigan, Ann Arbor, Mich.
Beachem, Katherine, 211 N. Manheim Blvd., New Paltz, N.Y.
Beahm, W. I., Donegal Area Joint Sch. Sys., Mount Joy, Pa.
Beaird, Roberta E., 3727 Sheridan Blvd., Lincoln, Neb.
Beamer, George C., North Texas State College, Denton, Tex.
Bear, David E., Southern Illinois University, Alton, Ill.
Beard, Richard L., 1621 Bruce Ave., Charlottesville, Va.
Beasley, Mrs. Eleanor C., 278 Ocean Ave., Portland, Me.
Beaton, Daniel W., Educ. Improv. Centre, 11669 Santa Monica, Los Angeles, Calif.
Beattie, Alfred W., 5501 Grubbs Rd., Gibsonia, Pa.
Beattie, George W., P.O. Box 100, Aptos, Calif.
Beatty, Walcott H., 209 Kensington Way, San Francisco, Calif.

Beaty, Betty, Tchrs. Col., University of Cincinnati, Cincinnati, Ohio
Beaubier, Edward W., 2431 Rockinghorse Rd., San Pedro, Calif.
Beauchamp, George A., Sch. of Educ., Northwestern University, Evanston, Ill.
Beaumont, Urville J., Tenney High School, Methuen, Mass.
Beaver, Eugene H., Roosevelt High School, 3436 Wilson Ave., Chicago, Ill.
Bebb, Randall R., State College of Iowa, Cedar Falls, Iowa
Bebell, Clifford S., Grad. Sch. of Educ., Rutgers Univ., New Brunswick, N.J.
Beck, Hubert Park, Sch. of Educ., City College, 523 W. 121st St., New York, N.Y.
Beck, Hugo E., Dept. of Educ., Univ. of Chicago, Chicago, Ill.
Beck, John M., 5832 Stony Island Ave., Chicago, Ill.
Beck, Norman W., Supt., Monroe County Schls., Waterloo, Ill.
Beck, Ralph Lea, Bowling Green State University, Bowling Green, Ohio
Beck, Robert H., 233 Burton Hall, University of Minnesota, Minneapolis, Minn.
Becker, George, 1100 Elm Ave., Brooklyn, N.Y.
Becker, Harry A., Superintendent of Schools, Norwalk, Conn.
Becker, Millie A., 7637 S. Loomis Blvd., Chicago, Ill.
Bedell, Ralph, Office of Educ., Dept. of H.E.W., Washington, D.C.
Beebe, Nelson, Jr., Pennsville Memorial High School, Pennsville, N.J.
Beggs, David W., III, University High School, Bloomington, Ind.
Behal, Rose, 9812 Broadview Rd., Brecksville, Ohio
Behrens, Herman D., 811 S. Johnson St., Ada, Ohio
* Behrens, Minnie S., 901 Sherman Ave., Denver, Colo.
Beiderman, David D., Dept. of Educ., Chico State Col., Chico, Calif.
Beitler, Roger T., Merrill Hall, Kent State Univ., Kent, Ohio
Belcher, Eddie W., Louisville Public Schls., 501 W. Hill St., Louisville, Ky.
Bell, Arthur P., Agricultural and Technical Col., Greensboro, N.C.
Bell, Dorothy M., Bradford Junior College, Bradford, Mass.
Bell, Keith A., 3155 S.W. Grace Lane, Portland, Ore.
Bell, Millard D., Superintendent of Schools, 738 Tenth St., Wilmette, Ill.
Bell, Richard H., Radio-TV Section, Univ. of Colorado, Boulder, Colo.
Bell, Robert N., 2819 W. Sherwin Ave., Chicago, Ill.
Bell, Wilmer V., 702 Kingston Rd., Baltimore, Md.
Bellack, Arno A., Tchrs. Col., Columbia University, New York, N.Y.
Bemis, Eaton O., Millikan High School, 2800 Snowden Ave., Long Beach, Calif.
Bemis, James R., 19041 Tango Ave., Yorba Linda, Calif.
Benben, John S., New York University, Washington Sq., New York, N.Y.
Benda, Harold, Educ. Dept., West Chester State College, West Chester, Pa.
Bengston, L. H., Minnehaha Academy, Minneapolis, Minn.
Bennett, Doris, Jacksonville State College, Jacksonville, Ala.
Bennett, Robert N., Greene Central School, Greene, N.Y.
Bennett, William R., Olivet Nazarene College, Kankakee, Ill.
Bennie, William A., 4803 Balcones Dr., Austin, Tex.
Bentall, Grace, 4712 S.E. River Dr., Portland, Ore.
Bentivegna, Joseph J., St. Francis College, Loretto, Pa.
Bentley, Harold, Northern Essex Community Col., Haverhill, Mass.
Bentley, Mrs. Harriett P., 2985 Wooster Rd., Rocky River, Ohio
Benyon, Robert P., Div. of Research, State Dept. of Education, Columbus, Ohio
Beran, D. L., USAID/RC, APO 676, New York, N.Y.
Berg, Arthur D., 5117 Reuter St., Dearborn, Mich.
Berg, Pauline G., Odebolt, Iowa
Berg, Selmer H., 240 Leimert Blvd., Oakland, Calif.
Berge, Marvin L., Superintendent of Schools, DeKalb, Ill.
Bergen, Morris C., Whittier Area Jr. Col. Dist., Whittier, Calif.
Bergeson, Clarence O., Pennsylvania State University, University Park, Pa.
Berggren, T. N., Bd. of Educ., City School Dist., Shaker Heights, Ohio
Berkihise, Frances, Evangel College, Springfield, Mo.
Berkowitz, Edward, 2 Loretta Dr., Syosset, L.I., N.Y.
Berlin, Pearl W., Wayne State University, Detroit, Mich.
Berlin, Robert S., 383 Grand St., New York, N.Y.
Bernard, Alpha E., State Teachers College, Clarion, Pa.
Bernard, Harold W., 1985 S.W. Warwick Ave., Portland, Ore.

Bernd, John M., Col. of Educ., Wayne State University, Detroit, Mich.
Bernstein, Abbot A., Children's Bureau, Columbia Ave. & Van Buren St.,
    Passaic, N.J.
Bernstein, Norman, State University College, Buffalo, N.Y.
Bernstein, Abraham, Dept. of Educ., Brooklyn College, Brooklyn, N.Y.
Berry, Henry W., P.O. Box 266, Normal, Ala.
Berry, John R., Sch. of Educ., University of Miami, Coral Gables, Fla.
Berryman, Charles, Col. of Educ., University of Georgia, Athens, Ga.
Berson, Mrs. Minnie, 311 Orchard Hills, S.E., Grand Rapids, Mich.
Bertermann, Helen A., 1339 Cryer Ave., Cincinnati, Ohio
Bertness, Henry J., 3701 N. Adams, Tacoma, Wash.
Bertrand, John R., Berry College, Mt. Berry, Ga.
Best, Mrs. Drusilla, 1148—8th Ave., S.W., Faribault, Minn.
Bettelheim, Bruno, 1365 E. 6oth St., Chicago, Ill.
Bettencourt, Mildred, Dept. of Educ., Texas Tech. College, Lubbock, Tex.
Better, Morris, Los Angeles State College, Los Angeles, Calif.
Betts, Emmett A., Sch. of Educ., University of Miami, Coral Gables, Fla.
Bevan, Harold Todd, University of San Francisco, San Francisco, Calif.
Beyer, Fred C., Superintendent of County Schools, Modesto, Calif.
Bickel, Lawrence G., Concordia Teachers College, Seward, Neb.
Bidstrup, Anna, Baker Ranch, Foresthill, Calif.
Bieber, Mrs. Ida P., 7357 Cornell Ave., University City, Mo.
Bigelow, Karl W., Tchrs. Col., Columbia University, New York, N.Y.
* Bigelow, M. A., Litchfield, Conn.
Bigelow, Roy G., Mississippi Southern College, Hattiesburg, Miss.
Biggs, Sarah Dorothy, 804 Court, Fulton, Mo.
Biggy, M. Virginia, 10 Alcott St., Acton, Mass.
Bigsbee, Earle M., Junior College of Connecticut, Bridgeport, Conn.
Bilhorn, J. Chester, 3846 N. Kedvale Ave., Chicago, Ill.
* Billig, Florence G., 2008 Melrose St., Rockford, Ill.
Billington, Lillian, San Jose College, San Jose, Calif.
Bills, Mark W., Superintendent of Schools, Peoria, Ill.
Bilterman, Kathryn Smith, 3445 Ybarra Rd., Spring Valley, Calif.
Binford, George H., Central High School, Charlotte Courthouse, Va.
Binford, Linwood T., J. Andrew Bowler School, Richmond, Va.
Bingham, Alma, Portland State College, Portland, Ore.
Birch, Tom, 20 Alexander Ave., White Plains, N.Y.
Bird, A. O., Superintendent of Schools, Gonzales, Tex.
Bird, Charles A., 23 Fraser Pl., Hastings on Hudson, N.Y.
Birkmaier, Emma Marie, Col. of Educ., Univ. of Minnesota, Minneapolis, Minn.
Bishop, Clifford L., State College of Iowa, Cedar Falls, Iowa
Bishop, Martha D., Dept. of Educ., Winthrop College, Rock Hill, S.C.
Bishop, W. E., Superintendent of Schools, Englewood, Colo.
Bjork, Alton J., Dept. of Educ., Univ. of North Dakota, Grand Forks, N.D.
Black, Hugh C., Dept. of Educ., Univ. of California, Davis, Calif.
Black, Leo P., Office of Instructional Services, State Office Bldg., Denver, Colo.
Black, Mrs. Marian W., Sch. of Educ., Florida State Univ., Tallahassee, Fla.
Black, Millard H., 10031 Vecino Lane, La Habra, Calif.
Blackburn, Cleo W., 146 E. Washington St., Indianapolis, Ind.
Blackburn, Clifford S., North Texas University, Denton, Tex.
Blackledge, Mrs. Helen V., Southern Heights School, 950 Fairfax, Fort Wayne,
    Ind.
Blackman, Charles A., 361 Educ. Bldg., Michigan State University, East Lansing,
    Mich.
Blackshear, John S., 3066 Bethune Ave., Macon, Ga.
Blackwell, Lewis F., Jr., Box 1026, University, Ala.
Blaine, Russell K., 1816 Park Ave., S.E., Cedar Rapids, Iowa
Blanchard, Marion U., 190 E. Mosholy Pkwy., So., New York, N.Y.
Blank, Stanley S., 853 Vermont St., Oakland, Calif.
Blanke, Virgil E., Superintendent of Schools, Massillon, Ohio
Blankenship, A. H., Superintendent of Schools, Gary, Ind.

Blanton, Roy R., Jr., Appalachian High School, Boone, N.C.
Blessington, John P., Whitby School, Greenwich, Conn.
Bliesmer, Emery P., McGuffy Read. Clinic, Univ. of Virginia, Charlottesville, Va.
Bligh, Harold F., 81 Lincoln Ave., Ardsley, N.Y.
Blodgett, Darrell R., Superintendent of Schools, Wheaton, Ill.
Blomenberg, Gilbert, 345 North 2nd St., Seward, Neb.
Blommers, Paul, East Hall, State University of Iowa, Iowa City, Iowa
Blomquist, Maryls, 3231 Aquila Lane, St. Louis Park, Minn.
Bloom, Royal F., Bethel College, St. Paul, Minn.
Bloomer, Richard H., Sch. of Educ., University of Connecticut, Storrs, Conn.
Boario, Dora A., 422 Third St., Leechburg, Pa.
Bodkin, Raymond C., Southampton High School, Courtland, Va.
Bock, R. Darrell, University of North Carolina, Chapel Hill, N.C.
Boeck, Clarence H., 5101 Ewing Ave., So., Minneapolis, Minn.
Boenig, Robert W., State University College of Education, Fredonia, N.Y.
Boger, D. L., Morehouse College, Atlanta, Ga.
Boggs, Doyle W., Hartsville High School, Hartsville, S.C.
Bogle, Frank P., Superintendent of Schools, Millville, N.J.
Bohlander, Frank M., 109 S. Third St., Arkansas City, Kan.
Boland, Michael P., St. Joseph's College, 54th & City Line, Philadelphia, Pa.
Bolton, Dale L., Dept. of Educ., Univ. of Washington, Seattle, Wash.
* Bolton, Frederick E., 4514—16th Ave., N.E., Seattle, Wash.
Bonar, Hugh S., Lewis College, Joliet, Ill.
Bond, George W., R.F.D. 2, Box 444B, New Paltz, N.Y.
Bond, Horace M., Sch. of Educ., Atlanta University, Atlanta, Ga.
Bondley, G. B., 1406 Griffith Ave, Las Vegas, Nev.
Bonk, Edward C., North Texas University, Denton, Tex.
Bonsall, Marcella Ryser, 137 Warwick Pl., South Pasadena, Calif.
Booker, Mrs. Ann, 1388 Prospect Ave., Bronx, N.Y.
Booker, Ivan A., N.E.A., 1201 Sixteenth St., N.W., Washington, D.C.
Bookwalter, Karl W., Indiana University, Bloomington, Ind.
Booth, Delores C., 6604 Tremont St., Oakland, Calif.
Borg, Robert L., Scott Hall, University of Minnesota, Minneapolis, Minn.
Bormuth, John R., 10635 Cushdon Ave., Los Angeles, Calif.
Bossard, Grace, Route 3, Box 6, Seaford, Del.
Bossier, Antonia M., 1661 No. Roman St., New Orleans, La.
Bossing, Nelson L., Col. of Educ., Southern Ill. Univ., Carbondale, Ill.
Bothell, John E., Colorado State College, Greeley, Colo.
Bottino, Louis F., Joliet Public Schools, Joliet, Ill.
Bottrell, Harold R., Col. of Educ., University of Houston, Houston, Tex.
Bouchard, John B., State Teachers College, Fredonia, N.Y.
Boula, James A., Office of Public Instrn., State Office Bldg., Springfield, Ill.
Bower, Robert K., 1905 E. Loma Alta Dr., Altadena, Calif.
Bowers, Norman D., Sch. of Educ., Northwestern Univ., Evanston, Ill.
Bowman, George A., Kent State University, Kent, Ohio
Bowyer, Vernon, 225 Millbridge Rd., Riverside, Ill.
Boyajy, Robert J., 154 Park Ave., West Caldwell, N.J.
Boyce, Floyd A., 3316 Scenic Dr., Austin, Tex.
Boyd, Laurence E., Sch. of Educ., Atlanta University, Atlanta, Ga.
Boyd, Rachel E., Cecil County Board of Education, Elkton, Md.
Boykin, Leander L., Florida A. & M. University, Tallahassee, Fla.
Boylston, Marie G., Portland State College, Portland, Ore.
Bozeman, Herman H., Virginia State College, Norfolk, Va.
Braam, L. S., Syracuse Univ. Reading Center, 508 Univ. Pl., Syracuse, N.Y.
Bracewell, George, Southern Illinois University, Carbondale, Ill.
Bradtmueller, Weldon G., Univ. of Mich. Flint College, Flint, Mich.
Brady, Elizabeth H., 9218 Shoshone Ave., Northridge, Calif.
Brady, Florence A., 186 Oakland Rd., Maplewood, N.J.
Brady, John C., Bemidji State College, Bemidji, Minn.
Bragdon, Clifford R., 41 Harrison Ave., Northampton, Mass.
Brainard, Lois, San Jose State College, San Jose, Calif.

Brandsmeier, Elvira, 2236—4th St. "A", East Moline, Ill.
Brandt, Harry A., Menaul School, 301 Menaul Blvd., N.E., Albuquerque, N.M.
Brandt, Willard J., University of Wisconsin-Milwaukee, Milwaukee, Wis.
Branom, Wayne T., Superintendent of Schools, Hillside, N.J.
Brantley, Mabel, 343 Linden Pl., DeKalb, Ill.
Brauer, Walter L., Rufus King High School, Milwaukee, Wis.
Braum, Gertrude, Danbury State College, Danbury, Conn.
Braun, Frank, Burton Hall, University of Minnesota, Minneapolis, Minn.
Breaux, Jerome E., 244 Aurora Ave., Metairie, La.
Breen, Lelwyn C., 1314 Wright, Richland, Wash.
Bregman, Mrs. Sydell, 17 Bodnarik Dr., Fords, N.J.
Brehm, Mrs. Marie E., 10187 Toelle Lane, St. Louis, Mo.
Breihan, Edna, 920 Madison St., Lockport, Ill.
Brener, Mrs. Olga, Lincoln Elem. School, Shawano, Wis.
Brenner, Anton, Merrill-Palmer School, 71 Ferry E., Detroit, Mich.
Bresina, Bertha M., Arizona State University, Tempe, Ariz.
Breslin, Frederick D., Glassboro State College, Glassboro, N.J.
Bretsch, Howard S., Sch. of Educ., University of Michigan, Ann Arbor, Mich.
Bretz, Frank H., 1999 Arlington Ave., Columbus, Ohio
Brewer, Curtis E., Superintendent of Schools, DeSoto, Mo.
Breyfogle, Mary E., R. 1, Box G, Hazelwood, Mo.
Brickman, Benjamin, Dept. of Educ., Brooklyn College, Brooklyn, N.Y.
Brickman, William W., University of Pennsylvania, Philadelphia, Pa.
Bridges, C. M., Col. of Educ., University of Oklahoma, Norman, Okla.
Bridges, Mrs. Julia W., 110 West End Ave., Westwood, N.J.
Bridges, Lonnie H., Box 10194, Southern University, Baton Rouge, La.
Bridges, Raymond H., Box 10194, Southern University, Baton Rouge, La.
Brigham, Bruce W., 909 Edgewood Rd., Havertown, Pa.
Bright, John H., 628 Cuesta Ave., San Mateo, Calif.
* Bright, Orville T., 516½ Prospect Ave., Lake Bluff, Ill.
Bright, Walter W., Superintendent of Schools, Escanaba, Mich.
Brimhall, Mrs. Alice, 111 Monticello Ave., Piedmont, Calif.
Briner, Conrad, Claremont University College, Claremont, Calif.
Brink, William G., Sch. of Educ., Northwestern University, Evanston, Ill.
Brinkman, A. John, 9929 S. Maplewood Ave., Chicago, Ill.
Brinkman, Albert R., Superintendent of Schools, Dobbs Ferry, N.Y.
Brinkmeier, Oria, 2203 Carter Ave., St. Paul, Minn.
Brish, William M., Superintendent of Schools, Washington County, Hagerstown,
    Md.
Brislawn, Maurice J., 1508—25th Ave., Longview, Wash.
Bristol, Stanley T., Joseph Sears School, Kenilworth, Ill.
Bristow, William H., Cur. of Curric. Res., Bd. of Educ., New York, N.Y.
Britt, Laurence V., University of Detroit, Detroit, Mich.
Brittain, Clay V., Div. of Tchr. Educ., Emory University, Atlanta, Ga.
Britton, Edward C., 6000 J St., Sacramento, Calif.
Britton, Ernest R., Superintendent of Schools, Midland, Mich.
Broderick, Catherine M., Girl Scouts of U.S.A., 830—3rd Ave., New York, N.Y.
Broderick, Mary P., 209 S. Camden Dr., Beverly Hills, Calif.
Broening, Angela M., Baltimore Public Schls., 3 East 25th St., Baltimore, Md.
Bromwich, Mrs. Rose M., 18111 Nordoff St., Northridge, Calif.
Bronars, Joseph C., 5200 Glennon Dr., St. Louis, Mo.
Bronson, Homer D., Chico State College, Chico, Calif.
Bronson, Moses L., 290 Ninth Ave., New York, N.Y.
Brooks, Mary B., Georgia State Col. for Women, Milledgeville, Ga.
Brookins, Jack E., 19740 Louise Ct., Castro Valley, Calif.
Brostoff, Theodore M., 3334 Bonnie Hill Dr., Hollywood, Calif.
Brother Adelbert James, Manhattan College, New York, N.Y.
Brother Julius Edgar, St. Mary's College, Winona, Minn.
Brother Luke, 2101 Maplewood Ave., Montreal, Canada
Brother Omer Cormier, St. Joseph's University, New Brunswick, Canada
Brother Roger, Christian Brothers College, Memphis, Tenn.

Brother U. Cassian, St. Mary's College, St. Mary's College, Calif.
Brother William Mang, St. Edward's University, Austin, Tex.
Brottman, Marvin A., 8926 Bellefort, Morton Grove, Ill.
Brougher, John F., Shippensburg State College, Shippensburg, Pa.
Brousseau, Sandy E., 186 Fairview Dr., Arroyo Grande, Calif.
Brower, George, Eastern Michigan University, Ypsilanti, Mich.
Brown, Aaron, Phelps-Stokes Fund, 297 Park Ave. So., New York, N.Y.
Brown, Alma, 6301 West 78th St., Overland Park, Kan.
Brown, Anna Beth, 2151 S.W. Crest Dr., Lake Oswego, Ore.
Brown, Charles I., Bennett College, Greenboro, N.C.
Brown, Cynthiana Ellen, 6644 Wildlife Rd., Malibu, Calif.
Brown, Douglas M., Superintendent of Schools, Shorewood, Wis.
Brown, Mrs. Edith F., Star Route, Erwinna, Pa.
Brown, Fred A., Col. of Educ., University of Maryland, College Park, Md.
Brown, George I., Univ. of Calif. at Santa Barbara, Santa Barbara, Calif.
Brown, George W., Superintendent of Schools, Webster Groves, Mo.
Brown, Gerald W., Educ. Dept., University of California, Riverside, Calif.
Brown, Gerald William, 2009 Paseo del Sol, Palos Verdes Estates, Calif.
Brown, Gertrude E., 2835 Milan St., New Orleans, La.
Brown, Helen I., University of Maryland, College Park, Md.
Brown, Howard L., Schl. Admin. Center, 49 E. College Ave., Springfield, Ohio
Brown, I. C., 36 Bethune Court, Columbia, S.C.
Brown, Jeremy, Windham College, Putney, Vt.
Brown, Kenneth B., University of Missouri, Columbia, Mo.
Brown, Kenneth G., Mankato State College, Mankato, Minn.
Brown, Kenneth R., California Tchrs. Assn., 1705 Murchison Dr., Burlingame, Calif.
Brown, Lawrence D., Sch. of Educ., Indiana University, Bloomington, Ind.
Brown, Lawrence L., Superintendent of Schools, Dedham, Mass.
Brown, Louis P., 2333 Brook Rd., Richmond, Va.
Brown, Marjorie, Sch. of Home Econ., University of Minnesota, St. Paul, Minn.
Brown, Mrs. Marjorie D., 4455 West 64th St., Los Angeles, Calif.
Brown, Perry, 1101—93rd St., Niagara Falls, N.Y.
Brown, Roy A., Kutztown State College, Kutztown, Pa.
Brown, Susan C., Box 129, McArthur, Calif.
Brown, Thomas, Hofstra College, Hempstead, N.Y.
Brown, Walter R., 1700 Republic Rd., Silver Spring, Md.
Brown, Woodrow W., Superintendent of Schools, York, Pa.
Browne, Rose Butler, North Carolina College at Durham, Durham, N.C.
Brownell, Samuel M., Superintendent of Schools, Detroit, Mich.
Brownell, William A., Tolman Hall, Univ. of California, Berkeley, Calif.
Browning, Roy W., Ottawa University, Ottawa, Kan.
Brownrigg, Helen R., Dept. of Guid. & Res., Pub. Schls., Belmont, Mass.
Brubaker, Leonard A., 202 Knollwood Dr., DeKalb, Ill.
Bruce, William C., Bruce Publishing Co., Milwaukee, Wis.
Brueckner, Leo J., 10790 Clarmon Pl., Culver City, Calif.
Brunelle, Paul E., 31 Herring Ave., Biddeford, Me.
Brunner, Henry S., U.S. Office of Educ., Dept. of H.E.W., Washington, D.C.
Brunning, Charles R., University of Minnesota-Morris, Morris, Minn.
Brunson, Mrs. DeWitt, P.O. Box 237, Ellis Ave. School, Orangeburg, S.C.
Bryan, Ray, 220 Curtis Hall, Iowa State University, Ames, Iowa
Bryant, Mrs. B. Carleton, 1426 Eighth St., West Palm Beach, Fla.
Bryant, Hayden C., State Department of Education, Macon, Ga.
Bryant, Ira B., Kashmere Gardens High Sch., Houston, Tex.
Bryant, Merle L., Univ. of Minnesota Dem. Laboratory School, Duluth, Minn.
Bryner, James R., 1498 Galbraith Rd., Cincinnati, Ohio
Buchanan, Alfred K., Mulberry St., Plantsville, Conn.
Buchanan, Paul G., 19 Elmdale St., Dorchester, Mass.
Buckley, J. L., Superintendent of Schools, Lockhart, Tex.
Buckner, John D., 4246 W. North Market St., St. Louis, Mo.
Buckner, William N., 2643—15th St., N.W., Washington, D.C.

Buda, Mrs. Mary C., Julia Richman High School, 317 E. 67th St., New York, N.Y.
Budde, Harold H., Southwestern State College, Weatherford, Okla.
Bueker, Armin H., Superintendent of Schools, Marshall, Mo.
Buelke, John A., Western Michigan University, Kalamazoo, Mich.
Bullis, Ella, 2656 N. 68th St., Wauwatosa, Wis.
Bullock, Portia C., 408 Tea St., N.W., Washington, D.C.
Bullock, William J., Superintendent of Schools, Kannapolis, N.C.
Bunger, Marianne, Wesleyan College, Macon, Ga.
Bunker, James G., Supt., Novato Unified Sch. Dist., Novato, Calif.
Bunnell, Robert, 3 Ferguson Pl., Glen Rock, N.J.
Burch, Charles H., 1602 S. Anderson St., Urbana, Ill.
Burdett, C. Fred., Burdett College, 160 Beacon St., Boston, Mass.
Burdette, Mrs. Elmyra, Box 231, Damascus, Md.
Burdick, A. E., Arkansas State Teachers College, Conway, Ark.
Burdick, Richard L., Educ. Dept., Carroll College, Waukesha, Wis.
Burdine, D. I., Prairie View A. & M. College, Prairie View, Tex.
Burg, Mrs. Mary, 2259 Wolfangle Rd., Cincinnati, Ohio
Burgdorf, Otto P., 36-12—210th St., Bayside, N.Y.
Burgess, Mrs. Evangeline, 714 W. California Blvd., Pasadena, Calif.
Burgess, Thomas C., Counseling Cen., Portland State College, Portland, Ore.
Burk, R. Burdett, 5940 E. Walton St., Long Beach, Calif.
Burke, Arvid J., New York State Tchrs. Assn., 152 Washington Ave., Albany, N.Y.
Burke, Eileen M., 649 Rahway Ave., Woodbridge, N.J.
* Burke, Gladys, 244 Outlook, Youngstown, Ohio
Burke, Henry R., 126 McGuire St., Menlo Park Terrace, Metuchen, N.J.
Burke, Paul J., 1 Lookout Pl., Ardsley, N.Y.
Burke, Thomas O., 424 Bayberry Dr., Plantation, Fla.
Burke, Thomas S., 6926 S. Wolcott Ave., Chicago, Ill.
Burkett, Mrs. Cecile C., Box 266, Arkansas Rd., West Monroe, La.
Burkholder, Kenneth, 4323 N. 37th St., Omaha, Neb.
Burks, Herbert M., Jr., 137 Burton Hall, Univ. of Minnesota, Minneapolis, Minn.
Burks, John B., Jersey City State College, Jersey City, N.J.
Burns, Hobert W., Sch. of Educ., Hofstra University, Hempstead, N.Y.
Burns, James W., 704 S. Sparks St., State College, Pa.
Buros, Francis C., 207 Davis Ave., White Plains, N.Y.
Burr, Elbert W., Monsanto Chemical Co., Lindbergh and Olive, St. Louis, Mo.
Burrell, E. William, Classical High School, Providence, R.I.
Burrell, Natelkka E., 6840 Eastern Ave., N.W., Washington, D.C.
Burrough, Rudolph V., Louisiana Polytechnic Institute, Ruston, La.
Burrows, Alvina Treut, 117 Nassau Ave., Manhasset, N.Y.
Burt, Lucile, Lincoln School, 338 Forest Ave., Fond du Lac, Wis.
Burton, William H., Dedbroke Hall, 3512 Willamette Ave., Corvallis, Ore.
Bush, Clifford L., Newark State College, Union, N.J.
Bushnell, Allan C., 2324 Loma Prieta Lane, Menlo Park, Calif.
Buswell, Guy T., 1836 Thousand Oaks Blvd., Berkeley, Calif.
Butler, Laurence, 630 Leonard St., Ashland, Ore.
Butler, Paul W., Roosevelt Junior College, West Palm Beach, Fla.
Butler, Thomas M., 1217 Madison Ave., Edwardsville, Ill.
Butts, Franklin A., Gov. George Clinton School, Poughkeepsie, N.Y.
Butts, R. Freeman, Tchrs. Col., Columbia University, New York, N.Y.
Buyse, R., Sch. of Educ., University of Louvain, Tournai, Belgium
Buzash, G. A., Baldwin-Wallace College, Berea, Ohio
Byerly, Carl L., 5057 Woodward Ave., Detroit, Mich.
Byram, Harold M., Sch. of Educ., Michigan State Univ., East Lansing, Mich.
Byrne, John, Sullivan High School, 6631 N. Bosworth, Chicago, Ill.
Byrne, Richard Hill, Col. of Educ., Univ. of Maryland, College Park, Md.

Caccavo, Emil, 123 Willow St., Roslyn Heights, N.Y.
Cadd, Ayrles, 271 Halcyon Rd., Arroyo Grande, Calif.
Cadwalder, Maurice, Southwestern Agricultural College, Waxahachie, Tex.

Cadwell, Herbert M., 265 N. San Rafael Ave., Pasadena, Calif.
Cahan, Mrs. Ruth, 1916 Overland Ave., Los Angeles, Calif.
Cain, Ralph W., Sutton Hall, University of Texas, Austin, Tex.
Caird, Mrs. Florence B., Joyce Kilmer Sch., 6700 N. Greenview Ave., Chicago, Ill.
Caldwell, Cleon C., Lewis-Clark Normal School, Lewiston, Idaho
Caldwell, O. K., Fostoria High School, Fostoria, Ohio
Califf, Stanley N., Augustana College, Rock Island, Ill.
Call, Mrs. Ardell, Utah Educ. Assn., Box 2159, Salt Lake City, Utah
Callahan, Carol, Creole Petrol. Corp., Cabimas, Edo, Zulia, Venezuela
Callahan, William T., Washington School, New Milford, N.J.
Callan, John H., Sch. of Educ., Seton Hall University, Newark, N.J.
Callas, Eliza E., 7080 Oregon Ave., N.W., Kensington, Md.
Callaway, Bryon, Col. of Educ., University of Georgia, Athens, Ga.
Calmes, Robert E., 2201 E. LaMadera Dr., Tucson, Ariz.
Camhi, Paul S., 4119 Levelside Ave., Lakewood, Calif.
Camien, Laiten L., P.O. Box 157, University Park, N.M.
Campbell, Douglas A., 819 Virginia Ct., Arroyo Grande, Calif.
Campbell, Jack L., Kearney State College, Kearney, Neb.
Campbell, Joe W., L. S. Rugg School, Alexandria, La.
Campbell, L. L., Knoxville College, Knoxville, Tenn.
Campbell, R. Lee, Campbellsville College, Campbellsville, Ky.
Campbell, Roald F., Midwest Adm. Center, Univ. of Chicago, Chicago, Ill.
Campbell, T. J., 109 Hughes Ave., Attalla, Ala.
Campbell, Thomas C., Superintendent, Sch. Dist., No. 834, Stillwater, Minn.
Campos, Mrs. M. A. Pourchet, Caixa Postal 8216, Sao Paulo S.P., Brazil
Canar, Donald A., Supt. Central YMCA Schls., 19 S. LaSalle St., Chicago, Ill.
Canfield, James K., Long Beach State College, Long Beach, Calif.
Cannon, Wendell E., Sch. of Educ., Univ. of Southern California, Los Angeles, Calif.
Canuteson, Richard L., State Univ. College of Education, Brockport, N.Y.
Capehart, Bertis E., 120 Squire Hill Rd., Upper Montclair, N.J.
Caple, Mrs. Charlotte M., Maxwell, Iowa
Capocy, John S., 4628 Seeley St., Downers Grove, Ill.
Cappa, Dan, Los Angeles State College, Los Angeles, Calif.
Cappalonga, Philip B., Sabine and Essex Aves., Narberth, Pa.
Capps, Lelon R., Bailey Hall, University of Kansas, Lawrence, Kan.
Capps, Mrs. Marian P., Virginia State College, Norfolk, Va.
Capron, Clara, 301 Olive St., West Palm Beach, Fla.
Carbaugh, Gaile A., Campus Sch., State Univ. Tchrs. College, Geneseo, N.Y.
Carden, William L., Wheaton College, Wheaton, Ill.
Cardina, Philip J., Box 269, R.D. 2, Farmingdale, N.J.
Cardwell, Robert H., Park Junior High School, Bertrand St., Knoxville, Tenn.
Carey, Clarence B., Jones Commerical High School, 607 Plymouth Ct., Chicago, Ill.
Carey, Elizabeth B., 489 State St., Albany, N.Y.
Carey, Justin P., 110 Echo Ave., New Rochelle, N.Y.
Carey, Wendell, Dept. of Educ., Park College, Parkville, Mo.
Carle, Richard F., Div. of Gen. Educ., Boston University, Boston, Mass.
Carline, Donald E., Read. Center, Kansas State Tchrs. Col., Emporia, Kan.
Carlson, Cecil V., 808 West 10th St., McCook, Neb.
Carlson, Mrs. Evelyn F., 6899 N. Wildwood, Chicago, Ill.
Carlson, F. Roy, Mt. Ida Junior College, Newton Centre, Mass.
Carlson, Mrs. Ruth K., 1718 LeRoy Ave., Berkeley, Calif.
Carlson, Thorston R., 415 Monte Vista Lane, Santa Rosa, Calif.
Carlson, W. H., Campus School, State University College, Oswego, N.Y.
Carnahan, Eleanor, 11 Forest Rd., Oakmont, Wheeling, W.Va.
Carne, Vernon E., 1383 Dorothy Dr., Decatur, Ga.
Carney, Thomas, 2107 Morningside Dr., Mineral Wells, Tex.
Carnochan, John L., Jr., Folly Quarter Rd., Ellicott, Md.
Carpenter, Aaron C., P.O. Box 387, Grambling, La.

Carpenter, N. H., Superintendent, City Schools, Elkin, N.C.
Carr, Carolyn Jane, 227 Whitemarsh Rd., Ardmore, Pa.
Carr, Julian W., 795 Kinderkamack Rd., River Edge, N.J.
Carrithers, Lura M., University of Wisconsin-Milwaukee, Milwaukee, Wis.
Carroll, Clifford, Gonzaga University, Spokane, Wash.
Carroll, John B., Grad. Sch. of Educ., Harvard University, Cambridge, Mass.
Carroll, John S., 16 S. Dunning St., Ventura, Calif.
Carroll, Katherine M., Western Washington State College, Bellingham, Wash.
Carroll, Margaret L., 208 Fairmont Rd., DeKalb, Ill.
Carron, Malcolm, Col. of Arts and Sci., University of Detroit, Detroit, Mich.
Carsello, Carmen J., 2154 N. Nordica Ave., Chicago, Ill.
Carson, H. Maude, 6025 N. Mason, Chicago, Ill.
Carstater, Eugene D., 606 Jackson Dr., Falls Church, Va.
Carter, Gordon, Superintendent Sch. Dist. 501, Bellingham, Wash.
Carter, Harold D., Sch. of Educ., University of California, Berkeley, Calif.
Carter, Homer L. J., Western Michigan University, Kalamazoo, Mich.
Carter, Richard C., Box 1250, Fairbanks Public Schools, Fairbanks, Alaska
Carter, Sims, 214 Spalding Dr., Beverly Hills, Calif.
Carter, Vincent, San Jose City Schools, San Jose, Calif.
Cartwright, H. William, Dept. of Educ., Duke University, Durham, N.C.
Cash, Harry T., Hamilton High School, 1478 Wilson St., Memphis, Tenn.
Caskey, Helen C., Tchrs. Col., University of Cincinnati, Cincinnati, Ohio
Casserly, Catherine M., Public Schls., 170 Pond St., Providence, R.I.
Cassidy, Rosalind, University of California, 405 Hilgard Ave., Los Angeles, Calif.
Castaneda, Alfred, 110 East End Ave., New York, N.Y.
Castelli, Albert, 2933 Shawnee Lane, Drayton Plains, Mich.
Caton, W. Barnie, Superintendent, Gallup-McKinley County Schls., Gallup, N.M.
Catrambone, A. R., Superintendent of Schools, Camden, N.J.
Caudle, Jean I., Wisconsin State College, Oshkosh, Wis.
Caughran, Alex M., 93 N. Main St., Orono, Me.
Caulfield, Patrick J., Dept. of Educ., St. Peter's College, Jersey City, N.J.
Cavanaugh, Alfred D., Dept. of Educ., University of Detroit, Detroit, Mich.
Cawrse, Robert C., 40 Maple Hill Dr., Chagrin Falls, Ohio
Chadderdon, Hester, Home Econ. Div., Iowa State University, Ames, Iowa
Chaffee, Charles E., Superintendent of Schools, Bethlehem, Pa.
Chaikin, Milton, 224 East 28th St., New York, N.Y.
Chall, Jeanne, City University of New York, New York, N.Y.
Chambers, J. Richard, 61 Patricia Lane, South Weymouth, Mass.
Chambers, Lyle David, 5175 Union Ave., San Jose, Calif.
Chambers, William M., 267 Liverpool, Lexington, Ky.
Champlin, George R., P.O. Box 2219, Hartford, Conn.
Chandler, H. E., 1320 Haskell Ave., Lawrence, Kan.
Chang, Alvin K., 3642 S. Court St., Palo Alto, Calif.
Chang, Jen-chi, Florida Normal and Ind. Mem. College, St. Augustine, Fla.
Chang, Lynette Y. C., 1947 Makiki St., Honolulu, Hawaii
Chansky, Norman M., North Carolina State Col. of Univ. of N.C., Raleigh, N.C.
Chao, Sankey C., 85½ Douglas Ave., St. Augustine, Fla.
Chapline, Elaine Burns, 168 Bergen Rd., Jersey City, N.J.
Chapman, Catherine, Weatherford College, Weatherford, Tex.
Chappell, Bartlett E. S., New York Military Academy, Cornwall-on-Hudson, N.Y.
Charles, Harvey, Dept. of Educ., John Carroll University, University Heights, Ohio
Charles, Ramon L., 327 Nickell Rd., Topeka, Kan.
Charlton, Huey E., 3785 Wisteria Lane, S.W., Atlanta, Ga.
Chase, Francis S., Dept. of Educ., University of Chicago, Chicago, Ill.
Chase, Naomi C., University of Minnesota, Minneapolis, Minn.
Chasnoff, Robert, Newark State College, Union, N.J.
Cheeks, L. E., 213 McFarland St., Kerrville, Tex.
Chell, Elsie M., 116 Steel St., Algoma, Wis.
Chellevold, John O., Wartburg College, Waverly, Iowa
Chenoweth, Margaret, Admin. Center, 315 S. Jackson St., Janesville, Wis.

Chern, Mrs. Nona E., 492 Concord Rd., Broomall, Pa.
Chidekel, Samuel J., 9124 Somoset Blvd., Skokie, Ill.
Chidester, Charles B., 6650 Jackson Ave., Hammond, Ind.
Chievitz, Gene L., Bldg. 12, University of New Mexico, Albuquerque, N.M.
Childress, Jack R., Sch. of Educ., Boston University, Boston, Mass.
Chinitz, Ben S., 15055 Hubbell Ave., Detroit, Mich.
Chipman, R. S., Superintendent of Schools, N. Summit Dist., Coalville, Utah
Chirhart, Mrs. Virginia, 608—6th St., North, St. Cloud, Minn.
Chitwood, R. B., Superintendent, Lakeside Schools, Lake Village, Ark.
Chivers, Naomi R., Spelman College, Atlanta, Ga.
Chiverton, William S., Moreland Sch. Dist., Murray Ave., Huntingdon Valley, Pa.
Choate, Ernest A., Germantown High School, Philadelphia, Pa.
Christenson, Mrs. Bernice M., 450 N. Grand Ave., Los Angeles, Calif.
Christian, Leo M., El Camino College, Via Torrance, Calif.
Christman, Paul S., Superintendent of Schools, Schuylkill Haven, Pa.
Chu, May Koo, Wittenberg University, Springfield, Ohio
Chuck, Harry C., 265 Kanoelani Dr., Hilo, Hawaii
Chudler, Albert A., 3540 Summerfield Dr., Sherman Oaks, Calif.
Cianciolo, Patricia J., 2116 S. 108th St., West Allis, Wis.
Cioffi, Joseph M., 652 Doriskill Ct., River Vale, N.J.
Clabaugh, R. E., Superintendent of Schools, Arlington Heights, Ill.
Clark, David L., Col. of Educ., Ohio State University, Columbus, Ohio
Clark, Edward F., St. Peter's College, Hudson Blvd., Jersey City, N.J.
Clark, Elmer J., Laboratory Sch., Indiana State College, Terre Haute, Ind.
Clark, Mrs. Esmer Knudson, 2274 Cedar St., Berkeley, Calif.
Clark, Francis E., Dept. of Educ. Psych., Univ. of Hawaii, Honolulu, Hawaii
Clark, Franklin B., District Superintendent of Schools, Athens, N.Y.
Clark, Herbert E., Dept. of Educ., Purdue University, Lafayette, Ind.
Clark, John F., 507 Marview Lane, Solana Beach, Calif.
Clark, Leonard II., 240 Van Nostrand Ave., Jersey City, N.J.
Clark, Lewis E., 3000 S.W. Flower Terrace, Portland, Ore.
Clark, Lois M., National Education Assn., 1201—16th St., N.W., Washington, D.C.
Clark, Maurice P., Superintendent of Schools, 4335 Howard Ave., Western
    Springs, Ill.
Clark, Max R., Superintendent of Schools, Dubuque, Iowa
Clark, Richard M., State University College of Education, Oneonta, N.Y.
Clark, Stephen C., 3424 Wilshire Blvd., Los Angeles, Calif.
Clark, Thomas H., 525 Plymouth St., Missoula, Mont.
Clark, Mrs. Willa B., 1224—16th St., Parkersburg, W.Va.
Clark, Woodrow Wilson, William Carey College, Hattiesburg, Miss.
Clarke, Albert T., Stephen F. Austin State College, Nacogdoches, Tex.
Clarke, Stanley C. T., 11615—78th Ave., Edmonton, Alba., Canada
Clarkston, Emmerine A., 8216 Eberhart Ave., Chicago, Ill.
Classon, Marion E., 412 Harrison Ave., Highland Park, N.J.
Claster, Barbara Leiner, R.D. 1, Box 547, Mill Hall, Pa.
Clayton, Harold, 317 W. Lamar St., Americus, Ga.
Clayton, Thomas E., 7 Kelly Dr., Manlius, N.Y.
Clegg, Ambrose A., Jr., Sch. of Educ., Univ. of North Carolina, Chapel Hill, N.C.
Cleland, Donald L., Sch. of Educ., Univ. of Pittsburgh, Pittsburgh, Pa.
Clem, William W., Southern University, Baton Rouge, La.
Cleveland, Ernest D., Superintendent of Schools, Palestine, Tex.
Clifford, Paul I., Sch. of Educ., Atlanta University, Atlanta, Ga.
Clift, Virgil A., Sch. of Educ., New York University, New York, N.Y.
Cline, Marion, Jr., Texas Western College, El Paso, Tex.
Clinton, Robert, Jr., Snyder High School, Snyder, Tex.
Clouser, John J., 200 N. Elm St., Mt. Prospect, Ill.
Clouthier, Raymond P., St. Norbert College, West DePere, Wis.
Clymer, Theodore W., Col. of Educ., University of Minnesota, Minneapolis, Minn.
Cobb, Beatrice M., Cambell Shore Rd., Gray, Me.
Cobb, Jacob E., Indiana State College, Terre Haute, Ind.
Cobban, Margaret R., 9 William St., Stamford, Conn.

* Cochran, J. Chester, 2413 Albans St., Houston, Tex.
Cochran, John R., Kalamazoo Public Schools, 1220 Howard St., Kalamazoo, Mich.
Cochran, Russell T., 27551 Drexel Way, Hayward, Calif.
Codwell, John E., Jack Yate Sr. High School, 3703 Sampson St., Houston, Tex.
Coen, Alban Wasson, II, Central Michigan University, Mt. Pleasant, Mich.
Coetzee, J. Christian, Potchefstroom University, Potchefstroom, South Africa
Cofell, William L., St. John's University, Collegeville, Minn.
Coffee, James M., Clark University, 950 Main St., Worcester, Mass.
Coffey, Thomas F., George Washington Sch., 3535 E. 114th St., Chicago, Ill.
Coffey, Warren, 1720 Bellamy Dr., Champaign, Ill.
Coffin, Edwin, III, Monterey County Schools, Box 851, Salinas, Calif.
Cogger, Robert V., 471 Viola Rd., Spring Valley, N.Y.
Cohen, George, 8 Etheride Pl., Park Ridge, N.J.
Cohen, S. Alan, 11 Priscilla Rd., Brighton, Mass.
Cohen, Samuel, 60 Everit Ave., Hewlett, N.Y.
Cohler, Milton J., 330 Diversey Parkway, Chicago, Ill.
Cohodes, Aaron, 1050 Merchandise Mart, Chicago, Ill.
Colbath, Edwin H., 101-40—117th St., Richmond Hill, N.Y.
Colburn, A. B., Rte. 5, Box 678E, Everett, Wash.
Cole, James C., Educ. Div., AID, APO 254, New York, N.Y.
Cole, Mary I., Western Kentucky State College, Bowling Green, Ky.
Coleman, F. Basil, 435 W. 119th St., New York, N.Y.
Coleman, Mary Elizabeth, Univ. of Pennsylvania, 3944 Walnut St., Philadelphia,
    Pa.
Colla, Frances S., 49 Regina St., Trumbull, Conn.
Collier, Mrs. Anna K., 903 Fourth St., Liverpool, N.Y.
Collier, Calhoun C., Michigan State University, East Lansing, Mich.
Collier, Richard E., Montgomery County Public Schools, Rockville, Md.
Collings, Miller R., 9201 W. Outer Dr., Detroit, Mich.
Collins, Helen C., 1203 Gilpin Ave., Wilmington, Del.
Collins, James D., St. John's Prep. School, 82 Lewis Ave., Brooklyn, N.Y.
Collins, Kathleen M., 5410 Connecticut Ave., N.W., Washington, D.C.
Collins, Mildred, 37725 Harlow Dr., Willoughby, Ohio
Collins, Paul W., Box 119, Lucasville, Ohio
Collins, Robert E., Deephaven Junior High School, Excelsior, Minn.
Conan, Mrs. Beatrice, 2063—74th St., Brooklyn, N.Y.
Conaway, Mrs. Freda Yanit, West Liberty State College, West Liberty, W.Va.
Congreve, Willard J., Lab. Schls., University of Chicago, Chicago, Ill.
Conley, William H., Marquette University, Milwaukee, Wis.
Connor, E. Faye, Huntington College Library, Huntington, Ind.
Connor, William H., Washington Univ. Grad. Inst. of Education, St. Louis, Mo.
Converse, David T., 1976 "A" St., Lincoln, Neb.
Conway, Marie M., Jefferson Court No. 31, 4925 Saul St., Philadelphia, Pa.
Cook, Ben J., Superintendent of Schools, South Plainfield, N.J.
Cook, Raymond M., Chicago Teachers College, 6800 Stewart Ave., Chicago, Ill.
Cooke, Dan B., High Point College, High Point, N.C.
Cooke, Dorothy E., State Education Department, Albany, N.Y.
Cooling, Elizabeth, 93 Cottage Ave., North Providence, R.I.
Coon, Alice B., 303 W. North St., Manteca, Calif.
Cooper, Bernice, Peabody Hall, University of Georgia, Athens, Ga.
Cooper, George H., 2913 Washington Blvd., Chicago, Ill.
Cooper, Shirley, Amer. Assn. of School Adm., 1201—16th St., N.W., Washington,
    D.C.
Corbally, John E., 202D Educ. Hall, University of Washington, Seattle, Wash.
Cordasco, Francesco, 6606 Jackson St., West New York, N.J.
Corey, Stephen M., Teachers Col., Columbia University, New York, N.Y.
Corley, Clifford L., Oregon College of Education, Monmouth, Ore.
Corman, Bernard R., Michigan State University, East Lansing, Mich.
Cornell, Francis G., 7 Holland Ave., White Plains, N.Y.
Cornish, Dale, 5770 Dudley St., Arvada, Colo.
Cornish, Robert L., Sch. of Educ., Kansas University, Lawrence, Kan.

Cortage, Cecelia, 2053 Illinois Ave., Santa Rosa, Calif.
Cortner, Frederick D., University of North Carolina, Chapel Hill, N.C.
Cory, N. Durward, 908 W. North St., Muncie, Ind.
Coss, Mrs. Carrie B., Prairie View A. & M. College, Prairie View, Tex.
Coster, John K., Dept. of Educ., Purdue University, Lafayette, Ind.
Cotter, Katharine C., South Main St., Osterville, Mass.
Cottone, Sebastian C., 2534 S. Colorado St., Philadelphia, Pa.
Couche, Martha E., Rust College, Holly Springs, Miss.
Coulson, John R., Parkside School, 6938 East End Ave., Chicago, Ill.
Coulson, Roger W., Col. of Educ., Butler University, Indianapolis, Ind.
Coulter, Myron L., Col. of Educ., Pennsylvania State Univ., University Park, Pa.
* Courtis, S. A., 9110 Dwight Ave., Detroit, Mich.
Courtney, Robert W., 10 Olcott St., Middlebush, N.J.
Cousins, E. H., 8 Upper Sandringham Ave., Half-way Tree P.O., Jamaica, B.W.I.
Cousins, John, High Street School, West Chester, Pa.
Covell, Merle O., California State College, California, Pa.
Cowan, Persis H., 1612 Fair Oaks Ave., South Pasadena, Calif.
Coward, Gertrude, 401 East 9th St., Charlotte, N.C.
Cowles, Clifton V., Jr., 919 West H. St., Ontario, Calif.
Cowley, W. H., Cubberley Hall, Stanford University, Stanford, Calif.
Cox, Edwin A., Superintendent of Schools, North Parade, Stratford, Conn.
Cox, Frank, 3118 Lucinda Lane, Santa Barbara, Calif.
Cox, John A., 735 N. Allen St., State College, Pa.
Cox, Johnnye, V., Col. of Educ., University of Georgia, Athens, Ga.
Cox, Velma V., Eastern Illinois University, Charleston, Ill.
Cozine, June, Oklahoma A. & M. College, Stillwater, Okla.
Crabtree, Charlotte, Sch. of Educ., University of California, Los Angeles, Calif.
* Craig, Gerald S., Tchrs. Col., Columbia University, New York, N.Y.
Craig, James C., 4821 Camelot St., Rockville, Md.
Craig, Robert C., Dept. of Educ., Marquette University, Milwaukee, Wis.
Craig, Mrs. Ruth B., State Department of Education, Concord, N.H.
Cramer, Beatrice E., 1365 Weaver St., Scarsdale, N.Y.
Crandell, W. B., 301 W. Jackson St., Villa Park, Ill.
Craney, Wayne A., 926 Ferdinand Ave., Forest Park, Ill.
Crannell, Clarke W., 120 S. Main St., Oxford, Ohio
Craton, Edward J., 1777 Glenwood Ct., Bakersfield, Calif.
Crawford, Dorothy M., 212 W. Washington St., Ottawa, Ill.
Crawford, Ernest A., Sch. of Educ., University of Dublin, Dublin, Ireland
Crawford, Robert T., 713 Maple Ave., Rockville, Md.
Crawford, T. James, Sch. of Business, Indiana University, Bloomington, Ind.
Creason, Frank, Valley View School, 8101 W. 95th St., Overland Park, Kan.
Crescimbeni, Joseph, University of Bridgeport, 126 Park Ave., Bridgeport, Conn.
Creswell, Mrs. Rowena C., 305 Montclair Ave., So., College Station, Tex.
Crews, Roy L., Aurora College, Aurora, Ill.
Crocker, Richard F., Jr., Superintendent of Schools, Caribou, Me.
Crook, Robert R., Queens College, Flushing, N.Y.
Crosby, G. J., Queens College, Flushing, N.Y.
Cross, William C., New Mexico State University, University Park, N.M.
Crossley, John B., 1621 Keller Rd., Honolulu, Hawaii
Crosslin, Barbara, 14 N. 11th Ave., Yakima, Wash.
Crosson, Robert Henry, 4463 Clay St., Denver, Colo.
Crow, A. L., Superintendent of Schools, Kirkwood, Mo.
Crow, Lester D., Brooklyn College, Bedford Ave. and Ave. H., Brooklyn, N.Y.
Crowder, Orvel C., Box 65, Milligan College, Tenn.
Crowe, James W., Chicago Vocational High School, 2100 E. 87th St., Chicago, Ill.
Crowell, R. A., Col. of Educ., University of Arizona, Tucson, Ariz.
Crowley, Mary C., 4636 Firestone No. 3, Dearborn, Mich.
Crowley, W. B., 823 Stebondale Rd., Columbia, S.C.
Crull, Howard D., Superintendent of Schools, Port Huron, Mich.
Crum, Clyde E., Div. of Educ., San Diego State College, San Diego, Calif.
Crumb, Frederick W., State University Tchrs. College, Potsdam, N.Y.

Culbertson, Jack A., Ohio State University, 65 S. Oval Dr., Columbus, Ohio
Culliton, Thomas E., Jr., 805 W. Pennsylvania St., Urbana, Ill.
Culver, Mrs. Erleen, 930 West Acres Rd., West Sacramento, Calif.
Cummings, Mabel Anna, 6044 Linden St., Brooklyn, N.Y.
Cummings, Mrs. Reta, 120 S. Prospect St., Orange, Calif.
Cummiskey, Cletus J., 226 Weaver St., Mankato, Minn.
Cunningham, George S., 3555 Riedham Rd., Shaker Heights, Ohio
Cunningham, Luvern L., Col. of Educ., Univ. of Minnesota, Minneapolis, Minn.
Cunningham, Myron, Col. of Educ., University of Florida, Gainesville, Fla.
Currier, Mrs. Lynor O., 713 Giddings Ave., Annapolis, Md.
Currier, Richard L., R. D., Yardley-Newtown Rd., Yardley, Pa.
Curry, Mrs. Alma M., 1330 New Hampshire Ave., N.W., Washington, D.C.
Curry, John F., Box 6765, North Texas State College, Denton, Tex.
Curtin, James R., Col. of Educ., University of Minnesota, Minneapolis, Minn.
Curtin, Wylma R., 9600 Culver St., Kensington, Md.
Curtis, E. Louise, Macalester College, St. Paul, Minn.
Curtis, H. A., Florida State University, Tallahassee, Fla.
Curtis, James E., 720 Garland Dr., Palo Alto, Calif.
Curtis, Thomas E., 205 Donna Dr., Carbondale, Ill.
Cusick, Ralph J., 6443 N. Wayne Ave., Chicago, Ill.

Daddazio, Arthur H., Bd. of Educ., 98 Grand St., Newburgh, N.Y.
Daeufer, Carl J., Univ. High Sch., Univ. of Hawaii, Honolulu, Hawaii
Dafoe, Don M., Superintendent of Schools, Anchorage, Alaska
Dahl, Mrs. Barbara, 1330 Cedar St., Santa Monica, Calif.
Dahle, C. O., Superintendent of Schools, Highland Park, Ill.
Daines, Mrs. Delva, 411—13th Ave. So., Nampa, Idaho
Dale, Arbie Myron, Sch. of Commerce, New York University, New York, N.Y.
Dale, Edgar, Sch. of Educ., Ohio State University, Columbus, Ohio
Daly, Edmund B., 1839 N. Richmond St., Chicago, Ill.
Daniel, A. A., Box 5451, North Texas Station, Denton, Tex.
Daniel, George T., 123 N. Wilbur St., Walla Walla, Wash.
Daniel, Sheldon C., 3783 Richlawn Rd., West Richfield, Ohio
Daniels, Paul R., 8411 Widener Rd., Philadelphia, Pa.
Danielson, Mrs. Hope F., Northeastern University, Boston, Mass.
Danielson, Paul J., Col. of Educ., University of Arizona, Tucson, Ariz.
Darcy, Natalie T., Dept. of Educ., Brooklyn College, Brooklyn, N.Y.
Darnowski, Vincent S., 164 Driggs Ave., Brooklyn, N.Y.
Darroch, Frank W., 27 Princeton Rd., Toronto, Ont., Canada
D'Ascoli, Louis N., 5 Hughes Ter., Yonkers, N.Y.
Davenport, William R., Col. of Educ., Butler University, Indianapolis, Ind.
Davey, Mrs. Elizabeth P., 5748 Harper Ave., Chicago, Ill.
Davidson, Mrs. Elizabeth W., Johnson Rd., Clarksburg, Md.
Davidson, Mrs. Evelyn K., Dept. of Educ., Kent State University, Kent, Ohio
Davidson, R. L., Texas Technological College, Lubbock, Tex.
Davies, Daniel R., Col. of Educ., Univ. of Arizona, Tucson, Ariz.
Davies, Don, NCTEPS (NEA), 1201—16th St., N.W., Washington, D.C.
Davies, Gordon F., 3070 Cromwell Pl., Hayward, Calif.
Davies, J. Leonard, Col. of Educ., State Univ. of Iowa, Iowa City, Iowa
Davies, Mrs. Lillian S., Dept. of Educ., Western Reserve Univ., Cleveland, Ohio
Davis, Benjamin F., 10 Lahey St., New Hyde Park, L.I., N.Y.
Davis, David Carson, 902 Cornell Ct., Madison, Wis.
Davis, Dwight M., 1110—17th St., Moline, Ill.
Davis, Guy C., Trinidad State Junior College, Trinidad, Colo.
Davis, H. Curtis, 1605 Park Ave., San Jose, Calif.
Davis, Hazel A., Hofstra College, Hempstead, N.Y.
Davis, J. Pinckney, 516 N.W. 21st Ave., Fort Lauderdale, Fla.
Davis, J. Sanford, Box 646, Madison, Conn.
Davis, James M., 2872 Glacier Way, Ann Arbor, Mich.
Davis, Joseph H., 8300 Jackson St., St. Louis, Mo.
Davis, Milton J., 725 West 18th St., North Chicago, Ill.

Davis, Nancy B., Indiana University, Bloomington, Ind.
Davis, O. L., Jr., Kent State University, Kent, Ohio
Davis, Ron W., 1745 Hillside Rd., Southampton, Pa.
Davis, Warren C., 65 S. Plymouth Ave., Rochester, N.Y.
Davoren, David, Superintendent of Schools, Milford, Mass.
Dawald, V. F., Dept. of Educ., Millikin University, Decatur, Ill.
Dawkins, M. B., 1110 Izard St., Little Rock, Ark.
Dawson, W. Read, Baylor University, Waco, Tex.
Day, James F., Dept. of Educ., Texas Western College, El Paso, Tex.
Dease, E. Richard, 413 Lorraine Rd., Wheaton, Ill.
DeBernardis, Amo, 1814 Dekum St., N.E., Portland, Ore.
Debin, Louis, 83-37—247th St., Bellerose, N.Y.
DeBoer, Mrs. Dorothy L., 3930 N. Southport Ave., Chicago, Ill.
DeBoer, John J., Col. of Educ., University of Illinois, Urbana, Ill.
DeBus, Raymond L., 666 Malabar Rd., Maroubra, N.S.W., Australia
DeClore, Beatrice Ann, 626 Pico Place, Santa Monica, Calif.
Deever, Merwin, Col. of Educ., Arizona State University, Tempe, Ariz.
DeJung, John E., Sch. of Educ., University of Oregon, Eugene, Ore.
DeKeni, Sara L., State Education Department, Tallahassee, Fla.
DeKock, Henry C., Col. of Educ., State Univ. of Iowa, Iowa City, Iowa
Delaney, Eleanor C., Sch. of Educ., Rutgers University, New Brunswick, N.J.
Dell, Daryl L., Ball State Teachers College, Muncie, Ind.
DeLong, Arthur R., University of Delaware, Newark, Del.
Delmare, Mrs. Maxine, State University of Iowa, Iowa City, Iowa
DeLuca, E. Albert, St. Vincent College, Latrobe, Pa.
Demming, John A., Bldg. S-502, Palm Beach Air Force Base, West Palm Beach, Fla.
DeMoraes, Maria P. Tito, WHO, Palais des Nations, Geneva, Switzerland
Denecke, Marie G., Col. of Educ., Univ. of Maryland, College Park, Md.
Denemark, George W., University of Wisconsin-Milwaukee, Milwaukee, Wis.
Dennis, Ronald T., Sch. of Educ., Louisiana Tech., Ruston, La.
Denny, Mrs. Alma G., 7418 Poplar Ave., Baltimore, Md.
Denny, Terry, Sch. of Educ., Purdue University, West Lafayette, Ind.
Denson, Lucille D., W. Ramapo Rd., Garnerville, N.Y.
Derby, Orlo L., State University Teachers College, Brockport, N.Y.
DeShazo, Willard, 6117 Brookside Dr., Alexandria, Va.
Desiderato, Otello, Dept. of Psych., Connecticut Col., New London, Conn.
Desoe, Hollis L., Board of Educ., 51 Route 100, Briarcliff Manor, N.Y.
Deutschman, Mrs. Marilyn L., 90-59—56th Ave., Elmhurst 73, Queens, L.I., N.Y.
DeVault, M. Vere, University of Wisconsin, Madison, Wis.
Devine, Florence E., 4822 Central Ave., Western Springs, Ill.
Devine, Thomas F., College of Our Lady of the Elms, Chicopee, Mass.
Devine, Thomas G., Rhode Island College, Providence, R.I.
Devor, J. W., 6309 E. Holbert Rd., Bethesda, Md.
Deyell, J. Douglas, Provincial Teachers College, North Bay, Ont., Canada
Dezelle, Walter, Jr., 3205 Allison Ave., Groves, Tex.
Dickerson, James L., 180 South View Dr., Athens, Ga.
Dickey, Otis M., Cherry Creek Sch. Dist. No. 5, Englewood, Colo.
Dickmeyer, Mrs. K. H., Fairfax, Minn.
Dickson, George E., Col. of Educ., University of Toledo, Ohio
Dickson, Paul, Sch. of Educ., Florida State Univ., Tallahassee, Fla.
* Diederich, A. F., St. Norbert College, West DePere, Wis.
Diedrich, Richard C., 17609 Oakwood Dr., Hazel Crest, Ill.
Diefenderfer, Omie T., 828 Third St., Fullerton, Pa.
Diener, Russell E., Eastern Michigan University, Ypsilanti, Mich.
Dierzen, Mrs. Verda, Community Cons. School Dist. 10, Woodstock, Ill.
Dieterle, Louise E., 10700 S. Avenue F, Chicago, Ill.
Dietz, Elizabeth H., 1093 Northern Blvd., Baldwin, N.Y.
Diffley, Jerome, St. Bernard College, St. Bernard, Ala.
Diggs, Kermit H., St. Paul's College, Lawrenceville, Va.
DiGiacento, Mrs. Rose, 68 Pilgrim Ave., Yonkers, N.Y.

Digman, John M., 382 Auwinala Rd., Kailua, Hawaii
Dil, Anwar S., Educ. Extn. Service Center, Gulberg, Lahore, West Pakistan
DiLeonarde, Joseph H., 6309 N. Cicero Ave., Chicago, Ill.
DiLieto, Ray Marie, 4 Bayberry Lane, Westport, Conn.
Dillinger, Claude M., Illinois State University, Normal, Ill.
Dillon, Frances H., Minnesota State College, Moorhead, Minn.
Dillon, Jesse D., Jr., 7425 Holabird Ave., Dundalk, Md.
DiLorenzo, Louis T., New York State Education Dept., Albany, N.Y.
Dimond, Ray A., Jr., 4034 E. Cambridge, Phoenix, Ariz.
Dimond, Stanley E., 2012 Shadford Rd., Ann Arbor, Mich.
DiNapoli, Peter J., Public School 90, Sheridan Ave., New York, N.Y.
DiNardo, V. James, Massachusetts State College, Bridgewater, Mass.
DiPace, William, 316 Jordan Court, Martinez, Calif.
DiPietro, Rocco R., Superintendent of Schools, Wayne, N.J.
Disko, Michael, 16 Briarwood Dr., Athens, Ohio
Dittmer, Daniel G., 1647 Francis Hammond Pkwy., Alexandria, Va.
Dittmer, Jane E., Kouts High School, Kouts, Ind.
Dix, M. S., North Shore School, 1217 Chase Ave., Chicago, Ill.
Dixon, Mrs. Glendora M., Oregon College of Education, Monmouth, Ore.
Dixon, James T., 24 Arrow Wood Lane, Huntington Sta., L.I., N.Y.
Dixon, W. Robert, Sch. of Educ., University of Michigan, Ann Arbor, Mich.
Doak, Helen, 124—26th St., Santa Monica, Calif.
Dobbs, Edith, Fort Hays Kansas State College, Hays, Kan.
Dobbs, Louis H., 3841 Mockingbird Lane, Dallas, Tex.
Dodd, John M., State University College of Education, Buffalo, N.Y.
Dodds, A. Gordon, Superintendent of Schools, Edwardsville, Ill.
Dodson, Dan W., New York University, Washington Sq., New York, N.Y.
Dodson, Robert G., St. Gregory's College, Shawnee, Okla.
Doherty, Thomas B., 1115 N. El Paso St., Colorado Springs, Colo.
Dolan, Francis, LaSalle-Peru Twp. High School, LaSalle, Ill.
Doll, Ronald C., 17 Rossmore Ter., Livingston, N.J.
Domian, E. O., 1595 Northrop, St. Paul, Minn.
Donat, G. M., Dept. of Psych., Concordia College, Moorhead, Minn.
Donchi, Mrs. Celia B., 118 Oakview Ave., Maplewood, N.J.
Donner, Arvin N., Col. of Educ., University of Houston, Houston, Tex.
Donoghue, Mildred R., Orange State College, Fullerton, Calif.
Donovan, Charles F., Sch. of Educ., Boston College, Chestnut Hill, Mass.
Doody, Louise E., 1697 Beacon St., Waban, Mass.
Dorricott, H. J., Western State College, Gunnison, Colo.
Doss, Paul, 12631 Fletcher Dr., Garden Grove, Calif.
Dotson, John M., 154 Jones Dr., Pocatello, Idaho
Dougherty, Denis, Immaculate Conception Seminary, Conception, Mo.
Douglass, Harl R., Col. of Educ., University of Colorado, Boulder, Colo.
Douglass, Malcolm P., Claremont Graduate School, Claremont, Calif.
Dowd, Robert J., Southern Connecticut State College, New Haven, Conn.
Dowling, Thomas I., Superintendent, Dist. No. 50, Greenwood, S.C.
Downing, Mrs. Gertrude L., 87 Huron Rd., Bellerose Village, N.Y.
Doyle, Andrew McCormick, 1106 Bellerive Blvd., St. Louis, Mo.
Doyle, E. A., Loyola University, New Orleans, La.
Drag, Francis L., Chula Vista City Schools, Chula Vista, Calif.
Dragositz, Anna, 215 Ewing St., Princeton, N.J.
Drees, Frank J., Dept. of Public Instr., P.O. Box 2360, Honolulu, Hawaii
Dreikurs, Rudolf, 6 N. Michigan Ave., Chicago, Ill.
Dressel, Paul L., Michigan State University, East Lansing, Mich.
Drew, Gladys J., 2505 Thirteenth St., N.W., Washington, D.C.
Drew, Robert E., Community Unit School Dist. 303, St. Charles, Ill.
Driver, Cecil E., Oslo Dependents School, APO 85, New York, N.Y.
Dropkin, Stanley, Queens College, Flushing, N.Y.
Drotter, Stephen J., Drury High School, North Adams, Mass.
Drummond, Harold D., Hodgin Hall, University of New Mexico, Albuquerque, N.M.

Drummond, William H., 223 North 9th St., Cheney, Wash.
Ducanis, Alex J., 62 Grandview Ter., Albany, N.Y.
Duckers, Ronald L., 616 W. Central Rd., Arlington Heights, Ill.
Duckworth, Alice, Board of Education, Reef Rd., Fairfield, Conn.
Duff, Franklin L., School of Educ., Miami University, Oxford, Ohio
Duffey, Robert V., 9225 Limestone Pl., College Park, Md.
DuFour, Stuart, Hartnell College, Salinas, Calif.
Duker, Jan, 210 Pattee Hall, Univ. of Minnesota, Minneapolis, Minn.
Dumler, Marvin J., Concordia Teachers College, River Forest, Ill.
Dunathan, Homer, Libbey Hall, University of Toledo, Toledo, Ohio
Duncan, Neal, 810 No. Spring St., LaGrange, Ill.
Duncan, William B., Miami Edison Senior High School, Miami, Fla.
Dunham, Amelia K., 2340 Auburn Ave., Cincinnati, Ohio
Dunham, Ralph E., 1302 Popkins Lane, Alexandria, Va.
Dunkel, Harold B., Dept. of Educ., University of Chicago, Chicago, Ill.
Dunkle, Maurice Albert, Superintendent, Calver Co. Schls., Prince Frederick, Md.
Dunlap, John T., Superintendent of Schools, Pueblo, Colo.
Dunlop, G. M., Div. of Educ., University of Alberta, Edmonton, Alba., Canada
Dunn, Ruth, 210 Breckinridge Lane, Louisville, Ky.
Dunning, Frances E., 125 Owre Hall, Univ. of Minnesota, Minneapolis, Minn.
Durant, Adrian J., Jr., 1115 Holiday Park Dr., Champaign, Ill.
Durante, Spencer E., Second Ward High School, Charlotte, N.C.
Durflinger, Glenn W., 5665 Cielo Ave., Goleta, Calif.
Durkee, Frank M., 183 Union Ave., Belleville, N.J.
Durost, Walter N., 2181 Indian Rocks Rd., Largo, Fla.
Durr, William K., Col. of Educ., Michigan State Univ., East Lansing, Mich.
Durrell, Donald D., Boston University, 332 Bay State Rd., Boston, Mass.
Dutton, Eugene, Rhode Island College, Providence, R.I.
Dutton, Wilbur H., 1913 Greenfield Ave., Los Angeles, Calif.
Duval, Joan E., 3911 Argyle Ter., N.W., Washington, D.C.
Duyser, Emma, Highland Rd., New Hartford, Conn.
Dwyer, John E., Superintendent of Schools, Elizabeth, N.J.
Dwyer, Roy E., University of Tampa, Tampa, Fla.
Dyer, Frank E., 1331 Cecil Ave., Delano, Calif.
Dyke, Elwood E., Southport Elem. Sch., 723—76th St., Kenosha, Wis.
Dykes, Mrs. Alma, 9755 Cincinnati-Columbus Rd., Cincinnati, Ohio
Dykes, Mrs. Eunice, 119 Woodbine St., Kirkwood, Mo.
Dykstra, Robert, 248 Burton Hall, Univ. of Minnesota, Minneapolis, Minn.
Dziak, Suzanne S., 2203—42nd St., N.W., Washington, D.C.

Eargle, Zane E., 247 Jackson Circle, Chapel Hill, N.C.
Earl, Rhea W., 1660 Shawnee Rd., Lima, Ohio
Early, Margaret J., 508 University Pl., Syracuse, N.Y.
Eash, Maurice J., Dept. of Educ., Ball State Tchrs. Col., Muncie, Ind.
Easley, Harriet, San Fernando State College, Northridge, Calif.
Ebel, Robert L., Michigan State University, East Lansing, Mich.
Eberle, August W., University of Chattanooga, Chattanooga, Tenn.
Eberly, J. Wilgus, Texas Woman's University, Denton, Tex.
Eberman, Paul W., 285 Forrest Ave., Elkins Park, Pa.
Eccles, Mrs. J. K., University of Alberta, Calgary, Alba., Canada
Echols, Jack, P.O. Box 660, Farmington, N.M.
Eckert, Ruth E., Col. of Educ., University of Minnesota, Minneapolis, Minn.
Eckhardt, John W., 13 Panorama Gardens, Bakersfield, Calif.
Eden, Donald F., Adams State College, Alamosa, Colo.
Edelfelt, Roy A., NCTEPS, National Education Assn., Washington, D.C.
Edelmann, Anne M., 7614 Garden Rd., Cheltenham, Pa.
Edgar, Robert W., Dept. of Educ., Queens College, Flushing, N.Y.
Edick, Helen, 55 Elizabeth St., Hartford, Conn.
Edson, William H., 206 Burton Hall, Univ. of Minnesota, Minneapolis, Minn.
Edstrom, A. E., Senior High School, 1001 State Hwy., Hopkins, Minn.
Edwards, Andrew S., Georgia Southern College, Statesboro, Ga.

Edwards, Arthur U., Eastern Illinois University, Charleston, Ill.
Edwards, Mrs. Barbara F., 217 N.W. 34th Dr., Gainesville, Fla.
Edwards, G. N., Board of Education, City Hall, Stratford, Ont., Canada
Edwards, Gerald F., Box 55A, Yellow Springs, Ohio
Edwards, Mrs. Inettie B., 2512 Orcutt Ave., Newport News, Va.
Edwards, Marcia, Burton Hall, University of Minnesota, Minneapolis, Minn.
Edwards, T. Bentley, Sch. of Educ., Univ. of California, Berkeley, Calif.
Effron, Michael P., John Adams High Sch., 3817 E. 116th St., Cleveland, Ohio
Egge, Donald E., Hoquiam High School, 625 Emerson Ave., Hoquiam, Wash.
Ehlers, Henry J., Duluth Branch, University of Minnesota, Duluth, Minn.
Ehrlich, Emanuel, 622 East 20th St., New York, N.Y.
Eichholz, Gerhard C., University of Southern Florida, Tampa, Fla.
Eikaas, Alf I., Dept. of Psych., West. Washington State Col., Bellingham, Wash.
Einolf, W. L., Birchrunville, Pa.
Eisenbise, Merlin E., Citrus Junior College, Azusa, Calif.
Eiserer, Paul E., Tchrs. Col., Columbia University, New York, N.Y.
Eklund, Paul A., Lake View School, 22nd and Bethesda Blvd., Zion, Ill.
Elam, Sophie L., 676 Riverside Dr., New York, N.Y.
Elder, Richard D., 301 W. Cross St., Ypsilanti, Mich.
Elder, Ruth E., Univ. Sch., University of Oklahoma, Norman, Okla.
Elderson, Marquitta B., 15521 Oakbury, LaMirada, Calif.
Elkin, Sol, 17457 Manderson, Detroit, Mich.
Elland, A. H., Hutchinson Junior College, 1300 Plum, Hutchinson, Kan.
Elle, Martin J., Southern Oregon College, Ashland, Ore.
Ellerbrook, Louis W., Box 276, Stephen F. Austin Sta., Nacogdoches, Tex.
Ellingson, Mark, Rochester Institute of Technology, Rochester, N.Y.
Elliott, A. R., 520 Campbell Ave., Geneva, Ill.
Elliott, David L., Box 120, Tchrs. Col., Columbia Univ., New York, N.Y.
Elliott, Ella Mary, Northern Montana Col., 526—4th St., Havre, Mont.
Elliott, John A., 61 N. McLean Blvd., Memphis, Tenn.
Ellis, Mrs. Celia Diamond, 1125 S. LaJolla Ave., Los Angeles, Calif.
Ellis, Frederick E., University of British Columbia, Vancouver, B.C., Canada
Ellis, G. W., P.O. Box 526, Lake City, Fla.
Ellis, John F., 4271 Highland Blvd., North Vancouver, B.C., Canada
Ellis, Joseph R., Dept. of Educ., Indiana State Tchrs. Col., Terre Haute, Ind.
Ellis, Robert L., 1125 S. LaJolla Ave., Los Angeles, Calif.
Ellis, U. Berkley, Bristol Township Schools, Levittown, Pa.
Ellison, Alfred, 1 Joseph St., New Hyde Park, N.Y.
Ellison, F. Robert, 1354 Laurel St., Casper, Wyo.
Ellsworth, Ruth E., 630 Merrick St., Detroit, Mich.
Elmer, Mrs. Marion Short, 131 Ullman St., Buffalo, N.Y.
Emmet, Thomas, 4001 W. McNichols Rd., Detroit, Mich.
Endres, Mary P., Purdue University, Lafayette, Ind.
Engel, Barney M., Southern Illinois Univ., Carbondale, Ill.
Engelhardt, Jack E., 1500 Maywood Ave., Ann Arbor, Mich.
Engelhardt, Nickolaus L., Jr., Purdy Station, N.Y.
England, Byron, Box 1710, El Paso, Tex.
Engle, Arthur W., Amherst Central Sch., 474 Church St., Amherst, Ohio
English, John W., Superintendent of Schools, Southfield, Mich.
English, Marvin D., 23 West 270th St., St. Charles Rd., Glen Ellyn, Ill.
Enzinger, Philip, Jr., 5975 N. Points Blvd., St. Louis, Mo.
Epstein, Bertram, City College, 139th St. and Convent Ave., New York, N.Y.
Erbe, Wesley A., Western Reserve University, Cleveland, Ohio
Erdman, Robert L., Univ. of Wisconsin-Milwaukee, Milwaukee, Wis.
Erickson, Harley E., State College of Iowa, Cedar Falls, Iowa
Erickson, L. W., Sch. of Educ., Univ. of California, Los Angeles, Calif.
Erickson, Marilyn, Psych. Dept., N.C. Mem. Hospital, Chapel Hill, N.C.
Erickson, Ralph J., 1326 W. Wincrest Dr., Winona, Minn.
Erickson, Ralph W., College Sta., Columbus, Miss.
Erskine, Mrs. Mildred R., 2096 Watson Ave., St. Paul, Minn.
Ersted, Ruth, State Department of Education, St. Paul, Minn.

Ervin, John B., 5933 Enright St., St. Louis, Mo.
Ervin, William B., 1 Midland Pl., Newark, N.J.
Erxleben, Arnold C., 157 Bemis Dr., Seward, Neb.
Eson, Morris E., State University of New York, Albany, N.Y.
Ettinger, Mrs. Bernadette C., 474 Brooklyn Blvd., Brightwaters, L.I., N.Y.
Eurich, Alvin C., 477 Madison Ave., New York, N.Y.
Evans, Edgar Ernest, P.O. Box 111, Alabama State College, Montgomery, Ala.
Evans, John C., Jr., 6325 South, 550 East, Bountiful, Utah
Evans, John W., Superintendent of Schools, 1020—7th St., Lorain, Ohio
Evans, Ralph F., Fresno State College, Fresno, Calif.
Evans, Rupert N., Col. of Educ., Univ. of Illinois, Urbana, Ill.
Evans, Warren D., Pennsylvania State College, Ebensburg, Pa.
Evenson, Warren L., 1528 S. Douglas St., Springfield, Ill.
Everett, Millard S., Oklahoma State University, Stillwater, Okla.
Evertts, Eldonna L., 147 Wedgewood Dr., Lincoln, Neb.
Ewart, Mrs. Annie G., Shorewood Public Schools, Shorewood, Wis.
Ewert, W. G., Box 428, Biggar, Sask., Canada
* Ewigleben, Mrs. Muriel, 3727 Weisser Park Ave., Ft. Wayne, Ind.
Ewing, Parmer L., Sch. of Educ., New York Univ., Washington Sq., New York, N.Y.
Eyermann, Louis M., 7740 N. Marshfield Ave., Chicago, Ill.

Faddis, Mrs. Gabrielle J., Col. of Educ., Temple University, Philadelphia, Pa.
Faerber, Louis J., University of Dayton, Dayton, Ohio
Fairbanks, Gar, Div. of Educ., Hofstra College, Hempstead, L.I., N.Y.
Fairfield, Mrs. Ethel D., 6316 Riverview, Houston, Tex.
Falk, Conrad, Conception Seminary, Conception, Mo.
Falk, Philip H., 3721 Council Crest, Madison, Wis.
Fallon, Berlic J., Dept. of Educ., Texas Technological Col., Lubbock, Tex.
Farber, Evan Ira, Earlham College, Earlham, Ind.
Fargen, J. Jerome, 1284 Cherokee Rd., Louisville, Ky.
Farley, Gilbert J., Sch. of Educ., University of Miami, Coral Gables, Fla.
Farley, John A., Univ. of Detroit, 4001 W. McNichols Rd., Detroit, Mich.
Farr, S. David, Educ. Res. Center, University of Buffalo, Buffalo, N.Y.
Fasan, Walter R., 3401 West 65th Pl., Chicago, Ill.
Faunce, Roland C., Wayne State University, Detroit, Mich.
Fawley, Paul C., Dept. of Educ., University of Utah, Salt Lake City, Utah
Fay, Leo C., Sch. of Educ., Indiana University, Bloomington, Ind.
Fea, Henry Robert, University of Washington, Seattle, Wash.
Fedorczyk, Viola S., Sch. of Educ., Univ. of Connecticut, Storrs, Conn.
Feelhaver, Carl T., Supt. of Schools, 5 North 16th St., Fort Dodge, Iowa
Feingold, S. Norman, 1640 Rhode Island Ave., N.W., Washington, D.C.
Feldhusen, John, Purdue University, Lafayette, Ind.
Feley, Ruth A., North Main St., East Granby, Conn.
Felix, Morton, Rhode Island College, Providence, R.I.
Feller, Dan, 9951-B Robbins Dr., Beverly Hills, Calif.
Felton, Ralph D., 35 High St., Montrose, Pa.
Fenollosa, George M., Houghton Mifflin Co., 2 Park St., Boston, Mass.
Fenske, Arthur S., 2739 Lincoln Rd., Kenosha, Wis.
Ferran, Rose M., 3515 Napoleon Ave., New Orleans, La.
Ferrier, William K., 6517 S.W. 35th Ave., Portland, Ore.
Ferris, Donald R., San Jose State College, San Jose, Calif.
Ferris, Newell D., Columbia Bible College, Columbia, S.C.
Fessier, Mrs. Margery, 3336 Josephine St., Lynwood, Calif.
Feuers, Stelle, 2372 Nalin Dr., Los Angeles, Calif.
Ficken, Clarence E., 39 Forest Ave., Delaware, Ohio
Fiedler, E. L., Superintendent of Schools, Abilene, Kan.
Fiedler, Ernest G., Sch. of Educ., Univ. of Chicago, Chicago, Ill.
Fiedler, William G., Superintendent of Schools, Union City, N.J.
Field, Robert L., 1415 Wisconsin St., Oshkosh, Wis.
Fields, Clarence J., Coppin State Teachers College, Baltimore, Md.

Fields, Ralph R., Tchrs. Col., Columbia University, New York, N.Y.
Fielstra, Clarence, Sch. of Educ., Univ. of California, Los Angeles, Calif.
Feilstra, Helen, San Fernando Valley State College, Northridge, Calif.
Fieman, Marvin, 307 S. Arnoz Dr., Los Angeles, Calif.
Figurel, J. Allen, 2430 Tanglewood Dr., Allison Park, Pa.
Filbeck, Orval, Abilene Christian College, Abilene, Tex.
Filosa, Mary G., Maple Lane, Mtd. Rte., Bound Brook, N.J.
Fina, Robert P., 522 Fourth St., Catasauqua, Pa.
Finch, F. H., 105 Gregory Hall, University of Illinois, Urbana, Ill.
Findlay, Stephen W., Delbarton School, Morristown, N.J.
Findley, Warren G., Col. of Educ., University of Georgia, Athens, Ga.
Findley, William H., Jr., 210—191st Ter., Miami Beach, Fla.
Fine, Huldah, 2970 Blaine Ave., Detroit, Mich.
Fink, Abel K., Educ. Dept., College of Education, Buffalo, N.Y.
Fink, Herbert J., Von Steuben High School, 5039 N. Kimball Ave., Chicago, Ill.
Fink, Martin B., 1557 Mendocino Dr., Concord, Calif.
Fink, Paul J., 31 S. Penn St., Allentown, Pa.
Fink, Stuart D., Northern Illinois University, DeKalb, Ill.
Finlay, Mrs. Helen K., 4521 N. Dittmar Rd., Arlington, Va.
Finster, Mrs. Virginia, P.O. Box 714, Raceland, La.
Fischer, Mrs. Cora I., 176 Grove Park, Fort Dix, N.J.
Fischer, John H., Tchrs. Col., Columbia University, New York, N.Y.
Fischer, William G., Bd. of Educ., 228 N. LaSalle St., Chicago, Ill.
Fischoff, Ephraim, 15 Riverview Pl., Lynchburg, Va.
Fishback, Woodson W., Southern Illinois University, Carbondale, Ill.
Fishell, Kenneth N., Col. of Educ., University of Rochester, Rochester, N.Y.
Fisher, Hazel, Hartford Co. Bd. of Educ., 45 E. Gordon St., Bel Air, Md.
Fisher, James A., Boston University, 688 Boylston, Boston, Mass.
Fisher, Joseph T., University of South Dakota, Vermillion, S.D.
Fisher, Lawrence A., University of Illinois, 1853 W. Polk St., Chicago, Ill.
Fisher, Mrs. Ljourie S., Miami Dade Junior College, Miami, Fla.
* Fisher, Mrs. Welthy H., Literacy Village, P.O. Singar Nagar, Lucknow, U.P.,
    India
Fisk, Robert S., Sch. of Educ., University of Buffalo, Buffalo, N.Y.
Fitch, Viola K., 12330 Middlebelt Rd., Livonia, Mich.
Fitz, John Allen, 8 Verde Court, Alexandria, Va.
* Fitzgerald, James A., 1103 Pine St., Scranton, Pa.
Fitzgerald, Louis A., Reading Clinic, Purdue Univ., Lafayette, Ind.
Fitzgibbon, Walter C., 206 N. Lansing, Mt. Pleasant, Mich.
Fitzpatrick, E. D., Southern Illinois University, Carbondale, Ill.
Fitzsimons, Frank P., 2467 Ocean Ave., Brooklyn, N.Y.
Fitzwater, James P., 3333 West 31st St., Chicago, Ill.
Flagg, E. Alma, 44 Stengel Ave., Newark, N.J.
Flaggert, James J., Jr., USA Leghorn Genl. Depot, APO 19, New York, N.Y.
Flamand, Ruth K., 72 Goldenridge Dr., Levittown, Pa.
Flamme, Wayne H., Junior-Senior High School, Antigo, Wis.
Flanagan, John C., Amer. Inst. for Res., 410 Amberson Ave., Pittsburgh, Pa.
Flanagan, William F., 100 Tanner Ave., Warwick, R.I.
Flanders, Ned A., Sch. of Educ., Univ. of Mich., Ann Arbor, Mich.
Fleck, Henrietta, H.E. Dept., New York Univ., Washington Sq., New York, N.Y.
Fleming, Harold D., Div. of Educ., State College, Bemidji, Minn.
Fleming, Lora, Idaho State University, Pocatello, Idaho
Fleming, Robert S., State Dept. of Educ., 175 W. State St., Trenton, N.J.
Fliegler, Louis A., University of Denver, Denver, Colo.
Fligor, R. J., Southern Illinois University, Carbondale, Ill.
Flint, Jack M., Highland Junior College, Highland, Kan.
Floren, Marcella A., 114 N.E. Fourth St., Little Falls, Minn.
Flores, Vetal, Drawer M, Bronte, Tex.
Flower, George Edward, Ontario Col. of Educ., 371 Bloor St. W., Toronto,
    Canada
Focht, James R., Educ. Dept., State Teachers College, Salisbury, Md.

Fogg, William E., Long Beach State College, Long Beach, Calif.
Fonacier, Andres Medina, Ilocos Norte Normal Sch., Laoag, I. Norte, Philippines
Fonner, Jean B., 4710 Vantage Ave., North Hollywood, Calif.
Foote, Lawrence E., Superintendent of Schools, Huntington, Ind.
Foran, Joseph A., Superintendent of Schools, Milford, Conn.
Foran, Mary Ellen, 2018 W. Greenleaf Ave., Chicago, Ill.
Foran, Thomas G., The Seigniory Club, Province of Quebec, Canada
Force, Dewey G., Jr., Pattee Hall, Univ. of Minnesota, Minneapolis, Minn.
Ford, LeRoy H., Jr., State Univ. of New York, Buffalo, N.Y.
Ford, Roxana R., Sch. of Home Econ., Univ. of Minnesota, St. Paul, Minn.
Forrester, Carl M., Lake Park High School, Medinah, Ill.
Forrester, Gertrude, 71 Overpeck Ave., Ridgefield Park, N.J.
Fortess, Lillian, 96 Bay State Rd., Boston, Mass.
Fosback, Alta B., 6025 S.E. 39th St., Portland, Ore.
Foshay, Arthur W., Tchrs. Col., Columbia University, New York, N.Y.
Fossieck, Theodore H., Milne Sch., State Col. for Tchrs., Albany, N.Y.
Foster, E. M., Fresno State Col., 4021 Mt. Vernon Ave., Bakersfield, Calif.
Foster, Mrs. Mardis, 2368—16th Ave., San Francisco, Calif.
Foster, Zeph H., Evergreen Trailer Park, Rt. 1, Moscow, Idaho
Fournier, Edmond A., 2215 Opdyke Rd., Bloomfield Hills, Mich.
Fowler, Raymond D., Jr., Box 6142, University, Ala.
Fowlkes, John Guy, 111 Educ. Bldg., Univ. of Wisconsin, Madison, Wis.
Fox, James H., Sch. of Educ., George Washington Univ., Washington, D.C.
Fox, Marion W., 705 Kensington Ave., Plainfield, N.J.
Fox, Robert S., 102 Univ. Sch., University of Michigan, Ann Arbor, Mich.
Frain, Thomas J., Superintendent, Diocese of Trenton, Trenton, N.J.
Francis, Ida L., P.O., Box 243, Somerville, N.J.
Frandsen, Arden N., Utah State University, Logan, Utah
Frankland, Elizabeth M., 1406 S. Prospect Ave., Marshfield, Wis.
Franklin, Jesse E., East Texas State Teachers College, Commerce, Tex.
Franklin, Ruby Holden, Roosevelt University, 430 S. Michigan Ave., Chicago, Ill.
Franson, Arthur H., 50 N. Spring St., LaGrange Park, Ill.
* Franzen, Carl G. F., Dept. of Educ., Marycrest College, Davenport, Iowa
Franzen, William L., Col. of Educ., Univ. of Toledo, Toledo, Ohio
Frase, H. Weldon, 1635 Hutchinson, S.E., Grand Rapids, Mich.
Fraser, Mrs. Dorothy McClure, R.R. 1, West Redding, Conn.
Fred, Bernhart G., 108 McCormick Dr., DeKalb, Ill.
Fredrick, James R., Arizona State College, Flagstaff, Ariz.
Frederick, Pauline M., Kamahameha Schools, Honolulu, Hawaii
Frederick, Orie I., Western Michigan University, Kalamazoo, Mich.
Freeman, Kenneth H., 403 Christian College Ave., Columbia, Mo.
Freeman, Ruges Richmond, Jr., 4582 Aldine St., St. Louis, Mo.
Fremont, Herbert, Queens College, Flushing, N.Y.
French, Joseph L., Hill Hall, University of Missouri, Columbia, Mo.
French, William M., Muhlenberg College, Allentown, Pa.
Frenzel, Norman J., Wisconsin State College, Oshkosh, Wis.
Fretwell, Elbert K., Jr., State Education Dept., Albany, N.Y.
Freund, Evelyn, 5954 Guilford, Detroit, Mich.
Fridlund, John V., Supt., Dist. 98, 1427 S. Oak Park Ave., Berwyn, Ill.
Frieberg, Carter N., Loyola University, 820 N. Michigan Ave., Chicago, Ill.
Friedhoff, Walter H., Illinois State University, Normal, Ill.
Frisbie, Mrs. Babette, Gloversville Public Schools, Gloversville, N.Y.
Frisk, John A., 394 Eureka St., San Francisco, Calif.
Fristoe, Wallace H., Morgan Park High School, Chicago, Ill.
Fritts, J. Scott, P.O. Box 361, Condon, Ore.
Fritzsche, Bertha M., Univ. of Southern Mississippi, Hattiesburg, Miss.
Froehlich, Gustave J., Bur. of Inst. Res., Univ. of Illinois, Urbana, Ill.
Frost, George E., Holyoke Junior College, 291 Pine St., Holyoke, Mass.
Frost, Ralph J., Jr., Maine Twp. High School East, Park Ridge, Ill.
Frost, S. E., Jr., Brooklyn Col., Bedford and Ave. H., Brooklyn, N.Y.
Frutchey, Fred P., U.S. Department of Agriculture, Washington, D.C.

Fujita, Shirley Y., 3279 Huelani Dr., Honolulu, Hawaii
Fulcher, Catherine, 3611 Beier St., Richmond, Mich.
Fulchino, Albert R., Revere High School, Revere, Mass.
Full, Harold, 30 Beekman Pl., New York, N.Y.
Fullagar, William A., Col. of Educ., Univ. of Rochester, Rochester, N.Y.
Fuller, John J., Winona State College, Winona, Minn.
Fullerton, Craig K., 2712 North 52nd St., Omaha, Neb.
Fulton, Helen, 9000 Westview Dr., Houston, Tex.
Fultz, Dan A., 3671 Inglewood Blvd., Los Angeles, Calif.
Fultz, Mrs. Jane N., Col. of Educ., Univ. of Hawaii, Honolulu, Hawaii
Furey, Mary Z., 8301 S.W. 32nd St., Miami, Fla.
Furlow, Florine D., 1047 Simpson St., N.W., Atlanta, Ga.
Furst, Norma, 885 Easton Rd., Glenside, Pa.
Futch, Olivia, Woman's College, Furman University, Greenville, S.C.

Gadbury, Mrs. Nada M., 2401 New York Ave., Muncie, Ind.
Gaines, Berthera E., 3418 S. Claiborne Ave., New Orleans, La.
Gaines, Rosslyn, 1740 Sunset Blvd., Los Angeles, Calif.
Gaiser, P. F., Sch. of Tch. Arts, Univ. of Portland, Portland, Ore.
Gall, Harold, Senior High School, Lancaster, Wis.
Gallagher, Dora Agnes, 400 S. Hauser Blvd., Los Angeles, Calif.
Gallagher, Erwin A., Superintendent of Schools, Westwood, Mass.
Gallen, Albert A., 54 Fern Hill Lane, West Chester, Pa.
Gallicchio, Francis A., 667 Madison Ave., Meadville, Pa.
Galloway, Geraldine, 111 Northwest Tenth St., Fairfield, Ill.
Gambert, Charles A., 607 Walnut Ave., Niagara Falls, N.Y.
Gamble, Karl W., California State College, California, Pa.
Gambrill, Bessie Lee, 201 Armory St., New Haven, Conn.
Gamelin, Francis C., 151 Sylvan Ave., Leonia, N.J.
Gammill, James R., Educ. Dept., Texas Technological Col., Tech Sta., Tex.
Gans, Leo, 4300 West 62nd St., Indianapolis, Ind.
Gansberg, Lucille, 2255-C Goodrich St., Sacramento, Calif.
Garbe, Lester, 2110 W. Marne Ave., Milwaukee, Wis.
Garbel, Marianne, 6732 Crandon Ave., Chicago, Ill.
Garber, Lee O., 3810 Walnut St., Philadelphia, Pa.
Garber, M. Delott, Northwest-Jones Sch., 485 Woodland St., Hartford, Conn.
Gardner, D. Bruce, Iowa State University, Ames, Iowa
Gardiner, Marian J., 415 N. Felton St., Philadelphia, Pa.
Garlich, Marvin O., 8901 McVicker Ave., Morton Grove, Ill.
Garinger, Elmer H., 2625 Briarcliff Pl., Charlotte, N.C.
Garoutte, Bill Charles, Univ. of California Medical Center, San Francisco, Calif.
Garrett, Charles G., 837 N. Cline St., Griffith, Ind.
Garvey, Reba, Allegheny College, Meadville, Pa.
Garvin, Fannie, 606 Ohio St., Wichita, Kan.
* Gates, Arthur I., Tchrs. Col., Columbia University, New York, N.Y.
Gates, Thomas J., Grad. Sch. of Educ., Rutgers Univ., New Brunswick, N.J.
Gathercole, F. J., Superintendent of Schools, Saskatoon, Sask., Canada
Gauerke, Warren E., Wayne State University, Detroit, Mich.
Gauvey, Ralph E., Urbana Junior College, Urbana, Ohio
Gazelle, Hazel N., 1255 N. Michillinda, Pasadena, Calif.
Gebbart, James W., USAID, APO 271, New York, N.Y.
Geer, Owen C., Sch. of Educ., University of Bridgeport, Bridgeport, Conn.
Geiken, Lloyd A., Evanston Twp. High School, Evanston, Ill.
Gelerinter, Alfred, 82 Meigs St., Rochester, N.Y.
Geller, Molly S., 344 Buckingham Rd., Cedarhurst, L.I., N.Y.
Gemmell, C. L., Dept. of Educ. and Psych., Union College, Lincoln, Neb.
Geng, George, Glassboro State College, Glassboro, N.J.
Gentry, George H., P.O. Box 30, Baytown, Tex.
Gentry, Ira A., Jr., Tennessee A. & I. State University, Nashville, Tenn.
George, Howard A., Northwest Missouri State College, Maryville, Mo.
George, Zale R., Jr., 309 Church Rd., Bethel Park, Pa.

Georgiades, William, Univ. of Southern California, Los Angeles, Calif.
Georgiady, Nicholas P., Asst. Supt. of Pub. Instrn., Lansing, Mich.
Geraty, T. S., 7422 Hancock Ave., Takoma Park, Md.
Gephart, Woodrow W., Old Orchard Dr., Geneva, Ohio
Gerber, Wayne J., Bethel College, Mishawaka, Ind.
Gerberich, J. Raymond, 2601 Woodley Pl., N.W., Washington, D.C.
Gerlach, Vernon, A-V Center, Arizona State University, Tempe, Ariz.
Gerletti, John D., USOM, APO 271, New York, N.Y.
Gerlock, D. E., Dept. of Educ., Valdosta State College, Valdosta, Ga.
Germann, Ruth Ann, Apt. 1212-S, 4250 Marine Dr., Chicago, Ill.
Gernert, H. F., Jr., 522 North 24th St., Allentown, Pa.
Gesler, Harriet L., 70 Agnes Dr., Manchester, Conn.
Gest, Mrs. Viola S., P.O. Box 254, Seguin, Tex.
Getzels, J. W., Dept. of Educ., University of Chicago, Chicago, Ill.
Ghalib, Hanna, P.O. Box, Beirut, Lebanon
Giannuzzi, John P., 482 Iris St., Los Alamos, N.M.
Gibbs, E. Delmar, College of Puget Sound, Tacoma, Wash.
Gibbs, Edward, III, 1145 Clinton Ter., South Plainfield, N.J.
Gibbs, Wesley, Superintendent, Dist. No. 68, 9300 N. Kenton, Skokie, Ill.
Gibert, James M., Randolph-Macon Woman's College, Lynchburg, Va.
Gibson, Mrs. Kathryn Snell, Prairie View A. & M. Col., Prairie View, Tex.
Gibson, Mrs. Norma Boyle, 902 S. Manhattan Pl., Los Angeles, Calif.
Giertz, Margaret E., 816 Taylor St., Joliet, Ill.
Giesy, John P., 1017 Blanchard, Flint, Mich.
Gilbert, Mrs. Doris Wilcox, 1044 Euclid Ave., Berkeley, Calif.
Gilbert, Floyd O., Minnesota State College, St. Cloud, Minn.
Gilbert, Jerome H., 11155 S. Depot St., Worth, Ill.
Gilbert, John H., Dept. of Educ., Monmouth College, West Long Branch, N.J.
Gilberts, Robert D., Superintendent of Schools, Madison, Wis.
Giles, LeRoy H., University of Dubuque, Dubuque, Iowa
Gilk, Edwin John, P.O. Box 642, Columbia Falls, Mont.
Gilkey, Richard, 424 Willamette Ave., Medford, Ore.
Gill, Bernard I., Moorhead State Tchrs. College, Moorhead, Minn.
Gill, Margaret, ASCD, 1201 Sixteenth St., N.W., Washington, D.C.
Gilland, Thomas M., 327 Wood St., California, Pa.
Gillanders, Dorothy F., 752 Orange St., Tempe, Ariz.
Gilligan, Michael B., Jersey City State College, Jersey City, N.J.
Gilman, Alice, C. W. Post College, Greenvale, L.I., N.Y.
Gilmore, Douglas M., 5721 Perryton St., Wichita, Kan.
Gilstrap, Robert L., University of Florida, Gainesville, Fla.
Gingerich, Mrs. Julia B., R. 1, Box 193-B, Bettendorf, Iowa
Giventer, Edwin B., 1250 Post Rd., Scarsdale, N.Y.
Glade, Melba, 2610 Highland Dr., Salt Lake City, Utah
Glaeser, Mrs. Louise M., 1409 Spaulding, Alton, Ill.
Glaess, Herman L., Concordia Teachers College, Seward, Neb.
Glas, Marie, Thoheper Theme School, R.D. 2, Napier, New Zealand
Glaser, Robert, Salk Hall, University of Pittsburgh, Pittsburgh, Pa.
Glasow, Ogden L., P.O. Box 143, Macomb, Ill.
Glauser, Alfred J., 309 S.E. 33rd Ave., Portland, Ore.
Glenn, Edward E., 1130 E. Epler Ave., Indianapolis, Ind.
Glenn, J. Curtis, 1531 West 103rd St., Chicago, Ill.
Glock, Marvin D., Stone Hall, Cornell University, Ithaca, N.Y.
Glogau, Arthur H., Oregon College of Education, Monmouth, Ore.
Gnagey, Thomas David, State University of New York, Geneseo, N.Y.
Gnifkowski, Kathleen, 267 East 15th Ave., Columbus, Ohio
Gobetz, Wallace, 540 East 22nd St., Brooklyn, N.Y.
Goble, Robert I., McGuffey No. 360, Miami University, Oxford, Ohio
Godfrey, Mary E., Pennsylvania State University, University Park, Pa.
Godwin, Joseph, Boiling Springs, N.C.
Goebel, Edmund J., Archdiocese of Milwaukee, 437 W. Galena St., Milwaukee, Wis.

Gold, Milton J., Hunter College, 695 Park Ave., New York, N.Y.
Goldberg, Miriam L., Tchrs. Col., Columbia University, New York, N.Y.
Goldberg, Nathan, 75-47—196th St., Flushing, N.Y.
Goldhammer, Keith, Sch. of Educ., University of Oregon, Eugene, Ore.
Goldman, Bert A., 1311 Dandridge St., Fredricksburg, Va.
Goldner, Ralph H., Sch. of Educ., New York University, New York, N.Y.
Goldstein, Mrs. Gertrude H., Woodward Sch., 321 Clinton Ave., Brooklyn, N.Y.
Goldstein, Helen H., 5325 Meadow Lane, Downers Grove, Ill.
Goldstein, Herbert, Yeshiva University, 110 W. 57th St., New York, N.Y.
Goleman, Clarence E., Box 149, College Sta., Hammond, La.
Goltry, Keith, Dept. of Educ., Parsons College, Fairfield, Iowa
Gomberg, Adeline W., Beaver College, Glenside, Pa.
Gonnelly, Ellen M., James R. Lowell Sch., 3320 W. Hirsch, Chicago, Ill.
Gonzalez, Alice M., University of Puerto Rico, Rio Piedras, Puerto Rico
Good, Carter V., Tchrs. Col., University of Cincinnati, Cincinnati, Ohio
Good, Richard M., 12521 Eastbourne Dr., Silver Spring, Md.
Good, Warren R., 1604 Stony Run Dr., Northwood, Wilmington, Del.
Goodlad, John I., Sch. of Educ., University of California, Los Angeles, Calif.
Goodman, Kenneth S., 18900 Prairie St., Detroit, Mich.
Goodpaster, Robert L., University of Kentucky-Ashland Center, Ashland, Ky.
Goodside, Samuel, Ramaz Upper School, 22 East 82nd St., New York, N.Y.
Goodson, Max R., H.S. Div., Ginn and Co., Boston, Mass.
Goodwin, Helen J., 2507 Beverly Rd., Brooklyn, N.Y.
Googins, Duane G., 2964—116th Ave., N.W., Coon Rapids, Minn.
Goossen, Carl V., 220 Burton Hall, University of Minnesota, Minneapolis, Minn.
Gordon, Alice S., Einstein School, 3830 Cottage Grove Ave., Chicago, Ill.
Gordon, Ira J., Col. of Educ., Univ. of Florida, Gainesville, Fla.
Gordon, Ted E., 317 N. Lucerne, Los Angeles, Calif.
Gore, Lillian L., U.S. Office of Education, Dept. of HEW, Washington, D.C.
Gorham, Marion, 10 Alcott St., Acton, Mass.
Gorman, Frank H., Col. of Educ., University of Omaha, Omaha, Neb.
Gorman, William J., 219-40—93rd Ave., Queens Village, N.Y.
Gormley, Charles L., Dept. of Educ., Alabama College, Montevallo, Ala.
Gorton, Harry B., Rte. No. 1, New Cumberland, Pa.
Gossard, Paul, Superintendent of Schools, Quincy, Mass.
Gottfried, F. J., Superintendent of Schools, Elyria, Ohio
Gottfried, Nathan W., Psych. Dept., Miami University, Oxford, Ohio
Gottschalk, G. R., 464 Brattle Rd., Syracuse, N.Y.
Gould, George, Cathedral of Learn., Univ. of Pittsburgh, Pittsburgh, Pa.
Gould, W. S., Graceland College, Lamoni, Iowa
Gowan, John Curtis, Educ. Div., State College, Northridge, Calif.
Gowin, D. Bob, Stone Hall, Cornell University, Ithaca, N.Y.
Graber, Eldon W., Dept. of Educ., Bluffton College, Bluffton, Ohio
Grabowski, A. A., 2512 Southport Ave., Chicago, Ill.
Grado, Louis M., USOM/Nicaragua, Dept. of State, Washington, D.C.
Grady, Joseph E., St. Bernard's Seminary, 2260 Lake Ave., Rochester, N.Y.
Graetz, Ralph C., 2532 Woodland Lane, Garden Grove, Calif.
Graff, George E., State Dept. of Educ., 41 Hale St., Rockville, Conn.
Graff, Orin B., Col. of Educ., University of Tennessee, Knoxville, Tenn.
Graffam, Donald T., Dickinson College, Carlisle, Pa.
Grandy. L. Munro, Superintendent of Schools, Scituate, Mass.
Granskog, Mrs. Dorothy, 1402 First Ave., So., Escanaba, Mich.
Grant, Eugene B., Northern Illinois University, DeKalb, Ill.
Grant, Wayman R. F., Booker T. Washington Junior High School, Mobile, Ala.
Grau, Mary, Montgomery County Schls., 12 W. Burke Ave., Towson, Md.
Grau, R. T., Clinton Public Schls., Box 110, Clinton, Iowa
Graves, Jack A., 7135th Sch. Group, Det. 306, APO 84, New York, N.Y.
Graves, Linwood D., 115 Leathers Circle, N.W., Atlanta, Ga.
Gray, Dorothy, Dept. of Educ., Queens College, Flushing, N.Y.
Graybeal, William S., 1203 Byrd Ave., Richmond, Va.
Graye, Mytrolene L., 825 Fairview St., High Point, N.C.

Grayson, William H., Jr., 21-71—34th Ave., Long Island City, N.Y.
Green, Donald Ross, 1419 Cornell Rd., N.E., Atlanta, Ga.
Green, John A., Educ. Field Service, Univ. of Idaho, Moscow, Idaho
Green, Ruth E., University of Minnesota, Duluth, Minn.
Greenberg, Mrs. Gilda M., 5435 N. Kennebec Lane, Tucson, Ariz.
Greenberg, Mrs. Judith W., Sch. of Educ., City College, New York, N.Y.
Greenblatt, Edward L., 211 Calle de Arboles, Redondo Beach, Calif.
Greene, Bert I., 717 Charles St., Ypsilanti, Mich.
Greene, Charles E., P.O. Box 185, East Side Sta., Santa Cruz, Calif.
Greene, John G., 107 Chestnut St., Boston, Mass.
Greene, Mrs. Maxine, 1080—5th Ave., New York, N.Y.
Greene, Mrs. Minnie S., 1121 Chestnut St., San Marcos, Tex.
Greenfield, Curtis O., 345 W. Windsor Ave., Phoenix, Ariz.
Greenman, Mrs. Margaret H., Country Fair, Champaign, Ill.
Greenwood, Edward D., Menninger Clinic, Box 829, Topeka, Kan.
Greer, Donald R., University of Missouri, Columbia, Mo.
Greer, Evelyn, Fayette County Schls., 400 Lafayette Dr., Lexington, Ky.
Gregg, Russell T., Sch. of Educ., University of Wisconsin, Madison, Wis.
Greif, Ivo P., Illinois State University, Normal, Ill.
Greivell, Richard, Waukesha Public Schls., South Campus, Waukesha, Wis.
Grennell, Robert L., State University College, Fredonia, N.Y.
Grey, Mrs. Emylu D., 2565 Duke Ave., Richmond, Calif.
Grib, Thomas F., St. Norbert College, West DePere, Wis.
Griffith, Coleman R., 105 Gregory Hall, University of Illinois, Urbana, Ill.
Griffith, Harry E., P.O. Box 427, Arcata, Calif.
Griffiths, Daniel E., 54 Clarendon Rd., Scarsdale, N.Y.
Griffiths, John A., Superintendent of Schools, Monongahela, Pa.
Griffiths, Ruth, 184 Middlesex St., North Andover, Mass.
Grigg, Charles B., Litchfield Junior-Senior High School, Litchfield, Ill.
Grimes, Leslie K., Superintendent of Schools, Greeley, Colo.
Grizzard, Mabel Youree, 711 W. Main St., Waxahachie, Tex.
* Grizzell, E. Duncan, 640 Maxwelton Ct., Lexington, Ky.
Groesbeck, Hulda, Fort Hays Kansas State College, Hays, Kan.
Groff, Frank E., New Hope-Solebury Joint School Dist., New Hope, Pa.
Grogan, M. Lucille, 7638 S. Wood St., Chicago, Ill.
Gronlund, Norman E., Col. of Educ., University of Illinois, Urbana, Ill.
Grose, Robert F., Amherst College, Amherst, Mass.
Gross, Lydia, Lock Haven State Tchrs. College, Lock Haven, Pa.
Gross, Neal, 8 Prescott St., Cambridge, Mass.
Gross, Robert Dean, Sacramento State College, Sacramento, Calif.
Gross, Wilma, 3750 Harrison Blvd., Ogden, Utah
Grossman, Eileen, 2207 W. Rosemont Ave., Chicago, Ill.
Grossnickle, Foster E., 38 Elm Pl., Nutley, N.J.
Grotberg, Mrs. Edith H., Northern Illinois University, DeKalb, Ill.
Grote, Donald V., 2604 Central St., Evanston, Ill.
Grove, Robert N., Superintendent of Schools, Midland Park, N.J.
Grover, Burton L., Manitowoc Public Schools, Manitowoc, Wis.
Groves, Vernon T., Olivet Nazarene College, Kankakee, Ill.
Gruber, Frederick C., Eisenlohr Annex, Univ. of Pennsylvania, Philadelphia, Pa.
Grudell, Regina C., 45 Chadwick Rd., Teaneck, N.J.
Guba, Egon G., Arps Hall, Ohio State University, Columbus, Ohio
Guest, Elizabeth Alice, 14664 East 4th St., Whittier, Calif.
Guillet, N. J., Midwest University, Wichita Falls, Tex.
Gulutsan, Metro, University of Alberta, Edmonton, Alba., Canada
Guss, Carolyn, R.R. 2, Box 139, Bloomington, Ind.
Gussner, William S., Superintendent of Schools, Jamestown, N.D.
Gustafson, A. M., Alice Vail Junior High Sch., 5350 E. 16th St., Tucson, Ariz.
Gustafson, Alma L., 1211 North 5th St., East Grand Forks, Minn.
Guthrie, John A., University of Pittsburgh, Pittsburgh, Pa.
Guttchen, Robert S., 137-16 231st St., Laurelton, N.Y.
Gwynn, J. Minor, 514 North St., Chapel Hill, N.C.

Guzzetta, Charles, Jr., Temple University, Philadelphia, Pa.

Haage, Catherine M., College of New Rochelle, New Rochelle, N.Y.
Haagen, C. Hess, Wesleyan University, Middletown, Conn.
Haas, Richard J., Jr., 119 Stubbs Dr., Trotwood, Ohio
Haberer, Maureen H., 365 Canterbury Dr., Ramsey, N.J.
Hackmann, Jane, 38 Signal Hill Blvd., East St. Louis, Ill.
Hackney, Ben H., Jr., 400 Latimer Rd., Raleigh, N.C.
Haffner, Hyman, 6229 Nicholson St., Pittsburgh, Pa.
Hagarty, Edward M., 3908 Lancaster Pike, Wilmington, Del.
Hagen, Elizabeth, Tchrs. Col., Columbia University, New York, N.Y.
Hagen, C. Larry, College of Idaho, Caldwell, Idaho
Hagenson, C. H., University of Southern Mississippi, Hattiesburg, Miss.
Hager, Walter E., 1785 Massachusetts Ave., N.W., Washington, D.C.
Haggerson, Nelson L., 132 W. Balboa Dr., Tempe, Ariz.
Haggerty, Helen Ruth, 110 N. George Mason Dr., Arlington, Va.
Hagglund, Oliver C., Gustavus Adolphus College, St. Peter, Minn.
Hagstrom, Ellis A., Seipsville Rd., Box 76, R.D. #1, Bethlehem, Pa.
Hahn, Albert R., Veterans' Administration Hospital, Phoenix, Ariz.
Haight, Wilbur T., 314 S. DuPont Blvd., Milford, Del.
Haimbach, David, Lab. Sch., Fresno State College, Fresno, Calif.
Halbert, Bernice, East Texas Baptist College, Marshall, Tex.
Haldiman, Carl G., Central Missouri State College, Warrensburg, Mo.
Hale, Gifford G., Sch. of Educ., Florida State University, Tallahassee, Fla.
Hale, Jordan, 2267 Renfrew Rd., Elmont, L.I., N.Y.
Haley, Charles F., Col. of Educ., Northeastern University, Boston, Mass.
Haley, Elizabeth, 1938 Channing Ave., Palo Alto, Calif.
Haley, Gerald J., 5625 N. Natoma Ave., Chicago, Ill.
Haley, Mrs. Margaret T., 1405 E. Grace St., Richmond, Va.
Halfter, Mrs. Irma Theobald, 134 W. St. Charles Rd., Elmhurst, Ill.
Hall, Barbara C., Illinois State University, Normal, Ill.
Hall, James A., Superintendent of Schools, Port Washington, N.Y.
Hall, Joseph I., Holt, Rinehart & Winston, Inc., 383 Madison Ave., New York, N.Y.
Hall, Leon P., Bd. of Educ., 1200 N. Telegraph Rd., Pontiac, Mich.
Hall, M. E., College of the Desert, Palm Desert, Calif.
Hall, Thelma, R.D. No. 1, Fishkill, N.Y.
Hall, William Frank, Elem. Sch. Dist. No. 1, 125 E. Lincoln St., Phoenix, Ariz.
Hallenbeck, Edwin F., University of Rhode Island, Kingston, R.I.
Hallett, Mrs. Robert L., Jr., 8 Old Shawnee Rd., Milford, Del.
Halliwell, Joseph, 347 Sunset Rd., Pompton Plains, N.J.
Hallman, George H., 434 Windermire Rd., Clarksville, Ind.
Halstrom, Frances J., Bradley University, Peoria, Ill.
Halvorsen, H. M., Ginn & Co., Statler Bldg., Boston, Mass.
Hamalainen, Arthur E., 306 Third Ave., East Northport, N.Y.
Hamilton, DeForest S., 2406 Mendota Way, Santa Rosa, Calif.
Hamilton, Gene E., Edgewood Elementary School, Minneapolis, Minn.
Hamilton, Herbert M., Sch. of Bus. Adm., Miami Univ., Oxford, Ohio
Hamilton, Homer H., Jackson State College, Jackson, Miss.
Hamilton, Hope J., 7 Highgate Ave., Buffalo, N.Y.
Hamilton, Lester L., Box 5285, North Charleston, S.C.
Hamilton, Robert J., Dundee School, Riverside, Conn.
Hamlin, Elizabeth, 802 Semmes St., Memphis, Tenn.
Hammel, John A., 740 Cadieux Ave., Grosse Pointe, Mich.
Hammer, Eugene L., Dept. of Educ., Wilkes College, Wilkes-Barre, Pa.
Hammock, Robert C., 3812 Walnut St., Philadelphia, Pa.
Hammond, Granville S., USOM/Educ., Box 32, APO 143, San Francisco, Calif.
Hammond, Sarah Lou, Florida State University, Tallahassee, Fla.
Hancock, Joseph T., 21 Ethel Street, Metuchen, N.J.
Hand, Harold C., Col. of Educ., University of Illinois, Urbana, Ill.
Handley, W. Harold, Olympus High School, Salt Lake City, Utah

Hanigan, Levin B., Superintendent, Echobrook School, Mountainside, N.J.
Hanitchak, John Joseph, USAID, APO 271, New York, N.Y.
Hankerson, M. R., Superintendent of Schools, Thief River Falls, Minn.
Hanley, James L., Superintendent of Schools, Providence, R.I.
Hanna, Alvis N., John Tyler High Schools, 331 S. College St., Tyler, Tex.
Hanna, Ben M., Baylor University, Waco, Tex.
Hanna, Geneva, University of Texas, Austin, Tex.
Hanna, Paul R., Stanford University, Stanford, Calif.
Hannifin, Mrs. Blanche B., 5259 Strohm Ave., North Hollywood, Calif.
Hannon, Elizabeth H., 1432 S. Crescent Ave., Park Ridge, Ill.
Hansen, Mrs. Dorothy Gregg, 1913 Kitty Hawk Pl., Alameda, Calif.
Hansen, G. G., Superintendent of County Schools, Aurora, Neb.
Hansen, Helge E., Public Schools, 5757 Neckel St., Dearborn, Mich.
Hansen, Paul J., 1626 South 13th St., East, Salt Lake City, Utah
Hansen, R. G., 1333 West Maynard Dr., St. Paul, Minn.
Hansen, Robert E., Cherry Hill High School, Cherry Hill, N.J.
Hansen, Stewart R., St. John's University, Collegeville, Minn.
Hanson, Donald L., 1205 Normal Ave., Cape Girardeau, Mo.
Hanson, Earl H., Superintendent of Schools, Rock Island, Ill.
Hanson, Frances F., Washington State College, Bellingham, Wash.
Hanson, Gordon C., University of Wichita, Wichita, Kan.
Hanway, Hannah F., 8011 Eastern Ave., Silver Spring, Md.
Harbo, L. S., Augsberg College, Minneapolis, Minn.
Hardee, Melvene D., Florida State University, Tallahassee, Fla.
Hardesty, Cecil D., 6401 Linda Vista Rd., San Diego, Calif.
Hardin, Mrs. Marjorie, 2421 El Camino, Turlock, Calif.
Hardy, J. Garrick, Alabama State College, Montgomery, Ala.
Hargett, Earl F., Freeport Community College, Freeport, Ill.
Hargrave, Ruth M., Div. of Educ., Central State College, Wilberforce, Ohio
Harkness, Donald E., Curriculum Service Center, Manhasset, N.Y.
Harlow, James G., Col. of Educ., University of Oklahoma, Norman, Okla.
Harmon, Ruth E., 1720 Commonwealth Ave., West Newton, Mass.
Harms, Irene, Pennsylvania State University, University Park, Pa.
Harnack, Robert S., Sch. of Educ., University of Buffalo, Buffalo, N.Y.
Harney, Paul J., University of San Francisco, San Francisco, Calif.
Harrington, Edmund Ross, 509 A St., Taft, Calif.
Harrington, Mrs. Edna B., 901 Savannah Rd., Lewes, Del.
Harrington, Frances J., 12½ Lafayette St., Attleboro, Mass.
Harrington, Johns H., 7615 McGroarty St., Tujunga, Calif.
Harris, Albert J., Educ. Clinic, Queens College, Flushing, N.Y.
Harris, Ben M., 325 Sutton Hall, University of Texas, Austin, Tex.
Harris, C. W., P.O. Box 1487, Deland, Fla.
Harris, Claude C., 201 North 15th St., Muskogee, Okla.
Harris, Dale B., Burrowes Bldg., Pennsylvania State Univ., University Park, Pa.
Harris, Fred E., Baldwin-Wallace College, Berea, Ohio
Harris, Janet C., 121 Allerton Rd., Newton Highlands, Mass.
Harris, Lewis E., 3752 N. Hight St., Columbus, Ohio
Harris, Mary Jo, Northwestern State College, Natchitoches, La.
Harris, Raymond P., Mt. Vernon Public Schools, Mt. Vernon, N.Y.
Harris, Ruby Dean, Univ. Hall, University of California, Berkeley, Calif.
Harris, Samuel D., Jr., 4047 Meek Dr., Jacksonville, Fla.
Harris, Theodore L., Sch. of Educ., University of Wisconsin, Madison, Wis.
Harris, Wylie V., Superintendent of Schools, Shawnee Mission, Kan.
Harry, David P., Jr., Grad. Sch., Western Reserve University, Cleveland, Ohio
Hart, Mrs. Lawrence W., P.O. Box 14, Rock Falls, Ill.
Hart, Richard H., 220 W. Forest St., Hillsboro, Ore.
Hart, Ruth M. R., 1100 Douglas Ave., Minneapolis, Minn.
Hartke, Ruth E., 4760 Roemer Ave., Dearborn, Mich.
Hartley, James R., Univ. Extn., University of California, Riverside, Calif.
Hartness, Helen Thun, 1825 N.E. Clackamas, Portland, Ore.
Hartsig, Barbara, Orange County State College, Fullerton, Calif.
Hartstein, Jacob I., 11-25 Virginia St., Far Rockaway, N.Y.

Hartung, Maurice L., Dept. of Educ., University of Chicago, Chicago, Ill.
Harwell, John Earl, East Texas Baptist College, Marshall, Tex.
Hasan, Syed, Frostburg State College, Frostburg, Md.
Hasanen, Kenneth L. C., 4491 West 8th Ave., Vancouver, B.C.
Hasenpflug, Thomas R., Barrington Public Schools, Barrington, Ill.
Haskell, Charlotte L., 89 Royal Rd., Bangor, Me.
Haskew, Laurence D., Col. of Educ., University of Texas, Austin, Tex.
Hasman, Richard H., 61 Oakwood Ave., Farmingdale, N.Y.
Hassel, Carl W., Moorestown School Dist., Moorestown, N.J.
Hastie, Reid, University of Minnesota, Minneapolis, Minn.
Hatchett, Ethel L., Dept. of Educ., Hardin-Simmons University, Abilene, Tex.
Hatfield, Donald M., Dept. of Educ., University of California, Berkeley, Calif.
Hastings, Glen R., 2117 South 12th St., Chickasha, Okla.
Haubrich, Vernon F., Dept. of Educ., Hunter College, New York, N.Y.
Hauck, Barbara B., 537 Tenth Ave., Kirkland, Wash.
Hauer, William H., State University College, New Paltz, N.Y.
Haupt, Leonard R., 2801 Glenview Rd., Glenview, Ill.
Hauschild, Mrs. J. R., 211 Bompart Ave., Webster Groves, Mo.
* Havighurst, Robert J., Dept. of Educ., University of Chicago, Chicago, Ill.
Hawkes, Thomas, 5419 University Ave., Chicago, Ill.
Hawkinson, Mabel, 11 Gregory St., Oswego, N.Y.
Hawley, Leslie R., 94 Walden Dr., RFD No. 1, Lakeview, Erie Co., N.Y.
Hawley, Ray C., Superintendent of County Schools, Ottawa, Ill.
Haws, Nina, 315 N. Lorraine, Wichita, Kan.
Hayden, Alice H., Miller Hall, University of Washington, Seattle, Wash.
Hayden, James R., 166 William St., New Bedford, Mass.
Hayden, Velma D., Sch. of Educ., Univ. of South Carolina, Columbia, S.C.
Hayes, Allen P., 1504—4th Ave., Tuscaloosa, Ala.
Hayes, Mrs. Betty M., 725 Hawthorne Dr., Tiburon, Calif.
Hayes, Denis A., Paterson Diocesan Schls., 24 DeGrasse St., Paterson, N.J.
Hayes, Mary T., Aroostook State Tchrs. Col., Presque Isle, Me.
Hayes, Paul C., 3761 Mayfair Dr., Grove City, Ohio
Hays, Harry N., 407 Jesse St., Philipsburg, Pa.
Hays, Warren S., 3218 N. Reno Ave., Tucson, Ariz.
Hayward, W. George, 27 Grant Ave., East Orange, N.J.
Hazan, Sam, 4930 Fulton Ave., Sherman Oaks, Calif.
Hazen, Oliver M., Renton School Dist. No. 403, Renton, Wash.
Hazleton, Edward W., Bogan High School, Chicago, Ill.
Headd, Pearl Walker, Box 362, Tuskegee Institute, Ala.
Headley, Ross A., 97-30 57th Ave., Corona, N.Y.
Heagney, Genevieve, State Teachers College at Towson, Baltimore, Md.
Heald, James E., 1512 Woodwide, East Lansing, Mich.
Healey, Margaret L., Rt. No. 1, Box 255, Taft, Calif.
Healy, Ann Kirtland, Valdosta State College, Valdosta, Ga.
Healy, Mary, 8459 Dante Ave., Chicago, Ill.
Heavenridge, Glen G., P.O. Box 836, Garden City, Mich.
Hebeler, Jean R., University of Maryland, College Park, Md.
Hecht, Irvin Sulo, Girls High School, 475 Nostrand Ave., Brooklyn, N.Y.
Heck, Theodore, St. Meinrad Seminary, St. Meinrad, Ind.
Hecker, Izora, 1486 Woodrow, Wichita, Kan.
Hedden, Gerald W., 3320 Jade Ave., Bakersfield, Calif.
Hedges, William D., Peabody Hall, University of Virginia, Charlottesville, Va.
Heding, Howard W., Col. of Educ., Univ. of Missouri, Columbus, Mo.
Heffernan, Helen, State Department of Education, Sacramento, Calif.
Heffernan, Mary, 296 Norwood Ave., Warwick, R.I.
Heftel, Winifred W., Read. and Speech Clinic, 116 S. Michigan, Chicago, Ill.
Hegman, M. Marian, 332 South Ave., Medina, N.Y.
Heideman, Paul J., Concordia College, St. Paul, Minn.
Heimann, Robert A., Arizona State University, Tempe, Ariz.
Heiney, John F., 14 Wollaston Rd., Wilmington, Del.
Heintzelman, Harvey A., 116 North 25th St., Camp Hill, N.J.

Heisner, H. Fred, Redlands Unified Sch. Dist., Redlands, Calif.
Heist, Paul H., 4606 Tolman Hall, Univ. of California, Berkeley, Calif.
Held, John T., 240 Steinwehr Ave., Gettysburg, Pa.
Helland, Philip C., Junior High School, 611 West 5th St., Willmar, Minn.
Heller, Melvin P., Dept. of Educ., Loyola University, Chicago, Ill.
Hellman, Walter H., 100 Reef Rd., Fairfield, Conn.
Helmick, Russell E., Peabody Hall, Louisiana State Univ., Baton Rouge, La.
* Helms, W. T., 1109 Roosevelt Ave., Richmond, Calif.
Heming, Hilton P., 12 Leonard Ave., Plattsburgh, N.Y.
Hemingway, William C., Western Apts., Billings, Mont.
Hemink, Lyle H., 1300 Elmwood Ave., Buffalo, N.Y.
Henderson, Algo D., 4205 Univ. H.S., Univ. of Michigan, Ann Arbor, Mich.
Henderson, Edmund H., University of Delaware, Newark, Del.
Henderson, Edward, New York University, Washington Sq., New York, N.Y.
Hendrickson, Gordon, University of Cincinnati, Cincinnati, Ohio
Hendrix, Holbert H., Southern Reg. Div., Univ. of Nevada, Las Vegas, Nev.
Hengesbach, Alice R., Willoughby-Eastlake Schls., Center St., Willoughby, Ohio
Henion, Ethel S., 435 N. Central Ave., Ramsey, N.J.
Henkel, Milford F., Malone College, Canton, Ohio
Henle, R. J., 221 N. Grand Blvd., St. Louis, Mo.
Henry, George H., Alison Hall, Univ. of Delaware, Newark, Del.
* Henry, Nelson B., Dept. of Educ., University of Chicago, Chicago, Ill.
Herbst, Leonard A., 3550 Crestmoor Dr., San Bruno, Calif.
Herchek, Michel, Kent State University, Kent, Ohio
Herge, Henry C., Sch. of Educ., Rutgers University, New Brunswick, N.J.
Herman, Myrl G., Board of Educ., Sch. Dist. #45, Villa Park, Ill.
Herman, Wayne L., Jr., 13 Riverview Apts., Laurel, Md.
Herr, Ross, 3452 W. Drummond Pl., Chicago, Ill.
Herr, William A., 536 W. Maple St., Hazleton, Pa.
Herrington, Mrs. Evelyn F., Sch. of Educ., Univ. of Texas, Austin, Tex.
Herriott, M. E., 8921 S. Sepulveda Blvd., Los Angeles, Calif.
Herrmann, D. J., College of William and Mary, Williamsburg, Va.
Hertel, Robert, Illinois State University, Normal, Ill.
Hertert, Patricia C., 221 Moraga Way, Orinda, Calif.
* Hertzler, Silas, 303 S. Washington St., Hillsboro, Kan.
Hesla, Arden E., Mankato State College, Mankato, Minn.
Hess, Clarke F., Marshall College, Huntington, W.Va.
Hess, Glenn C., 44 W. Wheeling St., Washington, Pa.
Hesse, Alexander N., 90 Salisbury Ave., Garden City, L.I., N.Y.
Hetrick, J. B., Grove City Joint Consolidated Schools, Grove City, Pa.
Hetzel, Walter L., 1004 Murray Dr., Ames, Iowa
Heuer, Josephine C., 8444 Edna St., St. Louis, Mo.
Heusner, William W., Michigan State University, East Lansing, Mich.
Heussman, John W., Concordia Seminary, Springfield, Ill.
Hibbs, M. Gregg, Superintendent of Schools, Red Bank, N.J.
Hickey, Bernard, 7 Digren Rd., Natick, Mass.
Hickey, Philip J., Curriculum Lab., 1517 S. Theresa Ave., St. Louis, Mo.
Hicks, Mrs. Aline Black, 812 Lexington St., Norfolk, Va.
Hicks, Samuel I., Col. of Educ., Ohio University, Athens, Ohio
Hicks, Victor H., East Central State College, Ada, Okla.
Hidy, Mrs. Elizabeth Willson, Box 287, Gila Bend, Ariz.
Hieronymus, Albert N., East Hall, State Univ. of Iowa, Iowa City, Iowa
Hiers, Mrs. Turner M., 5661 S.W. Second Court, Fort Lauderdale, Fla.
Higgins, Mrs. Ardis, 1527 E. Mountain Dr., Santa Barbara, Calif.
Hightower, Emory A., 520 S. Pascack Rd., Spring Valley, N.Y.
Hilgard, Ernest R., Dept. of Psych., Stanford University, Stanford, Calif.
Hill, Alberta D., Office of Education, Dept. of H.E.W., Washington, D.C.
Hill, Charles E., 529 Fifth St., S.W., Rochester, Minn.
Hill, George E., Dept. of Educ., Ohio University, Athens, Ohio
Hill, Mrs. Ione A., 107 Filer St., Monroe, La.

Hill, Joseph K., Downstate Medical Center, Brooklyn, N.Y.
Hill, Katherine E., Press 23, New York Univ., Washington Sq., New York, N.Y.
Hill, Mary C., 1302—20th St., Rock Island, Ill.
Hill, Mrs. Ruth E., 1255 Sandalwood Dr., El Centro, Calif.
Hillerby, Ruth C., 212 E. Live Oak St., San Gabriel, Calif.
Hillerich, Robert L., 950 Huber Lane, Glenview, Ill.
Hilliard, Herbert S., Bates High School, Annapolis, Md.
Hillson, Maurie, Linden Campus, Fairleigh Dickinson Univ., Teaneck, N.J.
Himler, Leonard E., 1225 Fair Oaks Pkwy., Ann Arbor, Mich.
Hinds, Jean, 2460 Sixth St., N.W., Washington, D.C.
Hinds, Lillian R., 932 W. Mackenzie Dr., Phoenix, Ariz.
Hindsman, Edwin, 1901 Windsor Dr., Bloomington, Ind.
Hines, Vynce A., 1220 S.W. Ninth Rd., Gainesville, Fla.
Hinkley, William C., Superintendent of Schools, Aurora, Colo.
Hinman, Marie, Westover Park Apts., Durham, N.C.
Hissong, Clyde, Urbana College, Urbana, Ohio
Hitchcock, Catharine, 1837 E. Erie Ave., Lorain, Ohio
Hites, Christopher, 302 Portola Rd., Portola Valley, Calif.
Hitt, Harold H., 802 Lawson St., Midland, Tex.
Hittinger, Mrs. Martha E., 914 W. Whitley, Whittier, Calif.
Ho, Thomas C. K., 72 Distler Ave., West Caldwell, N.J.
Hobbs, Earl W., Mamaroneck Public Schools, Mamaroneck, N.Y.
Hobbs, Mrs. Edith E., 119 Parsonage St., Bennettsville, S.C.
Hochstetler, Ruth, 225 S. Nichols, Muncie, Ind.
Hock, Louise E., Sch. of Educ., New York Univ., Washington Sq., New York,
    N.Y.
Hodgins, George W., Paramus High School, Paramus, N.J.
Hodgkins, George W., 1832 Biltmore St., N.W., Washington, D.C.
Hoeltgen, Alice, 4333 Benton Blvd., Kansas City, Mo.
Hoerauf, William E., 2701 W. Chicago Blvd., Detroit, Mich.
Hoffman, Charles L., East High School, 214 High St., Waterloo, Iowa
Hoffman, Joseph L., Chaminade College, 3140 Waialae Dr., Honolulu, Hawaii
Hofstrand, John M., San Jose State College, San Jose, Calif.
Hogan, Ursula, 2213-D Dresden Ct., Sacramento, Calif.
Hohl, George W., Superintendent of Schools, Waterloo, Iowa
Holda, Frederick W., 26 Hampden Rd., Monson, Mass.
Holland, Benjamin F., Sutton Hall, University of Texas, Austin, Tex.
Holland, Donald F., 11320 S. Prairie Ave., Chicago, Ill.
Holland, Gertrude I., 3160 E. Church St., Xenia, Ohio
Holley, Marian J., 120 Sexton St., Struthers, Ohio
Holliday, Jay N., P.O. Box 563, Canoga Park, Calif.
Hollis, Virgil S., Superintendent of County Schools, San Rafael, Calif.
Holloway, George E., Jr., Cooke Hall, Univ. of Buffalo, Buffalo, N.Y.
Holman, W. Earl, Jackson High School, 544 Wildwood Ave., Jackson, Mich.
Holmblade, Amy Jean, Dept. of H.E., University of Minnesota, St. Paul, Minn.
Holmer, Mrs. Helen, 515 Buchanan St., Gary, Ind.
Holmes, Daniel L., Willett School, Attleboro, Mass.
Holmes, Emma E., Orange County State College, Fullerton, Calif.
Holmes, Jack A., Sch. of Educ., Univ. of California, Berkeley, Calif.
Holmquist, Emily, Indiana Univ. School of Nursing, Indianapolis, Ind.
Holmstedt, Raleigh W., Indiana State Teachers College, Terre Haute, Ind.
Holstein, Louise V., 7130 Union Ave., Chicago, Ill.
Holston, M. J., 1128 Valley Dr., Borger, Tex.
Holton, Samuel M., University of North Carolina, Chapel Hill, N.C.
Homer, Francis R., 4800 Conshohocken Ave., Philadelphia, Pa.
Hood, Edwin Morris, The Claridge, 101 Old Mamaroneck Rd., White Plains, N.Y.
Hooker, Clifford P., Col. of Educ., Univ. of Minnesota, Minneapolis, Minn.
Hooper, George J., Sidney Lanier Sch., 1727 S. Harvard Ave., Tulsa, Okla.
Hoops, Robert C., Washington School, Bergen Ave., New Milford, N.J.
Hoover, Louis H., 1027 Dunlop Ave., Forest Park, Illinois
Hoover, Norman K., Pennsylvania State University, University Park, Pa.

Hopkins, Kenneth D., 12772 Oak Way Dr., Los Alamitos, Calif.
Hopkins, Monroe, Hannibal-LaGrange College, Hannibal, Mo.
Hopman, Anne B., 5935 Hohman Ave., Hammond, Ind.
Hopmann, Robert P., 210 N. Broadway, St. Louis, Mo.
Hoppock, Anne, State Department of Education, Trenton, N.J.
Horn, Ernest, East Hall, State University of Iowa, Iowa City, Iowa
Horn, Thomas D., Sutton Hall, University of Texas, Austin, Tex.
Hornburg, Mabel C., 118 Champlain Ave., Ticonderoga, N.Y.
Horowitz, Norman H., 3625 Purdue Ave., Los Angeles, Calif.
Horrocks, John E., Ohio State University, Columbus, Ohio
Horsman, Ralph D., Superintendent of Schls., 735 Washington Rd., Pittsburgh, Pa.
Horwich, Frances R., 1810 Rittenhouse Sq., Philadelphia, Pa.
Hosford, Marian H., Stirling Rd., Warren Twp., Plainfield, N.J.
Hoskins, Glen C., Southern Methodist University, Dallas, Tex.
Hotaling, Mrs. Muriel P., 140 Jensen Rd., R.D. No. 1, Vestal, N.Y.
Hough, John M., Jr., Mars Hill College, Mars Hill, N.C.
Hough, Robert E., Arthur L. Johnson Regional High School, Clark, N.J.
Houghton, John J., Superintendent of Schools, Ferndale, Mich.
Houlahan, F. J., Catholic University of America, Washington, D.C.
Houle, Cyril O., Dept. of Educ., University of Chicago, Chicago, Ill.
House, Ralph W., State Teachers College, Kirksville, Mo.
Houston, James, Jr., 300 Pompton Rd., Wayne, N.J.
Houston, W. Robert, 1104—16th St., Port Huron, Mich.
Hovet, Kenneth O., University of Maryland, College Park, Md.
Howard, Alexander H., Jr., Central Washington Col. of Educ., Ellensburg, Wash.
Howard, Daniel D., Pestalozzi-Froebel Tchrs. College, Chicago, Ill.
Howard, Elizabeth Z., Col. of Educ., Univ. of Rochester, Rochester, N.Y.
Howard, George, University of Alabama, University, Ala.
Howard, Glenn W., Queens College, Flushing, N.Y.
Howard, Marjorie M., 3201 Wisconsin Ave., N.W., Washington, D.C.
Howard, Opalmae, Hardin-Simmons University, Abilene, Tex.
Howd, M. Curtis, 200 Winthrop Rd., Muncie, Ind.
Howe, Mrs. Flora S., 271 S. Tradewinds Ave., Lauderdale-by-the-Sea, Fla.
Howe, Walter A., 6840 Eastern Ave., N.W., Washington, D.C.
Howland, Adelene E., Pennington School, Mount Vernon, N.Y.
Hoyle, Dorothy, Temple University, Philadelphia, Pa.
Hoyt, Cyril J., Burton Hall, Univ. of Minnesota, Minneapolis, Minn.
Huber, H. Ronald, 723 Portland Ave., Huntingdon, Pa.
Hubert, Frank W. R., Texas A. & M. College, College Station, Tex.
Hucksoll, William J., 1332 Heather Hill Rd., Baltimore, Md.
Hudson, Bruce M., 9908 Fairfield Ave., Livonia, Mich.
Hudson, Douglas, 212 Brouse Dr., Wadsworth, Ohio
Hudson, L. P., Huddleston High School, Huddleston, Va.
Hudson, Margaret, P.O. Box 260, Bella Vista Rd., Watsonville, Calif.
Hudson, Robert I., Bemidji State College, Bemidji, Minn.
Huebner, Dwayne E., Tchrs. Col., Columbia University, New York, N.Y.
Huebner, Mildred H., Southern Connecticut State College, New Haven, Conn.
Huehn, Kermith S., Superintendent of County Schools, Eldora, Iowa
Huelsman, Charles B., Jr., 203 Selby Blvd., West, Worthington, Ohio
Huff, Jack F., P.O. Drawer A., Elk Grove, Calif.
Huffaker, Dixie, 4310 E. Lancaster, Fort Worth, Tex.
Hufford, G. N., Dept. of Educ., Lewis College, Lockport, Ill.
Hughes, James W., State University College of Education, Geneseo, N.Y.
Hughes, McDonald, 1715—32nd Ave., Tuscaloosa, Ala.
Hughes, Thomas G., Ventura College, Ventura, Calif.
Hughes, Vergil H., San Jose State College, San Jose, Calif.
Hughson, Arthur, 131 East 21st St., Brooklyn, N.Y.
Hult, Esther, State College of Iowa, Cedar Falls, Iowa
Hultgren, Robert B., Joliet Public Schools, Joliet, Ill.
Hummel, Mrs. H. E., Paterson State College, Paterson, N.J.
Humelsine, Martha, Roberts Wesleyan College, North Chili, N.Y.

Humphrey, Charles, 6001 Berkeley Dr., Berkeley, Mo.
Hunsader, R. W., Senior High School, 409 S. High St., Fort Atkinson, Wis.
Hunt, Dorothy D., 2000 East 46th St., N., Kansas City, Mo.
Hunt, Herold C., Grad. Sch. of Educ., Harvard University, Cambridge, Mass.
Hunt, William A., Dept. of Psych., Northwestern University, Evanston, Ill.
Hunter, Eugenia, Woman's Col., Univ. of North Carolina, Greensboro, N.C.
Hunter, James J., Jr., San Diego State College, San Diego, Calif.
Hunter, Lavinia, Western Kentucky State College, Bowling Green, Ky.
Hunter, Robert W., Grambling College, Grambling, La.
Hunter, William, P.O. Box 938, Tuskegee, Ala.
* Huntington, Albert H., 736 Fairview Ave., Webster Groves, Mo.
Huntington, Elizabeth A., 45 Morris Ave., Springfield, N.J.
Hurd, Blair E., 4900 Heatherdale Lane, Carmichael, Calif.
Hurd, Paul DeH., Sch. of Educ., Stanford University, Stanford, Calif.
Hurlburt, Allan S., Duke University, Col. Sta., Durham, N.C.
Hurlburt, Lydia Delpha, 311 Richmond, S.E., Salem, Ore.
Hurt, Mary Lee, Office of Education, Dept. of H.E.W., Washington, D.C.
Husmann, John L., 256 Ash St., Crystal Lake, Ill.
Huss, Francis G., North Penn Vocational School, Lansdale, Pa.
Husson, Chesley H., Husson College, 157 Park St., Bangor, Me.
Husted, Inez M., Luzerne County Schools, Wilkes-Barre, Pa.
Hutaff, Lucile W., Bowman Gray School of Medicine, Winston-Salem, N.C.
Hutchison, James M., 4231 West 59th St., Los Angeles, Calif.
Hutson, Percival W., University of Pittsburgh, Pittsburgh, Pa.
Hutto, Jerome A., Los Angeles State College, Los Angeles, Calif.
Hutton, Harry K., Pennsylvania State University, University Park, Pa.
Hyde, Edith I., University of California at L.A., Los Angeles, Calif.
Hyde, LaMorris, University of Missouri, Columbia, Mo.
Hyram, George H., 4436 N. Market St., St. Louis, Mo.

Iannaccone, Laurence, 424 Melville Ave., University City, Mo.
Iglesias-Borges, Ramon, P.O. Box 226, San Lorenzo, Puerto Rico
Ihara, Teruo, 111 Wist Hall, University of Hawaii, Honolulu, Hawaii
Ilowit, Roy, C. W. Post College, Greenvale, L.I., N.Y.
Imes, Orley B., 3985 La Cresenta Rd., El Sobrante, Calif.
Imhoff, Myrtle M., Orange County State College, Fullerton, Calif.
Impellizzeri, Irene H., Dept. of Educ., Brooklyn Col., Brooklyn, N.Y.
Inabnit, Darrell J., 9220 S.W. 48th St., Miami, Fla.
Incardona, Joseph S., 325 Busti Ave., Buffalo, N.Y.
Ingebritson, Kasper I., 2790 Sunny Grove Ave., Arcata, Calif.
Ingle, Robert, 5321 N. Hollywood, Whitefish Bay, Wis.
Ingram, Mrs. Mildred, Danville High School, Danville, Ill.
Ingrelli, Anthony V., University of Wisconsin-Milwaukee, Milwaukee, Wis.
Inlow, Gail M., Sch. of Educ., Northwestern University, Evanston, Ill.
Inquai, Solomon, 38 East 12th Ave., Columbus, Ohio
Inskeep, James E., Jr., 6155 Lubbock Ave., La Mesa, Calif.
Ireland, Robert S., Superintendent of Schools, Stow St., Concord, Mass.
Irish, Elizabeth, University of California, Santa Barbara, Goleta, Calif.
Ironside, Roderick A., College of William and Mary, Williamsburg, Va.
Irsfeld, H. L., Superintendent of Schools, Mineral Wells, Tex.
Irving, James Lee, 5713 Ogontz Ave., Philadelphia, Pa.
Irwin, Alice M., Dept. of Spec. Classes, Public Schls, New Bedford, Mass.
Isaacs, Ann F., 409 Clinton Spring Ave., Cincinnati, Ohio
Isacksen, Roy O., Como Park Junior High School, 740 W. Rose Ave., St. Paul, Minn.
Isenberg, Robert M., N.E.A., 1201 Sixteenth St., N.W., Washington, D.C.
Iversen, Jack R., State University College, Oneonta, N.Y.
Ivie, Claude, Public Schools, P.O. Box 470, Meridian, Miss.
Ivins, George H., Roosevelt College, 430 S. Michigan Ave., Chicago, Ill.
Izzo, Raymond J., 12 Girard Rd., Winchester, Mass.

Jack, Maude E., P.O. Box 16, McLean, Ill.
Jackson, Philip W., Dept. of Educ., Univ. of Chicago, Chicago, Ill.
Jackson, Ronald, Taipei American School, APO 63, San Francisco, Calif.
Jackson, Virginia E., 9 Stratford Lane, Brentwood, Mo.
Jackson, Mrs. Wilda S., 6403 Shoal Creek Blvd., Austin, Tex.
Jackson, William H., Hampton Junior College, Ocala, Fla .
Jacobs, Robert, Southern Illinois University, Carbondale, Ill.
Jaeckel, Solomon, 13701 Bracken St., Pacoima, Calif.
Jaeger, Alan Warren, 14296 Buckner Dr., San Jose, Calif.
Jaeger, Eloise M., Norris Gym., University of Minnesota, Minneapolis, Minn.
Jaeger, Herman F., Amer. Dependents Sch., 50th Combat Sup. Grp., APO 109, New York, N.Y.
James, Mrs. Bernice O., 822 Avenue L., Galveston, Tex.
James, Carl A., Superintendent of Schools, Emporia, Kan.
James, Grace R., University of North Carolina, Greensboro, N.C.
James, J. I., Superintendent of Schools, Box 280, Eagle Pass, Tex.
* James, Preston E., Dept. of Geog., Syracuse University, Syracuse, N.Y.
James, Viola, Administration Library, 1800 Grand Ave., Des Moines, Iowa
James, Virginia White, Box 1981, University, Ala.
James, W. Raymond, Illinois State University, Normal, Ill.
Jameson, Sanford F., Superintendent of Schools, Warren, Ohio
* Jansen, William, 900 Palmer Rd., Bronxville, N.Y.
Jansen, Udo H., Col. of Educ., Univ. of Arizona, Tucson, Ariz.
Jansic, Anthony F., Educ. Clinic, City College of New York, New York, N.Y.
Jardine, Alex, 228 S. St. Joseph St., South Bend, Ind.
Jarman, B. H., Pikeville College, Pikeville, Ky.
Jarvis, Galen, Devonshire School, Skokie, Ill.
Jeffers, Jay W., Box 551, Las Vegas, Nev.
Jefferson, James L., 866 Lincoln St., S.W., Birmingham, Ala.
Jelinek, James J., Col. of Educ., Arizona State University, Tempe, Ariz.
Jellins, Miriam H., 2849 Dale Creek Dr., N.W., Atlanta, Ga.
Jemison, T. H., Dept. of Educ., Andrews University, Berrien Springs, Mich.
Jenkins, Clara Barnes, Dept. of Educ., Shaw University, Raleigh, N.C.
Jenkins, David S., Anna Arundel County Schools, Annapolis, Md.
Jenkins, James J., University of Minnesota, Minneapolis, Minn.
Jenks, William F., Holy Redeemer College, Washington, D.C.
Jennings, Wayne B., 1947 Malvern St., St. Paul, Minn.
Jensen, Arthur M., Tuttle School, 1042—18th Ave., Minneapolis, Minn.
Jensen, Arthur R., University of California, Berkeley, Calif.
Jensen, Gale E., 3055 Lakewood Dr., Ann Arbor, Mich.
Jensen, Grant W., South High School, 1101 Planz Rd., Bakersfield, Calif.
Jensen, John A., Col. of Educ., Univ. of Rochester, Rochester, N.Y.
Jenson, T. J., Ohio State University, Columbus, Ohio
Jetton, Clyde T., 720 Amherst, Abilene, Tex.
Jewell, R. Ewart, Superintendent of Schools, 547 Wall St., Bend, Ore.
Jewett, Arno, Office of Education, Dept. of H.E.W., Washington, D.C.
Jex, Frank B., Dept. of Educ. Psych., Univ. of Utah, Salt Lake City, Utah
Jobe, Mrs. Mildred, Moffat County High School, Craig, Colo.
Johns, O. D., Col. of Educ., Univ. of Oklahoma, Norman, Okla.
Johns, Edward B., Dept. of P.E., University of California, Los Angeles, Calif.
Johnson, Mrs. Alice N., 2635 Springfield Rd., Broomall, Pa.
Johnson, B. Lamar, Sch. of Educ., Univ. of California, Los Angeles, Calif.
Johnson, Bruce E., 3623 Prospect, Riverside, Calif.
Johnson, Carl E., 420 N. Elmhurst Ave., Mt. Prospect, Ill.
Johnson, Charles E., Col. of Educ., University of Illinois, Urbana, Ill.
Johnson, Charles E., 722 S. Van Ness, San Francisco, Calif.
Johnson, Mrs. Dorothea N., 670 Bell Ave., Elyria, Ohio
Johnson, Mrs. Dorothy K., 7 Dalston Circle, Lynbrook, N.Y.
Johnson, Douglas A., 3750 Esperanzo Dr., Sacramento, Calif.
Johnson, Eleanor M., Box 360, Middletown, Conn.

Johnson, Ellen V., State Teachers College, Minot, N.D.
Johnson, Evelyn Lawlah, Dept. of Soc., Kentucky State Col., Frankfort, Ky.
Johnson, G. Orville, 805 S. Crouse Ave., Syracuse, N.Y.
Johnson, Gladys V., 3229—4th Ave., South, Great Falls, Mont.
Johnson, Harry C., Duluth Branch, Univ. of Minnesota, Duluth, Minn.
Johnson, Harry O., 11411 Ingram, Livonia, Mich.
Johnson, Harry W. II, Municipal University of Omaha, Omaha, Neb.
Johnson, John N., 6191 Vereker Dr., Oxford, Ohio
Johnson, Leighton H., San Francisco State College, San Francisco, Calif.
Johnson, Leland I., 24—5th Ave., N.E., Osseo, Minn.
Johnson, Leonard E., L. H. Bugbee Sch., 1943 Asylum Ave., West Hartford,
    Conn.
Johnson, Mrs. Lois S., 29 S. Hillside Ter., Madison, Wis.
Johnson, Lois V., Los Angeles State College, Los Angeles, Calif.
Johnson, Margaret E., Alpine School District, American Fork, Utah
Johnson, Mrs. Marjorie Seddon, 61 Grove Ave., Flourtown, Pa.
Johnson, Minnie R., Crane Campus, Chicago Teachers College, Chicago, Ill.
Johnson, Paul E., Livonia Public Schools, Livonia, Mich.
Johnson, Philip G., Stone Hall, Cornell University, Ithaca, N.Y.
Johnson, Robert Leonard, 2500 South 118th St., West Allis, Wis.
* Johnson, Roy Ivan, 2333 Southwest Eighth Dr., Gainesville, Fla.
Johnson, Mrs. Shiela K., Sixth Ave. and A. St., Taft, Calif.
Johnson, Mrs. Stanley F., 1925 Thornwood Ave., Wilmette, Ill.
Johnson, Theodore D., 5236 N. Bernard St., Chicago, Ill.
Johnson, Walter F., Col. of Educ., Michigan State Univ., East Lansing, Mich.
Johnson, Walter R., Libertyville High School, Libertyville, Ill.
Johnson, Wynne E., 10261 Rinda Dr., Rancho Cordova, Calif.
Johnston, Aaron Montgomery, Col. of Educ., Univ. of Tennessee, Knoxville,
    Tenn.
Johnston, Betty Barker, University of Arizona, Tucson, Ariz.
Johnston, Edgar G., Waterford Twp. Schls., 3101 W. Walton Blvd., Pontiac,
    Mich.
Johnston, Lillian B., 538 W. Vernon Ave., Phoenix, Ariz.
Joll, Leonard W., Mulberry St., Plantsville, Conn.
Jonas, Russell E., Black Hills Teachers College, Spearfish, S.D.
Jones, A. Quinn, Lincoln High School, Gainesville, Fla.
Jones, Annie Lee, Sch. of Educ., Univ. of North Carolina, Chapel Hill, N.C.
* Jones, Arthur J., 407 Swarthmore Ave., Swarthmore, Pa.
Jones, Charles L., Gullett School, 6310 Treadwell Ave., Austin, Tex.
Jones, Clifford V., 189 Columbia Ave., Passaic, N.J.
Jones, Clyde A., University of Connecticut, Storrs, Conn.
Jones, Dilys M., 316 S. Fayette St., Shippensburg, Pa.
Jones, Donald W., 508 W. North St., Muncie, Ind.
Jones, Elvet Glyn, Western Washington Col. of Educ., Bellingham, Wash.
Jones, Franklin Ross, 121 Mullen Dr., Ashland, Va.
Jones, Harvey E., Northeastern State College, Tahlequah, Okla.
Jones, Hildred B., Ohio Northern University, Ada, Ohio
Jones, Howard Robert, State University of Iowa, Iowa City, Iowa
Jones, Joseph F., Christian College, Dearborn, Mich.
Jones, Lewis C., Jr., P.O. Box 98, Langley, S.C.
Jones, Lloyd Meredith, Hofstra College, Hempstead, N.Y.
Jones, Mary Elliott, 131 Grand Ave., Englewood, N.J.
Jones, Olwen M., 5 Putnam Hill, Greenwich, Conn.
Jones, Reginald L., 1808 Morena St., Nashville, Tenn.
Jones, Richard N., Carroll Rd., Monkton, Md.
Jones, Ronald D., Bowling Green State University, Bowling Green, Ohio
Jones, Samuel T., MacDonald Knolls School, Tenbrook Dr., Silver Spring, Md.
Jones, Vyron Lloyd, R. 7, Box 346, Terre Haute, Ind.
Jones, Wendell P., Sch. of Educ., Univ. of California, Los Angeles, Calif.
Joneson, Della, Washington School, Marseilles, Ill.
Jonsson, Harold, Div. of Educ., San Francisco State Col., San Francisco, Calif.

Jordan, A. B., 5811 Riverview Blvd., St. Louis, Mo.
Jordan, Benjamin W., Educ. Bldg., Wayne State Univ., Detroit, Mich.
Jordan, Laura, 1003 W. Nevada St., Urbana, Ill.
Jordan, Lawrence V., West Virginia State College, Institute, W.Va.
Jordan, Wayne, Antioch Public Schls., ABC Bldg., Antioch, Calif.
Joselyn, Edwin G., 4068 Hampshire Ave., N., Crystal, Minn.
Joyce, Bruce R., Sch. of Educ., Univ. of Chicago, Chicago, Ill.
Joyce, James M., Box 77, Mellette, S.D.
Joyce, William W., 550 S. Ridge Rd., Lake Forest, Ill.
Juan, K. C., Bishop College, Dallas, Tex.
Judenfriend, Harold, 21 Nutting Pl., Caldwell, N.J.
Julstrom, Eva, 7647 Colfax Ave., Chicago, Ill.
June, Elmer D., Middlesex High School, Bound Brook, N.J.
Jung, Christian W., Sch. of Educ., Indiana University, Bloomington, Ind.
Junge, Charlotte W., Col. of Educ., Wayne University, Detroit, Mich.
Junge, Ruby M., Col. of Educ., Michigan State College, East Lansing, Mich.
Junker, Margaret, 9138 S. Claremont Ave., Chicago, Ill.
Jurjevich, J. C., Jr., Dept. of Educ., Mankato State College, Mankato, Minn.
Justice, Kenneth, Centralia Senior High School, Centralia, Wash.
Justman, Joseph, Board of Education, 110 Livingston St., Brooklyn, N.Y.
Juvancic, William A., Eli Whitney Elem. Sch., 2815 S. Komensky Ave., Chicago,
   Ill.

Kaar, Mrs. Galeta M., 7050 Ridge Ave., Chicago, Ill.
Kaback, Goldie Ruth, 375 Riverside Dr., New York, N.Y.
Kabrud, Margaret, State Teachers College, Ellendale, N.D.
Kahler, Carol, St. Louis University, St. Louis, Mo.
Kahrs, Mary V., Mankato State College, Mankato, Minn.
Kandyba, Bernard S., Lincoln Estates, Frankfort, Ill.
Kane, James L., Stratford School, Garden City, L.I., N.Y.
Kantor, Bernard R., 117 S. Poinsettia Pl., Los Angeles, Calif.
Kaplan, Louis, 111 Via Monte de Oro Ave., Redondo Beach, Calif.
Karlin, Robert, Southern Illinois University, Carbondale, Ill.
Karlsen, Bjorn, Pattee Hall, Univ. of Minnesota, Minneapolis, Minn.
Karr, Johnston T., Gary Public Schools, 620 E. 10th Pl., Gary, Ind.
Karrel, Oscar, Lord & Taylor, 424 Fifth Ave., New York, N.Y.
Karwiel, Mrs. Lela S., 723 Steves Ave., San Antonio, Tex.
Kasdon, Lawrence, Department of Public Instruction, Honolulu, Hawaii
Kass, Corrine E., Calvin College, Grand Rapids, Mich.
Kata, Joseph J., Redbank Valley Joint Schools, New Bethlehem, Pa.
Katenkamp, Theodore W., Jr., Augsburg Home, Baltimore, Md.
Katkovsky, Walter, Counsel. Cen., Fordham University, New York, N.Y.
Katz, Mrs. Florine, Educ. Clinic, City College, New York, N.Y.
Katz, Joseph, University of British Columbia, Vancouver, B.C., Canada
Kauffman, Merle M., Col. of Educ., Bradley University, Peoria, Ill.
Kavanaugh, J. Keith, 8437 Karlov, Skokie, Ill.
Kawalek, Thaddens P., 700 N. LaGrange Rd., LaGrange, Ill.
Kaya, Esin, 520 Main Bldg., New York Univ., Washington Sq., New York, N.Y.
Kearl, Jennie W., State Department of Education, Salt Lake City, Utah
Kearney, George G., Rt. No. 1, Box 1108, Morgan Hill, Calif.
Keating, Barry J., 107 Somerset Ave., Garden City, N.Y.
Keaveny, T. Leo, 810 St. Germain St., St. Cloud, Minn.
Keck, Winston B., Superintendent of Schools, Springfield, Vt.
Keffer, Eugene R., 603 N. College Ave., Warrensburg, Mo.
Kehas, Chris D., Dept. of Educ., Univ. of Chicago, Chicago, Ill.
Keleher, Gregory C., Dept. of Educ., St. Anselm's College, Manchester, N.H.
* Keliher, Alice V., 2039 Hudson Blvd., Jersey City, N.J.
Kelleher, William J., Hirsch High School, Chicago, Ill.
* Keller, Franklin J., 333 E. Mosholu Pkwy., New York, N.Y.
Keller, Robert J., Peik Hall, Univ. of Minnesota, Minneapolis, Minn.
Kelley, Claude, Col. of Educ., University of Oklahoma, Norman, Okla.

Kelley, Mrs. Dorothy J., Willard Sch., 4915 St. Lawrence Ave., Chicago, Ill.
Kelley, H. Paul, University of Texas, Austin, Tex.
Kelley, Victor H., University of Arizona, Tucson, Ariz.
Kelley, William F., Marquette Univ., 1131 W. Wisconsin Ave., Milwaukee, Wis.
Kellogg, E. G., Superintendent of Schools, West Allis, Wis.
Kelly, Dean, 175 Tamarack Dr., Berea, Ohio
Kelly, Edward J., 2215 Ninth Ave., Greeley, Colo.
Kelly, James A., 1665-B Catalpa Dr., Anaheim, Calif.
Kelly, John W., 139 Emerson Ave., Croton-on-Hudson, N.Y.
Kelly, Shaun, Jr., Central School Dist. No. 2, Box 192, Cold Spring Harbor, N.Y.
Kelner, Bernard G., 1804 Ashurst Rd., Philadelphia, Pa.
Kelsey, Roger R., Educ. Annex, University of Maryland, College Park, Md.
Kemp, Edward L., Sch. of Educ., New York Univ., Washington Sq., New York, N.Y.
Kendall, Lloyd, Col. of Educ., San Diego State College, San Diego, Calif.
Kennard, Andrew J., 3511 Oakdale Ave., Houston, Tex.
Kennedy, Clephane A., Benjamin Franklin University, Washington, D.C.
Kennedy, Helen, 101 N. Grand Ave., Pasadena, Calif.
Kentner, Harold M., Rochester Institute of Technology, Rochester, N.Y.
Keohane, Robert E., Shimer College, Mt. Carroll, Ill.
Kephart, N. C., Dept. of Educ., Purdue University, Lafayette, Ind.
Kephart, Ruby G., Allen County Elementary Schools, Memorial Hall, Lima, Ohio
Keppers, George L., University of New Mexico, Albuquerque, N.M.
Kerns, LeRoy, Lab. Sch., Colorado State College, Greeley, Colo.
Kerr, Everett F., Superintendent of Schools, Blue Island, Ill.
Kersh, Bert Y., 260 Sacre Lane, Monmouth, Ore.
Kerst, Mrs. Marjorie, Campus Sch., Wisconsin State College, Stevens Point, Wis.
Keshian, Jerry G., 10 Kilburn Rd., Garden City, L.I., N.Y.
Kesselring, Ralph, 22 Sentul Rd., Kuala Lumpur, Malaya
Ketcherside, William J., Dept. of Educ., Univ. of Missouri, Columbia, Mo.
Kevane, Eugene, 120 Curley Hall, Catholic University, Washington, D.C.
Keys, Samuel P., Sch. of Educ., New York University, New York, N.Y.
Kidder, William W., 216 Walton Ave., South Orange, N.J.
Kies, Michael S., Superintendent of County Schools, Milwaukee, Wis.
Kilbourn, Robert W., 4902 Argyle, Dearborn, Mich.
Kilburn, H. Parley, Evening Div., Bakersfield College, Bakersfield, Calif.
Kilpatrick, Arnold R., Northeastern Louisiana State College, Monroe, La.
* Kilpatrick, William H., 106 Morningside Dr., New York, N.Y.
Kincheloe, James B., University of Kentucky, Lexington, Ky.
Kind, Dan E., Ginn & Co., Statler Bldg., Boston, Mass.
Kindred, Leslie W., Temple University, Philadelphia, Pa.
King, Charles T., 374 Millburn Ave., Millburn, N.J.
King, George G., Montclair State College, Springfield, N.J.
King, Kent H., 103 Thayer Ave., Mankato, Minn.
King, Lloyd H., College of the Pacific, Stockton, Calif.
King, Thomas C., Col. of Educ. and Nursing, Univ. of Vermont, Burlington, Vt.
Kingdon, Frederick H., Western State College, Gunnison, Colo.
Kingsley, Mrs. Iva Marie, Box 177, Kayehta, Ariz.
Kinsella, John J., Sch. of Educ., New York Univ., Washington Sq., New York, N.Y.
Kinsellar, Frances M., Rye St., Broad Brook, Conn.
Kinser, Mrs. Opha, Lisbon, Md.
Kinsman, Kephas Albert, 2009 Appleton St., Long Beach, Calif.
Kinzer, John R., Col. of Educ., Univ. of Arizona, Tucson, Ariz.
Kirby, Inabell T., 2002 E. Main St., Decatur, Ill.
Kirk, Samuel A., University of Illinois, Urbana, Ill.
Kirkland, Mrs. Eleanor R., 8707 Mohawk Way, Fair Oaks, Calif.
Kirkland, J. Bryant, North Carolina State College, Raleigh, N.C.
Kirkman, Ralph E., Mobile College, Mobile, Ala.
Kirkpatrick, J. E., Black Hills Teachers College, Spearfish, S.D.
Kissinger, Doris C., 34 Roosevelt St., Glen Head, L.I., N.Y.

Kitch, Donald E., 721 Capitol Ave., Sacramento, Calif.
Kitts, Harry W., U.S.O.M., APO 146, San Francisco, Calif.
Klaus, Catherine, 1295 Alta Vista St., Dubuque, Iowa
Klausmeier, Herbert J., Sch. of Educ., University of Wisconsin, Madison, Wis.
Klein, Philip, Harcum Junior College, Bryn Mawr, Pa.
Klein, Richard K., Department of Public Instruction, Bismarck, N.D.
Kleinpell, E. H., Wisconsin State College, River Falls, Wis.
Klevan, Albert, Col. of Educ., Univ. of Maryland, College Park, Md.
Kleyensteuber, Carl J., Northland College, Ashland, Wis.
Klimes, Rudolf E., Superintendent of Schools, Seoul, Korea
Klinckmann, Evelyn, San Francisco Col. for Women, San Francisco, Calif.
Kline, Donald F., F. E. Compton & Co., 1000 N. Dearborn St., Chicago, Ill.
Kline, Frances F., 152—72nd St., Brooklyn, N.Y.
Kling, Martin, 1232 Sunset Loop, Walnut Creek, Calif.
Klipfer, Leopold E., Sch. of Educ., Univ. of Chicago, Chicago, Ill.
Klofta, Norbert J., 2186 North 74th St., Milwaukee, Wis.
Klohr, Paul R., Arps Hall, Ohio State University, Columbus, Ohio
Klopf, Gordon, Tchrs. Col., Columbia University, New York, N.Y.
Kluwe, Mary Jean, 468 W. Hancock St., Detroit, Mich.
Knape, Clifford S., 1024 North 18-A St., Waco, Tex.
Knapp, Dale L., Los Angeles State College, Los Angeles, Calif.
Knapp, Royce H., Admin. Bldg., University of Nebraska, Lincoln, Neb.
Knight, Reginald R., 4338 Heather Rd., Long Beach, Calif.
Knoeppel, LeRoy J., Proviso Township High School, Maywood, Ill.
Knolle, Lawrence M., Chatham College, Pittsburgh, Pa.
Knowlden, Gayle E., 3003 Laurel Ave., Manhattan Beach, Calif.
Knox, Carl S., 1400 Massachusetts St., Lawrence, Kan.
Knox, Stanley C., St. Cloud State College, St. Cloud, Minn.
Knuti, Leo Leonard, Montana State College, Bozeman, Mont.
Knutson, Helen A., 106 Second Ave., S.W., Austin, Minn.
Koch, Mrs. Sylvia L., 539 N. Highland Ave., Los Angeles, Calif.
Koehring, Dorothy, State College of Iowa, Cedar Falls, Iowa
Koenig, Adolph J., 612 Cedar Hill Rd., Ambler, Pa.
Koenig, Vernon H., 1318 S. Central Ave., Lodi, Calif.
Koenigsberg, Lewis A., Bowling Green State University, Bowling Green, Ohio
Koerber, Walter F., Scarborough Board of Education, Scarborough, Ont., Canada
Koester, George A., San Diego State College, San Diego, Calif.
Koff, Robert H., 1219 Hyde Park Blvd., Chicago, Ill.
Kohler, Lewis T., 7659 Whitsett Ave., North Hollywood, Calif.
Kohlmann, Eleanor L., 169 MacKay Hall, Iowa State University, Ames, Iowa
Kohn, Martin, 35 West 92nd St., New York, N.Y.
Kohn, Nathan, Jr., 9827 Clayton Rd., St. Louis, Mo.
Kohs, Samuel C., 620 Plymouth Way, Burlingame, Calif.
Komarek, Henrietta, 508 Rex Blvd., Elmhurst, Ill.
Konen, Robert C., 1535 Monroe Ave., River Forest, Ill.
Konsh, Adeline, 101 East 16th St., New York, N.Y.
Kontos, George, Jr., Superintendent of Elementary Schls., Sweet Home, Ore.
Koos, Leonard V., Route 2, Newago, Mich.
Kopel, David, Chicago Teachers College, 6800 S. Stewart Ave., Chicago, Ill.
Koppin, Lawrence L., Otero Junior College, LaJunta, Colo.
Korey, Harold, 5000 S. Cornell Ave., Chicago, Ill.
Kornberg, Leonard, 137-30 Geranium Ave., Flushing, N.Y.
Korntheuer, Gerhard A., St. Johns College, Winfield, Kan.
Kough, Blachford, 1632 W. Wrightwood Ave., Chicago, Ill.
Koy, Arnold C., Little Fort School, 1775 Blanchard Rd., Waukegan, Ill.
Kraft, Milton Edward, Earlham College, Richmond, Ind.
Kramer, William A., Lutheran Church, Mo. Synod, 210 N. Broadway, St. Louis,
   Mo.
Krathwohl, David R., Michigan State University, East Lansing, Mich.
Kraus, Howard F., 512 Alameda de las Pulgas, Belmont, Calif.
Kraus, Philip E., 215 West 78th St., New York, N.Y.

Krautle, Hilda E., 3599 Werk Rd., Cincinnati, Ohio
Kravetz, Nathan, 328 Skyewiay Rd., Los Angeles, Calif.
Kravetz, Sol., 7642 Lena Ave., Canoga Park, Calif.
Krawitz, Harris, 431 Oakdale Ave., Chicago, Ill.
Krebs, Stephen O., State University College, Plattsburgh, N.Y.
Kreitlow, Burton W., Dept. of Educ., University of Wisconsin, Madison, Wis.
Kress, Roy A., 800 Moredon Rd., Meadowbrook, Pa.
Krich, Percy, Long Beach State College, Long Beach, Calif.
Krippner, Stanley, R.R. No. 1, Fort Atkinson, Wis.
Kroenke, Richard G., Valparaiso University, Valparaiso, Ind.
Kropp, Russell P., Florida State University, Tallahassee, Fla.
Krueger, Louise W., 1520 Laburnum Ave., Chico, Calif.
Krug, Edward, Dept. of Educ., University of Wisconsin, Madison, Wis.
Krumboltz, John D., Sch. of Educ., Stanford University, Stanford, Calif.
Kruszynski, Eugene S., Dept. of Educ., Beloit College, Beloit, Wis.
Kubik, Edmund J., 9741 S. Leavitt St., Chicago, Ill.
Kubis, Joseph F., Fordham University, New York, N.Y.
Kugler, Mrs. Ida C., Aiyepe Girls High School, Aiyepe via Odogbolu, W. Nigeria
Kuhn, Doris Y., Dept. of Educ., Purdue University, Lafayette, Ind.
Kuhn, Joseph A., 99 Buffalo Ave., Long Beach, N.Y.
Kuhnen, Mrs. Mildred, 2106 Park Ave., Chico, Calif.
Kulberg, Janet M., Easton Schools Admn. Bldg., Easton, Pa.
Kullman, N. E., Jr., 153 Murray Ave., Delmar, N.Y.
Kumpf, Carl H., Superintendent of Schools, Clark, N.J.
Kunimoto, Mrs. Tadako, 734—16th Ave., Honolulu, Hawaii
Kuntz, Allen H., 72 Lombardy St., Lancaster, N.Y.
Kunz, Mrs. Jean T., University of Maryland, College Park, Md.
Kurtz, John J., Inst. for Child Study, Univ. of Maryland, College Park, Md.
Kusmik, Cornell J., 7400 Augusta St., River Forest, Ill.
Kutz, Frederick B., Newark High School, Newark, Del.
Kuykendall, D. W., Trinity University, San Antonio, Tex.
Kvaraceus, W. C., Tufts University, Medford, Mass.
Kyle, Helen F., Sch. of Educ., University of Colorado, Boulder, Colo.
Kyzar, Barney L., 518 Norma, Nacogdoches, Tex.

Labaj, J. J., Creighton Prep. School, 7400 Western Ave., Omaha, Neb.
Labecki, Geraldine, 4004 Vailwood Dr., Nashville, Tenn.
Lacy, David W., Box 761, Converse, Ind.
Lacy, Susan M., W-215 Eddy Ave., Spokane, Wash.
Ladd, Edward T., Emory University, Atlanta, Ga.
LaDue, Donald C., Illinois State University, Normal, Ill.
LaFauci, Horatio M., 688 Boylston St., Boston, Mass.
Lafferty, Charles W., P.O. Box 1250, Fairbanks, Alaska
Lafferty, H. M., East Texas State Teachers College, Commerce, Tex.
LaForce, Charles L., 426 Malden Ave., LaGrange Park, Ill.
Lafranchi, W. E., Stabley Library, State College, Indiana, Pa.
LaGrone, Herbert F., 8614 Irvington Ave., Bethesda, Md.
Lahaderne, Henriette M., Dept. of Educ., Univ. of Chicago, Chicago, Ill.
Laird, A. W., 3705 Overton Park East, Fort Worth, Tex.
Laird, Byron F., Indiana University, Jeffersonville, Ind.
Lake, Mrs. Doris S., 145 East St., Oneonta, N.Y.
Laliberte, Richard A., Hinsdale Public Schools, Hinsdale, Ill.
Lamb, George S., Burton Hall, University of Minnesota, Minneapolis, Minn.
Lamb, Howard E., Sch. of Educ., University of Delaware, Newark, Del.
Lambert, Pierre D., Sch. of Educ., Boston College, Chestnut Hill, Mass.
Lambert, Ronald T., University of Minnesota, Minneapolis, Minn.
Lambert, Sam M., N.E.A., 1201 Sixteenth St., N.W., Washington, D.C.
Lammel, Rose, Wayne State University, Detroit, Mich.
Lampard, Dorothy M., University of Alberta, Edmonton, Alba., Canada
Landskov, N. L., Mississippi Southern College, Station A., Hattiesburg, Miss.
Lane, Mrs. Elizabeth Miller, 4390 Hyland Ave., Dayton, Ohio

Lane, Frank T., 42 St. Clair Dr., Delmar, N.Y.
Lane, Mrs. Mary B., 10 Lundy's Lane, San Mateo, Calif.
Lane, Olive, Sydney Teachers College, Newtown, Sydney, New South Wales, Australia
Lane, Ulysses S., State Teachers College, Elizabeth City, N.J.
Lange, Lorraine, State University College of Education, Buffalo, N.Y.
Lange, Paul W., Dept. of Educ., Valparaiso University, Valparaiso, Ind.
Lange, Phil C., Tchrs. Col., Columbia University, New York, N.Y.
Langenbach, Louise, 1359 Union Ridge Rd., Placerville, Calif.
Langeveld, M. J., Prins Hendriklaan 6, Bilthoven, Holland
Langland, Lois E., 332 Banhill Rd., Los Angeles, Calif.
Langman, Muriel Potter, 913 Congress St., Ypsilanti, Mich.
Langston, Roderick G., 1451 S. Loma Verde St., Monterey Park, Calif.
Lanham, Frank W., Sch. of Educ., University of Michigan, Ann Arbor, Mich.
Lankton, Robert S., Detroit Public Schls., 5057 Woodward, Detroit, Mich.
Lanning, Frank W., Northern Illinois University, DeKalb, Ill.
Lansu, Walter J., 6036 Metropolitan Plaza, Los Angeles, Calif.
Lant, Kenneth A., Jericho Public Schools, Jericho, L.I., N.Y.
Lantz, Donald, University of Southern Florida, Tampa, Fla.
Lantz, Ralph G., Pennsylvania State University, University Park, Pa.
Laramy, William J., Haverford Junior High School, Havertown, Pa.
Larkin, Joseph B., San Jose State College, San Jose, Calif.
Larkin, Lewis B., 15818 Westbrook, Detroit, Mich.
Larsen, Arthur Hoff, Illinois State University, Normal, Ill.
Larsen, Jack L., St. Joseph High School, St. Joseph, Mich.
Larson, Clifford E., Bethel College, St. Paul, Minn.
Larson, Eleanor E., Educ. Bldg., University of Wisconsin, Madison, Wis.
Larson, L. C., Audio-Visual Center, Indiana University, Bloomington, Ind.
Larson, Rolf W., NCATE, 17th and Penn Ave., N.W., Washington, D.C.
Larson, Vera M., 1331 N.E. 111th Ave., Portland, Ore.
Lassanske, Paul A., 2917 W. McLean, Chicago, Ill.
Lathrop, Irvin T., Long Beach State College, Long Beach, Calif.
Lathrop, Ross W., 5428 Woodlawn Ave., Chicago, Ill.
Laudico, Minerva G., Centro Escolar University, Manila, Philippines
Laurier, Blaise V., Les Clercs de Saint-Viateur, Montreal, Quebec, Canada
Lautenschlager, Harley, Lab. School, Indiana State College, Terre Haute, Ind.
Lavelle, Robert J., Xavier University, Cincinnati, Ohio
Lavenburg, F. M., Public Schls., 155 Broad St., Bloomfield, N.J.
Law, L. E., Superintendent of Schools, Alliance, Ohio
Lawhead, Victor B., Ball State Teachers College, Muncie, Ind.
Lawler, Marcella R., Tchrs. Col., Columbia University, New York, N.Y.
Lawrence, Mrs. Bessie F., LeMoyne School, 851 Waveland Ave., Chicago, Ill.
Lawrence, Clayton G., Marion College, Marion, Ind.
Lawrence, Edna R., 299 West 12th St., New York, N.Y.
Lawrence, Richard E., AACTE, 1201 Sixteenth St., N.W., Washington, D.C.
Lawrence, Ruth E., 627 Grove St., Denton, Tex.
Lawski, A. J., Edsel Ford High School, 20601 Rotunda Dr., Dearborn, Mich.
Lawson, John H., Hingham Public Schls., 229 North St., Hingham, Mass.
Layne, Fay, 1235 First St., Webster City, Iowa
Lazar, Alfred L., 6274 Del Rosa Ave., San Bernardino, Calif.
Lazarus, Arnold, Purdue University Station, Lafayette, Ind.
Lazow, Alfred, 138 Asbury, Evanston, Ill.
Leach, Marian E., 1227 The Alameda, Berkeley, Calif.
Leamy, Cora M., Gardner Junior High School, Gardner, Mass.
Leavitt, Jerome E., Portland State College, Portland, Ore.
Lee, Annabel, University of Puget Sound, Tacoma, Wash.
Lee, Dorris May, Portland State College, Portland, Ore.
Lee, Ernest C., Rainbow High School, Victoria, Australia
Lee, Harold Fletcher, Box 38, Lincoln University, Jefferson City, Mo.
Lee, Howard D., Atwater School, Shorewood, Wis.
Lee, J. Murray, Southern Illinois University, Carbondale, Ill.

Lee, James Michael, University of Notre Dame, Notre Dame, Ind.
Lee, John J., Col. of Educ., Wayne State University, Detroit, Mich.
Lee, John R., Northwestern University, Evanston, Ill.
Lee, William C., Box 327, Tusculum College, Greeneville, Tenn.
Leeds, Don S., 560 College Ave., Niagara Falls, N.Y.
Leeds, Willard L., 4620 N. Woodburn, Milwaukee, Wis.
Leese, Joseph, New York State College for Teachers, Albany, N.Y.
Leeseberg, Norbert H., 663 Manor Rd., Staten Island, N.Y.
Lefcourt, Ann, Anthony Apartments, Muncie, Ind.
Lefever, David Welty, 4251 Don Felipe Dr., Los Angeles, Calif.
* Lefforge, Roxy, 1945 Fruit St., Huntington, Ind.
Lehman, James L., 26255 Schoolcraft, Detroit, Mich.
Lehmann, Irvin J., Michigan State University, East Lansing, Mich.
Lehmann, William, Jr., Concordia Teachers College, River Forest, Ill.
Leib, Joseph A., 2416 Summit Ter., Linden, N.J.
Leibert, Robert, B1, L3, Slocum Heights, Syracuse, N.Y.
Leiman, Harold I., 526 Clinton Ave., Newark, N.J.
Leland, Allen O., Mt. Clef Village, Thousand Oaks, Calif.
Leland, Simeon E., Col. of L.A., Northwestern University, Evanston, Ill.
Lennon, Joseph L., Providence College, Providence, R.I.
Lennon, Lawrence J., 310 N. Webster Ave., Scranton, Pa.
Lensmire, Warren J., Wood County Teachers College, Wisconsin Rapids, Wis.
Lepera, Alfred G., 254 Franklin St., Newton, Mass.
LePere, Jean M., Michigan State University, East Lansing, Mich.
Lepore, Albert R., 2614 Lancaster Rd., Hayward, Calif.
Lerner, Arthur, Los Angeles City College, Los Angeles, Calif.
Letson, Charles T., 315 Whitney Ave., New Haven, Conn.
Letson, John W., Superintendent of Schools, 224 Central Ave., Atlanta, Ga.
Levin, J. Joseph, 221 N. Cuyler Ave., Oak Park, Ill.
Levine, Helen A., Bureau of Jewish Education, Cleveland, Ohio
Levine, Murray, Dept. of Psych., Yale University, New Haven, Conn.
Levine, Stanley L., 158 S. Westgate, Los Angeles, Calif.
Levinson, Boris M., Yeshiva University, New York, N.Y.
Levit, Martin, University of Kansas City, Kansas City, Mo.
Levitt, Eugene E., Indiana Univ., Medical Center, Indianapolis, Ind.
Lewis, Arthur J., Makerere College, Kampala, Uganda, Africa
Lewis, Edward R., 5293 Greenridge Rd., Castro Valley, Calif.
Lewis, Elizabeth V., University of Alabama Center, Mobile, Ala.
Lewis, Gertrude M., U.S. Office of Education, Dept. of H.E.W., Washington, D.C.
Lewis, Mrs. J. R., Batesville, Miss.
Lewis, Maurice S., Col. of Educ., Arizona State University, Tempe, Ariz.
Lewis, Philip, 6900 S. Crandon Ave., Chicago, Ill.
Lewis, Robert, 915 N. Union St., Natchez, Miss.
Lewis, Roland B., Eastern Washington State College, Cheney, Wash.
Leyton, Mario, 1318 E. Hyde Park Blvd., Chicago, Ill.
L'Heureux, Leon, Jr., Superintendent of Schools, Foster Center, R.I.
Libby, Mildred P., 7 Riverside Rd., Simsbury, Conn.
Lichtey, E. A., Illinois State University, Normal, Ill.
Lichty, John C., Paradise Township Elementary School, Paradise, Pa.
Lifton, Eli, Winthrop Junior High School, Brooklyn, N.Y.
Light, Alfred B., 93 Bailey Ave., Plattsburgh, N.Y.
Lighthall, Frederick, Dept. of Educ., Univ. of Chicago, Chicago, Ill.
Ligon, Mary Gilbert, Hofstra College, Hempstead, N.Y.
Liljeblad, Maynard T., P.O. Box 1067, Hanford, Calif.
* Lincoln, Edward A., Thompson St., Halifax, Mass.
Lind, Arthur E., 1422 Johnston Ave., Richland, Wash.
Lindberg, Lucile, Queens College, Flushing, N.Y.
Lindeman, Richard H., Tchrs. Col., Columbia University, New York, N.Y.
Lindemann, Erich, Massachusetts General Hospital, Fruit St., Boston, Mass.
Lindemer, George Charles, Seton Hall University, South Orange, N.J.

Lindgren, Henry Clay, 1975—15th Ave., San Francisco, Calif.
Lindsey, Robert V., 3207 Baker Dr., Concord, Calif.
Lindvall, C. Mauritz, Sch. of Educ., University of Pittsburgh, Pittsburgh, Pa.
Linehan, Mrs. Louise W., 4 Bolton Pl., Fair Lawn, N.J.
Lipham, James M., Dept. of Educ., University of Wisconsin, Madison, Wis.
Lipscomb, William A., Box 505, Wilder, Idaho
Lipsitz, Herbert J., Asst. Superintendent of Schls., Paterson, N.J.
Lisle, Mrs. H. G., 1559 Kinney Ave., Cincinnati, Ohio
Litin, Annette, 5218 North 18th Pl., Phoenix, Ariz.
Little, J. Kenneth, Bascom Hall, University of Wisconsin, Madison, Wis.
Little, Lawrence C., Cath. of Learn., Univ. of Pittsburgh, Pittsburgh, Pa.
Litzky, Leo, 11 Pomona Ave., Newark, N.J.
Livingston, Mrs. Esta H., 1747—48th St., Brooklyn, N.Y.
Livingston, Thomas B., Box 4060, Texas Tech. Station, Lubbock, Tex.
Lizotte, Mrs. Oneita B., 126 N. East St., Medina, Ohio
Lloyd Francis V., Jr., 5844 Stony Island Ave., Chicago, Ill.
Lloyd-Jones, Esther, 525 West 120th St., New York, N.Y.
Lobdell, Lawrence O., Union Free School Dist. 30, Valley Stream, N.Y.
LoBuglio, Armand Steven, 24 Audrey Ct., Malverne, L.I., N.Y.
Lockett, B. T., 1848 Tiger Flowers Dr., N.W., Atlanta, Ga.
Lodeski, Frank J., 124 S. East Ave., Oak Park, Ill.
Loew, Climmont C., 1733 North 76th Ct., Elmwood Park, Ill.
Lofgren, Mrs. Marie Luise S., 687 Cambridge, Santa Clara, Calif.
Logdeser, Mrs. Thomas, 11616 Woodview Blvd., Parma Heights, Ohio
Logsdon, J. D., Thornton Twp. H.S. and Jr. Col., Harvey, Ill.
Lola, Justita, Bicol Teachers College, Legaspi City, Philippines
Lomax, James L., Lomax Junior High School, Valdosta, Ga.
London, Jack, 2328 Derby St., Berkeley, Calif,
Long, F. P., Jr., R. D. No. 1, Valencia, Pa.
Long, Isabelle, 4343 Harriet Ave., S., Minneapolis, Minn.
Lonsdale, Mrs. Maxine deLappe, 1405 Campbell Lane, Sacramento, Calif.
Lonsdale, Richard C., 1339 Westmoreland Ave., Syracuse, N.Y.
Loomis, Arthur K., 917 W. Bonita Ave., Claremont, Calif.
Loomis, Chester M., 15443 Grandville, Detroit, Mich.
Looney, William F., State Teachers College, 625 Huntington Ave., Boston, Mass.
Loop, Alfred B., 2619 Franklin St., Bellingham, Wash.
Loree, M. Ray, Box 742, University of Alabama, University, Ala.
Lorenz, Donald W., Lutheran High School East, Harper Woods, Mich.
Loretan, Joseph O., Bd. of Educ., 110 Livingston St., Brooklyn, N.Y.
Lott, Jurelle, Col. of Educ., University of Georgia, Athens, Ga.
Loudon, Mrs. Mary Lou, 1408 Stephens Ave., Baton Rouge, La.
Loughlin, Leo J., 257 Rolfe Rd., DeKalb, Ill.
Loughrea, Mildred, 716 City Hall and Court House, St. Paul, Minn.
Lourie, Samuel, 185 Hall St., Brooklyn, N.Y.
Lowe, A. J., Loyola University, New Orleans, La.
Lowe, Alberta L., Col. of Educ., University of Tennessee, Knoxville, Tenn.
Lowe, Mary G., University of Utah, Salt Lake City, Utah
Lowe, Paul F., Southern Connecticut State College, New Haven, Conn.
Lowe, R. N., Sch. of Educ., University of Oregon, Eugene, Ore.
Lowe, William T., Stone Hall, Cornell University, Ithaca, N.Y.
Lowery, Zeb A., Rutherford County Schools, Rutherford, N.C.
Lowes, Ruth, 2004 Seventh Ave., Canyon, Tex.
Lowry, Carmen, Huston-Tillotson College, Austin, Tex.
Lowther, William L., 434 Lathrop Ave., Boonton, N.J.
Lubbock-Evans, Catherine, P.O. Box 57, Houston, Tex.
Lubell, Richard M., 2 Stoddard Pl., Brooklyn, N.Y.
Lucas, J. H., 2006 Fayetteville St., Durham, N.C.
Lucas, Mrs. May, Oregon College of Education, Monmouth, Ore.
Lucash, Benjamin, 1219 Robbins Ave., Philadelphia, Pa.
Lucio, William H., Sch. of Educ., University of California, Los Angeles, Cailf.
Lucito, Leonard J., George Peabody College for Tchrs., Nashville, Tenn.

Luckey, Bertha M., 1310 West 104th St., Cleveland, Ohio
Lucy, Herbert E., 503 Canal Ave., Cleveland, Miss.
Ludes, Titus H., Quincy College, Quincy, Ill.
Ludwig, Adela E., 2453 N. Grant Blvd., Milwaukee, Wis.
Luebke, Martin F., 1508 Whittier, Springfield, Ill.
Luecke, Mrs. Carl, 411 Sergeant Ave., Joplin, Mo.
Luhmann, Philip R., 5752 Maryland Ave., Chicago, Ill.
Luihn, Mrs. Martha Bruckner, 1027 N.E. Schuyler, Portland, Ore.
Luker, Arno Henry, Colorado State College, Greeley, Colo.
Lund, S. E. Torsten, Haviland Hall, University of California, Berkeley, Calif.
Lunney, Gerald H., 1070 E. County Rd. D., White Bear Lake, Minn.
Lunt, Robert, Superintendent, School Union Ten, Cape Elizabeth, Me.
Luther, Vincent A., St. Agnes Church, Lloydell, Pa.
Lutz, Frank W., 14824 Larchburr, Bridgeton, Mo.
Lutz, Jack, Plymouth-Whitemarsh Jt. High School, Plymouth Meeting, Pa.
Luvaas, Clarence B., 2326 Bever Ave., S.E., Cedar Rapids, Iowa
Lyman, Howard B., University of Cincinnati, Cincinnati, Ohio
Lynch, Katherine D., 203 West 93rd St., New York, N.Y.
Lynch, James M., Superintendent of Schools, Rt. No. 9, East Brunswick, N.J.
Lynch, Mary Elizabeth, 23 Winborough St., Mattapan, Boston, Mass.
Lynch, Patrick D., Hodgin Hall, University of Albuquerque, N.M.
Lynch, Viola M., 1401 East 55th St., Chicago, Ill.
Lyon, Margaret C., Livingston State College, Livingston, Ala.
Lyons, Mrs. Cora E., 25 N. Jefferson St., Amboy, Ill.
Lyons, John H., Box 216, Thompsonville, Conn.
Lyons, John Wesley, 349 Angell St., Providence, R.I.

Maag, Raymond E., 3553 Hennepin Ave., Minneapolis, Minn.
Macbeth, Ruby, 69 Cannon St., Charleston, S.C.
MacDonald, Donald V., University of Scranton, Scranton, Pa.
MacDougall, Mary Ann, Carolina Apts., Charlottesville, Va.
MacGown, Paul C., 3128 N. Ash St., Spokane, Wash.
Mack, Esther, San Jose State College, San Jose, Calif.
* MacKay, James L., 1105 W. Mulberry St., San Antonio, Tex.
MacKay, Vera A., Col. of Educ., Univ. of British Columbia, Vancouver, B.C.
MacKay, William R., 521—17th St., Bellingham, Wash.
Mackenzie, Donald M., 505 Lake Ave., Webster Groves, Mo.
MacKenzie, Elbridge G., Anderson College, Anderson, Ind.
Mackenzie, Gordon N., Tchrs. Col., Columbia University, New York, N.Y.
Mackintosh, Helen K., U.S. Office of Education, Dept. of H.E.W., Washington,
    D.C.
MacNaughton, Mrs. John F., St. John's School, Sugarland, Tex.
MacVicar, Robert, Oklahoma State University, Stillwater, Okla.
Madden, Richard, 410 Stonecrest Ct., Santa Rosa, Calif.
Maddox, Clifford Rhea, Cedarville College, Cedarville, Ohio
Madore, Normand William, Illinois State University, Normal, Ill.
Maehara, Oei, 3535 Pinao St., Honolulu, Hawaii
Maffeo, Pasquale E., Mercer University, Macon, Ga.
Magary, James F., Jersey City State College, Jersey City, N.J.
Magoon, Thomas M., 9521 Woodley Ave., Silver Spring, Md.
Mahar, Robert J., Col. of Educ., Wayne State University, Detroit, Mich.
Maher, Trafford P., St. Louis University, 15 N. Grand Blvd., St. Louis, Mo.
Maia, Celeste, USAID/Liberia, State Dept. Mailroom, Washington, D.C.
Mailey, James H., University of Southern Mississippi, Hattiesburg, Miss.
Mains, Mrs. Susie T., Box 145, Guilford, Me.
Malan, Russell, Superintendent of Schools, Harrisburg, Ill.
Mallery, Adele, 801 Kirby Pl., Shreveport, La.
Mallery, Kenneth P., Superintendent of Schools, Centralia, Wash.
Mallory, Berenice, Office of Education, Dept. of H.E.W., Washington, D.C.
Malmquist, M. L., Superintendent, School Dist. 318, Grand Rapids, Minn.
Malone, James W., Diocese of Youngstown, 144 W. Wood St., Youngstown, Ohio

Maloof, Mitchell, 63 Main St., Williamstown, Mass.
Malsky, Stanley J., 85-09—167th St., Jamaica Hills, L.I., N.Y.
Mangum, G. C., P.O. Box 494, Darlington, S.C.
Manley, Francis J., Frontier Central Sch., Bay View Rd., Hamburg, N.Y.
Mann, Maxine, Whitewater State College, Whitewater, Wis.
Mann, Vernal S., Box 266, State College, Miss.
Mannello, George, 26 Regis Pl., Hempstead, N.Y.
Manning, Edward, Superintendent of Schools, Pearl River, N.Y.
Manoil, Adolph, Sch. of Educ., Boston University, Boston, Mass.
Manolakes, Theodore, Col. of Educ., University of Illinois, Urbana, Ill.
Manone, Carl, Abington Township Schools, Abington, Pa.
Mantor, Lyle E., State Teachers College, Kearney, Neb.
Manuel, Herschel T., University of Texas, Austin, Tex.
Manwiller, Lloyd V., Glassboro State College, Glassboro, N.J.
Mapes, Cecil S., 29 Payne Ave., Chatham, N.Y.
Mapes, Elmer S., Superintendent of Schools, East Weymouth, Mass.
Marable, Mrs. Florence, Spring Avenue School, 1001 Spring Ave., LaGrange, Ill.
Marburger, Carl L., 17430 Denby St., Detroit, Mich.
Marc-Aurele, Paul, 162 Marois Blvd., Laval-des-Rapids, Montreal, Quebec
Margolin, Mrs. Edythe, 12013 Rose Ave., Los Angeles, Calif.
Margolis, Isidor, Yeshiva University, 1495 Morris Ave., New York, N.Y.
Marinaccio, Anthony, Superintendent of Schools, Davenport, Iowa
Markarian, Robert E., Springfield College, Springfield, Mass.
Markle, David H., Ohio Northern University, Ada, Ohio
Marksberry, Mary Lee, Sch. of Educ., Univ. of Kansas City, Kansas City, Mo.
Marksheffel, Ned D., Oregon State University, Corvallis, Ore.
Marquis, Francis Norwood, Sch. of Educ., Miami University, Oxford, Ohio
Marquis, R. L., Jr., Box 5282, North Texas Station, Denton, Tex.
Marsden, W. Ware, 2217 West 5th St., Stillwater, Okla.
Marsh, Mrs. Augusta B., 30 Bronner Ave., Prichard, Ala.
Marsh, Marian, 115 Ivy St., Nampa, Idaho
Marshall, B. F., Pleasantville Jt. Schools, Pleasantville, Pa.
Marshall, Beth, 1526 Catherine Dr., Anaheim, Calif.
Marshall, Daniel W., North Hall, Tufts University, Medford, Mass.
Marshall, Stuart A., Sch. of Educ., Boston University, Boston, Mass.
Marshall, Thomas O., 17 Mill Rd., Durham, N.H.
Marshall, Wayne P., 704 East 36th St., Kearney, Neb.
Marston, Mrs. Marjorie, 860 Lake Shore Dr., Chicago, Ill.
Martin, Edwin D., 2341 Quenby, Houston, Tex.
Martin, Elaine, 608 S. Norwood Ave., Green Bay, Wis.
Martin, F. Gerald, Sacred Heart Seminary, Detroit, Mich.
Martin, Frieda, 2428½ Wabash, Terre Haute, Ind.
Martin, George Berry, Salem Public Schools, P.O. Box 87, Salem, Ore.
Martin, Ignatius A., Supt., Diocese of Lafayette, Drawer E., Lafayette, La.
Martin, Jackson J., 661 Grace St., Livermore, Calif.
Martin, John Henry, Superintendent of Schools, Freeport, N.Y.
Martin, Kathryn J., 2208 Fairhill Ave., Glenside, Pa.
Martin, Mavis D., Oklahoma State University, Stillwater, Okla.
Martin, R. Lee, State University Teachers College, Oswego, N.Y.
Martin, William R., 320 N.W. 19th Ave., Fort Lauderdale, Fla.
Martini, Angiolina A., 2524 Benvenue Ave., Berkeley, Calif.
Martinson, Ruth A., 7614 Brunache, Downey, Calif.
Martire, Harriette A., St. Joseph College, West Hartford, Conn.
Martorana, Sebastian V., State Education Dept., Albany, N.Y.
Marvin, John H., 101 Manchester, Arlington, Va.
Marx, George L., Col. of Educ., University of Maryland, College Park, Md.
Marzolf, Stanley S., Illinois State University, Normal, Ill.
Masiko, Peter, Dade County Junior College, Miami, Fla.
Mason, George E., 138 Sims Rd., Syracuse, N.Y.
Mason, John M., Michigan State University, East Lansing, Mich.
Masoner, Paul H., University of Pittsburgh, Pittsburgh, Pa.

Massey, William J., 209 E. Hamilton Ave., Silver Spring, Md.
Massingill, Richard A., 15905 Harrison, Livonia, Mich.
Masters, Harry V., Albright College, Reading, Pa.
Masterson, John A., Selma Public Schools, 917 Lapsley St., Selma, Ala.
Mathews, C. O., 6501 El Greco Rd., Goleta, Calif.
Mathias, C. Wilbur, State Teachers College, Kutztown, Pa.
Mathias, John A., Moorefield High School, Moorefield, W.Va.
Mathiasen, O. F., Antioch College, Yellow Springs, Ohio
Mathis, Claude, Sch. of Educ., Northwestern University, Evanston, Ill.
Matthew, Eunice Sophia, 340 Riverside Dr., New York, N.Y.
Matthews, Ethel B., Box 83, Bowling Green, Ky.
Matthews, William P., 1114 N. Centennial, High Point, N.C.
Mattila, Mrs. Ruth Hughes, 2702 E. Drachman St., Tucson, Ariz.
Mattison, Robert James, Plymouth Teachers College, Plymouth, N.H.
Matzner, G. C., Eastern Illinois University, Charleston, Ill.
Mauch, James E., Office of Educ., Dept. of H.E.W., Washington, D.C.
Maucker, James William, State College of Iowa, Cedar Falls, Iowa
Mauk, Gertrude, 2880 S.W. First St., Ft. Lauderdale, Fla.
Mauk, Mrs. R. I., 623-A E. South Broadway, Lombard, Ill.
Maurer, Marion V., 1119 Bonnie Brae, River Forest, Ill.
Maurer, Robert L., California State Polytechnic College, Pomona, Calif.
Mauth, Leslie J., Ball State Teachers College, Muncie, Ind.
Maw, Wallace H., Sch. of Educ., University of Delaware, Newark, Del.
Maxwell, Ida E., Box 34, Cheyney, Pa.
May, Charles R., Dept. of Educ., Ohio State University, Columbus, Ohio
May, John B., State Teachers College, Salisbury, Md.
Mayer, Lewis F., 4507 West 213th St., Cleveland, Ohio
Mayer, Ronald W., 131 Garfield St., San Francisco, Calif.
Mayfield, L. B., Superintendent of Schools, 500 Monroe St., Medford, Ore.
Mayo, Samuel T., Sch. of Educ., Loyola University, Chicago, Ill.
Maziraz, Edward A., St. Joseph's College, Collegeville, Ind.
Mazyck, Harold E., Jr., 2007 Chelsea Lane, Greensboro, N.C.
McAdam, J. E., State University of Iowa, Iowa City, Iowa
McAllister, David, USAID, APO 205, New York, N.Y.
McArthur, L. C., Jr., Drawer 1191, Sumter, S.C.
McAuliffe, M. Eileen, 5649 N. Kolmar Ave., Chicago, Ill.
McBirney, Ruth, Boise Junior College, Boise, Idaho
McBride, James H., Superintendent of Schools, Norwalk, Ohio
McBride, William B., Ohio State University, Columbus, Ohio
McBurney, Mrs. Doris, 1641 West 105th St., Chicago, Ill.
McCaffrey, Austin J., Amer. Textbook Publ. Inst., 432 Fourth Ave., New York,
    N.Y.
McCain, Paul M., Arkansas College, Batesville, Ark.
McCallum, Gladys, 207 W. Wesley, Jackson, Mich.
McCann, Thomas W., 19 Jeffery Pl., Trumbull, Conn.
McCartin, William B., Superintendent, Catholic Schools, Tucson, Ariz.
McCartney, Hilda, 2916 Redwood Ave., Costa Mesa, Calif.
McCartney, Mrs. Virginia, Stonehouse Farm, R.F.D., Colon, Mich.
McCarty, Henry R., San Diego County Bd. of Educ., San Diego, Calif.
McClain, Warren J., Superintendent of Schools, Woodbury, N.J.
McClean, Donald E., P.O. Box 702, Menlo Park, Calif.
McClendon, LeRoy, Box 715, Stephen F. Austin Station, Nacogdoches, Tex.
McClintock, James A., Drew University, Madison, N.J.
McCluer, V. C., Superintendent of Schools, Ferguson, Mo.
McClure, L. Morris, Col. of Educ., Univ. of Maryland, College Park, Md.
McClure, Nancy, Col. of Educ., Univ. of Kentucky, Lexington, Ky.
McClure, Robert M., 22838 Epsilon St., Woodland Hills, Calif.
McClurkin, W. D., George Peabody College for Teachers, Nashville, Tenn.
McClusky, Howard Yale, Elem. Sch., University of Michigan, Ann Arbor, Mich.
McCollum, Elinor C., 619 Ridge Ave., Evanston, Ill.
McConnell, Gaither, Cen. for Tchr. Educ., Tulane Univ., New Orleans, La.

McConnell, John C., Windward School, Inc., White Plains, N.Y.
McConnell, T. R., Center for Study of Higher Educ., Univ. of Calif., Berkeley, Calif.
McCook, T. Joseph, 32 Spring St., Springfield, Mass.
McCorkle, C. Howard, Superintendent of Schools, Johnson City, Tenn.
McCormick, Ethel M., 31 S. Penn St., Allentown, Pa.
McCormick, G. A., Thiel College, Greenville, Pa.
McCracken, Oliver, Jr., Superintendent of Schools, Skokie, Ill.
McCrimmon, James M., 1109 S. Douglas, Urbana, Ill.
McCue, L. H., Jr., E. C. Glass High School, Lynchburg, Va.
McCue, Robert E., 715½ W. Locust St., Davenport, Iowa
McCullough, Constance M., APO 675, New York, N.Y.
McCully, Clyde C., Antelope Valley College, Lancaster, Calif.
McCurdy, Charles M., 933 S.W. Avenue B., Belle Glade, Fla.
McDaniel, Ernest D., Univ. Test. Service, Univ. of Kentucky, Lexington, Ky.
McDavit, H. W., South Orange-Maplewood Public Schools, South Orange, N.J.
McDermott, John C., 165 Chapel Road, Manhasset, N.Y.
McDonald, Arthur S., Reading Center, Marquette University, Milwaukee, Wis.
McDonald, L. R., Woodruff Senior High School, Peoria, Ill.
McEwen, Gordon B., 545 E. Walnut St., Whittier, Calif.
McFarland, Donald F., Jr., Wayne State University, Detroit, Mich.
McFeaters, Margaret M., 608 Brown's Lane, Pittsburgh, Pa.
McGavern, John H., University of Hartford, Hartford, Conn.
McGeever, John F., 13025 Morene St., Poway, Calif.
McGeoch, Dorothy M., Tchrs. Col., Columbia University, New York, N.Y.
McGinnis, Frederick A., Wilberforce University, P.O. Box 22, Wilberforce, Ohio
McGinnis, James H., Knoxville College, Knoxville, Tenn.
McGlasson, Maurice A., Sch. of Educ., Indiana University, Bloomington, Ind.
McGrath, Earl J., 525 West 120th St., New York, N.Y.
McGrath, G. D., Col. of Educ., Arizona State University, Tempe, Ariz.
McGrath, John W., Superintendent of Schools, Belmont, Mass.
McGuire, George K., 7211 Merrill Ave., Chicago, Ill.
McGuire, J. Carson, Col. of Educ., University of Texas, Austin, Tex.
McHugh, Walter J., Alameda County State College, Hayward, Calif.
McIlfatrick, Mrs. Edna M., 140 W. Englewood Ave., Teaneck, N.J.
McInerney, George K., 88-42—210th St., Jamaica, N.Y.
McIntosh, Lucy J., Box 242, Grambling, La.
McIntosh, William Ray, Superintendent of Schools, Rockford, Ill.
McIntyre, Margaret, George Washington University, McLean, Va.
McIntyre, Richmond E., 809 Carver St., Burlington, N.C.
McIsaac, John S., 2829 Fourth Ave., Beaver Falls, Pa.
McKay, Jean W., Board of Education, Manassas, Va.
McKean, Robert C., Col. of Educ., University of Colorado, Boulder, Colo.
McKee, Richard C., Office of Educ., Dept. of H.E.W., Washington, D.C.
McKelpin, Joseph P., North Carolina College, Durham, N.C.
McKenna, John J., Superintendent, Princeton Twp. Schls., Princeton, N.J.
McKenney, James L., Grad. Sch. of Business, Harvard Univ., Boston, Mass.
McKenney, Thomas K., Creighton University, Omaha, Neb.
McKenzie, Francis W., Board of Educ., 1025 Post Rd., Darien, Conn.
McKercher, Mrs. Berneth N., 1600 Dryden Rd., Metamora, Mich.
McKinley, Mrs. Elva, 219 Oak St., Fond du Lac, Wis.
McKinley, S. Justus, Emerson College, 130 Beacon St., Boston, Mass.
* McKinney, James, 505 Aragon Blvd., San Mateo, Calif.
McKinney, Lorella A., 4251 Orchard Ave., Willoughby, Ohio
McKown, George W., 2603 S. Forest Ave., Palatine, Ill.
McKune, Esther J., State University Teachers College, Oneonta, N.Y.
McLaren, Dallas C., 3240 Manoa Rd., Honolulu, Hawaii
McLaughlin, Edward R., Superintendent of Schools, Lead, S.D.
McLaughlin, Eleanor T., Albion College, Albion, Mich.
McLaughlin, Kenneth F., 871 N. Madison, Arlington, Va.
McLaughlin, Rita E., 242 Marlborough St., Boston, Mass.

McLean, Harvard W., Wayne State College, Wayne, Neb.
McLendon, Jonathon C., Sch. of Educ., Northwestern Univ., Evanston, Ill.
McLeod, Mrs. Jeanne, 29540 Bernice Dr., San Pedro, Calif.
McMahan, F. J., St. Ambrose College, 518 W. Locust St., Davenport, Iowa
McMahan, John Julia, State Univ. of Agric., Engr., and Sci., State College, N.M.
McMahon, Charles W., 22439 Gregory, Dearborn, Mich.
McMahon, Mrs. Edna T., 2418 Cochran St., Blue Island, Ill.
McMahon, Frances E., 6233A Loran, St. Louis, Mo.
McManamon, James, Quincy College, Quincy, Ill.
McManus, Robert P., State University College, Oswego, N.Y.
McManus, William E., Supt. of Catholic Schls., 205 Wacker Dr., Chicago, Ill.
McMaster, Blanche E., 102 Hull St., Bristol, Conn.
McMath, James G., Box 3912, Odessa, Tex.
McMillian, Nathaniel B., 242 Tarragona Way, Daytona Beach, Fla.
McMullen, Charles B., Sakonnet Point Rd., Little Compton, R.I.
McMurtrey, Violet, 3365 S.W. 103rd, Beaverton, Ore.
McNally, Harold J., Teachers Col., Columbia University, New York, N.Y.
McNamee, L. V., Waco Independent School Dist., P.O. Drawer 27, Waco, Tex.
McNeil, Alvin J., P.O. Box 66, Grambling, La.
McNelis, Francis A., Supt., Diocesan Schools, 1406—12th Ave., Altoona, Pa.
McNiel, Guy, El Paso Public Schools, El Paso, Tex.
McNutt, C. R., 116 Ridge Rd., Woodbridge, Va.
McPherson, Virgil L., Adams State College, Alamosa, Colo.
McPherson, W. N., Darke County Superintendent of Schools, Greenville, Ohio
McSharry, John T., Vailsburg High School, Newark, N.J.
McSwain, E. T., Sch. of Educ., Northwestern University, Evanston, Ill.
McTeer, Blanche R., 803 Lafayette St., Beaufort, S.C.
McWilliams, Earl M., Winchester-Thurston Sch., 4721—5th Ave., Pittsburgh, Pa.
* Mead, Arthur R., 1719 N.W. 6th Ave., Gainesville, Fla.
Meador, Bruce, Arizona State University, Tempe, Ariz.
Meadows, Jack H., Texas Western College, El Paso, Tex.
Mease, Clyde D., Superintendent of Schools, Humboldt, Iowa
Mecham, George P., Texas Technological College, Lubbock, Tex.
Mednick, Martha T., 523 Sunset Rd., Ann Arbor, Mich.
Medsker, Leland L., Ctr., Study of Higher Educ., Univ. of Calif., Berkeley, Calif.
Medved, A. A., Cherry Lawn School, Darien, Conn.
Meer, Samuel J., 631 Lafayette Ave., Mt. Vernon, N.Y.
Meier, Frederick A., State Teachers College, Salem, Mass.
Meier, Willard H., 5144 Alice Ct., LaSierra, Calif.
Meissner, Harley W., 13 Devonshire, Pleasant Ridge, Mich.
Melberg, Merritt E., 1222 W. 22nd St., Cedar Falls, Iowa
Melby, Ernest O., Michigan State University, East Lansing, Mich.
Mellott, Malcolm E., Prentice-Hall, Inc., P.O. Box 900, Englewood Cliffs, N.J.
Melnick, Curtis C., Supt., Dist. 14, Chicago Public Schls., Chicago, Ill.
Melnik, Amelia, Col. of Educ., University of Arizona, Tucson, Ariz.
Melnyk, Maria, 4432 S. Christiana Ave., Chicago, Ill.
Melton, Arthur W., Dept. of Psychol., Univ. of Michigan, Ann Arbor, Mich.
Melton, C. Y., Anderson Hall, University of Florida, Gainesville, Fla.
Melvin, Keith L., Peru State College, Peru, Neb.
Mendenhall, Alan D., 5205 Sunny Point Pl., Palos Verdes, Calif.
Mendenhall, C. B., Col. of Educ., Ohio State University, Columbus, Ohio
Mendoza, Romulo Y., 17 Iba, Sta. Mesa Heights, Quezon City, Philippines
Menge, Carleton P., University of New Hampshire, Durham, N.H.
Menge, Joseph W., Wayne University, Detroit, Mich.
Merchant, Vasant V., 2667 S. Ellendale Pl., Los Angeles, Calif.
Meredith, Cameron W., Southwestern Illinois Campus, Alton, Ill.
Merenda, Peter F., 258 Negansett Ave., Warwick, R.I.
Merideth, Howard V., Central Sch. Dist. No. 2, Syosset, L.I., N.Y.
Merkle, Paul M., Phoenixville Area High School, Phoenixville, Pa.
Merrihew, James L., Superintendent of Schools, Richmond, Calif.
Merrill, Dale O., 1002 N. Indian Hill Blvd., Claremont, Calif.

Merrill, Helen L., Jacksonville University, Jacksonville, Fla.
Merritt, C. B., Col. of Educ., Univ. of Arizona, Tucson, Ariz.
Merritt, Frances L., Div. of Educ., Howard Payne College, Brownwood, Tex.
Merry, Mrs. Frieda Kiefer, 2108 Kanawha Ave., S.E., Charleston, W.Va.
Mersand, Joseph, Jamaica High Sch., 168th St. and Gothic Dr., Jamaica, N.Y.
Merwin, Jack C., Eddy Hall, University of Minnesota, Minneapolis, Minn.
Metcalf, Harold H., Bloom Township High School, Chicago Heights, Ill.
Metcalfe, William W., 68 Blue Hills Rd., Amherst, Mass.
Metzner, William, John B. Stetson Junior High School, Philadelphia, Pa.
Meyer, Ammon B., Route 1, Fredericksburg, Pa.
Meyer, George A., University of Hawaii, Honolulu, Hawaii
Meyer, Lorraine V., 4501 N. 41st St., Milwaukee, Wis.
Meyer, Mrs. Marie, Douglass Col., Rutgers Univ., New Brunswick, N.J.
Meyer, Michael, Dept. of Educ., Centennial Bldg., St. Paul, Minn.
Meyer, Warren G., 5829 Portland Ave., So., Minneapolis, Minn.
Meyer, William T., Adams State College, Alamosa, Colo.
Meyers, Max B., 324 E. 59th St., Brooklyn, N.Y.
Michael, Calvin B., Col. of Educ., East. Mich. Univ., Ypsilanti, Mich.
Michael, Lloyd S., Evanston Township High School, Evanston, Ill.
Michael, Lois, 10967 Roebling Ave., Los Angeles, Calif.
Michaelis, John U., Sch. of Educ., Univ. of California, Berkeley, Calif.
Micheels, William J., Stout State College, Menomonie, Wis.
Michelson, John M., Sch. of Educ., Temple University, Philadelphia, Pa.
Mickelson, I. T., Superintendent of Schools, Austin, Minn.
Middledorf, Carl W., St. Peter's Lutheran School, East Detroit, Mich.
Middleton, C. A., 2216 Iowa St., Cedar Falls, Iowa
Middleton, Mildred L., 1944 Park Ave., S.E., Cedar Rapids, Iowa
Middleton, Ray F., 2910 Charlotte Dr., Merrick, L.I., N.Y.
Miles, Arnold A., 11500 Hamilton Ave., Detroit, Mich.
Miles, Mrs. V. G., Baylor Station, Belton, Tex.
Milheim, Robert Porter, 925 Cedar Dr., Oxford, Ohio
Milhollan, Frank E., 3325 Starr St., Lincoln, Neb.
Millar, Allen R., Mankato State College, Mankato, Minn.
Miller, Arthur L., 5625 Rosa Ave., St. Louis, Mo.
Miller, Benjamin, 251 Ft. Washington Ave., New York, N.Y.
Miller, Carroll H., Dept. of Educ., Northern Illinois Univ., DeKalb, Ill.
Miller, Carroll L., Howard University, Washington, D.C.
Miller, Charles, 1 Essex Ave., Maplewood, N.J.
Miller, Doris I., Sch. of Nursing, University of California, San Francisco, Calif.
Miller, Eliza Beth, Catskill High School, Catskill, N.Y.
Miller, Ethel B., Butler University, Indianapolis, Ind.
Miller, G. Harold, Gastonia City Schools, Gastonia, N.C.
Miller, George E., Univ. of Illinois Col. of Medicine, Chicago, Ill.
Miller, Harold E., Westmont College, Santa Barbara, Calif.
Miller, Mrs. Helen H., 1471 Westhaven Rd., San Marino, Calif.
Miller, Henry, Sch. of Educ., City College of New York, New York, N.Y.
Miller, Howard G., North Carolina State College, Raleigh, N.C.
Miller, Ingrid O., Edina-Morningside Senior High School, Edina, Minn.
Miller, Ira E., Eastern Mennonite College, Harrisonburg, Va.
Miller, Mrs. Ivy, 4280 Van Slyke Rd., Flint, Mich.
Miller, Mrs. J. Winona, 1961 Center St., Salem, Ore.
Miller, Jack W., Div. of Surveys, Peabody College, Nashville, Tenn.
Miller, Jacob W., Brooke Rd., Saybrooke Park, Pottstown, Pa.
Miller, John L., 345 Lakeville Rd., Great Neck, N.Y.
Miller, Leon F., Northwest Missouri State College, Maryville, Mo.
Miller, Lyle L., Col. of Educ., University of Wyoming, Laramie, Wyo.
Miller, Mrs. Mildred T., Box 215, Mooresville, N.C.
Miller, Paul A., Superintendent of Schools, Omaha, Neb.
Miller, Ralph, Superintendent of Schools, Georgetown, Ill.
Miller, Ward I., Board of Public Education, 511 W. 8th St., Wilmington, Del.
Millhollen, Lloyd F., Board of Education, Dist. No. 4, Eugene, Ore.

Millikin, R. M., 301 South State St., Geneseo, Ill.
Milling, Euleas, 227 N. Spring St., Concord, N.C.
Mills, Charles L., Superintendent of Schools, Box 2017, Hobbs, N.M.
Mills, Donna M., 530 Taft Place, Gary, Ind.
Mills, Forrest L., Racine Public Library, Racine, Wis.
Mills, Henry C., University of Rochester, Rochester, N.Y.
Mills, Marjorie F., Flower Vocational High School, Chicago, Ill.
Mills, Robert E., Mills Center, 1512 E. Broward Blvd., Fort Lauderdale, Fla.
Mills, Ruth I., State St., Richmond, Mass.
Mills, William H., Univ. School, Univ. of Michigan, Ann Arbor, Mich.
Milner, Ernest J., Sch. of Educ., Syracuse University, Syracuse, N.Y.
Miner, George D., 1108 Bissel Ave., Richmond, Calif.
Miniclier, Gordon E., 1965 Laurel Ave., St. Paul, Minn.
Minnis, Roy B., U.S. Office of Education, Dept. of H.E.W., Washington, D.C.
Minock, Mrs. Daniel F., 5520 Donna Ave, Tarzana, Calif.
Minogue, Mildred M., 612 Ridge Ave., Evanston, Ill.
Misner, Paul J., Superintendent, Glencoe Public Schools, Glencoe, Ill.
Mitchell, Donald P., 58 Woodridge Rd., Wayland, Mass.
Mitchell, Guy Clifford, Sch. of Educ., Baylor University, Waco, Tex.
Mitchell, Mrs. Leona, 3310 S.W. 192nd St., Aloha, Ore.
Mitchell, Mrs. Marian A., 1331 Bernard St., N.W., Atlanta, Ga.
Mitchell, Mary Frances, 9305 Ewing Dr., Bethesda, Md.
Mitzel, Harold E., 928 S. Sparks St., State College, Pa.
Mobley, M. D., 1010 Vermont Ave., N.W., Washington, D.C.
Modiste, Charles J., 3221 Southmore Blvd., Houston, Tex.
Moffatt, Maurice P., Montclair State College, Upper Montclair, N.J.
Moffitt, John Clifton, Superintendent of Schools, Provo, Utah
Mohr, Raymond E., 2050 South 108th St., Milwaukee, Wis.
Mohr, Robert L., University of Tampa, Tampa, Fla.
Molenkamp, Alice, 5 Homeside Lane, White Plains, N.Y.
Moll, Boniface E., St. Benedict's College, Atchison, Kan.
Monell, Ira H., 2714 Augusta Blvd., Chicago, Ill.
Monell, Ralph P., Superintendent of Schools, Canon City, Colo.
Monroe, Charles R., Wilson Junior College, 6800 S. Stewart Ave., Chicago, Ill.
Montesano, Edmund J., Carteret School No. 6, Bloomfield, N.J.
Montgomery, John F., Greenbrier College, Lewisburg, W.Va.
Montz, Doyle F., 2532 Sierra Way, LaVerne, Calif.
Moore, Alexander M., 1140 Northwest St., Indianapolis, Ind.
Moore, Arnold J., Dept. of Educ., Creighton University, Omaha, Neb.
Moore, Charles W., Murray State College, Murray, Ky.
Moore, Clyde B., Sch. of Educ., Cornell University, Ithaca, N.Y.
Moore, Dewey J., Indiana State College, Terre Haute, Ind.
Moore, Fletcher, Dept. of Fine Arts, Box 313, Elon College, N.C.
Moore, Harold E., Superintendent of Schools, Littleton, Colo.
Moore, Hollis A., Jr., Col. of Educ., University of Arizona, Tucson, Ariz.
Moore, Mrs. Patricia S., 2119 Guilford Rd., Hyattsville, Md.
Moore, Robert Ezra, 20 Tapia Dr., San Francisco, Calif.
Moore, W. J., Eastern Kentucky State College, Richmond, Ky.
Moore, Wilhelmina E., C. D. Hine Library, State Office Bldg., Hartford, Conn.
Moorhead, Sylvester A., Sch. of Educ., Univ. of Mississippi, University, Miss.
Moreau, Jules L., Seabury-Western Theological Seminary, Evanston, Ill.
Moreland, Kenneth O., Box 119, McLean, Ill.
Moreskine, Wallace R., 7802 Burns Ct., El Cerrito, Calif.
Moretz, Elmo E., Col. of Educ., Univ. of Southern Florida, Tampa, Fla.
Morgan, Esther M., New York State University, New Paltz, N.Y.
Morgan, Muriel, Newark State College, Newark, N.J.
Morgan, Raymond W., 1110 Milford St., Johnstown, Pa.
Morgan, Roland R., Superintendent, Mooresville City Schls., Mooresville, N.C.
Moriarty, Margaret C., 1220 Powderhorn Ter., Minneapolis, Minn.
Moriarty, Mary J., 92 Birch St., Bridgewater, Mass.
Morley, Franklin P., 101 Arthur Ave., Webster Groves, Mo.

Morris, James L., 577 W. College St., Yellow Springs, Ohio
Morris, M. B., 1133 Westridge, Abilene, Tex.
Morris, Mrs. Marjorie S., 16225 Moorpark, Encino, Calif.
Morrison, Coleman, 32 Hillcrest Circle, Watertown, Mass.
Morrison, D. A., East York Bd. of Educ., 670 Cosburn Ave., Toronto, Ont.
* Morrison, J. Cayce, 13 Cherry Tree Rd., Loudonville, N.Y.
Morrison, Leger R., 16 Brown St., Warren, R.I.
Morrison, Louis E., Superintendent of Schools, Alliance, Neb.
Morrow, Robert O., Col. of Educ., Univ. of Tennessee, Knoxville, Tenn.
Morse, Horace T., Nicholson Hall, University of Minnesota, Minneapolis, Minn.
Morse, Richard N., 16154 Via Lupine, San Lorenzo, Calif.
Morse, William C., Sch. of Educ., Univ. of Michigan, Ann Arbor, Mich.
Morton, Harold L., Cowen High School, Cowen, W.Va.
Morton, R. Clark, 210 Drummond St., Wattensburg, Mo.
Mosbo, Alvin O., Colorado State College, Greeley, Colo.
Moseley, S. Meredith, 424 N.W. 15th Way, Fort Lauderdale, Fla.
Moser, William G., 95 Concord Rd., Chester, Pa.
Moses, Morgan, 310 Garland Ave., Garland, Tex.
Mosher, Frank K., 2 Haskell Ave., Suffern, N.Y.
Mosier, Earl E., 28 Woodhampton Dr., Trenton, N.J.
Moss, Theodore C., 88 Sixth Ave., Oswego, N.Y.
Mother Anne Martina, St. Joseph Provincial House, Crookston, Minn.
Mother Beth Nothomb, San Francisco Col. for Women, San Francisco, Calif.
Mother Margaret Burke, Barat Col. of the Sacred Heart, Lake Forest, Ill.
Mother Marie Louise Martinez, Duchesne College, Omaha, Neb.
Mother Mary Aimee Rossi, San Diego Col. for Women, San Diego, Calif.
Mother M. Gonzaga, Blessed Sacrament College, Cornwells Heights, Pa.
Mother M. Gregory, Marymount College, Palos Verdes Estates, Calif.
Mother Mary Inez, Dept. of Educ., Holy Family College, Manitowoc, Wis.
Mother M. Irene Cody, Marymount College, 331 E. 71st., New York, N.Y.
Mother St. Lawrence, Rosemont College, Rosemont, Pa.
Mother St. Rita Marie, Notre Dame College, Staten Island, N.Y.
Motyka, Agnes L., 6311 Utah Ave., N.W., Washington, D.C.
Moulton, Gerald L., 600 S. Ruby St., Ellensburg, Wash.
Muck, Mrs. Ruth E. S., 1091 Stony Point Rd., Grand Island, N.Y.
Mudge, Evelyn L., Box 842, Hood College, Frederick, Md.
Muellen, T. K., 3606 Spruell Dr., Silver Spring, Md.
Mulhern, Joseph C., Spring Hill College, Mobile, Ala.
Muller, Philippe, Reulle Dofeyronz, Neuchatel, Switzerland
Mulliner, John H., 421 Richmond Rd., Kenilworth, Ill.
Mullins, William H., Antioch College, Yellow Springs, Ohio
Mulrooney, Thomas W., Board of Public Education, Wilmington, Del.
Mulry, Verna, 213 Tenny Ave., Waukesha, Wis.
Muns, Arthur C., Superintendent of Schools, Sycamore, Ill.
Munshaw, Carroll, 555 Byron St., Plymouth, Mich.
Munster, T., 2219 N. Kenmore Ave., Chicago, Ill.
Muntyan, Milosh, Michigan State University, East Lansing, Mich.
Murdick, Olin J., Superintendent, Diocesan Schools, Saginaw, Mich.
Murdock, Mrs. Ruth, Andrews University, Berrien Springs, Mich.
Murphy, Anne P., 480 S. Jersey St., Denver, Colo.
Murphy, Mrs. Carol M., 1117 McDaniel St., Evanston, Ill.
Murphy, Daniel A., Seton Hall University, South Orange, N.J.
Murphy, Forrest W., Sch. of Educ., University of Mississippi, University, Miss.
Murphy, Helen A., Boston University, 332 Bay State Rd., Boston, Mass.
Murphy, John A., 21-10—33rd Rd., Long Island City, N.Y.
Murphy, Loretta, 303 Lime St., Joliet, Ill.
Murphy, Robert A., 93 Clark St., Clinton, Mass.
Murray, C. Merrill, State University Col. of Educ., Geneseo, N.Y.
Murray, Robert E., 1916 S. Signal Hill Dr., Kirkwood, Mo.
Musgrave, Ray S., Univ. of Southern Mississippi, Hattiesburg, Miss.
Mussen, Paul, Dept. of Psych., Univ. of California, Berkeley, Calif.

Myer, Marshall E., Jr., 2329 S. Rose St., Kalamazoo, Mich.
Myers, Donald A., 1370 Northumberland Dr., St. Louis, Mo.
Myers, Garry Cleveland, 968 Main St., Honesdale, Pa.
Myles, William C., Campbellsville College, Campbellsville, Ky.

Nafziger, Mary K., Goshen College, Goshen, Ind.
Nagel, Roberta F., 3207—54th St., Moline, Ill.
Nagel, Wilma I., 1849 Warwick Ave., Warwick, R.I.
Nagle, Robert J., 289 Rock St., Fall River, Mass.
Nagy, Richard, North Junior High School, Bloomfield, N.J.
Nahm, Helen, Sch. of Nursing, University of Calif., Med. Center, San Francisco, Calif.
Nahshon, Samuel, Bureau of Jewish Educ., 2030 S. Taylor Rd., Cleveland, Ohio
Nally, Thomas P., University of Rhode Island, Kingston, R.I.
Nance, Mrs. Afton Dill, State Educ. Bldg., 721 Capitol Ave., Sacramento, Calif.
Nance, Helen M., 6 Donna Dr., Normal, Ill.
Nardelli, Robert, Campus Lab. Sch., San Diego State Col., San Diego, Calif.
Narkis, William F., 4921 W. Ferdinand St., Chicago, Ill.
Naslund, Robert A., Sch. of Educ., Univ. of So. California, Los Angeles, Calif.
Nason, Doris E., University of Connecticut, Storrs, Conn.
Nason, Leslie J., 216 Euclid Ave., Long Beach, Calif.
Nasser, Sheffield, Sarasota County Schls., 2405 Hatton St., Sarasota, Fla.
Nault, William H., Field Enterprises Educational Corp., Chicago, Ill.
Naus, Grant, 911 Seventh St., Coronado Unified Schl. Dist., Coronado, Calif.
Neal, Mrs. Bernice E., 7510 Richmond Dr., Omaha, Neb.
Neale, Daniel C., Col. of Educ., University of Minnesota, Minneapolis, Minn.
Nebel, Dale, Bethel College, North Newton, Kan.
Nees, Ruth, 1220 N. Reymond St., Las Cruces, N.M.
Neiderhiser, F. J., Superintendent of Schools, McClure, Ohio
Nelson, Carl B., New York State University College, Cortland, N.Y.
Nelson, Edith I., 8 Waterford St., Edinboro, Pa.
Nelson, Esther Marion, Col. of Educ., Univ. of Houston, Houston, Tex.
Nelson, Ethel C., 692 Des Plaines Ave., Des Plaines, Ill.
Nelson, Florence A., Univ. of South Carolina, 825 Sumter St., Columbia, S.C.
Nelson, Harvey D., 1473 Queen City Ave., Tuscaloosa, Ala.
Nelson, John M., Dept. of Educ., Purdue University, Lafayette, Ind.
Nelson, Kenneth G., 511 Glasgow Rd., Alexandria, Va.
Nelson, L. Warren, Miami University, Oxford, Ohio
Nelson, Mrs. Lois Ney, 13506 Rye St., Sherman Oaks, Calif.
Nelson, Margaret B., State College of Iowa, Cedar Falls, Iowa
Nelson, Orville W., Route No. 1, Stanchfield, Minn.
Nelson, Pearl Astrid, Boston University, 332 Bay State Rd., Boston, Mass.
Nelson, Sylvia, 415 W. 8th St.,Topeka, Kans.
Nemzek, Claude L., Univ. of Detroit, 4133 W. McNichols Rd., Detroit, Mich.
Nerbovig, Marcella, Northern Illinois University, DeKalb, Ill.
Nesi, Carmella, 906 Peace St., Pelham Manor, N.Y.
Netsky, Martin G., Dept. of Path., University of Virginia, Charlottesville, Va.
Neuner, Elsie Flint, 2 Atlas Place, Mt. Vernon, N.Y.
Neville, Donald, Child Study Center, Peabody College, Nashville, Tenn.
Newman, Herbert M., Educ. Dept., Brooklyn College, Brooklyn, N.Y.
Newman, Robert E., 1401 East 55th St., Chicago, Ill.
Newman, Wilfred, West High School, Rochester, N.Y.
Newsom, A. Carolyn, Louisiana State University, Baton Rouge, La.
Newsom, Herman A., P.O. Box 5243, North Texas Station, Denton, Tex.
Newton, Eunice S., Howard University, Washington, D.C.
Nicholas, William T., 609 Nevada St., Susanville, Calif.
Nichols, J. Herbert, Frankfort, Del.
Nichols, Richard J., Ball State Teachers College, Munice, Ind.
Nicholson, Alice, 1009 E. Hatton St., Pensacola, Fla.
Nicholson, Lawrence E., Psych. Dept., Harris Tchrs. Col., St. Louis, Mo.
Niehaus, Philip C., Sch. of Educ., Duquesne University, Pittsburgh, Pa.

Niemeyer, John H., Bank Street College of Education, New York, N.Y.
Nikoloff, Sayra B., 234 Woodmere Dr., Tonawanda, N.Y.
Niland, William P., 1858 Tacoma Ave., Berkeley, Calif.
Nimroth, William T., Sch. of Educ., Stanford University, Stanford, Calif.
Nix, J. Gordon, Jr., Harlingen Senior High School, Harlingen, Tex.
Nixon, Clifford L., East Carolina College, Greenville, N.C.
Nixon, John Erskine, Sch. of Educ., Stanford University, Stanford, Calif.
Nixon, W. D., Sch. of Educ., Univ. of South Carolina, Columbia, S.C.
Noar, Gertrude, 195 Adams St., Brooklyn, N.Y.
Noe, Samuel V., 506 West Hill St., Louisville, Ky.
Noel, Edward W., 5443 S. Cornell Ave., Chicago, Ill.
Noll, Frances E., 1810 Taylor St., N.W., Washington, D.C.
Noll, Victor H., Col. of Educ., Michigan State Univ., East Lansing, Mich.
Nonnamaker, Eldon R., 153 Student Services Bldg., East Lansing, Mich.
Noonan, Joseph D., Jr., 34 Holden St., Worcester, Mass.
Norcross, Claude E., 301 E. Lucard, Taft, Calif.
Nordberg, H. Orville, Sacramento State College, Sacramento, Calif.
Norem, Grant M., State Teachers College, Minot, N.D.
Norman, Ralph Paul, 18395 Clemison Ave., Saratoga, Calif.
Norman, Robert H., 315—4th Ave., N.W., Faribault, Minn.
Norris, Ralph C., 216 S.W. First St., Des Moines, Iowa
Northey, Ethel May, 224 Iowa Ave., Muscatine, Iowa
Northrup, Sunbeam Ann, Off. of Supt. of Sch. Dist. VI, c/o USAREUR (rear)
    Com. Z, APO 58, New York, N.Y.
Norton, Frank E., Jr., 3608 Dryden Rd., Fort Worth, Tex.
Nosofsky, William, Junior High School 178, 2163 Dean St., Brooklyn, N.Y.
Now, H. O., Findlay College, Findlay, Ohio
Nowell, Mrs. Lillian D., 2500—25th Ave., San Francisco, Calif.
Nunnally, Nancy, 5916 Monticello Ave., Cincinnati, Ohio
Nutter, H. E., Norman Hall, University of Florida, Gainesville, Fla.
Nutterville, Catherine, W2923 Euclid Ave., Spokane, Wash.
Nutting, William C., University of Utah, Salt Lake City, Utah
Nye, Robert E., Sch. of Music, University of Oregon, Eugene, Ore.
Nystrom, J. W., Jr., American University of Beirut, Beirut, Lebanon

Oaks, Ruth E., B-104 Haverford Villa, Haverford, Pa.
Oberholtzer, Kenneth E., Superintendent of Schools, Denver, Colo.
Obourn, L. C., Superintendent of Schools, East Rochester, N.Y.
O'Brien, Cyril C., 9120—118 St., Windsor Park, Edmonton, Alba., Canada
O'Connor, Clarence D., Lexington School for Deaf, 904 Lexington Ave., New
    York, N.Y.
O'Connor, John D., Maple Park, Ill.
O'Connor, Joseph F., Spring Gardens Institute, Philadelphia, Pa.
O'Connor, Mrs. Marguerite O., Maple Park, Ill.
Odland, Norine, Burton Hall, University of Minnesota, Minneapolis, Minn.
O'Donnell, Beatrice, Michigan State University, East Lansing, Mich.
O'Donnell, John F., Box 1086, Tupper Lake, N.Y.
O'Fallon, O. K., Sch. of Educ., Kansas State University, Manhattan, Kan.
O'Farrell, John J., Loyola University, 7101 W. 80th St., Los Angeles, Calif.
Ogden, Lowell K., Bakersfield Center, Fresno State College, Bakersfield, Calif.
O'Hare, Mary Rita, 212 Hollywood Ave., Crestwood, N.Y.
Ohlsen, Merle M., Col. of Educ., University of Illinois, Urbana, Ill.
Ohnmacht, Fred W., Col. of Educ., University of Maine, Orono, Me.
Ojemann, R. H., Child Welfare Res. Sta., State Univ. of Iowa, Iowa City, Iowa
Olander, Herbert T., University of Pittsburgh, Pittsburgh, Pa.
Oldendorf, Mrs. Dorothy, Superintendent of Schools, Wilmette, Ill.
* Oldham, Mrs. Birdie V., 621 W. Silver St., Lakeland, Fla.
Olieker, Isidore I., Hofstra University, Hempstead, N.Y.
Olivari, Irene M., 80 LaSalle St., New York, N.Y.
Olivas, Romeo A., Univ. of the Philippines, Diliman, Rizal, Philippines
Oliver, George J., Richmond Professional Institute, Richmond, Va.

Olmsted, M. D., Geneseo Central School, Geneseo, N.Y.
Olphert, Warwick Bruce, University of New England, Armidale, New South Wales
Olsen, George L., Wessels Library, Newberry College, Newberry, S.C.
Olsen, Hans C., Jr., Col. of Educ., Wayne State University, Detroit, Mich.
Olsen, Marion G., 462 Grider St., Buffalo, N.Y.
Olson, R. A., Ball State Teachers College, Muncie, Ind.
* Olson, Willard C., Sch. of Educ., University of Michigan, Ann Arbor, Mich.
Olson, William L., 1946 Sharondale Ave., St. Paul, Minn.
O'Malley, Sarah, 1130 Washington Blvd., Oak Park, Ill.
O'Mara, Arthur P., Lane Tech. High School, Chicago, Ill.
O'Mara, J. Francis, 29 Snowling Rd., Uxbridge, Mass.
O'Neal, John F., Dept. of Educ., Lehigh University, Bethlehem, Pa.
O'Neill, John H., Dept. of Educ., DePaul University, Chicago, Ill.
O'Neill, John J., State College of Boston, 625 Huntington Ave., Boston, Mass.
O'Neill, Leo W., Jr., Col. of Educ., University of Maryland, College Park, Md.
O'Neill, Patrick J., Superintendent, Diocesan Schools, Fall River, Mass.
Oppenheim, Alan, 5200 Blackstone Ave., Chicago, Ill.
Oppenheimer, J. J., Belknap Campus, University of Louisville, Louisville, Ky.
Oppleman, Dan L., Iowa Wesleyan College, Mt. Pleasant, Iowa
Ore, Malvern L., Div. of Educ., Huston-Tillotson Col., Austin, Tex.
O'Reilly, Robert C., Morningside College, Sioux City, Iowa
Orlich, Donald C., Idaho State University, Pocatello, Idaho
Orlovich, Joseph, Jr., 554 Clay St., Joliet, Ill.
Ormsby, Lelia Ann, Sacramento State College, Sacramento, Calif.
O'Rourke, J. Mel, Central Y.M.C.A. High School, Chicago, Ill.
O'Rourke, Joseph, 3197 Gerbert Rd., Columbus, Ohio
Orr, Beryl, 308 Stanley St., Middletown, Ohio
Orr, Charles W., R. 3, Box 492, Fayette Rd., Durham, N.C.
Orr, Louise, 925 Crockett St., Amarillo, Tex.
Ort, Lorrene Love, Bowling Green State University, Bowling Green, Ohio
Orton, Don A., Lesley College, Cambridge, Mass.
Orton, Kenneth D., Southern Illinois University, Carbondale, Ill.
Osborn, Wayland W., 2701 Hickman Rd., Des Moines, Iowa
O'Shea, John T., 3233 Main St., Buffalo, N.Y.
Osibov, Henry, Oregon Educ. Assn., 1530 S.W. Taylor St., Portland, Ore.
Oskamp, Stuart, Claremont Graduate School, Claremont, Calif.
Ostheimer, George F., Genl. Superintendent of Education, Indianapolis, Ind.
Ostrander, Raymond H., 15 Winter St., Weston, Mass.
Ostrom, Gerald, 291 Wagner Rd., Northfield, Ill.
Ostrovsky, Everett S., Newark State College, Union, N.J.
Ostwalt, Jay H., P.O. Box 387, Davidson, N.C.
Osuch, A. E., 6636 N. Odell, Chicago, Ill.
Osuna, Pedro, Sch. of Educ., College of the Pacific, Stockton, Calif.
Oswalt, Edna Rickey, Dept. of Spec. Educ., Westminster Col., New Wilmington, Pa.
Oswalt, Howard C., 1518 N. McAllister Ave., Tempe, Ariz.
Oswalt, William W., Jr., Lehigh County Schools, 445 Hamilton St., Allentown, Pa.
Otomo, Aiko, 1510-A Evelyn St., Honolulu, Hawaii
Otterness, June, Public Schools, Hutchinson, Minn.
Otto, Henry J., University of Texas, Austin, Tex.
Otts, John, University of North Carolina, Chapel Hill, N.C.
Overfield, Ruth, State Educ. Bldg., 721 Capitol Ave., Sacramento, Calif.
Overholt, Elbert D., University of Kansas, Lawrence, Kan.
Overstreet, George Thomas, 811 S. Frances St., Terrell, Tex.
Owen, Jason C., P.O. Box 537, Tech. Station, Ruston, La.
Owen, John M., Burma Road School, Wasilla, Alaska
Owen, Mary E., F. A. Owen Publishing Co., Dansville, N.Y.
Owens, John, Roslyn Public Schools, Roslyn, N.Y.
Owens, Robert G., State University of New York, Buffalo, N.Y.
Owings, Ralph S., Mississippi Southern College, Hattiesburg, Miss.

Pace, C. Robert, Sch. of Educ., University of California, Los Angeles, Calif.
Packer, C. Kyle, 629 Deerfield Dr., Tonawanda, N.Y.
Padget, Mattie Bell, 704 N. Chestnut St., Carlsbad, N.M.
Page, Ellis B., Bur. of Educ. Res., Univ. of Connecticut, Storrs, Conn.
Page, Richard H., Psych. Dept., Skidmore College, Saratoga Springs, N.Y.
Pagel, Betty Lou, 304 E. 5th Ave., Cheyenne, Wyo.
Paine, Harry W., 5436 North Woods Lane, Norwood, Cincinnati, Ohio
Painter, Fred B., Superintendent, Brighton School Dist. No. 1, Rochester, N.Y.
Palliser, G. C., Central P.O. Box 1525, Wellington, New Zealand
Palmer, Albert, Stockton College, Stockton, Calif.
Palmer, Anne M. H., 22277 Cass Ave., Woodland Hills, Calif.
Palmer, Frank J., 208 Church St., North Syracuse, N.Y.
Palmer, John C., Tufts University, Medford, Mass.
Palmer, Lulu, State Department of Education, Montgomery, Ala.
Pangburn, Margaret C., 104 Glenwood Ave., Leonia, N.J.
Panos, Robert J., 196 Park Rd., Park Forest, Ill.
Papanek, Ernst, 1 West 64th St., New York, N.Y.
Pappas, George, 26 Keith St., Parkdale S. 12, Victoria, Australia
Paquin, Laurence G., Board of Education Bldg., New Haven, Conn.
Parisho, Mrs. Eugenia G., 10109 Lake Ave., Cleveland, Ohio
Park, Maxwell G., 44 Clayton Ave., Cortland, N.Y.
Parke, Margaret B., 430 West 118th St., New York, N.Y.
Parker, Don H., Science Research Associates, Chicago, Ill.
Parker, James R., 210 Thornbrook Rd., DeKalb, Ill.
Parker, Marjorie H., 4919 Sixteenth St., N.W., Washington, D.C.
Parkinson, Daniel S., 725 Melissa Dr., Oxford, Ohio
Parkyn, George William, Southern Cross Bldg., Wellington, New Zealand
Parmelee, Elizabeth, Calhoun School, 309 West 92nd St., New York, N.Y.
Parr, Kenneth E., Box 1348, c/o Tapline, Beirut, Lebanon
Parry, O. Meredith, William Penn Senior High School, York, Pa.
Parsey, John M., 305 Droste Circle, East Lansing, Mich.
Parsley, Kenneth M., University of Alabama, University, Ala.
Parsons, Brooks A., Superintendent of Schools, Norwood, Ohio
Parsons, David, Univ. of British Columbia, Woollahra, N.S.W., Australia
Parsons, Seth Hamilton, 1114 Seventh St., Las Vegas, N.M.
Parton, Daisy, Box 1882, University, Ala.
Paschal, Harland L. R., 5675 Carr St., Arvada, Colo.
Pascoe, David D., LaMesa Spring Valley Sch. Dist., LaMesa, Calif.
Pasquale, Vincent C. D., Superintendent, Valley Central School System, Mont-
    gomery, N.Y.
Passow, Aaron Harry, Teachers College, Columbia University, New York, N.Y.
Paster, G. Nicholas, 117 W. Center College St., Yellow Springs, Ohio
Paster, Julius, 867 Barbara Dr., Teaneck, N.J.
Patacsil, Gregorie C., Sec. Educ. Div., Bur. of Public Schools, Manila, Philippines
Patch, Robert B., 4 Carleton Dr., Glens Falls, N.Y.
Pate, Mildred, 1806 East 6th St., Greenville, N.C.
Paterson, John J., 1008 Happy Hollow, West Lafayette, Ind.
Paton, James M., Ontario College of Education, Toronto, Ont., Canada
Paton, William, Superintendent of Schools, Oconomowoc, Wis.
Patrick, Robert B., 433 W. Park Ave., University Park, Pa.
Patt, Jack M., Soc. Sci. Div., San Jose State College, San Jose, Calif.
Pattee, Howard H., P.O. Box 5215, Carmel, Calif.
Patterson, Gordon E., New Mexico Highlands Univ., Las Vegas, N.M.
* Patterson, Herbert, 406 S. Stallard Ave., Stillwater, Okla.
Pattison, Mattie, Home Econ. Hall, Iowa State University, Ames, Iowa
Patton, Earl D., Superintendent of Schools, Culver City, Calif.
Paul, Marvin S., 6743 N. California Ave., Chicago, Ill.
Paulsen, Gaige B., 36 Fairview Ave., Athens, Ohio
Paulson, Alice T., 125 W. Eighth St., Blue Earth, Minn.
Pautz, Wilmer, Wisconsin State College, Eau Claire, Wis.
Pavel, Mrs. Harriet M., 6343 N. Kildare Ave., Chicago, Ill.
Paxton, J. Hall, 1405 Pine St., St. Louis, Mo.

Payne, Arlene, Univ. of Kansas Medical Center, Kansas City, Kan.
Payne, Donald T., 221 East 7th St., Bloomington, Ind.
Payne, Joe D., Box 2261, Sam Houston College Station, Huntsville, Tex.
Paynovich, Nicholas, Rt. 4, Box 840, Tucson, Ariz.
Peacock, A. E., Superintendent of Schools, Moose Jaw, Sask., Canada
Pearson, Jim, 4350 Neo St., Pierrefonds, Que., Canada
Pearson, Lois, State University College, Buffalo, N.Y.
Pearson, Millie V., 215 S. Monroe St., Stillwater, Okla.
Peavey, Samuel B., Educ. Dept., University of Louisville, Louisville, Ky.
Peavy, R. Vance, Central Oregon College, Bend, Ore.
Pebley, Wilson A., 310 Lincoln Way East, McConnellsburg, Pa.
Peccola, Charles, 2456 Hobbs Dr., Manhattan, Kan.
Pederson, Arne K., Pacific Lutheran University, Tacoma, Wash.
Pederson, Clara A., Dept. of Educ., Univ. of North Dakota, Grand Forks, N.D.
Pedigo, Louise, Lynchburg College, Lynchburg, Va.
Peiffer, Paul D., 5902 Jonestown Rd., Harrisburg, Pa.
Pell, Richard E., 409 S. Swain Ave., Bloomington, Ind.
Pella, Milton O., Wisconsin High School, Univ. of Wisconsin, Madison, Wis.
Pellegrin, Lionel, 945 E. River Oaks Dr., Baton Rouge, La.
Pelton, Frank M., Dept. of Educ., Univ. of Rhode Island, Kingston, R.I.
Penn, Floy L., Mt. Lebanon Public Schls., 735 Washington Rd., Pittsburgh, Pa.
Pennetta, Gerardo, 841—80th St., North Bergen, N.J.
Penta, A. H. Della, Superintendent of Schools, Lodi, N.J.
Perdew, Philip W., Sch. of Educ., University of Denver, Denver, Colo.
Peregoy, C. G., Woodrow Wilson High School, Beckley, W.Va.
Perry, Arthur V., Superintendent of Schools, Batavia, Ill.
Perry, James Olden, 2919 Wheeler St., Houston, Tex.
Perry, Leland M., 3180 W. Rome Ave., Anaheim, Calif.
Perry, T. Edward, 2080 Alton Rd., East Cleveland, Ohio
Perry, W. D., University of North Carolina, Chapel Hill, N.C.
Pescosolido, John R., Central Connecticut State College, New Britain, Conn.
Peters, J. V., Dept. of Educ., Walla Walla College, College Place, Wash.
Peters, Jon S., State Col. for Alameda County, Hayward, Calif.
Peters, Mary Magdalene, 950 West "D" St., Ontario, Calif.
Petersen, Clarence E., 19 Fulton St., Redwood City, Calif.
Petersen, Fred J., University of South Dakota, Vermillion, S.D.
Petersen, Paul G., Long Beach State College, Long Beach, Calif.
Peterson, Basil H., Orange Coast Col., 2701 Fairview Rd., Costa Mesa, Calif.
Peterson, Carl H., 9807 S. Seeley Ave., Chicago, Ill.
Peterson, Donald W., 1817—16th St., Rock Island, Ill.
Peterson, Dorothy G., Trenton State College, Trenton, N.J.
Peterson, Douglas W., Dept. of Educ., Kalamazoo College, Kalamazoo, Mich.
Peterson, Dwain F., 202-D Huskerville, Lincoln, Neb.
Peterson, Elmer T., Col. of Educ., State Univ. of Iowa, Iowa City, Iowa
Peterson, Evelyn F., East High School Bldg., Waterloo, Iowa
Peterson, Grace, Nebraska State Teachers College, Kearney, Neb.
Peterson, Herbert H., 828 Circle Dr., High Point, N.C.
Peterson, LeRoy, University of Wisconsin, Madison, Wis.
Peterson, Miriam E., 5422 Wayne Ave., Chicago, Ill.
Peterson, Vianna, 300 Humphrey St., Logansport, Ind.
Pethick, Wayne M., 6136 Northwest Hwy., Chicago, Ill.
Petor, Andrew, East Dear-Frazer Union High School, Creighton, Pa.
Pettersch, Carl A., 200 Southern Blvd., Danbury, Conn.
Petterson, Mrs. Muriel, County Schls. Serv. Center, San Luis Obispo, Calif.
Pettinga, R. C., North Fourth St. Christian School, Paterson, N.J.
Pettiss, J. O., Dept. of Educ., Louisiana State University, Baton Rouge, La.
Petty, Edgar L., Jr., Eastern New Mexico University, Portales, N.M.
Petty, Mary Clare, Col. of Educ., University of Oklahoma, Norman, Okla.
Petty, Walter T., 3632 Tolenas Ct., Sacramento, Calif.
Pezzullo, Thomas J., 268 Greenville Ave., Johnston, R.I.
Phay, John E., Bur. of Educ. Res., University of Mississippi, University, Miss.

Phearman, Leo Thomas, Long Beach State College, Long Beach, Calif.
Phelan, William F., 67 S. Windsor Ave., Brightwaters, N.J.
Phelps, H. Vaughn, 8727 Shamrock Rd., Omaha, Neb.
Phelps, Harold R., Illinois State University, Normal, Ill.
Phelps, Roger P., 4 Barnes Ave., Baldwin, L.I., N.Y.
Phillips, Cecil K., State College of Iowa, Cedar Falls, Iowa
Phillips, Don O., 1158 S. Harris Ave., Columbus, Ohio
Phillips, James A., Jr., Col. of Educ., Kent State University, Kent, Ohio
Phillips, Paul, 520 W. Palmer Ave., Morrisville, Pa.
Phillips, Richard C., Univ. of North Carolina, Chapel Hill, N.C.
Phillips, Thomas Arthur, 1536 S. Sixth St., Terre Haute, Ind.
Philp, William A., 440 Williams Ave., Natchitoches, La.
Phipps, Mrs. H. W., 133 Summit Ave., Summit, N.J.
Phoenix, William D., 28 W. Winthrope Rd., Kansas City, Mo.
Piazza, Frank, Board of Education, 51 Aldine Ave., Bridgeport, Conn.
Pickett, Louis L., County Supt. of Schools, Court House, Davenport, Iowa
Piekarz, Josephine A., Sch. of Educ., New York University, New York, N.Y.
Pierce, Arthur E., Hanover School District, Hanover, N.H.
Pikunas, Justin, Psych. Dept., University of Detroit, Detroit, Mich.
Pilch, Mrs. Mary M., State Dept. of Education, Centennial Bldg., St. Paul, Minn.
Pinkston, Dow G., 105 E. Madison, Yates Center, Kan.
Pitkin, Royce, Goddard College, Plainfield, Vt.
Pittillo, Robert A., Jr., Raleigh Public Schools, Raleigh, N.C.
Pittman, DeWitt Kennieth, 6800 Monroe Rd., Charlotte, N.C.
Pitts, Clara L., 4700 Upton St., N.W., Washington, D.C.
Pitts, F. N., 435 S. Fifth St., Louisville, Ky.
Pivnick, Isadore, 135 Van Ness Ave., San Francisco, Calif.
Plana, Juan F., Andrés Sánchez 306, Vigía. Camagüey, Cuba
Pledger, Maude M., 3481 College Station, Commerce, Tex.
Plimpton, Blair, Superintendent of Schools, 400 S. Western Ave., Park Ridge, Ill.
Pliska, Stanley R., 1022 Hanover Ave., Norfolk, Va.
Plotnick, Morton, 31860 Beverly St., Oak Park, Mich.
Plumb, Mary Louise, Bennington High School, Bennington, Vt.
Plumb, Valworth R., University of Minnesota, Duluth Branch, Duluth, Minn.
Plummer, Violin G., Oakwood College, Huntsville, Ala.
Podell, Mrs. Harriett A., Dept. of Educ., Univ. of California, Berkeley, Calif.
Podlich, William F., Jr., 1630 College Ave., Tempe, Ariz.
Poehler, W. A., Concordia College, St. Paul, Minn.
Pogue, E. Graham, Ball State Teachers College, Muncie, Ind.
Pogue, Pauline C., Colorado State College, Greeley, Colo.
Polansky, Leon, 33-47 Fourteenth St., Long Island City, N.Y.
Pole, E. John, Ball State Teachers College, Munice, Ind.
Polglase, Robert J., 10 Army Dr., Westfield, N.J.
Pond, Millard Z., Superintendent of Schools, Dist. No. 4, Eugene, Ore.
Poole, Albert E., 214 N. Washington Cir., Lake Forest, Ill.
Pooley, Robert C., University of Wisconsin, Madison, Wis.
Porter, M. Roseamonde, University of Hawaii, Honolulu, Hawaii
Porter, R. H., The Steck Co., Box 16, Austin, Tex.
Porter, Willis P., Sch. of Educ., Indiana University, Bloomington, Ind.
Potell, Herbert, 1719—48th St., Brooklyn, N.Y.
Potts, John F., Voorhees Junior College, Denmark, S.C.
Poulos, Thomas H., Michigan School for the Deaf, Flint, Mich.
Poulter, James R., Superintendent of Schools, Anamosa, Iowa
Pound, Clarence A., Educ. Bldg., Purdue University, Lafayette, Ind.
Pounds, Ralph L., Tchrs. Col., University of Cincinnati, Cincinnati, Ohio
Pourchot, Leonard L., 2490 Simms Circle, Sparks, Nev.
Powell, Mrs. Ruth Marie, 611 Young's Lane, Nashville, Tenn.
Powell, William R., Ball State Teachers College, Muncie, Ind.
Powers, F. R., 262 Cornell Ave., Amherst, Ohio
Powers, Francis P., Sch. of Educ., Boston College, Chestnut Hill, Mass.
Powers, Philander, Ventura College, 4667 Telegraph Rd., Ventura, Calif.

Prasch, John, Superintendent of Schools, Racine, Wis.
Preil, Joseph J., 189 Shelley Ave., Elizabeth, N.J.
Prentice, Warren L., Sacramento State College, Sacramento, Calif.
Preseren, Herman J., Box 7266, Reynolds Sta., Winston-Salem, N.C.
Preston, Ralph C., Sch. of Educ., University of Pennsylvania, Philadelphia, Pa.
Prestwood, Elwood L., 426 Righters Mill Rd., Gladwyne, Pa.
Pricco, Ernest, Melrose Park School, Melrose Park, Ill.
Price, Alvin H., University of Minnesota, Minneapolis, Minn.
Price, Louis E., University of Massachusetts, Amherst, Mass.
Price, Rebecca W., Norristown Public Schls., Norristown, Pa.
Price, Robert Diddams, 7819 Pinemeadow Lane, Cincinnati, Ohio
Prince, Mrs. Virginia Faye, P.O. Box 4015, St. Louis, Mo.
Pringle, Glenn L., Wheaton College, Wheaton, Ill.
Pritchett, John P., Trenton Junior College, 101 W. State St., Trenton, N.J.
Pritzkau, Philo T., University of Connecticut, Storrs, Conn.
Procunier, Robert W., 600 N. Elmhurst Ave., Mt. Prospect, Ill.
Propsting, Mrs. M., 44 Henrietta St., Waverley, N.S.W., Australia
Prouse, Peter, 414 Aliso, S.E., Albuquerque, N.M.
Pruitt, Robert E., Superintendent of Schools, Quincy, Mass.
Prutzman, Stuart E., County Superintendent of Schools, Jim Thorpe, Pa.
Pudlowski, Victor, 2321 Russell St., Berkeley, Calif.
Pugmire, Jean, Edith Bowen Sch., Utah State University, Logan, Utah
Purdy, Ralph D., Miami University, Oxford, Ohio
Puryear, Ada P., P.O. Box 1243, Tuskegee Institute, Ala.
Puryear, Royal W., Florida Normal and Ind. Mem. College, St. Augustine, Fla.
Putnam, John F., Office of Education, Dept. of H.E.W., Washington, D.C.

Quall, Alvin B., Whitworth College, Spokane, Wash.
Quanbeck, Martin, Augsburg College, Minneapolis, Minn.
Quanbeck, Thor H., Augustana College, Sioux Falls, S.D.
Quaranta, Joseph L., 555 Harley Dr., Columbus, Ohio
Queen, Renee, Brooklyn College, Brooklyn, N.Y.
Quesenberry, Virginia C., Fresno County Schls., 2314 Mariposa St., Fresno, Calif.
Quick, Henry E., 293 Main St., Box 279, Oswego, Tioga County, N.Y.
Quick, Otho J., Northern Illinos University, DeKalb, Ill.
Quiller, Gordon F., Colorado State University, Fort Collins, Colo.
Quinn, Villa H., State Department of Education, Augusta, Me.
Quish, Bernard A., 2601 W. 81st Pl., Chicago, Ill.

Rabb, Willynne, Kingsville Public Schools, Kingsville, Tex.
Rabin, Bernard, Bowling Green State University, Bowling Green, Ohio
Raciti, C. Stephen, Pennington-Titusville Rd., Pennington, N.J.
Radhakrishna, Rajghat, Varanasi 1, U.P., India
Raffone, Alexander M., 44 Paramount Ave., Hamden, Conn.
Ragan, William Burk, University of Oklahoma, Norman, Okla.
Ragsdale, Elva Mae, Dept. of Educ., Anderson College, Anderson, Ind.
Ragsdale, Ted R., 301 W. College St., Carbondale, Ill.
Ramer, Earl M., University of Tennessee, Knoxville, Tenn.
Ramig, Clifford, Ball State Teachers College, Muncie, Ind.
Ramos, John P., Jr., Morris Ave., Union, N.J.
Ramsey, J. W., Superior-Maitland School, Northfork, W.Va.
Ramseyer, John A., Ohio State University, Columbus, Ohio
Ramseyer, Lloyd L., Blufften College, Blufften, Ohio
Rand, E. W., Texas Southern University, Houston, Tex.
Randall, Edwin H., Western State College, Gunnison, Colo.
Randall, William M., Wilmington College, 1220 Market St., Wilmington, N.C.
Randolph, Katharine G., Colorado Woman's College, Denver, Colo.
Rankin, Earl F., Jr., 3921 Lynncrest Dr., Fort Worth, Tex.
Rankin, Paul T., 16823 Plainview Rd., Detroit, Mich.
Rapp, Don W., University of Georgia, Athens, Ga.
Rappaport, David, 2747 Coyle Ave., Chicago, Ill.

Rappaport, Mary B., State Education Department, Albany, N.Y.
Rasmussen, Elmer M., Dana College, Blair, Neb.
Rasmussen, Glen R., Carthage College, Kenosha, Wis.
Rasmussen, H. L., 427 S.W. Bade Ave., College Place, Wash.
Raubinger, F. M., State Dept. of Educ., 175 W. State St., Trenton, N.J.
Rausch, Richard G., Sch. Adm. Bldg., Mill Ridge, Danbury, Conn.
Rawson, Kenneth O., Superintendent of Schools, Clintonville, Wis.
Ray, Rolland, State University of Iowa, Iowa City, Iowa
Razik, Taher A., State University of New York, Buffalo, N.Y.
Rea, Thelma M., 1406 Brown Ave., W., Fresno, Calif.
Read, Edward M., St. Paul Academy, 1712 Randolph Ave., St. Paul, Minn.
Reak, Jack E., Ball State Teachers College, Muncie, Ind.
Reas, Herbert D., Sch. of Educ., Seattle University, Seattle, Wash.
Red, S. B., University of Houston, 3801 Cullen Blvd., Houston, Tex.
Reddin, Estoy, Trenton State College, Trenton, N.J.
* Reddy, Anne L., 117 E. 34th St., Savannah, Ga.
Rediger, Milo A., Taylor University, Upland, Ind.
Reed, Earl J., Superintendent of Schools, Longview, Wash.
Reed, Flo, Department of Education, Carson City, Nev.
Reed, Lula B., County Superintendent of Schools, Red Oak, Iowa
Reed, William S., 3105 W. University Ave., Gainesville, Fla.
Reed, Zollie C., Birmingham Southern College, Birmingham, Ala.
Reeves, Emily D., Centre College of Kentucky, Danville, Ky.
Reeves, Glenn D., Superintendent of Schools, Littlefield, Tex.
Reeves, James H., University of Minnesota, Minneapolis, Minn.
Reeves, Wilfred, Washington Junior High School, Olympia, Wash.
Regner, Olga W., 116 South 4th St., Darby, Pa.
Rehage, Kenneth J., Dept. of Educ., University of Chicago, Chicago, Ill.
Reichart, Sanford, 10 Forest Dr., Chagrin Falls, Ohio
Reid, C. E., Jr., 6225 N. Circuit Dr., Beaumont, Tex.
Reid, L. Leon, 517 Clemson Dr., Pittsburgh, Pa.
Reilley, Albert G., 28 Long Ave., Framingham, Mass.
Reiner, William B., 130 W. 55th St., New York, N.Y.
* Reinhardt, Emma, Pittsfield, Ill.
Reisman, Diana J., 223 N. Highland Ave., Merion Station, Pa.
Reisman, Morton, Anshe Emet Day Sch., 3760 N. Pine Grove Ave., Chicago, Ill.
Reiter, Mrs. Anne, 51 Buchanan Pl., Bronx, N.Y.
Reitz, Donald J., Loyola College, 4501 N. Charles St., Baltimore, Md.
Reitz, Louis M., St. Thomas Seminary, 7101 Brownsboro Rd., Louisville, Ky.
Reitze, Arnold W., 3 Lienau Pl., Jersey City, N.J.
Reller, Theodore L., Sch. of Educ., Univ. of California, Berkeley, Calif.
Rempel, P. J., State College of Washington, Pullman, Wash.
Renard, John N., Oxnard Evening High School, Oxnard, Calif.
Renouf, Edna M., 116 Yale Square, Swarthmore, Pa.
Resek, E. Frederick, 913 Garden St., Park Ridge, Ill.
Reuter, George S., Jr., 1806 E. Lilac Ter., Arlington Heights, Ill.
Reuther, Carolyn A., Mills College, Oakland, Calif.
Reuwsaat, Emily A., Col. of Educ., Univ. of New Mexico, Albuquerque, N.M.
Revie, Virgil A., Long Beach State College, Anaheim, Calif.
Rex, Ronald G., Michigan State University, East Lansing, Mich.
Reyna, L. J., 227 Beacon St., Boston, Mass.
Reynolds, Dorothy S., 414—14th St., Denver, Colo.
Reynolds, James Walton, Box 7998, University of Texas, Austin, Tex.
Reynolds, M. C., University of Minnesota, Minneapolis, Minn.
Rhoads, Jonathan E., 3400 Spruce St., Philadelphia, Pa.
Rhodes, Gladys L., State University College, Geneseo, N.Y.
Ricciardi, Richard S., Dept. of Education, 100 Reef Rd., Fairfield, Conn.
Rice, Arthur H., The Nation's Schools Pub. Co., Chicago, Ill.
Rice, David, Ball State Teachers College, Muncie, Ind.
Rice, John E., Jenkintown High School, Jenkintown, Pa.
Rice, Roy C., Arizona State University, Tempe, Ariz.

Rice, Theodore D., 33963 N. Hampshire, Livonia, Mich.
Richards, Eugene, Sol R. Crown Elem. School, 2123 S. St. Louis, Chicago, Ill.
Richardson, Canute M., Paine College, Augusta, Ga.
Richardson, George M., 1422 S. Queen St., Arlington, Va.
Richardson, John S., 4079 Overlook Dr., East., Columbus, Ohio
Richardson, L. S., 1615 West 4th St., Freeport, Tex.
Richardson, Orvin T., Washington University, St. Louis, Mo.
Richardson, Sybil K., 18111 Nordhoff, Northridge, Calif.
Richardson, Thomas H., 200 Summitt Rd., Elizabeth, N.J.
Richardson, William R., R. 1, Box 362, Chapel Hill, N.C.
Richey, Herman G., Dept. of Educ., University of Chicago, Chicago, Ill.
Richey, Robert W., Sch. of Educ., Indiana University, Bloomington, Ind.
Richmond, John D., P.O. Box 1311, Martinsville, Va.
Ricketts, Robert E., 490 Park Ave., Paterson, N.J.
Riedel, Mark T., 210 S. Edgewood, LaGrange, Ill.
Riederer, L. A., 3114—14th Ave., Regina, Sask.
Riegel, Samuel A., Biddle Street Area School, West Chester, Pa.
Riegle, H. Edgar, Superintendent of Schools, Gettysburg, Pa.
Riehm, Carl L., 8531 Devon St., Norfolk, Va.
Riese, Harlan C., 511 North Ave., East, Missoula, Mont.
Riethmiller, Gorton, Olivet College, Olivet, Mich.
Riggio, Ines, 2967 Perry Ave., New York, N.Y.
Riggle, Earl L., 160 E. Main St., New Concord, Ohio
Riggs, Edwon L., 2702 E. Flower St., Phoenix, Ariz.
Riggs, William J., East 38 Hoffman, Spokane, Wash.
Righter, Charles L., 419 Lee Pl., Frederick, Md.
Rigney, Mrs. Margaret G., Hunter College, Park Ave. and 68th St., New York, N.Y.
Rikkola, V. John, Dept. of Educ., State Teachers College, Salem, Mass.
Riley, Garland G., 910 Colby Ct., DeKalb, Ill.
Riley, Kenneth, Shepherd College, Shepherdstown, W.Va.
Rinehart, John, Oakfield Rd., St. James, L.I., N.Y.
Ripple, Richard E., Stone Hall, Cornell University, Ithaca, N.Y.
Risinger, Robert G., Col. of Educ., University of Maryland, College Park, Md.
Risk, Thomas M., 105½ Fourth St., S.W., Orange City, Iowa
Ritchie, Harold L., Superintendent of Schools, West Paterson, N.J.
Ritchie, Harold S., 725 E. 26th St., Paterson, N.J.
Ritscher, Richard C., General Beadle State Tchrs. College, Madison, S.D.
Ritsema, Louise, 231 Wildwood, Ann Arbor, Mich.
Ritter, William E., 2910 E. State St., Sharon, Pa.
Rivard, Thomas L., Superintendent of Schools, Chelmsford, Mass.
Rivlin, Harry N., 535 East 80th St., New York, N.Y.
Roaden, Arliss, Dept. of Education, Ohio State University, Columbus, Ohio
Robbins, Edward T., Alamo Heights Sch. Dist., San Antonio, Tex.
Robbins, Melvyn Paul, 6500 W. Irving Park, Chicago, Ill.
Robbins, Rintha, Office of County Supt. of Schools, Madera, Calif.
Roberson, James A., 1802 Lincoln Dr., Abilene, Tex.
Roberts, Dodd Edward, Oakland County Schools, Pontiac, Mich.
Roberts, Jack D., Dept. of Educ., Queens College, Flushing, N.Y.
Roberts, James B., Dept. of Educ., West Texas State Col., Canyon, Tex.
Robertson, Anne McK., Tchrs. Col., Columbia University, New York, N.Y.
Robertson, Robert L., 101 Virginia Ave., Springfield, Kan.
Robinette, Walter R., University of Louisiana, Lafayette, La.
Robinson, Alice, Board of Educ., 115 E. Church St., Frederick, Md.
Robinson, Alvin E., 255 Palm Drive, Oxnard, Calif.
Robinson, Charles R., County Admin. Center, 2555 Mendocina Ave., Santa Rosa, Calif.
Robinson, H. Alan, Dept. of Educ., University of Chicago, Chicago, Ill.
Robinson, Mrs. Helen M., Dept. of Educ., University of Chicago, Chicago, Ill.
Robinson, Phil C., 8635 Dexter Blvd., Detroit, Mich.
Robinson, Richard M., 6808—16th St., N.E., Seattle, Wash.

Robinson, Thomas L., 3224 McElvy St., Montgomery, Ala.
Robinson, W. L., Norfolk City Schools, Norfolk, Va.
Roche, Lawrence A., Duquesne University, Pittsburgh, Pa.
Rockwell, Perry J., Jr., Sch. of Educ., Indiana University, Bloomington, Ind.
Roden, Aubrey H., Sch. of Educ., Univ. of California, Berkeley, Calif.
Rodgers, John O., 6402 Wilbur Dr., Austin, Tex.
Rodgers, Margaret, Lamar State College of Technology, Beaumont, Tex.
Rodgers, Paul R., Board of Education, Dist. No. 102, LaGrange Park, Ill.
Rodriguez-Diaz, Manlo, Alfred University, Alfred, N.Y.
Roe, Anne, 8 Prescott St., Cambridge, Mass.
Roemmich, Herman, San Diego State College, San Diego, Calif.
Roenigk, Elsie Mae, R.D. No. 1, Box 311, Cabot, Pa.
Roens, Bert A., Superintendent of·Schools, Arlington, Mass.
Roeper, George A., City and Country School, Bloomfield Hills, Mich.
Roers, James P., Appleton-Century-Crofts, Inc., New York, N.Y.
Roff, Mrs. Rosella Zuber, 4410 S. 148th St., Seattle, Wash.
Rogers, John D., 735 Washington Rd., Pittsburgh, Pa.
Rogers, Virgil M., 2500 Q St., N.W., Washington, D.C.
Rogers, William R., San Jose State College, San Jose, Calif.
Rogoldsy, Saul, Northeastern University, Boston, Mass.
Rohan, William, 5683 N. Rogers Ave., Chicago, Ill.
Rolens, Robert E., 295 S. Arcade St., Ventura, Calif.
Rolfe, Howard C., 1344 Studebaker Rd., Long Beach, Calif.
Rollins, William B., Jr., 7772 Otto St., Downey, Calif.
Romano, Frank E., 588 Broadway, Newark, N.J.
Romano, Louis, 1701 E. Capitol Dr., Shorewood, Wis.
Rome, Samuel, 9852 Cerritos Ave., Anaheim, Calif.
Romoser, D. Richard C., 2155 S. Race St., Denver, Colo.
Rondinella, Orestes R., 48 Sheridan Ave., West Orange, N.J.
Rooney, Edward B., Jesuit Educ. Assn., 49 E. 84th St., New York, N.Y.
Roossinck, Esther P., Alameda State College, Hayward, Calif.
Rosamilia, M. T., 183 Union Ave., Belleville, N.J.
Roschy, Mrs. Bertha B., 1807 Gildner Rd., Hampton, Va.
Rose, Gale W., Dept. of Educ., University of Chicago, Chicago, Ill.
Rose, Mrs. Ruth R., 1251 S.W. 42nd Ave., Fort Lauderdale, Fla.
Roseberry, Minnie, Box 545, Flagstaff, Ariz.
Rosebrock, Allan F., State Dept. of Educ., 175 W. State St., Trenton, N.J.
Rosecrance, Francis C., Col. of Educ., Wayne State University, Detroit, Mich.
Rosen, Sidney, Col. of Educ., University of Illinois, Urbana, Ill.
Rosenberg, Marguerite G., 216 Conroy Ave., Scranton, Pa.
Rosenberger, David S., 5827 Garden Park Dr., Sylvania, Ohio
Rosenberger, Russell S., Dept. of Educ., Gettysburg Col., Gettysburg, Pa.
Rosenbloom, Alfred A., Jr., 6829 S. Crandon Ave., Chicago, Ill.
Rosenbluh, Benjamin J., Central High School, Bridgeport, Conn.
Rosenfeld, Babette F., 22 Prospect Park, West, Brooklyn, N.Y.
Rosenstein, Pearl, 124 Sheldon Ter., New Haven, Conn.
Rosenthal, Alan G., 18 Homeside Lane, White Plains, N.Y.
Rosenthal, Lester, 94 Stirling Ave., Freeport, N.Y.
Rosenthal, Samuel, 5213 N. Moody Ave., Chicago, Ill.
Rosenzweig, Celia, 6239 N. Leavitt St., Chicago, Ill.
Ross, Mrs. Alice M., 1446 Wilbraham Rd., Springfield, Mass.
Ross, John G., Haviland Hall, University of California, Berkeley, Calif.
Rossmiller, Richard, Sch. of Educ., University of Wisconsin, Madison, Wis.
Rost, Nellie, Tabor College, Hillsboro, Kan.
Roswell, Florence G., 38 Bon Air Ave., New Rochelle, N.Y.
Roth, Bernice, 520 Woodley Rd., DeKalb, Ill.
Roth, Mrs. Frances, 21598 Ellacott Pkwy., Cleveland, Ohio
Roth, Lois H., Midland College, Fremont, Neb.
Rothstein, Arnold M., 27 Rellim Dr., Glen Cove, N.Y.
Rothstein, Jerome H., San Francisco State College, San Francisco, Calif.
Rothwell, Angus B., State Superintendent of Public Instruction, Madison, Wis.

Roush, Donald C., New Mexico State University, University Park, N.M.
Rousseve, Charles B., 2040 Humanity St., New Orleans, La.
Rousseve, Ronald J., Prairie View A. and M. College, Prairie View, Tex.
Row, Howard E., 207 Orchard Ave., Dover, Del.
Rowe, Ernest Ras, 512 East Flower St., Phoenix, Ariz.
Rubadean, Duane O., State University College, Geneseo, N.Y.
Rubke, Walter C., 6325 Camden St., Oakland, Calif.
Ruch, Mary A. R., R.F.D. No. 1, Tower City, Pa.
Rucker, W. Ray, East Texas State College, Commerce, Tex.
Ruckman, Stanley Van, 394 S. Monmouth Ave., Monmouth, Ore.
Ruddell, Arden K., Sch. of Educ., Univ. of California, Berkeley, Calif.
Rudman, Herbert C., Col. of Educ., Michigan State Univ., East Lansing, Mich.
Rudolf, Kathleen Brady, 53 Cook St., Rochester, N.Y.
Rudolph, Mrs. Jean, 12211 W. Lincoln Ave., West Allis, Wis.
Rugen, Mabel E., Sch. of Pub. Health, Univ. of Michigan, Ann Arbor, Mich.
Rugen, Myrtle L., 2240 Pfingsten Rd., Northbrook, Ill.
Rule, Philip, East Otero School Dist., Rt. 1, LaJunta, Colo.
Rulon, Phillip J., Harvard Grad. School of Education, Cambridge, Mass.
Rummel, J. Francis, USAID/Cambodia, APO 153, San Francisco, Calif.
Runyan, Charles S., Marshall University, Huntington, W.Va.
Rusch, Reuben R., State University Teachers College, Oneonta, N.Y.
Rushdoony, Haig A., Stanislaus State College, Turlock, Calif.
Russel, John H., Office of Educ., Dept. of H.E.W., Washington, D.C.
Russell, Mrs. Audrey B., Admin. Bldg., 228 W. Franklin St., Elkhart, Ind.
Russell, David H., Sch. of Educ., Univ. of California, Berkeley, Calif.
Russell, David L., Dept. of Psych., Ohio University, Athens, Ohio
Russell, Earle Stone, Superintendent of Schools, Windsor, Conn.
* Russell, John Dale, R.R. 10, Russell Rd., Bloomington, Ind.
Russo, Anthony J., Dept. of Public Schools, 211 Veazie St., Providence, R.I.
Ruthenberg, Donald B., 2185 S. Vine St., Denver, Colo.
Rutledge, James A., Univ. High School, Univ. of Nebraska, Lincoln, Neb.
Ryan, Carl J., 5418 Moeller Ave., Cincinnati, Ohio
Ryan, J. Joseph, Dept. of Educ., College of the Holy Cross, Worcester, Mass.
Ryan, Margaret R., 23-22—36th St., Long Island City, N.Y.
Ryan, Suler E., Sam Houston State Teachers College, Huntsville, Tex.
Ryan, Thomas A., 719 Bullock Ave., Yeadon, Pa.
Ryan, W. Carson, 1303 Mason Farm Rd., Chapel Hill, N.C.
Rye, Howard H., 6 Kent Dr., Normal, Ill.
Rzepka, Louis, DePaul University, Chicago, Ill.

Sabath, Mildred R., Alameda State College, Alameda, Calif.
Sabik, Adolph J., Franklin School, 4215 Alder St., East Chicago, Ind.
Sack, Saul, Grad. Sch. of Educ., Univ. of Pennsylvania, Philadelphia, Pa.
Sadler, Vera J., 15587 Inverness, Detroit, Mich.
Safford, George R., 6444 Leonard Dr., Redding, Calif.
Sagen, H. Bradley, Bur. of Inst. Res., Univ. of Illinois, Urbana, Ill.
Sain, Leonard F., 2959 Lakeview Ave., Ann Arbor, Mich.
Salinger, Herbert E., 3740 Hamilton Ave., Napa, Calif.
Salisbury, Arnold W., Superintendent of Schools, Cedar Rapids, Iowa
Sallee, Mrs. Mozelle T., 4401 North Ave., Richmond, Va.
Salmons, George B., Tamworth Academy, Wonalancet, N.H.
Salser, G. Alden, 207 S. Sheridan St., Wichita, Kan.
Salten, David G., 10 The Esplanade, New Rochelle, N.Y.
Saltz, Martin, Broad Brook School, Broad Brook, Conn.
Saltzman, Irving J., Dept. of Psych., Indiana Univ., Bloomington, Ind.
Salyer, Guy, Stout State College, Menomonie, Wis.
Sample, William J., 45 Van Ethel Dr., Matawan, N.J.
Samson, Gordon E., Dept. of Educ., Fenn College, Cleveland, Ohio
Sand, Ole, Natl. Educ. Assn., 1201 Sixteenth St., N.W., Washington, D.C.
Sander, Paul J., 3139 E. Monterosa, Phoenix, Ariz.
Sanders, David C., Sutton Hall, University of Texas, Austin, Tex.

Sanders, Richard H., 10639 Drew St., Chicago, Ill.
Sanders, Mrs. Ruby, P.O. Box 1956, Waco, Tex.
Sanderson, J. Wesley, Bakersfield College, Bakersfield, Calif.
Sanderson, Jesse O., Superintendent of Schools, Raleigh, N.C.
Sandilos, James C., Hopewell Twp. Board of Education, Pennington, N.J.
Sandilos, Peter C., Superintendent of Schools, West Long Branch, N.J.
Sandin, Adolph A., Sch. of Educ., University of Oregon, Eugene, Ore.
Sando, Wilbur B., Bethel College, 1000 W. McKinley Ave., Mishawaka, Ind.
Sangster, Cecil Henry, 6012 Elbow Dr., Calgary, Alba., Canada
Santigian, Marty, 2624 University Ave., Fresno, Calif.
Sarafian, Armen, Pasadena City College, Pasadena, Calif.
Sartain, Harry W., Falk Lab. Schls., Univ. of Pittsburgh, Pittsburgh, Pa.
Sarto, Angeline, 1210 Superior Ave., Sheboygan, Wis.
Satterfield, Martha A., 40 N. Summit Ave., Gaithersburg, Md.
Saunders, Jack O. L., New Mexico Western College, Silver City, N.M.
Saunders, Margaret, Colorado College, Colorado Springs, Colo.
Sauvain, Walter H., R.D. No. 2, Buffalo Rd., Lewisburg, Pa.
Savage, Russell H., 4409 Pomona, La Mesa, Calif.
Sawin, Ethel, Shrewsbury Junior-Senior High School, Shewsbury, Mass.
Sax, Gilbert, Dept. of Educ., University of Hawaii, Honolulu, Hawaii
Saxe, Richard W., 11351 S. Fairfield St., Chicago, Ill.
Saylor, Charles F., Superintendent of Schools, New Wilmington, Pa.
Saylor, Galen, Tchrs. Col., University of Nebraska, Lincoln, Neb.
Scally, Mary Irene, 2722 Cheswolde Rd., Baltimore, Md.
Scanlan, William J., Wilson High School, 631 N. Albert, St. Paul, Minn.
Scanlon, Kathryn I., Sch. of Educ., Fordham University, New York, N.Y.
Schaadt, Mrs. Lucy G., Cedar Crest College, Allentown, Pa.
Schaefer, Frances M., 9946 S. Campbell Ave., Chicago, Ill.
Schaefer, Judith B., 40 Linden Ter., Leonia, N.J.
Schaefer, Reed N., Sch. of Educ., Parsons College, Fairfield, Iowa
Schaefer, Wilbert S., 194 Hillside Ave., Mineola, L.I., N.Y.
Schaibly, Colon L., Waukegan Township High School, Waukegan, Ill.
Scharf, Louis, 350 Sterling St., Brooklyn, N.Y.
Scharf, Mary C., St. Cloud State College, St. Cloud, Minn.
Schenke, Lahron H., 2010 E. Harrison Ave., Charleston, Ill.
Schifreen, Edward B., 314 Iris Rd., Cherry Hill, N.J.
Schimmel, Ethel, 157 Bulkley St., Kalamazoo, Mich.
Schlegel, Miriam A., 1610 Moore St., Huntingdon, Pa.
Schleif, Mabel, 1908 Hennepin Ave., Minneapolis, Minn.
Schlessinger, Fred R., 1945 N. High St., Columbus, Ohio
Schmidt, Florence, 785 Temple St., Long Beach, Calif.
Schmidt, L. G. H., J. J. Cahill Mem. Sch., Mascot P.O., Rosebery, New So. Wales
Schmidt, Lyle D., Dept. of Psych., Ohio State Univ., Columbus, Ohio
Schmidt, Ralph L. W., 568 Magnolia Wood Dr., Baton Rouge, La.
Schmidt, William S., County Superintendent of Schools, Upper Marlboro, Md.
Schmitt, Irvin H., 4808 S. 30th St., Arlington, Va.
Schnabel, Robert V., 6902 S. Calhoun St., Fort Wayne, Ind.
Schneider, Erwin H., Sch. of Music, Ohio State University, Columbus, Ohio
Schneider, Samuel, 315 West 70th St., New York, N.Y.
Schnell, Fred, 1625 Wilson Ave., Sheboygan, Wis.
Schnell, Rodolph L., Educ. Dept., University of Detroit, Detroit, Mich.
Schnepf, Virginia, 2516½ College Ave., Cedar Falls, Iowa
Schneyer, J. Wesley, 7454 Ruskin Rd., Philadelphia, Pa.
Schnitzen, Joseph P., University of Houston, Houston, Tex.
Schoeller, Arthur W., 8626 W. Lawrence Ave., Milwaukee, Wis.
Schoeppe, Aileen, Sch. of Educ., New York University, New York, N.Y.
Schooler, Virgil E., Sch. of Educ., Indiana University, Bloomington, Ind.
Schooling, Herbert W., Superintendent of Schools, Webster Groves, Mo.
Schor, Theodore, 149 N. Fifth Ave., Highland Park, N.J.
Schott, Marion S., Central Missouri State College, Warrensburg, Mo.
Schramm, John S., 201 Third Ave., New Town Square, Pa.

Schreiber, Herman, 80 Clarkson Ave., Brooklyn, N.Y.
Schritchfield, Floyd C., South Div., University of Nevada, Las Vegas, Nev.
Schroeder, Carl N., 6 Atkins Ave., Cortland, N.Y.
Schroeder, Marie L., 3125 N. Spangler St., Philadelphia, Pa.
Schroeder, W. P., State Polytechnic College, San Luis Obispo, Calif.
Schueler, Herbert, Hunter College, 295 Park Ave., New York, N.Y.
Schuker, Louis A., Jamaica High School, 168-01 Gothic Dr., Jamaica, N.Y.
Schuller, Charles F., Michigan State University, East Lansing, Mich.
Schulte, Emerita S., 1110 Jefferson, Celina, Ohio
Schultz, Frederick, Box 931, G.P.O., New York, N.Y.
Schultz, Kenneth M., 454 E. Locust St., Middletown, Ind.
Schulze, Herbert, 2766 Stoneybrook, West, Anaheim, Calif.
Schumann, Myrtle G., Orono School Dist. 278, Long Lake, Minn.
Schumann, Victor, 3355 N. 23rd St., Milwaukee, Wis.
Schutz, Richard E., Arizona State University, Tempe, Ariz.
Schwanholt, Dana B., Valparaiso University, Valparaiso, Ind.
Schwartz, Alfred, Drake University, Des Moines, Iowa
Schwartz, Emanuel, 193 Sullivan Pl., Brooklyn, N.Y.
Schwartz, William P., 273 Ave. P., Brooklyn, N.Y.
Schwarz, A. R., J. D. Pierce Lab. Sch., Northern Mich. College, Marquette, Mich.
Schwarzenberger, Alfred J., 5943 North 42nd St., Milwaukee, Wis.
Schwertfeger, Mary Jane, 6 Parkview Pl., Ann Arbor, Mich.
Scobey, Mary-Margaret, San Francisco State College, San Francisco, Calif.
Scott, Cecil Winfield, Rutgers University, New Brunswick, N.J.
Scott, Guy, Larned State Hospital, Larned, Kan.
Scott, Thomas B., University of Tennessee, Knoxville, Tenn.
Scott, Waldo I., 21 Second Ave., Port Washington, N.Y.
Scott, Walter W., 340 Pine Ave., Holland, Mich.
Scott, William Owen Nixon, 275 Milledge Terrace, Athens, Ga.
Seaberg, Dorothy I., 119 Stadium, Stockton, Calif.
Seagoe, May V., Sch. of Educ., University of California, Los Angeles, Calif.
Seaman, B. E., Northwest Nazarene College, Nampa, Idaho
Sear, C. E., General Beadle State Teachers College, Madison, S.D.
Searle, Herbert A., 761 Mt. Vernon Ave., Haddonfield, N.J.
Searles, Warren B., 97 Surrey Lane, Hempstead, L.I., N.Y.
Sears, Jesse B., 40 Tevis Pl., Palo Alto, Calif.
Seaton, Donald F., Superintendent of Schools, Boone, Iowa
Seay, Maurice F., Kellogg Foundation, Battle Creek, Mich.
Sebaly, A. L., Western University of Michigan, Kalamazoo, Mich.
Sechler, Hazel B., 800 West 8th St., Silver City, N.M.
Seckinger, Richard K., Sch. of Educ., University of Pittsburgh, Pittsburgh, Pa.
Seedor, Marie M., 1401 Lincoln Ave., Prospect Park, Pa.
Seely, Gordon M., Jr., P.O. Box 533, Redwood City, Calif.
Sehmann, Henry R., 6101 East 7th St., Long Beach, Calif.
Seifert, George G., 1719 East 116th Pl., Cleveland, Ohio
Seifert, Leland B., Haverstraw-Stony Point School Dist., Stony Point, N.Y.
Sellery, Austin R., 344 Sunset Way, Palm Springs, Calif.
Selzer, Edwin, 168-06 Jewel Ave., Flushing, N.Y.
Sentman, Everette E., United Educators, Inc., Lake Bluff, Ill.
Servey, Richard E., San Diego State College, San Diego, Calif.
Serviss, Trevor K., L. W. Singer Co., 249 W. Erie Blvd., Syracuse, N.Y.
Seubert, Eugene E., Washington University, St. Louis, Mo.
Severson, John, Salinas High School, Salinas, Calif.
Seville, George C., 134 Newcomb Rd., Tenafly, N.J.
Seyfert, Warren C., 6423 N. Santa Monica, Milwaukee, Wis.
Shack, Jacob H., 127 Remsen St., Brooklyn, N.Y.
Shafer, B. Henry, 1885 Grand Blvd., Wyomissing, Pa.
Shafer, Robert E., Tchrs. Col., Columbia University, New York, N.Y.
Shane, Harold G., Sch. of Educ., Indiana University, Bloomington, Ind.
Shankman, Mrs. Florence, 20 Garner St., South Norwalk, Conn.
Shannon, E. Boyd, Pasadena College, Pasadena, Calif.

Shannon, MacRae, Ottawa Twp. High School, 211 E. Main St., Ottawa, Ill.
Shaplin, Judson T., 182 Upland Rd., Cambridge, Mass.
Shattuck, George E., Norwich Free Academy, Norwich, Conn.
Shaw, Frances, 4717 Central Ave., Indianapolis, Ind.
Shaw, M. Luelle, 1126 N.W. Eighth Ave., Miami, Fla.
Shaw, Robert C., Superintendent of Schools, Columbia, Mo.
Shay, Carleton B., Los Angeles State College, Los Angeles, Calif.
Shea, James T., San Antonio Ind. School Dist., 141 Lavaca St., San Antonio, Tex.
Sheehan, T. Joseph, 5835 Kimbark Ave., Chicago, Ill.
Sheeley, Vernon L., Box 659, Topanga, Calif.
Sheerin, James S., Sarah D. Ottiwell Sch., Diman St., New Bedford, Mass.
Sheldon, Dorothy R., Bethany Nazarene College, Bethany, Okla.
Sheldon, Muriel Inez, Los Angeles City Board of Educ., Los Angeles, Calif.
Sheldon, William Denley, 508 University Pl., Syracuse, N.Y.
Shelton, Nollie W., 328 Blowing Rock Rd., Boone, N.C.
Shemky, Robert W., St. Joseph's College, Rensselaer, Ind.
Shepard, Samuel, Jr., 4633 Moffitt Ave., St. Louis, Mo.
Sheppard, Lawrence E., Antioch Unified School Dist., Antioch, Calif.
Sherer, Lorraine, 1109 Magnolia Ave., Los Angeles, Calif.
Sheridan, William C., Board of Education, Scotch Plains, N.J.
Sherman, Mrs. Helene, 350 Central Park West, New York, N.Y.
Sherman, Neil, School Dist. No. 1, 125 E. Lincoln, Phoenix, Ariz.
Sherwood, Virgil, P.O. Box 836, Westminster, Md.
Shiflet, R. B., Lamar Elementary School, Mineral Wells, Tex.
Shinaberry, Charles G., Box 114, Slippery Rock, Pa.
Shipley, Thomas E., Jr., Dept. of Psych., Temple Univ., Philadelphia, Pa.
Shive, Mrs. Mae L., 600 Michael Rd., Newton, Kan.
Shnayer, Sidney W., Chico State College, Chico, Calif.
Shoemaker, F. L., 15 Woodside Dr., Athens, Ohio
Shohen, Samuel S., 229 Friends Lane, Westbury, L.I., N.Y.
Sholund, Milford, Gospel Light Press, 725 E. Colorado, Glendale, Calif.
Shope, Nathaniel H., Superintendent of Schools, Goldsboro, N.C.
Shores, J. Harlan, 805 W. Pennsylvania Ave., Urbana, Ill.
Short, D. Robert, Wessington Springs College, Wessington Springs, S.D.
Short, Robert Allen, 17059 Fifth N.E. St., Seattle, Wash.
Shrum, John W., 97 E. Lane Ave., Columbus, Ohio
Shuff, Robert V., 20 Price Dr., Edison, N.J.
Shugert, Walter C., Jr., 120 Circle Dr., Redwood City, Calif.
Shultz, Mrs. Dona, R. R. 1, Grabill, Ind.
Shuman, Elsie, 805 S. Florence St., Kirksville, Mo.
Shyryn, E. Layne, Queen Elizabeth High School, Calgary, Alberta
* Sias, A. B., Route 3, Box 459B, Orlando, Fla.
Siebert, Edna M., 5742 N. Kingsdale Ave., Chicago, Ill.
Siebrecht, Elmer B., 3019 Queen Anne Ave., Seattle, Wash.
Siegel, Martin, 1807 Randolph Rd., Schenectady, N.Y.
Siegfried, Paul V., 892 W. Boston Blvd., Detroit, Mich.
Siemers, Allan A., Wisconsin State College, River Falls, Wis.
Siemons, Alice E., San Francisco State College, San Francisco, Calif.
Sievert, Erich H., 31 Waldheim Dr., New Ulm, Minn.
Sieving, Eldor C., Concordia Teachers College, River Forest, Ill.
Siewers, Karl, 2301 Estes Ave., Chicago, Ill.
Sigel, Irving, Merrill Palmer Institute, Detroit, Mich.
Silvaroli, Nicholas J., Arizona State University, Tempe, Ariz.
Silverman, Susan B., 5337 S. Harper Ave., Chicago, Ill.
Silvern, Leonard Charles, 979 Teakwood Rd., Los Angeles, Calif.
Silverstein, Paul C., 364 Sackman St., Brooklyn, N.Y.
Simmons, D. D., Oregon State University, Corvallis, Ore.
Simmons, I. F., Howard College, Birmingham, Ala.
Simmons, Marian Alice, 2118 East 50th St., Kansas City, Mo.
Simmons, Virginia Lee, 1207 Essex House, Indianapolis, Ind.
Simms, Naomi, 333 College Ct., Kent, Ohio

Simms, Thelma, 80 Waddell Ave., Elm Grove, W.Va.
Simms, V. James, Col. of Educ., Idaho State Univ., Pocatello, Idaho
Simon, Dan, Superintendent of Schools, East Chicago, Ind.
Simon, Eric, Sherman, Conn.
Simpson, Elisabeth P., 140 Evergreen Dr., Dover, Del.
Simpson, Mrs. Elizabeth A., 5627 Blackstone Ave., Chicago, Ill.
Simpson, Frederick W., University of Tulsa, Tulsa, Okla.
Simpson, Mrs. Hazel D., Col. of Educ., University of Georgia, Athens, Ga.
Simpson, Ray H., Col. of Educ., University of Illinois, Urbana, Ill.
Sims, H. H., Superintendent of Schools, Bristow, Okla.
Sims, Harold W., 9423 Harvard Ave., Chicago, Ill.
Singer, Harry, Div. of Soc. Sci., Univ. of California, Riverside, Calif.
Singh, Mrs. Kirpal T., 2994/4 Ranjeet Nagar, New Delhi, India
Singletary, James Daniel, USOM/Kabul, State Dept. Mail Room, Washington, D.C.
Singleton, Stanton J., Col. of Educ., University of Georgia, Athens, Ga.
Sipay, Edward R., 173 Franklin St., Ansonia, Conn.
Sires, Ely, 5018 LaCrosse Lane, Madison, Wis.
Sister Agnes Cecilia, Nazareth Academy, 1001 Lake Ave., Rochester, N.Y.
Sister Ann Augusta, 400 The Fenway, Boston, Mass.
Sister Anna Clare, College of St. Rose, Albany, N.Y.
Sister Anna Marie, Presentation Junior College, Aberdeen, S.D.
Sister Anne Martina, St. Joseph's Junior College, Crookston, Minn.
Sister Barbara Geoghegan, Col. of Mt. St. Joseph-on-the-Hudson, Mt. St. Joseph, Ohio
Sister Celine, 57 Lincoln Ave., Port Chester, N.Y.
Sister Clare Mary, Xavier University, Palmetto and Pine Sts., New Orleans, La.
Sister Dorothy Marie Riordan, College of St. Elizabeth, Convent Station, N.J.
Sister Elizabeth Ann, Immaculate Heart College, Los Angeles, Calif.
Sister Eugenia Marie, Mercy College, 8200 W. Outer Dr., Detroit, Mich.
Sister Irene Elizabeth, 1 Main St., Groton, Mass.
Sister James Claudia, Siena Heights College, Adrian, Mich.
Sister James Edward, Brescia College, Owensboro, Ky.
Sister Justa McNamara, Dept. of Educ., St. Joseph College, Emmitsburg, Md.
Sister Margaret Mary O'Connell, College of Notre Dame of Maryland, Baltimore, Md.
Sister Marie Claudia, Barry College, Miami Shores, Fla.
Sister Marie Gabrielle, Diocesan Sisters College, Woodstock, Conn.
Sister Mary Agnello, Regis College, Weston, Mass.
Sister Mary Agnes Hennessey, Mount Mercy College, Cedar Rapids, Iowa
Sister Mary Alma, St. Mary's College, Notre Dame, Ind.
Sister M. Angela Betke, Cantalician Ctr. for Child., 3233 Main St., Buffalo, N.Y.
Sister Mary Antonius, St. Mary College, Hooksett, N.H.
Sister Mary Basil, Good Counsel College, White Plains, N.Y.
Sister Mary Basil, Notre Dame of the Lake, Nequon, Wis.
Sister Mary Benedict Phelan, Clarke College, Dubuque, Iowa
Sister Mary Bernard, Diocesan Educ. Office, Charleston, S.C.
Sister Mary Bernice, Mt. Angel College, Mt. Angel, Ore.
Sister Mary Bernice, St. John College, Cleveland, Ohio
Sister Mary Bonnita, Felician College, Chicago, Ill.
Sister M. Brideen Long, Holy Family College, Manitowoc, Wis.
Sister M. Camille Kliebhan, Cardinal Stritch College, Milwaukee, Wis.
Sister Mary Chrysostom, College of Our Lady of the Elms, Chicopee, Mass.
Sister Mary Clarissa, Dominican College of Blauvelt, Blauvelt, N.Y.
Sister Mary Conleth, Mount Alvernia College, Chestnut Hill, Mass.
Sister M. Consolata, St. Hedwig High School, 5680 Konkel St., Detroit, Mich.
Sister Mary David, College of St. Benedict, St. Joseph, Minn.
Sister Mary de Lourdes, Saint Joseph College, West Hartford, Conn.
Sister Mary Dolores, College of St. Francis, Joliet, Ill.
Sister Mary Dorothy, Educ. Dept., Siena Heights College, Adrian, Mich.
Sister Mary Dorothy, Queen of Apostles Library, Harriman, N.Y.

Sister Mary Edward, College of St. Catherine, St. Paul, Minn.
Sister Mary Edward, Comstock Hall, University of Minnesota, Minneapolis, Minn.
Sister Mary Edwina, 5286 South Park Ave., Hamburg, N.Y.
Sister Mary Elaine, College of St. Mary, 1901 S. 73rd St., Omaha, Neb.
Sister Mary Elizabeth, Sister Mary's High School, Rutherford, N.J.
Sister M. Felicitas, Regina Heights, 4830 Salem Ave., Dayton, Ohio
Sister Mary Fidelia, Bartlett, Ill.
Sister M. Francis Regis, 444 Centre St., Milton, Mass.
Sister Mary Fridian, Dept. of Educ., St. Francis College, Fort Wayne, Ind.
Sister Mary Gabrielle, Nazareth College, Nazareth, Mich.
Sister Mary Giles, Mariam College, Indianapolis, Ind.
Sister M. Harriet Sanborn, Aquinas College, Grand Rapids, Mich.
Sister Mary Hugh, Fontbonne College, St. Louis, Mo.
Sister Mary Hyacinth, Mount Senario College, Ladysmith, Wis.
Sister Mary Imeldine, Marylhurst College, Marylhurst, Ore.
Sister Mary Innocenta, The Felician College, 3800 Peterson Ave., Chicago, Ill.
Sister Mary Irmina Saelinger, Villa Madonna College, Covington, Ky.
Sister Mary James, Mt. St. Vincent College, Rockingham, Nova Scotia
Sister Mary Jamesetta, 1001 Lake Ave., Rochester, N.Y.
Sister Mary Joachim, Benedictine Heights College, Tulsa, Okla.
Sister Mary John Francis, Mount Mary College, Milwaukee, Wis.
Sister M. Josephina, Xavier University, 7325 Palmetto St., New Orleans, La.
Sister Mary Judith, Dept. of Educ., Briar Cliff College, Sioux City, Iowa
Sister Mary Kathleen, Mt. St. Agnes College, Mt. Washington, Baltimore, Md.
Sister M. Laurina, Mount Mary College, Yankton, S.D.
Sister Mary Lawrence, Mary Manse College, Toledo, Ohio
Sister Mary Lawrence Huber, Mt. St. Joseph Teachers College, Buffalo, N.Y.
Sister Mary Leo, Immaculata College, Immaculata, Pa.
Sister M. Leonella, St. Mary of the Wasatch, Salt Lake City, Utah
Sister Mary Liguori, Mercyhurst College, Erie, Pa.
Sister Mary Lucille, Mercy College, 8200 W. Outer Dr., Detroit, Mich.
Sister M. Margarita, Rosary College, River Forest, Ill.
Sister M. Matthew, Sacred Heart Dominican College, Houston, Tex.
Sister Mary Mercita, St. Mary College, Xavier, Kan.
Sister M. Merici, Educ. Dept., Ursuline College, Louisville, Ky.
Sister M. Muriel Gallagher, Mt. Mercy College, Pittsburgh, Pa.
Sister Mary Muriel Hogan, Ottumwa Heights College, Ottumwa, Iowa
Sister Mary Nila, Cardinal Cushing Education Clinic, Boston, Mass.
Sister M. Petrine, So. Cent. Prov. House, 2110 Cooper Dr., Irving, Tex.
Sister M. Philomene Schiller, Webster College, Webster Groves, Mo.
Sister M. Pierre, Marian College of Fond du Lac, Fond du Lac, Wis.
Sister Mary Priscilla, Notre Dame College, Cleveland, Ohio
Sister M. Ronalda, St. Margaret Hospital, Hammond, Ind.
Sister Mary Rosalia, Salve Regina College, Newport, R.I.
Sister Mary Rose Agnes, Our Lady of Cincinnati College, Cincinnati, Ohio
Sister M. Rose Alice, St. Paul's Priory, 301 Summit Ave., St. Paul, Minn.
Sister M. Roselyn, 45 Sixth Ave., Le Mars, Iowa
Sister M. Rosine, Dunbarton College, Washington, D.C.
Sister Mary of St. Michael, College of the Holy Names, Oakland, Calif.
Sister Mary Theodine, Viterbo College, LaCrosse, Wis.
Sister M. Theodore, Educ. Dept., Dominican College, Racine, Wis.
Sister M. Veronice Engelhardt, Maria Regina College, Syracuse, N.Y.
Sister Mary Vianney, St. Xavier College, 103rd and Central Park, Chicago, Ill.
Sister Mary Vincent Therese Tuohy, 245 Clinton Ave., Brooklyn, N.Y.
Sister Mary Zeno, Notre Dame College, 320 E. Ripa Ave., St. Louis, Mo.
Sister Maureen, College of Great Falls, Great Falls, Mont.
Sister Mildred Clare, Nazareth College, Bardstown, Ky.
Sister Nesta Feldman, 136 West 75th St., New York, N.Y.
Sister Rosemarie Julie, Educ. Dept., College of Notre Dame, Belmont, Calif.
Sittler, Mrs. Fannie Ruth, 1000 W. Rollins St., Box 458, Moberly, Mo.

Sizemore, Robert A., 2602 Glendale Ave., Toledo, Ohio
Skaggs, Darcy A., 3699 N. Holly Ave., Baldwin Park, Calif.
Skalski, John M., Sch. of Educ., Fordham University, New York, N.Y.
Skard, Mrs. Aase Gruda, Fjellvn 2, Lysaker, Norway
Skatzes, D. H., P.O. Box 105, Old Washington, Ohio
Skawski, John, Superintendent of Schools, Peekskill, N.Y.
Skibbens, Charles P., 3732 N. Kildare Ave., Chicago, Ill.
Skinner, Richard C., Clarion State College, Clarion, Pa.
Skipper, Mrs. Dora Sikes, Florida State University, Tallahassee, Fla.
Skogsberg, Alfred H., Bloomfield Junior High School, Bloomfield, N.J.
Skonberg, Mrs. Madelon, 2601 Sunnyside Ave., Chicago, Ill.
Sligo, Joseph R., 102 N. Lancaster St., Athens, Ohio
Slobetz, Frank, St. Cloud State College, St. Cloud, Minn.
Slocum, Helen M., 202 Morris Gym, University of Minnesota, Minneapolis, Minn.
Smail, Robert W., USOM, APO 153, San Francisco, Calif.
Smallenburg, Harry W., County Schools, 808 N. Spring St., Los Angeles, Calif.
Smedstad, Alton O., Superintendent, Elem. Schools, Hillsboro, Ore.
Smerling, William H., 710 N. Main St., Ada, Ohio
Smiley, Marjorie B., Hunter College, 695 Park Ave., New York, N.Y.
Smith, A. Edson, East Alton–Wood River High School, Wood River, Ill.
Smith, Mrs. Adean M., 2519 North 41st St., Milwaukee, Wis.
Smith, Alexander F., Southern Connecticut State College, New Haven, Conn.
Smith, Alvin H., Hampden-Sydney College, Hampden-Sydney, Va.
Smith, Ara K., 609 Lafayette St., Michigan City, Ind.
Smith, Arthur E., National Merit Scholarship Corp., Evanston, Ill.
Smith, B. Othanel, Col. of Educ., University of Illinois, Urbana, Ill.
Smith, C. C., 4801 Tremont St., Dallas, Tex.
Smith, Calvin S., 5705 South 1700 West, Murray, Utah
Smith, Dorothy D., 1721 E. Third St., Duluth, Minn.
Smith, Emmitt D., Box 745, West Texas Station, Canyon, Tex.
Smith, Garmon B., Austin College, Sherman, Tex.
Smith, Gary R., 14520 Asbury Park, Detroit, Mich.
Smith, H. Hayes, 326 Tower Dr., East Alton, Ill.
Smith, Hannis S., State Office Annex, 117 University Ave., St. Paul, Minn.
Smith, Henry P., Sch. of Educ., University of Kansas, Lawrence, Kan.
Smith, Ida T., Col. of Educ., Oklahoma State University, Stillwater, Okla.
Smith, Inez L. New York University, Washington Square, New York, N.Y.
Smith, James O., R.R. 2. Wilson St., Rising Sun, Ind.
Smith, Joseph M., 422 Willard Ave., Newington, Conn.
Smith, Katie P., Claflin College, Orangeburg, S.C.
Smith, Lawrence J., Central Michigan University, Mt. Pleasant, Mich.
Smith, Leslie F., 705 N. Killingsworth, Portland, Ore.
Smith, Lloyd L., Col. of Educ., State University of Iowa, Iowa City, Iowa
Smith, Lloyd N., Dept. of Educ., Indiana State Teachers Col., Terre Haute, Ind.
Smith, Mary Alice, State College, Lock Haven, Pa.
Smith, Mary Thomas, Queens College, Charlotte, N.C.
Smith, Menrie M., Rte. 4, Hamilton, Ala.
Smith, Nila Banton, 1111 S. Broadway, Pitman, N.J.
Smith, Paul E., Board of Education, Wilmington, Del.
Smith, Paul M., 7271 East Ave., U-3, Littlerock, Calif.
Smith, Philip John, Box 13, P.O. Cottesloe, Western Australia
Smith, Robert M., Sch. of Educ., Univ. of Pittsburgh, Pittsburgh, Pa.
Smith, Sara E., Western Maryland College, Westminster, Md.
Smith, Sisera, 115 South 54th St., Philadelphia, Pa.
* Smith, Stephen E., East Texas Baptist College, Marshall, Tex.
Smith, W. Holmes, El Camino College, El Camino College, Calif.
Smith, Walter Douglas, Winthrop College, Rock Hill, S.C.
Snader, Daniel W., State University Col. of Education, Fredonia, N.Y.
Snider, Glenn R., Col. of Educ., University of Oklahoma, Norman, Okla.
Snider, Hervon Leroy, Sch. of Educ., University of Idaho, Moscow, Idaho
Sniderman, S. M., Barber School, 45 E. Buena Vista, Highland Park, Mich.

Snowden, Terrence J., Campus Sch., Wisconsin State Col., Stevens Point, Wis.
Snyder, Agnes, 50 Central Ter., Clifton Park, Wilmington, Del.
Snyder, Harvey B., Pasadena College, 1539 E. Howard St., Pasadena, Calif.
Snyder, Helen I., 1030 W. Beaver Ave., State College, Pa.
Snyder, Jerome R., 1114 Mogford St., Midland, Tex.
Snyder, Mrs. Marjorie Sims, Col. of Educ., Univ. of Florida, Gainesville, Fla.
Snyder, Ralph E., 50 Howell Ave., Larchmont, N.Y.
Snyder, Robert D., Superintendent of Schools, Wayzata, Minn.
Snyder, Ruth C., 1217 Walnut St., Utica, N.Y.
Snyder, Walter E., 362 N. Craven St., Monmouth, Ore.
Soares, Anthony T., 224 Parish Rd., Needham Heights, Mass.
Sobel, Morton J., Suite 300, 515 Madison Ave., New York, N.Y.
Sobel, Stuart W., 135 Hawthorne St., Brooklyn, N.Y.
Sobin, Gloria A., 370 Seymour Ave., Derby, Conn.
Soeberg, Mrs. Dorothy, 106 Ridge Rd., Whittier, Calif.
Soffin, Alan L., Col. of Educ., Temple University, Philadelphia, Pa.
Soles, Stanley, San Francisco State College, San Francisco, Calif.
Solomon, Ruth H., 91 N. Allen St., Albany, N.Y.
Sommers, Mildred, Board of Educ., 290 W. Michigan Ave., Jackson, Mich.
Sommers, Wesley S., 820 Sixth St., Menomonie, Wis.
Sonntag, Ida May, 5101 Norwich Rd., Toledo, Ohio
Sonstegard, Manford A., Southern Illinois University, Alton, Ill.
Sorenson, A. Garth, Moore Hall., University of California, Los Angeles, Calif.
Sorensen, Helmer E., Oklahoma A. and M. College, Stillwater, Okla.
Sorenson, Katherine, Burton Hall, University of Minnesota, Minneapolis, Minn.
Sorgatz, Walter C., 1845 E. Hubbell St., Phoenix, Ariz.
Sosulski, M. C., St. John Fisher College, Rochester, N.Y.
Soucy, Leo, Central School, Dist. No. 1, 27 Cayuga St., Union Springs, N.Y.
Southall, Maycie K., Peabody College for Teachers, Nashville, Tenn.
Sowards, G. Wesley, Sch. of Educ., Stanford University, Stanford, Calif.
Spalding, Willard B., 455 Golden Gate Ave., San Francisco, Calif.
Spalke, E. Pauline, P.O. Box 405, Salem Depot, N.H.
Sparks, J. E., Beverly Hills Unified School Dist., Beverly Hills, Calif.
Sparling, Edward J., Roosevelt University, 430 S. Michigan Ave., Chicago, Ill.
Spaulding, Robert L., RFD 6, Carlls Straight Path, Huntington, N.Y.
Spaulding, Seth, Sch. of Educ., Univ. of Pittsburgh, Pittsburgh, Pa.
Spear, William G., 7233 W. Lunt Ave., Chicago, Ill.
Spears, William, Superintendent of Schools, Appleton, Wis.
Speer, Hugh W., University of Kansas City, Kansas City, Mo.
Spence, Ralph B., Tchrs. Col., Columbia University, New York, N.Y.
Spencer, Doris U., Johnson State College, Johnson, Vt.
Spencer, Edward M., Fresno State College, Fresno, Calif.
Spencer, Elizabeth, Ball State Teachers College, Muncie, Ind.
Spencer, James E., 261 Sea Vale St., Chula Vista, Calif.
Spencer, Lyle M., Science Research Associates, Inc., 259 E. Erie, Chicago, Ill.
Spencer, Peter L., 5550 Gravois Ave., Los Angeles, Calif.
Sperber, Robert I., 6552 Rosemoor St., Pittsburgh, Pa.
Spielman, Lester, 2970 Sheridan Rd., Chicago, Ill.
Spieseke, Alice W., Tchrs. Col., Columbia University, New York, N.Y.
Spigle, Irving, Superintendent of Schools, Park Forest, Ill.
Spinola, A. R., Superintendent, Denville School Dist. No. 1, Denville, N.J.
Spitzer, Herbert F., Col. of Educ., State University of Iowa, Iowa City, Iowa
Spooner, Donald W., 935 Waukegan Rd., Deerfield, Ill.
Sprietsma, Lewis R., 1031 Princeton Ave., Modesto, Calif.
Springman, John H., 1215 Waukegan Rd., Glenview, Ill.
Spruill, Betty Anne, 241 Langdon St., Madison, Wis.
Squire, James R., 805 W. Indiana Ave., Urbana, Ill.
Staats, Arthur W., Dept. of Psych., Arizona State Univ., Tempe, Ariz.
Staats, Pauline G., Chas. Hay Elem. Sch., 3185 S. Lafayette, Englewood, Colo.
Stabler, Ernest, Wesleyan University, Middletown, Conn.
Stachenfeld, Emanuel, Marine Park Junior High School, Brooklyn, N.Y.

Stack, Eileen C., 937 N. Linden Ave., Oak Park, Ill.
Stack, Mrs. Thelma D., 2209 E. Park Pl., Milwaukee, Wis.
Stafford, H. D., P.O. Box 21, Murrayville, B.C., Canada
Staggs, Jack, Sam Houston Teachers College, Huntsville, Tex.
Stahlecker, Lotar V., Kent State University, Kent, Ohio
Stahly, Harold L., 1401 Randol Ave., Cape Girardeau, Mo.
Staiger, Ralph C., 701 Dallam Rd., Newark, Del.
Staiger, Roger P., Dept. of Chem., Ursinus College, Collegeville, Pa.
Stalnaker, John M., 1580 Sherman Ave., Evanston, Ill.
Stanchfield, Jo M., Occidental College, Los Angeles, Calif.
Stanford, Madge, 3336 Rankin, Dallas, Tex.
Stanley, Calvin, Texas Southern University, Houston, Tex.
Stanley, Charles J., Jr., Florida A. and M. University, Tallahassee, Fla.
Stanton, William A., 3037 Garfield Ave., Costa Mesa, Calif.
Stapleton, Mary Ellen, Jonathan Maynard Training School, Framingham, Mass.
Starner, Norman Dean, Wyalusing Valley Joint High School, Wyalusing, Pa.
Stathopulos, Peter H., Elem. School, Second Ave. and Manavon St., Phoenixville, Pa.
Stauffer, Richard F., Horton Watkins High School, St. Louis, Mo.
Stauffer, Russell G., University of Delaware, Newark, Del.
Staven, LaVier L., 1304 MacArthur Rd., Hays, Kan.
Steadman, E. R., 277 Columbia, Elmhurst, Ill.
Stedje, Raynard L., 3146 Minnehaha Ave., So., Minneapolis, Minn.
Stedman, Edith, 600 University Ave., S.E., Minneapolis, Minn.
Steel, Wade A., Leyden High School, Franklin Park, Ill.
Steele, Lysle H., P.O. Box 66, Beloit, Wis.
Steeves, Frank L., University of Vermont, Burlington, Vt.
Steg, Mrs. Loreen E., 4114 Fountain Green, Lafayette Hill, Pa.
Stegall, Alma L., Virginia State College, Petersburg, Va.
Stegeman, William H., Educ. Ctr., San Diego City Schools, San Diego, Calif.
Steider, Alma T., 207 S. Walnut St., Eureka, Ill.
Steige, Robert, Eastern New Mexico University, Portales, N.M.
Stein, Jay W., Drake University, Des Moines, Iowa
Stein, Michael W., Western Junior High School, Byram, Conn.
Steinberg, Paul M., Hebrew Union Sch. of Educ., 40 W. 68th St., New York, N.Y.
Steinberg, Walter F., Luther High School South, 3130 W. 87th St., Chicago, Ill.
Steinberg, Warren L., 2737 Dunleer Pl., Los Angeles, Calif.
Steiner, William F., Superintendent of Schools, Cliffside Park, N.J.
Steinhagen, Margaret J., 107 McKendree Ave., Annapolis, Md.
Steininger, Earl W., 535 West 5th St., Dubuque, Iowa
Steinkellner, Robert H., Southern Illinois Univ., S.W. Campus, East St. Louis, Ill.
Stelmachowicz, Michael J., Jr., Concordia Teachers Col., Seward, Neb.
Stephens, Bertha L., 1765 Gilpin St., Denver, Colo.
Stephens, Darleen, East. Montana College of Educ., Billings, Mont.
Stephens, J. M., Dept. of Educ., University of California, Berkeley, Calif.
Stephens, Kenton E., 276 Nuttall, Riverside, Ill.
Stephens, Lester D., Col. of Educ., Univ. of Georgia, Athens, Ga.
Sterling, A. M., P.O. Box 213, Northville, N.Y.
Sternberg, William N., Public Sch. 114, 1155 Cromwell Ave., New York, N.Y.
Stetson, Ethel A., 47 West Chester Ave., North Babylon, N.Y.
Steudler, Mary Margaret, 70 Grove Hill, New Britain, Conn.
Stevens, J. H., 320 S. Highland St., Murfreesboro, Tenn.
Stevens, Paul C., Rapid City Public Schools, Rapid City, S.D.
Stewart, Frederick H., P.O. Box 3, Jarrettown, Pa.
Stibbs, R. B., Supt., School Dist 43, New Westminster, British Columbia
Stickler, W. Hugh, Florida State University, Tallahassee, Fla.
Stiemke, Eugenia A., Valparaiso University, Valparaiso, Ind.
Stier, Lealand D., 14675 Aloha St., Saratoga, Calif.
Stiles, Cordelia L., 403 West 154th St., New York, N.Y.
Stiles, Grace Ellen, Box 34, Kingston, R.I.
Stirzaker, Norbert A., 323 South 32nd St., Terre Haute, Ind.

Stitt, Sam C., Superintendent of Schools, Ellinwood, Kan.
Stoddard, George D., 14 Washington Mews, New York, N.Y.
Stofega, Michael E., 271 State St., Perth Amboy, N.J.
Stokes, Maurice S., Savannah State College, Savannah, Ga.
Stolee, Michael J., 66-8 San Vicente Ave., Coral Gables, Fla.
Stoller, Nathan, Hunter College, 695 Park Ave., New York, N.Y.
Stolurow, Lawrence M., 809 Dodds Dr., Champaign, Ill.
Stone, Chester D., 549 Westwood Ct., Vacaville, Calif.
Stone, Ernest, 403 Edgewood Dr., Jacksonville, Fla.
Stone, George P., Union College, Lincoln, Neb.
Stone, Gladys, Superintendent, Monterey County Schools, Salinas, Calif.
Stone, Mode L., Sch. of Educ., Florida State University, Tallahassee, Fla.
Stone, Paul T., Huntingdon College, Montgomery, Ala.
Stonehocker, D. Doyle, 1515 Oakdale St., Burlington, Iowa
Stoneking, Lewis W., George Peabody College for Tchrs., Nashville, Tenn.
Stoneman, Mrs. Nora C., Lincoln School, 1821 Lincoln Rd., Wickliffe, Ohio
Stoops, John A., Dept. of Educ., Lehigh University, Bethlehem, Pa.
Stordahl, Kalmer E., MPATI, Mem. Center, Purdue Univ., Lafayette, Ind.
Storen, Helen F., Dept. of Educ., Queens College, Flushing, N.Y.
Storlie, Theodore R., 3400 Rose St., Franklin Park, Ill.
Storm, Jerome F., 22 Grand Ave., Northport, L.I., N.Y.
Storr, Mrs. Maude L., 2001 N.W. Third Ct., Fort Lauderdale, Fla.
Stottler, Richard H., University of Maryland, College Park, Md.
Stoughton, Robert W., State Department of Education, Hartford, Conn.
Stover, G. Franklin, Box 385, RD 3, Somerset, N.J.
Straight, Mrs. Madeline J., 312 S. Scoville Ave., Oak Park, Ill.
Strain, Mrs. Sibyl M., 2236 Los Lunas St., Pasadena, Calif.
Strand, Helen A., Luther College, Decorah, Iowa
Strand, William H., 170 Mimosa Way, Menlo Park, Calif.
* Strang, Ruth, Col. of Educ., University of Arizona, Tucson, Ariz.
Stratemeyer, Florence B., Tchrs. Col., Columbia University, New York, N.Y.
Strathairn, Pamela L., Women's Phy. Ed. Dept., Stanford Univ., Stanford, Calif.
Strauss, John F., Jr. College of St. Thomas, St. Paul, Minn.
Strayer, George D., Jr. Col. of Educ., University of Washington, Seattle, Wash.
Strebel, Jane D., Bd. of Educ., 807 N.E. Broadway, Minneapolis, Minn.
Strei, Kenneth G., 2112 DuPont Ave., So., Minneapolis, Minn.
Strem, Bruce E., 222 W. Gardner St., Long Beach, Calif.
Streng, Alice, University of Wisconsin-Milwaukee, Milwaukee, Wis.
Strickland, C. G., Sch. of Educ., Baylor University, Waco, Tex.
Strickland, Mrs. Helen B., Arlington High School, Arlington, Tex.
* Strickler, Robert E., 3815 Flod, St. Louis, Mo.
Strickling, Cloria Ann, 6904 Calverton Dr., Hyattsville, Md.
Strohbehn, Earl F., 12151 Mellowood Dr., Saratoga, Calif.
Strole, Lois E., R.R. No. 2, West Terre Haute, Ind.
Strong, Ethel, 815 East St., Iola, Kan.
Stroud, James B., Col. of Educ., State University of Iowa, Iowa City, Iowa
Stuardi, J. Edwin, 550 Dauphin St., Mobile, Ala.
Stuart, Alden T., 81 Rose Ave., Patchogue, L.I., N.Y.
Stuart, Chester J., Canisius Hall, Fairfield University, Fairfield, Conn.
Stuenkel, Walter W., Concordia College, 3126 W. Kilbourn Ave., Milwaukee, Wis.
Stutz, F. H., Sch. of Educ., Cornell University, Ithaca, N.Y.
Suber, James W., Woodrow Wilson High School, Washington, D.C.
Sugden, W. E., Superintendent of Schools, 7776 Lake St., River Forest, Ill.
Sullivan, Daniel C., Sch. of Educ., St. John's University, Jamaica, N.Y.
Sullivan, F. W., 1012 Lena St., N.W., Atlanta, Ga.
Sullivan, Helen Blair, 106 Elm St., Belmont, Mass.
Sullivan, Robert E., Notre Dame Col., Cotabato City, Philippines
Sullivan, Ruth E., 885 Easton Rd., Glenside, Pa.
Sullivan, Sheila R., Ohio State University, Columbus, Ohio
Sulzer, Edward Stanton, University of Minnesota, Minneapolis, Minn.

Sun, Huai Chin, 7123 Sycamore Ave., Takoma Park, Md.
Sunderlin, Edith M., Child Dev. Cent., Iowa State Univ., Ames, Iowa
Suskowitz, Min, 81-31—188th St., Jamaica, N.Y.
Sutherland, J. K., Col. of Educ., Univ. of Saskatchewan, Saskatoon, Sask.
Sutherland, Jack W., San Jose State College, San Jose, Calif.
Sutherland, Margaret, Col. of Educ., University of California, Davis, Calif.
Sutter, Belva, Friends University, 732 Beverly Dr., Wichita, Kan.
Sutton, Elizabeth, 1825 Jackson Bluff Rd., Tallahassee, Fla.
Svolopoulos, Christos, 24 Sarantaporou St., Salonica, Greece
Swann, Mrs. A. Ruth, 2713 Mapleton Ave., Norfolk, Va.
Swann, Reginald L., Central Connecticut State College, New Britain, Conn.
Swanson, Mrs. Arlene C., 23 Wolden Rd., Ossining, N.Y.
Swanson, Gordon L., Dept. of Agric. Educ., Univ. of Minnesota, St. Paul, Minn.
Swanson, J. Chester, Sch. of Educ., University of California, Berkeley, Calif.
Swanson, Reynold A., Board of Education, 100 N. Jefferson, Green Bay, Wis.
Swartout, Sheridan G., State University College of Education, Brockport, N.Y.
Swartzmiller, Jean, 90 Ridge Ave., North Plainfield, N.J.
Swauger, Velora V., 1314 Potomac Ave., Hagerstown, Md.
Swearingen, Mildred E., 930 N. Wildwood Dr., Tallahassee, Fla.
Sweet, Harmon C., Rochester Business Inst., 172 Clinton Ave., Rochester, N.Y.
Swenson, Esther J., Box 1942, University, Ala.
Swertfeger, Floyd F., Route 3, Box 16, Farmville, Va.
Swindall, Wellington, Palmdale School, 3000 E. Wier Ave., Phoenix, Ariz.
Syverson, Genevieve B., Northern Illinois University, DeKalb, Ill.

Taba, Hilda, San Francisco State College, San Francisco, Calif.
Tackman, Mary C., P.O. Box 6, Damascus, Md.
Tadena, Tomas, Philippine Normal College, Manila, Philippines
Tag, Herbert G., University of Connecticut, Storrs, Conn.
Taggart, Leo R., Superintendent of Schools, Ambridge, Pa.
Tajima, Yuri, 1918 N. Bissell, Chicago, Ill.
* Tallman, Russell W., 2024 Avalon Rd., Des Moines, Iowa
Tamura, Kunihiko, No. 16, 2 Chome, Hachimandori, Sibuya-ku, Tokyo, Japan
Tancil, Sallie E., 5823 Dix St., N.E., Washington, D.C.
Tanger, Frederick, Media Borough School District, Media, Pa.
Tanner, B. William, 650 S. Detroit Ave., Toledo, Ohio
Tanner, Daniel, Northwestern University, Evanston, Ill.
Tanner, Wilbur H., Northwestern State College, Alva, Okla.
Tanruther, Edgar M., Indiana State Teachers College, Terre Haute, Ind.
Tant, Norman, Morehead State College, Morehead, Ky.
Tarbox, Florence H., D'Youville College, Buffalo, N.Y.
Tardif, Fernand R., La Salette Seminary, Enfield, N.H.
Tarver, K. E., John P. Odom School, 3445 Fannett Rd., Beaumont, Tex.
Tate, Virginia, 1440—7th St., Charleston, Ill.
Taylor, Mrs. Emily C., Mayo Elementary School, Edgewater, Md.
Taylor, Faith, 3681B Alabama Ave., S.E., Washington, D.C.
Taylor, George E., Council Rock High School, Newton, Pa.
Taylor, Kenneth I., West Leyden High School, Northlake, Ill.
Taylor, L. O., 4314 Dodge St., Omaha, Neb.
Taylor, M. Ruth, Hillcrest School, Drexel Hill, Pa.
Taylor, Marvin J., St. Paul School of Theology, 5110 Cherry, Kansas City, Mo.
Taylor, Marvin T., Div. of Educ., Queens College, Flushing, N.Y.
Taylor, Mrs. Mary C., Box 164, Rt. No. 1, New Lenox, Ill.
Taylor, Robert E., 1835 Riverhill Rd., Columbus, Ohio
Taylor, Wayne, 160 Kenberry, East Lansing, Mich.
Teague, Carroll, Pasadena Ind. School District, Pasadena, Tex.
Teare, B. R., Jr., Carnegie Institute of Technology, Pittsburgh, Pa.
Teigen, B. W., Bethany Lutheran College, Mankato, Minn.
Telford, Charles W., San Jose State College, San Jose, Calif.
Temp, George E., 10 Solona Ct., Santa Barbara, Calif.
Tempero, Howard E., Teachers Col., University of Nebraska, Lincoln, Neb.

Temple, F. L., Box 2185, University, Ala.
Templin, Mildred C., Inst. of Child Welfare, Univ. of Minnesota, Minneapolis, Minn.
Tennessee, Mrs. Hyacinth B., 1123—28th St., Newport News, Va.
Tenny, John W., 630 Merrick Ave., Detroit, Mich.
Terrill, Maymie I., 2477 Overlook Rd., Cleveland Heights, Ohio
Tetz, Henry E., Oregon College of Education, Monmouth, Ore.
Thevaos, Deno G., 575 Westview Ave., State College, Pa.
Thomann, Don F., Dept. of Educ., Ripon College, Ripon, Wis.
Thomas, Cleveland A., Francis Parker School, 330 Webster Ave., Chicago, Ill.
Thomas, Granville S., Superintendent of Schools, Salem, N.J.
Thomas, John, 4 Washington Manor, Hunting Lodge Rd., Storrs, Conn.
Thomas, R. Irene, Col. of Educ., Kent State University, Kent, Ohio
Thomas, Wade F., Santa Monica City College, Santa Monica, Calif.
Thomassen, Henry S., Webster Pub. Co., 1154 Reco Ave., St. Louis, Mo.
Thompson, Mrs. Annie B., 705 Apple St., Burlington, N.C.
Thompson, Anton, Long Beach Public Schls., 715 Locust Ave., Long Beach, Calif.
Thompson, Ben, Dept. of Educ., Antioch College, Yellow Springs, Ohio
Thompson, Charles H., Grad. Sch., Howard University, Washington, D.C.
Thompson, Elton Noel, City Schools, 133 Mission St., Santa Cruz, Calif.
Thompson, Franklin J., South Pasadena High School, South Pasadena, Calif.
Thompson, Fred R., Col. of Educ., Univ. of Maryland, College Park, Md.
Thompson, Helen M., Chapman College, Orange, Calif.
Thompson, J. M., Elgin Academy, Elgin, Ill.
Thompson, James H., 511 Harley Dr., Columbus, Ohio
Thompson, John D., Box 635 Seminole Public Schools, Seminole, Tex.
Thompson, Olive L., 1541 Iroquois Ave., Long Beach, Calif.
Thompson, Orrin G., Superintendent of Schools, Elgin, Ill.
Thompson, Ralph H., Western Washington College of Education, Bellingham, Wash.
Thompson, Ray, North Carolina College, Durham, N.C.
Thomson, Procter, Pitzer Hall, Claremont Men's College, Claremont, Calif.
Thorn, Burton K., Michigan State University, East Lansing, Mich.
Thorndike, Robert L., Tchrs. Col., Columbia University, New York, N.Y.
Thorne, Edmund H., 7 Whiting Lane, West Hartford, Conn.
Thornton, James W., Jr., San Jose State College, San Jose, Calif.
Thorp, Mary T., 84 Eleventh St., Providence, R.I.
Thorpe, Louis P., Sch. of Educ., University of California, Los Angeles, Calif.
Threlkeld, A. L., Jamaica, Vt.
Throne, Elsie M., 306 Lincoln Ave., Avon-by-the-Sea, N.J.
Thursby, Mrs. Ruth, 310 W. Francis St., Corona, Calif.
Thyberg, Clifford S., 1717 W. Merced Ave., West Covina, Calif.
Tidrow, Joe, Dept. of Educ. and Phil., Texas Tech. College, Lubbock, Tex.
Tidwell, R. E., Stillman College, Tuscaloosa, Ala.
Tiedeman, Herman R., Illinois State University, Normal, Ill.
Tiedt, Sidney W., Educ. Div., San Jose State College, San Jose, Calif.
Tierney, Marie, Chicago Teachers College, 6800 Stewart Ave., Chicago, Ill.
Tillan, Lynn, 417 Hillsboro Pkwy., Syracuse, N.Y.
Tillman, Rodney, Minneapolis Pub. Schls., 807 N.E. Broadway, Minneapolis, Minn.
Timberlake, Walter B., Jr., 715 N.W. Military Dr., San Antonio, Tex.
Timko, Irene H., 6153 Fletcher St., Chicago, Ill.
Timmons, F. Alan, 230 East 12th St., Long Beach, Calif.
Tinari, Charles, Shackamaxon School, Scotch Plains, N.J.
Tingle, Mary J., Col. of Educ., University of Georgia, Athens, Ga.
Tink, Albert K., 18 Wendall Pl., DeKalb, Ill.
Tinker, Miles A., 991 Winther Way, Santa Barbara, Calif.
Tipton, Elis M., 941 East Bel Air, Merced, Calif.
Tisdall, William J., Cath. of Learn., Univ. of Pittsburgh, Pittsburgh, Pa.
Tittle, Carol Kehr, 5453 Everett Ave., Chicago, Ill.
Tobias, S., Sch. of Educ., City College of New York, New York, N.Y.

Tobin, Albert J., 611 Helen St., Garden City, Mich.
Todd, G. Raymond, R.D. No. 3, Bethlehem, Pa.
Toles, Caesar F., Bishop Junior College, 4527 Crozier St., Dallas, Tex.
Tollinger, William P., Superintendent, Wilson Borough Schls., Easton, Pa.
Tomes, Cornelia A., 1584 Koch Lane, San Jose, Calif.
Toops, Herbert A., 1430 Cambridge Blvd., Columbus, Ohio
Topp, Robert F., Col. of Educ., Northern Illinois University, DeKalb, Ill.
Torbet, David P., Butler University, Indianapolis, Ind.
Torchia, Joseph, State Teachers College, Millersville, Pa.
Torkelson, Gerald M., Pennsylvania State University, University Park, Pa.
Torrance, E. Paul, Bur. of Educ. Res., Univ. of Minnesota, Minneapolis, Minn.
Tostberg, Robert E., Dept. of Educ., University of Washington, Seattle, Wash.
Totten, W. Fred, Mott Sci. Bldg., 1401 E. Court St., Flint, Mich.
Toussaint, Isabella H., 101 Olive Dr., Level Green, Trafford, Pa.
Towles, Lena Ruth, 2104 Murray Ave., Louisville, Ky.
Towne, Ruth, Col. of Educ., Temple University, Philadelphia, Pa.
Trabue, M. R., 306 Strathmore Rd., Lexington, Ky.
Tracy, Edward, Easton-Forks and Easton Area Joint Sch. System, Easton, Pa.
Tracy, Elaine M., St. Olaf College, Northfield, Minn.
Traeger, Carl, 375 N. Eagle St., Oshkosh, Wis.
Traiber, Frank, USAID Mission, Guatemala, Dept. of State Mail Rm., Washington, D.C.
Traill, Robert R., 84 Argyle Rd., KEW, Victoria, Australia
Travelstead, Chester C., Col. of Educ., Univ. of New Mexico, Albuquerque, N.M.
Travers, John F., Sch. of Educ., Boston College, Chestnut Hill, Mass.
Travis, Vaud A., Dept. of Educ., Northeastern State College, Tahlequa, Okla.
Traxler, Arthur E., Educational Records Bureau, 21 Audubon Ave., New York, N.Y.
Treece, Marion B., Southern Illinois University, Carbondale, Ill.
Tremaine, Donahue L., Roosevelt University, 430 S. Michigan Ave., Chicago, Ill.
Trice, J. A., Superintendent of Schools, Pine Bluff, Ark.
Triggs, Frances, Mountain Home, N.C.
Trinkaus, William K., Southern Connecticut State Col., New Haven, Conn.
Tripp, Philip A., U.S. Office of Educ., Dept. of H.E.W., Washington, D.C.
Trippe, Matthew J., George Peabody College for Teachers, Nashville, Tenn.
Trippensee, Arthur E., Col. of Educ., University of Bridgeport, Bridgeport, Conn.
Trow, William Clark, Sch. of Educ., University of Michigan, Ann Arbor, Mich.
Truher, Helen Burke, 245 Hillside Rd., South Pasadena, Calif.
Trumble, Verna J., 42 West St., Johnson City, N.Y.
Trump, J. Lloyd, National Educ. Assn., 1201 Sixteenth St., N.W., Washington, D.C.
Trump, Paul L., American Col. Test. Program, Box 168, Iowa City, Iowa
Truncellito, Louis, M-239 Arlington Towers, Arlington, Va.
Tsugé, Haruko, 5570 Tsujido, Fujisawa, Kanagawa, Japan
Tucker, Mrs. Sylvia B., 30929 Rue Langlois, Palos Verdes Estates, Calif.
Tudyman, Al, 9333 Murillo Ave., Oakland, Calif.
Tully, Glover E., Educ. Dept., Florida State University, Tallahassee, Fla.
Turansky, Isadore, Western Michigan University, Kalamazoo, Mich.
Turner, Delia F., 3310 Edgemont, Tucson, Ariz.
Turner, Howard, Southern Louisiana Institute, Lafayette, La.
Turner, James W., Box 5431 North Texas Station, Denton, Tex.
Turner, Mrs. Nell B., 3431 Sangamon Ave., Dayton, Ohio
Turney, David T., Univ. School, Kent State University, Kent, Ohio
Tuseth, Alice, 1500 N. Washburn, Minneapolis, Minn.
Tuttle, Edwin A., Jr., 3620 Woodbridge Lane, Wantagh, N.Y.
Twombly, John J., Northern Illinois University, DeKalb, Ill.
Tyler, Fred. T., Sch. of Educ., University of California, Berkeley, Calif.
Tyler, I. Keith, Ohio State University, Columbus, Ohio
Tyler, John M., Mulberry Rd., Mansfield Center, Conn.
Tyler, Louise L., University of California, Los Angeles, Calif.
Tyler, Priscilla, Eng. Dept., University of Illinois, Urbana, Ill.

Tyler, Ralph W., 202 Junipero Serra Blvd., Stanford, Calif.
Tyler, Robert, Educ. Dept., Southwestern State College, Weatherford, Okla.
Tyrrell, Francis M., Immaculate Conception Seminary, Huntington, N.Y.
Tyson, Ivernia M., Arizona State College, Flagstaff, Ariz.
Tystad, Edna, Thoreau Public Schools, Thoreau, N.M.

Ulmer, T. H., Superintendent of Schools, Hartville, S.C.
Umansky, Harlan L., Emerson High School, Union City, N.J.
Umbarger, Helen D., East Chicago Public Schools, East Chicago, Ind.
Umholtz, Mrs. Anne K., 292 N. Fifth Ave., Highland Park, N.J.
Umstattd, James G., Sutton Hall, University of Texas, Austin, Tex.
Underwood, Mrs. Anna, Box 72, Southard, Okla.
Underwood, Mrs. Frances A., 5900 Hilltop Rd., Pensacola, Fla.
Underwood, Helen B., 1920 Madrona, Napa, Calif.
Underwood, William J., 116 Madison, Lee's Summit, Mo.
Unger, Mrs. Dorothy Holberg, 99 Lawton Rd., Riverside, Ill.
Unruh, Adolph, Washington University, St. Louis, Mo.

* Vakil, K. S., 119, Marzbanabad, Andheri, Bombay, India
Valentine, Mrs. M., 138 Highland, Highland Park, Mich.
Van Bruggen, John A., 549 Benjamin Ave., Grand Rapids, Mich.
Vandenberg, E. M., Hirsch High School, 7740 S. Ingleside Ave., Chicago, Ill.
Vander Horck, Karl J., 1417 Sunnymede, South Bend, Ind.
Vander Linde, Louis F., 29676 Milton Ave., Madison Heights, Mich.
Vanderlinden, J. S., Whiting Community Schools, Whiting, Iowa
Vander Meer, A. W., 627 W. Hamilton, University Park, Pa.
Vanderpol, Jeanette A., 10 Huron Ave., Jersey City, N.J.
Vanderpool, J. Alden, 1125 West 6th St., Los Angeles, Calif.
Vander Werf, Lester S., Col. of Educ., Northeastern University, Boston, Mass.
Van Devander, Donald M., Superintendent of Schools, Overland Park, Kan.
Van Loo, Eleanor, South Macomb Com. College, Detroit, Mich.
Van Ness, Paul H., 380 Mt. Prospect Ave., Newark, N.J.
Van Slyke, Valerie R., 4130 Monteith Dr., Los Angeles, Calif.
Van Wagenen, Marvin J., 1729 Irving Ave., South, Minneapolis, Minn.
Van Zanten, Mrs. Hazel, 4822 Division Ave., Grand Rapids, Mich.
Van Zwoll, James A., Col. of Educ., University of Maryland, College Park, Md.
Varn, Guy L., Superintendent of Schools, 1311 Marion St., Columbia, S.C.
Vasey, Hamilton G., Superintendent of Schools, Fargo, N.D.
Vaughan, Elaine P., 1433 Teller Ave., Bronx, N.Y.
Vaughan, Larry, Nebraska Wesleyan University, Lincoln, Neb.
Vaughan, Verdry D., Gallaudet College, Washington, D.C.
Vaughan, W. Donald, Centennial Joint Schools, Johnsville, Pa.
Veach, Jeannette, Pennsylvania State University, University Park, Pa.
Veltman, Peter, 600 College Ave., Wheaton, Ill.
Venable, Douglas, 118 Aztec Ave., White Rock, N.M.
Verger, Don, P.O. Box 5273, Eugene, Ore.
Veroff, Joseph, University of Michigan, Ann Arbor, Mich.
Verseput, Robert Frank, 8 South St., Dover, N.J.
Vigilante, Nicholas J., 181 Cornell Ct., Westerville, Ohio
Vignos, Dorothy Z., 718 Hermosa Ave., Hermosa Beach, Calif.
Vikner, Carl F., Gustavus Adolphus College, St. Peter, Minn.
Villano, George R., 1415 Pearl St., Denver, Colo.
Vilscek, Elaine C., University of Pittsburgh, Pittsburgh, Pa.
Vineyard, Jerry J., Superintendent of Schools, Arkansas City, Kan.
Vinson, Mrs. Etta Mary, 434 Newman Ave., Huntsville, Ala.
Vitalo, Nicholas F., Jr., 262 Blacksmith Rd., Levittown, N.Y.
Voelker, Paul Henry, Detroit Public Schools, 453 Stimson Ave., Detroit, Mich.
Voigt, Harry R., St. Paul's College, Concordia, Mo.
Voigt, Virginia E., 9 East Clark Pl., South Orange, N.J.
Vonk, Paul Kenneth, 508 E. Burlington Ave., Fairfield, Iowa
Vopni, Sylvia, Col. of Educ., University of Washington, Seattle, Wash.

Voris, George A., 291 Seward Pl., Schenectady, N.Y.
Votava, Arthur J., 5401 S. Nordica Ave., Chicago, Ill.
Votaw, Daniel C., 3535 Sterne St., San Diego, Calif.

Wade, D. E., 38 Stuyvesant Manor, Geneseo, N.Y.
Wagner, Carl E., 7421 Zephyr Pl., Maplewood, Mo.
Wagner, Eva, 6 Barberry Rd., Convent, N.J.
Wagner, Robert W., 1885 Neil Ave., Ohio State University, Columbus, Ohio
Wagner, Victor H., Green Vale School, Glen Head, N.Y.
Waimon, Morton D., Illinois State University, Normal, Ill.
Waine, Sidney I., 312 West 24th St., Deer Park, N.Y.
Wainscott, Carlton O., 301 Hawthorne, Abilene, Tex.
Walby, Grace S., 330 Anderson Ave., Winnipeg, Manitoba
Walcott, Fred G., University High School, Univ. of Michigan, Ann Arbor, Mich.
Walden, James, 1714 Oxford Dr., Bloomington, Ind.
Waldron, Margaret L., St. Mary-of-the-Woods College, St. Mary-of-the-Woods, Ind.
Walker, Charles Lynn, San Jose State College, San Jose, Calif.
* Walker, Ernest T., Bigfork, Mont.
Walker, Jerry L., 1703 Tara Dr., Champaign, Ill.
Walker, John S., Storer Junior High School, 3111 W. Euclid Ave., Muncie, Ind.
Walker, K. P., Superintendent of Schools, Jackson, Miss.
Walker, Mary Louise, 502 Rio Vista Dr., Daytona Beach, Fla.
Walker, Robert N., 2629 Pocomoke St., North, Arlington, Va.
Wall, Harry V., 17013 Alwood St., West Covina, Calif.
Wall, Jessie, Mississipi Southern College, Hattiesburg, Miss.
Wall, John L., North Texas State College, Denton, Tex.
Wall, T. H., Jr., Lowndes County High School, Valdosta, Ga.
Wallace, Donald G., Col. of Educ., Drake University, Des Moines, Iowa
Wallace, Elsie H., Florida State University, Tallahassee, Fla.
Wallace, James O., 1300 San Pedro Ave., San Antonio, Tex.
Wallace, Morris S., Dept. of Educ., Texas Tech. College, Lubbock, Tex.
Wallar, Gene A., San Jose State College, San Jose, Calif.
Wallen, Carl J., Sch. of Educ., Oregon State University, Corvallis, Ore.
Waller, Raymond L., 31 S. Penn St., Allentown, Pa.
Wallis, C. Lamar, 258 McLean Blvd., Memphis, Tenn.
Walmsley, Louise J., Southern Sem. Junior College, Buena Vista, Va.
Walsh, J. Hartt, Col. of Educ., Butler University, Indianapolis, Ind.
Walter, Raymond L., Box 201, Millbrook, Ala.
Walter, Robert B., 434 N. DelMar Ave., San Gabriel, Calif.
Walters, Mrs. Maxine Oyler, 12 S. High St., Mt. Sterling, Ohio
Walther, Herbert K., USOM/Education, American Embassy, APO 143, San Francisco, Calif.
Walvoord, Anthony C., Box 2845, University Hill Station, Denton, Tex.
Walz, Edgar, Concordia Senior College, Fort Wayne, Ind.
Walz, Garry R., 1718 Arbordale, Ann Arbor, Mich.
Wampler, W. Norman, Superintendent of Schools, Bellflower, Calif.
Wantling, G. K. Dale, TCM/American Embassy, New Delhi, India
Wantoch, Mrs. Ardell H., McNeal Hall, University of Minnesota, St. Paul, Minn.
Ward, Mrs. Annie W., Volusia County Schools, DeLand, Fla.
Ward, John C., Supt., Diocese of New Ulm, Hutchinson, Minn.
Ward, John Henry, Texas College, Tyler, Tex.
Ward, Ted, Michigan State University, East Lansing, Mich.
Ward, Virgil S., Sch. of Educ., University of Virginia, Charlottesville, Va.
Wardeberg, Helen L., Stone Hall, Cornell University, Ithaca, N.Y.
Ware, Mrs. Dorothy, 109 Touraine Rd., Grosse Pointe Farms, Mich.
Warner, Doris E., 4C Sandra Ct., Niagara Falls, N.Y.
Warren, John H., 623 Commonwealth Ave., Boston, Mass.
Warriner, David A., 514 Division St., East Lansing, Mich.
Warshavsky, Mrs. Belle, 35 Cooper Dr., Great Neck, N.Y.
Warshavsky, Bernard, 910 West End Ave., New York, N.Y.

Warwick, Raymond, 627 Elm Terrace, Riverton, N.J.
Washington, B. T., Williston School, 401 South 10th St., Wilmington, N.C.
Washington, Mrs. Justine W., 1228 Kent St., Augusta, Ga.
Washington, Walter, Utica Junior College, Utica, Miss.
Wasserman, Mrs. Lillian, 1684 Meadow Lane, East Meadow, N.Y.
Wasson, Margaret, 3705 University Blvd., Dallas, Tex.
Wasson, Roy J., 1115 N. El Paso St., Colorado Springs, Colo.
Waterman, Floyd T., 540 West 122nd St., New York, N.Y.
Waters, E. Worthington, Maryland State College, Princess Anne, Md.
Watkins, Ralph K., Hill Hall, University of Missouri, Columbia, Mo.
Watkins, Ray H., Decatur Baptist College, 1401 S. Trinity, Decatur, Tex.
Watkins, Thomas W., South Lehigh School District, Coopersburg, Pa.
Watson, David Roland, Elm Place School, 2031 Sheridan Rd., Highland Park, Ill.
Watson, N. E., Supt., Glenbrook High School, Northbrook, Ill.
Watson, Norman E., Orange Coast College, Costa Mesa, Calif.
Watson, Mrs. Robert, 22 Burlington St., Bordentown, N.J.
Watson, William Crawford, 29 Woodstock Rd., Mt. Waverly, Victoria, Australia
Watt, John Stewart, Col. of Educ., University of Akron, Akron, Ohio
Watt, Ralph W., 1206 Parker Ave., Hyattsville, Md.
Wattenberg, William W., Wayne University, Detroit, Mich.
Watters, Velma V., Savannah State College, Savannah, Ga.
Watts, Ann Rorem, 1508 N.W. 37th St., Oklahoma City, Okla.
Watts, Morrison L., Dept. of Educ., Province of Alberta, Edmonton, Alberta
Waxwood, Howard B., Jr., Witherspoon School, Quarry St., Princeton, N.J.
Way, Gail W., 1232 Henderson St., Chicago, Ill.
Wayson, William W., 5659 S. Drexel Ave., Chicago, Ill.
Weakley, Mrs. Mary L., 1426 Center St., Geneva, Ill.
Weaks, R. H., 22 Heather Hill Lane, St. Louis, Mo.
Weaver, Gladys C., 4708 Tecumseh St., College Park, Md.
Weaver, James Frederick, Sch. of Educ., Boston University, Boston, Mass.
Webb, Mrs. E. Sue, 216 W. Fifth St., Shawano, Wis.
Webb, Holmes, Dept. of Educ., Texas Tech. College, Lubbock, Tex.
Webber, Warren L., Music Dept., Cedarville College, Cedarville, Ohio
Weber, Clarence A., N. Eagleville Rd., Storrs, Conn.
Weber, Martha Gesling, Bowling Green State University, Bowling Green, Ohio
Webster, Bill R., Mankato State College, Mankato, Minn.
Weddington, Rachel T., Queens College, 65-30 Kissena Blvd., Flushing, N.Y.
Wedul, Melvin O., Minnesota State College, Winona, Minn.
Weeks, James S., Sch. of Educ., Univ. of Colorado, Boulder, Colo.
Wegrzyn, Helen A., 5240 W. Newport Ave., Chicago, Ill.
Wegstein, Mrs. Joseph L., 3027 Morehead Ave., El Paso, Tex.
Wehner, Freda, 723 Woodland Ave., Oshkosh, Wis.
Wehrer, Charles S., Jr., 2909 East 13th St., Des Moines, Iowa
Weidig, Phyllis D., 33 North St., Ramsey, N.J.
Weilbaker, Charles R., Tchrs. Col., University of Cincinnati, Cincinnati, Ohio
Weiner, Max, Brooklyn College, Brooklyn, N.Y.
Weinrich, Ernest F., Board of Coop. Educ. Services, P.O. Box 338, Huntington,
    N.Y.
Weintraub, Sam, Dept. of Educ., University of Chicago, Chicago, Ill.
Weis, Harold P., 437—23rd Ave., Moline, Ill.
Weisberg, Patricia H., 9411 S. Pleasant Ave., Chicago, Ill.
Weisiger, Louise P., 312 N. Ninth St., Richmond, Va.
Weiss, George D., Kutztown State College, Kutztown, Pa.
Weiss, M. Jerry, Jersey City State College, Jersey City, N.J.
Weiss, Morris H., Public School 215, Ave. S. and East 2nd St., Brooklyn, N.Y.
Weissmann, Paul, 18 Crocus St., Woodbridge, N.J.
Welcenbach, Frank J., Trombly School, Grosse Pointe, Mich.
Welch, Cornelius A., St. Bonaventure University, St. Bonaventure, N.Y.
Welch, Ronald C., Sch. of Educ., Indiana University, Bloomington, Ind.
Weld, Mary D., 9407 Corsica Dr., Bethesda, Md.
Welker, Latney C., Jr., 3704 Eastbrook Rd., Natchez, Miss.

Wellck, A. A., 724 Solano Dr., N.E., Albuquerque, N.M.
Welling, Helen F., 64 E. Arndt St., Fond du Lac, Wis.
Welliver Paul W., 1613 Walker Ave., Greensboro, N.C.
Welsh, Walter C., School of Indust. Art, 211 E. 79th St., New York, N.Y.
Wendt, Paul R., Southern Illinois University, Carbondale, Ill.
Wenger, Roy E., Kent State University, Kent, Ohio
Wenner, Harry W., 40 Mills St., Morristown, N.J.
Wenrich, Ralph C., Sch. of Educ., University of Michigan, Ann Arbor, Mich.
Wentz, Howard A., Nether Providence School District, Wallingford, Pa.
Wernick, Leo J., 3500 W. Douglas Blvd., Chicago, Ill.
Wesley, Emory Jones, 316 N. Eighth St., Arkadelphia, Ark.
West, Mrs. Lorraine W., Bakersfield Ctr., Fresno State Col., Bakersfield, Calif.
West, William H., County Union Schools, 7 Bridge St., Elizabeth, N.J.
Westbrook, Charles Hart, 17 Towana Rd., Richmond, Va.
Westbrooks, Sadye Wylena, 1433 Sharon St., N.W., Atlanta, Ga.
Westby-Gibson, Dorothy, San Francisco State College, San Francisco, Calif.
Westlund, Hildur L., 920 North 22nd St., Superior, Wis.
Wetter, Allen H., Superintendent of Schools, 21st and Parkway, Philadelphia, Pa.
Wetzel, Alma E., R.D. No. 1, Green Lane, Pa.
Wewer, William P., 638 Buttonwood St., Anaheim, Calif.
Whalen, Mary Margaret, 2734 Michigan Ave., Fresno, Calif.
Wharton, William P., Allegheny College, Meadville, Pa.
Whayland, Charles W., Glen Burnie High School, Glen Burnie, Md.
Wheat, Leonard B., Southern Illinois University, Alton, Ill.
Wheeler, Eldon G., East Alton-Wood River Community High School, Wood
    River, Ill.
Wheeler, Elizabeth, University of Wisconsin-Milwaukee, Milwaukee, Wis.
Wheeler, Mrs. Olive Boone, Box 818, Austin, Tex.
Whelhan, Amelia, State University College of Education, Oswego, N.Y.
Whetton, Mrs. Betty B., 1810 N. Mitchell St., Phoenix, Ariz.
Whigham, E. L., Oak Ridge Board of Education, P.O. Box Q, Oak Ridge, Tenn.
Whilt, Selma E., 49 Norfolk Rd., Island Park, N.Y.
Whipple, Carl E., 28 Franklin St., Warren, Pa.
White, Andrew William, St. Michael's College, Cerrillos Rd., Sante Fe, N.M.
White, George L., Harcourt, Brace & Co., 383 Madison Ave., New York, N.Y.
White, J. B., Col. of Educ., University of Florida, Gainesville, Fla.
White, John C., Edison School, Mesa, Ariz.
White, Kenneth B., New Jersey State Teachers College, Paterson, N.J.
White, Kenneth E., Central Michigan College, Mt. Pleasant, Mich.
White, Vern A., 26720 Grayslake Rd., Palos Verdes Estates, Calif.
Whitehead, Willis A., 3692 Traynham Rd., Shaker Heights, Ohio
Whiteside, Mrs. I .H., County Superintendent of Education, Ashland, Miss.
Whittier, C. Taylor, Rt. 3, Box 285, Gaithersburg, Md.
Wickenden, Roma C., 542 N. Main St., Ada, Ohio
Wickes, Mrs. Una Southard, 141 N. Bonnie, Pasadena, Calif.
Wiebe, Joel A., 1717 S. Chestnut St., Fresno, Calif.
Wieden, Clifford O. T., 181 Main St., Presque Isle, Me.
* Wieder, Beth Joyce, 161 West 86th St., New York, N.Y.
Wiens, Ben J., Rutgers University, New Brunswick, N.J.
Wiggin, Richard G., 1426 N. Quincy St., Arlington, Va.
Wildebush, Sarah W., 125 Hobart Ave., Rutherford, N.J.
Wiley, Russell, Board of Public Instruction, Sarasota, Fla.
Wilkerson, Bernice, 2726 Wauwatosa Ave., Milwaukee, Wis.
Wilkinson, H. A., Station ACC, Box 565, Abilene, Tex.
Willard, Robert L., Utica College, Utica, N.Y.
Willey, Lawrence V., Jr., 259 E. Erie St., Chicago, Ill.
Williams, Aimee, 1136 East 48th St., Chicago, Ill.
Williams, Alma V., Educ. Dept., University of California, University, Calif.
Williams, Arloff L., St. John's Military Academy, Delafield, Wis.
Williams, Arthur E., Dillard Comprehensive High School, Fort Lauderdale, Fla.
Williams, Byron B., University of Rochester, Rochester, N.Y.

Williams, Catharine M., 1945 N. High St., Columbus, Ohio
Williams, Charles C., North Texas State College, Denton, Tex.
Williams, Chester Spring, UNESCO, Min. of Educ., Apia, Repub. of West. Samoa
Williams, Clarence M., Col. of Educ., University of Rochester, Rochester, N.Y.
Williams, Cyrus Paul, 903 Peach St., El Campo, Tex.
Williams, Emmet D., 1261 Highway 36, St. Paul, Minn.
Williams, Fannie C., 1633 St. Bernard Ave., New Orleans, La.
Williams, Fountie N., 505 Pennsylvania Ave., Clarksburg, W.Va.
Williams, Frances I., Lab. Sch., Indiana State Teachers Col., Terre Haute, Ind.
Williams, G. A., Walnut Hill High School, Shreveport, La.
Williams, Harold A., Flat Top, W.Va.
Williams, Herman, 40 Elmwood St., Tiffin, Ohio
Williams, Howard Y., Jr., 2298 Doswell Ave., St. Paul, Minn.
Williams, James Harry, Armstrong High School, Richmond, Va.
Williams, John D., Long Beach State College, Long Beach, Calif.
Williams, Mrs. Lois, 200 North 18th St., Montebello, Calif.
Williams, Malcolm, Sch. of Educ., Tennessee A. & I. University, Nashville, Tenn.
Williams, Nat, Superintendent of Schools, Lubbock, Tex.
Williams, Richard H., 380 Moseley Rd., Hillsborough, Calif.
Williams, Robert Alan, 1945 Berkeley Way, Berkeley, Calif.
Williams, Robert Bruce, 710 Locust St., Roselle, N.J.
Williams, W. Morris, USOM/K, TC ED, APO 301, San Francisco, Calif.
Williams, Wilbur A., Moorhead State College, Moorhead, Minn.
Williamson, Jane, Morehead State College, Morehead, Ky.
Wills, Benjamin G., 1550 Bellamy St., Santa Clara, Calif.
Wilson, Alan S., Hillyer Col., University of Hartford, Hartford, Conn.
Wilson, David H., Lodi, N.Y.
Wilson, Dustin W., Community Cons. School District 10, Rt. 2, Woodstock, Ill.
Wilson, Harold M., 3006 N. Trinidad St., Arlington, Va.
Wilson, Herbert B., University of Arizona, Tucson, Ariz.
Wilson, Irma B., 809 Catalina Ave., Redondo Beach, Calif.
Wilson, J. A. R., University of California, Goleta, Calif.
Wilson, James W., Rochester Institute of Technology, Rochester, N.Y.
Wilson, Jean Alice, 715 Tidball Ave., Grove City, Pa.
Wilson, Joseph E., 2635—79th Ave., Baton Rouge, La.
Wilson, Merle A., 2800—62nd St., Des Moines, Iowa
Wilson, Roy K., Natl. Sch. Pub. Relations Assn., Washington, D.C.
Wilson, Roy R., Jr., Central Washington State Col., Ellensburg, Wash.
Wilson, Ulrey K., Dept. of Educ. and Psych., Univ. of Chattanooga, Chattanooga,
 Tenn.
Wilson, William G., Briar Wood, Wolf Road, Mokena, Ill.
Wilstach, Mrs. Ilah M., 2127 N. Eastern Ave., Los Angeles, Calif.
Wiltse, Earl W., Superintendent of Schools, H.S. Dist. 207, Park Ridge, Ill.
Wimpey, John A., The Citadel, Charleston, S.C.
Winfield, Kenneth, P.O. Box 151, Hannawa Falls, N.Y.
Wing, Lucy, State University College, Oswego, N.Y.
Wing, Richard L., North. Westchester Tech. and Educ. Center, Yorktown
 Heights, N.Y.
Wingerd, Harold H., Superintendent of Schools, West Chester, Pa.
Winkley, Mrs. Carol K., 1815 Kenilworth Pl., Aurora, Ill.
Winsor, Mrs. Charlotte B., Bank Street College, 4 East 74th St., New York, N.Y.
Winston, Bertha H., 730 Oakwood Blvd., Chicago, Ill.
Winter, Stephen S., Sch. of Educ., University of Buffalo, Buffalo, N.Y.
Wise, Harold L., Western Reserve University, Cleveland, Ohio
Wiseman, Rex M., 808 Genoa St., Monrovia, Calif.
Wishart, James S., 1638 Ridge Rd., West, Rochester, N.Y.
Witherspoon, W. H., P.O. Box 527, Rockhill, S.C.
Witt, Paul W. F., Tchrs. Col., Columbia University, New York, N.Y.
Witte, Cyril M., Loyola College, 4501 N. Charles St., Baltimore, Md.
Witter, Sanford C., Superintendent of Schools, Dist. 202, Kansas City, Kan.
Wittick, Mildred Letton, 300 Pompton Rd., Wayne, N.J.

Wittmer, Arthur E., 2112 Broadway, Rm. 401, New York, N.Y.
Witty, Paul A., Sch. of Educ., Northwestern University, Evanston, Ill.
Wixted, William G., Marymount College, Boca Raton, Fla.
Wochner, Raymond E., Arizona State University, Tempe, Ariz.
Woerdehoff, Frank J., Dept. of Educ., Purdue University, Lafayette, Ind.
Woestehoff, Orville W., Oak Park Elementary Schls., 122 Forest Ave., Oak Park, Ill.
Wohlers, A. E., Ohio State University, Columbus, Ohio
Wolbrecht, Walter F., 316 Parkwood, Kirkwood, Mo.
Wolf, Dan B., P.O. Box 367, Bloomington, Ind.
Wolf, Lloyd L., 605 N. McLean Ave., Lincoln, Ill.
Wolf, Richard, 3208 Western Ave., Park Forest, Ill.
Wolf, William C., Jr., Coop. Res. Br., USOE, 400 Maryland, Washington, D.C.
Wolfe, Deborah P., 62 S. Union Ave., Cranford, N.J.
Wolfe, Josephine B., 793B Erford Rd., Camp Hill, Pa.
Wolfram, Donald J., 1845 Champ St., Denver, Colo.
Wolfson, Bernice J., University of Wisconsin-Milwaukee, Milwaukee, Wis.
Wolinsky, Gloria F., 69-52 Groton St., Forest Hills, N.Y.
Wong, William T. S., 1640 Paula Dr., Honolulu, Hawaii
Wood, Donald I., Dept. of Educ., Houston, Tex.
Wood, Harvey, Dimondale Area Schools, Dimondale, Mich.
Wood, Helen A., Dept. of Educ., Brooklyn College, Brooklyn, N.Y.
Wood, Joseph E., 18 Duryea Rd., Upper Montclair, N.J.
Wood, Mrs. Marion, 783 Watertown St., West Newton, Mass.
Wood, Roi S., Superintendent of Schools, Joplin, Mo.
Wood, W. Clement, Fort Hays Kansas State College, Hays, Kan.
Woodard, Prince B., Col. of Educ., Temple University, Philadelphia, Pa.
Woodburn, A. C., Alamogordo Public Schools, Alamogordo, N.M.
Woodburn, John H., Walter Johnson High School, Rockville, Md.
Wooden, Maurice L., West Covina High School, West Covina, Calif.
Woodhull, James E., USAID to Colombia, American Consulate, Cali, Colombia
Woodruff, Olive, Kent State University, Kent, Ohio
Woods, Robert Keith, 103 W. Hickory St., Platteville, Wis.
Woodson, C. C., 435 S. Liberty St., Spartanburg, S.C.
Woodson, Grace I., West Virginia State College, Institute, W.Va.
Woodson, Marshall Scott, Jr., 16 Cypress Ter., Boonton, N.J.
Woodward, Mrs. Etta K., 927 Cayuga Heights Rd., Ithaca, N.Y.
Woodworth, Denny, Col. of Educ., Drake University, Des Moines, Iowa
Woodworth, William O., 999 Kedzie Ave., Flossmoor, Ill.
Woofter, James, 412 S. Union St., Ada, Ohio
Woolbright, William J., 2329 W. Borchard Ave., Santa Ana, Calif.
Woolf, Kenneth A., Hunterdon County Schools, Flemington, N.J.
Woolson, Edith L., Box 203, Imperial, Calif.
Worden, J. William, Gordon College, Wenham, Mass.
Workman, Charlotte B., State University of New York Col., Oswego, N.Y.
Wozencraft, Marian, State University College of Education, Geneseo, N.Y.
Wrenn, C. Gilbert, Burton Hall, University of Minnesota, Minneapolis, Minn.
Wrenn, Michael P., 6544 Greenview Ave., Chicago, Ill.
Wright, Adele J., 275 S. Glencoe St., Denver, Colo.
Wright, C. O., Kansas State Teachers Assn., Topeka, Kan.
Wright, C. P., Guthrie High School, Guthrie, Okla.
Wright, Dorothy L., Sch. of Educ., New York University, New York, N.Y.
Wright, Eleanore B., Little Silver Public Schools, Little Silver, N.J.
Wright, Floyd K., 1432 Price Dr., Cape Girardeau, Mo.
Wright, John R., San Jose State College, San Jose, Calif.
Wright, William H., Jr., 602 Starbuck St., Whittier, Calif.
Wrightstone, J. Wayne, Board of Educ., 110 Livingston St., Brooklyn, N.Y.
Wronski, Stanley P., Col. of Educ., Michigan State Univ., East Lansing, Mich.
Wubben, Horace J., Mesa County Junior College, Grand Junction, Colo.
Wuolle, Mrs. Ethel, P.O. Box 173, Pine City, Minn.

Wyeth, E. R., 18111 Nordhoff St., Northridge, Calif.
Wyllie, Eugene D., Sch. of Bus., Indiana University, Bloomington, Ind.
Wynn, Willa T., 1122 N. St. Clair St., Pittsburgh, Pa.

Yamashiro, Margaret H., 1720 Ala Moana Blvd., Honolulu, Hawaii
Yaple, Graydon W., 664 Timber Lane, Wilmington, Ohio
Yates, Mrs. Flora R., R.F.D. 1, Box 43, Elkton, Va.
Yates, J. W., Curric. Lab., Kansas University, Lawrence, Kan.
Yates, Virginia D., 5318 Troost, Kansas City, Mo.
Yauch, Wilbur A., Northern Illinois University, DeKalb, Ill.
Yavicoli, Mildred,, 3067 Orleans Ave., Niagara Falls, N.Y.
Yeager, Paul M., Sheridan School, Second and Liberty Sts., Allentown, Pa.
Yoder, Samuel L., Goshen College, Goshen, Ind.
Yoshimori, Alice S., 1801 University Ave., Honolulu, Hawaii
Young, Albert T., Jr., National Science Foundation, Washington, D.C.
Young, Gordon Mawson, 23 The Lowlands, Hailsham, Sussex, England
Young, Harold L., Central Missouri State College, Warrensburg, Mo.
Young, Horace A., Jr., Texas Southern University, Houston, Tex.
Young, J. E. M., Macdonald College Post Office, Quebec
Young, Jean A., San Francisco College for Women, San Francisco, Calif.
Young, John J., 519 Clay St., Mishawaka, Ind.
Young, Lloyd P., Keene Teachers College, Keene, N.H.
Young, William E., New York State Education Department, Albany, N.Y.
Young, William Howard, 1460 Tampa Ave., Dayton, Ohio
Youngblood, Chester E., P.O. Box 413, College, Alaska
Younglund, Donald E., 3831 S. Fees St., Wichita, Kan.
Yourd, John L., 1104—2nd Ave., Fargo, N.D.
Yuhas, Theodore Frank, Educ. Dept., Ball State Teachers College, Muncie, Ind.
Yunghans, Ernest E., Wartburg College, Waverly, Iowa

Zahm, Bernice S., 4422 Sherman Oaks Circle, Sherman Oaks, Calif.
Zahn, D. Willard, Col. of Educ., Temple University, Philadelphia, Pa.
Zahorsky, Mrs. Metta, San Francisco State College, San Francisco, Calif.
Zakrzewski, Aurelia R., 4806 Chovin St., Dearborn, Mich.
Zambite, Stephen C., 616 North River, Ypsilanti, Mich.
Zawadski, Bohdan, 106 East 85th St., New York, N.Y.
Zbornik, Joseph J., 3219 Clarence Ave., Berwyn, Ill.
Zdanowicz, John Paul, 71 Spring Hill Ave., Bridgewater, Mass.
Zebrowski, Kenneth M., USA DEG, Dist. V., APO 58, New York, N.Y.
Zeiler, E. J., Superintendent of Schools, Whitefish Bay, Wis.
Zepper, John Thomas, Hodgin Hall, University of New Mexico, Albuquerque, N.M.
Ziebold, Edna B., 6401 Linda Vista Rd., San Diego, Calif.
Ziemba, Walter J., St. Mary's College, Orchard Lake, Mich.
Zim, Herbert Spencer, Box 34, Tavernier, Fla.
Zimmerman, Katherine A., 619½ East 3rd St., Northfield, Minn.
Zimmerman, William G., Jr., Hanover Public Schools, Hanover, N.H.
Zimnoch, Frances J., West Tresper Clark High School, Westbury, L.I., N.Y.
Zinn, Lawrence A., 2560 Lorain Ct., Columbus, Ohio
Zintz, Miles V., 3028 Marble Ave., N.E., Albuquerque, N.M.
Zipper, Joseph H., 1569 West 41st St., Erie, Pa.
Zumsteg, Frederick C., 109 Michigan Dr., Terrace Park, Ohio
Zweig, Richard L., Reading Guid. Center, Inc., 9200 Colima Rd., Whittier, Calif.

INFORMATION CONCERNING THE NATIONAL SOCIETY FOR THE STUDY OF EDUCATION

1. PURPOSE. The purpose of the National Society is to promote the investigation and discussion of educational questions. To this end it holds an annual meeting and publishes a series of yearbooks.

2. ELIGIBILITY TO MEMBERSHIP. Any person who is interested in receiving its publications may become a member by sending to the Secretary-Treasurer information concerning name, title, and address, and a check for $8.00 (see Item 5), except that graduate students, on the recommendation of a faculty member, may become members by paying $6.00 for the first year of their membership. Dues for all subsequent years are the same as for other members (see Item 4).

Membership is not transferable; it is limited to individuals, and may not be held by libraries, schools, or other institutions, either directly or indirectly.

3. PERIOD OF MEMBERSHIP. Applicants for membership may not date their entrance back of the current calendar year, and all memberships terminate automatically on December 31, unless the dues for the ensuing year are paid as indicated in Item 6.

4. DUTIES AND PRIVILEGES OF MEMBERS. Members pay dues of $7.00 annually, receive a cloth-bound copy of each publication, are entitled to vote, to participate in discussion, and (under certain conditions) to hold office. The names of members are printed in the yearbooks.

Persons who are sixty years of age or above may become life members on payment of fee based on average life-expectancy of their age group. For information, apply to Secretary-Treasurer.

5. ENTRANCE FEE. New members are required the first year to pay, in addition to the dues, an entrance fee of one dollar.

6. PAYMENT OF DUES. Statements of dues are rendered in October for the following calendar year. Any member so notified whose dues remain unpaid on January 1, thereby loses his membership and can be reinstated only by paying a reinstatement fee of fifty cents.

School warrants and vouchers from institutions must be accompanied by definite information concerning the name and address of the person for whom membership fee is being paid. Statements of dues are rendered on our own form only. The Secretary's office cannot undertake to fill out special invoice forms of any sort or to affix notary's affidavit to statements or receipts.

Cancelled checks serve as receipts. Members desiring an additional receipt must enclose a stamped and addressed envelope therefor.

7. DISTRIBUTION OF YEARBOOKS TO MEMBERS. The yearbooks, ready prior to each February meeting, will be mailed from the office of the distributors, only to members whose dues for that year have been paid. Members who desire yearbooks prior to the current year must purchase them directly from the distributors (see Item 8).

8. COMMERCIAL SALES. The distribution of all yearbooks prior to the current year, and also of those of the current year not regularly mailed to members in exchange for their dues, is in the hands of the distributor, not of the Secretary. For such commercial sales, communicate directly with the University of Chicago Press, Chicago 37, Illinois, which will gladly send a price list covering all the publications of this Society. This list is also printed in the yearbook.

9. YEARBOOKS. The yearbooks are issued about one month before the February meeting. They comprise from 600 to 800 pages annually. Unusual effort has been made to make them, on the one hand, of immediate practical value, and, on the other hand, representative of sound scholarship and scientific investigation.

10. MEETINGS. The annual meeting, at which the yearbooks are discussed, is held in February at the same time and place as the meeting of the American Association of School Administrators.

Applications for membership will be handled promptly at any time on receipt of name and address, together with check for $8.00 (or $7.50 for reinstatement). Applications entitle the new members to the yearbook slated for discussion during the calendar year the application is made.

5835 Kimbark Ave.   HERMAN G. RICHEY, *Secretary-Treasurer*
Chicago 37, Illinois

PUBLICATIONS OF THE NATIONAL SOCIETY FOR THE STUDY OF EDUCATION

NOTICE: Many of the early Yearbooks of this series are now out of print. In the following list, those titles to which an asterisk is prefixed are not available for purchase.

POSTPAID
PRICE

*First Yearbook, 1902, Part I—*Some Principles in the Teaching of History.* Lucy M. Salmon . . . .
*First Yearbook, 1902, Part II—*The Progress of Geography in the Schools.* W. M. Davis and H. M. Wilson . . . .
*Second Yearbook, 1903, Part I—*The Course of Study in History in the Common School.* Isabel Lawrence, C. A. McMurry, Frank McMurry, E. C. Page, and E. J. Rice . . . .
*Second Yearbook, 1903, Part II—*The Relation of Theory to Practice in Education.* M. J. Holmes, J. A. Keith, and Levi Seeley . . . .
*Third Yearbook, 1904, Part I—*The Relation of Theory to Practice in the Education of Teachers.* John Dewey, Sarah C. Brooks, F. M. McMurry, et al. . . . .
*Third Yearbook, 1904, Part II—*Nature Study.* W. S. Jackman . . . .
*Fourth Yearbook, 1905, Part I—*The Education and Training of Secondary Teachers.* E. C. Elliott, E. G. Dexter, M. J. Holmes, et al. . . . .
*Fourth Yearbook, 1905, Part II—*The Place of Vocational Subjects in the High-School Curriculum.* J. S. Brown, G. B. Morrison, and Ellen Richards . . . .
*Fifth Yearbook, 1906, Part I—*On the Teaching of English in Elementary and High Schools.* G. P. Brown and Emerson Davis . . . .
Fifth Yearbook, 1906, Part II—*The Certification of Teachers.* E. P. Cubberley $0.64
*Sixth Yearbook, 1907, Part I—*Vocational Studies for College Entrance.* C. A. Herrick, H. W. Holmes, T. deLaguna, V. Prettyman, and W. J. S. Bryan . . . .
*Sixth Yearbook, 1907, Part II—*The Kindergarten and Its Relation to Elementary Education.* Ada Van Stone Harris, E. A. Kirkpatrick, Marie Kraus-Boelté, Patty S. Hill, Harriette M. Mills, and Nina Vandewalker . . . .
*Seventh Yearbook, 1908, Part I—*The Relation of Superintendents and Principals to the Training and Professional Improvement of Their Teachers.* Charles D. Lowry
*Seventh Yearbook, 1908, Part II—*The Co-ordination of the Kindergarten and the Elementary School.* B. J. Gregory, Jennie B. Merrill, Bertha Payne, and Margaret Giddings . . . .
Eighth Yearbook, 1909, Part I—*Education with Reference to Sex: Pathological, Economic, and Social Aspects.* C. R. Henderson 85
*Eighth Yearbook, 1909, Part II—*Education with Reference to Sex: Agencies and Methods.* C. R. Henderson and Helen C. Putnam . . . .
*Ninth Yearbook, 1910, Part I—*Health and Education.* T. D. Wood . . . .
*Ninth Yearbook, 1910, Part II—*The Nurse in Education.* T. D. Wood, et al. . . . .
*Tenth Yearbook, 1911, Part I—*The City School as a Community Center.* H. C. Leipziger, Sarah E. Hyre, R. D. Warden, C. Ward Crampton, E. W. Stitt, E. J. Ward, Mrs. E. C. Grice, and C. A. Perry . . . .
*Tenth Yearbook, 1911, Part II—*The Rural School as a Community Center.* B. H. Crocheron, Jessie Field, F. W. Howe, E. C. Bishop, A. B. Graham, O. J. Kern, M. T. Scudder, and B. M. Davis . . . .
*Eleventh Yearbook, 1912, Part I—*Industrial Education: Typical Experiments Described and Interpreted.* J. F. Barker, M. Bloomfield, B. W. Johnson, P. Johnson, L. M. Leavitt, G. A. Mirick, M. W. Murray, C. F. Perry, A. L. Safford, and H. B. Wilson . . . .
*Eleventh Yearbook, 1912, Part II—*Agricultural Education in Secondary Schools.* A. C. Monahan, R. W. Stimson, D. J. Crosby, W. H. French, H. F. Button, F. R. Crane, W. R. Hart, and G. F. Warren . . . .
*Twelfth Yearbook, 1913, Part I—*The Supervision of City Schools.* Franklin Bobbitt, J. W. Hall, and J. D. Wolcott . . . .
*Twelfth Yearbook, 1913, Part II—*The Supervision of Rural Schools.* A. C. Monahan, L. J. Hanifan, J. E. Warren, Wallace Lund, U. J. Hoffman, A. S. Cook, E. M. Rapp, Jackson Davis, and J. D. Wolcott . . . .
*Thirteenth Yearbook, 1914, Part I—*Some Aspects of High-School Instruction and Administration.* H. C. Morrison, E. R. Breslich, W. A. Jessup, and L. D. Coffman . .
*Thirteenth Yearbook, 1914, Part II—*Plans for Organizing School Surveys, with a Summary of Typical School Surveys.* Charles H. Judd and Henry L. Smith . . . . .
*Fourteenth Yearbook, 1915, Part I—*Minimum Essentials in Elementary School Subjects—Standards and Current Practices.* H. B. Wilson, H. W. Holmes, F. E. Thompson, R. G. Jones, S. A. Courtis, W. S. Gray, F. N. Freeman, H. C. Pryor, J. F. Hosic, W. A. Jessup, and W. C. Bagley . . . .
Fourteenth Yearbook, 1915, Part II—*Methods for Measuring Teachers' Efficiency.* Arthur C. Boyce 79
*Fifteenth Yearbook, 1916, Part I—*Standards and Tests for the Measurement of the Efficiency of Schools and School Systems.* G. D. Strayer, Bird T. Baldwin, B. R. Buckingham, F. W. Ballou, D. C. Bliss, H. G. Childs, S. A. Courtis, E. P. Cubberley, C. H. Judd, George Melcher, E. E. Oberholtzer, J. B. Sears, Daniel Starch, M. R. Trabue, and G. M. Whipple . . . .

Distributed by
THE UNIVERSITY OF CHICAGO PRESS, CHICAGO 37, ILLINOIS
1964